GENERAL EQUILIBRIUM, GROWTH, AND TRADE II

This is a volume in
ECONOMIC THEORY, ECONOMETRICS, AND MATHEMATICAL ECONOMICS
A Series of Monographs and Textbooks

Consulting Editor: KARL SHELL, *Cornell University*

A list of recent titles in this series appears at the end of this volume.

GENERAL EQUILIBRIUM, GROWTH, AND TRADE II

The Legacy of Lionel McKenzie

EDITED BY

Robert Becker

Department of Economics
Indiana University
Bloomington, Indiana

Michele Boldrin

MEDS-KGSM
Northwestern University
Evanston, Illinois

Ronald Jones

Department of Economics
University of Rochester
Rochester, New York

William Thomson

Department of Economics
University of Rochester
Rochester, New York

Academic Press, Inc.
A Division of Harcourt Brace & Company
San Diego New York Boston London Sydney Tokyo Toronto

This book is printed on acid-free paper. 

Academic Press, Inc.
1250 Sixth Avenue, San Diego, California 92101-4311

United Kingdom Edition published by
Academic Press Limited
24–28 Oval Road, London NW1 7DX

Library of Congress Cataloging-in-Publication Data
(Revised for vol. 2)

General equilibrium, growth, and trade.

(Economic theory, econometrics, and mathematical economics)
Vol. 2 edited by Robert Becker ... [et al.]
Includes bibliographies and index.
1. Economics, Mathematical. 2. Equilibrium (Economics) 3. Economic development. 4. Commerce.
5. McKenzie, Lionel W. I. McKenzie, Lionel W.
II. Green, Jerry R. III. Scheinkman, Jose Alexandre.
IV. Series.
HB135.G445 330'.01'51 79-50216
ISBN 0-12-298750-0 (v. 1)
ISBN 0-12-084655-1 (v. 2)

PRINTED IN THE UNITED STATES OF AMERICA
93 94 95 96 97 98 QW 9 8 7 6 5 4 3 2 1

LIONEL McKENZIE

Curriculum Vitae

BORN:

January 26, 1919, Montezuma, Georgia

EDUCATION:

Montezuma Public School	1925–1935
Middle Georgia College	1935–1937
Duke University (A.B.)	1937–1939
Princeton University (M.A., Ph.D.)	1939–1942
Oxford University (B. Litt.)	1946–1948
University of Chicago	1950–1951

PROFESSIONAL EXPERIENCE:

Junior Economist, War Production Board	1942
Officer (Ensign to Lieutenant) United States Naval Reserve	1943–1945
Instructor in Economics, Massachusetts Institute of Technology	1946
Assistant Professor, Associate Professor, Duke University	1948–1957
Research Associate, Yale University	1956
Visiting Associate Professor, University of Michigan, Spring Semester	1957
Leader, Summer Workshop in Mathematical Economics for Social Science Research Council at Stanford University	1957
Professor of Economics and Department Chairman, University of Rochester	1957–1966
John Munro Professor of Economics, University of Rochester	1964–1967
Wilson Professor of Economics, University of Rochester	1967–1989

Wilson Professor of Economics, Emeritus, University of Rochester	1989–
Representative of the Econometric Society to the Mathematics Division of the National Research Council	1961–1963
Representative of the American Economic Association to the Behavioral Sciences Division of the National Research Council	1964–1969
Leader, Summer Conference on Mathematical Models of Economic Growth for Social Science Research Council at the University of Rochester	1964
Economics Member of Mathematical Social Science Board of Center for Advanced Research in Behavioral Sciences	1964–1970
Chairman	1968–1970
Associate Editor, International Economic Review	1964–
Journal of Economic Theory	1970–1973
Journal of International Economics	1971–1984
Vice President, Econometric Society	1975–1976
President, Econometric Society	1977
Taussig Research Professor, Harvard University	1980–1981

HONORS:

Highest Honors in Politics, Economics, and Philosophy at Duke University	1939
Phi Beta Kappa at Duke University	1939
Rhodes Scholar from Georgia	1939
Fellowship at Princeton	1939–1942
Fellowship at Chicago	1950–1951
Social Science Research Council Fellow at Oxford	1946–1948
Social Science Research Council Supplementary Research Grant (unsolicited award)	1959
Elected Fellow of the Econometric Society	1958
Elected Fellow of the American Academy of Arts and Sciences	1967
Guggenheim Fellow	1973–1974
Fellow of Center for Advanced Research in Behavioral Sciences	1973–1974
Elected to the National Academy of Sciences	1978
Honorary Doctor of Laws from University of Chicago	1991

PUBLICATIONS:

A method for drawing marginal curves. *Journal of Political Economy*, October 1950, pp. 434–435.

Ideal output and the interdependence of firms. *Economic Journal*, December 1951, pp. 785–803.

On equilibrium in Graham's model of world trade and other competitive systems. *Econometrica*, April 1954, pp. 147–161.

Specialization and efficiency of world production. *Review of Economic Studies*, June 1954, pp. 165–180.

Equality of factor prices in world trade. *Econometrica*, July 1955, pp. 239–257.

Competitive equilibrium with dependent consumer preferences. "Second Symposium in Linear Programming," vol. I, edited by H. A. Antosiewicz. National Bureau of Standards, Washington, D.C. 1956, pp. 277–294.

Specialization in production and the production possibility locus. *Review of Economic Studies*, October 1955, vol. XXIII (1), pp. 56–64.

Demand theory without a utility index. *Review of Economic Studies*, June 1957, vol. XXIV (3), pp. 185–189.

An elementary analysis of the Leontief system. *Econometrica*, July 1957, pp. 456–462.

Review of R. G. D. Allen, "Mathematical Economics." *American Economic Review*, March 1958, pp. 139–147.

On the existence of general equilibrium for a competitive market. *Econometrica*, January 1959, pp. 54–71.

Matrices with dominant diagonals and economic theory. In "Mathematical Methods in the Social Sciences," edited by K. J. Arrow, S. Karlin, and P. Suppes. Stanford University Press, 1959, pp. 47–62.

Stability of equilibrium and the value of excess demand. *Econometrica*, July 1960, pp. 606–617.

On the existence of general equilibrium: Some corrections. *Econometrica*, April 1961, pp. 247–248.

The Dorfman–Samuelson–Solow turnpike theorem. *International Economic Review*, January 1963, pp. 29–43.

Turnpike theorems for a generalized Leontief model. *Econometrica*, January–April 1963, pp. 165–180.

Turnpike theorem of Morishima. *Review of Economic Studies*, June 1963, pp. 169–176.

Review of R. E. Kuenne, "The Theory of General Economic Equilibrium." *American Economic Review*, December 1964, pp. 1096–1103.

Maximal paths in the von Neumann Model. In "Activity Analysis in the Theory of Growth and Planning," edited by E. Malinvaud and M. O. L. Bacharach. Macmillan, London, 1967, pp. 43–63.

The inversion of cost functions: A counter-example. *International Economic Review*, October 1967, pp. 271–278.

Theorem and counter example. *International Economic Review*, October 1967, pp. 279–285.

Accumulation programs of maximum utility and the von Neumann facet. In "Value, Capital, and Growth," edited by J. N. Wolfe. Edinburgh University Press, 1968, pp. 353–383.

International trade, II, mathematical theory. In "International Encyclopedia of the Social Sciences," 1968, vol. 8, pp. 96–104.

Capital accumulation optimal in the final state. In "Contributions to the von Neumann Growth Model," edited by G. Bruckmann and W. Weber. Springer-Verlag, New York, 1971, pp. 107–120.

Turnpike theorems with technology and welfare function variable. In "Mathematical Models in Economics," edited by J. Los and M. Los. North Holland, Amsterdam, 1974, pp. 271–288.

Review of H. Scarf, "The Computation of Economic Equilibria." *Review of Economic Literature*, June 1975, pp. 511–513.

Why compute competitive equilibria? In "Computing Equilibria: How and Why," edited by J. Los and M. Los. North Holland, Amsterdam, 1976, pp. 3–19.

Turnpike theory. *Econometrica*, September 1976, pp. 841–865.

A new route to the turnpike. In "Mathematical Economics and Game Theory," edited by R. Henn and O. Moeschlin. Springer-Verlag, New York, 1977, pp. 683–694.

Turnpike theory: Some corrections, with Makoto Yano. *Econometrica*, November 1980, pp. 1839–1840.

The classical theorem on existence of competitive equilibrium. Presidential address to the Econometric Society. *Econometrica*, July 1981, pp. 819–841.

A primal route to the turnpike and Liapounov stability. *Journal of Economic Theory*, June 1982, vol. 27, pp. 194–209.

Turnpike theory, discounted utility, and the von Neumann facet. *Journal of Economic Theory*, August 1983, vol. 30, pp. 330–352.

A note on comparative statics and dynamics of stationary states, with S. Dasgupta. *Economics Letters*, 1985, vol. 18, 333–338.

Optimal economic growth, turnpike theorems, and comparative dynamics. In "Handbook of Mathematical Economics," edited by K. J. Arrow and M. D. Intriligator. North Holland, Amsterdam, 1986, vol. III, pp. 1281–1355.

General equilibrium. In "The New Palgrave Dictionary of Economics," edited by J. Eatwell, M. Milgate, and P. Newman. Stockton Press, New York, 1987, vol. 2, pp. 566–569.

Gross substitutes. *Op. cit.*, vol. 2, pp. 498–512.

Turnpike theory. *Op. cit.*, vol. 4, pp. 712–720.

A limit theorem on the core. *Economics Letters*, 1988, vol. 27, pp. 7–9.

Discussion of H. Atsumi, "On the Rate of Interest in a 'Neo-Austrian' Theory of Capital;" also Introduction, with S. Zamagni. In "Value and Capital: Fifty Years Later," edited by L. McKenzie and S. Zamagni. Macmillan, London, 1990, pp. 410–420, pp. xvii–xxix

A limit theorem on the core: Addendum. *Economics Letters*, 1990, vol. 32, pp. 109–110.

The comparative statics and dynamics of stationary states, with S. Dasgupta. In "Preferences, Uncertainty and Optimality," edited by J. S. Chipman, D. McFadden, and M. K. Richter. Frontier Press, Boulder, Colo., 1990, pp. 346–377.

A limit theorem on the core: Addendum II. *Economics Letters*, 1991, vol. 37, pp. 331–332.

The existence of competitive equilibrium over an infinite horizon with production and general consumption sets, with J. H. Boyd III. *International Economic Review*, February, 1993, vol. 34, pp. 1–20.

CONTENTS

Preface xvii

PART **I** **GENERAL EQUILIBRIUM**

LIONEL McKENZIE ON THE EXISTENCE OF COMPETITIVE EQUILIBRIUM

M. Ali Kahn

1. Introduction 3
2. Existence in Graham's Model: 1954 4
3. Existence with Externalities: A Year Later 15
4. Interiority, Irreducibility, and Irreversibility: Four Years Later 22
5. Classical Theorem in Its Fully Developed Form: 22 Years Later 36
6. An Overview 44

   References 46

McKENZIE AND THE SLUTSKY COEFFICIENTS **51**

S. N. Afriat

References 55

REAL INDETERMINACY FROM IMPERFECT FINANCIAL MARKETS: TWO ADDENDA

David Cass

1. Introduction 56
2. The Setting 57
3. Outside Money 61
4. Small Imperfections 67

   References 71

IRREDUCIBILITY, RESOURCE RELATEDNESS, AND SURVIVAL IN EQUILIBRIUM WITH INDIVIDUAL NONCONVEXITIES

Peter J. Hammond

1. Introduction 73
2. Preliminaries 77
3. Cheaper Points for Individuals 81
4. Nonoligarchic Allocations 90
5. Interdependent Agents and Irreducible Economies 96
6. Continuum Economies 104
7. Proofs of Propositions 107
8. Concluding Remarks 112
References 113

INCOMPLETE FINANCIAL MARKETS WITH AN INFINITE HORIZON

Alejandro Hernández D. and Manuel S. Santos

1. Introduction 116
2. Definitions 120
3. Bankruptcy Condition and Continuity of the Budget Set 127
4. Price Space 138
5. Indeterminacy 141
6. Conclusions 146
References 147

COMMODITY PAIR DESIRABILITY AND THE CORE EQUIVALENCE THEOREM

Aldo Rustichini and Nicholas C. Yannelis

1. Introduction 150
2. Preliminaries 152
3. The Model and a Preliminary Theorem 155
4. Extremely Desirable Commodities and Commodity Pair Desirability 160
5. Core–Walras Equivalence in Banach Lattices Whose Positive Core Has an Empty Interior 162
6. Concluding Remarks 164
References 166

LUMP-SUM TAXATION: THE STATIC ECONOMY

Yves Balasko and Karl Shell

1. Introduction 168
2. Preliminaries 169

3. Bonafide Fiscal Policies 172
4. The Set of Equilibrium Money Prices 176
5. Extensions 178
References 179

EQUILIBRIUM, STABILITY, AND PRICE ADJUSTMENTS IN COMPETITIVE MARKETS

Edward Zabel

1. Introduction 181
2. Examples of Competitive Economies 185
3. Price Choices with an Optimizing Price Maker 187
4. Scarf's Economy: Single-Period Horizon 189
5. Scarf's Economy: Multiperiod Horizon 193
6. Gale's Economy 197
7. Concluding Comments 200
References 202

ASYMPTOTIC BEHAVIOR OF ASSET MARKETS: ASYMPTOTIC INEFFICIENCY

William R. Zame

1. Introduction 203
2. The Model 206
3. Existence of Securities Market Equilibrium 209
4. Asymptotics 213
5. Genericity 221
6. Unconstrained Consumption 227
7. Concluding Remarks 230
References 232

PART II GROWTH

ENDOGENOUS FERTILITY AND GROWTH

Jess Benhabib and Kazuo Nishimura

1. Introduction 237
2. The Model and Assumptions 238
3. Characterization of Fertility Rate Changes 241
4. The Model with Schooling 246
References 247

A VINTAGE CAPITAL MODEL OF INVESTMENT AND GROWTH: THEORY AND EVIDENCE

Jess Benhabib and Aldo Rustichini

1. Introduction 248
2. The Model: Description and General Properties 251
3. Some Technical Results 256
4. Nonmonotonicity Properties of the Optimal Path 259
5. The Steady State 260
6. The Policy Function 262
7. The Stochastic Model 272
8. Empirical Results 274
Appendix 285
References 300

THOUGHTS OF VOLATILITY TESTS OF THE INTEMPORAL ASSET PRICING MODEL

Truman F. Bewley

1. Introduction 302
2. Definition of Market Efficiency 303
3. A Quick Review of Tests of Market Efficiency 305
4. The Model 307
5. Asset Prices with Insurance 312
6. Asset Prices without Insurance 317
7. A Possible Explanation of Volatility 327
References 329

STATIONARY MARKOVIAN STRATEGIES IN DYNAMIC GAMES

Rose-Anne Dana and Luigi Montrucchio

1. Introduction 331
2. A Dynamic Game Model of Resource Exploitation 332
3. Cyert–deGroot–Maskin–Tirole Duopoly Games 339
4. Reaction Function Equilibria 344
5. Concluding Remarks 349
Appendix 349
References 351

TURNPIKE PROPERTIES AND COMPARATIVE DYNAMICS OF GENERAL CAPITAL ACCUMULATION GAMES

Engelbert J. Dockner and Harutaka Takahashi

1. Introduction 352
2. Formulation and Notation 355
3. Existence and Stability Properties 358

4. Comparative Statics and Dynamics 362
5. Conclusions 363
Appendix 364
References 365

EXPERIMENTAL CONSUMPTION FOR A GENERAL CLASS OF DISTURBANCE DENSITIES
Jerry M. Fusselman and Leonard J. Mirman
1. Introduction 367
2. The Model 370
3. Main Results 375
4. An Extension 382
5. Examples 385
References 392

THE FIRM AND THE PLANT IN GENERAL EQUILIBRIUM THEORY
Andreas Hornstein and Edward C. Prescott
1. Introduction 393
2. The Firm in General Equilibrium Theory 395
3. The Plant in General Equilibrium Theory 397
4. Existence of Competitive Equilibrium 403
References 410

A NOTE ON BOUNDARY OPTIMAL PATHS
Henry Wan, Jr.
1. Motivation 411
2. Our Basic Model 413
3. Key Assumptions and Their Implications 418
4. Additional Results 423
5. Conclusion 426
References 426

PART **III** **INTERNATIONAL TRADE**

THE STOLPER–SAMUELSON THEOREM: LINKS TO DOMINANT DIAGONALS
Ronald W. Jones, Sugata Marjit, and Tapan Mitra
1. The Strong Factor-Intensity Condition 430
2. A Dominant Diagonal Matrix 434
3. The Willoughby Theorem 435

4. The Produced Mobile Factor (PMF) Structure 438
5. Concluding Remarks 439
References 440

LABOR MOBILITY AND WAGE RATE EQUALIZATION

Eric Bond

1. Introduction 442
2. One Immobile Factor 444
3. Two Immobile Factors 452
4. Conclusions 458
References 458

BORROWING CONSTRAINTS AND INTERNATIONAL COMOVEMENTS

Antoine Conze, Jean-Michel Lasry, and José Scheinkman

1. Introduction 460
2. The Model 462
3. The Stationary Distribution of Asset Holding 475
4. Simulations of the Model 477
5. Conclusion 480
Appendix 481
References 489

MULTINATIONAL CORPORATIONS AND ABSOLUTE ADVANTAGE: THE ASYMMETRIC CASE

Fumio Dei

1. Introduction 490
2. The Basic Structure of the Model 491
3. The World Transformation Curve 497
4. Concluding Remarks 503
Appendix: The World Transformation Curves with No MNCs or MNCs of One Type Only 504
References 505

VARIABLE RETURNS TO SCALE AND DYNAMIC ADJUSTMENTS: THE MARSHALL–LERNER CONDITION RECONSIDERED

T. Ide and A. Takayama

1. Introduction 507
2. Model 509
3. Stability of Temporary and Long-Run Equilibrium 512

4. Output Adjustment and Capital Adjustment Processes 516
5. Rehabilitation of the Marshallian Approach 517
6. A Shift in Tastes 524
7. The Transfer Problem 525
8. Some Further Discussions 532
Appendix A 533
Appendix B 535
References 539

TARIFF PROTECTION WITH IMPERFECT COMPETITION AND EXISTENCE OF THE GENERAL EQUILIBRIUM SOLUTION WITH INTRAINDUSTRY TRADE

Yasuo Uekawa

1. Introduction 541
2. Model 542
3. Existence of General Equilibrium Solution with Intraindustry Trade between Two Countries 543
4. Tariff and Individual Countries 548
5. Tariff and World Welfare 551
References 554

INTERNATIONAL TRANSFER IN DYNAMIC ECONOMIES

Makoto Yano

1. Introduction 555
2. Model 557
3. Comparative Dynamics and Statics: Main Theorems 561
4. Interpretation of the Theorems 565
5. Proof of Theorems 570
Appendix 579
References 581

Index 583
Previous Volumes in the Series 607

PREFACE

Lionel McKenzie is one of the most influential economic theorists of the post-war period. His research has been instrumental in the development of three of the most important fields of modern economics: general equilibrium, optimal growth, and international trade. To those (like ourselves) who have been lucky enough to meet him and learn in his classroom, Lionel McKenzie appears in many roles: as an influential scholar, as a superb teacher, and as the mentor who shaped the vision and the research interests of more than one generation of economic theorists. His dedication to students is matched only by his continuous enthusiasm for economic theory.

It is difficult to exaggerate the impact of his contributions on modern economics. Most of the progress in applied economic fields has been, from the fifties onward, grounded in the general equilibrium framework. This is particularly true in the areas of international trade, financial asset pricing, public finance, and macroeconomics. The latter, in particular, has flourished during the past twenty years by applying, enriching, and merging the methods and ideas of the theory of optimal growth and general equilibrium, a theme that has always been at the core of Lionel's interests. His continued focus on the reduced form optimal growth model supplied the framework for analyzing dynamic competitive economies underlying many of the new applications. This strong impact on applied fields is not coincidental: McKenzie's work was from its inception motivated by applied problems originating in international trade. The needs of applications remained central to motivating Lionel's research throughout his career as his students and colleagues saw so well in his classroom, through his writings, dissertation advising, and comments during workshops.

In 1988, together with a group of other colleagues and friends, we set out to organize a conference to celebrate Lionel McKenzie's seventieth birthday and his (fortunately only formal) retirement from active teaching duties. That he had no plans to quit being the active scholar we all knew was confirmed by a couple of new contributions to general equilibrium theory, only recently published in journals, that he circulated. The original organization of the conference did not include a plan to publish a festschrift volume because one had already been produced ten years before [Jerry Green and José Scheinkman (eds.), *General Equilibrium, Growth, and Trade*, Academic Press, 1979], and the quality of the contributions contained there set a standard that seemed hard to match.

The conference was held at the University of Rochester over a three-day period in May 1989. It proved to be a great success. Almost two hundred friends, colleagues, and students of Lionel came to town from the four corners of the earth to honor and celebrate the career of their friend and master. The days were spent debating a number of fascinating topics in economic theory, with the nights given over to some equally serious celebrations—Buz Brock's "tap dance" performance at the banquet honoring Blanche and Lionel being singled out as the most remarkable moment. Rochester also reminded us of its unique climate when five inches of snow fell on the last day of the meeting.

It was at this point that, not without some effort on his part, Karl Shell managed to convince the four of us that another volume, containing some of the best papers presented at that conference, would be a proper completion of our tribute to Lionel's lifetime achievements.

Thus the enterprise was undertaken in January of the following year and, in the wave-like form that characterizes these projects, it has kept us busy for the last three years—without any doubt a time much longer than we had ever planned or desired. We can only apologize for this delay, in particular to those contributors who always respected our deadlines and whose completed papers have been awaiting publication for nearly two years. We hope that the quality of the final product will be sufficient compensation for the patience of a few too many scholars.

Given the success of the first festschrift, we found it natural to follow the Green and Scheinkman model by organizing the book around the three areas of economic theory that characterize Lionel's research output. There are twenty-four articles in this volume: nine in the general equilibrium section, eight in the optimal growth section, and seven in the section dedicated to international trade. Twenty-four contributions is far too many for us to try to review here; we trust that the reader will be able to make a good selection even without our guidance.

While most of the papers originate from presentations given at the Rochester conference, for a variety of circumstances the correspondence between the two events is less than perfect. Some articles included here are from authors who were unable to attend the conference; there are no written contributions for a few lectures included in the conference program.

All in all we are quite happy with the outcome and, we hope, Lionel will also be pleased. Nevertheless, aware as we are that his academic wit has not diminished with age, we all look forward to his forthcoming comments and criticisms. We trust they will be no less sharp than those we all had the pleasure to experience during our past years of acquaintance—beautiful years of which we are still proud. It is with this pride that we submit this book to you, Professor McKenzie.

Robert Becker
Michele Boldrin
Ronald Jones
William Thomson

PART I

GENERAL EQUILIBRIUM

LIONEL McKENZIE ON THE EXISTENCE OF COMPETITIVE EQUILIBRIUM

M. Ali Khan
Department of Political Economy
The Johns Hopkins University
Baltimore, Maryland 21218

1. INTRODUCTION

Over a period spanning 35 years, Lionel McKenzie has published four papers on the question of the existence of competitive equilibrium in an economy with a finite number of agents and commodities. His first contribution was presented to the Econometric Society in 1952 and published in 1954, a year that also saw the publication of independent work on the same question by Arrow and Debreu (1954). The next two years were distinguished by a flurry of seminal activity; in addition to the independent work of Nikaido, there were papers from Gale and Kuhn, as well as further contributions from Debreu and McKenzie themselves. Since then the subject has mushroomed and Debreu's recent overview lists a bibliography of 356 items.[1]

In this expository paper we focus on McKenzie's four contributions to the subject and attempt to bring into somewhat bolder relief economic and mathematical ideas that were particularly original with him. Furthermore, by looking at all his contributions to this subject under one rubric and with a unified notation, we get a deeper understanding of the evolution of his ideas, and also gain insight into problems of current research interest, such as economies with increasing returns to scale, with an infinite number of commodities, and/or with a continuum of traders. It is of some interest that such connections can be made despite the fact that McKenzie himself

[1]See Debreu (1982).

GENERAL EQUILIBRIUM, GROWTH, AND TRADE II

never wrote on any of these topics. Finally, our examination also brings to light the powerful geometric emphasis in McKenzie's work. This leads us directly into mathematical subjects of current interest such as *nonsmooth analysis* and *approximation theory*.

The paper is organized into four basic sections, each section devoted to a particular paper of McKenzie. In each section we present the results, the basic ideas of the proofs, and the relation to subsequent work. We conclude with an overview.

2. EXISTENCE IN GRAHAM'S MODEL: 1954

We begin with some preliminary notation. Let $\mathbb{R}^l$ denote the l-dimensional Euclidean space. For any $x \in \mathbb{R}^l$, let x_i refer to the ith coordinate of x, $i = 1, \ldots, l$. For any $x, y \in \mathbb{R}^l$, $x \gg y$, $x > y$ and $x \geq y$ will have their usual meaning. e^i refers to a vector with one in the ith coordinate and zero everywhere else. We shall use S to refer to the $(l - 1)$-dimensional simplex, i.e., $S = \{x \in \mathbb{R}^l\colon \Sigma_{i=1}^l x_i = 1\}$. The positive orthant of $\mathbb{R}^l$ is denoted by $\mathbb{R}^l_+$. For any subset A of $\mathbb{R}^l$, A^o denotes the interior of A in $\mathbb{R}^l$, $\text{Int}_{\mathbb{R}^l_+} A$ the interior of A in $\mathbb{R}^l_+$, A^{ro} the relative interior of A in the sense of convex analysis,[2] cl(A) the closure of A, con A the convex hull of A, A^c the complement of A, $\text{Proj}_i A$ the projection of A onto the ith coordinate, and $\mathbb{R}^l_{++}$ the interior of $\mathbb{R}^l_+$. / denotes set-theoretic subtraction and $\prod_j$ the Cartesian product.

2.1 The Result

Definition 1. A Graham–McKenzie economy consists of a pair (f, Y) such that

1. $f\colon \mathbb{R}^l_{++} \to \mathbb{R}^l_+$ is positively homogeneous of degree zero, continuous on its domain and such that

(a) For any $p \in \mathbb{R}^l_{++}$, $pf(p) = \text{Max}_{y \in Y}\, py \equiv r(p)$.

(b) For any sequence $\{p^n\} \in \mathbb{R}^l_{++}$ with $p^n_i \to 0$, $f_i(p^n) \to \zeta_i$ where

$$\zeta_i = (1 + \text{Max}\,\text{Proj}_i\, Y).$$

2. $Y \subseteq \mathbb{R}^l_+$ is closed, bounded, and convex and $0 \in \text{Int}_{\mathbb{R}^l_+} Y$.

In words, a Graham–McKenzie economy consists of an aggregate demand function that is defined only at strictly positive prices and a production possibility set. From this production possibility set one can derive an aggregate income function r that can be defined at any price

[2]See Rockafellar (1970) for a precise definition.

level. Given the emphasis in the earlier part of the paper on an interpretation of the model as one pertaining to a world economy, and also the emphasis on specific demands and on the depiction of the technology in terms of linear activities, it is natural to ask how loyal I have been to McKenzie's own description. I can only refer the reader to Section 6 of his paper where an interpretation in terms of trade theory or activity analysis is explicitly avoided.

DEFINITION 2. A competitive equilibrium for a Graham–McKenzie economy consists of a pair $(p^*, y^*) \in S^o \times Y$ such that

1. $y^* \in \text{Argmax}_{y \in Y}\, p^* y$.
2. $f(p^*) = y^*$.

In words, a competitive equilibrium is a price system and an aggregate production plan such that this production plan is a profit maximizing plan at the given price system and is equal to aggregate demands evaluated at the same price system.

THEOREM 1. *There exists a competitive equilibrium for a Graham–McKenzie economy.*

2.2 The Proof

The proof is an application of the Kakutani fixed-point theorem to a mapping that takes the simplex S into itself. However, before going into the details of the proof, I refer you to Figure 1, which is reproduced from

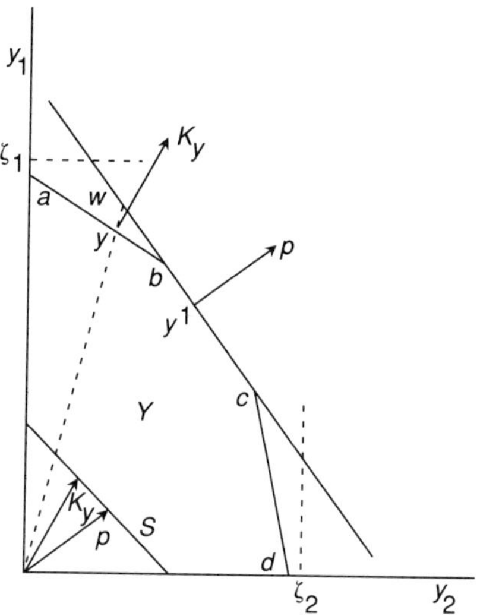

FIGURE 1

McKenzie and gives a transparent "bird's eye" view of the basic idea of the proof. I follow McKenzie's notation. Given the homogeneity of the functions $r(\cdot)$ and $f(\cdot)$, and the desirability assumption on $f(\cdot)$, in our search for an equilibrium price system, we may without any loss of generality confine ourselves to the interior of the simplex S. Start with any price p from S^o and compute the demands w and the income. If w is in the production possibility set, we have an equilibrium. If not, project the demand w onto the efficiency frontier to obtain the production plan y. Compute the efficiency price K_y and normalize it to lie in S. Note that at production plans such as b and c, the efficiency prices do not constitute a singleton set. When the normalized set of efficiency prices includes the price with which we began the procedure, we are done.

In more formal terms, we want to establish the existence of a fixed point of the mapping F, which is a composite of the following mappings.

1. The *extended demand mapping* f^* that takes the simplex S into the cube $\Xi = \{x \in \mathbb{R}^l_+ : x_i \leq \zeta_i, \ i = 1, \ldots, l\}$ and is given by $p \to f^*(p)$, where

$$f_i^*(p) = \begin{cases} f_i(p) & \text{if } f_i(p) \leq \zeta_i \text{ with } p \in S^o \\ \zeta_i & \text{if } f_i(p) > \zeta_i \text{ or } p_i = 0. \end{cases}$$

2. The *intersection mapping* h that takes $\Xi/\text{Int}_{\mathbb{R}^l_+} Y$ into the efficiency frontier ∂Y of Y and is given by $w \to h(w) = \{\alpha w \in Y : \alpha \leq 1, \ k > \alpha \Rightarrow kw \notin Y\}$.

3. The *efficiency price mapping* g that takes the efficiency frontier ∂Y into the simplex S and is given by $y \to g(y) = \{p \in S : py \geq py' \forall y' \in Y\}$.

Let $F = g \circ h \circ f^*$. In order to apply Kakutani's theorem, we need only verify that F is a nonempty, upper hemicontinuous, convex valued mapping that takes the nonempty, compact, convex set S into itself.

Now let us suppose that p^* is such a fixed point of F. We have to show that $(p^*, f(p^*))$ is a competitive equilibrium. Let $y^* = h(f^*(p^*))$. The first point to be noted is that the definition of the intersection mapping yields $y^* \in Y$. This implies, given the definition of the efficiency price mapping g, that

$$p^* y^* = \text{Max}_{y \in Y} \, p^* y = r(p^*). \tag{1}$$

By the assumption explicit in the definition of the demand mapping f that all income is spent, and by the construction of the extended demand mapping f^*, we have

$$p^* f^*(p^*) \leq p^* f(p^*) = r(p^*) = p^* y^*. \tag{2}$$

However, by definition of the intersection mapping h, we have

$$y^* = \alpha f^*(p^*), \text{ which implies } p^* y^* = \alpha p^* f^*(p^*). \tag{3}$$

On putting (2) and (3) together, we obtain the fact that

$$\alpha = 1, \text{ which implies } y^* = f^*(p^*). \tag{4}$$

All that remains to be shown is that $p^* \in S^o$. But this is a direct consequence of (4) and the construction of the extended demand mapping.

In terms of the economics, the first point to be noted is that the centerpiece on which the proof hangs is the sustaining of efficient production plans as profit maximizing plans. McKenzie himself understands this very clearly. He writes[3]

> Gerard Debreu and Kenneth Arrow have been working, independently, along similar lines. Their method seems closely related to the theory of competitive games developed by John Nash, while my motivation comes directly from the work of Abraham Wald and Tjalling Koopmans. The essential idea of the present proof is the conjunction of a fixed point theorem and the notion, familiar in activity analysis, of an efficiency frontier to the convex set of attainable outputs.

Two other ideas are noteworthy. The first is the explicit recognition of problems relating to continuity of demands when the price of a commodity goes to zero. The second is the resolution of this difficulty by the interiority assumption on the production possibility set and the consequent uniform boundedness away from zero of the aggregate income function.

We shall have more to say on all of this as we proceed. Let us now turn to the mathematics in the proof. The fact that S is a nonempty, convex, compact subset of $\mathbb{R}^l$ is straightforward. The continuity of the extended demand mapping is not difficult under the given assumptions once its construction is conceived. McKenzie himself dismisses it as[4] "a technical point in the proof." The motivation for the intersection mapping is purely geometric once the insight of the proof is in place and the proof of its continuity, along with that of the income function $r(\cdot)$, is relegated by McKenzie to an appendix. In this appendix, both results are established as a consequence of an interesting lemma that deserves to be made explicit.

LEMMA 1. *Any real-valued function H on a finite-dimensional vector space*[5] *is continuous if it is positively homogeneous of degree zero and superadditive, i.e.,* $H(x+y) \geq H(x) + H(y)$.

Proof. See McKenzie (1954; page 160); the original proof is ascribed to Bateman (1951). ∎

[3]See footnote 2 in McKenzie (1954).

[4]Last paragraph on page 155 in McKenzie (1954).

[5]Also assumed to be endowed with its natural topology.

The application of this lemma to the continuity of $r(\cdot)$ is a straightforward consequence of the properties of the max operator;[6] the argument pertaining to that of $h(\cdot)$ is a little more subtle. Rewrite this mapping as

$$h(w) \equiv w\phi(w) \equiv w\,\mathrm{Sup}_{\{\lambda \in \mathbb{R}:\ \lambda w \in Y\}}\,\lambda \equiv w\,\mathrm{Sup}_{F(w,Y)}\,\lambda,$$

and observe that the continuity of $h(\cdot)$ hinges on the continuity of $\phi(\cdot)$. Fans of Berge's (1963) theorem will have a natural inclination to reduce the question to that of the lower hemicontinuity of the correspondence $F(\cdot, Y)$, and readers raised on Debreu's (1959) proof of the lower hemicontinuity of the budget set will look for an interior point in $F(w, Y)$ to finish the argument. McKenzie's route is different; he observes that (i) $\phi(\cdot)$ is positively homogeneous of degree one, (ii) for any $w \in \Xi/\mathrm{Int}_{\mathbb{R}^l_+} Y$, $\phi(w) > 0$, and (iii) for any $w \in Y$, $\phi(w) \geq 1$. Only (ii) is not trivial; it uses the relative interiority of 0 in an essential way. Now for any two points w, w' in $\Xi/\mathrm{Int}_{\mathbb{R}^l_+} Y$, $w\phi(w)$ and $w'\phi(w')$ are in Y. By (ii) and the convexity of Y, we obtain

$$\left[\frac{\phi(w)}{\phi(w)+\phi(w')} w\phi(w) + \frac{\phi(w')}{\phi(w)+\phi(w')} w'\phi(w')\right] \in Y.$$

On appealing to (iii) and then to (i), we establish the superadditivity of $\phi(\cdot)$ and complete the proof. Figures 2a and 2b show the importance to the argument of the interiority and convexity assumptions on Y.

It is, however, the efficiency price mapping g that is the most interesting. McKenzie appeals to the convexity of Y and the separating hyperplane theorem to establish the nonemptiness of this mapping. The fact that it is closed and convex valued is established in the text while the fact that it is upper hemicontinuous constitutes the only lemma in the paper. I stress all the properties of the efficiency price mapping because I want to emphasize that these properties were studied later by convexity theorists as properties of the normal cone to a convex set at a particular point.[7] It is interesting that it finally took Clarke, a mathematician, to generalize the properties of the efficiency price mapping to the nonconvex case and in so doing, to pioneer the subject of *nonsmooth analysis*.[8] Indeed, the following notions and results were to follow.

Definition 3. Let $Y \subseteq \mathbb{R}^l$ and $y \in Y$. Then the tangent cone $T_Y(y)$ in the sense of Clarke is given by the set $\{x \in \mathbb{R}^l\colon \forall t^k \downarrow 0, \forall y^k \to y\ \exists x^k \to x$ such that $y^k + t^k x^k \in Y\}$. The normal cone $N_Y(y)$ in the sense

[6]Terminologically inclined readers will also find amusing McKenzie's reference to *support functions* as *tac-functions*; see footnote 22 in McKenzie (1954). Bateman (1951) has a section on *tac-functions*.

[7]See, for example, Chapter 23 in Rockafellar (1970). It is interesting in this connection that McKenzie apparently does not have access to Fenchel's (1953) notes but refers instead to those of Bateman (1951).

[8]See Clarke (1975, 1983).

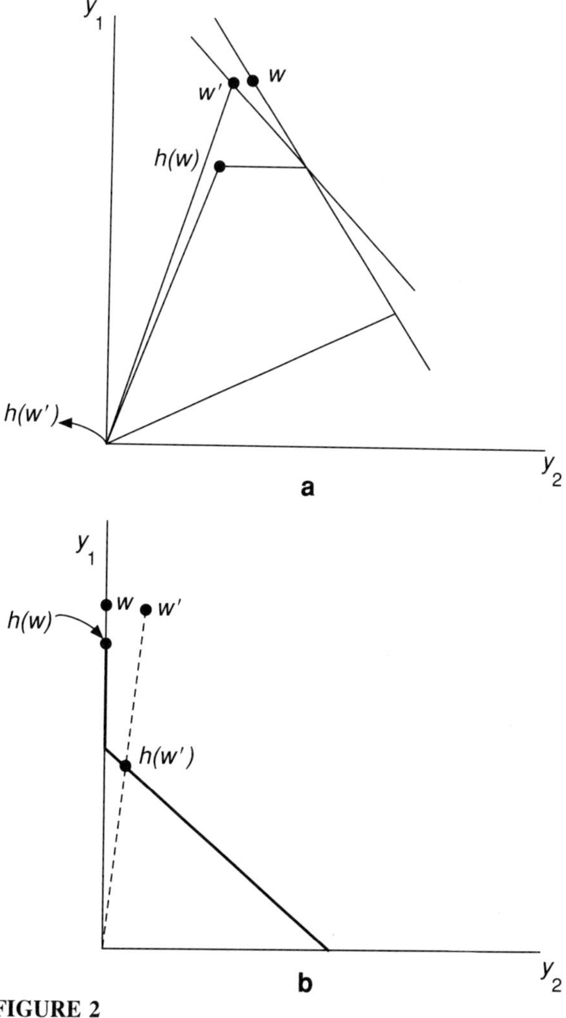

FIGURE 2

of Clarke[9] is given by the polar of the tangent set, i.e., $\{x \in \mathbb{R}^l\colon px \leq 0 \ \forall x \in T_Y(y)\}$.

THEOREM 2 (*Clarke–Rockafellar*[10])

(*i*) *$y \in Y^o$ if and only if $N_Y(y) = 0$ or equivalently $T_Y(y) = \mathbb{R}^l$. Thus Y has at least one nonzero normal vector at each of its boundary points.*

[9] For an expository treatment of how this concept formalizes marginal rates of substitution, see, for example, Khan and Vohra (1987a).

[10] For the proofs of (i)–(iii), see Rockafellar (1979); and for the proofs of (iv)–(v), see Proposition 3.3 in Clarke (1975). The statement of Theorem 2 itself has been reproduced from Brown et al. (1986).

(ii) $T_Y(y)$ *is nonempty and convex.*

(iii) Let $y \in Y$ *be such that* $(T_Y(y))^o \neq \emptyset$, *i.e.,* $N_Y(y)$ *is pointed in the sense that* $N_Y(y) \cap (-N_Y(y)) = \{0\}$. *Then the correspondence* $N_Y(\cdot)$ *has a closed graph.*

(iv) Let Y be a C^1 *manifold. Then* $N_Y(y)$ *coincides with the usual space of normals at y.*

(v) Let Y be convex. Then $N_Y(y) = \bigcup_{\lambda \geq 0} \lambda(Y - \{y\})$, *i.e., it coincides with the cone of normals at y in the sense of convex analysis.*

The point I make, of course, is that $N_Y(\cdot)$ is none other than McKenzie's mapping $g(\cdot)$ and that it arises naturally in his proof.

2.3 Influence on Subsequent Work

The freshness and modernity of the 1954 paper is evident when one looks at recent work on the existence of marginal cost pricing equilibria in economies with increasing returns to scale.[11] This is, of course, not surprising in view of McKenzie's own emphasis on production. However, the fact that that road was already so clearly and systematically laid out may be a source of surprise. I shall illustrate my point by using two papers, that of Beato (1982) and that of Vohra (1988). The former was the first of several subsequent papers, while the latter represents, along with contemporaneous work of others, a more or less finished state of the subject.[12]

Let me recall informally the definition of a marginal cost pricing equilibrium. It represents a price system and consumption and production plans such that (i) the prices are the marginal cost prices at the production plans of each of the nonconvex technologies, (ii) the production plans of the convex technologies are profit maximizing at the given price system, (iii) the consumption plans are utility maximizing at the given price system, and (iv) the aggregate excess demands of the convex sector equal the quantities at which the nonconvex production subsector is regulated.

Beato (1982) formulates[13] this equilibrium notion and proves its existence; first in the case when the efficiency frontiers of the individual production sets are differentiable and subsequently to the case when they are not. In both cases, Beato confines herself to a setting where demands are single-valued continuous functions of strictly positive prices. I shall not go into the details of her proof other than to refer you to Figure 3, which is reproduced from her paper.[14] The essential difference from McKenzie's

[11]See Cornet's (1988) introduction to the *Symposium on Increasing Returns* for an overview and detailed references.

[12]See the references in Cornet (1988).

[13]Also see Beato (1979) and Mantel (1979).

[14]Similar diagrams occur in Brown and Heal (1982) and Mantel (1979).

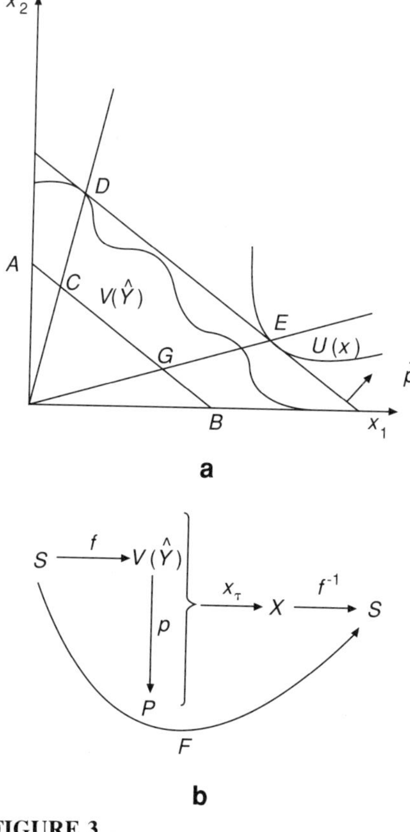

FIGURE 3

Figure 1 is the nonconvex (but smooth-frontiered) production possibility set and this is handled by a homeomorphism between the frontier and the simplex. We may point out here that the arguments[15] establishing the existence of this homeomorphism bear more than a superficial resemblance to those establishing the continuity of the intersection mapping—indeed, Figures 2a and 2b are relevant to both issues.[16] Next, note that it is the nondifferentiable case that is the source of the difficulty in McKenzie's proof. It is precisely the presence of "kinks" in the production possibility set that causes the mapping F to lose its single-

[15]For these, also see Chipman and Moore (1968), Moore (1975), and the relevant sections in the papers in Cornet (1988).

[16]Figures 3 and 4 in Chipman and Moore (1968) are particularly noteworthy in this connection.

valuedness; this necessitates the use of Kakutani's fixed-point theorem rather than that of Brouwer; a point of some interest in view of subsequent work of McKenzie's.

In the nonconvex setting of Beato, nondifferentiability forces one to confront the question of how marginal cost prices should be defined. Beato does this by adopting the Dubovickii–Milyutin *cone of interior displacement*,[17] which is simply a fancier way of asking one to take *normals* to the local approximation to the production possibility set at the given production plan. This works when the approximation is a convex set, and Beato, in keeping with earlier work of Guesnerie (1974), simply assumes this. Subsequent work uses the normal cone of Clarke, already referred to above, and dispenses with this assumption. The point, however, is clear. Whatever notion of marginal cost prices one chooses, it has to satisfy all the properties which McKenzie verified for his efficiency price mapping (and Clarke and Rockafellar for the Clarke normal cone).

This fact is explicitly brought out in Vohra's (1988) paper. He proves the existence of equilibria in an economy with several nonconvex technologies Y^j under five assumptions, two of which are particularly noteworthy. The first can be stated formally:[18] *For all* $j, \mu_j\colon\ S \times \prod_j \partial(Y_j) \to S$ *is nonempty, convex-valued, and upper hemicontinuous*. Vohra refers[19] to μ_j as "a pricing rule for firm j," emphasizes that "in many cases μ_j will actually depend only on y_j," and interprets his assumption as one which requires "that the pricing rule for each firm is well behaved."

Vohra's second assumption that is of interest from the point of view of this paper relates the size of the attainable production possibility sets, the production sets themselves, and the pricing rules to the sign of the income mappings, r_i, one for each consumer i, and now taking $S \times \prod_j Y_j$ to $\mathbb{R}$. I shall not go into the details of this assumption other than to point out that McKenzie's assumptions on incomes and the size of the production possibility set, as reflected in the parameters ζ_i, are a precursor to this assumption in a sense that is hardly superficial. Such parallels can also be drawn with reference to the other papers in Cornet (1988).

So far, we have confined our discussion to work on the existence question in economies with increasing returns to scale. I would now like to discuss the extended demand mapping in light of Schmeidler's (1969) proof of the existence of competitive equilibrium in economies with a continuum of agents. Schmeidler limited himself to an exchange economy, but the way he handles the question of the unboundedness of the consumption set, and consequent lack of continuity (upper hemicontinuity in his case) of demands at the point where prices become zero, is of interest.

[17]See Guesnerie (1975) and Khan and Vohra (1987a) for exposition and further references.
[18]Recall that $\partial(Y_j)$ denotes the efficiency frontier of Y_j.
[19]See page 181 in Vohra (1988).

Schmeidler truncates the consumption set to a cube whose size depends on the aggregate (integral) of the initial endowments. An extended demand mapping is defined that equals the original demands if they lie inside the truncated set, but equal to the truncation levels if they do not or if any price is zero. Upper hemicontinuity is preserved. Monotonicity of preferences guarantees that truncations can be made so that truncated demands are infeasible and this fact is used to show that no price system can lie in the boundary of the simplex. But in this case the entire budget set lies inside the truncated consumption set and the extended demands are identical to the original demands. There are a lot of points of contact of this argument with that used by McKenzie; zero prices for any commodity are excluded in equilibrium; initial endowments take the place of maximum possible production; global monotonicity takes the place of McKenzie's desirability assumption on demands as prices tend to zero. All of this is, of course, not surprising—Schmeidler was following Aumann (1966), a paper on which we shall have more to say in the exposition below.

The assumption that aggregate demands tend to infinity as prices tend to the boundary of the simplex is made explicit in Debreu's (1970) paper. Debreu does present an existence theorem based on this assumption, but his primary concern is, of course, totally different.[20] In this connection, I would like to remind the reader that McKenzie is also concerned with sufficient conditions for the uniqueness of competitive equilibrium, but that topic is outside the scope of my review.

I would like to close this subsection by drawing attention to the assumption of Y having zero as an interior point. This assumption has already been made by Debreu (1954) in another context—in some form or another, it continues to be emphasized,[21] and it will play a prominent role in the sequel. It is interesting that McKenzie himself justifies this assumption, as did Debreu, by the presence of free disposal.[22]

2.4 A Second Look

In this subsection, I would like to take a second look at the proof, especially with a view toward assumptions that seem essential to the argument but without going into aspects that come later.

The first surely pertains to the assumption of single-valued demands. Once this is violated, we would have a set, each of whose elements would have to be projected to the efficiency frontier. An extension of the

[20]It is worth stating in this context that Debreu (1974) sights McKenzie (1954) as an antecedent of Dierker (1974).

[21]In terms of more recent work, see, for example, Jones (1987) and Khan and Peck (1989).

[22]See the last sentence of the Appendix in McKenzie (1954). Note that for the treatment above, free disposal is stronger than necessary.

efficiency price mapping to one that takes the efficiency prices at all of these production plans into account would fail on account of a union of convex sets not necessarily being convex. An alternative would be to break the mapping F into two parts, neither of which is single-valued, and map a product space of prices *and* quantities into itself. This procedure has been followed in Vohra's (1983) work and undoubtedly in those of others,[23] but it goes against the spirit of McKenzie's mappings, which typically take a set in the price space to itself.

Next, we turn to the assumption of a single production possibility set. If we had several convex technologies, the most obvious procedure would be to work with the aggregate and then appeal to the elementary fact that corresponding to an aggregate profit maximizing production plan, there exist individual production plans, also profit maximizing at the same prices, which sum to the aggregate plan. However, if we have several firms, some of which are not convex, the argument can be salvaged by an additional map of the Nash (1950) variety that brings these various efficiency prices into line with each other.[24]

2.5 Miscellany

I would like to conclude this section with two further quotations. The first pertains to an open problem that was solved by Uzawa (1962) but on which research persists:[25]

> I should conjecture that elementary proofs do not exist of [the] theorem unless the demand functions are drastically restricted.[26]

The second pertains to a question to which McKenzie returns later—that of the continuity of demands.

> It is impossible that the demand functions should be continuous at a . . . zero price for some final outputs and . . . for a primary good, if some consumers depend entirely on this primary good for income, while they do consume some of the free goods. Since these consumers have no income at p, their demand for a free good will be entirely cut off at any positive price, however small.[27]

In this context, the following quotation from Arrow is also of interest.

> Debreu and I sent our manuscripts to each other and so discovered our common purpose. We also detected the same flaw in each other's work; we had ignored the possibility of discontinuity when prices vary in such a way that some consumers' incomes approach zero.[28]

[23]See Cornet (1988). Of course, one has to limit oneself to proofs of existence using the efficiency price mapping.

[24]See Beato and Mas-Colell (1985) and Khan and Vohra (1988) for this kind of argument.

[25]See Gwinner (1981) and references cited therein.

[26]See last line on page 155 in McKenzie (1954).

[27]Last paragraph on page 159 in McKenzie (1954).

[28]See prefatory note to Chapter IV in Arrow (1983).

3. EXISTENCE WITH EXTERNALITIES: A YEAR LATER

McKenzie's (1955) paper departs from his earlier piece in three essential ways; there is disaggregation on the demand side, general externalities are introduced, and all of $\mathbb{R}^l$ is utilized rather than only the nonnegative orthant.

3.1 The Results

DEFINITION 4. An economy with externalities consists of a pair $((X^i, f^i)_{i=1}^m, A)(\equiv ((\chi, f), A))$ such that

1. For all consumers i, $X^i \subseteq \mathbb{R}^l$ is nonempty, convex, closed, and bounded from below and with $X \equiv \sum_{i=1}^m X^i$.

2. A is an $(l \times d)$-matrix and $Y \equiv \{y = A\delta\colon\ \delta \in \mathbb{R}_+^d\} \subseteq \mathbb{R}^l$ is such that (i) $\exists \bar{x} \in Y^o \cap X$, (ii) $Y \cap \mathbb{R}_+^l = \{0\}$, (iii) $Y \cap (-Y) = \{0\}$.

3. For all i, $f^i\colon S \to \mathbb{R}^l$ is continuous on its domain and such that for any[29] $z \in S$, $z_p f^i(z) \leq 0$ with equality if $f_k^i(z) \leq \xi_k$, where

$$\xi_k = \left(1 + \text{Max Proj}_k\left(X^j \cap \left(Y - \sum_{i \neq j} X^i\right)\right)\right),$$

$$S = \left(P \times \chi \times \mathbb{R}_+^d\right) \cap \left(P \times \left\{((x^i), \delta) \in \left(\chi \times \mathbb{R}_+^d\right)\colon \sum_{i=1}^m x^i = A\delta\right\}\right),$$

$$P \equiv \left\{p \in \mathbb{R}^l\colon py \leq 0,\ y \in Y, \text{ and } p\bar{x} = -1\right\}.$$

It is interesting to contrast an economy with externalities with a Graham–McKenzie economy. The aggregate demand function of the latter is replaced by m consumption sets and m demand functions, each defined on prices that are not necessarily nonnegative and on an "attainable set" derived from the consumption sets and the technology. The nonsatiation assumption on aggregate demands at zero prices is replaced by a similar assumption with ξ_i taking the place of ζ_i. Furthermore, there is now an explicit depiction of the technology in terms of linear activities. For later reference, we shall say that an economy is *strongly viable* if Condition 2(i) holds.

[29]For any $z \in S$, let z_p and z_δ denote the projections on P and $\mathbb{R}_+^d$, respectively.

DEFINITION 5. A competitive equilibrium for an economy with externalities consists of a triple $(p^*, x^*, \delta^*) \in P \times \chi \times \mathbb{R}^d_+$ such that

1. For all consumers i, $x^{*i} = f^i(p^*, x^*, \delta^*)$,
2. $\sum_{i=1}^m f^i(p^*, x^*, \delta^*) = A\delta^*$.

In words, a competitive equilibrium is a price system, m consumption plans and d activity levels such that aggregate production at these activity levels equals aggregate demands and each individual demand is evaluated at the price system, at the demands of the other consumers, and at the activity levels. What is striking about this definition is the apparent absence of any maximizing hypotheses. Of course, they are built into the definition of the demand functions and, on the production side, into the fact that the prices are being chosen from the polar cone of Y.

THEOREM 3. *There exists a competitive equilibrium for an economy with externalities.*

Next, we present a modification of this result.

DEFINITION 6. A McKenzie economy is an economy with externalities but in which the continuity condition on the demands f^i in Condition 3 in Definition 4 is replaced by

f^i is continuous at a point z in its domain if $\exists \bar{x}^i \in X^i$ such that $z_p \bar{x}^i < 0$.

DEFINITION 7. A McKenzie economy is said to satisfy the survival assumption if for all consumers i, $X^i \cap Y \neq \varnothing$. It is said to be productive if for all consumers i, $\exists \tilde{x}^i \in (X^i \cap Y)$, $\exists \delta > 0$, $\exists k \in G \cup D$ such that $(\tilde{x}^i - \delta e_k) \in (X^i \cap Y)$, where

$$D = \{k \in (1, \cdots, l) \colon \forall p \in P,\ p_k \leq 0 \Rightarrow \xi^i_k > \xi_k \text{ for all } i\}$$

$$G = \{k \in (1, \cdots, l) \colon \forall y \in Y\ \exists y' \in Y \text{ such that } y' \lhd_k y\}$$

$$y' \lhd_k y \quad \text{if} \begin{cases} y'_k < y_k & \\ y'_i > y_i & \text{for some } i \in D \\ y'_i = y_i & \text{all other indices.} \end{cases}$$

In words, *productivity* demands that each consumer possesses some desirable commodities, i.e., those commodities whose indices are in D, or commodities that can be used to produce desirable commodities, i.e., those whose indices are in G. Note that this is an assumption[30] on both the preferences as well as on the technology.

[30]McKenzie ascribes this assumption to Arrow and Debreu (1954). It is also reminiscent of Malinvaud's (1953) *non-tightness* assumption on technology.

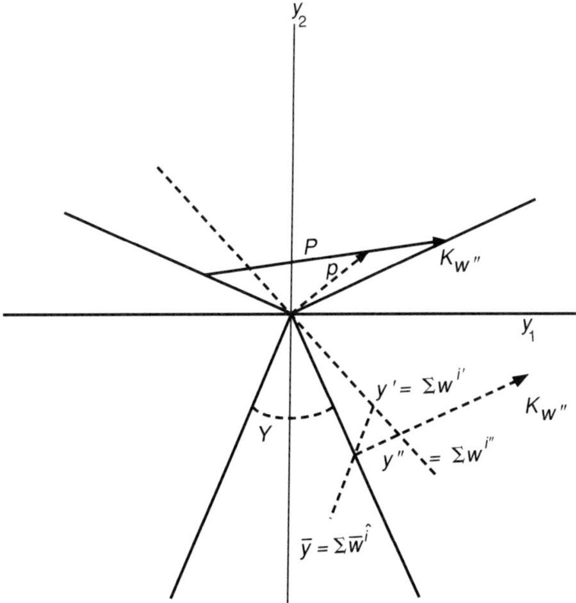

FIGURE 4 The mapping F is represented here without the explicit mention of the set X.

On defining a competitive equilibrium for a McKenzie economy exactly as in Definition 4, we can now present the following.

THEOREM 4. *There exists a competitive equilibrium for a McKenzie economy if it is productive and satisfies the survival assumption.*

3.2 The Proofs

We begin with Theorem 3. However, before going into the details of the proof, I refer you to Figure 4, which is reproduced from McKenzie[31] and gives, rather than an overall view, an important part of the "action." Start with any point z from the set S and note that it is a tuple of prices, consumption plans, and activity levels. Compute the demands x^i and the aggregate demand x and note the activity levels δ for future reference. Project x onto the efficiency frontier by utilizing the interior point $\bar{x}$ to obtain the production plan y. Compute the efficiency prices K_y and normalize them to lie in P. The final values of the mapping consist of these prices along with the tuple of demands and activity levels that we did not use for the range of the inverse supply mapping. Since this tuple was

[31]There is a slight change of notation in that demands are now indicated by x rather than by w.

part of a vector chosen from S, the final values also belong to S. When these final values include the point z with which we began the procedure, we are done. Note that, as in Section 2, the efficiency prices do not constitute a singleton set at "kinks." However, these can no longer be shown in a two-dimensional diagram. Note also that, unlike Section 2, we now have a mapping from the Cartesian product of several sets to itself, something that is natural given the interdependence in the actions of the various agents.

More formally, the proof is an application of the Kakutani fixed-point theorem applied to a mapping F that takes S into itself and is a composite of the following mappings.

1. The *modified demand mapping* $\hat{f}$ that takes S into $(X \times \chi \times \mathbb{R}^d_+)$ and is given by $z \to (\Sigma_i f^i(z), f(z), z_\delta)$.
2. The *inverse supply mapping* s that takes X into P and is given by $x \to s(x) = g(h(x))$, where

$$h\colon X \to Y,\ x \to h(x)$$
$$= \{(\bar{x} + \alpha(x - \bar{x})) \in Y\colon k > \alpha \Rightarrow (\bar{x} + k(x - \bar{x}) \notin Y\},$$

$g\colon Y \to P$, the efficiency price mapping of Section 2 but normalized in a different way.

3. The *identity mapping* i that takes $\chi \times \mathbb{R}^l_+$ into itself.

Let $F = (s \circ \hat{f}, i)$. In order to apply Kakutani's theorem, we need only verify that F takes S into itself, that it is upper hemicontinuous and convex-valued, and that its domain is a nonempty, compact, convex set.

Let us suppose, to begin with, that (p^*, x^*, δ^*) is such a fixed point of F. Let $y^* = A\delta^*$. All that needs to be shown is that $y^* = x^*$. This follows from the mapping h if we can show that α in $h(x^*)$ equals unity. But this is easy. Given that Y is a cone, by the definition of the efficiency mapping, $p^* y^* = 0$. This implies

$$0 = p^*(\bar{x}(1 - \alpha) + \alpha x^*)$$
$$= (1 - \alpha)p^*\bar{x} + \alpha p^* x^*.$$

By (3) in Definition 3, p^*x^* is zero and by definition of P, $p^*\bar{x} = -1$. Hence $\alpha = 1$.

In view of the work discussed in Section 2, all that remains is the compactness of S and the nonemptiness and upper semicontinuity of s. For the latter, McKenzie simply observes that[32] "it is provided by the fact

[32]See page 136 in McKenzie (1955).

that Y has an interior point." As regards the former, for later reference we can isolate the following lemma.

LEMMA 2. *If $\bar{x} \in Y^o$, P is compact.*

The compactness of S now hinges crucially on the boundedness of the production plans within the attainable set. We can extract the following lemma, which swiftly became part of the standard results in the subject.[33]

LEMMA 3. *If Y is a nonempty, closed, convex set that contains 0 and is such that $Y \cap \mathbb{R}^l_+ = \{0\}$, then a subset of Y that is bounded from below is also bounded from above.*

Proof.[34] If not, we can find a sequence in this subset whose positive coordinates increase without bound. Normalize this sequence so that each of its elements has unit length. Given inaction and convexity, this normalized sequence belongs to Y. Given that we work in $\mathbb{R}^l$, this sequence has a convergent subsequence. Since Y is closed, this limit is in Y. But, given the assumption of boundedness from below, we have produced something from nothing. ■

In terms of the economics, the first point to be noted is that problems relating to continuity of demands are brought to the fore. A section is devoted to the issue and the difficulty clearly brought out. I quote:[35]

> To convince oneself of the need for some such assumption, consider a price vector which leaves the ith consumer with no commodities having a positive price, which he can supply, but enough free goods to allow him to subsist. Neighboring price vectors may exist in P with some of these commodities having positive prices. The ith consumer will have to cease consuming such commodities abruptly, if his resources continue to be free. But this is quite possible.

It is this concern with continuity problems that is the motivation behind Theorem 4. McKenzie deduces it from Theorem 3. It is clear that Theorem 4 follows as a direct corollary of Theorem 3 if

$$X^i \cap Y^o \neq \emptyset \text{ for all consumers } i, \tag{5}$$

but "this is very restrictive [because it] requires [every] consumer [to] have a positive supply of every unproduced commodity."[36] We shall refer to (5) as the *strong survival* assumption. The reader should note the difference between *survival*, *strong survival*, and *strongly viable*.

[33] See, for example, the footnote on page 106 in Hahn and Matthews (1965).

[34] This is an almost symbol-free rendering of the argument on page 133 in McKenzie (1955). Note the importance of convexity in the proof; a generalization to the nonconvex case is available in Hurwicz and Reiter (1973).

[35] See the footnote on page 287 in McKenzie (1955). Also footnote 18 above.

[36] See the footnote on page 288 in McKenzie (1955).

The proof of Theorem 4 then proceeds in the following steps.

1. Embed Y in a set Y^t, t a positive integer, such that $Y^t \to Y$ as $t \to \infty$ and the resulting economy $\mathscr{E}^t$ satisfies *strong survival* and all the other conditions in the definition of an economy with externalities. Given the *survival* assumption and that Y has an interior, this can be done.

2. Observe that Theorem 3 guarantees an equilibrium $(p^*(t), x^*(t), \delta^*(t))$ for $\mathscr{E}^t$. Since the sequence of equilibria are in S, a subsequence will have a limit, say, (p^*, x^*, δ^*).

3. We can check that $p^* \in P$ and hence the profit maximizing condition is satisfied. All that remains to be checked is that the other conditions for this limit to be a competitive equilibrium are satisfied.

Toward this end, observe that *productivity* implies that

$$p_k^* > 0 \text{ for all } k \in D \Rightarrow p_h^* > 0 \text{ for all } h \in G. \tag{6}$$

Since $X \cap Y^o \neq \emptyset \Rightarrow \exists$ a consumer i and $\bar{x}^i \in X^i \cap Y^o$, we obtain that $p^*\bar{x}^i < 0$. Hence f^i is continuous at z^*. This implies that $f^i(z^*) \leq \xi$; otherwise we contradict $f^i(z^{*t}) \leq \xi$ for sufficiently large t. Since $D \neq \emptyset$, there exists a commodity k such that $p_k^* > 0$. By (6), this implies that $p_h^* > 0$ for all $h \in G$. We can now appeal again to *productivity* to assert that for all consumers $i, p^*\tilde{x}^i < 0$. But this gives us continuity of $f^i(\cdot)$ at z^* for all i and the proof can be routinely completed.

3.3 Subsequent Work

It is of interest that in their paper on the existence of competitive equilibrium, Arrow and Debreu (1954) did not use the full power of Debreu's (1952) theorem on the existence of Cournot–Nash equilibria. It was left to McKenzie (1955) to study externalities but present an existence proof that was not explicitly patterned on the game-theoretic result. Debreu's result in this context was used by Shafer and Sonnenschein (1975), who also allowed for price-dependent preferences but without the dependence of consumer actions on those of the producers, as in McKenzie (1955). Shafer and Sonnenschein's treatment of externalities has been extended to infinite commodities and to economies with a continuum of traders.[37] This research continues.

McKenzie works with demand functions and thus it is difficult to disentangle the price effects on preferences. He does discuss preference relations in the last section of the paper but these are not explicitly assumed to be interdependent and are defined on each consumer's own

[37]See, in particular, Yannelis and Prabhakar (1983), Khan (1984), Toussaint (1984), and Tulcea (1988) for the former and Khan and Vohra (1984) and Yannelis (1987) for the latter. The fact that all of this work deals with nonordered preferences need not concern us here.

consumption set. In any case, the full power of Arrow's insight[38] on the creation of artificial markets in coping with externalities, and in particular, public goods, was to be realized 12 years later by Foley (1967, 1970). Starrett's (1972) observation that externalities introduce nonconvexities was to follow a year later.

The work stemming from Scarf (1973) also belongs in this section. In this literature, the specification of an economy is along the lines of a McKenzie economy without externalities, with the technology formalized as a set of linear activities and with demand functions.

Finally, it is tempting to trace the influence of the line of proof, in particular, the composed mappings on McKenzie's own subsequent work in capital theory. This is a temptation that we shall resist.[39]

3.4 Miscellany

In our discussion of the 1954 paper, we emphasized the assumptions of single valued demands and that of the single production possibility set. In the 1955 paper, McKenzie considers the former and writes[40]

> It is possible to allow for set valued demand functions which are upper semicontinuous, but the proof is somewhat complicated thereby, and a more powerful fixed point theorem has to be used.

This is an interesting statement in view of McKenzie's later work, which utilized a simpler fixed point theorem in a setting with demand correspondences.[41]

Regarding the formalization of technology, we also get an explicit defense of the constant returns to scale assumption. The following statement[42] deserves to be quoted in full. Over time, this will emerge to be the key difference between an Arrow-Debreu economy and a McKenzie economy.[43]

> Arrow and Debreu assume each firm to have available a convex set of possible input-output vectors, including the origin. The entrepreneurial resources can be treated as always sold by their owners to the firms where each firm can dispose of them without cost if necessary. The convex set of possible input-output vectors then becomes a cone in a space which includes a dimension for each firm's entrepreneurial resources. The fact that a firm has to use its entire batch of entrepreneurial resources, no more and no less, and the batch may, indeed, be

[38]See Arrow (1969).

[39]But see McKenzie (1986; last paragraph on page 1302).

[40]See the footnote on page 290 in McKenzie (1955).

[41]In his comment on the first draft of this paper, McKenzie writes in this context, "In any case when Arrow said he didn't see how and I tried to prove it I did not succeed (using the projection method and trying to show that $g(h(f(p)))$ is a retractible set."

[42]See the footnote on page 278 in McKenzie (1955).

[43]See McKenzie (1987).

indivisible, does not interfere with the proof. Of course, if the batches could be broken up and reorganized, the problem might be greatly complicated.

I cannot help observing that decreasing returns to scale are accommodated in the Ricardo-Viner model of trade theory precisely in this way by introducing a nonshiftable factor of production.[44]

4. INTERIORITY, IRREDUCIBILITY, AND IRREVERSIBILITY: FOUR YEARS LATER

McKenzie introduces his 1959 paper in the following words.

The postulates are weaker in three ways:

(i)... there are no restrictions on the dimensionality of the production and consumer sets. In earlier papers,... the production set was directly assumed to have an interior point or else free disposal... was assumed, which implies the interior point. (ii)... the assumption that there are always desired goods and always productive goods is replaced by the assumption that the economy is irreducible. (iii)... production processes may be reversible. The argument uses the most elementary of the fixed point theorems. As in my [1955] paper, I first [assume] constant returns to scale of production and then show that the general case can be handled through an appropriate introduction of entrepreneurial factors. Again as in [the 1955 paper], I do not define a utility function but proceed directly from the preference ordering.[45]

McKenzie departs from his own earlier (1955) piece in two ways; there are no externalities and, more essentially, preferences are not assumed to be strictly convex.

4.1. The Result

Definition 8. An abstract market consists of a pair $((X^i, \succsim_i)_{i=1}^m, Y)$ such that

1. For all i, $X^i \subseteq \mathbb{R}^l$ is nonempty, convex, closed, and bounded from below.
2. $Y \subseteq \mathbb{R}^l$ is a closed, convex cone such that (i) for all i, $Y \cap X^i \neq \varnothing$, (ii) $\exists \bar{x} \in Y^{ro} \cap X^{ro}$, (ii) $Y \cap \mathbb{R}^l_+ = \{0\}$.
3. For all i, $\succsim_i$ is a complete, transitive, reflexive, convex, closed relation on $X^i \times X^i$.

Note that the condition of *strong viability* in Definition 4 has been weakened to Condition 2(ii). We shall say that an economy is *viable* if it satisfies this condition.

[44]See Samuelson (1971), Jones (1975), and the subsequent literature.

[45]See McKenzie (1959, pp. 54–55). I have introduced the numbering and the text within brackets [ ].

DEFINITION 9. An allocation (of resources) of an abstract market is the pair $((x^*), y^*) \equiv ((x^{*i})_{i=1}^m, y^*) \in (\chi, Y)$ such that $\Sigma_{i=1}^m x^* = y^*$.

DEFINITION 10. A competitive equilibrium for an abstract market consists of a price, allocation pair $(p^*, (x^{*i})_{i=1}^m, y^*) \in \Delta \times \chi \times Y$, $\Delta \equiv \{p \in \mathbb{R}_+^l\colon\ py \leq 0\ \forall y \in Y,\ \|p\| = 1\}$, such that (i) For all i, x^{*i} is a maximal element for $\succcurlyeq_i$ in the set $H^i(p^*) \equiv \{x \in X^i\colon\ p^*x \leq 0\}$, (ii) For all $y \in Y$, $p^*y \leq p^*y^* = 0$. This definition is, by now, completely standard. The reader should only note that the inequality in (ii) is redundant on account of the way that (the nonconvex set) Δ is defined. For our next definition, we denote Ψ for the set of all twofold partitions of the set of traders $(1,\cdots,m)$.

DEFINITION 11. An abstract market is said to be irreducible if for any $(I_1, I_2) \in \Psi$ and for any allocation $((x), y)$, there exist $(\tilde{x}^i)_{i \in I_1}$ such that $(x^i + \tilde{x}^i)_{i \in I_1} \in \Pi_{i \in I_1} X^i$, $w \in \Sigma_{i \in I_2} X^i$, $\tilde{y} \in Y$ with $\Sigma_{i \in I_1} \tilde{x}^i = (\tilde{y} - y - w)$ and

$$x^i + \tilde{x}^i \succcurlyeq_i x^i \text{ for all } i \in I_1,$$

$$\succ_i x^i \text{ for at least one } i \in I_1.$$

THEOREM 5. *There exists a competitive equilibrium for an abstract market if it is irreducible.*

4.2 A Digression on Irreducibility[46]

We cannot do better than to begin this subsection with McKenzie's[47] description of Definition 11.

> This assumption says that however we may partition the consumers into two groups if the first group receives an aggregate trade which is an attainable output for the rest of the market, the second group has within its feasible aggregate trades one which, if *added* to the goods already obtained by the first group, can be used to improve the position of someone in that group, while damaging the position of none there. Of course, this implies immediately that some member of the first group is not satiated.

The parallel with core theory is suggestive. However, unlike the definition of blocking in core theory, the bundles we use to improve the position of a particular coalition do not constitute an allocation. This can be easily seen in the context of a two-person, two-good economy in which each good is desired by each trader and the initial endowment consists of

[46]I am indebted to Leo Hurwicz for encouraging me to write this subsection and to Rajiv Vohra for many clarifying examples which considerations of space forbid me to reproduce.

[47]See pages 58–59 in McKenzie (1959). The formal statement of the assumption, however, relies on McKenzie (1961, 1981).

each trader having the total amount of one of the two commodities. In order to check if this economy is *irreducible*, pick a partition consisting of two single-agent coalitions and an allocation where consumer 1 has all of the initial endowment. If we have to make 1 better off, we certainly cannot do it through another allocation. Fortunately, this is not what Definition 11 asks us to do. We have to find an increment $\tilde{x}^1$ that need not be in X^1 but whose negative (w in the definition) must be in X^2. Since consumer 2 also has a nonzero endowment, such an increment can always be found. Note that y and $\tilde{y}$ are both zero. Note also that desirability is crucial here; if 1 did not desire the commodities held by 2, the economy would not be *irreducible*.

At this point, one may profitably mention Arrow and Hahn's (1971) related notion of *resource relatedness*. Here the parallel with core theory is more explicit. Arrow and Hahn keep the nomenclature of an allocation but one that pertains to a *different* and an incompletely specified economy. Specifically, what they require in the context of our example above is that 1 be made better off and 2 not be made worse off by an allocation of a different economy in which the *aggregate* endowments have been increased by all commodities held by 2. The point is that the new bundles do not constitute an allocation of the original economy.

Definition 11 is based on McKenzie's 1961 correction; I turn next to the alternative definition of *irreducibility* given in the original paper.

DEFINITION 12. An abstract market is said to be irreducible if for any $(I_1, I_2) \in \Psi$ and for any allocation $((x), y)$, there exist $(\tilde{x}^i)_{i \in I_1}$ such that $(x^i + \tilde{x}^i)_{i \in I_1} \in \prod_{i \in I_1} X^i$, $w \in \sum_{i \in I_2} X^i$, $\tilde{y} \in Y$ with $\sum_{i \in I_1} \tilde{x}^i = (\tilde{y} - w)$ and

$$\begin{aligned} x^i + \tilde{x}^i &\succcurlyeq_i x^i \text{ for all } i \in I_1, \\ &\succ_i x^i \text{ for at least one } i \in I_1. \end{aligned}$$

The fact that the two definitions are identical in the context of an exchange economy is clear enough. More generally, under Definition 12 the resources that one is allowed to take from I_2 consist not only of their endowments but also what they can do with their endowments using the social production set Y. This is given by the expression $\sum_{i \in I_1} \tilde{x}^i = (\tilde{y} - w)$. Under Definition 11, on the other hand, we also include the original production plan y in the preceding expression. This additional wrinkle means that one should be able to make the agents in I_1 better off through the resources of I_2 and the use of Y but with the initial production levels y guaranteed. Alternatively, we may observe that in Definition 11 one is limited to the set $Y - \{y\}$ in an attempt to improve the coalition I_1. Reversing the initial production plan may turn out to be advantageous, since the technology may satisfy irreversibility, but of course this does not necessarily obtain under decreasing returns to scale. We now leave the verification of the following claim to the reader.

Claim 1. Under free disposal and/or monotonicity of preferences, an economy irreducible in the sense of Definition 11 is irreducible in the sense of Definition 12. When Y is a convex cone with vertex 0, irreducibility in the sense of Definition 12 implies that in the sense of Definition 11.

Under constant returns to scale, Definition 12 may be strictly stronger than Definition 11. Consider a two-consumer economy in which $Y = \{y \in \mathbb{R}^2 | y_1 + y_2 = 0;\ y_1 \leq 0\}$, $X_1 = X_2 = \mathbb{R}^2_+$, $\omega_1 = (1, 0)$, $\omega_2 = (0, 1)$, $u_1(x_1, x_2) = x_1$. Consider the allocation $x_1 = (0, 1)$, $x_2 = (0, 1)$, $y = (-1, 1)$. Certainly, it is impossible to make consumer 1 better off by getting commodity 2 from consumer 2 and using the technology, i.e., *irreducibility* in terms of Definition 12 is not satisfied. It is of course possible to move in the direction $(\tilde{y} - y)$, and increase 1's utility.

If we do not have constant returns to scale, it is entirely possible that *irreducibility* in terms of Definition 12 is satisfied by not in terms of Definition 11; we leave this verification to the interested reader and turn to the raison d'etre of the concept.

The following argument constitutes a proof of the claim that for a constant returns to scale technology, under *irreducibility* (either kind!), if one agent has positive income, every other agent has positive income.

LEMMA 4. *Let $((x^{*i}), y^*)$ constitute an allocation in which x^{*i} is a maximal element in the budget set of trader i if this trader has income at p^*. Then under irreducibility (Definition 11 or 12), if one trader has income, all traders have income at p^*.*

Proof. We shall work with Definition 11 and leave the other case for the reader. Let there exist a consumer i_0, and $x^{i_0} \in X^{i_0}$ such that $p^* x^{i_0} < 0$. This is simply the statement that i_0 has income. Let $I_2 \equiv \{i\colon p^* x \geq 0\ \forall x \in X^i\}$ and $I_1 = (I_2)^c$. Since $((x^{*i}), y^*)$ is an allocation, we can appeal to the assumption of *irreducibility* in the sense of Definition 11 to assert that there exist $(\tilde{x}^i)_{i \in I_1}$ with $(\tilde{x}^i + x^{*i})_{i \in I_1} \in \prod_{i \in I_1} X^i$, $\omega \in \sum_{i \in I_2} \overline{X}^i$, $\tilde{y} \in Y$ with $\sum_{i \in I_1} \tilde{x}^i = (\tilde{y} - y^* - w)$ such that

$$x^{*i} + \tilde{x}^i \succcurlyeq_i \quad x^{*i} \quad \text{for all } i \in I_1,$$

$$\succ_i \quad x^{*i} \quad \text{for at least one } i \in I_1.$$

By the definition of maximality in the budget set at prices p^*,

$$p^*(x^{*i}) \leq 0 \quad \text{and} \quad p^*(x^{*i} + \tilde{x}^i) \geq 0, \qquad \forall i \in I_1$$

with strict inequality for at least one i. This implies that $p^*(\sum_{i \in I_1} \tilde{x}^i) > 0$ and hence $p^*(\tilde{y} - y^* - w) > 0$. Since $p^* \in P$, $p^* w < 0$. But this allows us to assert the existence of a consumer $i_0 \in I_2$, and $x^{i_0} \in X^{i_0}$ such that $p^* x^{i_0} < 0$. This is a contradiction to the construction of I_2. ∎

Note that the argument did not use the constant returns to scale assumption; this is required in the case of Definition 12 to guarantee $p^* \tilde{y} \leq 0$. This underlines the fact that some of the observations pertaining to Definition 12 and preceeding Lemma 4 above are not useful for the case of decreasing returns to scale technologies.

We end this subsection by referring to Debreu (1962), who presents an assumption that finesses the problem that *irreducibility* is designed to solve.

> (e) *If, in a quasi-equilibrium,* $p \cdot x_i = \min p \cdot X^i$ *occurs for some consumer, then it occurs for every consumer.*

Of course, *irreducibility* is a stronger assumption and Debreu (1962) proves this. Note, however, that (e) involves quasiequilibria and unlike the analogous but much stronger assumption in Debreu (1959), not one on the primitive, individual data of the economy. One can look on *irreducibility* more as an assumption on the relationship between agents, although one should avoid the rather fruitless question as to which of these assumptions is the "more primitive."

One may also mention Spivak's (1978) note in this connection. She shows that (e) is indeed weaker than irreducibility (this is her second figure); and that there is a partial converse.

4.3 The Proof

The proof is an application of the Brouwer fixed-point theorem to a mapping that takes the price space P into itself. However, before going into the details of the proof, we need to consider the set

$$C(p) = \sum_{i=1}^{m} C^i(p) = \sum_{i=1}^{m} \left\{ x'^i \in X^i \colon x'^i \succcurlyeq_i x^i \; \forall x^i \in H^i(p) \right\}.$$

The set $C^i(p)$ is, in Koopmans terminology,[48] the *no-worse-than-*x^i set for consumer i but with x^i the $\succcurlyeq_i$ maximal element in his budget set. McKenzie refers[49] to $C(p)$ as the "generalized preferred set in the sense of Pareto" and describes it as "the set of combinations of goods that can be distributed so that no one is worse off than when he trades freely at these prices."

I now refer you to Figure 5, which is reproduced from McKenzie.[50] Start with any point p from the set P and compute the sets $C^i(p)$ and

[48]See Koopmans (1957).

[49]See pages 55 and 57 in McKenzie (1959). Also page 55 for the quotation below.

[50]There is a minor change in that I have substituted P for S.

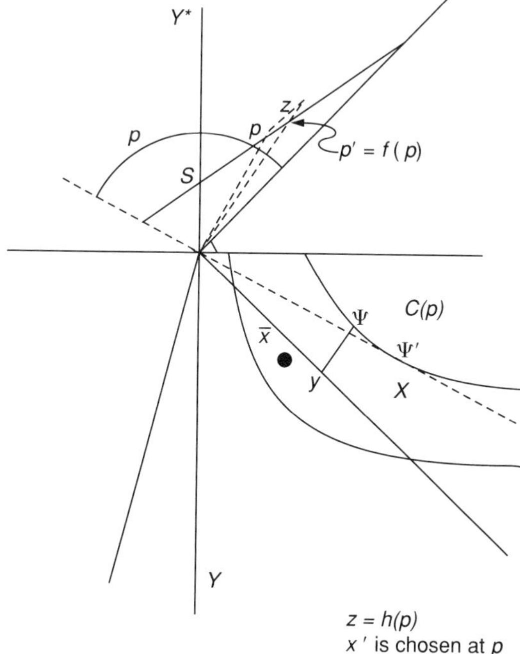

FIGURE 5

hence $C(p)$. Let the shortest distance between $C(p)$ and Y be attained at the respective points x and y. As in Figure 5, let $h(p) = z = x - y$ and consider the vector $p + z$. Normalize this vector to lie in P. However, when z equals zero, we end up with the p we began with and are done.

The basic idea of the proof can best be stated in McKenzie's own words. On considering a Pareto optimum allocation that can be sustained as, in modern terminology, an efficiency equilibrium,[51] he writes:

> The value of net output in this equilibrium is maximized, at the equilibrium prices, over the production set Y and minimized over the preferred set $C(p)$. But the shortest vector reaching from Y to $C(p)$ has a similar property. It has a maximum inner product over Y at the point where it starts, and a minimum inner product over $C(p)$ at the point where it ends. This suggests a mapping of prices by shifting them towards the shortest vector joining [these two sets].

Let us now turn to the technical details of the proof. We want to show the existence of a fixed point of F that may be referred to as the *McKenzie*

[51]To my knowledge, a term first used by Shitovitz (1973).

mapping, takes P into itself and is given by

$$p \to F(p) = -(p + h(p))/(p + h(p))\bar{x}$$
$$= -(p + h(p))/(-1 + h(p)\bar{x}),$$

where

$$h: P \to \mathbb{R}^l,\ p \to h(p) = \left\{z \in C(p) - Y: z \in \operatorname{Argmin}_{z' \in C(p) - Y} \|z'\|\right\}.$$

In order to apply Brouwer's theorem, we need only verify that F takes P into itself, that it is a function, that it is continuous, and that its fixed point is a competitive equilibrium. The compactness of P has been asserted in the context of the proof of Theorem 3 (Lemma 2 above) to hinge crucially on the nonempty interiority of Y. In the first stage of the argument, following McKenzie, let us assume more; namely, *strong survival*, $X^i \cap Y^o \neq \varnothing$.

The mapping $h(\cdot)$ is the "heart of the show." We have to establish first what is implicit in Figures 5 and 6; namely, that $h(\cdot)$ is a single-valued, continuous map, and that for any p in P, and with $h(p) = x - y$,

$$\text{(a) } h(p)x \leq h(p)x'\ \forall x' \in C(p); \quad \text{(b) } h(p)y' \leq h(p)y = 0\ \forall y' \in Y.$$

McKenzie establishes these properties in Lemmas 6–10 in his paper and rather than reproduce them here, it might be more valuable to place his mathematical techniques in a broader context. Toward this end, I borrow[52] the following notions from *Approximation Theory*.

DEFINITION 13. Let (E, ρ) be a metric space, $G \subseteq E$ and $x \in E$. An element $g_0 \in G$ is called an element of best approximation of x (by the elements of the set G) if we have $\rho(x, g_0) = \operatorname{Inf}_{g \in G} \rho(x, g)$. Let $\mathscr{P}_G(x) = \{g_0 \in G: \rho(x, g_0) = \operatorname{Inf}_{g \in G} \rho(x, g)\}$. A selection from the correspondence $\mathscr{P}_G(\cdot)$ is denoted by $\pi_G(\cdot)$ and referred to as the metric projection.

In words, $\mathscr{P}_G(x)$ ($\pi_G(x)$) is the set of points (a point) in G *nearest* to x.

DEFINITION 14. A set G in a metric space (E, ρ) is said to be proximinal if every element $x \in E$ has at least one element of best approximation in G, i.e., $\mathscr{P}_G(x) \neq \varnothing\ \forall x \in E$. G is said to be a semi-Chebyshev set if every element $x \in E$ has at most one element of best approximation in G, i.e., $x \in E$, $g_1, g_2 \in \mathscr{P}_G(x)$ imply $g_1 = g_2$. A Chebyshev set is a set that is simultaneously proximinal and semi-Chebyshev.

We can now recall the following results.

THEOREM 6. *Every closed convex set G in a Banach space E is a Chebyshev set if and only if E is reflexive and strictly convex. If E is an inner*

[52] See, for example, Holmes (1972) or Singer (1974).

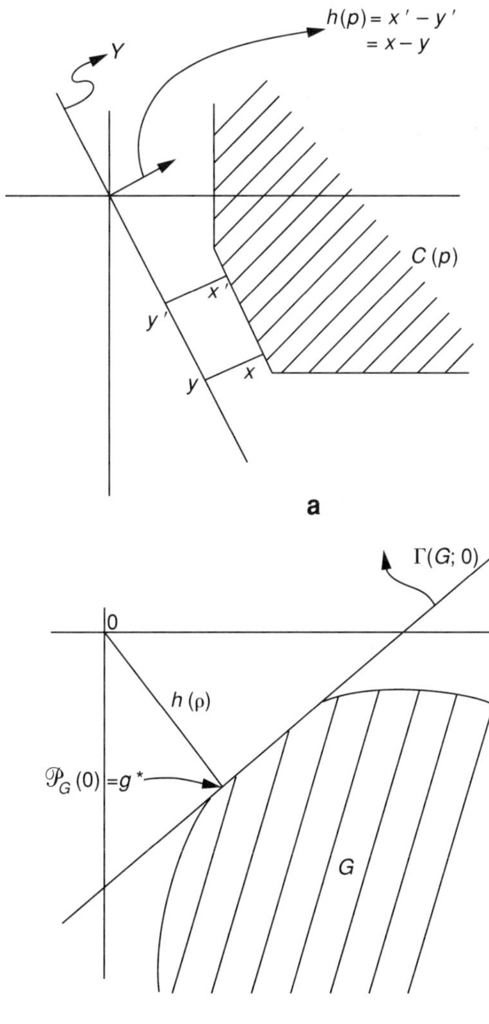

FIGURE 6

product space and G is a complete convex set in E, then G is a Chebyshev set and the metric projection is a contraction with Lipschitz constant unity, i.e.,

$$\|\pi_G(x) - \pi_G(y)\| \leq \|x - y\|, \quad \textit{for all } x, y, \in E,$$

and monotone, i.e.,

$$\mathscr{R}(x - y, \pi_G(x) - \pi_G(y)) \geq \|\pi_G(x) - \pi_G(y)\|^2 \geq 0 \quad \textit{for all } x, y, \in E.$$

Moreover, either of these properties of π_G *characterizes inner product spaces among general normed linear spaces.*[53]

Under the assumption that $0 \notin G(\cdot) \equiv (C(\cdot) - Y)$, $h(\cdot) = \mathscr{P}_{G(\cdot)}(0)$; see Figure 6. Since McKenzie is in the setting of a Euclidean space, the single valuedness of $h(\cdot)$ follows once we show that $G(\cdot)$ is a nonempty, closed set. But on appealing to Lemma 3, we can show that the attainable set is bounded and hence one can restrict oneself to bounded subsets of X^i. But then closedness of $C^i(\cdot)$ (McKenzie's Lemma 3) implies its compactness and hence the compactness of $C(\cdot)$ and the consequent closedness of $G(\cdot)$.

Next, we turn to the continuity of $h(\cdot)$.

THEOREM 7 (*Brosowski et al.*). *Let A be a topological space, E a metric space, $x \in E$, and for each $a \in A$, let K_a be a nonempty compact subset of E. If the mapping $a \to K_a$ is Hausdorff continuous at a_0, then the parameter mapping $a \to \mathscr{P}_{K_a}(x)$ is upper hemicontinuous at a_0.*

This is a recent result,[54] and it establishes the continuity of the metric projection as the underlying set changes in a "continuous" manner. The relevance of this result to the problem at hand is clear. McKenzie establishes in his Lemma 10 the continuity of $h(\cdot)$ as $G(\cdot)$ changes continuously. Of course, the continuity of the latter hinges on the continuity of the correspondence $C(\cdot)$, and this follows from the continuity of the budget set $H^i(\cdot)$ (McKenzie's Lemma 4) for which *strong survival* is a sufficient condition.

Next, we turn to the characterization of the metric projection.[55] Let E^* denote the set of continuous linear functions on E.

THEOREM 8. *Let G be a convex set in a normed linear space E, and let $x \in E/cl(G)$, $g_0 \in G$. Then $g_0 \in \mathscr{P}_G(x)$ iff $\exists f \in E^*$ with the following properties*:

(*i*) $\|f\| = 1$, (*ii*) $\mathscr{R}f(g_0 - g) \geq 0 \; \forall g \in G$, (*iii*) $\mathscr{R}f(x - g_0) = \|x - g_0\|$.

Denote the set of these functionals f by $\Gamma(x; G)$.

The point that I wish to make with these theorems is clear. As in 1954, McKenzie in 1959 is working with mathematical objects that arise natu-

[53]See page 79 for the first statement and page 67 for the others in Singer (1974). $\mathscr{R}$ denotes the real part; since we deal with real spaces throughout, $\mathscr{R}$ can be simply ignored in the sequel.

[54]See Browoski *et al.* (1980). Of course, if we replace Hausdorff continuity by the conventional notion of continuity of correspondences, this is a simple consequence of Berge's (1963) maximum theorem.

[55]Singer (1974, p. 65) attributes the following theorem to independent work of five authors around 1967. Out of these Deutsch and Maserick (1967) is the only reference in English.

rally in the context of his economic problem and that thrive in mathematics later.

Once the properties of the mapping h are established, we can turn our attention to the mapping F and show that its fixed point is a competitive equilibrium. However, an alternative approach that repackages McKenzie's ideas in light of these basic results from approximation theory, is of interest. I first reproduce the following consequence of the intermediate value theorem (McKenzie's Lemma 2).

LEMMA 5. *If the ith consumer is not satiated at* $p \in P$, $px \geq 0$ $\forall x \in C^i(p)$.

Proof. Rewrite $C^i(p)$ as $\{x^i \in X^i: \nexists x \in H^i(p)$ such that $x \succ_i x^i\}$. Suppose $\exists \tilde{x} \in C^i(p)$ such that $p\tilde{x} < 0$. By nonsatiation $\exists \vec{x} \succ_i \tilde{x}$. By definition of $C^i(p)$, $p\vec{x} > 0$. Now consider the function χ: $[0,1] \to \mathbb{R}$ such that $\chi(t) = p(t\tilde{x} + (1-t)\vec{x}) \equiv px(t)$ and note that $\exists \bar{t} \in]0,1[$ such that $px(\bar{t}) = 0$. By convexity of $\succcurlyeq_i$, $x(\bar{t}) \succcurlyeq_i \tilde{x}$. Hence $\tilde{x} \notin C^i(p)$ and we have our required contradiction. ■

We can now get on with the proof. For any $p \in P$, let $G(p) \equiv C(p) - Y$. Suppose that there exists $\tilde{p} \in P$ such that $0 \in G(p)$. Then there exist $((\tilde{x}^i)_{i=m}^m, \tilde{y})$ such that $((\tilde{x}, \tilde{y})$ is an allocation. By definition of P, $\tilde{p}y \leq 0$ $\forall y \in Y$. By Lemma 5, $\tilde{p}\tilde{x}^i \geq 0$ for all i. Hence $\tilde{p}\tilde{y} \geq 0$. Hence $\tilde{p}\tilde{y} = 0$. Hence $p\tilde{x}^i = 0$ for all i, and therefore $(\tilde{p}, (\tilde{x}), \tilde{y})$ is a competitive equilibrium.

Hence suppose that for all $p \in P$, $0 \notin G(p)$. Note that $p \to \Gamma(0; G(p))$ takes P into elements of $\mathbb{R}^l$ with unit norm. We consider the mapping $p \to \tilde{F} \equiv \{-(q/q\bar{x}): q \in \Gamma(0; G(p))\}$. On putting $x = 0$, $f = q$ and $G = C(p) - Y$, we obtain that $qg \leq 0$ $\forall (x - y) \in C(p) - Y$. Since $0 \in C(p)$, certainly $qy \geq 0$ and $q\bar{x} \neq 0$. Hence $\tilde{F}$ takes P into P and by virtue of the fact that $G(p)$ is a closed set, Theorems 6 and 8 guarantee that $\tilde{F}$ is well defined. It is straightforward to check that it is convex-valued. All that remains is to check upper hemicontinuity. But this follows easily from Theorem 7 and the fact that we are in finite-dimensional Euclidean space. We can now apply Kakutani's theorem to assert that $\tilde{F}$ has a fixed point in P, say p^*. Let $z^* \equiv (x^* - y^*) = \mathscr{P}_{\mathscr{P}(p^*)}(0)$. From the definition of $\tilde{F}(p^*)$, there exists $\hat{p} \in \Gamma(0, G(p^*))$ such that $p^* = -(\hat{p}/p\bar{x})$. Now, from the definition of $\Gamma(0, G(p^*))$, $\hat{p}z^* \geq \hat{p}g$ $\forall g \in G(p^*)$. This implies that

$$\hat{p}(x^* - y^*) \geq \hat{p}(x - y) \quad \text{for all } x \in C^i(p^*), \quad \text{for all } y \in Y. \quad (7)$$

We can now rewrite the above equation as

$$p^*(x^* - y^*) \leq p^*(x - y) \quad \text{for all } x \in C^i(p^*), \quad \text{for all } y \in Y. \quad (8)$$

On choosing x to equal x^*, we obtain

$$p^* y^* \geq p^* y \quad \text{for all } y \in Y. \tag{9}$$

Similarly, on choosing y to equal y^*, we obtain

$$p^* x^* \leq p^* x \quad \text{for all } x \in C^i(p^*). \tag{10}$$

Since Y is a cone, $p^* y^* = 0$. But from (iii) of Theorem 8, $p^*(x^* - y^*) = \|y^* - x^*\|$. Since the latter is positive by hypothesis, $p^* x^* > 0$. This implies from (10), that

$$p^* x > 0 \quad \text{for all } x \in C^i(p^*). \tag{11}$$

But $C^i(p) \cap H^i(p^*) \neq \emptyset$ and we have a contradiction to our hypothesis.

Why is this repackaging of any use? The answer lies in the fact that, unlike the mapping F, we avoid the summation of a point p from the price space to a point $h(p)$ in the quantity space. In doing this, McKenzie is using an essential property of Euclidean space, or more generally Hilbert space, that every continuous linear function on the space can be represented as a point in the space.[56] In our repackaging, we use the finite dimensionality of the commodity space only in establishing the upper hemicontinuity of $\tilde{F}$.

The assumption of nonsatiation in Lemma 5 is a consequence of *irreducibility*; one needs work to dispense with the assumption of *strong survival* [used in establishing the compactness of P and the continuity of $C^i(\cdot)$]. McKenzie reverts to the techniques in the 1955 paper. We confine ourselves to the case when Y is not a linear subspace [see McKenzie (1981, p. 836) for modifications when it is], and limit ourselves, without any loss of generality, to the smallest linear subspace, L, containing Y and all the X^i. For $t \in \mathbb{R}_+$, let

$$\tilde{Y}(t) = \operatorname{cl}\operatorname{con}\big(\{Y\} \cup \{x \in \mathbb{R}^l : d(x, \bar{x}) < t\}\big),$$

$$\tilde{X}^i(t) = \{t\bar{x} + (1-t)x^i : x^i \in X^i, t < 1\}.$$

1. For any $t > 0$, let $\mathscr{E}^t$ be an economy with $(\tilde{X}^i(t), \succcurlyeq_{ti}, \tilde{Y}(t))$ substituted for $(X^i, \succcurlyeq_i, Y(t))$. Since $\tilde{x} \in \tilde{X}^i(t)$ implies that there exists a unique $x \in X^i$ such that $t\bar{x}^i + (1-t)x = \tilde{x}$, we can extend $\succcurlyeq_i$ to $\succcurlyeq_{ti}$ on $\tilde{X}^i(t)$ in the obvious way. Let $P(t)$ be the analogue of P with reference to $\tilde{Y}(t)$, i.e., the set $\{p \in \mathbb{R}^l : py \leq 0\ \forall y \in \tilde{Y}(t);\ p\bar{x} = -1\}$.

[56]This is the celebrated Reisz representation theorem; see, for example, Chapter II.16 in the text of Akhiezer and Glazman (1978).

2. Observe that for any small enough t, the economy $\mathscr{E}^t$ satisfies all the assumptions, in particular interiority and non-satiation, required for the argument above, and hence we can assert the existence of a competitive equilibrium $(p^*(t), ((x^*(t)), y^*(t)))$ for the economy $\mathscr{E}^t$ with $p^*(t) \in P(t)$.

3. Since $\bar{x} \in (\tilde{Y}(t))^o$ but not necessarily in Y^o, P is not necessarily compact. Since $p^*(t)\bar{x} = -1$, we can normalize $p^*(t)$ to lie in Δ.

4. As in Section 3, this normalized sequence of equilibria has a convergent subsequence as $t \to 0$. Let the limit of this subsequence be $(p^*, ((x^*), y^*))$.

5. We can check that $p^* \in \Delta$, that the profit maximizing conditions on technology are satisfied and that $((x^*), y^*)$ is an allocation. All that remains to be checked is that $x^{*i} \in C^i(p^*)$.

Toward this end, we need two results. The first relies on a geometric argument and the second is a consequence of the viability assumption.

LEMMA 6. $\mathrm{Int}_L(\mathrm{con}(\{X\} \cup \{Y\})) \neq \emptyset$.

Proof. Let M be the smallest linear subspace containing $\mathrm{con}(\{X\} \cup \{Y\})$. Certainly $M \subseteq L$. For any consumer i_0, $X^{i_0} \subseteq (X - Y)$. Pick any $x \in X^{i_0}$. Given the *survival* assumption that $X^i \cap Y \neq \emptyset$, $\exists x^i \in X^i$, $i \neq i_0$, such that $x^i \in Y$. Since Y is a convex cone, certainly $\vec{x} \equiv \sum_{i \neq i_0} x^i \in Y$. Also, by construction, $(x + \vec{x}) \in X$. This implies that $x \in X - Y$.

Since $X \subseteq \mathrm{con}\, X \subseteq \mathrm{con}(X \cup Y) \subseteq M$ and $Y \subseteq M$, we have shown that $X^{i_0} \subseteq M$ and hence $L \subseteq M$. Moreover, Rockafellar (1970, Theorem 6.2) and the convexity of X^{i_0} imply that X^{i_0} has a nonempty interior in its affine hull.[57] But an affine space containing Y contains 0 and hence it is a linear subspace. Since $X^{i_0} \subseteq (\mathrm{con}(\{X\} \cup \{Y\}))$, we are done. ■

LEMMA 7. *For any $p \in \Delta$, there exists $x \in X$ such that $px < 0$.*

Proof. Suppose there exists $p \in \Delta$ such that $px \geq 0$ for all $x \in X$. By definition of Δ, $py \leq 0$ for all $y \in Y$. Let $H = \{x \in \mathbb{R}^l : px = 0\}$. If $X \subseteq H$ and $Y \subseteq H$, certainly $\mathrm{con}(\{X\} \cup \{Y\}) \subseteq H$ and we obtain a contradiction to the above lemma. Hence, $Y^{ro} \cap X^{ro} = \emptyset$, a contradiction to the *viability* condition 2(ii) in the definition of an abstract market. ■

We can now proceed to show that $x^{*i} \in C^i(p^*)$. From Lemma 7, there exists a consumer i_0, and $x^{i_0} \in X^{i_0}$ such that $p^* x^{i_0} < 0$. We can now simply appeal to Lemma 4 above to show that all traders have income and complete the proof.

[57]Following Fenchel (1953), McKenzie refers to this as a "flat." Rockafellar's (1970) book was to appear 11 years later.

4.4 Influence on Subsequent Work

The influence of the 1959 paper on Aumann's (1966) proof of the existence of competitive equilibrium is well known. Aumann writes[58]

> The proof is based on McKenzie's beautiful existence proof. The differences between this proof and McKenzie's are caused by the different initial equipment: we have no convexity assumption to work with, and we have a continuum of traders rather than a finite number. McKenzie needs the convexity assumption in only one place, to show the aggregate preferred set is convex [and] to define $h(p)$ uniquely. Because of the presence of a continuum of traders, ... the continuity of the aggregate preferred set as a function of the price vector [does not] follow trivially from the continuity of the individual preferred sets. Another significant difference... is in the matter of boundedness [of the individual consumption sets].

It is of interest that Aumann patterned his proof on McKenzie despite the fact that he was limiting himself to an exchange economy. It is not surprising that subsequent work of Schmeidler (1969) and others reverts to proofs based on Debreu (1956). Three other observations in this connection. Aumann assumes monotonicity of preferences and hence establishes the existence of strictly positive equilibrium prices. This is important, as discussed in Section 2 in the context of Schmeidler (1969), for handling unboundedness of the consumption sets. Second, he also assumes *strong survival* in the assumption that initial endowments $i(t) \gg 0$ for almost all consumers t. Finally, it is worth pointing out that Aumann follows McKenzie's mapping F to the letter and confines the[59] "methods of functional analysis (Banach spaces) and topology" solely to problems raised by the continuum of traders.

The conjunction of Brouwer's fixed-point theorem and the separating hyperplane theorem that is at the heart of McKenzie's 1959 proof raises the question whether his technique can be used to give an alternative proof of the (so-called) Debreu–Gale–Nikaido lemma. Such a proof has been offered in several recent contributions.[60] The basic idea is simple. If the excess demand set does not intersect with the negative orthant at any price, the two sets, being closed and convex, can be strictly separated. Consider the set of these normalized separating hyperplanes, one set for each price we began with. This correspondence has a continuous selection and hence a fixed point. But this furnishes a contradiction to Walras' law. The point of contact with McKenzie's 1959 proof is that he, too, is selecting continuously a unique hyperplane and this selection is obtained, as in McCabe, by construction. Mehta and Tarafdar use the more power-

[58]Pages 2 and 15 in Aumann (1966).

[59]See page 15 in Aumann (1966).

[60]See, in particular, McCabe (1981), Florenzano (1982), Tarafdar and Mehta (1984), Yannelis (1985), and Mehta and Tarafdar (1987).

ful Tarafdar fixed-point theorem, and Yannelis offers, and relies on, a more sophisticated selection theorem.

We conclude this subsection by showing the relevance of McKenzie's proof to recent work on economies with infinite commodities. The idea of approximating a given economy by "better behaved" ones and then taking the limits of their equilibria finds full expression in Bewley's (1972) work. The importance of the interiority assumption for the compactness of P goes back to 1955 (see Lemma 2 above); it is a standard result in functional analysis.[61] More generally, the importance of interiority can be seen, for example, in the remark of Khan (1984) and in Jones (1987). If we want to set our repackaged version of McKenzie's proof in an infinite-dimensional context and rely on the 1952 Fan–Glicksberg fixed-point theorem, the difficult step is to show the upper hemicontinuity of the map Γ without any interiority assumptions. The problem, as pointed out by Bewley (1970), is that the evaluation functional is no longer continuous and that the weak * limit of a sequence of prices with unit norm may be zero.[62] Mas-Colell (1986), and following him, Yannelis and Zame (1986), Zame (1987), and subsequent literature[63] does this by "bounding the marginal rates of substitution." The point is that our version of McKenzie's proof brings this out in a natural way because the range of the map Γ is precisely the *efficiency prices* and hence reflects the marginal rates in production or in consumption. If one can limit oneself to a norm bounded subset of P on account of the boundedness of these marginal rates, there is here the possibility of a proof of the existence of competitive equilibrium in infinite-dimensional spaces that follows McKenzie (1959) rather than Negishi (1960) and Arrow and Hahn (1971). Similar to McKenzie (1954), the proof would hang on the sustaining of the boundary points of $G(p)$ as efficiency equilibria and for this the closedness of $G(p)$ seems essential. Recent work offers sufficient conditions for the sum of closed sets to be closed in the context of the second welfare theorem.[64]

4.5 Miscellany

So far we have made no reference in this section to the assumption of Y being a cone. McKenzie shows how to accommodate the apparently (!) general case in Section 7 of his 1959 paper on "Concordance with [the] Hicksian model." The reader should also see McKenzie (1961).

[61] See, for example, Jameson (1970, page 123) and Alfsen (1971, p. 72).

[62] This is really the same issue as ensuring the compactness of P; see Yannelis (1985) and the references cited in footnote 6 (above).

[63] See Aliprantis *et al.* (1989) for references.

[64] See Khan and Vohra (1987b, 1988).

5. CLASSICAL THEOREM IN ITS FULLY DEVELOPED FORM: 22 YEARS LATER

In 1981, McKenzie integrates into his 1959 set-up the fact that the *survival* assumption as well as that of completeness and transitivity of preferences can simply be dropped.[65] He also returns to the question of dispensing with the interiority assumption on the technology, and considers, in particular, the case when it is a linear subspace.

In the absence of the *survival* assumption, X^i does not necessarily contain 0. McKenzie works with, and hence needs the notation, $\bar{X}^i \equiv \text{con}(\{X^i\} \cup \{0\})$.

5.1 Results

We begin with a result inspired by Moore (1975).

DEFINITION 15. An abstract market is said to be weakly irreducible if in Definition 10 of an irreducible market,

$$w \in \sum_{i \in I_2} \bar{X}^i \text{ is substituted for } w \in \sum_{i \in I_2} X^i.$$

THEOREM 9. *Theorem 5 is valid if the survival condition 2(ii) in the definition of an abstract market is eliminated and weak irreducibility is substituted for irreducibility.*

Next we turn to a result inspired by Mas-Colell (1974) and Gale and Mas-Colell (1975). It also incorporates the relaxation of convexity assumption on the *better-than-sets* by Shafer and Sonnenschein (1975). This represents "the classical theorem in its fully developed form."

DEFINITION 16. An ADMMM-economy[66] consists of a pair $((X^i, P^i)_{i=1}^m, Y)$ such that

1. For all i, $X^i \subseteq \mathbb{R}^l$ is nonempty, convex, closed, and bounded from below.
2. $Y \subseteq \mathbb{R}^l$ is a closed, convex cone such that

$$\text{(i) } \exists \bar{x} \in Y^{ro} \cap X^{ro}, \qquad \text{(ii) } Y \cap \mathbb{R}^l_+ = \{0\}.$$

3. For all i, P^i is a correspondence from X^i to X^i such that P^i is (i) open-valued relative to X^i, (ii) lower semicontinuous, and with (iii) $x^i \notin \text{con}\, P^i(x^i)$.

[65]He refers to the former as "perhaps the most dramatic innovation since 1959;" see McKenzie (1981, p. 83).

[66]ADMMM for Arrow, Debreu, McKenzie, Mas-Colell, and Moore.

DEFINITION 17. An ADMMM-economy is said to be strongly irreducible if for any $(I_1, I_2) \in \Psi$ and any allocation $((x), y)$ obtained with $\overline{X}^i$ substituted for X^i, $i \in I_2$, there exist $(\tilde{x}^i)_{i \in I_1}$ such that $(x^i + \tilde{x}^i)_{i \in I_1} \in \prod_{i \in I_1} X^i$, $w \in \sum_{i \in I_2} \overline{X}^i$, $\tilde{y} \in Y$ with $\sum_{i \in I_1} \tilde{x}^i = (\tilde{y} - y - w)$ and

$$(x^i + \tilde{x}^i) \in P^i(x^i) \quad \text{for all } i \in I_1.$$

Note that *strong irreducibility* does not insist on $((x), y)$ being an allocation but rather that everyone in I_1 be made better off.[67] On defining a competitive equilibrium for an ADMMM-economy in the obvious way, we can present Theorem 10.

THEOREM 10. *There exists a competitive equilibrium for an ADMMM-economy if it is strongly irreducible.*

5.2 Proofs

We begin with the proof of Theorem 9. Note that the principal difficulty in the proof lies in the fact that we can no longer use the *survival* condition $X^i \cap Y \neq \emptyset$. As the first stage of the argument, McKenzie assumes, as in 1959, *strong viability* ($X \cap Y^o \neq \emptyset$) and works with the sets $\overline{X}^i$ for all consumers i. Since $0 \in Y$ and also in $\overline{X}^i$, the *survival* assumption is met.

The proof shows the strong influence of McKenzie (1955) and Debreu (1962). As in the 1955 paper, McKenzie works with a modified demand mapping from prices to quantities and an inverse supply mapping from quantities to prices but unlike the earlier paper, a composition of these mappings is not taken but they are "kept separate" in the form of a Cartesian product. Moreover, the demand mapping is now modified as in Debreu (1962). Figure 7, reproduced from McKenzie's paper, gives an overview of the proof, and its resemblance to Figure 4 bears emphasis.

In more concrete terms, we work with a mapping F that takes $P \times \overline{X}$ to itself and is given by $f \times s$, where s is just the *inverse supply mapping* of Section 3 but $f\colon P \to \overline{X}$, $f(p) = \sum_{i=1}^{m} \psi^i(p)$, where

$$\psi^i(p) = \begin{cases} \xi^i(p) & \text{if } \exists x \in X^i \text{ with } px < 0 \\ \{x \in \overline{X}^i : px = 0\} & \text{otherwise} \end{cases}$$

$$\xi^i(p) = \{x \in X^i : px \leq 0 \quad \text{and} \quad x \succcurlyeq_i z \ \forall z \in X^i \text{ such that } pz \leq 0\}.$$

[67] In his comment on the first draft of this paper, McKenzie writes, "If one considers the application of this assumption, one sees that what is really needed is that the improving change in I_1's consumption should lie in the cone from the origin spanned by $Y - y$ and $-X_{I_2}$. Perhaps this is the proper form of the assumption; it can be applied equally easily to the case of constant returns and to the case of diminishing returns."

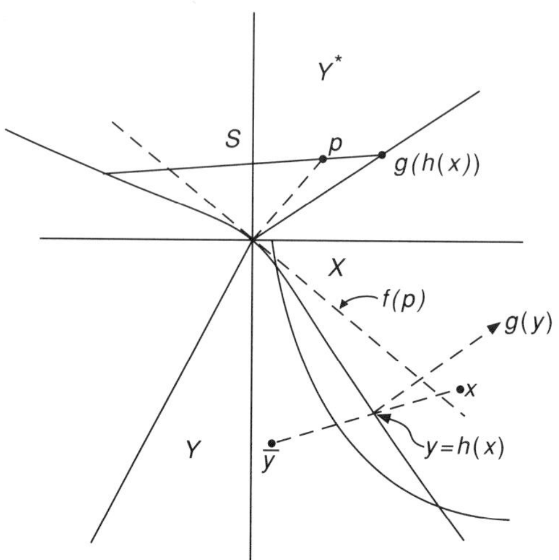

FIGURE 7(a) For $(p, x) \in S \times \overline{X}$, $F(p, x) = (g(h(x)), f(p)) \subset S \times \overline{X}$, where $\overline{X}$ is the convex hull of X and 0.

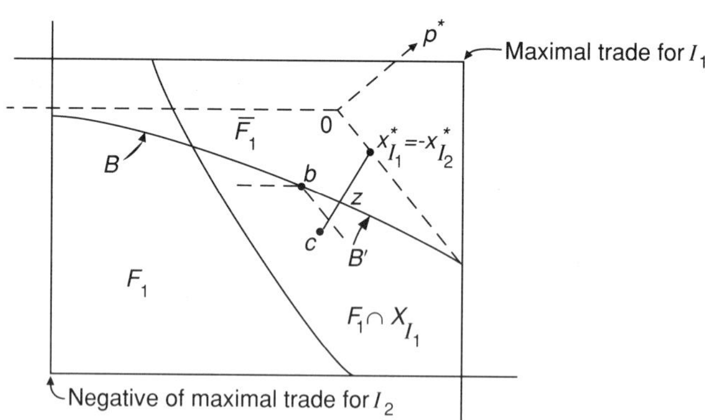

FIGURE 7(b):

$$v(x^*_{I_1}) > v(b).$$

$$v(c) \geq v(b).$$

$$\therefore v(z) > v(b).$$

$\therefore b$ does not max v on B'.

I_2 cannot survive without trade. $Y = -R^n$, $F_1 = R^n_- - X_{I_2}$. No equilibrium exists in F_1, but $(p^*, x^*_i, i = 1, \ldots, m)$ is an equilibrium with $\Sigma^m_1 x^*_i = x^* \in \overline{F}_1 - F_1$. v has no maximum on $B' = B \cap X_{I_1}$. This may be viewed as an Edgeworth box with the initial allocation at 0.

The fact that the mapping F has a fixed point is straightforward given the discussion in Sections 2–4 above. The difficult part of the proof is to show that the fixed point is an equilibrium. For this, one has to rule out the case that at the fixed point (p^*, x^*), $\psi^i(p^*) \neq \xi^i(p^*)$ for any consumer i. This requires one to establish that each consumer has a positive income at p^*. The argument is a nontrivial modification of the one used by McKenzie in 1959, and part of it is illustrated in Figure 7b. We present the salient points of the argument.

From *strong viability*, there exists a consumer i_0, and $x^{i_0} \in X^{i_0}$ such that $p^* x^{i_0} < 0$. Let $I_2 \equiv \{i: p^* x \geq 0 \ \forall x \in X^i\}$ and $I_1 = (I_2)^c$. Now suppose that

$$f(p^*) \cap (X \cap Y) \neq \emptyset. \tag{12}$$

This allows us to appeal to *weak irreducibility* and to Lemma 4 to show that $I_2 = \emptyset$ and to finish the proof.

The pièce de résistance of the proof is the validity of (12). However, before we consider this, we need to take an excursion into some simple but useful geometry.[68]

A Geometric Problem

Let $\mathscr{F}$ be a nonempty convex subset of a linear space that does not contain zero. Let $\overline{\mathscr{F}}$ be the convex hull of $\mathscr{F}$ and zero. Let $x^* \in \overline{\mathscr{F}}/\mathscr{F}$ and $b \in \mathscr{F}$. If there exists $c \in \mathscr{F}$, $c \neq b$ and with $(c - b) \in \overline{\mathscr{F}}$, can c be a "point of first contact of rays drawn from x^*." Formally, is $c \in \mathscr{F}_{x^*} \equiv \{x \in \mathscr{F}: ((1 - \lambda)x^* + \lambda x) \notin \mathscr{F}, 0 \leq \lambda \leq 1\}$?

The problem can be illustrated in Figure 8. The quadrilateral *ABCD* is the set $\mathscr{F}$ and $\overline{\mathscr{F}}$ is the triangle *OAD*. The set $\mathscr{F}_{x^*}$ is the line segment *CD*. The question is whether we can find a point c in *CD* such that $(c - b)$ remains in the triangle *OAD*. Before we establish McKenzie's negative answer to this question, we need an additional concept and an additional piece of notation.

For any subset $\mathscr{F}$ of a linear space and $x^* \notin \mathscr{F}$, let cone $(x^*, \mathscr{F}) \equiv \{(1 - \lambda)x^* + \lambda x: \lambda \geq 0, x \in \mathscr{F}\}$ denote the "smallest cone originating from x^* and containing $\mathscr{F}$." This is the cone spanned by the rays x^*D and x^*C in Figure 8. Now all we need to do is to substitute $(c - b)$ for m in Lemma 8 and appeal to it and Lemma 9 below to solve the problem.

Before plunging the reader into the details of the lemmata, one gains some intuition by illustrating them in terms of Figure 8. Lemma 8 simply says that one cannot find m in the triangle *OAD* without it being contained in the cone $(x^*, \mathscr{F})$ shifted to the origin. Lemma 9 says that

[68] I am not aware of a reference to these results in the convexity literature. McKenzie introduces these notions in the context of closed subsets of $\mathbb{R}^l$ but they generalize, word for word, to linear spaces.

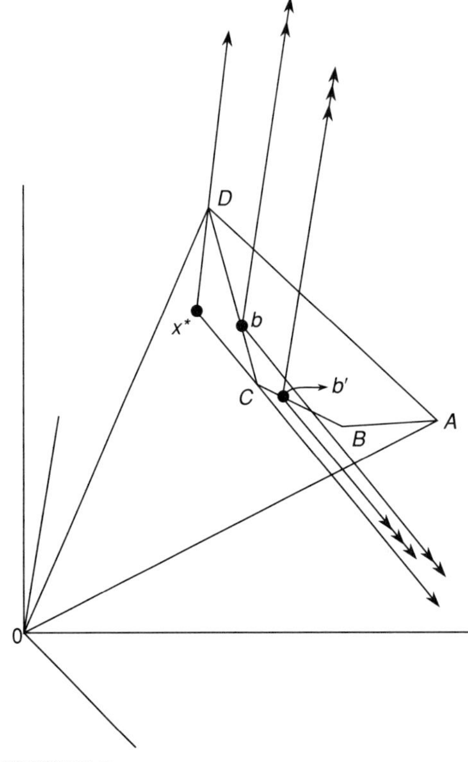

FIGURE 8

one cannot find a point in CD different from b, which is in the cone $(x^*, \mathscr{F})$ shifted to b. If b is not in CD and (say) at b', this is all the more evident.

LEMMA 8. *If $\mathscr{F}$ is convex, $m \in \overline{\mathscr{F}}$ and $x^* \notin \mathscr{F}$, then $(x^* + m) \in$ cone $(x^*, \mathscr{F})$.*

Proof. If $m = 0$, there is nothing to prove. Since $m \in \overline{\mathscr{F}} = \text{con}(\{0\} \cup \mathscr{F})$, and $m \neq 0$, $\exists \gamma > 0$ such that $\gamma m \in \mathscr{F}$. Since $x^* \in \overline{\mathscr{F}}/\mathscr{F}$, $\exists \beta \geq 1$ such that $\beta x^* \in \mathscr{F}$. Since $\mathscr{F}$ is convex, $\forall \delta \in [0, 1]$, $\tau(\delta) \equiv (\delta \beta x^* + (1 - \delta)\gamma m) \in \mathscr{F}$. Certainly, $\forall \alpha \geq 0$, $\alpha \tau(\delta) + (1 - \alpha)x^* \in$ cone $(x^*, \mathscr{F})$. But now on choosing δ to be $1/\beta$ and α to be $1/(1 - (1/\beta))\gamma$ we complete the proof of the claim. ■

LEMMA 9. *If $\mathscr{F}$ is convex, $\forall b \in \mathscr{F}$, $\forall c \in \mathscr{F}_{x^*}$, $b \neq c$, $(x^* + c - b) \notin$ cone $(x^*, \mathscr{F})$.*

Proof. Suppose there exist $b \in \mathscr{F}$ and $c \in \mathscr{F}_{x^*}$, $b \neq c$, such that $(x^* + c - b) \in$ cone $(x^*, \mathscr{F})$. Then by the definition of cone $(x^*, \mathscr{F})$, there exist $z \in \mathscr{F}$ and $\lambda \geq 0$ such that $(1 - \lambda)x^* + \lambda z = x^* + c - b$. If $\lambda = 0$, we contradict the hypothesis that $b \neq c$. We can thus write $z = x^* + (1/\lambda)(c - b)$. Since $\mathscr{F}$ is convex and z, b are in $\mathscr{F}$, for any $t \in [0, 1]$, we obtain that $((1 - t)x^* + (1/\lambda)(c - b) + tb) \in \mathscr{F}$. On choosing t to be equal to $\bar{t} \equiv 1/1 + \lambda$, we obtain that $((1 - \bar{t})x^* + \bar{t}c) \in \mathscr{F}$. This contradicts the fact that $c \in \mathscr{F}_{x^*}$ and completes the proof. ∎

We can now get back to the question at hand—recall that the issue was to show the validity of (12). We begin with a simple but very useful observation whose routine verification we leave to the reader.

LEMMA 10. $f(p^*) \cap (X \cap Y) = \emptyset \Leftrightarrow \Sigma_{i \in I1}\xi^i(p^*) \cap (Y - X_{I_2}) = \emptyset$.

Lemma 10 implies that if (12) does not hold, there exists $x^*(I_1) \in \Sigma_{i \in I_1}\xi^i(p^*)$ such that

$$x^*(I_1) \in \left(Y - \sum_{i \in I_2} \bar{X}^i\right) \Big/ \left(Y - \sum_{i \in I_2} X^i\right) \equiv \bar{\mathscr{F}}_1/\mathscr{F}_1.$$

Note that by the definition of I_1, $x^*(I_1) \in \Sigma_{i \in I_1}X^i$. Let $\Sigma_{i \in I_1}x^{*i} = x^*(I_1)$.

In order to get an overview of the argument, let us assume that I_1 is a singleton set and correspondingly abbreviate $x^*(I_1)$ to x^*, $\mathscr{F}_1$ and $\bar{\mathscr{F}}_1$ to $\mathscr{F}$ and $\bar{\mathscr{F}}$. The basic steps are then as follows.

1. $x^* \in \bar{\mathscr{F}}/\mathscr{F}$. $x^* \notin \mathscr{F}$ by hypothesis and $x^* \in \bar{\mathscr{F}}$ by definition of $f(p^*)$.

2. Let B be the boundary of $\mathscr{F}_1$ in the relative topology of $\bar{\mathscr{F}}_1$ and $B' = B \cap \Sigma_{i \in I_1}X^i$. B' is nonempty compact and therefore has a maximum (say, b) with respect to the preference relation $\succcurlyeq_1$. From *strong viability*, $\exists \bar{x} \in \mathscr{F}$. Convexity of $\mathscr{F}$, $\bar{\mathscr{F}}$ and $\Sigma_{i \in I_1}X^i$ implies that the line segment joining $\bar{x}$ and x^* has a point of intersection with B'. The rest is straightforward.

3. $x^* \succcurlyeq_1 b$. If not, $b \succcurlyeq_1 x^*$. Since $b \in \mathscr{F}$, $p^*b \leq 0$. Hence $b \in \xi^1(p^*)$ and we contradict the fact that $\xi^1(p^*) \cap \mathscr{F} = \emptyset$.

4. Since $b \in \mathscr{F}$, there exists $y \in Y$ and $x^i \in X^i$, $i \in I_2$ such that $((b, x^i)), y)$ constitute an allocation. By *weak irreducibility*, there exists $\tilde{y} \in Y$ and $w \in \bar{X}_{I_2}$ such that $(b + \tilde{y} - w) \succcurlyeq_1 b$. Let $c = (b + \tilde{y} - w) \equiv (b + m)$. Note that $c \in \mathscr{F}$ and $m = (c - b) \in \bar{\mathscr{F}}$.

5. All the conditions of our geometric problem are fulfilled, and hence we may conclude that $c \notin \mathscr{F}_{x^*}$. Hence there exists $\mu \in]0, 1[$ such that $z \equiv \mu x^* + (1 - \mu)c$ is in B'.

6. We now use convexity of $\succcurlyeq_1$ to get a contradiction to the fact that b is a maximal element for $\succcurlyeq_1$ in B'.

The question remains as to what happens when I_1 is not a singleton. In this case, McKenzie constructs a social utility function $v(\cdot)$ pertaining to the traders in I_1 and then essentially follows Steps 1–6 above with the necessary modifications. Toward this end, let u^i represent $\succcurlyeq_i$ with $\sup_{x \in X^i} u^i(x) = 1$ and $\inf_{x \in X^i} u^i(x) = 0$. From Debreu (1959, pp. 56–59), we know that this can be done. Let $u^{*i} = u^i(x^{*i})$, v: $\Sigma_{i \in I_1} X^i \to \mathbb{R}$, $v(x) = \text{Max}_{\alpha \in \mathscr{A}(x)}\, \alpha$ and $\mathscr{A}(x) = \{\alpha \in \mathbb{R}$: For all $i \in I_1$, $u^i(x^i) \geq \alpha u^{*i}$, $x^i \in X^i$ with $\Sigma_{i \in I_1} x^i = x\}$.

Claim 2. $v(\cdot)$ is continuous and quasiconcave.

Proof. This is straightforward; see McKenzie (1981, p. 828). ■

Let U_1 be the utility possibility frontier for the consumers in I_1 over $\mathscr{F}_1$.

Claim 3. $u^* \notin U_1$, where $u^* \equiv ((u^{*i})_{i \in I_1})$.

Proof. If any consumer in I_1 is satiated, it follows from *weak irreducibility* that u^* is not obtained from a feasible allocation for I_1, and hence $u^* \notin U_1$. If no consumer in I_1 is satiated, and $u^* \in U_1$, $\exists x \in \mathscr{F}_1$ and $x^i \in X^i$ such that $u^i(x^i) = u^*(x^{*i})$ for all $i \in I_1$. But this validates (12) above and furnishes a contradiction. ■

Claim 4. $v(b) < 1$ where b is the maximum of $v(\cdot)$ over B'.

Proof. If not, $\exists b^i \in X^i$ with $\Sigma_{i \in I_1} b^i = b$ and $u^i(b^i) \geq u^i(x^{*i})$. But this contradicts Claim 2. ■

Claim 5. There exists $m \in \overline{\mathscr{F}}_1$, $m \neq 0$ such that $v(m + b) \equiv v(c) \geq v(b)$.

Proof. A consequence of *weak irreducibility* essentially as in Step 4 above. Note that $c \in \Sigma_{i \in I_1} X^i$ and $c \in \mathscr{F}_1$. ■

Now we again appeal to the solution of our geometric problem and construct z that is different from b and is a convex combination of $x^*(I_1)$ and c. The quasiconcavity of $v(\cdot)$ then allows us to conclude that $v(z) > v(b)$ and obtain the necessary contradiction.

As in the proof of Theorem 5, once we have equilibrium under the assumption of *strong viability*, we can rely on the embedding methods first used in 1959 to obtain an equilibrium using only the *viability* and *irreducibility* conditions on the economy. A point that should be made in the context of Theorem 8, however, is that some care has to be taken when Y is a linear subspace as in the pure exchange case without free disposal. This requires the introduction of a fictitional commodity which facilitates the embedding but is not used in equilibrium. I refer to Section 4 in McKenzie (1981) for details.

Next we consider the proof of Theorem 10. McKenzie is influenced by Shafer (1974) and Shafer and Sonnenschein (1975) in defining a pseudoutility function to generate pseudodemand functions. These pseudo-demands are then used along with the inverse supply mapping to generate a correspondence from $P \times \prod_{i=1}^{m} \overline{X}^i$ to itself as in the 1955 paper. Kakutani's fixed-point theorem applied to this correspondence yields prices and quantities which, with further work, can be shown to be an equilibrium. However, rather than reproduce the arguments, it might be more worthwhile to ask how relevant are the methods of McKenzie (1959) to the problem at hand. We turn to this.

Except for a slight change in the definition of the aggregate preferred set $C(p)$, we retain the notation of Section 4. The idea is to apply Kakutani's fixed point theorem to a mapping F given by $((F^i)_{i=1}^m, F^{m+1})$ where

$$F^i: P \times \chi \to X^i, (p,(x)) \to F^i(p,x) = \operatorname{con} C^i(p,x),$$

$$C^i(p,x) = \left\{ w \in X^i : w \in \operatorname{Argmax}_{z \in H^i(p)} u^i(z, x^i) \text{ and } pw \geq 0 \right\},$$

$$u^i: X^i \times X^i \to \mathbb{R}, u^i(y,x) = \operatorname{Inf}_{z \in (\text{graph } P^i)^c} d((y,x),z),$$

$$F^{m+1}: P \times \chi \to P, F^{m+1}(p,x) = \begin{cases} \Gamma\left(\sum_{i=1}^{m} x^i; Y\right) & \text{if } \sum_{i=1}^{m} x^i \notin Y \\ P & \text{if } \sum_{i=1}^{m} x^i \in Y. \end{cases}$$

We first verify that for any $(p,x) \in P \times \chi$, $C^i(p,x) \neq \emptyset$. Since $u^i(\cdot, x^i)$ is a continuous function and $H^i(p,x)$ is a compact set, $\operatorname{Argmax}_{z \in H^i(p)} u^i(z, x^i) \neq \emptyset$. Let $u^i(w, x^i) \geq u^i(z, x^i)\ \forall z \in H^i(p)$. Suppose that $u^i(w, x^i) = 0$. Then $u^i(z, x^i) = 0\ \forall z \in H^i(p)$. Now any $z \in H^i(p,x)$ with $pz = 0$ finishes the verification. Thus suppose that $u^i(w, x^i) > 0$ and $pw < 0$. The first implies that $w \in P^i(x^i)$. Given that the set $P^i(x^i)$ is open, there exists $\varepsilon_1 > 0$ such that $B_{\varepsilon_1}(w) \subseteq P^i(x^i)$. Since $pw < 0$, there exists $\varepsilon_2 > 0$ such that $pz < 0\ \forall z \in B_{\varepsilon_2}(w)$. Let $\varepsilon = \operatorname{Min}(\varepsilon_1, \varepsilon_2)$. We can now find a $\hat{z} \in H^i(p)$ such that $u^i(\hat{z}, x^i) > 0$ i.e.,

$$d\left((\hat{z}, x^i), (\text{graph } P^i)^c\right) > d\left((w, x^i), (\text{graph } P^i)^c\right),$$

a contradiction to the maximality of w.

We leave it to the reader to check the remaining conditions for the validity of Kakutani's fixed-point theorem. Let us suppose that (p^*, x^*) is a fixed point of the map F and that $\exists z \in (P^i(x^*) \cap H^i(p^*))$. Then $u^i(\hat{z}, x^{*i}) > 0$. Since $x^{*i} \in \operatorname{con} C^i(p^*, x^*)$,

$$\exists \lambda_j \geq 0, \sum_j \lambda_j = 1, x^{*i}(j) \in C^i(p^*, x^*) \text{ such that } \sum_j \lambda_j x^{*i}(j) = x^{*i}.$$

But this implies that

$$p^* x^{*i}(j) \geq 0 \quad \text{and} \quad u^i\big(x^{*i}(j), x^{*i}\big) \geq u^i(z, x^{*i}) \forall z \in H^i(p^*). \quad (13)$$

By (13) $u^i(x^{*i}(j), x^{*i}) > 0$ for all j. But this implies that for all j, $x^{*i}(j) \in P^i(x^{*i})$ and hence $x^{*i} \in \text{con } P^i(x^{*i})$. But this is a contradiction.

Now suppose that $x^* = \Sigma_{i=1}^m x^{*i} \in Y$, i.e., $\exists y^* \in Y$ such that $x^* = y^*$. Since $p^* \in P$, $p^* y^* \leq 0$. Hence $p^* x^* \leq 0$. Since $x^* \in \Sigma_{i=1}^m \text{con } P^i(p^*, x^*)$, $p^* x^* \geq 0$. Hence $p^* x^* = 0$. This implies

$$0 = p^* y^* \leq p^* y \ \forall y \in Y \quad \text{and} \quad p^* x^{*i} = 0 \ \forall i.$$

Hence $(p^*, (x^*), y^*)$ is a competitive equilibrium.

Suppose, on the other hand, that $x^* \notin Y$. Let $y^* \in \mathscr{P}_Y(x^*)$. By definition of Γ,

$$\| y^* - x^* \| = p^*(y^* - x^*) \geq p^*(y - x^*) \ \forall y \in Y.$$

This implies that $p^* y^* = 0$. Since $p^* x^* \geq 0$, $\| y^* - x^* \| \leq 0$. Hence $\| y^* - x^* \| = 0$, and we are done.

5.3 Influence on Subsequent Work

It is surely too early to tell; if the 1954 paper and the literature on marginal cost pricing equilibria is any guide, we may have to wait another 15 years!

6. AN OVERVIEW

We began this paper by referring to the emphasis on geometry in McKenzie's work. We can now be more specific. Except for the 1959 paper, all the proofs make use of *intersection mappings*, which involve projecting points onto the production sets. In addition, all these proofs make use of *efficiency price mappings*, which involve *tangent spaces* and their *normal cones*. In the 1959 paper, McKenzie exploits the observation that the difference of the vectors at which the distance between two closed convex sets is attained, is a singleton. This allows him to use the more elementary fixed-point theorem of Brouwer. However, as we have seen in our repackaged version of McKenzie's proof, even here there is implicit a projection and a normal cone. Euclidean n-space simply allows them to be given a simpler representation.

The counterpoint to this emphasis on geometry is the sparse use of ordered structures. Other than in the assumption of consumption sets being bounded from below, and of course, in the specification of preferences, no use is made of the binary relation. Thus, prices are not required to be nonnegative, monotonicity assumptions on preferences are explicitly avoided and free disposal is seen synonymously with the question of interiority.[69] This goes against the grain of modern work with its heavy use of lattice and Reisz space structures.[70] However, as we have argued in the context of the ideas stemming from the 1959 paper, the potential of convexity and of topology in the context of an infinite-dimensional setting without ordered structures seems hardly exhausted.[71]

The lack of emphasis on order is mirrored in the total avoidance of measure-theoretic structures or those relying on nonstandard analysis. This is interesting in light of the early recognition of economic negligibility as an essential underpinning of the formalization of perfect competition. McKenzie writes[72]

> The presence of competition means that everyone accepts prices as given and beyond the scope of his influence. The assumption that market participants take prices as independent of their actions fails to describe many markets and describes very few exactly.

Here again the full potential of the interplay between geometry and measure theory which began with Aumann, seems hardly realized.

A final point as regards the proofs. Starting from 1954, McKenzie sees the primitives of his theorems as limits of objects for which the results can be more easily proved. The general result is then obtained by taking the limit of the results for the special case. This technique is most finely tuned in the 1981 paper when *strong survival* and *strong viability* is relaxed to viability in the presence of *weak irreducibility*, but, in essentials, its roots lie in the extended demands of 1954.

Finally, we turn to the emphasis on constant returns to scale and on the *survival assumption*, i.e., guaranteeing income to everyone in a *viable* economy. The latter is a constant theme ever since 1955, and as regards the former, McKenzie writes[73]

> It is an unusual characteristic of my contributions to the theory of existence of equilibrium that the social production set has been represented by a convex cone. The linear model is intended to represent free entry into any line of production by cooperating factors, however organized in a legal sense, where economies of scale are sufficiently small to allow approximate linearity to be achieved by the multiplication of producing units. The lumpiness which is present is compared to that resulting from goods which are in fact indivisible, although they are treated as divisible. Of course, it has to be recognized that in real economies some sectors

[69]See Section 4 in McKenzie (1981).

[70]See Aliprantis *et al.* (1989) and references cited therein.

[71]See Khan and Peck (1989) for the relation between interiority assumptions and those on supporting functionals of a convex set.

[72]See page 152 in McKenzie (1954) and page 29 in McKenzie (1987).

[73]See page 836 in McKenzie (1981) and pages 10–11 in McKenzie (1987).

cannot be approximated in this way. However, when linearity becomes a bad approximation to the production sector, convexity has in all likelihood become an equally bad approximation to the production sets of firms.

It is of some interest that the 1954 paper in which the technology is not assumed to be a cone has proved so influential for the work on the existence of marginal cost pricing equilibria in economies with increasing returns to scale.

Acknowledgments

A first version of this paper was presented at the Conference on *General Equilibrium and Growth: The Legacy of Lionel McKenzie* held at Rochester on May 5–7, 1989. This final version is respectfully dedicated to the memory of Tjalling C. Koopmans.

It is a pleasure to acknowledge the detailed suggestions of Lionel McKenzie, Hugh Rose, Jane Shieh, and Rajiv Vohra as well the many valuable conversations I had with them and with John Chipman, Tadashi Hamano, Joe Harrington, Tatsuo Hatta, Leo Hurwicz, Ron Jones, Lou Maccini, Mukul Majumdar, Tapan Mitra, Peter Newman, Ed Prescott, Kali Rath, S. Takekuma, Akira Yamazaki, and Nicholas Yannelis. Finally, I am grateful to an anonymous referee for her or his comments—I am sorry that I could not take up her or his suggestion "to explore the connections and interplay between Professor McKenzie's work in capital theory and on the existence problem." Errors, particularly of fact or of interpretation, are all mine.

References

Akhiezer, N. I., and I. M. Glazman (1978). *Theory of Linear Operators in Hilbert Space*, Vol. 1 (Frederick Ungar Publishing Co., New York).

Alfsen, E. M. (1971). *Compact Convex Sets and Boundary Integrals* (Springer-Verlag, Berlin).

Aliprantis, C. D., D. J. Brown, and O. Burkinshaw (1989). *Existence and Optimality of Competitive Equilibrium* (Springer-Verlag, Berlin).

Arrow, K. J., and G. Debreu (1954). "Existence of an equilibrium for a competitive economy," *Econometrica* **22**, 265–290.

Arrow, K. J. (1969). "The organization of economic activity: Issues pertinent to the choice of market versus non-market allocation," in *Joint Economic Committee*, *The Analysis and Evaluation of Public Expenditures*, *The PBB System* (Govt. Printing Office, Washington, D.C.).

Arrow, K. J. (1983). *Collected Papers*, Vol. 2 (Belknap Press, Massachusetts).

Arrow, K. J., and F. H. Hahn (1971). *General Competitive Analysis* (Holden-Day, San Francisco).

Aumann, R. J. (1966). "Existence of competitive equilibria in markets with a continuum of traders," *Econometrica* **34**, 1–17.

Bateman P. T. (1951). "Introductory material on convex sets in Euclidean space," *Seminar on Convex Sets*, mimeographed, Princeton, N.J.

Beato, P. (1979). "Marginal cost pricing and increasing returns," Ph.D dissertation (University of Minnesota, Minneapolis).

Beato, P. (1982). "The existence of marginal cost pricing with increasing returns," *Quart. J. Econ*. **100**, 669–688.

Beato, P., and A. Mas-Colell (1985). "On marginal cost pricing with given tax-subsidy rules," *J. Econ. Theory* **37**, 356–365.

Berge, C. (1963). *Topological Spaces* (Macmillan, New York).

Bewley, T. F. (1970). "A very weak theorem on the existence of equilibria in economies with an atomless space of agents and infinitely many commodities," Chapter V of Ph.D dissertation (University of California, Berkeley).

Bewley, T. F. (1972). "Existence of equilibria in economies with infinitely many commodities," *J. Econ. Theory* **4**, 572–592.

Brosowski, B., F. Deutsch, and G. Nurnberger (1980). "Parametric approximation," *J. Approximation Theory* **29**, 261–277.

Brown, D. J., and G. M. Heal (1982). "Existence, local uniqueness and optimality of a marginal cost pricing equilibrium in an economy with increasing returns," Social Science Working Paper No. 415, Caltech, Pasadena.

Brown, D. J., G. M. Heal, M. Ali Khan, and R. Vohra (1986). "On a general existence theorem for marginal cost pricing equilibria," *J. Econ. Theory* **38**, 371–379.

Chipman, J., and J. Moore (1968). "The compensation principle in welfare economics," pp. 1–77 in A. M. Zarley (ed.). *Papers in Quantitative Economics*, Vol. 2 (The University Press of Kansas, Lawrence, Kansas).

Clarke, F. (1975). "Generalized gradients and applications," *Trans. Am. Math. Soc.* **205**, 247–262.

Clarke, F. (1983). *Optimization and Nonsmooth Analysis* (Wiley, New York).

Cornet, B. (1988). "General Equilibrium Theory and Increasing Returns," *J. Math. Econ.* 17.

Debreu, G. (1952). "A social equilibrium existence theorem," *Proc. Nat. Acad. Sci., USA* **38** (1952), 886–893.

Debreu, G. (1954), Valuation equilibrium and Pareto optimum, *Proc. Nat. Acad. Sci., USA* **40**, 588–592.

Debreu, G. (1956). "Market equilibrium," *Proc. Nat. Acad. Sci., USA* **42**, 876–878.

Debreu, G. (1959). *Theory of Value* (Wiley, New York).

Debreu, G. (1962). "New concepts and techniques for equilibrium analysis," *Internat. Econ. Rev.* **3**, 257–273.

Debreu, G. (1970). "Economies with a finite set of equilibria," *Econometrica* **38**, 387–392.

Debreu, G. (1974). "Four aspects of the mathematical theory of economic equilibrium," *Proceedings of the International Congress of Mathematicians* **1**, 65–77.

Debreu, G. (1982). "Existence of competitive equilibria," pp. 697–743 in K. J. Arrow and M. Intrilligator (eds.). *Handbook of Mathematical Economics*, Vol. II (North Holland, Amsterdam).

Deutsch, F. R., and P. H. Maserick, 1967, Applications of the Hahn-Banach theorem in approximation theory, *Siam Rev.* **9**, 516–530.

Dierker, E. (1974). *Topological Methods in Walrasian Economics*, Vol. 92 (Springer-Verlag, Berlin).

Fan, Ky (1952). "Fixed points and minimax theorems in locally convex spaces," *Proc. Nat. Acad. Sci., USA* **38**, 121–126.

Fenchel, W. (1953). *Convex Cones, Sets and Functions*, mimeographed, Princeton Univ., Princeton, N.J.

Florenzano, M. (1982). "The Gale-Nikaido-Debreu lemma and the existence of transitive equilibrium with or without the free-disposal assumption," *J. Math. Econ.* **9**, 113–134.

Foley, D. (1967). "Resource allocation and the public sector," *Yale Economic Essays*, New Haven, Conn.

Foley, D. (1970). "Lindahl's solution and the core of an economy with public goods," *Econometrica* **38**, 66–72.

Gale, D., and A. Mas-Colell (1975). "An equilibrium existence theorem for a general model without ordered preferences," *J. Math. Econ.* **2**, 9–15.

Glicksberg, I. (1952). "A further generalization of the Kakutani fixed point theorem with applications to Nash equilibrium points," *Proc. Am. Math. Soc.* **3**, 170–174.

Guesnerie, R. (1975). "Pareto optimality in non-convex economies," *Econometrica* **43**, 1–29.

Gwinner, J. (1981). "On fixed points and variational inequalities—a circular tour," *Nonlinear Analysis* **5**, 565–583.

Hahn, F. H., and R. C. O. Matthews (1965). "The theory of economic growth: A survey," *Econ. J.* **74**, 779–902.

Holmes, R. B. (1972). *A Course on Optimization and Best Approximation*, *Lecture Notes in Mathematics No. 257* (Springer-Verlag, New York).

Hurwicz, L., and S. Reiter (1973). "On the boundedness of the feasible set without convexity assumptions," *Int. Econ. Rev.* **14**, 580–586.

Jameson, G. (1970). *Ordered Linear Spaces* (Springer-Verlag, Berlin).

Jones, L. E., (1987). "Existence of equilibria with infinitely many commodities: Banach lattices reconsidered," *J. Math. Econ.* **16**, 89–94.

Jones, R. W. (1975). "Income distribution and effective protection in a multi-commodity trade model," *J. Econ. Theory* **11**, 1–15.

Khan, M. Ali (1984). "A remark on the existence of equilibria in markets without ordered preferences and with a Reisz space of commodities," *J. Math. Econ.* **13**, 165–169.

Khan, M. Ali, and N. T. Peck (1989). "On the interiors of production sets in infinite dimensional spaces," *J. Math. Econ.* **18**, 29–39.

Khan, M. Ali, and R. Vohra (1984). "Equilibrium in abstract economies without ordered preferences and with a measure space of agents," *J. Math. Econ.* **13**, 133–142.

Khan, M. Ali, and R. Vohra (1987a). "An extension of the second welfare theorem to economies with non-convexities and public goods," *Quart. J. Econ.* **102**, 223–245.

Khan, M. Ali, and R. Vohra (1987b). "On sufficient conditions for the sum of two weak * closed convex sets to be weak * closed," *Archiv der Mathematik* **48**, 328–330.

Khan, M. Ali, and R. Vohra (1987c). "On the existence of Lindahl–Hotelling equilibria," *J. Public Econ.* **34**, 143–158.

Khan, M. Ali, and R. Vohra (1988). "On approximate decentralization of Pareto Optimal allocations in locally convex spaces," *J. Approximation Theory* **52**, 149–165.

Koopmans, T. C. (1957). *Three Essays on the State of Economic Science* (McGraw-Hill, New York).

Malinvaud, E. (1953). "Capital accumulation and the efficient allocation of resources," *Econometrica* **21**, 233–268.

Mantel, R. (1979). "Equilibrio con rendimento crecientes a escala," *Anales de la Asociation Argentiana de Economia Politica* **1**, 271–283.

Mas-Colell, A. (1974). "An equilibrium existence theorem without complete or transitive preferences," *J. Math. Econ.* **1**, 237–246.

Mas-Colell, A. (1986). "The price equilibrium existence problem in topological vector lattices," *Econometrica* **54**, 1039–1055.

McCabe, P. J. (1981). "On two market equilibrium theorems," *J. Econ. Theory* **8**, 167–171.

McKenzie, L. W. (1954). "On equilibrium in Graham's model of world trade and other competitive systems," *Econometrica* **22**, 147–161.

McKenzie, L. W. (1955). "Competitive equilibrium with dependent consumer preferences," *Second Symposium on Linear Programming* (National Bureau of Standards, Washington, D.C.), pp. 277–294. Reprinted in *Readings in Mathematical Economics*, P. K. Newman (ed.) (Johns Hopkins University Press, Baltimore), pp. 129–146.

McKenzie, L. W. (1956). "Application of activity analysis to the theory of general equilibrium," unpublished Ph.D dissertation submitted to Princeton University.

McKenzie, L. W. (1959). "On the existence of general equilibrium for a competitive market," *Econometrica* **27**, 54–71. Reprinted in *Selected Readings in Economic Theory from Econometrica*, K. J. Arrow (ed.), (MIT Press, Cambridge, Mass.), pp. 339–356.

McKenzie, L. W. (1961). "On the existence of general equilibrium: Some corrections," *Econometrica* **29**, 247–248.

McKenzie, L. W. (1981). "The classical theorem on the existence of general equilibrium," *Econometrica* **49**, 819–841.

McKenzie, L. W. (1986). "Optimal economic growth, turnpike theorems and comparative dynamics," pp. 1281–1355 in K. J. Arrow and M. Intrilligator (eds.). *Handbook of Mathematical Economics*, Vol. III (North Holland, Amsterdam).

McKenzie, L. W. (1987). "General equilibrium," in *The New Palgrave: A Dictionary of Economics*, J. Eatwell *et al.* (eds.), (Macmillan Press, London). Reprinted in *General Equilibrium*, J. Eatwell *et al.* (eds.), (Macmillan Press, London), pp. 1–61.

Mehta, G., and E. Tarafdar (1987). "Infinite dimensional Gale-Nikaido-Debreu theorem and the Tarafdar fixed point theorem," *J. Econ. Theory* **41**, 333–339.

Moore, J. (1975). "The existence of compensated equilibrium and the structure of the Pareto efficiency frontier," *Int. Econ. Rev.* **16**, 267–300.

Nash, J. F. (1950). "Equilibrium points in N-person games," *Proc. Nat. Acad. Sci. USA* **36**, 48–59.

Negishi, T. (1960). "Welfare economics and existence of equilibrium for a competitive economy," *Metroeconomica* **12**, 92–97.

Rockafellar, R. T. (1970). *Convex Analysis* (Princeton University Press, N.J.).

Rockafellar, R. T. (1979). "Clarke's tangent cones and the boundaries of closed sets in R^n," *Nonlinear Analysis* **3**, 145–154.

Samuelson, P. A. (1971). "Ohlin was right," *Swedish J. Econ.* **13**, 365–389.

Scarf, H. E. (with the collaboration of T. Hansen) (1973). *The Computation of Economic Equilibria* (Yale University Press, New Haven, Conn.).

Schmeidler, D. (1969). "Competitive equilibria in markets with a continuum of traders and incomplete preferences," *Econometrica* **37**, 578–585.

Shafer, W. J. (1974). "The nontransitive consumer," *Econometrica* **42**, 913–919.

Shafer, W. J. and H. Sonnenschein (1975). "Equilibrium in abstract economies without ordered preferences," *J. Math. Econ.* **2**, 345–348.

Shitovitz, B. (1973). "Oligopoly in markets with a continuum of traders," *Econometrica* **41**, 467–505.

Singer, I. (1974). *The Theory of Best Approximation and Functional Analysis*, *Regional Conference Series in Applied Mathematics No. 13* (Soc. Ind. Appl. Math., Philadelphia).

Spivak, A. (1978). "A note on Arrow–Hahn's resource-relatedness (or McKenzie's irreducibility)," *Int. Econ. Rev.* **19**, 527–531.

Starrett, D. (1972). "Fundamental non-convexities in the theory of externalities," *J. Econ. Theory* **4**, 180–199.

Tarafdar, E. and G. Mehta (1984). "The existence of quasi-equilibria in a competitive economy," *Int. J. Sci. Eng.* **1**, 1–12.

Toussaint, S. (1984). "On the existence of equilibria in economies with infinitely many commodities and without ordered preferences," *J. Econ. Theory* **33**, 98–115.

Tulcea, C. I. (1988). "On the approximation of upper semi-continuous correspondences and the equilibriums of generalized games," *J. Math. Analysis and Applications* **136**, 267–287.

Uzawa, H. (1962). "Walras' existence theorem and Brouwer's fixed point theorem," *Economic Studies Quart.* **13**, 59–62.

Vohra, R. (1983). "Increasing returns, public goods and general equilibrium theory," Ph.D dissertation (Johns Hopkins University Baltimore, Md.).

Vohra, R. (1988). "On the existence of equilibria in economies with increasing returns," *J. Math. Econ.* **17**, 179–192.

Yannelis, N. C. (1985). "On a market equilibrium theorem with an infinite number of commodities," *J. Math. Analysis and Applications* **108**, 595–599.

Yannelis, N. C. (1987). "Equilibria in noncooperative models of competition," *J. Econ. Theory* **41**, 96–111.

Yannelis, N. C., and N. Prabhakar (1983), Existence of maximal elements and equilibria in linear topological spaces, *Journal of Mathematical Economics* 12, 233–245.

Yannelis, N. C., and W. R. Zame (1986). "Equilibria in Banach lattices without ordered preferences," *J. Math. Econ.* **15**, 85–110.

Zame, W. R. (1987). "Equilibria in production economies with an infinite dimensional commodity space," *Econometrica* **55**, 1075–1108.

McKENZIE AND THE SLUTSKY COEFFICIENTS

S. N. Afriat
Economics Department
Bilkent University
06533 Bilkent/Ankara, Turkey

It is a pleasure to take part in honoring Lionel McKenzie. As with so many others present, he has been a favorite of mine, so my approach may be somewhat personal besides mathematical. I encounter him in areas associated with Walras, von Neumann, and Slutsky. Attention in this conference to the first two is intensive but for my particular indebtedness I should give attention to the third, where his contribution (McKenzie, 1957a, b, 1958; see also Afriat, 1980) should be marked even though we may be taken up with other branches of his work.

Following McKenzie, differentiate a utility–cost function twice, and we have a negative semidefinite symmetric matrix of Slutsky coefficients. The important conditions are obtained simultaneously, in one short stroke. With Slutsky and others, after some pages of calculus, we find more is asked. Something extra, and in fact spurious, has entered unnoticed. This is brought out in Afriat (1972), which involves an acceptable demand function, with continuous derivatives and a utility function. But all the coefficients are zero—an impossibility in the original account.

A null matrix is certainly symmetric, but it is without the other requirement wanted by others, intermediate between the matrix being negative definite and semidefinite. Here is evidence that the usually offered conditions are more than necessary. The conditions obtained by McKenzie, besides being necessary for the existence of a utility, appear good candidates for being sufficient also, as in fact they are.

GENERAL EQUILIBRIUM, GROWTH, AND TRADE II

We will review the question Slutsky's theory is about. With prices p, and an amount M of money to be spent on some bundle of goods x, there is the budget constraint $px = M$.[1] Given a function $x = F(p, M)$ that determines the unique maximum of a function ϕ under any budget constraint, F is a *demand function* that *has* ϕ *as a utility function*, or is *derived* from ϕ.

Now with any given function F it may be asked whether it is such a function so associated with a utility function. The function F first must have the properties

$$pF(p, M) = M, \qquad F(p, M) = F(M^{-1}p, 1),$$

usually associated with demand functions. Then a function ϕ is sought for which, for all p and M, $x = F(p, M)$ is the unique maximum of ϕ under the constraint $px = M$, that is,

$$py = M, \quad y \neq x \Rightarrow \phi(y) < \phi(x).$$

Slutsky (1915) considered this question with reference to a demand function $x = F(p, M)$, with continuous derivatives, and coefficients

$$s_{ij} = \partial x_t / \partial p_j + (\partial x_i / \partial M) x_j$$

formed from these, or elements of the matrix

$$s = x_p + x_M x'.$$

From the assumption that F has a utility with continuous second derivatives, by a method with the first order Lagrange conditions, he obtained the *Slutsky symmetry* condition

$$s_{ij} = s_{ji},$$

in terms of these coefficients, that is,

$$s = s'.$$

Then from second-order conditions, involving bordered Hessians and so forth, the symmetric matrix s is required to be something more than negative semidefinite, toward its being negative definite, although it cannot possibly be that since $ps = 0$ is an identity. The appropriate *Slutsky negativity* condition is that

$$q \nparallel p \Rightarrow qsq' < 0,$$

where $q \| p$ means $q = tp$ for some $t \neq 0$, and $q \nparallel p$ is the denial. It has

[1]In present notation, with Ω as the positive numbers, $B = \Omega_n$ is the *budget space* (nonnegative row vectors), and $C = \Omega^n$ is the *commodity space* (column vectors). Then any $p \in B$, $x \in C$ determine $px \in \Omega$ for the value of the commodity bundle x at the prices p.

been a cumbersome matter with heavy calculus, largely unnecessary if we are to follow McKenzie.

For simplification, introduce the *budget vector* $u = M^{-1}p$, so the budget constraint $px = M$ is stated $ux = 1$. The *standard* demand function F determines the *normal* demand function f, its *normalization*, given by

$$f(u) = F(u, 1),$$

with the property

$$uf(u) = 1,$$

from which it is recovered as

$$F(p, M) = f(M^{-1}p).$$

Modified by a factor M, which alters nothing important, the Slutsky matrix is

$$s = M(x_p + x_M x'),$$

Then put in terms of the normal function $x = f(u)$, it admits the factorization

$$s = x_u(1 - u'x'),$$

into the product of a Jacobian and a projector.

With a utility order R, there is the *utility–cost function*[2]

$$\rho(p, x) = \min[\, py : yRx\,],$$

which tells the cost at prices p of attaining the utility of a commodity bundle x. Immediately from the form of its definition, this is concave conical in p. Also,

$$\rho(p, x) \leq px,$$

for all p and x, with equality for a demand (p, x) in the case of cost-efficiency.

McKenzie's approach is as follows. If f, with derivative matrix $g = f_u$, has this utility, then

$$x = f(u) \Rightarrow \rho(u, x) = 1, \qquad \rho_{u'}(u, x) = x,$$

[2]This form of definition with reference to an order, any reflexive transitive binary relation R in the commodity space, serves here to emphasize a complete absence of dependence on prior assumptions, even that utility has a numerical representation. The form is important also in other connections, as when $\rho(p, x)$ takes special forms, which cannot be stated with the perhaps more usual definition that involves a numerical utility level, for instance when $\rho(p, x) = \theta(p)\phi(x)$, which makes expansion paths to be rays and is significant in dealing with price indices, or $\rho(p, x) = \theta(p)\phi(x) + v(p)$, which makes them general lines; an account is in Afriat (1987).

and also, for any x,

$$\rho_{u'}(u, x) = f(\rho^{-1}u),$$

so that, with $\rho = \rho(u, x)$, we have

$$\rho_{u'u}(u, x) = g(\rho^{-1}u)(\rho^{-1}1 - \rho^{-2}u'\rho_u),$$

and consequently,

$$x = f(u) \Rightarrow \rho_{u'u} = g(1 - u'x') = s.$$

No explicit properties for R are required at all, even though there may be implicit ones just from its association with a demand function. Here f being derived from R ensures that ρ is differentiable in u, and so, because concave, it must be continuously differentiable. Then $\rho_{u'u}$ exists, and is continuous. From the continuity of $\rho_{u'u}$, the symmetry follows, and this matrix must be nonpositive definite, because ρ is concave in u, just from the form of its definition as a cost function. Hence the conclusion that *s is symmetric and nonpositive definite*.

The plan for proceeding backward has several steps, which can be stated briefly.[3] From the local integrability at any point in the budget space, provided by Frobenius from the symmetry of s, this being identified with the conditions in his theorem, we arrive at a *global integral* ψ. In any case monotonic, by a choice of sign the integral ψ is made a decreasing function. Then s being everywhere nonpositive definite is the condition for ψ to be quasiconvex. With ψ a decreasing function in the budget space,

$$\phi(x) = \min[\psi(u): ux \leq 1]$$

is an increasing quasiconcave function in the commodity space. Provided that ψ is quasiconvex, this a utility function with which ψ is associated as the corresponding indirect utility function, since it is recovered from ϕ by the formula

$$\psi(u) = \max[\phi(x): ux \leq 1].$$

Finally,

$$x = f(u) \Leftrightarrow \phi(x) = \psi(u), \qquad ux = 1,$$

from which there is the conclusion that f has utility ϕ.

From the expression $s = x_u(1 - u'x')$, the Slutsky matrix is expressed as a product of a Jacobian, and a factor that, because $ux = 1$, is idempo-

[3]Details, in particular the passage from local to global conditions, are laborious. An account is in Afriat (1980), with summary in Afriat (1987, pp. 158ff). The development depends on the identity in Afriat (1954), which connects symmetry of s with classical integrability conditions, and then on Slutsky negativity being connected with quasi-convexity of the integral.

tent and so a projector. This exposes otherwise obscured features about the Slutsky matrix; for instance, the rank is $n-1$ for the invertible case, and otherwise less. It also provides a way of viewing Hicks's distinction of *income* and *substitution effects*, using resolution of a budget differential du into components by means of the projector and its complement:

$$du' = (u'x')\,du' + (1 - u'x')\,du'.$$

With the elements x_i of x and $x_{ij} = \partial x_i/\partial u_j$ of x_u, we may form

$$x_{ijk} = x_i(x_{jk} - x_{kj}) + x_j(x_{ki} - x_{ik}) + x_k(x_{ij} - x_{ji}).$$

Such coefficients have a part in Frobenius' theorem on the integrability of linear differential forms. The identity

$$\sum_k x_{ijk}u_k = s_{ij} - s_{ji}$$

assists the discovery that

$$x_{ijk} = 0 \Leftrightarrow s_{ij} = s_{ji},$$

where the *symmetry of s* is identified with *classical integrability conditions* for the linear differential form with coefficients $x = f(u)$. This finding does seem significant. But the integral obtained is in the budget space, instead of the commodity space. How it should bear on the question of utility construction is shown by the further considerations we have described.

References

Afriat, S. N. (1954). On linear differential forms and the symmetry condition of Slutsky (mimeo). Department of Applied Economics, Cambridge.

Afriat, S. N. (1972). The case of the vanishing Slutsky matrix, *J. Econ. Theory* **5**, 208–223.

Afriat, S. N. (1980). *Demand Functions and the Slutsky Matrix*. (Princeton University Press, Princeton, NJ).

Afriat, S. N. (1987). *Logic of Choice and Economic Theory*. (Clarendon Press, Oxford), pp. 158ff.

Allen, R. G. D., and J. R. Hicks (1934). A reconsideration of the theory of value, I, II. *Economica* **1**, 52–75, 196–219.

Hicks, J. R. (1948). *Value and Capital* 2nd edition (Clarendon Press, Oxford).

McKenzie L. W. (1957a). A direct approach to the Slutsky equation. *Cowles Foundation Discussion Paper* **13**, Yale University.

McKenzie L. W. (1957b). Demand theory without a utility index. *Rev. Econ. Studies* **24**, 185–189.

McKenzie L. W. (1958). Further comments, *Rev. Econ. Studies* **25**, 200.

Slutsky, E. E. (1915). Sulla teoria del bilancio del consumatore. *Giornale degli Economisti* **51**, 1–26. Translation by O. Ragusa (1952). On the theory of the budget of the consumer, in G. J. Stigler and K. E. Boulding (eds), *Readings in Price Theory* (Richard D. Irwin, Chicago), pp. 27–56.

REAL INDETERMINACY FROM IMPERFECT FINANCIAL MARKETS: TWO ADDENDA

David Cass
Department of Economics,
University of Pennsylvania,
Philadelphia, Pennsylvania 19104-6297

1. INTRODUCTION

Recently there has been a great deal of interest in examining the properties of competitive equilibrium with incomplete—or, more generally, imperfect—financial markets.[1] An important branch of this research has focused on the fact that, in such economies, there is typically a large degree of price or *nominal* indeterminacy, over and above that analogous to choosing a numeraire in the standard Walrasian model, which also translates into allocation or *real* indeterminacy.[2] The principal aim of this paper is to present two analyses that are basically responses to criticism of this latter development.

One sort of criticism has been based on the idea that the "reason" for indeterminacy is simply that the future "price level" is not tied down, and that, in particular, introducing the institution of fiat or *outside* money

[1]Two somewhat diferent kinds of surveys of this literature can be found in Cass [4] and Geanakoplos [6]. Both contain extensive references.

[2]This branch developed from an example I constructed that emphasized the possible sunspot interpretation of this phenomenon [3]. Generalization and refinement (as of this date) can be found in Balasko and Cass [1], Balasko, Cass and Siconolfi [2], Geanakoplos and Mas-Colell [7], Mas-Colell [10], Pietra [11], Polemarchakis [12], Siconolfi and Villanacci [13] and Werner [15]; the list is not exhaustive. Cass [5] provides a more comprehensive survey and appraisal, as well as some intuition for the basic substantive results.

GENERAL EQUILIBRIUM, GROWTH, AND TRADE II

should ameliorate the problem. I will argue here that while there is some truth to this conjecture (see also Magill and Quinzii [9]), its validity depends crucially on how one conceives the operation of a monetary system and, more critically, on what one takes as variable (read "determined endogenously") in a monetary economy. My own ultimate conclusion is that extensive real indeterminacy persists despite (in the extreme case) simply imposing value to holding outside money balances, and that it will be necessary (in order to reduce or even eliminate the problem) to look much more closely at the structure of the institutions and behavior of the intermediaries that constitute the monetary—or, more generally, financial—sector.

A second sort of criticism has been based on the following observation. While there may be a large degree of real indeterminacy (measured, in particular, by the minimum possible dimension of the set of equilibrium allocations), this phenomenon may not be of much substantive importance (judged, for instance, against the prevalence of such indeterminacy in a comparable Walrasian environment). It is not at all obvious how one can usefully formulate this possibility in a tractable fashion. I investigate the issue by considering a sequence of economies in which relatively more and more households have access to complete financial markets. It turns out that (given my particular methodology) as the extent of market imperfection becomes insignificant, so does the substantive importance of real indeterminacy. (For a quite different approach, with a quite different result, see also Green and Spear [8] and Zame [16].) A caution is warranted here, however. Even if (nominal or real) indeterminacy is of little substantive importance, it still presents a very difficult practical hurdle for the rational expectations hypotheses: Why should one believe households capable of concentrating their undivided attention on just one among a plethora of conceptually indistinguishable, consistent market outcomes?

In the next section I outline the basic framework for my analyses. Then, in the two subsequent sections, I consider first, the introduction of institutionalized outside money, and second, the significance of small market imperfections. At the outset I should emphasize that I am purposely adopting several simplifying hypotheses (which I will highlight as I go along) in order to avoid getting entangled with needless technical complication, and that I am purposely stressing results rather than proofs, most of which are pretty simple in conception, but nonetheless pretty complex in execution.

2. THE SETTING

For my purposes here it is most convenient to utilize the model with *restricted participation* analyzed in Balasko *et al.* [2]. Concerning some of its finer points (for example, the justification for the assumption A1, or the interpretation of the alterntive assumptions A5′ and A5″ below) the reader is advised to consult that paper. (*Note*: Here I employ a more mnemonic notation than there; otherwise the models are identical.)

There are C types of physical commodities (labeled by superscript $c = 1, 2, \ldots, C$, and referred to as *goods*), and I types of credit or financial instruments (labeled by superscript $i = 1, 2, \ldots, I$, and referred to as *bonds*). Both goods and bonds are traded on a spot market today, while only goods will be traded on a spot market in one of S possible states of the world tomorrow (these markets are labeled by superscript $s = 0, 1, \ldots, S$, so that $s = 0$ represents today and $s > 0$ represents the possible states tomorrow, and are both referred to as *spots*). Thus, altogether there are $G = C(S + 1)$ goods, whose quantities and (spot) prices are represented by the vectors $x = (x^0, \ldots, x^s, \ldots, x^S)$ [with $x^s = (x^{s,1}, \ldots, x^{s,c}, \ldots, x^{s,C})$] and $p = (p^0, \ldots, p^s, \ldots, p^S)$ [with $p^s = (p^{s,1}, \ldots, p^{s,c}, \ldots, p^{s,C})$], respectively. The quantities and prices of bonds are represented by the vectors $b = (b^1, \ldots, b^i, \ldots, b^I)$ and $q = (q^1, \ldots, q^i, \ldots, q^I)$, respectively. (*Note*: All prices are measured in units of account, referred to as *dollars*. It will be convenient, for example, in representing dollar values of spot market transactions, to treat every price or pricelike vector as a row. Otherwise I maintain the standard convention.) The typical bond, which costs q^i dollars at spot $s = 0$, promises to return a yield of $y^{s,i}$ dollars at spot $s > 0$. Let

$$Y = \begin{bmatrix} y^{1,1} & \cdots & y^{1,i} & \cdots & y^{1,I} \\ \vdots & \ddots & & & \\ y^{s,1} & & y^{s,i} & & \\ \vdots & & & \ddots & \\ y^{S,1} & & & & y^{S,I} \end{bmatrix} = \begin{bmatrix} y^1 \\ \vdots \\ y^s \\ \vdots \\ y^S \end{bmatrix}.$$

$$= (S \times I)\text{-dimensional matrix of bond yields.}$$

There is no loss of generality in assuming that

A1. Rank $Y = I$, *(no redundancy)*
which implies that $I \leqq S$.

Finally, there are H households (labeled by the subscript $h = 1, 2, \ldots, H$), who are described by (i) consumption sets $X_h = \mathbb{R}^G_{++}$, (ii) utility functions u_h: $X_h \to \mathbb{R}$, (iii) goods endowments $e_h \in X_h$, and (iv) portfolio sets $B_h \subset \mathbb{R}^I$. I assume throughout that, for $h = 1, 2, \ldots, H$,

A2. u_h is C^2, differentiably strictly increasing [i.e., $Du_h(x_h) \gg 0$] and differentiably strictly quasiconcave [i.e., $Du_h(x_h)\,\Delta x = 0$ and $\Delta x \neq 0 \Rightarrow \Delta x^T D^2 u_h(x_h)\,\Delta x < 0$], and has indifference surfaces with closure in X_h; and

A3. B_h is an I_h-dimensional linear subspace, with $I_h < S$ for some h. *(restricted participation)*

Let

$$P = \{p \in \mathbb{R}^G_{++}\}$$

$$= \text{set of possible (no-free-lunch) spot goods prices,}$$

$$Q = \left\{q \in \mathbb{R}^I\text{: there is no } h \text{ with } b_h \in B_h \text{ such that } \begin{bmatrix} -q \\ Y \end{bmatrix} b_h > 0\right\}$$

$$= \text{set of possible (no-financial-arbitrage) bond prices,}$$

$$\mathbf{Y} = \{Y \in \mathbb{R}^{SI}\text{: rank } Y = I\}$$

$$= \text{set of possible bond yields,}$$

and

$$E = \{e = (e_1, \ldots, e_h, \ldots, e_H) \in (\mathbb{R}^G_{++})^H\}$$

$$= \text{set of possible goods endowments (as well as allocations).}$$

Then, given $(Y, e) \in \mathbf{Y} \times E$, $(p, q) \in P \times Q$ is a *financial equilibrium* if, when households optimize, i.e.,

$$\text{given } (p, q)\text{—and } Y\text{—}(x_h, b_h) = \big(f_h(p, q, Y, e_h), g_h(p, q, Y, e_h)\big) \quad (1)$$

solves the problem

$$\begin{aligned} &\text{maximize } u_h(x_h) \\ &\text{subject to } p^0\big(x_h^0 - e_h^0\big) = -qb_h, \\ &\qquad\qquad p^s(x_h^s - e_h^s) = y^s b_h, \qquad \text{for } s > 0, \\ &\text{and} \qquad (x_h, b_h) \in X_h \times B_h, \quad h = 1, 2, \ldots, H, \end{aligned}$$

both spot goods and bond markets clear, i.e.,

$$\sum_h (x_h^{s,c} - e_h^{s,c}) = \sum_h (f_h^{s,c}(p, q, Y, e_h) - e_h^{s,c}) = 0, \quad (2)$$

$$(s, c) = (0, 1), (0, 2), \ldots, (S, C),$$

and

$$\sum_h b_h^i = \sum_h g_h^i(p, q, Y, e_h) = 0, \qquad i = 1, 2, \ldots, I. \quad (3)$$

Remarks.

1. Several specific aspects of this formulation greatly facilitate the analysis of properties of financial equilibrium. Most notable among these are the assumptions that (i) there are only two periods, with no production (obviously the leading case); (ii) the financial structure is exogenous (for instance, the number of bonds is given a priori), and all financial instruments are inside assets (that is, bonds are issued and redeemed by households directly) whose yields are specified in terms of dollars (which is one polar case, usually contrasted to that in which asset yields are specified in terms of bundles of goods, a kind of generalized forward contract); and (iii) the only restrictions on portfolio holdings essentially take the form of simple linear equality constraints (rather than, say, more complicated bounds on borrowing that involve households' observable wealth, or even just outright prohibition of short sales in some bonds).

2. This model with restricted participation reduces to the more commonly recognized model with *incomplete markets* when $I < S$ and $B_h = \mathbb{R}^I$, $h = 1, 2, \ldots, H$. The reason I consider a more general formulation is that it easily encompasses permitting most—but not all—households having access to the same complete financial market when I later want to formalize the notion of small market imperfections.

The main result establishing extensive real indeterminacy in this setting requires two additional sorts of technical assumptions. The first concerns sufficiently disparate incentives for exchange of both goods and credit (in terms of numbers and also, implicitly, diversity of households); the second, sufficiently flexible opportunities for exchange of credit (within the confines of restricted participation). So suppose that some group of households, say, the first H_0, faces common portfolio restrictions, say,

$$B_h = B_0, \qquad h = 1, 2, \ldots, H_0.$$

Also, denote, for $h = 1, 2, \ldots, H_0$, $I_h = I_0$, and let $D_0 = S - I_0$, an indicator of this group's *deficiency* in access to the bond market. Now assume that

A4. $H_0 > D_0$; and $0 < I_0 < S$ (so $0 < D_0 < S$) and — *(sufficiently numerous households)*

A5′. There is $b^+ \in B_0$ such that $Yb^+ \gg 0$, or — *(possibility of positive wealth "accumulation")*

A5″. Y is in general position, or — *(possibility of maximum wealth "insurance")*

A5‴. Y is variable. — *("endogenous" determination of bond yields)*

Note that, under either assumption A5′ or assumption A5″, Y is taken to be exogenous or fixed. With some pair of assumptions A4 and A5$^{\bullet}$, given the maintained assumptions A1–A3, one can demonstrate a precise degree of real indeterminacy.

PROPOSITION 0. *Generically in endowments, the set of equilibrium allocations contains a smooth, D_0-dimensional manifold (under assumption A5′) or a smooth, $(S-1)$-dimensional manifold (under assumption A5″), or a smooth, $D_0 I_0$-dimensional manifold (under assumption A5‴).*[3]

3. OUTSIDE MONEY

In order to examine the potential role that outside money might play in reducing nominal and hence real uncertainty, I consider two of the simplest possible specifications, under what are (admittedly) the simplest possible assumptions. In the first model, outside money must be used to pay a terminal tax liability; in the second, terminal outside money balances have direct utility.

To be more specific, for $h = 1, 2, \ldots, H$, let

$$e_h^m = \left(e_h^{m,0}, \ldots, e_h^{m,s}, \ldots, e_h^{m,S}\right) \geqq 0$$

and

$$x_h^m = \left(x_h^{m,0}, \ldots, x_h^{m,s}, \ldots, x_h^{m,S}\right)$$

represent outside money endowments (at the beginning of the period) and outside money balances (at the end of the period), respectively. Also, assume the following.

- There is some initial outside money in the economy, i.e.,

$$\sum_h e_h^{m,0} > 0.$$

- Outside money balances must be nonnegative, i.e., by fiat

$$x_h^m \geqq 0, \qquad h = 1, 2, \ldots, H.$$

- The "price" of money is identically one (in units of account, naturally).

[3]This is essentially Theorem 5.1 in Balasko *et al.* [2]. The very last assertion, however, requires straightforward modification of the proof of Theorem 5.3 in Balasko and Cass [1]; it will be central to the argument in the subsequent section.

- Bond $i = 1$ is *inside* money, i.e., $y^{1,s} = s = 1, 2, \ldots, S$, and can be freely transacted by all households, i.e., if $b_h \in B_h$, then

$$b_h + (\Delta b_h^1, \ldots, 0, \ldots, 0) \in B_h \quad \text{for} \quad \Delta b_h^1 \in \mathbb{R},\ h = 1, 2, \ldots, H.$$

Thus, in this setting,

$$Y = [\mathbf{1}Y^{\setminus 1}] \qquad \Big(\text{identified with } Y^{\setminus 1} \in \mathbf{Y}^{\setminus 1}$$
$$= \{Y^{\setminus 1} \in \mathbb{R}^{S(I-1)}\text{:rank}\,[\mathbf{1}Y^{\setminus 1}] = I\}\Big),$$

where $Y^{\setminus 1}$ is the $[S \times (I-1)]$-dimensional matrix of bond yields exclusive of inside money, and the possibility of positive wealth "accumulation" is taken for granted.[4]

With outside money, the description of financial equilibrium must be modified, depending on how the monetary system impinges on households' preferences and opportunities. Under the first specification (say, the *terminal tax* model) (1) is replaced by

$$\text{given } (p, q)\text{—and } Y^{\setminus 1}\text{—}(x_h, x_h^m, b_h) \text{ solves} \tag{1^{tt}}$$

the problem

$$\text{maximize } u_h(x_h)$$
$$\text{subject to } p^0(x_h^0 - e_h^0) + (x_h^{m,0} - e_h^{m,0}) = -qb_h,$$
$$p^s(x_h^s - e_h^s) + (x_h^{m,s} - [x_h^{m,0} + e_h^{m,s}]) = y^s b_h, \quad \text{for } s > 0,$$
$$x_h^{m,s} \geqq t_h, \quad \text{for } s > 0,$$
$$\text{and} \qquad (x_h, x_h^m, b_h) \in X_h \times X_h^m \times B_h, \qquad h = 1, 2, \ldots, H,$$

where $t_h \geqq 0$ represents household h's terminal tax liability, and $X_h^m = \mathbb{R}_+^{S+1}$ by fiat, while under the second specification (say, the *terminal utility* model), (1) becomes

$$\text{given } (p, q)\text{—and } Y^{\setminus 1}\text{—}(x_h, x_h^m, b_h) \text{ solves} \tag{1^{tu}}$$

[4]Notice that postulating the existence of inside money is equivalent to assumption A5′ (for an appropriate choice of units of account), since the households' financial opportunities are unaffected by replacing any particular bond with a fixed portfolio that includes that bond (a sort of mutual fund). As far as I can see, this is a pretty innocuous assumption, taken by itself. Much less innocuous is the further assumption that all households can freely transact on the market for inside money.

the problem

$$\text{maximize } u_h(x_h, x_h^m)$$

$$\text{subject to } p^0(x_h^0 - e_h^0) + (x_h^{m,0} - e_h^{m,0}) = -qb_h,$$

$$p^s(x_h^s - e_h^s) + (x_h^{m,s} - [x_h^{m,0} + e_h^{m,s}]) = y^s b_h, \quad \text{for } s > 0,$$

$$\text{and} \qquad (x_h, x_h^m, b_h) \in X_h \times X_h^m \times B_h, \qquad h = 1, 2, \ldots, H,$$

where u_h: $X_h \times X_h^m \to \mathbb{R}$, with $X_h^m = \mathbb{R}_+ \times \mathbb{R}_{++}^S$, is assumed to be independent of $x_h^{m,0}$ (but otherwise to exhibit the same properties described by assumption A2). For both specifications, in addition to (2) and (3), outside money markets must also clear, i.e.,

$$\sum_h (x_h^{m,0} - e_h^{m,0}) = 0 \tag{4}$$

and

$$\sum_h (x_h^{m,s} - [x_h^{m,0} + e_h^{m,s}]) = \sum_h (x_h^{m,s} - [e_h^{m,0} + e_h^{m,s}]) = 0,$$

$$s = 1, 2, \ldots, S.$$

Proposition 0 is easily adapted to these two models.

PROPOSITION 1. *The terminal tax model. Suppose that*

$$e_h^{m,s} = 0, \quad \textit{for } s > 0, h = 1, 2, \ldots, H, \tag{5}$$

and

$$\sum_h (e_h^{m,0} + e_h^{m,s}) = \sum_h e_h^{m,0} = \sum_h t_h. \tag{6}$$

Then, generically in endowments (excluding $e^{m,0} = (e_1^{m,0}, \ldots, e_h^{m,0}, \ldots, e_H^{m,0})$*), the set of equilibrium allocations contains a smooth,* D_0*-dimensional manifold, or a smooth,* $(S-1)$*-dimensional manifold (when* $[1Y^{\setminus 1}]$ *is in general position) or a smooth,* $D_0 I_0$*-dimensional manifold (when* $Y^{\setminus 1}$ *is variable).*

Remarks.

1. Given (5), (1^{tt}) and (4) are only consistent also given (6). Of course, if the price of money were allowed to be different than one (which it surely should be!), then the terminal tax model would also be consistent when (6) is replaced by

$$\sum_h e_h^{m,0} \leqq \sum_h t_h; \tag{6'}$$

strict inequality would simply entail the price of money being identically zero in equilibrium. In this case the conclusions of Proposition 1 would clearly still obtain.

2. For an economy with incomplete markets, Villanacci [14] considers —among other things—the more general version of the terminal tax model in which (i) inside money may not be available, and (ii) terminal tax liabilities—interpreted as being net of second period outside money endowments, or, more simply, transfers—may be state dependent. Since, in this more general framework he must treat $p^{0,1}$ as variable (whereas, for simplicity, I treat it as fixed; see footnote 5 below), he finds an increase in the degree of "significant" nominal and hence real indeterminacy of one dimension (under assumption A5″).

PROPOSITION 2. *The terminal utility model. Suppose that*

$$e_h^{m,0} + e_h^{m,s} > 0, \quad \text{for } s > 0,\ h = 1, 2, \ldots, H. \tag{7}$$

Then, generically in endowments (including $e^m = (e_h^m, \ldots, e_h^m, \ldots, e_H^m)$*), equilibrium (and hence equilibrium allocation) is locally unique, or the set of equilibrium allocations contains a smooth,* $D_0(I_0 - 1)$*-dimensional manifold (when* $Y^{\setminus 1}$ *is variable).*

Proofs of Propositions 1 and 2. In either model the proof basically involves elementary accounting.

To begin with, observe that, in both models, for there to be no financial arbitrage opportunities, it must be true that $q^1 \leqq 1$ (since otherwise, if $q^1 > 1$, every household could immeasurably profit by selling inside money and buying outside money at spot $s = 0$), and for the initial outside money market to clear, it must be true that $q^1 \nless 1$ (since otherwise, if $q^1 < 1$, no household would be interested in buying outside money at spot $s = 0$). So $q^1 = 1$ in equilibrium.

Now consider the terminal tax model maintaining (5) and (6). Because terminal balances of outside money are useful only for meeting terminal tax liabilities, the optimal solution to (1^{tt}) must have

$$x_h^{m,s} = t_h, \quad \text{for } s > 0. \tag{8}$$

Thus, by employing the notational convention that if $z = (z^1, \ldots, z^i, \ldots, z^n)$, then $z^{\setminus 1} = (z_1^2, \ldots, z^i, \ldots, z^n)$ (introduced earlier for bond yields exclusive of inside money), and reintroducing a variable $q^1 > 0$, the budget constraints in (1^{tt}) can be rewritten

$$\begin{aligned} p^{0,1}\big(x_h^{0,1} - \big[e_h^{0,1} - \big(t_h - e_h^{m,0}\big)/p^{0,1}\big] &+ p^{0\setminus 1}\big(x_h^{0\setminus 1} - e_h^{0\setminus 1}\big) \\ &= -q^1\big(b_h^1 - \big[t_h - x_h^{m,0}\big]\big)/q^1 - \big(q^1 q^{\setminus 1}\big)b_h^{\setminus 1}/q^1 \end{aligned}$$

and

$$(p^s/q^1)(x_h^s - e_h^s) = \left(b_h^1 - \left[t_h - x_h^{m,0}\right]\right)/q^1 + y^{s\backslash 1}b_h^{\backslash 1}/q^1,$$
$$\text{for} \quad s > 0,$$

or, by letting $q' = (q^1, q^1q^{\backslash 1})$, $p^{s\prime} = p^s/q^1$, for $s > 0$,

$$e_h^{0,1\prime} = e_h^{0,1} - \left(t_h - e_h^{m,0}\right)/p^{0,1} \quad \text{and} \quad b_h' = \left(b_h^1 - \left[t_h - x_h^{m,0}\right], b_h^{\backslash 1}\right)/q^1$$

(and then, for simplicity, suppressing "′"), just as in (1). Moreover, the initial outside money market clearing condition can be presumed satisfied (by having households—who are indifferent between inside and outside money—hold suitable offsetting balances of inside money in their portfolios), while the terminal outside money market clearing conditions are, by virtue of (8), automatically satisfied. But this means that the terminal tax model effectively reduces to the original model of the preceding section (with $Y = [1Y^{\backslash 1}]$), and in fact, that the original version of Proposition 0 still applies.[5]

The argument for the terminal utility model is even more straightforward. Here the budget constraints in (1^{tu}) can be rewritten

$$p^0\left(x_h^0 - e_h^0\right) = -q^1\left(b_h^1 + \left[x_h^{m,0} - e_h^{m,0}\right]\right)/q^1 - (q^1q^{\backslash 1})b_h^{\backslash 1}/q^1$$

and

$$p^s(x_h^s - e_h^s) + \left(x_h^{m,s} - \left[e_h^{m,0} + e_h^{m,s}\right]\right)$$
$$= \left(b_h^1 + \left[x_h^{m,0} - e_h^{m,0}\right]\right)/q^1 + y^{s\backslash 1}b^{h\backslash 1}/q^1, \quad \text{for } s > 0,$$

or, by now letting $q' = (q^1, q^1q^{\backslash 1})$, $p^{s\prime} = p^s/q^1$, $e_h^{m,s\prime} = e_h^{m,0} + e_h^{m,s}$, for $s > 0$ and $b_h' = (b_h^1 + [x_h^{m,0} - e_h^{m,0}],\ b_h^{\backslash 1})/q^1$ (and again, for simplicity, suppressing "′"), just as in (1) when there C types of commodities at spot $s = 0$ but $C + 1$ at each spot $s > 0$, and (with appropriate relabeling of commodities at spots $s > 0$) spot goods prices are normalized so that

[5]Here two minor technical points need checking: First, in the transformed model, $p^{0,1}$ must be large enough to guarantee (implicitly) that $e_h^{0,1} > 0$ [i.e., in the terminal tax model itself, to guarantee that $e_h^{0,1}(t_h - e_h^{m,0})/p^{0,1} > 0$]. This interiority restriction can be satisfied by utilizing the fact that, in the original model of the preceding section, $p^{\cdot 1} = (p^{0,1}, \ldots, p^{s,1}, \ldots, p^{S,1})$ as well as e can be treated as parameters (see Balasko *et al.* [2], Section 4.3). Second, in the transformed model, appropriate perturbations of $p^{\cdot 1}$ and $Y^{\backslash 1}$ must still yield D_0I_0 "significant" degrees of nominal indeterminacy. This result, involving routine linear algebra, is verified along the lines sketched in the Appendix to Balasko *et al.* [5].

$p^{s,1} = 1$, for $s > 0$. So this model too effectively reduces to the original model of the preceding section (but now with both $p^{\cdot 1} = 1$ and $Y = [1Y^{\setminus 1}]$), and an appropriate modification of Proposition 0 again applies (a result also verified along the lines sketched in the Appendix to Balasko *et al.* [5]). ■

What do I conclude? Simply that institutionalized outside money of and by itself doesn't necessarily eliminate real indeterminacy, and may even provide a convincing rationale for a substantially greater degree than has been proposed in the bulk of the literature on this problem. It all depends on the nature of the (market clearing) equations added when characterizing the economy's monetary equilibria, as well as the variety of the (market-determined) variables introduced when characterizing the economy's monetary sector. In the almost trivial, extreme models I've considered here, either the additional equations are completely redundant —with terminal taxes—or they are completely determinant—with terminal utility[6]—*provided* that the monetary mechanism is presumed to have no connection with the determination of any nominal variables other than spot prices, for instance, interest rates (and thereby bond yields). Of course, this last proviso runs counter to long-standing tradition in (one might even say the essence of) monetary theory, which leads me to the position that in Propositions 1 and 2 it is precisely the case where $Y^{\setminus 1}$ is variable—and where extensive real indeterminacy is exhibited regardless of the direct consequences of institutionalized outside money—which is by far more natural and interesting.[7]

[6]An even more direct derivation of this seemingly strong conclusion follows upon just appending spot-by-spot price normalization to the original model—the crudest version of the venerable quantity theory of money—for instance, in the form of the additional equations

$$\sum_c \alpha^{s,c} p^{s,c} = \beta^s,$$

where $\alpha^s = (\alpha^{s,1}, \ldots, \alpha^{s,c}, \ldots, \alpha^{S,C}) > 0$ and $\beta^s > 0$, $s = 0, 1, \ldots, S$. This is, for all practical purposes, the route followed by Magill and Quinzii [9].

[7]I recognize that it makes sense to consider variation in

$$\begin{bmatrix} -q \\ Y \end{bmatrix}$$

as being limited by specific functional characteristics of the financial sector. Nonetheless, the fundamental conclusion, that endogenous bond yields—or, more generally, financial instruments—contribute to extensive real indeterminacy seems to me to be quite robust. My position receives some support from Proposition 2 itself: To be concrete, suppose that $S = 3$, $I = 2$, $H > 1$ and the market imperfection is purely incompleteness. When bond 1 is inside money, so that $y^{1,s} = 1$, $s = 1, 2, 3$, but bond 2 a variable rate loan, so that $y^{2,s} = 1 + r^s > 1$, $s = 1, 2, 3$, the set of equilibrium allocations will still typically contain a continuum.

4. SMALL IMPERFECTIONS

Now returning to the original model, assume that

- the bond market is (in principle) complete, i.e., that $I = S$, and
- there are two groups of households, the *unrestricted* households $h \in H^{u} \subset \{1, 2, \ldots, H\}$ who can freely transact on the bond market, so that

$$B_h = \mathbb{R}^I, \qquad h \in H^{u},$$

  and the *restricted* households $h \in H^{r} = \{1, 2, \ldots, H\} \setminus H^{u}$ who are effectively constrained in their transactions on that market, so that B_h is an I_h-dimensional linear subspace with $0 \leqq I_h < I$, $h \in H^{r}$.[8]

I will compare the financial equilibria of two distinct derivative economies. In the first, say, the *complete market* economy, only the H^{u} unrestricted households trade, while in the second, say, the *improved participation* economy, $j \geqq 1$ replicas of the H^{u} unrestricted households (totaling jH^{u} in number) together with just the original H^{r} restricted households trade.[9] The basic idea is to interpret j being sufficiently large as representing the situation in which there are only small imperfections on the bond market.

PROPOSITION 3. *As j goes to infinity, the financial equilibria in the improved participation economy converge uniformly to a subset of those in the complete market economy.*

Remark. This result explicitly pertains to equilibria, i.e., prices. To understand its ramifications for quantities, i.e., equilibrium allocations, focus on just the unrestricted households, who, for sufficiently small imperfections, carry essentially all the weight in the economy. Then applying two well-known results, we find that in the complete market economy, generically in endowments, equilibrium allocations are locally unique.[10] Thus, Proposition 3 basically means that in the improved partici-

[8] For simplicity, I will also denote the numbers of unrestricted and restricted households by H^{u} and H^{r}, respectively (and hereafter, for symmetry, also the set of all households by $H = H^{u} \cup H^{r}$). No confusion should result.

[9] Equivalently, in this second type of economy there are $J \geqq 1$ replicas of the H^{u} unrestricted households and $K \leqq J$ replicas of the H^{r} restricted households, and $j = J/K \geqq 1$.

[10] The two results required are that (i) equilibrium allocations in the complete market economy are identical to those in the corresponding Walrasian economy with the same fundamentals (i.e., preferences and endowments), and (ii) in a smooth Walrasian economy, generically in endowments, equilibria (up to price normalization) and hence equilibrium allocations are locally unique. (*Note*: Here and in the text, translating from prices to allocations only utilizes the underlying result that demand functions are smooth.)

pation economy, "typically" equilibrium allocations to just the unrestricted households are "almost" locally unique.[11] I don't know—and don't see why it is especially interesting to know—whether the "opposite" of this proposition is also true, namely, whether every equilibrium in the complete market economy can be arbitrarily closely approximated by some equilibrium in the improved participation economy (for sufficiently large j).

Proof of Proposition 3. The argument is considerably more technical than any other in the paper. It also requires, in order to distinguish between the two economies, introducing considerably more notation. So let the original model (with H replaced by H^{u} and $B_h = \mathbb{R}^I$, $h \in H^{\mathrm{u}}$) now describe the complete market econmy. Furthermore, let

$$\begin{aligned} M &= \{(p, q, e) \in P \times Q \times E: \\ &\qquad \sum_{h \in H^{\mathrm{u}}} (f_h(p, q, Y, e_h) - e_h, g_h(p, q, Y, e_h)) = 0\} \\ &= \text{equilibrium set}, \\ p^{\cdot 1} &= (p^{0,1}, \ldots, p^{s,1}, \ldots, p^{S,1}) \\ &= \text{vector of spot goods prices for just the first type of commodity} \\ &\qquad \text{(as introduced earlier, in footnote 5)}, \\ P^{\cdot 1} &= \{p^{\cdot 1} \in \mathbb{R}^{S+1}_{++}\} \end{aligned}$$

and

$$\Phi = \text{restriction to } M \text{ of the projection of } P \times Q \times E \text{ onto } P^{\cdot 1} \times E.$$

[*Note*: We know, in fact, that the set M is a smooth, $((S + 1) \times H^{\mathrm{u}}G)$-dimensional manifold, and, furthermore, that the mapping Φ is proper and surjective (so that, in particular, equilibria exist for every $(p^{\cdot 1}, e) \in P^{\cdot 1} \times E$); see Theorem 4.1 in Balasko *et al.* [2]]. For the improved

[11] "Typically" also refers to just endowments of the unrestricted households. I doubt that much can be inferred regarding the asymptotic behavior of equilibrium allocations to the restricted households. There is simply no reason to expect their goods demands to be systematically delimited on the sets of (financial) equilibrium prices

$$\{(p, q) \in P \times Q: p = (p^{0\prime}, p^{1\prime}/\lambda^1, \ldots, p^{s\prime}/\lambda^2, \ldots, p^{S\prime}/\lambda^S) \text{ with } \lambda = qY^{-1} \gg 0\}$$

associated with equilibrium prices p' in the corresponding Walrasian economy—as they certainly are for the unrestricted households (precisely the content of the first result mentioned in the preceding footnote).

participation economy with j replicas of the unrestricted households, adapt the same notation by affixing "(j)" where appropriate: For example, for this economy, spot goods prices will be denoted $p(j) \in P$, while endowments and the equilibrium set will be denoted

$$e(j) = \left(\overbrace{(e_h)_{h\in H^{\mathrm{u}}}, \ldots, (e_h)_{h\in H^{\mathrm{u}}}, \ldots, (e_h)_{h\in H^{\mathrm{u}}}}^{j \text{ times}}, (e_h)_{h\in H^{\mathrm{r}}}\right)$$

$$\in E(j) = \left\{e(j) \in \left(\mathbb{R}^G_{++}\right)^{jH^{\mathrm{u}}+H^{\mathrm{r}}}\right\}$$

$$\left(\text{identified with } E = \left\{e \in \left(\mathbb{R}^G_{++}\right)^H\right\}\right)$$

and

$$M(j) = \Big\{(p(j), q(j), e(j)) \in P \times Q \times E(j):$$

$$j \sum_{h\in H^{\mathrm{u}}} (f_h(p(j), q(j), Y, e_h) - e_h, g_h(p(j), q(j), Y, e_h))$$

$$+ \sum_{h\in H^{\mathrm{r}}} (f_h(p(j), q(j), Y, e_h) - e_h, g_h(p(j), q(j), Y, e_h)) = 0\Big\}.$$

[*Note*: Here too we know, by the same reasoning as in the proof of Theorem 4.1 in Balasko *et al.* [2], that $M(j)$ is a smooth, $((S + 1) \times HG)$-dimensional manifold and that $\Phi(j)$ is proper and surjective.]

Now the argument per se proceeds in four steps. (i) Pick $\tilde{e}_h \in X_h$, $h \in H$. (ii) Pick $\tilde{P}^{\cdot 1} \subset P^{\cdot 1}$ compact. (iii) Define

$$\tilde{A} = \{a = (p, q) \in P \times Q: p^{\cdot 1} \in \tilde{P}^{\cdot 1} \quad \text{and} \quad (p, q, \tilde{e}) \in M\},$$

$$\tilde{A}(j) = \{a(j) = (p(j), q(j)) \in P \times Q: p^{\cdot 1}(j) \in \tilde{P}^{\cdot 1}$$

$$\text{and} \quad (p(j), q(j), \tilde{e}(j)) \in M(j)\} \quad \text{for } j \geq 1$$

and

$$\alpha(j) = \sup_{a(j)\in A(j)} \min_{a\in\tilde{A}} \|a - a(j)\|.$$

Since Φ is proper, $\tilde{A}$ is compact, and $\min_{a\in\tilde{A}}\|a - a(j)\|$ is well defined.

(iv) Show that

$$\limsup_{j\to\infty} \alpha(j) = \lim_{j\to\infty} \alpha(j) = 0,$$

i.e., that it is not the case that

$$\limsup_{j\to\infty} \alpha(j) > \varepsilon > 0.$$

This last step is established as follows. Suppose that the assertion were false, i.e., that, without any loss of generality, there were a sequence $a(j) \in \tilde{A}(j)$, $j \geqq 1$, such that

$$\min_{a\in\tilde{A}} \|a - a(j)\| \geqq \varepsilon, \qquad j \geqq 1,$$

or

$$\|a - a(j)\| \geqq \varepsilon \qquad \text{for} \quad a \in \tilde{A}, \quad j \geqq 1. \tag{9}$$

From an argument basically identical to that used to show that $\Phi(j)$ is proper, or that, in particular, $\Phi^{-1}(j)(\tilde{P}^{\cdot 1} \times \{\tilde{e}(j)\})$ is compact, it follows that we can pick a subsequence, without any loss of generality the original sequence itself, such that

$$\begin{aligned}\lim_{j\to\infty} a(j) &= \lim_{j\to\infty} (p(j), q(j)) = a(\infty) \\ &= (p(\infty), q(\infty)) \in P \times Q \qquad \left(\text{with } p^{\cdot 1}(\infty) \in \tilde{P}^{\cdot 1}\right)\end{aligned}$$

and

$$\begin{aligned}&\lim_{j\to\infty} \left(f_h(p(j), q(j), Y, \tilde{e}_h), g(p(j), q(j), Y, \tilde{e})\right) \\ &\quad = \left(f_h(p(\infty), q(\infty), Y, \tilde{e}_h), g_h(p(\infty), q(\infty), Y, \tilde{e}_h)\right), \qquad h \in H.\end{aligned}$$

But since $(p(j), q(j), \tilde{e}(j)) \in M(j)$, $j \geqq 1$, this implies that

$$\begin{aligned}&\lim_{j\to\infty} \sum_{h\in H^{\mathrm{u}}} \left(f_h(p(j), q(j), Y, \tilde{e}_h) - \tilde{e}_h, g_h(p(j), q(j), Y, \tilde{e}_h)\right) \\ &\quad = \sum_{h\in H^{\mathrm{u}}} \left(f_h(p(\infty), q(\infty), Y, \tilde{e}_h) - \tilde{e}_h, g_h(p(\infty), q(\infty), Y, \tilde{e}_h)\right) \\ &\quad = \lim_{j\to\infty} (1/j) \sum_{h\in H^{\mathrm{r}}} \left(f_h(p(j), q(j), Y, \tilde{e}_h)\right. \\ &\qquad\qquad\qquad \left. -\tilde{e}_h, g_h(p(j), q(j), Y, \tilde{e}_h)\right) = 0,\end{aligned}$$

or that $(p(\infty), q(\infty), \tilde{e}) \in M$, or that $\lim_{j\to\infty} \|a(\infty) - a(j)\| = 0$ with $a(\infty) \in \tilde{A}$, which contradicts (9). ■

Two aspects of the foregoing merit brief comment. First, the argument actually applied only to the subsets of equilibria in the improved participation economy for which $p^{\cdot 1}(j) \in \tilde{P}^{\cdot 1}$, where $\tilde{P}^{\cdot 1}$ is an arbitrary compact subset of $P^{\cdot 1}$. I simply have no idea whether there can be some sort of "perverse" behavior if $p^{\cdot 1}(j)$ goes to $p^{\cdot 1}(\infty) \in \partial\tilde{P}^{\cdot 1}$ (i.e., the boundary of the closure of $P^{\cdot 1}$) as j goes to infinity. Second, while the argument was carried out for fixed or exogenous Y, it can be easily extended to cover the case of variable or endogenous Y (restricted to $\tilde{Y} \subset Y$ compact).

Acknowledgments

This paper, intended as a modest contribution to the theory of general competitive equilibrium, is dedicated to Lionel McKenzie. The importance of Lionel's seminal influence on the modern development of this fundamental discipline almost requires no elaboration (and is, anyway, very amply detailed elsewhere in this volume). More personally, Lionel has been an incomparable role model for me, as well as my friend and benefactor.

Research support from the NSF under grant SES 88-08524 is gratefully acknowledged, as are useful comments by numerous (supportive and yet critical) colleagues.

References

1. Y. Balasko and D. Cass (1989). "The structure of financial equilibrium with exogenous yields: The case of incomplete markets," *Econometrica* **57**, 135–162.
2. Y. Balasko, D. Cass, and P. Siconolfi (1990). "The structure of financial equilibrium with exogenous yields: The case of restricted participation," *J. Math. Econ.* **19**, 195–216.
3. D. Cass (1989). "Sunspots and incomplete financial markets: The leading example," in G. Feiwel (ed.), *The Economics of Imperfect Competition and Employment: Joan Robinson and Beyond*. Macmillan, London.
4. D. Cass (1991). "Perfect equilibrium with incomplete financial markets: An elementary exposition," in L. W. McKenzie and S. Zamagni (eds.), *Value and Capital Fifty Years Later* (Macmillan, London).
5. D. Cass (1992). "Incomplete financial markets and indeterminacy of competitive equilibrium," in J.-J. Laffont (ed.), *Advances in Economic Theory*, 6th World Congress (Cambridge University Press, Cambridge, U.K.).
6. J. Geanakoplos (1990). "An introduction to general equilibrium with incomplete asset markets," *J. Math. Econ.* **19**, 1–38.
7. J. Geanakoplos and A. Mas-Collel (1989). "Real indeterminacy with financial assets," *J. Econ. Theory* **47**, 22–38.
8. R. C. Green and S. E. Spear (1989). "Equilibria in large commodity spaces with incomplete financial markets," preliminary paper, Carnegie-Mellon University.
9. M. Magill and M. Quinzii (1992). "Real effects of money in general equilibrium," *J. Math. Econ.* **21**, 301–342.
10. A. Mas-Colell (1991). "Indeterminacy in incomplete market economies," *Econ. Theory* **1**, 45–61.
11. T. Pietra (1988). "Indeterminacy in general equilibrium models with incomplete financial markets: Mixed asset returns," *J. Math. Econ.* **21**, 155–172.
12. H. M. Polemarchakis (1988). "Portfolio choice, exchange rates and indeterminacy," *J. Econ. Theory* **46**, 414–421.

13. P. Siconolfi and A. Villanacci (1991). "Real indeterminacy in incomplete financial market economies without aggregate risk," *Econ. Theory* **1**, 265–276.
14. A. Villanacci (1991). "Indeterminacy of equilibria, taxes and outside money in exchange economies with incomplete financial markets," CARESS Working Paper, University of Pennsylvania.
15. J. Werner (1990). "Structure of financial markets and real indeterminacy of equilibria," *J. Math. Econ.* **19**, 217–232.
16. W. R. Zame (1988). "Asymptotic behavior of asset markets, I: Asymptotic inefficiency," preliminary paper, SUNY at Buffalo (Department of Mathematics).

IRREDUCIBILITY, RESOURCE RELATEDNESS, AND SURVIVAL IN EQUILIBRIUM WITH INDIVIDUAL NONCONVEXITIES

Peter J. Hammond
Department of Economics
Stanford University
Stanford, California 94305

1. INTRODUCTION

1.1 General Equilibrium Theory in the 1950s

The heyday of mathematical economics in general, and of general equilibrium theory in particular, was surely the decade of the 1950s. For the first time general logically consistent models of a competitive market economy were developed and existence of a competitive equilibrium was proved. First Arrow (1951) proved the two efficiency theorems of welfare economics. The first of these theorems shows that any competitive equilibrium is Pareto-efficient. The second shows that, under assumptions such as convexity and continuity which have since become standard, almost any Pareto-efficient allocation can be achieved through competitive markets in general equilibrium, provided that lump-sum redistribution is used to ensure that each individual has the appropriate amount of purchasing power.

After these efficiency theorems, the next step was to give a proper proof of the existence of equilibrium for a given exogenous distribution of purchasing power. McKenzie (1954a) gave such a proof for a world economy with continuous aggregate demand functions for each nation. This was done using newly available fixed-point theorems in mathematics such as Kakutani's (1941).[1] McKenzie's proof used arguments that were

[1]Despite considering demand correspondences rather than (single-valued) demand functions, in his later general existence proof McKenzie (1959) was able to use just Brouwer's fixed-point theorem for continuous functions, rather than Kakutani's theorem for correspondences. See Khan (this volume) for further details.

obviously capable of significant generalization. Also, since he was using Graham's (1948) model of international trade in which whole nations were being considered as economic units, McKenzie (1954a, 1954b) naturally saw no need to assume that each nation has the preferences of a representative national consumer. Indeed, Gorman's (1953) work the year before had already shown how restrictive such an assumption would be, even if it were possible to classify all individuals as nationals of their own nations in which they live permanently.

In the very next issue of *Econometrica*, Arrow and Debreu (1954) gave the first published general proof of existence for an economy in which preferences and endowments, rather than demand functions, are exogenous. Of course, one could well argue that this model is somewhat more appropriate for general existence proofs than Graham's, because one should perhaps consider a model of international trade in which each consumer in each nation is treated as a separate economic unit. Anyway, these results were then extended, in rapid succession, in such works as those of McKenzie (1955, 1959, 1961), Gale (1955), Nikaido (1956, 1957), and Debreu (1959, 1962).

Although no excuse for revisiting the 1950s is required on this occasion, I shall nevertheless provide one. It should come as no surprise that the arguments of these path-breaking papers can be somewhat streamlined 30 or more years later. Nor that the assumptions can be considerably relaxed. In the process of doing so, however, it has become very useful to adopt an approach first hinted at in Arrow and Debreu (1954), and then put into practice in Arrow and Hahn (1971).[2] This requires first demonstrating either that a particular Pareto-efficient or core allocation is a compensated equilibrium, or that such an equilibrium exists. Only at a second stage is it shown that the compensated equilibrium must be an ordinary or uncompensated equilibrium. An important part of this approach to extending the results of general equilibrium theory involves concepts closely related to McKenzie's (1959, 1961, 1981, 1987) irreducibility assumption. Yet the key role played by this assumption (or by Arrow and Hahn's similar notion of "resource relatedness") has often been neglected.[3] Nor has much attention been given to the different possible variations of this assumption, or even [apart from Spivak (1978)] to whether significant weakenings may still be possible.

1.2 From Compensated to Uncompensated Equilibrium

Indeed, following the approach of Arrow (1951), it is almost trivial to prove the first efficiency theorem. In its weak form, this states that, without any assumptions at all, any competitive equilibrium allocation is

[2]See also Moore (1975).

[3]For example, it is not discussed at all in Duffie and Sonnenschein's (1989) survey, or in Hildenbrand and Kirman's (1988) advanced textbook.

weakly Pareto-efficient, in the sense that there is no other physically feasible allocation which moves all agents simultaneously to a preferred allocation. In its stronger and more familiar form, the first efficiency theorem states that if agents have locally nonsatiated preferences, then any competitive equilibrium allocation is Pareto-efficient in the sense that there is no other physically feasible allocation that moves some agent or agents to a preferred allocation without simultaneously moving others to a dispreferred allocation. Equally trivial is the theorem that says that any competitive equilibrium allocation is in the core.

The departures from standard assumptions which interest us include nonconvexity of feasible sets or of preferences, the possible nonsurvival of some individuals, boundary problems, and exceptional cases such as that discussed by Arrow (1951). Such departures from standard assumptions can do nothing to perturb these very simple and robust results. They do, however, create serious difficulties for the existence of the competitive equilibrium that is predicated in the first efficiency theorem. They may also make the core empty, or lead to violations of the second efficiency and core equivalence theorems. One of the principal aims of our work, therefore, is to generalize the conditions under which these important results in general equilibrium theory retain their validity, especially in continuum economies for which individual nonconvexities may become smoothed out.

To this end, an approach that appears to be very helpful is to break the problem up into two parts. It turns out to be relatively easy to prove weak versions of the existence, second efficiency, and core equivalence theorems, using a weaker notion of *compensated* competitive equilibrium. This terminology is apparently due to Arrow and Hahn (1971), although the concept can be found in Arrow and Debreu (1954, Section 5.3.3). In compensated equilibrium every agent is minimizing expenditure at equilibrium prices, subject to not falling below an upper contour set associated with the preference relation (cf. McKenzie, 1957). Whereas uncompensated equilibrium is the more familiar and natural kind of equilibrium in which every agent is maximizing preferences subject to the budget constraint that net expenditure at equilibrium prices cannot be positive. This distinction is brought out in Section 2. The weak version of the existence theorem is simply that a compensated equilibrium exists. The weak version of the second efficiency theorem is that (almost) any Pareto-efficient allocation can be achieved as a compensated equilibrium, provided that appropriate lump-sum redistribution of wealth has occurred. The weak version of the core equivalence theorem is that any allocation in the core of a continuum economy must be a compensated equilibrium. These three weak theorems have been stated and proved in various ways by numerous different authors. The assumptions under which they are valid do not necessarily require individuals' feasible sets to be convex, nor do they require that all individuals survive in compensated equilibrium.

Of course, these weak theorems concerning compensated equilibrium still leave us with the problem of proving the existence of an uncompensated competitive equilibrium, as well as the usual versions of the second efficiency and core equivalence theorems, which refer to uncompensated equilibria. One way to prove these results, obviously, is to pass as directly as possible from a compensated equilibrium to an uncompensated equilibrium. This is precisely where irreducibility becomes important. Section 3 discusses some of the precursors to the idea of irreducibility, especially the extremely implausible interiority assumption used originally by Arrow (1951) and Arrow and Debreu (1954). As is well known, the main function of this assumption is to ensure directly that all agents have cheaper points in their feasible sets. If individuals have convex feasible sets and continuous preferences, this ensures that any compensated equilibrium is also an uncompensated equilibrium. But since this work is intended to allow nonconvex feasible sets, a different assumption concerning particular cones generated by the feasible set and by the set of preferred net trade vectors is used to establish this standard conclusion. This is also discussed in Section 3, along with an aggregate interiority condition which rules out Arrow's (1951) exceptional case by ensuring that at least one individual has a cheaper feasible net trade vector.

Thereafter, Section 4 presents a "convexified nonoligarchy" condition that proves adequate to show that a particular compensated equilibrium allocation is an uncompensated equilibrium. For the special case of "linear exchange" economies, in which each consumer's indifference map consists of parallel hyperplanes in the nonnegative orthant, this condition is virtually equivalent to irreducibility, according to Gale's (1957) and Eaves' (1976) definition, or to Gale's (1976) definition of "self-sufficiency." The results of this section confirm that an important part of a more appealing sufficient condition for compensated equilibria to become uncompensated equilibria involves considering the extent to which different agents in the economy are able to benefit from one another's resources. Moreover, a result due to Spivak (1978) is extended to show that this convexified nonoligarchy condition is necessary as well as sufficient for every agent to have a cheaper point in any compensated equilibrium with lump-sum redistribution.

The convexified nonoligarchy condition ensures that for a specific compensated equilibrium allocation and corresponding equilibrium price vector, every consumer has a cheaper feasible point and so, given the additional assumptions we shall make in Section 4, is actually in uncompensated equilibrium. To ensure existence of an uncompensated equilibrium, it would therefore be sufficient to have every allocation that is weakly Pareto-superior to autarky be convexified nonoligarchic. This sufficient condition is unnecessarily strong, however. For existence theorems it is enough to consider those compensated equilibria without lump-sum transfers in which the equilibrium allocation and price vector imply that each consumer's budget hyperplane passes through the autarky allocation. In order to ensure that at these equilibria each consumer has a cheaper point, it is enough to ensure that each consumer's endowment is not a cheapest point. To this end, McKenzie's concept of "irreducibility" considers the benefits of replicating the consumers in the economy so that their initial endowments can then be exploited by the existing agents. This is the topic of Section 5. It points out how McKenzie's fundamental contribution was incompletely anticipated in the latter part of Arrow and Debreu (1954). As mentioned above, an earlier paper by Gale (1957) contained a somewhat related idea for linear exchange economies. Irreducibility was duly recognized by Debreu (1962). Not surprisingly, Arrow and Hahn's (1971) later concept of resource relatedness also turns out to be closely related. Section 5 presents a generalized version of irreducibility which encompasses virtually all previous conditions of this kind,[4] and is also suitable for economies in which individuals may have nonconvex feasible sets. The new condition, moreover, is the weakest possible which guarantees that, in any compensated equilibrium without lump-sum transfers, each consumer has a cheaper point.

In addition, irreducibility was extended by Moore (1975) and McKenzie (1981, 1987) to finite economies in which consumers may have to rely on others to survive. The last part of Section 5 generalizes their sufficient conditions, which ensure that any compensated equilibrium in the economy is actually an uncompensated equilibrium in which all consumers are able to survive.

Finally, following Hildenbrand's (1972) modification of irreducibility, Section 6 shows how to extend the analysis to continuum economies. There is no need to consider convexified versions of the earlier nonoligarchy and interdependence conditions because the continuum of agents itself ensures convexity.

Proofs of many of the main results which are very similar to each other are gathered together in Section 7. Section 8 contains a few concluding remarks.

2. PRELIMINARIES

2.1 Basic Assumptions

2.1.1 A Finite Set of Agents

Assume that there is a finite set A of economic agents, with typical member denoted by a.

[4]The sole exception of which I am aware is Gale's (1976) special condition for linear exchange economies.

2.1.2 The Commodity Space

Assume that there is a fixed finite set G of physical commodities, so that the commodity space is the finite-dimensional Euclidean space $\mathscr{R}^G$.

2.1.3 Consumers' Feasible Sets

Next, assume that every agent $a \in A$ has a fixed feasible set $X_a \subset \mathscr{R}^G$ of net trade vectors x_a satisfying $0 \in X_a$. If agent $a \in A$ happens to have a fixed endowment $\omega_a \in \mathscr{R}^G$, then each $x_a \in X_a$ is equal to the difference $c_a - \omega_a$ between a feasible consumption vector c_a and this endowment vector. By following Rader (1964) and others, however, and considering only feasible net trade vectors, the formulation here allows domestic production activities such as storage, as well as the kind of economy with small farmers considered in Coles and Hammond (1994). Note the assumption that autarky is feasible, but note, too, that this does *not* imply that autarky enables an agent to survive.

2.1.4 Feasible Allocations

An *allocation* $\mathbf{x} := \langle x_a \rangle_{a \in A} \in \prod_{a \in A} X_a$ is a profile of net trade vectors that are individually feasible for all agents $a \in A$. A *feasible allocation* $\mathbf{x}$ also has the property that the aggregate net trade vector $\sum_{a \in A} x_a = 0$. Note that only an exchange economy is being considered, and that free disposal is assumed only to the extent that some individual agents can dispose of goods freely.

2.1.5 Consumers' Preferences

It is also assumed that every agent $a \in A$ has a (complete and transitive) weak *preference ordering* $\succsim_a$ on the set X_a, and an associated strict preference relation $\succ_a$ that is *locally nonsatiated*—i.e., for every $x_a \in X_a$ the *preferred set* $P_a(x_a) := \{x'_a \in X_a | x'_a \succ_a x_a\}$ is nonempty and includes the point x_a in its closure cl $P_a(x_a)$. Note especially that there is no assumption of monotonicity, free disposal, convexity, or even continuity.

In addition to the notation $P_a(x_a)$ introduced above, let

$$U_a(x_a) := \{x_a \in X_a | x'_a \succsim_a x_a\} \quad \text{and} \quad L_a(x_a) := \{x'_a \in X_a | x_a \succsim_a x'_a\}$$

denote the consumer's *upper* and *lower contour sets*, respectively.

2.1.6 The Classical Hypotheses

Some later results, however, will require standard convexity and continuity hypotheses. Indeed, say that agents' preferences *satisfy the classical hypotheses* provided that, for all $a \in A$, in addition to local nonsatiation, the following are true:

(i) The set X_a of feasible net trade vectors is convex.
(ii) Whenever $x'_a \succsim_a x_a, x''_a \succsim_a x_a$, and also $0 < \lambda \leq 1$, then $(1 - \lambda)x'_a + \lambda x''_a \succsim_a x_a$, and if also $x''_a \succ_a x_a$, then $(1 - \lambda)x'_a + \lambda x''_a \succ_a x_a$.
(iii) Both the feasible set X_a and, for every $x_a \in X_a$, the lower contour set $L_a(x_a)$, are closed sets.

These classical hypotheses are automatically satisfied when the set of all feasible allocations is convex, and when preferences are convex, continuous, and locally nonsatiated. Of course, these latter are standard assumptions in geneal equilibrium theory for finite economies; indeed, (iii) above is usually supplemented by the requirement that each upper contour set $U_a(x_a)$ is also closed.

2.1.7 The Price Domain

The set of all allowable price vectors will be $\{p \in \mathscr{R}^G | p \neq 0\}$. Note that negative prices are allowed because there has been no assumption of free disposal.

2.2 Equilibrium

2.2.1 The Budget, Demand, and Compensated Demand Correspondences

For each agent $a \in A$, wealth level w_a, and price vector $p \neq 0$, define the *budget set*

$$B_a(p, w_a) := \{x \in X_a | px \leq w_a\}$$

of feasible net trade vectors satisfying the budget constraint. Note that $B_a(p, w_a)$ is never empty when $w_a \geq 0$ because of the assumption that $0 \in X_a$.

Next define, for every $a \in A$ and $p \neq 0$, the following three demand sets:

(i) The *uncompensated demand set* is given by

$$\xi_a^U(p, w_a) := \{x \in B_a(p, w_a) | x' \in P_a(x) \Rightarrow px' > w_a\}$$
$$= \arg\max_x \{\succsim_a | x \in B_a(p, w_a)\}.$$

(ii) The *compensated demand set* is given by

$$\xi_a^C(p, w_a) := \{x \in B_a(p, w_a) | x' \in U_a(x) \Rightarrow px' \geq w_a\}.$$

(iii) The *weak compensated demand set* is given by

$$\xi_a^W(p, w_a) := \{x \in B_a(p, w_a) | x' \in P_a(x) \Rightarrow px' \geq w_a\}.$$

Evidently these definitions imply that $\xi_a^U(p,w_a) \cup \xi_a^C(p,w_a) \subset \xi_a^W(p,w_a)$. Establishing when $\xi_a^C(p,w_a) = \xi_a^U(p,w_a)$ at an equilibrium price vector p is, of course, one of the main topics of the paper. The following lemma shows that, because of local nonsatiation, demands of all three kinds always exhaust the budget, and also there is in fact never any need to consider weak compensated demands, since they become equal to compensated demands.

LEMMA. *Whenever preferences are locally nonsatiated, it must be true that (i)* $x \in \xi_a^W(p,w_a) \Rightarrow px = w_a$; *(ii)* $\xi_a^W(p,w_a) = \xi_a^C(p,w_a)$.

Proof.

(i) If $px < w_a$ then, since local nonsatiation implies that $x \in \text{cl } P_a(x)$, there must also exist $x' \in P_a(x)$ with $px' < w_a$, and so $x \notin \xi_a^W(p,w_a)$. Conversely, $x \in \xi_a^W(p,w_a)$ must imply that $px \geq w_a$. But since $x \in \xi_a^W(p,w_a)$ implies $x \in B_a(p,w_a)$ and so $px \leq w_a$, it must actually be true that $x \in \xi_a^W(p,w_a)$ implies $px = w_a$.

(ii) Suppose that $\hat{x} \in \xi_a^W(p,w_a)$. For any $x' \in U_a(\hat{x})$, local nonsatiation implies that $x' \in \text{cl } P_a(x')$. But $P_a(x') \subset P_a(\hat{x})$ because preferences are transitive, and so $x' \in \text{cl } P_a(\hat{x})$. Now, since $\hat{x} \in \xi_a^W(p,w_a)$ implies that $px \geq w_a$ for all $x \in P_a(\hat{x})$, the same must also be true for all $x \in \text{cl } P_a(\hat{x})$, including x'. Therefore $x' \in U_a(\hat{x})$ implies $px' \geq w_a$, and so $\hat{x} \in \xi_a^C(p,w_a)$. ∎

2.2.2 Compensated and Uncompensated Equilibria

An *uncompensated* (resp. *compensated*) *equilibrium* is a pair $(\mathbf{x}, p)$ consisting of a feasible allocation $\mathbf{x}$ and a price vector p such that, for all $a \in A$, both $px_a = 0$ and $x_a \in \xi_a^U(p,0)$ [resp. $\xi_a^C(p,0)$].

An *uncompensated* (resp. *compensated*) *equilibrium with transfers* is a pair $(\mathbf{x}, p)$ consisting of a feasible allocation $\mathbf{x}$ and a price vector p such that $x_a \in \xi_a^U(p, px_a)$ [resp. $\xi_a^C(p, px_a)$] for all $a \in A$.[5]

[5]Honkapohja (1987) has recently used a different definition of compensated equilibrium, based on the alternative (and often used) definition

$$D_a(p, x_a^*) := \arg\min_x \{px \mid x \in U_a(x_a^*)\}.$$

of the compensated demand set. Thus there is no reference whatsoever to the consumer's available wealth. Indeed, in the special case of an exchange economy in which each agent's consumption set is the nonnegative orthant, according to this definition there is always a trivial equilibrium in which all endowments get thrown away and each consumer has zero consumption. This is because Honkapohja allows free disposal, however. Duffie (1988, p. 44) also uses this definition of compensated demand, in effect, but his definition of compensated equilibrium turns out to be the same as the standard one given here because he does not allow free disposal. Also, these observations only apply to Honkapohja's discussion of compensated equilibrium, and not to his other results concerning compensated demand.

3. CHEAPER POINTS FOR INDIVIDUALS

3.1 Arrow's Exceptional Case

Recall that the second efficiency theorem states conditions under which a Pareto-efficient allocation is an uncompensated equilibrium with lump-sum redistribution—or, in a weaker version, under which such an allocation is a compensated equilibrium with lump-sum redistribution. Both Arrow (1951) and Debreu (1951) announced versions of this theorem in the same year. It seems clear that Arrow was the first to realize the nature of the problem of how to prove that a compensated equilibrium with expenditure minimization by agents is also an uncompensated equilibrium with preference maximization by agents. Indeed, in that paper he gave a famous example of an "exceptional case" in which expenditure minimization is insufficient to ensure preference maximization. On the other hand, Debreu (1951) simply passed from compensated to uncompensated equilibrium without any attempt at a proof. He was apparently unaware of the possibility of any exceptional case, even though he acknowledged having seen an early version of Arrow's paper. Of course this logical flaw was later set right in his succeeding works such as Debreu (1954, 1959, 1962).

3.2 Interiority

3.2.1 Interiority of a Particular Allocation

In fact, Arrow's paper was presented at the same symposium as Kuhn and Tucker's (1951) classic work on nonlinear programming. They also gave an example in which a constrained maximum could not be supported by shadow prices—something that is impossible for linear programs in finite-dimensional spaces, because for those the well-known duality theorem applies. The simplest instance of a constraint qualification is Slater's condition, requiring that a concave program have a point in the interior of its feasible set.

Arrow gave two alternative conditions that rule out exceptional cases. The first of these is a direct parallel of the Slater constraint qualification. This is the "interiority assumption," which simply assumes that the Pareto-efficient allocation being considered gives each agent a net trade vector in the interior of his feasible set. For the case of convex feasible sets and continuous preferences, this is certainly enough to convert a compensated equilibrium with lump-sum redistribution into an uncompensated equilibrium with identical lump-sum redistribution, and to make the second efficiency theorem true.

3.2.2 Interiority of Initial Endowments

A somewhat different interiority assumption was also used in the first existence theorem of Arrow and Debreu (1954), and in immediately suceeding works such as Gale (1955), Nikaido (1956), and Debreu (1959). For the second efficiency theorem, the interiority assumption could refer to the particular Pareto-efficient allocation whose competitive properties are being demonstrated. For an existence theorem, however, it makes no sense to refer to the equilibrium allocation until we know whether one exists. Nor should we assume that a compensated equilibrium allocation is an interior allocation, since there are many examples where it will not be —for instance, if some individuals are unconcerned about the consumption of some goods, compensated equilibrium at strictly positive prices implies that these individuals are at the lower boundaries of their consumption sets. For this reason, then, it seemed more natural to assume that all individuals had endowment vectors in the interior of their consumption sets—or, somewhat more generally, that the zero net trade vector was in the interior of each individual's set of feasible net trades. Since feasibility was nearly always assumed to imply survival, this was actually a kind of "strict survival" assumption. But in fact, as remarked above, there is actually no need to assume that feasibility implies survival. After making this survival assumption, as well as the usual assumptions that individuals' feasible sets are convex and their preferences are continuous, it becomes quite straightforward to show that any compensated equilibrium is actually an uncompensated equilibrium.

Of course, Debreu (1959) and many successors prefer to use the assumption that endowments are interior in order to demonstrate upper hemicontinuity of the uncompensated rather than of the compensated or of the quasidemand correspondence, and then go on to prove existence of an uncompensated equilibrium by applying a fixed-point theorem directly to the aggregate excess uncompensated demand correspondence. This approach, however, tends to obscure what role the objectionable interiority assumption plays in the proof of existence. More seriously, it may also make existence proofs harder than necessary, especially in "nonclassical" economies such as those where there is a continuum of consumers who may have nonconvex feasible sets. For such economies it is often easier to follow the techniques of Khan and Yamazaki (1981) and Yamazaki (1978, 1981) in order to prove existence of compensated equilibrium first, and then use their results or those of this paper in order to prove that a compensated equilibrium is also an uncompensated equilibrium.

The absurdity of this assumption that each consumer's endowments are interior was immediately apparent. Early writers would typically apologize for it and would sometimes seek to weaken it.[6] After all, in a model of

[6]Kenneth Arrow tells me that at first both he and Debreu, in independent unpublished work, had overlooked the need for some additional assumption such as interiority. Later they held up the publication of their joint paper Arrow and Debreu (1954) while they formulated a less unsatisfactory alternative to interiority. This alternative is discussed in Section 5.1 below.

competitive equilibrium international trade in the world economy, non-traded goods such as local construction and other labor services have to be differentiated by the country in which they are supplied. Then the interiority assumption requires each individual to be able to supply every non-traded good in every country of the world simultaneously. Not even internationally mobile professors of economics have this capability! Indeed, once commodities become distinguished by time and geographic location, as they should be, interiority requires all agents to be both omnipresent and immortal. This kind of consideration surely motivated Nikaido's (1957) ingenious relaxation of the interiority assumption. But he had to assume instead that all agents have the nonnegative orthant as their consumption set, that there is a positive total endowment of every commodity, and also that preferences are strictly monotone—in particular, that every good is strictly desirable.[7] The last assumption is hardly more acceptable than interiority when one considers goods differentiated by location. Chinese tea is wonderful almost anywhere at almost any time, but all the tea in China benefits only those who are actually there.

3.3 Cheaper Feasible Points

3.3.1 Introduction

Despite its evident absurdity, the interiority assumption remains the one that is most frequently encountered in the general equilibrium literature. Yet alternatives have been proposed, starting with a second assumption in Arrow (1951) that was weaker than the interiority condition he had used first. Whereas interiority requires the agent to be able to supply a little of every good, Arrow's second assumption is that every agent can supply a little of at least one good having a positive price in the compensated equilibrium price system. Unfortunately, however, this assumption has the obvious defect that it can only be checked after the compensated equilibrium price system has become known. Or at least it is necessary to know which goods have zero or even negative prices, and which goods have positive prices, in this system.

3.3.2 Cheaper Points for Nonconvex Feasible Sets

The usual demonstration that the existence of a cheaper feasible point for an individual converts a compensated into an uncompensated equilibrium for that individual depends on the feasible set being convex. To

[7]Actually, despite Nikaido's contribution, many subsequent papers in general equilibrium theory seem to combine nonnegative orthant consumption sets, strictly monotone preferences, and the interiority assumption which he showed to be unnecessary in the presence of the other two assumptions.

generalize this to nonconvex feasible sets requires an additional assumption. When some goods are indivisible, it has been common to assume that divisble goods are "overridingly desirable," meaning that any commodity bundle with indivisible goods can be improved by moving to another with only divisible goods. This assumption is discussed below in Section 3.3.3. An attempt to generalize it follows.

First, let $\operatorname{co} Y$ and $\operatorname{cl} Y$ denote respectively the convex hull and the closure of any set $Y \subset \mathscr{R}^G$. Then, for every $a \in A$ and $x_a \in X_a$, let

$$K_a(x_a) := \operatorname{co}\{x'_a \in \mathscr{R}^G | \exists \tilde{x}_a \in X_a \;\&\; \exists \lambda > 0 : x'_a = x_a + \lambda(\tilde{x}_a - x_a)\};$$

$$K_a^{\succ}(x_a) := \operatorname{co}\{x'_a \in \mathscr{R}^G | \exists \tilde{x}_a \in P_a(x_a) \;\&\; \exists \lambda > 0 : x'_a = x_a + \lambda(\tilde{x}_a - x_a)\}.$$

Thus $K_a(x_a)$ denotes the smallest convex cone with vertex x_a that is generated by the set X_a of feasible net trade vectors, while $K_a^{\succ}(x_a)$ denotes the corresponding cone that is generated by the set $P_a(x_a)$ of net trade vectors that are strictly preferred to x_a. Because $x_a \in X_a$, note that $K_a(x_a)$ is a *pointed cone* containing its own vertex x_a. On the other hand, $x_a \notin P_a(x_a)$, and so it may well be true that $x_a \notin K_a^{\succ}(x_a)$, in which case the cone $K_a^{\succ}(x_a)$ is *unpointed*—indeed, this will always be the case when agent a has convex preferences.

Assumption 1. For every agent $a \in A$ and net trade vector $x_a \in X_a$, if $x'_a \in K_a^{\succ}(x_a)$ and $\bar{x}_a \in K_a(x_a) \setminus \operatorname{cl} K_a^{\succ}(x_a)$, then the (relatively) open line segment $L := (x'_a, \bar{x}_a) \subset K_a(x_a)$ of points lying strictly between x'_a and $\bar{x}_a$ must have a nonempty intersection $L \cap K_a^{\succ}(x_a)$ with the convex cone $K_a^{\succ}(x_a)$.[8]

Note that often $K_a(x_a)$ will be the whole space $\mathscr{R}^G$, but this still makes Assumption 1 meaningful—in this case it simply requires $K_a^{\succ}(x_a)$ to be an open set. The convex cone $K_a^{\succ}(x_a)$ may also be the whole space $\mathscr{R}^G$ if preferences are nonconvex, in which case Assumption 1 is automatically satisfied at x_a.

Assumption 1 is perhaps not as easy to check as it should be. Nevertheless, it gives what is needed by ruling out such troublesome examples as those discussed in Broome (1972), Mas-Colell (1977), and Khan and Yamazaki (1981). In addition, it generalizes the more familiar condition which is the hypothesis of the following:

LEMMA. *Suppose that the feasible set X_a is convex and that the lower contour set $L_a(x_a)$ is closed for each $x_a \in X_a$. Then Assumption 1 is satisfied.*

[8]As stated here, Assumption 1 is strictly weaker than the requirement that the convex cone $K_a^{\succ}(x_a)$ should be open relative to the convex cone $K_a(x_a)$—i.e., that $K_a^{\succ}(x_a) = O \cap \bar{K}_a(x_a)$ for some set O that is open in $\mathscr{R}^G$.

Proof. Let x_a be any net trade vector in X_a. Suppose $x'_a \in K_a^{\succ}(x_a)$ and that $\bar{x}_a \in K_a(x_a) \setminus \text{cl}\, K_a^{\succ}(x_a)$. Then $L := (x'_a, \bar{x}_a) \subset K_a(x_a)$.

Because $x'_a \in K_a^{\succ}(x_a)$ and $\bar{x}_a \in K_a(x_a)$, there must exist finite sets of net trade vectors $x^j \in P_a(x_a)$, $y^i \in X_a$ and of associated positive scalars λ^j, μ^i ($j = 1$ to J; $i = 1$ to I) such that

$$x'_a - x_a = \sum_{j=1}^{J} \lambda^j (x^j - x_a) \quad \text{and} \quad \bar{x}_a - x_a = \sum_{i=1}^{I} \mu^i (y^i - x_a).$$

Let $\mu := \sum_{i=1}^{I} \mu^i$ and $y := \sum_{i=1}^{I} (\mu^i/\mu) y^i$. Then $y \in X_a$ because X_a is convex. Also $\bar{x}_a - x_a = \mu(y - x_a)$.

Now $x^j \in P_a(x_a)$ and $y \in X_a$ while X_a is convex and the lower contour set $L_a(x_a)$ is closed. So, for each $j = 1$ to J there must exist an ϵ^j with $0 < \epsilon^j \leq 1$ such that $x^j + \epsilon(y - x^j) \in P_a(x_a)$ whenever $0 < \epsilon < \epsilon^j$. Then, however, for the vector $x^\epsilon := x'_a + \epsilon(\bar{x}_a - x'_a) \in L$ it must be true that

$$\begin{aligned} x^\epsilon - x_a &= (1 - \epsilon)(x'_a - x_a) + \epsilon(\bar{x}_a - x_a) \\ &= (1 - \epsilon) \sum_{j=1}^{J} \lambda^j (x^j - x_a) + \epsilon\mu(y - x_a) \\ &= \sum_{j=1}^{J} \frac{(1 - \epsilon)\lambda^j}{1 - \delta} \left[x^j + \delta(y - x^j) - x_a \right] \end{aligned}$$

where $\epsilon\mu(1 - \delta) = (1 - \epsilon)\delta \sum_{j=1}^{J} \lambda^j$ and so $\delta = \epsilon\mu / [\epsilon\mu + (1 - \epsilon)\sum_{j=1}^{J} \lambda^j]$. This implies that $x^\epsilon \in K_a^{\succ}(x_a)$ as long as $0 < \delta < \epsilon^j$ and so $x^j + \delta(y - x^j) \in P_a(x_a)$ for $j = 1$ to J. This requires that

$$0 < \epsilon < \min_j \left\{ \frac{\epsilon^j \sum_{i=1}^{J} \lambda^i}{\mu(1 - \epsilon^j) + \sum_{i=1}^{J} \lambda^i} \right\}.$$

Since the interval of such values of ϵ is certainly nonempty, so is $L \cap K_a^{\succ}(x_a)$. ■

3.3.3 *Overriding Desirability of Divisible Goods*

Consider an economy with just one divisible and one indivisible good. Indeed, suppose that $X_a = \mathscr{R}_+ \times Z_+$ where Z_+ denotes the set of non-negative integers, representing quantities of the indivisible good. Suppose too that preferences are *strictly monotone* in the sense that, if $x_a = (y_a, z_a)$ and $x'_a = (y'_a, z'_a)$ are both members of X_a with $y'_a \geq y_a$ and $z'_a \geq z_a$, then $x'_a \succsim_a x_a$, with strict preference unless both $y'_a = y_a$ and $z'_a = z_a$.

Next, say that *divisible goods are overridingly desirable* if, whenever $x_a = (y_a, z_a)$ and $x'_a = (y'_a, z'_a)$ are both members of X_a, then there exists $\hat{y}_a \in \mathscr{R}_+$ such that $(\hat{y}_a, z'_a) \succ_a (y_a, z_a)$.[9] Thus, even though z'_a may involve much less of the indivisible good than z_a does, the move from z_a to z'_a can always be outweighed by a move from y_a to $\hat{y}_a$ in the divisible good.

Assumption 1 seems at first to be a significant weakening of overriding desirability. When some goods are indivisible, however, Assumption 1 often turns out to be no weaker than the assumption of overriding desirability, as is shown by the following.

LEMMA. *Under the hypotheses of the first paragraph of this section, Assumption* 1 *implies that divisible goods are overridingly desirable.*

Proof. Suppose that (y_a, z_a) is some member of X_a with $z_a > 0$. Then the hypotheses imply that the convex cone $K_a(y_a, z_a)$ with vertex (y_a, z_a) that is generated by the feasible set $X_a = \mathscr{R}_+ \times Z_+$ is either (i) the whole of $\mathscr{R}^2$, in case $y_a > 0$; or (ii) just the half-space $\{(y, z) \in \mathscr{R}^2 | y \geq 0\}$, in case $y_a = 0$.

Suppose it were true that $(y_a, z_a) \succsim_a (\tilde{y}_a, z_a - 1)$ whenever $\tilde{y}_a \geq 0$. Then the convex cone $K_a^{\succ}(y_a, z_a)$ with vertex (y_a, z_a) which is generated by the preference set $P_a(y_a, z_a)$ would be a subset of $\{(y, z) \in \mathscr{R}^2 | z \geq z_a\}$. Consider now any $(y^*, z^*) \in \mathscr{R}^2$ satisfying $y^* > y_a$ and $z^* = z_a$. By strict monotonicity of preferences one has $(y^*, z^*) \succ_a (y_a, z_a)$, implying that (y^*, z^*) would belong not only to $K_a^{\succ}(y_a, z_a)$ but also to the boundary of this set—which is (partly) illustrated as the shaded set in Figure 1. So, if L is the open line segment with endpoints (y^*, z^*) and $(y^*, 0)$, then $L \cap K_a^{\succ}(y_a, z_a)$ would be empty, thereby contradicting Assumption 1.

Therefore, for every $(y_a, z_a) \in X_a$ with $z_a > 0$, there must exist $\tilde{y}_a \geq 0$ for which $(\tilde{y}_a, z_a - 1) \succ_a (y_a, z_a)$. Because preferences are transitive, an easy argument by induction on the integer z_a then establishes that the one divisible good is overridingly desirable. ∎

Although this lemma has been proved only for the case of one divisible and one indivisible good, it is clear that the argument can be

[9]This assumption appears to have originated with Broome (1972). It has since been used by, amongst others, Mas-Colell (1977). Khan and Yamazaki (1981). and Hammond *et al.* (1989). Henry (1970) earlier formulated a condition that the divisible good be necessary for survival. However, this condition is stated in a way that appears to be inconsistent with his other assumptions. For, in the notation used here, it requires that, whenever $x_a = (y_a, z_a)$ and $x'_a = (y'_a, z'_a)$ are both members of X_a, then there should exist $\hat{y}_a \in \mathscr{R}_+$ such that $(y_a, z_a) \succ_a (\hat{y}_a, z'_a)$. This can never hold, of course, if $(y_a, z_a) = (0, 0)$, the worst point in X_a. If instead the condition is required to hold only for those $x_a = (y_a, z_a) \in \mathscr{R}_+ \times Z_+$ that satisfy $y_a > 0$, then there is no inconsistency, but the assumption becomes quite different from overriding desirability.

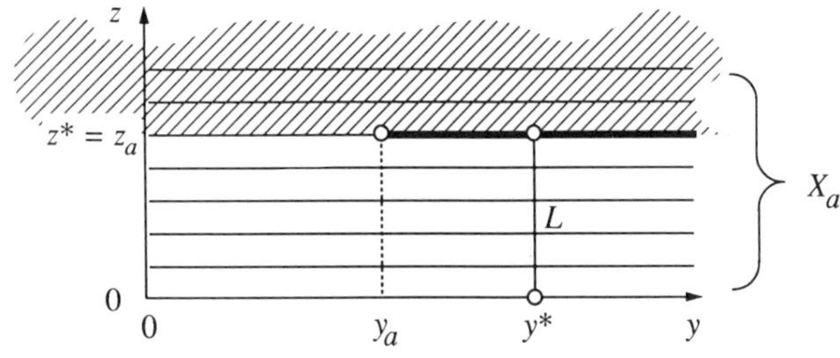

FIGURE 1

greatly generalized to allow many divisible and indivisible goods. The issue of whether there is an adequate weaker assumption than overriding desirability of divisible goods will be taken up in Section 3.3.5 below.

3.3.4 The Cheaper Point Theorem

PROPOSITION. *Suppose that* $\hat{x}_a \in \xi^C(p, w_a)$ *is any compensated equilibrium for agent a at the price vector* $p \neq 0$. *If Assumption* 1 *is satisfied, and if there also exists* $\bar{x}_a \in X_a$ *with* $p\bar{x}_a < w_a$, *then* $\hat{x}_a \in \xi^U(p, w_a)$—*i.e.,* $\hat{x}_a$ *is an uncompensated equilibrium.*

Proof. Suppose that $\hat{x}_a \in \xi^C(p, w_a) \setminus \xi^U(p, w_a)$. By Lemma 2.2.1, $p\hat{x}_a = w_a$. Because $\hat{x}_a \notin \xi^U(p, w_a)$, there exists $x'_a \in P_a(\hat{x}_a)$ such that $px'_a \leq w_a$. Since $\hat{x}_a \in \xi^C(p, w_a)$ it follows that $x_a \in U_a(\hat{x}_a)$ implies $px_a \geq p\hat{x}_a = w_a$ and so in fact $px'_a = w_a$. Also, one must have $px_a \geq w_a$ for all $x_a \in K_a^{\succ}(\hat{x}_a)$ and so for all $x_a \in \text{cl}\, K_a^{\succ}(\hat{x}_a)$.

Since $p\bar{x}_a < w_a = px'_a = p\hat{x}_a$, it must be true that $\bar{x}_a \in K_a(\hat{x}_a) \setminus \text{cl}\, K_a^{\succ}(\hat{x}_a)$. Let L denote the nonempty open line segment $(x'_a, \bar{x}_a) \subset K_a(\hat{x}_a)$. Suppose now that the set $L \cap K_a^{\succ}(\hat{x}_a)$ were nonempty, in which case there would exist an ϵ for which $0 < \epsilon < 1$ and

$$x_a^{\epsilon} := x'_a + \epsilon(\bar{x}_a - x'_a) \in K_a^{\succ}(\hat{x}_a).$$

Then there would be a finite collection of points $x_a^j \in P_a(\hat{x}_a)$ and of associated positive scalars λ_j ($j = 1$ to J) such that $x_a^{\epsilon} - \hat{x}_a = \sum_{j=1}^J \lambda_j(x_a^j - \hat{x}_a)$. Because $px'_a = w_a = p\hat{x}_a$ and $p\bar{x}_a < px'_a$, this would imply that

$$\sum_{j=1}^{J} \lambda_j p(x_a^j - \hat{x}_a) = p(x_a^{\epsilon} - \hat{x}_a) = p(x'_a - \hat{x}_a) + \epsilon p(\bar{x}_a - x'_a) < 0.$$

Since each scalar λ_j is positive, this would imply that there must be at least one j for which $p(x_a^j - \hat{x}_a) < 0$. But $x_a^j \in P_a(\hat{x}_a)$ and so this contradicts the hypothesis that $\hat{x}_a \in \xi^C(p, w_a)$. Therefore, $L \cap K_a^{\succ}(\hat{x}_a)$ must be empty, after all.

Thus, if $\hat{x}_a \in \xi^C(p, w_a) \setminus \xi^U(p, w_a)$, then Assumption 1 is violated. Conversely, if Assumption 1 is satisfied, then $\xi^C(p, w_a) = \xi^U(p, w_a)$. ∎

3.3.5 The Necessity of Assumption 1

Although Assumption 1 has some undesirable implications that were discussed in Section 3.3.3, the following result shows that there is a sense in which it is indispensable.

PROPOSITION. *Suppose that there exist net trade vectors $\hat{x}_a \in X_a$, $x'_a \in K_a^{\succ}(\hat{x}_a)$ and $\bar{x}_a \in K_a(\hat{x}_a) \setminus \text{cl}\, K_a^{\succ}(\hat{x}_a)$ for which the open line segment $L := (x'_a, \bar{x}_a)$ is disjoint from the convex cone $K_a^{\succ}(\hat{x}_a)$. Then there exists a price vector $p \neq 0$ and a wealth level $w_a := p\hat{x}_a$ such that $\hat{x}_a \in \xi_a^C(p, w_a)$ and yet $\hat{x}_a \notin \xi_a^U(p, w_a)$, even though $p\bar{x}_a < w_a$—i.e., the compensated equilibrium net trade vector $\hat{x}_a$ is not an uncompensated equilibrium, even though X_a has a cheaper point at the equilibrium price vector p.*

Proof.

1. The hypotheses of the proposition imply that the point $\bar{x}_a$ has an open and convex neighborhood V that is disjoint from cl $K_a^{\succ}(\hat{x}_a)$. Let K^0 be the smallest unpointed convex cone with vertex $\hat{x}_a$ that contains $L \cup V$. Evidently K^0 is nonempty, open, convex, and also disjoint from the convex cone $K_a^{\succ}(\hat{x}_a)$ with the same vertex $\hat{x}_a$. So there must be a price vector $p \neq 0$ and an associated hyperplane $px_a = \alpha$ that separates the two convex sets K^0 and $K_a^{\succ}(\hat{x}_a)$ in the sense that $x \in K^0 \Rightarrow px \leq \alpha$ and $x \in K_a^{\succ}(\hat{x}_a) \Rightarrow px \geq \alpha$.

2. Let $w_a := \alpha$. In fact, since the two points $\hat{x}_a$ and x'_a both lie in the intersection of the respective closures of the two convex cones $K_a^{\succ}(\hat{x}_a)$ and K^0, both these points must actually lie in the separating hyperplane, and so $p\hat{x}_a = px'_a = \alpha = w_a$.

3. Moreover, since K^0 is open and $x \in K^0 \Rightarrow px \leq \alpha$, it is actually true that $x \in K^0 \Rightarrow px < \alpha$. In particular, since $\frac{1}{2}x'_a + \frac{1}{2}\bar{x}_a \in L \subset K^0$ and $px'_a = \alpha$, one must have $p(\frac{1}{2}x'_a + \frac{1}{2}\bar{x}_a) < px'_a$ and so $p\bar{x}_a < px'_a = w_a$.

4. In addition, since $P_a(\hat{x}_a) \subset K_a^{\succ}(\hat{x}_a)$, it follows that $x_a \in P_a(\hat{x}_a)$ implies $px_a \geq w_a$.

5. Because (2) implies that $p\hat{x}_a = w_a$, and also because of local nonsatiation and Lemma 2.2.1, (4) shows that $\hat{x}_a \in \xi_a^C(p, w_a)$.

6. Finally, because $x'_a \in K_a^{\succ}(\hat{x}_a)$, there exists a finite collection of net trade vectors $x_a^j \in P_a(\hat{x}_a)$ and of associated positive scalars λ^j ($j = 1$ to J) for which $x'_a - \hat{x}_a = \sum_{j=1}^J \lambda^j (x_a^j - \hat{x}_a)$. But, by (2) and (4), $x_a \in P_a(\hat{x}_a)$ implies $px_a \geq w_a = p\hat{x}_a$, and so $px_a^j \geq p\hat{x}_a$ for $j = 1$ to J.

7. Also, since (2) implies that $p\hat{x}_a = px'_a$, it follows from (6) that

$$0 = p(x'_a - \hat{x}_a) = \sum_{j=1}^{J} \lambda^j p(x^j_a - \hat{x}_a) \geq 0$$

and so $\sum_{j=1}^{J} \lambda^j p(x^j_a - \hat{x}_a) = 0$.

8. Since $\lambda^j > 0$ and, by (6), $px^j_a \geq p\hat{x}_a$ ($j = 1$ to J), (2) and (7) together imply that $px^j_a = p\hat{x}_a = w_a$ for $j = 1$ to J. But (6) implies that $x^j_a \in P_a(\hat{x}_a)$ ($j = 1$ to J), and so $\hat{x}_a \notin \xi^U_a(p, w_a)$. ∎

3.4 Aggregate Interiority

3.4.1 The Interiority Assumption

In a finite economy, in order for some individual to have a cheaper feasible net trade, it is necessary that society as a whole should have some cheaper point. So assume the following.

Assumption 2. The origin $0 \in \mathscr{R}^G$ belongs to the interior of K_A, the convex hull of the set $X_A := \sum_{a \in A} X_a$.

This assumption can be motivated as follows. Back in Section 2.1.3 it was assumed that $0 \in X_a$ for all $a \in A$. So if Assumption 2 is false, it can only be because 0 is a boundary point of K_A. But then there would be a hyperplane $px = 0$ through 0 that supports the convex set K_A in the sense that $px \geq 0$ whenever $x \in K_A$. Note how $X_a \subset X_A \subset K_A$ (all $a \in A$) because $0 \in X_{a'}$ for all $a' \in A \setminus \{a\}$. So, for all $a \in A$, it would follow that $px \geq 0$ whenever $x \in X_a$. Thus almost no agent in the economy can trade in the open half-space H of directions x satisfying $px < 0$. If almost nobody can trade in any such direction, net demands for vectors in the opposite half-space $-H$ are completely ineffective. They are like asking for the moon—or at least, for a return trip there this year (1993). It therefore makes sense to restrict attention to the proper linear subspace of net trade vectors satisfying $px = 0$. Repeating this argument as many times as necessary results in a commodity space that is the linear space spanned by the relative interior of the convex set K_A. For this commodity space, of course, Assumption 2 is satisfied by construction.

3.4.2 Cheaper Points for Some Individuals

LEMMA. *Under Assumption 2, for every feasible allocation* $\mathbf{x}$ *and every price vector* $p \neq 0$, *the set*

$$\{a \in A | \exists \bar{x}_a \in X_a \quad \textit{such that} \quad p\bar{x}_a < px_a\}$$

of individuals with cheaper points is nonempty.

Proof. Assumption 2 implies that for every price vector $p \neq 0$ there exists $\tilde{x} \in K_A$ such that $p\tilde{x} < 0$. But then there must exist $\bar{x} \in \Sigma_{a \in A} X_a$ for which $p\bar{x} < 0$. Let $\bar{x} = \Sigma_{a \in A} \bar{x}_a$ where $\bar{x}_a \in X_a$ for all $a \in A$. Then, since aggregate feasibility implies that $\Sigma_{a \in A} x_a = 0$, it must be true that

$$\sum_{a \in A} p(\bar{x}_a - x_a) = \sum_{a \in A} p\bar{x}_a = p\bar{x} < 0.$$

This is only possible, however, if $p\bar{x}_a < px_a$ for at least one $a \in A$. ■

4. NONOLIGARCHIC ALLOCATIONS

4.1 Definitions

Suppose that $\mathbf{x}$ is a feasible allocation. Let C be any proper subset of A. Say that "$A \setminus C$ may strongly improve the condition of C in $\mathbf{x}$" if there exists an alternative feasible allocation $\mathbf{x}'$ such that $x'_a \succ_a x_a$ for all $a \in C$. And, as in Spivak (1978), say that "$A \setminus C$ may improve the condition of C in $\mathbf{x}$" if there exists an alternative feasible allocation $\mathbf{x}'$ such that $x'_a \succsim_a x_a$ for all $a \in C$, and $x'_{a^*} \succ_{a^*} x_{a^*}$ for some $a^* \in C$.

Next, C is said to be a *weak oligarchy* at $\mathbf{x}$ if $A \setminus C$ cannot strongly improve the condition of C in $\mathbf{x}$. Equivalently, C is a weak oligarchy at $\mathbf{x}$ if there is no other feasible allocation $\mathbf{x}'$ such that $x'_a \succ_a x_a$ for all $a \in C$—i.e., if

$$0 \notin \sum_{a \in C} P_a(x_a) + \sum_{a \in A \setminus C} X_a.$$

And C is said to be a *strong oligarchy* at $\mathbf{x}$ if $A \setminus C$ cannot improve the condition of C in $\mathbf{x}$. Equivalently, C is a strong oligarchy at $\mathbf{x}$ if there is no other feasible allocation $\mathbf{x}'$ such that $x'_a \succsim_a x_a$ for all $a \in C$, and $x'_{a^*} \succ_{a^*} x_{a^*}$ for some $a^* \in C$—i.e., if

$$0 \notin P_{a^*}(x_{a^*}) + \sum_{a \in C \setminus \{a^*\}} U_a(x_a) + \sum_{a \in A \setminus C} X_a$$

for all $a^* \in C$.

The last definitions receive their name because an omnipotent oligarchy would presumably choose a feasible allocation with the (strong oligarchy) property that no alternative feasible allocation could make some of its members better off without simultaneously making some other members worse off. Or it would at least choose a feasible allocation with the (weak oligarchy) property that no alternative feasible allocation could make all of its members better off simultaneously.

Conversely, the feasible allocation $\mathbf{x}$ is said to be *strongly* (resp. *weakly*) *nonoligarchic* if there is no weak (resp. strong) oligarchy at $\mathbf{x}$. Thus, $\mathbf{x}$ is strongly nonoligarchic if and only if, for every partition $A_1 \cup A_2$ of A into two disjoint nonempty sets A_1, A_2, there exists another feasible allocation $\mathbf{x}'$ such that $x'_a \succ_a x_a$ for all $a \in A_1$—i.e., if

$$0 \in \sum_{a \in A_1} P_a(x_a) + \sum_{a \in A_2} X_a.$$

And $\mathbf{x}$ is weakly nonoligarchic if and only if, for every partition $A_1 \cup A_2$ of A into two disjoint nonempty sets A_1, A_2, there exists another feasible allocation $\mathbf{x}'$ such that $x'_a \succsim_a x_a$ for all $a \in A_1$, and $x'_{a^*} \succ_{a^*} x_{a^*}$ for some $a^* \in A_1$—i.e., if there exists $a^* \in A_1$ such that

$$0 \in P_{a^*}(x_{a^*}) + \sum_{a \in A_1 \setminus \{a^*\}} U_a(x_a) + \sum_{a \in A_2} X_a.$$

Of course, any strongly nonoligarchic allocation is weakly nonoligarchic.

In a nonoligarchic allocation, by contrast to an oligarchic allocation, every coalition that is a proper subset of A, the set of all agents, does have an improvement available, provided it can suitably exploit the resources of the complementary coalition. The force of the nonoligarchy assumption is that the allocation leaves every coalition with some resources that the complementary coalition would like to exploit if it could. Provided that some agents are in uncompensated equilibrium, this will ensure that the other agents do have cheaper points, as Proposition 4.3 (i.e., the proposition in Section 4.3, below) demonstrates.

4.2 Gale's Linear Exchange Model

Gale (1957, 1976) considered a linear exchange model in which each agent a has a feasible set $X_a = \{x_a \in \mathscr{R}^G | x_a \geqq \underline{x}_a\}$ of net trades, and a preference ordering $\succsim_a$ represented by the linear utility function $V_a(x_a) := v_a x_a = \sum_{g \in G} v_{ag} x_{ag}$ for some semipositive vector v_a of coefficients. Typically the minimum net trade vector $\underline{x}_a$ of X_a is taken to be $-\omega_a$, where $\omega_a \in \mathscr{R}^G_+$ is agent a's fixed endowment vector. Then a's consumption set $X_a + \{\omega_a\}$ is the nonnegative orthant $\mathscr{R}^G_+$. But there is no need here for this specific assumption.

In this linear exchange economy, the allocation $\mathbf{x}$ is said to be *reducible* (Eaves, 1976) if there exist two partitions $A = A_1 \cup A_2$ and $G = G_1 \cup G_2$ into two nonempty subsets of both the set of agents A and the set of goods G with the property that

$$v_{ag} = 0 \; (a \in A_1; g \in G_1); \qquad x_{ag} - \underline{x}_{ag} = 0 \; (a \in A_2; g \in G_2).$$

Thus the only goods desired by the members of A_1 are in the set G_2, and none of these can be supplied by the members of A_2. Consequently, a Pareto-efficient allocation in this economy is reducible only if there exists an oligarchy (A_1) that cannot be made better off even with the resources of the complementary coalition (which are goods in G_1). Notice that the allocation $\mathbf{x}$ is reducible only if the matrix M defined by

$$M_{aa'} := \sum_{g \in G} v_{ag}(x_{a'g} - \underline{x}_{a'g}) \quad (\text{all } a, a' \in A)$$

is reducible in the sense of Gantmacher (1953, 1959) and Gale (1960)—i.e., there is a partition $A_1 \cup A_2$ of A into two nonempty subsets such that $M_{aa'} = 0$ for all $a \in A_1$ and all $a' \in A_2$. Of course, the element $M_{aa'}$ of this matrix represents the utility to a of agent a''s resources.

The converse statements are also true in this special economy. That is, if the proper subset C of A is an oligarchy at the allocation $\mathbf{x}$, then for all $a \in C$, $a' \in A \setminus C$ and $g \in G$ it must be true that

$$v_{ag} > 0 \Rightarrow x_{a'g} - \underline{x}_{a'g} = 0.$$

This is the condition which Gale (1976) calls "self-sufficiency," although that term could perhaps be applied better to feasible allocations rather than to ways of making a coalition better off. The same condition holds, of course, if the matrix M is reducible, with an independent subset C. In either case, define

$$G_2 := \{g \in G | x_{ag} - \underline{x}_{ag} = 0 \quad (\text{all } a \in A \setminus C)\}.$$

Note that G_2 is certainly nonempty because it contains any good g for which there exists some $a \in C$ with $v_{ag} > 0$. This construction shows that the economy is reducible except in the uninteresting special case when $x_a = \underline{x}_a$ for all $a \in A \setminus C$, so that the coalition $A \setminus C$ has no resources at all available for redistribution to the members of C.

Thus, for the special case of the linear exchange economy, the nonoligarchy condition is very closely related to irreducibility of the matrix M defined above.

4.3 Convexified Nonoligarchic Allocations

In fact only the convex combinations of potential changes turns out to matter. Accordingly, the proper subset C of A is said to be a *convexified oligarchy* at the feasible allocation $\mathbf{x}$ if, for every agent $a^* \in C$, one has

$$0 \notin \text{co}\left[P_{a^*}(x_{a^*}) + \sum_{a \in C \setminus \{a^*\}} U_a(x_a) + \sum_{a \in A \setminus C} X_a\right].$$

The feasible allocation $\mathbf{x}$ is said to be *convexified non-oligarchic* if, for every partition $A_1 \cup A_2$ of A into two disjoint non-empty sets A_1, A_2, neither subset is a convexified oligarchy—i.e., if there exists $a^* \in A_1$ such that

$$0 \in \text{co}\left[P_{a^*}(x_{a^*}) + \sum_{a \in A_1 \setminus \{a^*\}} U_a(x_a) + \sum_{a \in A_2} X_a\right].$$

Under the classical hypotheses of Section 2.1.6, any convexified nonoligarchic allocation $\mathbf{x}$ is obviously nonoligarchic. So "convexified" nonoligarchic allocations are only more general if the usual convexity hypotheses are violated. The following result is proved in Section 7.1.

PROPOSITION. *Under Assumptions* 1 *and* 2, *any convexified nonoligarchic allocation* $\mathbf{x}$ *that is a compensated equilibrium with transfers at some price vector* $p \neq 0$ *must be an uncompensated equilibrium with transfers at the same price vector* p.

4.4 Agents outside Convexified Oligarchies Are at Cheapest Points

Following Spivak's (1978) proof of a similar result for nonoligarchic allocations, one can show that an allocation must be convexified nonoligarchic if every agent is to have a cheaper point at every possible compensated equilibrium price vector. Indeed, the following is proved in Section 7.2.

PROPOSITION. *Let* $\hat{\mathbf{x}}$ *be a feasible allocation at which the coalition* C *is a convexified oligarchy. Then there exists a price vector* $p \neq 0$ *such that* $(\hat{\mathbf{x}}, p)$ *is a compensated equilibrium with transfers in which all agents outside* C *are at cheapest points—i.e., for all* $a \in A \setminus C$, *it must be true that* $x_a \in X_a \Rightarrow px_a \geq p\hat{x}_a$.

4.5 Two Instructive Examples

So far I have considered necessary and sufficient conditions for a particular compensated equilibrium allocation to have the property that each agent has a cheaper point at the equilibrium prices, thus assuring (under Assumptions 1 and 2) that the equilibrium is also uncompensated. Obviously, for any compensated equilibrium to be an uncompensated equilibrium, and so for the existence of some uncompensated equilibrium, it would be sufficient for every feasible allocation to be convexified nonoli-

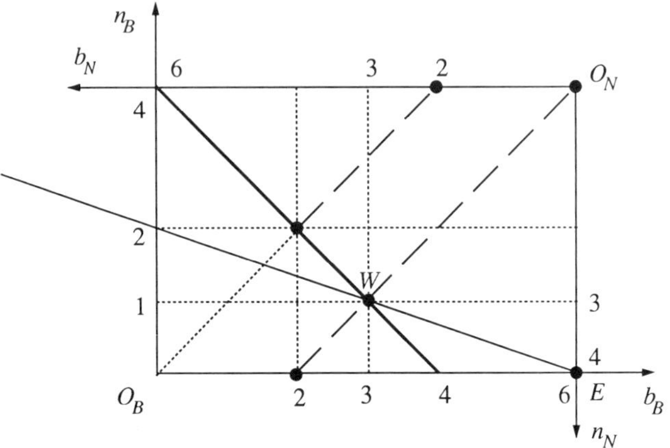

FIGURE 2

garchic. Yet this condition can never be satisfied, since there will always be extreme allocations that are oligarchic or even dictatorial. Instead one might think of assuming that at least every feasible allocation in which no agent is worse off than under autarky should be convexified nonoligarchic. This latter sufficient condition turns out to be unnecessarily strong, however, since it takes no account of the fact that the only relevant compensated equilibrium prices are those giving rise to a budget hyperplane for each agent that passes through the autarky allocation. An example to show this will now be provided.

Figure 2 illustrates a "clipped" Edgeworth box exchange economy. It is presumed that there are two perfectly complementary commodities—nuts and bolts, with quantities indicated by n and b, respectively. There are also two agents labeled mnemonically B and N whose initial endowments are $(\bar{b}_B, \bar{n}_B) = (6, 0)$ and $(\bar{b}_N, \bar{n}_N) = (0, 4)$, respectively. Both agents have the obvious utility function $u(b, n) \equiv \min\{b, n\}$. For some reason that I shall not try to justify, agent B's feasible set is assumed to be not the whole of $\mathscr{R}^2_+$, but only that part of the nonnegative orthant satisfying the additional constraint $b_B + n_B \geq 4$. This explains why the Edgeworth box has its corner clipped off, in effect.

Because there are more bolts than nuts, B has no market power. In fact, the unique (Walrasian) uncompensated equilibrium in this economy is at the allocation W, where $(b_B, n_B) = (3, 1)$ and $(b_N, n_N) = (3, 3)$, with corresponding prices $(1, 3)$ for nuts and bolts, respectively. This allocation is oligarchic—indeed, it is even "dictatorial"—because it is the best possible allocation for N given the need to respect the constraint that $b_B + n_B \geq 4$. Note that the initial endowment, however, is certainly not oligarchic because it is not even weakly Pareto-efficient. Thus having the autarky allocation be nonoligarchic does not rule out the possibility that the only equilibrium may be oligarchic.

The allocation W is not only a Walrasian equilibrium at the price vector $(1, 3)$. It is also a compensated equilibrium with transfers at any nonnegative price vector (p, q) with $0 \leq p \leq q$, including $(1, 1)$. For the particular compensated equilibrium price vector $(1, 1)$, of course, W is a cheapest point of B's feasible set. Since W is oligarchic, this is the compensated equilibrium price vector whose existence is assured by Proposition 4.4. Yet at the alternative compensated equilibrium price vector $(1, 3)$ even agent B has a cheaper point, and so this also gives an uncompensated equilibrium. Moreover, only this price vector is relevant to the existence of a Walrasian equilibrium, since it is only for the price vector $(1, 3)$ that the allocation W satisfies the budget constraint $pb_a + qn_a = p\bar{b}_a + q\bar{n}_a$ for each agent $a \in \{B, N\}$ and for the approprite endowment vector $(\bar{b}_a, \bar{n}_a)$.

This suggests that a weaker sufficient condition may still ensure existence of uncompensated equilibrium without transfers, since oligarchy by itself is not always an obstacle. Yet sometimes it certainly is, as illustrated by the alternative triangular Edgeworth box shown in Figure 3. The only difference from Figure 2 is that agent B's additional constraint has been changed from $b_B + n_B \geq 4$ to $b_B + n_B \geq 6$. This is enough, however, to prevent existence of uncompensated equilibrium without transfers. For the only compensated equilibrium without transfers occurs at C, where $(b_B, n_B) = (4, 2)$ and $(b_N, n_N) = (2, 2)$. This is indeed a cheapest point of B's feasible set at the only possible equilibrium price vector $(1, 1)$ that can be sustained without any transfers. It is not an uncompensated equilibrium, however, because at these prices agent B

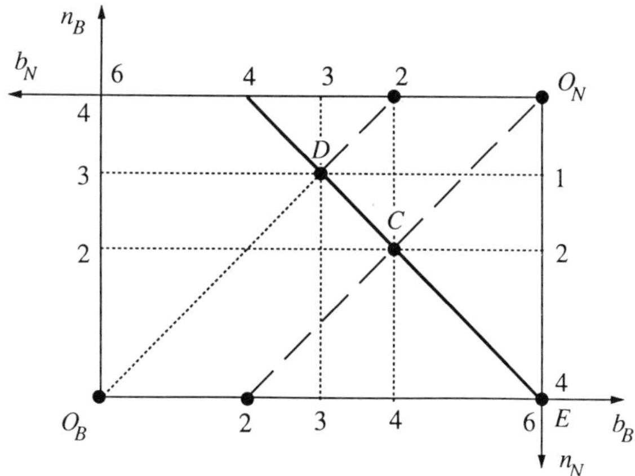

FIGURE 3

would like to move to the point D on the budget line DCE, where $(b_B, n_B) = (3, 3)$.

So we should look for a weaker sufficient condition that includes the oligarchic Walrasian allocation W in Figure 2, but excludes all allocations in the economy illustrated in Figure 3. Such a condition is the generalized form of irreducibility to be considered in the next section.

5. INTERDEPENDENT AGENTS AND IRREDUCIBLE ECONOMIES

5.1 Arrow and Debreu's Early Version of Irreducibility

It has already been pointed out that the first part of Arrow and Debreu (1954) relies on the implausible interiority assumption. But they do also present a different and more interesting second assumption. For this they assume that there is some set of goods $\mathscr{D}$ that all consumers desire. Also, that for any given feasible allocation, every consumer's endowment includes some kind of labor service that can be converted into an increased aggregate net supply of some good in $\mathscr{D}$, without any offsetting reduction in the aggregate net supply of any other good. In a finite economy, any such labor service is bound to command a positive wage provided that any consumers at all are maximizing preferences subject to their budget constraints.

Now, it was evident that with convex feasible sets and continuous preferences, for any consumer having a net trade vector of negative value —i.e., able to sell something of positive value—any compensated equilibrium must be an uncompensated equilibrium, as in the "cheaper point theorem" of Section 3.3.4 above, which actually requires only the weaker Assumption 1 of Section 3.3.2. So, in a finite economy, this second Arrow–Debreu assumption leaves just two possibilities. The first of these is that nobody has a cheaper point at the compensated equilibrium price vector, and that nobody is in uncompensated equilibrium. This is what happens in Arrow's exceptional case, but one could argue that the problem there is the attempt to price commodities such as return trips to the moon this year that cannot possibly be traded in any feasible allocation. The second possibility is more interesting. This is that every commodity can be traded, so every commodity can be supplied by somebody. Since at least one commodity should have a positive price, at least one consumer has a cheaper point, and so is in uncompensated equilibrium. But then, under the Arrow–Debreu assumption, all the desirable commodities in the set $\mathscr{D}$ must have positive prices, so everybody has a valuable labor service to supply, and therefore everybody has a cheaper feasible point.

This shows that, in a finite economy, the compensated equilibrium is an uncompensated equilibrium for everybody, as required.

Arrow and Debreu's second assumption was unnamed. Yet it is actually a special case of the much more general irreducibility assumption introduced a few years later by McKenzie.

5.2 McKenzie's Irreducibility

As McKenzie (1959, p. 58) points out, he was "able to dispense with the categories of always desired goods and always productive goods used by Arrow and Debreu. An always desired good appears particularly implausible. It requires that every consumer be insatiable in this good within the supplies attainable by the whole market." One can also note that Arrow and Debreu's second assumption cannot apply in the usual kind of exchange economy in which each consumer has a fixed endowment vector of consumer goods, so that labor services are of no use to anyone.

In the introduction to McKenzie (1959, p. 55), he writes, "In loose terms, an economy is irreducible if it cannot be divided into two groups of consumers where one group is unable to supply any goods which the other group wants." After stating the relevant assumption formally, this verbal description is expanded somewhat on pages 58–59:

> [The irreducibility] assumption says that however we may partition the consumers into two groups if the first group receives an aggregate trade which is an attainable output for the rest of the market, the second group has within its feasible aggregate trades one which, if *added* to the goods already obtained by the first group, can be used to improve the position of someone in that group, while damaging the position of none there.

Later, in McKenzie's (1961) "Corrections," the formal assumption is re-stated in a way which "actually corresponds better with the verbal discussion," and certainly seems easier to interpret. Indeed, the economy is said to be *irreducible* if and only if, for every feasible allocation $\mathbf{x}$ and every partition $A_1 \cup A_2$ of A into two disjoint nonempty sets A_1 and A_2, there exists a pair $\mathbf{x}' \in \prod_{a \in A_1} X_a$ and $\mathbf{y} \in \prod_{a \in A_2} X_a$ with

$$\sum_{a \in A_1} x'_a + \sum_{a \in A_2} x_a = \sum_{a \in A_1} (x'_a - x_a) = - \sum_{a \in A_2} y_a$$

such that $x'_a \succsim_a x_a$ for all $a \in A_1$, and $x'_a \succ_{a^*} x_{a^*}$ for some $a^* \in A_1$. Equivalently, irreducibility requires that, for every feasible allocation $\mathbf{x}$ and every partition $A_1 \cup A_2$ of A, there exists $a^* \in A_1$ for whom

$$\sum_{a \in A_1} x_a = - \sum_{a \in A_2} x_a \in P_{a^*}(x_{a^*}) + \sum_{a \in A_1 \setminus \{a^*\}} U_a(x_a) + \sum_{a \in A_2} X_a,$$

or equivalently, for whom

$$0 \in P_{a^*}(x_{a^*}) + \sum_{a \in A_1 \setminus \{a^*\}} U_a(X_a) + \sum_{a \in A_2} [X_a + \{x_a\}].$$

Thus, the economy is irreducible if and only if, at every feasible allocation $\mathbf{x}$, every coalition which is a proper subset A_1 of A would have a Pareto improvement available for its own members provided it could suitably exploit *additional* resources from outside the economy that duplicate those which the complementary coalition A_2 could supply at the initial (autarky) allocation, while leaving the members of A_2 with their net trade vectors in the allocation $\mathbf{x}$. The force of this assumption is that every coalition A_2 has some initial resources with which the complementary coalition A_1 would be able to improve the existing allocation if it could have access to these additional resources from outside the economy, while leaving the coalition A_2 where it is. Provided some consumers are in uncompensated equilibrium, this will ensure that all the other consumers do have cheaper points.

Notice that $x_a \in U_a(x_a)$ for all $a \in A_2$. A weaker condition than irreducibility can be derived, therefore, by replacing the point set $\{x_a\}$ with $U_a(x_a)$ for all $a \in A_2$. The result is the requirement that, for every feasible allocation $\mathbf{x}$ and every partition $A_1 \cup A_2$ of A into two disjoint subsets, there should exist $a^* \in A_1$ for whom

$$\begin{aligned} 0 &\in P_{a^*}(x_{a^*}) + \sum_{a \in A_1 \setminus \{a^*\}} U_a(x_a) + \sum_{a \in A_2} [X_a + U_a(x_a)] \\ &= P_{a^*}(x_{a^*}) + \sum_{a \in A \setminus \{a^*\}} U_a(x_a) + \sum_{a \in A_2} X_a. \end{aligned}$$

It is this weakened condition that suggests the apparently more general idea of resource relatedness, to be considered next.

5.3 Interdependent Agents and Resource Relatedness

5.3.1 Interdependent Agents

Suppose that $\mathbf{x}$ is a feasible allocation. Let C be any proper subset of A. Then the coaliation C is said to be *weakly independent* at $\mathbf{x}$ if and only if

$$0 \notin \sum_{a \in C} P_a(x_a) + \sum_{a \in A \setminus C} [U_a(x_a) + X_a].$$

And C is said to be *strongly independent* at $\mathbf{x}$ if and only if, for every $a^* \in C$, one has

$$0 \notin P_{a^*}(x_{a^*}) + \sum_{a \in A \setminus \{a^*\}} U_a(x_a) + \sum_{a \in A \setminus C} X_a.$$

Thus a coaliation C is independent at a given feasible allocation if there is no weakly Pareto-superior allocation in which C benefits from access to additional resources from outside the economy that the complementary coalition $A \setminus C$ could have made available at the initial (autarkic) allocation.

Conversely, the set A of all agents is said to be *strongly* (resp. *weakly*) *interdependent* at the feasible allocation $\mathbf{x}$ if there is no proper subset C of A that is weakly (resp. strongly) independent at $\mathbf{x}$. Thus, agents are strongly interdependent at $\mathbf{x}$ if and only if, for every partition $A_1 \cup A_2$ of A into two disjoint nonempty sets A_1 and A_2,

$$0 \in \sum_{a \in A_1} P_a(x_a) + \sum_{a \in A_2} [U_a(x_a) + X_a].$$

And agents are weakly interdependent at $\mathbf{x}$ if and only if, for every partition $A_1 \cup A_2$ of A into two disjoint nonempty sets A_1 and A_2, there exists $a^* \in A_1$ for whom

$$0 \in P_{a^*}(x_{a^*}) + \sum_{a \in A \setminus \{a^*\}} U_a(x_a) + \sum_{a \in A_2} X_a.$$

In an allocation $\mathbf{x}$ at which all agents are interdependent, every coalition that is a proper subset of A has an improvement available among those allocations which would be weakly Pareto-superior if the economy were able to exploit suitably *additional* resources that the complementary coalition could supply at the initial (autarky) allocation. The force of the interdependence assumption is that every coalition has some initial resources that the complementary coalition could use to reach an allocation that is weakly Pareto-superior to the existing one, if only it could have access to these additional resources. Provided some consumers are in uncompensated equilibrium, this will ensure that the other consumers do have cheaper points.

5.3.2 Direct and Indirect Resource Relatedness

At any Pareto-efficient allocation $\mathbf{x}$, the agent a^* is said to be *resource related* to $\bar{a}$ if there exists a pair $\mathbf{x}' \in \prod_{a \in A} X_a$ and $y_{\bar{a}} \in X_{\bar{a}}$, with $\sum_{a \in A} x'_a = -y_{\bar{a}}$, such that $x'_{a^*} \succ_{a^*} x_{a^*}$ and also $x'_a \succsim_a x_a$ for all $a \in A$.[10] And the agent a^* is said to be *indirectly resource related* to $\bar{a}$ if there exists

[10]This definition differs from Arrow and Hahn (1971, p. 117) in several ways, most of them unimportant. The main difference could be removed, however, provided that the requirement that $y_{\bar{a}} \in X_{\bar{a}}$ in the above definition were relaxed to the requirement that there exist corresponding finite sets of positive numbers λ^k and net trade vectors $x^k_{\bar{a}} \in X_{\bar{a}}$ ($k = 1$ to K) for which $y_{\bar{a}} = x_{\bar{a}} + \sum_{k=1}^{K} \lambda^k (x^k_{\bar{a}} - x_{\bar{a}})$. In other words, the main difference would be removed if the feasible set $X_{\bar{a}}$ were extended to the convex cone $K_{\bar{a}}(x_{\bar{a}})$ with vertex $x_{\bar{a}}$ that is generated by the feasible set $X_{\bar{a}}$. This difference would actually be irrelevant in an economy where every agent has convex preferences and a convex set of feasible net trades.

a chain $a_0, a_1, \ldots, a_n$ of agents in A, starting with $a_0 = a^*$ and ending with $a_n = \bar{a}$ such that, for $j = 1$ to n, agent a_{j-1} is resource related to a_j.

5.3.3 Strong Interdependence Implies Resource Relatedness

LEMMA. *If all agents are strongly interdependent at the feasible allocation* $\mathbf{x}$, *then all agents are resource related there.*

Proof. If $\mathbf{x}$ is strongly interdependent, then for each $\bar{a} \in A$, the coalition $A \setminus \{\bar{a}\}$ cannot be weakly independent. This implies that there exists a pair $\mathbf{x}' \in \prod_{a \in A} X_a$ and $y_{\bar{a}} \in X_{\bar{a}}$, with $\sum_{a \in A} x'_a = -y_{\bar{a}}$, such that $x'_a \succsim_a x_a$ for all $a \in A$, and also $x'_a \succ_a x_a$ for all $a \in A \setminus \{\bar{a}\}$. This shows that every agent $a^* \in A \setminus \{\bar{a}\}$ is resource related to $\bar{a}$. Since this is true for all $\bar{a} \in A$, all agents are indeed resource related at the allocation $\mathbf{x}$. ■

5.3.4 Indirect Resource Relatedness Implies Weak Interdependence

LEMMA. *If all agents are indirectly resource related at the feasible allocation* $\mathbf{x}$, *then all agents are weakly interdependent there.*

Proof. Suppose that some proper subset C of A were strongly independent at the allocation $\mathbf{x}$. Let a^* be any member of C, and let $\bar{a}$ be any member of $A \setminus C$. Then there cannot be any pair $\mathbf{x}' \in \prod_{a \in A} X_a$ and $\mathbf{y} \in \prod_{a' \in A \setminus C} X_{a'}$ with $\sum_{a \in A} x'_a = -\sum_{a' \in A \setminus C} y_{a'}$ such that $x'_a \succsim_a x_a$ for all $a \in A$, and also $x'_{a^*} \succ_{a^*} x_{a^*}$. But $C \subset A$ and $\bar{a} \in A \setminus C$ together imply that $C \subset A \setminus \{\bar{a}\}$. Therefore there is no pair $\mathbf{x}' \in \prod_{a \in A} X_a$ and $y_{\bar{a}} \in X_{\bar{a}}$ with $\sum_{a \in A} x'_a = -y_{\bar{a}}$, such that $x'_a \succsim_a x_a$ for all $a \in A$, and also $x'_{a^*} \succ_{a^*} x_{a^*}$. This proves that, for all $a^* \in C$ and all $\bar{a} \in A \setminus C$, agent a^* is not resource related to $\bar{a}$. This contradicts indirect resource relatedness of all agents at the feasible allocation $\mathbf{x}$. ■

5.3.5 Why Weak Interdependence Does Not Imply Strong Interdependence

Arrow and Hahn (1971, p. 119) provide a simple counterexample to illustrate how indirect resource relatedness does not imply (direct, or ordinary) resource relatedness. Since indirect resource relatedness implies weak interdependence, and strong interdependence implies resource relatedness, the same example shows that weak interdependence does not imply strong interdependence.

5.4 Generalized Interdependence

Having discussed earlier versions of irreducibility and resource relatedness, this section will now present the new generalized version to be used in the rest of the paper. To show the need for such generalizations, note that not even resource relatedness is weak enough to be satisfied at the equilibrium point W in the clipped Edgeworth box economy illustrated in

Figure 2 of Section 4.5. Additional resources duplicating those that can be supplied out of agent B's endowments include only bolts, and never any nuts. Yet more bolts are not enough for N, who also needs more nuts in order to become better off. The remedy is to allow N's *net trade vector* to be replicated as well. Since N can indeed be made better off when both agent B's endowment of bolts and N's compensated equilibrium net trade vector are replicated together, the sum of the two vectors must have positive value. Yet N's net trade vector must have zero value in compensated equilibrium,and so B's endowment must have positive value at the equilibrium price vector. This is precisely what we want to prove.

First recall that, at the feasible allocation $\mathbf{x}$, agents are weakly interdependent if and only if, for every partition $A_1 \cup A_2$ of A into two disjoint nonempty sets A_1 and A_2, there exists $a^* \in A_1$ for whom

$$0 \in P_{a^*}(x_{a^*}) + \sum_{a \in A \setminus \{a^*\}} U_a(x_a) + \sum_{a \in A_2} X_a.$$

For generalized interdependence, every set will be replaced by its convex hull, as in the definition of convexified oligarchy.[11] But an extra term $-\Sigma_{a \in A}\{0, x_a\}$ will be added, to allow agents in the set A_1 to exploit replicas of their own or others' net trade vectors, if that would be desirable. Of course, $\{0, x_a\}$ just denotes the pair set whose two members are 0 and x_a. In equilibrium without transfers, the value of such extra resources must be zero. Later in Proposition 5.5, the extra term will ensure that there are compensated equilibrium prices at which each agent's net trade vector has zero value.

Thus all agents are said to be *generalized interdependent* at the feasible allocation $\mathbf{x}$ if and only if, for every partition $A_1 \cup A_2$ of A into two disjoint nonempty sets A_1 and A_2, there exists $a^* \in A_1$ for whom

$$0 \in \operatorname{co}\left[P_{a^*}(x_{a^*}) + \sum_{a \in A \setminus \{a^*\}} U_a(x_a) + \sum_{a \in A_2} X_a - \sum_{a \in A} \{0, x_a\} \right].$$

This definition leads to the following result, proved in Section 7.1:

Proposition. *Under Assumptions* 1 *and* 2, *if* $(\mathbf{x}, p)$ *is a compensated equilibrium without transfers such that all agents are generalized interdependent at the allocation* $\mathbf{x}$, *then* $(\mathbf{x}, p)$ *must also be an uncompensated equilibrium*.

[11]The idea that only directions matter is embodied, to some extent, in Arrow and Hahn's definition of resource relatedness, and in versions of irreducibility used in Bergstrom (1976) and Coles and Hammond (1994). It seems only natural to adapt this idea by considering convex hulls, which indeed is suggested by the definitions in Moore (1975) and McKenzie (1981, 1987). Since the only issue is whether 0 does or does not belong to a convex hull, any further extensions to convex cones would make no difference.

Thus, in an economy satisfying both Assumptions 1 and 2, generalized interdependence of all agents is a sufficient condition for a particular compensated equilibrium to be an uncompensated equilibrium. So generalized interdependence at all feasible allocations is sufficient for every compensated equilibrium to be an uncompensated equilibrium. In this case it follows, of course, that existence of a compensated equilibrium also implies existence of an uncompensated equilibrium.

5.5 Generalized Irreducibility

When interdependence was introduced in Section 5.3, it was as a weakening of irreducibility. Yet it will now be shown how a generalized version of the stronger condition of irreducibility is necessary to avoid some consumers having cheapest points in compensated equilibrium. Since generalized irreducibility will imply generalized interdependence trivially, this means that the two conditions are actually equivalent.

Recall from Section 5.2 how irreducibility requires that, for every feasible allocation $\mathbf{x}$ and every partition $A_1 \cup A_2$ of A, there exists $a^* \in A_1$ for whom

$$0 \in P_{a^*}(x_{a^*}) + \sum_{a \in A_1 \setminus \{a^*\}} U_a(x_a) + \sum_{a \in A_2} [X_a + \{x_a\}].$$

Corresponding to the definition of generalized interdependence in the previous, section say that the feasible allocation $\mathbf{x}$ is *generalized irreducible* if, for every partition $A_1 \cup A_2$ of A into disjoint nonempty sets, there exists $a^* \in A_1$ for whom

$$0 \in \operatorname{co}\left[P_{a^*}(x_{a^*}) + \sum_{a \in A_1 \setminus \{a^*\}} U_a(x_a) + \sum_{a \in A_2} (X_a + \{x_a\}) - \sum_{a \in A} \{0, x_a\} \right].$$

This is indeed like generalized interdependence, except that the set $U_a(x_a)$ has been restricted to $\{x_a\}$ for all $a \in A_2$.

The following result, also proved in Section 7.2, is similar to Proposition 4.4. It shows how generalized irreducibility is a necessary condition for every agent to have a cheaper point at every compensated equilibrium price vector for which the value of each agent's net trade is zero.

PROPOSITION. *Let $\hat{\mathbf{x}}$ be a feasible allocation which is not generalized irreducible. Then there exists a coalition C and a price vector $p \neq 0$ such that $(\hat{\mathbf{x}}, p)$ is a compensated equilibrium without transfers in which all agents outside C are at cheapest points—i.e., for all $a \in A \setminus C$, it must be true that $x_a \in X_a \Rightarrow px_a \geq p\hat{x}_a = 0$.*

Since generalized interdependence is sufficient and generalized irreducibility is necessary for a compensated equilibrium without transfers to avoid all cheapest points, we are in the happy position of having a necessary condition that is stronger than the sufficient condition. Hence the two conditions must actually be both necessary and sufficient.

5.6 Sufficient Conditions for Survival

Recall how in Section 2.1.3 it was not assumed that each agent a can survive at every point of the set X_a of feasible net trades. Instead there will generally be a *survival set* $S_a \subset X_a$. Also, on the reasonable presumption that each agent prefes to survive, each preference ordering will satisfy the condition that $x'_a \succ_a x_a$ whenever $x'_a \in S_a$ but $x_a \in X_a \setminus S_a$. To ensure universal survival in equilibrium then requires additional assumptions, similar to those in McKenzie (1981, 1987) and Coles and Hammond (1994).[12] The first of these is the following obvious modification of the aggregate interiority Assumption 2.

Assumption 2S. 0 belongs to the interior of the convex hull of the set $S_A := \sum_{a \in A} S_a$.

In addition, a rather different version of generalized interdependence is required. Indeed, at the particular feasible allocation $\mathbf{x}$, all agents are said to be *generalized interdependent with survival* at the feasible allocation $\mathbf{x}$ if and only if, for every partition $A_1 \cup A_2$ of A into two disjoint non-empty sets A_1 and A_2, there exists $a^* \in A_1$ for whom

$$0 \in \text{co}\left[P_{a^*}(x_{a^*}) + \sum_{a \in A \setminus \{a^*\}} U_a(x_a) + \sum_{a \in A_1} \{0, x_a\} + \sum_{a \in A_2} S_a\right].$$

The difference from the earlier definition of generalized interdependence comes in the requirement that, for each agent $a \in A_2$, the feasible set X_a has been replaced by the corresponding survival set S_a.

This definition leads to the following strengthening of Proposition 5.4 that is also proved in Section 7.1.

PROPOSITION. *Under Assumptions* 1 *and* 2*S*, *if* $(\mathbf{x}, p)$ *is a compensated equilibrium without transfers such that all agents are generalized interdependent with survival at the allocation* $\mathbf{x}$, *then* $(\mathbf{x}, p)$ *must also be an uncompensated equilibrium in which* $x_a \in S_a$ *for all* $a \in A$*—i.e., all agents survive.*

[12]McKenzie (1981, 1987) actually treats the feasible set X_a as if it were the survival set S_a, but then dispenses with the assumption that $0 \in X_a$. Our approach is effectively equivalent.

6. CONTINUUM ECONOMIES

6.1 Preliminaries

6.1.1 A Measure Space of Consumers

As in Aumann (1964, 1966) and Hildenbrand (1974), it will now be assumed that there is a nonatomic measure space $(A, \mathscr{A}, \alpha)$ of economic agents in which A is the interval $[0, 1]$ of the real line $\mathscr{R}$, $\mathscr{A}$ is the σ-algebra of Borel sets, and α is the Lebesgue measure satisfying $\alpha(A) = 1$.

6.1.2 Consumers' Feasible Sets

In addition to the earlier assumption that every consumer $a \in A$ has a fixed feasible set $X_a \subset \mathscr{R}^G$ of net trade vectors x_a satisfying $0 \in X_a$, assume also that the graph $\{(a, x_a) \in A \times \mathscr{R}^G | x_a \in X_a\}$ of the feasible set correspondence $X: A \twoheadrightarrow \mathscr{R}^G$ is measurable when the space $A \times \mathscr{R}^G$ is equipped with its product σ-algebra.

6.1.3 Consumers' Preferences

In addition to the earlier assumption that every consumer $a \in A$ has a weak preference ordering $\succsim_a$ satisfying local nonsatiation on the set X_a, assume also that the preference relation $\succsim_a$ has a graph $\{(a, x_a, x'_a) \in A \times X_a \times X_a | x'_a \succsim_a x_a\}$ that is a measurable subset of the space $A \times \mathscr{R}^G \times \mathscr{R}^G$ equipped with its product σ-algebra.

6.1.4 Feasible Allocations

A *feasible allocation* $\mathbf{x}: A \to \mathscr{R}^G$ is a measurable function whose values satisfy $x_a \in X_a$ a.e. in A, with the additional property that the mean net trade vector $\int_A x_a \alpha(da) = 0$. Note once again that only an exchange economy with individual production is being considered, and that free disposal is possible only to the extent that some individuals can dispose of goods freely.

6.1.5 Compensated and Uncompensated Equilibrium

In a continuum economy, an *uncompensated* (resp. *compensated*) *equilibrium* is a pair $(\mathbf{x}, p)$ consisting of a feasible allocation $\mathbf{x}$ and a price vector p such that $px_a = 0$ and $x_a \in \xi_a^U(p, 0)$ [resp. $\xi_a^C(p, 0)$] a.e. in A.

An *uncompensated* (resp. *compensated*) *equilibrium with transfers* is a pair $(\mathbf{x}, p)$ consisting of a feasible allocation $\mathbf{x}$ and a price vector p such that $x_a \in \xi_a^U(p, px_a)$ [resp. $\xi_a^C(p, px_a)$] a.e. in A.

6.1.6 The Aggregate Interiority Assumption

The counterpart for continuum economies of our earlier Assumption 2 in Section 3.4.1 is as follows.

*Assumption 2**. 0 belongs to the interior of the set $\int_A X_a \alpha(da)$.

As in Section 3.4.2, this implies that, for any feasible allocation $\mathbf{x}$: $A \to \mathscr{R}^G$ and at any price vector $p \neq 0$, the set

$$\{a \in A | \exists \bar{x}_a \in X_a \text{ such that } p\bar{x}_a < px_a\}$$

of individuals having cheaper feasible net trade vectors at the price vector p must have positive measure.

6.2 Nonoligarchic Allocations

6.2.1 Definitions

A *coalition* in the continuum economy is a measurable set $C \in \mathscr{A}$ satisfying $0 < \alpha(C) < 1$. Such a coalition C is said to be an *oligarchy* at the feasible allocation $\mathbf{x}$ if, for every subset $A^* \subset C$ of positive measure, one has

$$0 \notin \int_{A^*} P_a(x_a)\alpha(da) + \int_{C \setminus A^*} U_a(x_a)\alpha(da) + \int_{A \setminus C} X_a \alpha(da).$$

The feasible allocation $\mathbf{x}$ in the continuum economy is said to be *nonoligarchic* if there is no oligarchy at $\mathbf{x}$. Note that there is no need to consider convexified oligarchies or convexified nonoligarchic allocations in a continuum economy.

6.2.2 Sufficiency of Nonoligarchy

The following result, showing how nonoligarchy ensures that a compensated equilibrium is an uncompensated equilibrium, is proved in Section 7.2.

PROPOSITION. *Under Assumptions* 1 *and* 2*, *if* $(\mathbf{x}, p)$ *is a compensated equilibrium with transfers in a continuum economy, and if the allocation* $\mathbf{x}$ *is nonoligarchic, then* $(\mathbf{x}, p)$ *must be an uncompensated equilibrium.*

6.2.3 Necessity of Nonoligarchy

The following result, proved in Section 7.2, is similar to Proposition 4.4.

PROPOSITION. *Let* $\hat{\mathbf{x}}$ *be a feasible allocation at which the coalition* C *is an oligarchy. Then there exists a price vector* $p \neq 0$ *such that* $(\hat{\mathbf{x}}, p)$ *is a compensated equilibrium with transfers in which almost all agents outside* C *are at cheapest points—i.e., for almost all* $a \in A \setminus C$, *it must be true that* $x_a \in X_a \Rightarrow px_a \geq p\hat{x}_a$.

6.3 Interdependence and Irreducibility

6.3.1 Irreducibility

The continuum economy is said to be *irreducible* (cf. Hildenbrand, 1972, p. 85) if, at every feasible allocation $\mathbf{x}$: $A \to \mathscr{R}^G$ and for every partition $A_1 \cup A_2$ of A into two disjoint measurable sets A_1 and A_2 of positive measure, there exist two measurable functions $\mathbf{x}'$: $A_1 \to \mathscr{R}^G$ and $\mathbf{y}$: $A_2 \to \mathscr{R}^G$ such that

(i) $\int_{A_1} x'_a \alpha(da) + \int_{A_2} x_a \alpha(da) = \int_{A_1}(x'_a - x_a)\alpha(da) = -\int_{A_2} y_a \alpha(d\alpha)$;
(ii) $x'_a \in X_a$ and $x'_a \succsim_a x_a$ a.e. in A_1, with $x'_a \succ_a x_a$ for almost all a in some subset A^* of A_1 which has positive measure;
(iii) $y_a \in X_a$ a.e. in A_2.

Equivalently, irreducibility requires that, at every feasible allocation $\mathbf{x}$: $A \to \mathscr{R}^G$, and for every partition $A_1 \cup A_2$ of A into two disjoint measurable sets A_1 and A_2 of positive measure, there exists $A^* \subset A_1$ such that $\alpha(A^*) > 0$ and

$$\int_{A_1} x_a \alpha(da) = -\int_{A_2} x_a \alpha(da)$$

$$\in \int_{A^*} P_a(x_a)\alpha(da) + \int_{A_1 \setminus A^*} U_a(x_a)\alpha(da) + \int_{A_2} X_a \alpha(da).$$

6.3.2 Generalized Interdependence and Irreducibility

The following definitions are obvious adaptations for continuum economies of those in Sections 5.3, 5.4, and 5.5 for finite economies.

All agents in the continuum economy are said to be *interdependent* at a particular feasible allocation $\hat{\mathbf{x}}$ if, for every partition $A_1 \cup A_2$ of A into two disjoint sets of positive measure,

$$0 \in \int_{A^*} P_a(\hat{x}_a)\alpha(da) + \int_{A \setminus A^*} U_a(\hat{x}_a)\alpha(da) + \int_{A_2} X_a \alpha(da)$$

for some $A^* \subset A_1$ that has positive measure. Agents in the continuum economy are said to be *generalized interdependent* at a particular feasible allocation $\hat{\mathbf{x}}$ if and only if, for every partition $A_1 \cup A_2$ of A into two disjoint sets of positive measure,

$$0 \in \int_{A^*} P_a(\hat{x}_a)\alpha(da) + \int_{A \setminus A^*} U_a(\hat{x}_a)\alpha(da) + \int_{A_2} X_a \alpha(da)$$

$$- \int_A \{0, \hat{x}_a\}\alpha(da)$$

for some $A^* \subset A_1$ that has positive measure. Finally, the feasible allocation $\hat{\mathbf{x}}$ in the continuum economy is said to be *generalized irreducible* if and only if, for every partition $A_1 \cup A_2$ of A into two disjoint sets of positive measure,

$$0 \in \int_{A^*} P_a(\hat{x}_a)\alpha(da) + \int_{A_1 \setminus A^*} U_a(\hat{x}_a)\alpha(da) + \int_{A_2} (X_a + \{\hat{x}_a\})\alpha(da) - \int_A \{0, \hat{x}_a\}\alpha(da)$$

for some $A^* \subset A_1$ that has positive measure.

6.3.3 Interdependent Agents and Uncompensated Equilibrium

For a continuum economy, the result corresponding to Proposition 5.4 is as follows.

PROPOSITION. *Under Assumptions* 1 *and* 2*, *if* $(\mathbf{x}, p)$ *is a compensated equilibrium without transfers such that all agents are generalized interdependent at the allocation* $\mathbf{x}$, *then* $(\mathbf{x}, p)$ *must also be an uncompensated equilibrium*.

6.3.4 Agents outside Independent Coalitions Are at Cheapest Points

The following last result is similar to Proposition 5.5.

PROPOSITION. *Let* $\hat{\mathbf{x}}$ *be a feasible allocation in the continuum economy that is not generalized irreducible. Then there exists a coalition* C *and a price vector* $p \neq 0$ *such that* $(\hat{\mathbf{x}}, p)$ *is a compensated equilibrium without transfers in which almost all agents outside* C *are at cheapest points—i.e., for almost all* $a \in A \setminus C$, *it must be true that* $x_a \in X_a \Rightarrow px_a \geq p\hat{x}_a = 0$.

7. PROOFS OF PROPOSITIONS

7.1 Sufficiency Theorems

PROPOSITION 4.3. *Under Assumptions* 1 *and* 2, *any convexified nonoligarchic allocation* $\mathbf{x}$ *which is a compensated equilibrium with transfers at some price vector* $p \neq 0$ *must be an uncompensated equilibrium with transfers at the same price vector* p.

Proof.

1. For the compensated equilibrium $(\mathbf{x}, p)$, let

$$C := \{a \in A | \exists x'_a \in X_a : px'_a < px_a\}$$

be the set of agents $a \in A$ with cheaper points $x'_a \in X_a$. Assumption 2 and Lemma 3.4.2 together imply that C is not empty. Assumption 1, together with the cheaper point Proposition 3.3.4, implies that $(\mathbf{x}, p)$ is an uncompensated equilibrium for the members of C.

2. Suppose that $A \setminus C$ is not empty. Since C cannot be a convexified oligarchy, there must exist an $a^* \in C$ for which

$$0 \in \mathrm{co}\left[P_{a^*}(x_{a^*}) + \sum_{a \in C\setminus\{a^*\}} U_a(x_a) + \sum_{a \in A\setminus C} X_a \right].$$

This implies the existence of net trade vectors $x_a^j \in X_a$ (for $a \in A$ and $j = 1$ to J), and of positive scalars λ^j ($j = 1$ to J) with $\sum_{j=1}^J \lambda^j = 1$, such that

(i) $0 = \sum_{j=1}^J \lambda^j \sum_{a \in A} x_a^j$;
(ii) $x_{a^*}^j \succ_{a^*} x_{a^*}$ for $j = 1$ to J;
(iii) $x_a^j \succsim_a x_a$ for all $a \in C\setminus\{a^*\}$ and for $j = 1$ to J.

3. Because $(\mathbf{x}, p)$ is a compensated equilibrium, (iii) implies that $px_a^j \geq px_a$ for all $a \in C\setminus\{a^*\}$ and for $j = 1$ to J. Because $(\mathbf{x}, p)$ is an uncompensated equilibrium for the members of C, including agent a^*, (ii) implies that $px_{a^*}^j > px_{a^*}$ for $j = 1$ to J. Then, because $\sum_{a \in A} x_a = 0$, (i) implies that

$$\sum_{j=1}^{J} \lambda^j \sum_{a \in A\setminus C} \left(px_a^j - px_a \right)$$
$$= -\sum_{j=1}^{J} \lambda^j \left[\left(px_{a^*}^j - px_{a^*} \right) + \sum_{a \in C\setminus\{a^*\}} \left(px_a^j - px_a \right) \right] < 0.$$

4. Since each λ^j is positive, there must be at least one $a \in A \setminus C$ and at least one $x_a^j \in X_a$ for which $px_a^j < px_a$.

5. This contradicts the assumption that no agent $a \in A\setminus C$ has any cheaper point in the feasible set X_a. Therefore $A \setminus C$ must be empty after all, and (x, p) must be an uncompensated equilibrium for all the members of A. ■

Proposition 5.4. *Under Assumptions* 1 *and* 2, *if* $(\mathbf{x}, p)$ *is a compensated equilibrium without transfers such that all agents are generalized interdependent at the allocation* $\mathbf{x}$, *then* $(\mathbf{x}, p)$ *must also be an uncompensated equilibrium.*

Proof.

1. For the compensated equilibrium without transfers $(\mathbf{x}, p)$, let C be the set of agents $a \in A$ with cheaper points $x_a' \in X_a$ satisfying $px_a' < 0$. As in (1) of the proof of Proposition 4.3, C must be nonempty and $(\mathbf{x}, p)$ must be an uncompensated equilibrium for the members of C.

2. Suppose that $A \setminus C$ is not empty. Since C cannot be generalized independent, there must exist an $a^* \in C$ for whom

$$0 \in \mathrm{co}\left[P_{a^*}(x_{a^*}) + \sum_{a \in A \setminus \{a^*\}} U_a(x_a) + \sum_{a \in A \setminus C} X_a - \sum_{a \in A} \{0, x_a\} \right].$$

This implies the existence of net trade vectors $x_a^j \in X_a$, $\bar{x}_a^j \in \{0, x_a\}$ (for $a \in A$) and $y_a^j \in X_a$ (for $a \in A \setminus C$), as well as of associated positive scalars $\lambda^j (j = 1 \text{ to } J)$ with $\sum_{j=1}^J \lambda^j = 1$, such that

(i) $0 = \sum_{j=1}^J \lambda^j [\sum_{a \in A} (x_a^j - \bar{x}_a^j) + \sum_{a \in A \setminus C} y_a^j]$;

(ii) $x_{a^*}^j \succ_{a^*} x_{a^*}$ for $j = 1$ to J;

(iii) $x_a^j \succsim_a x_a$ for $a \in A \setminus \{a^*\}$ and for $j = 1$ to J.

3. Because $(\mathbf{x}, p)$ is a compensated equilibrium without transfers, it must be true, as in part (3) of the proof of Proposition 4.3, that for $j = 1$ to J one has $px_a^j \geq 0$ for all $a \in A \setminus \{a^*\}$ and also $px_{a^*}^j > 0$. In addition, $px_a = 0$ implies that $p\bar{x}_a^j = 0$ for all $a \in A$ and for $j = 1$ to J. Therefore, (i) implies that

$$\sum_{j=1}^J \lambda^j \sum_{a \in A \setminus C} py_a^j = - \sum_{j=1}^J \lambda^j \sum_{a \in A} p\left(x_a^j - \bar{x}_a^j\right) < 0.$$

Thus there is at least one $a \in A \setminus C$ and at least one $y_a^j \in X_a$ for which $py_a^j < 0$. The proof is then completed as in part (5) of the proof of Proposition 4.3 above. ■

PROPOSITION 5.6. *Under Assumptions* 1 *and* 2S, *if* $(\mathbf{x}, p)$ *is a compensated equilibrium without transfers such that all agents are generalized interdependent with survival at the allocation* $\mathbf{x}$, *then* $(\mathbf{x}, p)$ *must also be an uncompensated equilibrium in which* $x_a \in S_a$ *for all* $a \in A$—*i.e., all agents survive.*

Proof. For the compensated equilibrium $(\mathbf{x}, p)$, let

$$C := \left\{ a \in A | \exists x'_a \in S_a : px'_a < px_a = 0 \right\}$$

be the set of agents $a \in A$ with cheaper points x'_a in their survival sets S_a.

The remainder of the proof is the same as that of Proposition 5.4, except that for each agent $a \in A \setminus C$ the feasible set X_a should be replaced by the corresponding survival set S_a. The concusion is that $A \setminus C$ is empty, from which it follows that $(\mathbf{x}, p)$ is not only an uncompensated equilibrium, but is also one in which all the members of A can afford to survive and so will choose to do so. ■

PROPOSITION 6.2.2. *Under Assumptions* 1 *and* 2*, *if* $(\mathbf{x}, p)$ *is a compensated equilibrium with transfers in a continuum economy, and if the* *allocation* $\mathbf{x}$ *is nonoligarchic, then* $(\mathbf{x}, p)$ *must be an uncompensated equilibrium.*

PROPOSITION 6.3.3. *Under Assumptions* 1 *and* 2*, *if* $(\mathbf{x}, p)$ *is a compensated equilibrium without transfers such that all agents are generalized interdependent at the allocation* $\mathbf{x}$, *then* $(\mathbf{x}, p)$ *must also be an uncompensated equilibrium.*

Proof. The proofs of both Propositions 6.2.2 and 6.3.3 are exactly the same as those for Propositions 4.3 and 5.4, respectively, except that (i) $J = 1$ and so $\lambda^1 = 1$, since convex hulls need not be considered; (ii) the single agent $a^* \in C$ should be replaced by a set $A^* \subset C$ of positive measure; (iii) sums should be replaced by integrals in the obvious way; (iv) the phrases "for all" and "for at least one" in connection with any given set of agents should be replaced by "for almost all" and "for a set of positive measure" respectively; and (v) every reference to the set $A \setminus C$ being empty or nonempty should be replaced by the measure $\alpha(A \setminus C)$ being zero or positive. ■

7.2 Necessity Theorems

PROPOSITION 4.4. *Let* $\hat{\mathbf{x}}$ *be a feasible allocation at which the coalition* C *is a convexified oligarchy. Then there exists a price vector* $p \neq 0$ *such that* $(\hat{\mathbf{x}}, p)$ *is a weak compensated equilibrium with transfers in which all agents outside* C *are at cheapest points—i.e., for all* $a \in A \setminus C$, *it must be true that* $x_a \in X_a \Rightarrow px_a \geq p\hat{x}_a$.

Proof.

1. For every $a^* \in C$, define the convex set

$$K_{a^*C}(\hat{x}) := \text{co}\left[P_{a^*}(\hat{x}_{a^*}) + \sum_{a \in C \setminus \{a^*\}} U_a(\hat{x}_a) + \sum_{a \in A \setminus C} X_a\right].$$

Because C is a convexified oligarchy at the feasible allocation $\hat{\mathbf{x}}$, it must be true that $0 \notin K_{a^*C}(\hat{\mathbf{x}})$ for every $a^* \in C$. Also $K_{a^*C}(\hat{\mathbf{x}})$ is nonempty because of nonsatiation.

2. Therefore there exists a price vector $p \neq 0$ and so a hyperplane $py = 0$ through the point $0 \in \mathscr{R}^G$ such that $py \geq 0$ for all $y \in K_{a^*C}(\hat{\mathbf{x}})$. In particular, because $\Sigma_{a \in A} \hat{x}_a = 0$, it follows that $0 \leq \Sigma_{a \in A} px_a = \Sigma_{a \in A} p(x_a - \hat{x}_a)$ whenever $x_{a^*} \in P_{a^*}(\hat{x}_{a^*})$, $x_a \in U_a(\hat{x}_a)$ (all $a \in C \setminus \{a^*\}$), and $x_a \in X_a$ (all $a \in A \setminus C$).

3. Because $\hat{x}_{a^*}$ is on the boundary of $P_{a^*}(\hat{x}_{a^*})$, because $\hat{x}_a \in U_a(\hat{x}_a)$ for all $a \in C \setminus \{a^*\}$, and because also $\hat{x}_a \in X_a$ for all $a \in A \setminus C$, it then follows that (i) $px_{a^*} \geq p\hat{x}_{a^*}$ whenever $x_{a^*} \in P_{a^*}(\hat{x}_{a^*})$; (ii) for all $a \in C \setminus \{a^*\}$, one has $px_a \geq p\hat{x}_a$ whenever $x_a \in U_a(\hat{x}_a)$; (iii) for all $a \in A \setminus C$, one

has $px_a \geq p\hat{x}_a$ whenever $x_a \in X_a$ and so also whenever $x_a \succsim_a \hat{x}_a$. Because of local nonsatiation and Lemma 2.2.1, it follows that $(\hat{\mathbf{x}}, p)$ is indeed a compensated equilibrium with transfers in which all agents outside C are at cheapest points. ■

PROPOSITION 5.5. *Let $\hat{\mathbf{x}}$ be a feasible allocation that is not generalized irreducible. Then there exists a coalition C and a price vector $p \neq 0$ such that $(\hat{\mathbf{x}}, p)$ is a compensated equilibrium without transfers in which all agents outside C are at cheapest points—i.e., for all $a \in A \setminus C$, it must be true that $x_a \in X_a \Rightarrow px_a \geq p\hat{x}_a = 0$.*

Proof. If $\hat{\mathbf{x}}$ is not generalized irreducible, then there must exist some coalition C such that $0 \notin K_{a^*C}(\hat{x})$ for every $a^* \in C$, where $K_{a^*C}(\hat{\mathbf{x}})$ denotes the convex hull of the nonempty set

$$P_{a^*}(\hat{x}_{a^*}) + \sum_{a \in C \setminus \{a^*\}} U_a(\hat{x}_a) + \sum_{a \in A \setminus C} (X_a + \{\hat{x}_a\}) - \sum_{a \in A} \{0, \hat{x}_a\}.$$

Arguing as in the proof of Proposition 4.4 above, there is a price vector $p \neq 0$ such that

$$\begin{aligned} 0 &\leq \sum_{a \in A} px_a + \sum_{a \in A \setminus C} p\hat{x}_a - \sum_{a \in A} py_a \\ &= \sum_{a \in A} p(x_a - \hat{x}_a) + \sum_{a \in A \setminus C} p\hat{x}_a - \sum_{a \in A} p(y_a - \hat{x}_a) \end{aligned}$$

whenever $x_{a^*} \in P_{a^*}(\hat{x}_{a^*})$, $x_a \in U_a(\hat{x}_a)$ (all $a \in C \setminus \{a^*\}$), $x_a \in X_a$ (all $a \in A \setminus C$), and $y_a \in \{0, \hat{x}_a\}$ (all $a \in A$). Since one can choose $y_a = 0$ and $y_{a'} = \hat{x}_{a'}$ for all $a' \in A \setminus \{a\}$, this implies in particular that $p\hat{x}_a \geq 0$ for all $a \in A$. Because $\Sigma_{a \in A} \hat{x}_a = 0$, it follows that $\Sigma_{a \in A} p\hat{x}_a = 0$ and so $p\hat{x}_a = 0$ for all $a \in A$.

The rest of the proof is similar to that of Proposition 4.4. ■

PROPOSITION 6.2.3. *Let $\hat{\mathbf{x}}$ be a feasible allocation at which the coalition C is an oligarchy. Then there exists a price vector $p \neq 0$ such that $(\hat{\mathbf{x}}, p)$ is a compensated equilibrium with transfers in which almost all agents outside C are at cheapest points—i.e., for almost all $a \in A \setminus C$, it must be true that $x_a \in X_a \Rightarrow px_a \geq p\hat{x}_a$.*

Proof. Because C is an oligarchy at the feasible allocation $\hat{\mathbf{x}}$, one has

$$0 \notin K_{A^*C}(\hat{\mathbf{x}}) := \int_{A^*} P_a^*(\hat{x}_a)\alpha(da) + \int_{C \setminus A^*} U_a(\hat{x}_a)\alpha(da) + \int_{A \setminus C} X_a \alpha(da)$$

for every measurable set $A^* \subset C$ such that $\alpha(A^*) > 0$. Note that, because α is a nonatomic measure, $K_{A^*C}(\hat{\mathbf{x}})$ is a convex set, and that it is nonempty because of nonsatiation.

The rest of the proof is an obvious modification of that of Proposition 4.4. ■

PROPOSITION 6.3.4. *Let* $\hat{\mathbf{x}}$ *be a feasible allocation in the continuum economy that is not generalized irreducible. Then there exists a coalition* C *and a price vector* $p \neq 0$ *such that* $(\hat{\mathbf{x}}, p)$ *is a compensated equilibrium without transfers in which almost all agents outside* C *are at cheapest points —i.e., for almost all* $a \in A \setminus C$, *it must be true that* $x_a \in X_a \Rightarrow px_a \geq p\hat{x}_a = 0$.

Proof. Because the feasible allocation $\hat{\mathbf{x}}$ is not generalized irreducible, there must be a coalition $C \subset A$ for which $0 < \alpha(C) < 1$ and also $0 \notin K_{A^*C}(\hat{\mathbf{x}})$ for every measurable $A^* \subset C$ such that $\alpha(A^*) > 0$, where $K_{A^*C}(\hat{\mathbf{x}})$ denotes the convex set

$$\int_{A^*} P_a(\hat{x}_a)\alpha(da) + \int_{C\setminus A^*} U_a(\hat{x}_a)\alpha(da) + \int_{A\setminus C} (X_a + \{\hat{x}_a\})\alpha(da)$$
$$- \int_A \{0, \hat{x}_a\}\alpha(da).$$

The rest of the proof is then almost identical to that of Proposition 5.5 above. ■

8. CONCLUDING REMARKS

McKenzie's assumption of irreducibility plays a crucial role in showing how compensated equilibria will be uncompensated equilibria because agents have cheaper net trade vectors in their feasible sets. This paper has considered several different versions of this assumption, including Arrow and Hahn's later notion of resource relatedness.

Actually, for considering a particular allocation that may be a compensated equilibrium with lump-sum transfers, the alternative simpler condition of nonoligarchy suffices, as was shown in Section 4. But the example of Section 4.5 illustrated how, in order to prove that every compensated equilibrium at which all agents are on their Walrasian budget constraint is an uncompensated equilibrium, it is enough to use more involved but weaker assumptions such as irreducibility and resource relatedness. This is because all individuals should have net trades whose value is zero at the equilibrium price vector. Survival of all individuals in compensated equilibrium without transfers can also be assured with a slight modification of these conditions.

Finally, these nonoligarchy and irreducibility assumptions were generalized to allow nonconvexities in agents' feasible sets, and also to produce necessary conditions, in the absence of which some compensated equilibria will inevitably put some agents at cheapest points of their feasible sets. Of course, compensated equilibra could still be uncompensated equilibria even if some agents are at cheapest points. This is certainly true when, for instance, there is a unique cheapest point in each agent's feasible set, as there will be in the case [considered by Nikaido (1956, 1957)] where prices are strictly positive and each agent's consumption set is the nonnegative orthant. But for the usual proofs of uncompensated equilibrium to be applicable, the important sufficient conditions of nonoligarchy and irreducibility are also necessary conditions. That is, there are no weaker assumptions that can be used to replace convexified nonoligarchy and generalized irreducibility in the standard proofs.

Acknowledgments

This paper has been developed from some of the results presented earlier in joint work with Jeffrey Coles (see Coles and Hammond, 1994). That work was in turn largely inspired by Lionel McKenzie's presidential address to the Econometric Society in Vienna, 1977 (see McKenzie, 1981). Much of the work reported here was carried out while I was at the European University Institute. I am grateful to Jeff for his encouragement, to an anonymous referee for several most valuable comments, and to Kenneth Arrow, David Gale, Robert Gilles, Alan Kirman, Andreu Mas-Colell, and the discussant Sidney Afriat for helpful suggestions. None of these are responsible for any remaining errors.

References

Arrow, K. J. (1951). "An extension of the basic theorems of classical welfare economics," in *Proceedings of the Second Berkeley Symposium on Mathematical Statistics and Probability*, J. Neyman (ed.) (University of California Press, Berkeley). pp. 507–532; reprinted in Newman (1968) and in Arrow (1983).

Arrow, K. J. (ed.) (1971). *Selected Readings in Economic Theory from Econometrica*, (MIT Press, Cambridge, Mass.).

Arrow, K. J. (ed.) (1983). *Collected Papers of Kenneth J. Arrow*, Vol. 2: *General Equilibrium* Belknap Press of Harvard University Press, Cambridge, Mass.

Arrow, K. J., and G. Debreu (1954). "Existence of an equilibrium for a competitive economy," *Econometrica* **22**, 265–290; reprinted in Arrow (1983) and Debreu (1983).

Arrow, K. J., and F. H. Hahn (1971). *General Competitive Analysis*. (Holden-Day, San Francisco).

Aumann, R. J. (1964). "Markets with a continuum of traders," *Econometrica*, **32**, 39–50; reprinted in Newman (1968).

Aumann, R. J. (1966). "Existence of competitive equilibria in markets with a continuum of traders," *Econometrica* **34**, 1–17.

Bergstrom, T. C. (1976). "How to discard 'free disposability'—at no cost," *J. Math. Econ.* **3**, 131–134.

Broome, J. (1972). "Existence of equilibrium in economies with indivisible commodities," *J. Econ. Theory*, **5**, 224–250.

Coles, J. L., and P. J. Hammond (1994). "Walrasian equilibrium without survival: Existence, efficiency, and remedial policy," to appear in *Development, Welfare, and Ethics: A Festschrift for Amartya Sen*, K. Basu, P. K. Pattanaik, and K. Suzumura (eds.) (Oxford University Press, Oxford).

Debreu, G. (1951). "The coefficient of resource utilization," *Econometrica* **19**, 273–292; reprinted in Debreu (1983) and Arrow (1971).

Debreu, G. (1954). "Valuation equilibrium and Pareto optimum," *Proc. Nat. Acad. Sci.* **38**, 588–592; reprinted in Debreu (1983).

Debreu, G. (1959). *Theory of Value: An Axiomatic Analysis of Economic Equilibrium* (Wiley, New York).

Debreu, G. (1962). "New concepts and techniques for equilibrium analysis," *Int. Econ. Rev.* **3**, 257–273; reprinted in Debreu (1983).

Debreu, G. (1983). *Mathematical Economics: Twenty Papers of Gerard Debreu*. (Cambridge University Press, Cambridge, U.K.).

Duffie, D. (1988). *Security Markets: Stochastic Models* (Academic Press, San Diego).

Duffie, D., and H. Sonnenschein (1989). "Arrow and general equilibrium theory," *J. Econ. Lit.* **27**, 565–598.

Eaves, B. C. (1976). "A finite algorithm for the linear exchange model," *J. Math. Econ.* **3**, 197–203.

Gale, D. (1955). "The law of supply and demand," *Mathematica Scandinavica*, **3**, 155–169; reprinted in Newman (1968).

Gale, D. (1957). "Price Equilibrium for Linear Models of Exchange," Technical Report P-1156, RAND Corporation.

Gale, D. (1960). *The Theory of Linear Economic Models*. (McGraw-Hill, New York).

Gale, D. (1976). "The linear exchange model," *J. Math. Econ.* **3**, 204–209.

Gantmacher, F. R. (1953; Engl. transl. 1959). *The Theory of Matrices* (2 vols.) (Chelsea, New York).

Gorman, W. M. (1953). "Community preference fields," *Econometrica* **22**, 63–80.

Graham, F. D. (1948). *The Theory of International Values*. (Princeton University Press, Princeton, N.J.).

Grandmont, J.-M., and D. McFadden (1972). "A technical note on the classical gains from trade," *J. Int. Econ.* **2**, 109–125.

Hammond, P. J., M. Kaneko, and M. H. Wooders (1989). "Continuum economies with finite coalitions: Core, equilibrium, and widespread externalities," *J. Econ. Theory* **49**, 113–134.

Henry, C. (1970). "Indivisibilités dans une économie d'échange," *Econometrica* **38**, 542–558.

Hildenbrand, W. (1972). "Metric measure spaces of economic agents," in *Proceedings of the Sixth Berkeley Symposium on Mathematical Statistics and Probability*, Vol. II, L. Le Cam, J. Neyman, and E. L. Scott (eds.) (University of California Press, Berkeley). pp. 81–95.

Hildenbrand, W. (1974). *Core and Equilibria of a Large Economy* (Princeton University Press, Princeton, N.J.).

Hildenbrand, W., and A. P. Kirman (1988). *Equilibrium Analysis: Variations on Themes by Edgeworth and Walras*. (North-Holland, Amsterdam).

Honkapohja, S. (1987). "On the continuity of compensated demand," *Int. Econ. Rev.* **28**, 545–557.

Kakutani, S. (1941). "A generalization of Brouwer's fixed point theorem," *Duke Math. J.* **8**, 457–459.

Khan, M. A., and A. Yamazaki (1981). "On the cores of economies with indivisible commodities and a continuum of traders," *J. Econ. Theory* **24**, 218–225.

Kuhn, H. W., and A. W. Tucker (1951). "Nonlinear Programming," in *Proceedings of the Second Berkeley Symposium on Mathematical Statistics and Probability*, J. Neyman (ed.) (University of California Press, Berkeley). pp. 481–492; reprinted in Newman (1968).

McKenzie, L. W. (1954a). "On equilibrium in Graham's model of world trade and other competitive systems," *Econometrica* **22**, 147–161.

McKenzie, L. W. (1954b). "Specialisation and efficiency in world production," *Rev. Econ. Studies* **21**, 165–180.

McKenzie, L. W. (1955). "Competitive equilibrium with dependent consumer preferences," in *Proceedings of the Second Symposium on Linear Programming*, Vol. I, H. A. Antosiewicz (ed.) (National Bureau of Standards and Directorate of Management Analysis, Washington, D.C.). pp. 277–294; reprinted in Newman (1968).

McKenzie, L. W. (1957). "Demand theory without a utility index," *Rev. Econ. Studies* **24**, 185–189.

McKenzie, L. W. (1959, 1961). "On the existence of general equilibrium for a competitive market," and "———: Some Corrections," *Econometrica* **27**, 54–71 and **29**; 247–248; reprinted in Arrow (1971).

McKenzie, L. W. (1981). "The classical theorem on existence of competitive equilibrium," *Econometrica* **49**, 819–841.

McKenzie, L. W. (1987). "General equilibrium," in *The New Palgrave*: *A Dictionary of Economics*, J. Eatwell, M. Milgate, and P. Newman (eds.) (Macmillan, London).

Mas-Colell, A. (1977). "Indivisible commodities and general equilibrium theory," *J. Econ. Theory* **16**, 443–456.

Moore, J. C. (1975). "The existence of 'compensated equilibrium' and the structure of the Pareto efficient frontier," *Int. Econ. Rev.* **16**, 267–300.

Newman, P. (ed.) (1968). *Readings in Mathematical Economics*, Vol I: *Value Theory* (Johns Hopkins University Press, Baltimore).

Nikaido, H. (1956, 1957). "On the classical multilateral exchange problem," and "A supplementary note to '———'," *Metroeconomica* **8**, 21–45 and **9**, 209–210.

Rader, T. (1964). "Edgeworth exchange and general economic equilibrium," *Yale Econ. Essays* **4**, 133–180.

Spivak, A. (1978). "A note on Arrow–Hahn's resource relatedness (or McKenzie's irreducibility)." *Int. Econ. Rev.* **19**, 527–531.

Yamazaki, A. (1978). "An equilibrium existence theorem without convexity assumptions," *Econometrica* **46**, 541–555.

Yamazaki, A. (1981). "Diversified consumption characteristics and conditionally dispersed endowment distribution: Regularizing effect and existence of equilibria," *Econometrica* **49**, 639–654.

INCOMPLETE FINANCIAL MARKETS WITH AN INFINITE HORIZON

Alejandro Hernández D.
Department of Economics
Instituto Tecnológico
Autónomo de México
Mexico City, Mexico 01000

Manuel S. Santos
Departamento de Economia
Universidad Carlos III, Madrid
28903 Getafe, Madrid, Spain

1. INTRODUCTION

In this paper we study some properties of competitive equilibria for dynamic exchange economies with an infinite horizon and incomplete financial markets. That is, we study stochastic economies where in every period agents participate in financial markets with an incomplete structure. By "incompleteness of the financial markets," we mean that the available borrowing and lending instruments are not sufficient in number to allow agents to freely transfer income across states of nature and fully insure themselves against adverse events. Our interest in this type of economy is twofold. First, we would like to develop the theoretical foundations that can lead to financial and macroeconomic studies for these economies from a general equilibrium approach. Second, we would like to extend the incomplete markets model with finitely many states to a fully dynamic model.

A significant amount of the effort devoted to understanding dynamic economies has been undertaken under the assumption that the economy is populated by a single representative agent. Alternatively, one could assume that there are several consumers but markets are complete. Both environments are equivalent in terms of the behavior of equilibrium aggregate variables. The complete markets assumption has been widely criticized. For example, the incompleteness of financial markets is a fact in the real world. Setting aside this methodological issue, the complete

GENERAL EQUILIBRIUM, GROWTH, AND TRADE II

market assumption imposes strong implications on the properties of dynamic equilibria, which lessen the explanatory power of the model. The possibility for full insurance implies that along the equilibrium path, the marginal utilities of income remain constant. There is mounting empirical evidence against such a characterization (Grossman and Shiller, 1981; Hansen and Singleton, 1983; Hayashi, 1985; Zeldes 1989). Some of these authors conclude that violations to the Euler equation with constant marginal utilities of income are evidence of liquidity constraints or credit rationing. Exactly on the same grounds one could argue that the results are generated by an incomplete asset market structure (see Duffie 1990; Hansen and Jaganathan, 1990). At an intuitive level, we would expect that the variability in marginal utilities of income, due to an incomplete asset market structure, should be reflected in additional volatility of prices and considerable differences in expected real rates of return of assets.

Most of the literature on incomplete markets assumes a simple two-period model. An initial period where agents trade in spot commodity markets and one-period asset markets, and a terminal period, after the uncertainty has been resolved, where agents pay or collect their debts and trade in spot commodity markets. The asset market structure is incomplete in the sense that the available assets are not enough to span the commodity space over states of nature. This simply amounts to say that the number of independent assets is less than the number of possible states of nature. Radner's original paper on existence with incomplete markets (Radner, 1972) as well as works by Duffie and Shafer (1986), Duffie (1987), and Werner (1990), study economies that live for more than two periods, and where some assets may have longer lives. However, in all of these papers the economy lives an arbitrary but finite number of periods.[1]

Our interest in infinite horizons is motivated by the observation that finite horizons often impose severe restrictions on economic models. Such is the case, for example, of monetary economies or models with repeated games, where the introduction of an infinite horizon generates equilibria that cannot arise in finite horizon models. In the monetary model (Bewley, 1980; Santos, 1990), if monetary endowments are positive, an equilibrium with a positive value of money can exist only if the planning horizon is infinite. In order to obtain monetary equilibria for finite horizons additional elements, such as taxes in the terminal period, must be introduced. However, these amendments introduce indeterminacy in the set of equilibrium relative prices [see, e.g., the introductory section of Geanakoplos and Mas-Colell (1989)].

[1]Recent extensions by Green and Spear (1987), Mas-Colell and Monteiro (1991), and Zame (1989) consider two-period models with an infinite-dimensional commodity space. In all these papers, however, there is a finite number of tradable assets.

Our model follows the same lines of Cass (1984), Werner (1985), and Duffie (1987) in the sense that we consider only purely financial assets. In every period and state of nature agents trade with a limited menu of financial assets that pay in units of account. The existence of equilibria with numeraire assets in a two-period economy was established by Geanakoplos and Polemarchakis (1986). These assets pay in units of a numeraire commodity. Essentially, these assets do not present further difficulties and our conjecture is that our methods should cover this case. Real assets are instruments that pay in vectors of commodities. Thus, their returns depend on relative prices. In addition to the discontinuity problems analyzed below, these assets present further complications for the existence of equilibria. Technically, the endogenous matrix of returns may be such that changes in commodity prices may cause drops in rank, generating a discontinuous demand function. As a consequence, an equilibrium may not exist. The available proofs of existence with this type of assets in finite economies include those of Radner (1972), who imposes ad hoc bounds on short sales, and Duffie and Shafer (1985, 1986), who provide a generic existence theorem. A generic result is the most we can expect; Hart (1975) provides an example where an equilibrium does not exist. An existence theorem for an infinite-dimensional economy has to be generic at most.

An infinite horizon economy with incomplete financial markets has been studied by Schmachtenberg (1989). The difference between his model and ours is that he assumes an overlapping generation structure where consumers live a finite number of periods. Independently of the economic significance of the two models, we would like to emphasize that the difficulties each model displays are fundamentally different. The central element in our model is the definition of the transversality conditions that consumers must face. We need to define the consumer problem in a way that rules out taking on new debt to pay back old debt. If such a scheme were feasible, consumers would be able to finance unlimited amounts of consumption by rolling their debts to infinity. In the overlapping generations scenario of Schmachtenberg, consumers live a finite number of periods and eventually must pay back their debts. The condition we impose is that at every moment consumers must be able to pay back their debts using their future savings. In this way, we rule out bankruptcy from our model without resorting to prior bounds on the quantities of traded assets (i.e., short sales constraints). There are other limiting restrictions that could be considered. Some of them are discussed in the paper. All these constraints, however, impose severe limitations on the continuity of the budget set. This is an important analytical difference with respect to the complete markets case.

To the best of our knowledge, the only paper that studies incomplete markets with infinitely lived agents is Levine (1989). The emphasis in his paper is on the characterization of an infinite equilibrium as a limit of finite-horizon equilibria, rather than on the existence question. In a way, Levine's paper is more general, since it allows both for real and financial assets, as well as money. Also, agents can live finitely or infinitely many periods. The stochastic structure is also more general. There are, however, some features in his model that make it significantly different from ours. The most important difference lies on the specification of the bankruptcy conditions. He imposes borrowing or short sales constraints. Instead, we allow for more flexible transactions by requiring agents to meet their financial obligations with future wealth. In his model, the state of the economy at any given time is fully characterized by the partial history of realizations. Consumers can borrow only against accumulated savings. The same phenomenon occurs in Duffie *et al.* (1988). In our model, the limitations to trade are determined by all possible future histories of realizations.

Besides the discontinuity problems embodied in the definition of the budget set of a consumer—and the corresponding difficulties involved in the existence of equilibria—we also investigate some dynamic properties of equilibria. First, we discuss the subspace of equilibrium prices. By way of example, we show that for economies with a single representative agent, it is possible to construct equilibrium prices that produce infinite wealth. Our conjecture is that the same result holds for any arbitrary number of consumers. If so, the infinite horizon model with incomplete markets possesses an interesting property. There is a multiplicity of equilibrium prices, some of which assign an infinite value of wealth but not necessarily all. This result distinguishes this model from the complete markets model where all equilibrium prices assign finite wealth to the consumers, and from the monetary model, where no equilibrium price vector can generate finite wealth.

It is not surprising to find equilibrium prices that produce infinite endowment values. Essentially what this means is that lifetime income at present value prices may be unbounded. Yet, this does not violate per se the equilibrium conditions. Because of the incomplete market structure, the consumer may find it impossible to use future wealth to finance unlimited initial period consumption without eventually violating a bankruptcy condition. Perhaps what is more surprising is the fact that under certain conditions there is always an equilibrium with finite wealth. [The proof of this assertion is rather involved and is shown in a more technical paper, Hernández and Santos (1992).]

One major limitation of the incomplete markets model in economies with a finite horizon is the indeterminacy of equilibria (Balasko and Cass, 1989; Geanakoplos and Mas-Colell, 1989; Werner, 1990). Without local uniqueness, the study of stability and comparative statics becomes awkward. However, the introduction of an infinite horizon offers a new interpretation to the indeterminacy in finite economies. If we consider a finite horizon equilibrium as the initial segment of an equilibrium for the infinite economy, then not every perturbation of the initial segment, which in itself may be a finite horizon equilibrium, will conform to an equilibrium for the infinite-horizon economy. Once we require this form of consistency for the finite equilibria, and assuming exogenous yields, the indeterminacy vanishes and equilibria are locally unique. A certain degree of indeterminacy remains, however, if nominal yields are endogenously formed. The formal treatment of indeterminacy for the infinite-horizon economy must analyze perturbations of the entire equilibrium path. In order to pursue this line of research, it may be necessary to develop new techniques for infinite-dimensional spaces.

The paper is structured as follows. Section 2 presents the model. Section 3 discusses alternative definitions of the bankruptcy condition and explores the discontinuity of the feasible budget set. Section 4 studies the equilibrium price space of a representative consumer economy, and illustrates the existence of equilibrium price vectors that generate infinite wealth. Section 5 analyses some results regarding the indeterminacy of equilibria. Section 6 concludes with some extensions. The problem of existence of a competitive equilibrium in our model is pursued in our companion paper, Hernández and Santos (1992).

2. DEFINITIONS

2.1 Stochastic Environment

The stochastic structure of the model is described by an infinite tree (S, σ), where S denotes the infinite set of nodes, s, and σ is a function from S to itself that denotes precedence. Formally, the set S admits a partition $S = \{S_0, S_1, \dots\}$ and $\sigma\colon S \to S$, with $\sigma(S_t) = S_{t-1}$, $t = 1, 2, \dots$. We shall denote by S^T the set of nodes up to (and including) time T, $S^T = \{S_0, \dots, S_T\}$. The finite tree (S^T, σ) describes the stochastic environment for the truncated economy that lives T periods.

For any $s \in S$, let $s^- = \sigma(s)$ denote the node that immediately precedes s, and let $\sigma^{-1}(s)$ be the set of immediate successors of s. Also, let $\tau(s)$ denote the time period in which s occurs, $s \in S_{\tau(s)}$.

We assume that the state of the economy in period $t = 0$ is common knowledge, $S_0 = \{0\}$, and, that for every $s \in S$, $\sigma^{-1}(s)$ has a finite number of elements. Denote by $N_s = \#\sigma^{-1}(s) < \infty$ the number of immediate successors of s.

Let $\Psi(s) \subset S$ be the infinite set of all successors of s, and let $\Theta(s) \subset S$ be the set of predecessors of s,

$$\Psi(s) = \{s'\colon s' \in \sigma^{-t}(s) \text{ for some } t = 1, 2, \dots\}, \tag{2.1}$$

$$\Theta(s) = \{s'\colon s' = \sigma^{t}(s) \text{ for some } t = 1, 2, \dots, \tau(s)\}. \tag{2.2}$$

Also, let

$$\tilde{\Psi}(s) = \Psi(s) \cup \{s\} \tag{2.3}$$

$$\tilde{\Theta}(s) = \Theta(s) \cup \{s\} \tag{2.4}$$

The stochastic structure implicitly assumes a sequence of realizations of a random variable. At any node, agents can make probability assessments about the future state of the world based exclusively on the history of realizations. Formally, the measurable space is defined as the set of infinite histories $\{s_t\}_{t=0}^{\infty}$, $s_t = \sigma(s_{t+1})$. An elementary date t event, is a t-measurable subset of infinite histories with identical partial histories up to period t. As such, an elementary date t event is the set of all partial histories contained in $\tilde{\Theta}(s) \cup \Psi(s)$, for some $s \in S_t$. Therefore, an elementary date t event is completely characterized by a node $s \in S_t$. We shall refer to a node s as a date-event. Notice that, although the measurable space is not countable, the set of date-events is.

2.2 Financial Structure

At every date-event, agents participate in financial and spot commodity markets. Let $\mathscr{I}_s$ be the set of financial instruments available at date-event s. We assume that at every date-event the number of available instruments, I_s, is finite, and that the only available financial assets are purely financial, one-period contingent securities. In other words, all financial assets have a single-period maturity, and pay a nominal return contingent on the state of the economy in the subsequent period and denominated in units of account. The assumption of one-period maturity of the securities is adopted here for convenience. Our analysis is easily extended to longer lifespans. Let $r_i(s')$ be the return that asset $i \in \mathscr{I}_s$ promises to pay at date-event $s' \in \sigma^{-1}(s)$. Denote by

$$R_s = \left[r_i(s')\right]_{i \in \mathscr{I}_s,\, s' \in \sigma^{-1}(s)}$$

the $N_s \times I_s$ matrix of returns that describes the financial structure at date-event s. Let r_i, $i \in \mathscr{I}_s$, denote a column of R_s, and let $r(s')$, $s' \in \sigma^{-1}(s)$, denote a row of R_s. Finally, let $R = \{R_s\}_{s \in S}$ denote the financial structure of the economy.

Assumption F1. For every $s \in S$, $1 \leq I_s \leq N_s$.

Assumption F2. For every $s \in S$, $\operatorname{rank}(R_s) = I_s$.

Assumption F3. For every $s \in S$, $R_s \geq 0$.

Assumption F4. For every $s \in S$ and every $s' \in \sigma^{-1}(s)$, there exists $i \in \mathscr{I}_s$ such that $r_i(s') > 0$.

Assumptions $F1$ and $F2$ simply state that assets are not redundant, in the sense that no date-event security payoff vector can be reproduced by a portfolio of the remaining date-event securities. The complete markets case, $I_s = N_s$ for all $s \in S$, is well understood. Also, the case $I_s = N_s$ for all but finitely many s, is an easy extension of the finite horizon models of Cass (1984), Werner (1985), and Duffie (1987). Hence, we shall assume that $I_s < N_s$ for infinitely many s. Assumption $F3$ is imposed merely for convenience. It guarantees the equilibrium asset prices are strictly positive. Without this assumption, asset prices can take either sign, but the no arbitrage conditions confine equilibrium prices to a well-defined cone (see Werner, 1985). Assumption $F4$ guarantees that all financial markets in the economy are connected, allowing agents to transfer wealth across states of nature. If such a condition did not hold, then the equilibrium for the subtree originating in s, may be independent of the equilibrium for the rest of the tree.

Let $q(s) \in \mathbf{R}^{I_s}$ denote a security price vector at date-event s. Equilibrium prices must preclude arbitrage opportunities. Let Q_s be the set of arbitrage-free security prices. Assumption $F3$ implies $Q_s \subset R^{I_s}_{++}$. Also, $q(s) \in Q_s$ implies $q(s) \cdot z > 0$ for every $z \in R^{I_s}$ such that $R_s z > 0$.[2]

2.3 Commodities

At every date-event s, there is a finite number of commodities M_s. Every commodity m is traded exclusively in spot commodity markets. Let $p(s) \in \mathbf{R}^{M_s}$ denote a commodity price vector at date-event s, and let $p = \{p(s)\}_{s \in S}$ be an infinite price sequence. Let $x = \{x(s)\}_{s \in S}$ be an infinite bundle of commodities. In order to simplify the notation, let

$$p \cdot x = \liminf_{T \to \infty} \sum_{s \in S^T} p(s)x(s)$$

2.4 Consumers

There is a finite number of infinitely lived consumers, $h = 1, \ldots, H$. Consumers are described by a consumption set X^h, a preference relation $\succcurlyeq_h$ on X^h and an endowment vector of commodities $\omega^h \in X^h$.

Assumption C1. For every h, $X^h = \times_{s \in S} \mathbf{R}^{M_s}_+$.

Assumption C2. For every h, every $s \in S$ and every $m = 1, \ldots, M_s$, $0 < \omega^h_m(s) < \overline{\omega}$, for some $\overline{\omega} > 0$.

[2]The vector inequalities used are $\geq$, $>$, and $\gg$.

Assumption C3. For every h, $\succcurlyeq_h$ can be represented by a time-additive, Von Neumann–Morgenstern utility function U_h,

$$U_h(x) = \sum_{s \in S} \beta^{\tau(s)} \pi(s) u_h(x(s)),$$

where $0 < \beta < 1$ is a discount factor and π defines a probability distribution over each S_T, $T = 0, 1, \ldots$. Furthermore, u_h is continuously differentiable and concave, and the partial derivatives $\partial_m u_h$ have the property $\kappa'' \geq \partial_m u_h \geq \kappa'$ for some positive scalars $\kappa'' > \kappa' > 0$.

We assume strictly positive endowments in order to guarantee a positive income for every consumer at every date-event. Presumably, it may be relaxed by imposing instead a sort of irreducibility condition. The uniform bound is imposed to guarantee that, under appropriate discounting, the present value of the aggregate resources available in the distant future is small. Let $\omega = \Sigma_h \omega^h$ denote the aggregate endowment.

Assumption $C3$ confines our analysis to a specific family of preferences. The additive structure of preferences and the differentiability assumption can be relaxed with a corresponding cost in notation. The continuity of the budget correspondence does require, however, a strong form of discounting, with respect to both future time and uncertainty. The assumption of uniform discounting and objective probabilities is fairly harmless. Heterogenous discount factors and subjective probabilities can be incorporated with little difficulty. The assumption on uniform bounds on marginal utilities is the strongest and most crucial for our analysis. In the next section we show that the budget correspondences are generally not continuous. However, a weak form of continuity of the budget constraints holds provided future prices fall at a sufficiently high rate.

At every date-event, consumers participate in financial and spot commodity markets. Let $x^h(s) \in \mathbf{R}^{M_s}$ denote a consumption vector by individual h at date-event s, and let $x^h = \{x^h(s)\}_{s \in S}$ be an infinite consumption plan for consumer h. Similarly, let $b^h(s) \in \mathbf{R}^{I_s}$ be a portfolio held by agent h in node s, and $b^h = \{b^h(s)\}_{s \in S}$ a portfolio plan.

The financial constraint that a consumer must meet at date-event s is determined by the state of the economy at date-event t and the history of past consumption and portfolio decisions, as summarized by the preceding portfolio $b^h(s^-)$, $s^- = \sigma(s)$:

$$p(0)x^h(0) + q(0)b^h(0) \leq p(0)\omega^h(0); \tag{2.5}$$

$$p(s)x^h(s) + q(s)b^h(s) \leq p(s)\omega^h(s) + r(s)b^h(s^-), \qquad s \in S \setminus S_0. \tag{2.6}$$

It should be observed that at a given date-event consumers face only current prices and form expectations about future prices. The set up resembles Arrow (1964) and Radner (1972), instead of an Arrow–Debreu-type model where consumers face initially all current value prices.

In addition to the budget constraints (2.5) and (2.6), consumers must meet a "transversality"-type condition that prevents them from rolling over their debts indefinitely. Such a condition is not necessary in finite horizon models, where consumers are required to pay back their debts in the final period. The condition we shall impose is a sort of bankruptcy condition that limits the amount an individual can borrow at any date-event. Roughly speaking, we require an individual's borrowing not to exceed that person's future wealth. Clearly, in order for this condition to be well defined, security and commodity prices must bear some relationship. Before defining the bankruptcy conditions, we shall normalize the nominal system of the economy.

2.5 Normalized Nominal Systems

As in the two period model of Cass (1984), we can invoke Farkas' lemma to characterize the no arbitrage condition as a linear relationship between security prices and returns.

FARKAS' LEMMA. *Let R_s be a real $N_s \times I_s$ matrix. Then, a vector $q(s) \in \mathbf{R}^{I_s}$ satisfies $q(s)z \geq 0$ for all $z \in \mathbf{R}^{I_s}$ with $R_s z \geq 0$ if and only if there exists a positive vector $\lambda_s \in \mathbf{R}^{N_s}$, $\lambda_s = (\lambda_s(s'))_{s' \in \sigma^{-1}(s)}$, such that $q(s)^T = \lambda_s^\top R_s$.*[3]

Notice that the vector λ_s from Farkas' lemma is not in general unique. The assumptions on R_s imply that for $q(s) \in Q_s$, the set of such vectors λ_s is given by the intersection of the $(N_s - I_s)$-dimensional hyperplane $q(s)^T = \lambda^\top R_s$ with the positive orthant.

Let (p, q) be a no-arbitrage price system for a given financial structure R, and let $\lambda = \{\lambda_s\}_{s \in S}$ be a sequence of N_s-dimensional vectors with $q(s)^T = \lambda_s^\top R_s$. Notice that a consumption and portfolio plan (x^h, b^h) satisfies the budget constraints (2.5) and (2.6) at prices (p, q) and financial structure R if and only if $(x^h, \bar{b}^h)$ satisfies those constraints at prices $(\bar{p}, q)$ and financial structure $\bar{R}$, where

$$\bar{p}(s') = \prod_{s \in \tilde{\Theta}(s')} [\lambda_{s^-}(s)]\, p(s'), \tag{2.7}$$

$$\bar{b}(s') = \prod_{s \in \tilde{\Theta}(s')} [\lambda_{s^-}(s)]\, b(s'), \tag{2.8}$$

and

$$\bar{R}_s = \Lambda_s R_s, \tag{2.9}$$

[3]The T superscript denotes a transpose matrix or row vector.

where Λ_s is the $N_s \times N_s$ diagonal matrix whose diagonal is given by λ_s. Hence, we can define equivalence classes of financial structures $\overline{R} \sim R$, if and only if there exists a sequence of positive diagonal matrices $\{\Lambda_s\}_{s \in S}$ such that $\overline{R}_s = \Lambda_s R_s$ for all $s \in S$.

The normalized financial structure $\overline{R}$ is such that for every available security, the sum of its payoffs equals the price of the security

$$q(s)^T = 1_{N_s}^{\top} \overline{R}_s, \qquad s \in S,$$

where 1_{N_s} is an N_s-dimensional vector of ones.

The normalized commodity prices, $\bar{p}$, represent "real" or current value terms of trade in the following sense. Adding the budget constraints over S^T, for any $T \geq 0$, it follows that

$$\sum_{s' \in S^T} p(s')x^h(s') + \sum_{s \in S_T} q(s)b^h(s) \leq \sum_{s' \in S^T} p(s')\omega^h(s').$$

Notice, however, that if $I_s < N_s$ for some s, the system of "real" prices depends on the particular λ_s chosen.

The no-arbitrage conditions imply that security prices are strictly positive. Thus, without loss of generality we shall assume that security prices are equal to one. The (normalized) financial structure satisfies, in addition to Assumptions $F1$–$F4$,

Assumption F5. For every $s \in S$ and every $i \in \mathcal{I}_s$, $\sum_{s' \in \sigma^{-1}(s)} r_i(s') = 1$.

Assumption F6. For every $s \in S$, $\{z \in \mathbf{R}^{I_s}: [-1_{I_s}^{\top} z, R_s z] > 0\} = \varnothing$.

Assumption $F6$ explicitly states the no-arbitrage condition. The financial structure must be such that, the exogenous security price precludes arbitrage opportunities, $1_{I_s} \in Q_s$ for all $s \in S$.

For a normalized financial structure, the date-event budget constraints are given by

$$p(0)x^h(0) + \sum_{i \in \mathcal{I}_0} b_i^h(0) \leq p(0)\omega^h(0); \tag{2.10}$$

$$p(s)x^h(s) + \sum_{i \in \mathcal{I}_s} b_i^h(s) \leq p(s)\omega^h(s) + r(s)b^h(s^-). \tag{2.11}$$

Notice that in order to perform these normalizations, we do not need to take the restrictive view that security yields (and commodity prices) *are* exogenously given to the model. Security yields may be endogenously formed. However, competitive agents *regard* these quantities as exogenously given.

In addition to the assumptions imposed so far, we need to impose a final assumption on the relationship between the financial structure and probability assessments by individual consumers. For any $s \in S$, let

$$\pi_s = \left(\frac{\pi(s')}{\pi(s)} \right)_{s' \in \sigma^{-1}(s)}$$

be the vector of conditional probabilities for date-events that immediately succeed s.

Assumption F7. The financial structure R is such that for every s,

$$\pi_s \in \text{span } \bar{R}_s,$$

for some $\bar{R} \sim R$.

Roughly speaking, this assumption states that after appropriately normalizing asset returns and commodity prices, it is possible to construct at every asset market a portfolio that pays at every subsequent date-event a return equal to the probability of occurrence. Notice that in view of the previous normalizations, this assumption is trivially satisfied in economies with a single security. In fact, in a companion paper (Hernández and Santos, 1992) we show that this assumption is generically true. The role of this assumption will become clear in Section 3. For the moment, let us say that it is sufficient to provide some form of continuity to the infinite dimensional consumer problem.

2.6 Bankruptcy Condition

In addition to the budget constraints at each date-event, (2.10) and (2.11), consumers must meet a bankruptcy condition that prevents them from rolling over their debts indefinitely. Basically, we require that a consumption and portfolio plan (x^h, b^h) be such that at every date-event s, the value of the excess demand over all nodes that follow s does not exceed the value of the portfolio at s. In other words, the consumer must be able eventually to finance future net purchases with current savings. Alternatively, the absolute value of the debt at s should not exceed all limiting values of future excess supply. Formally, for every $s \in S$,

$$\sum_{i \in \mathcal{I}_s} b_i^h(s) \geq \liminf_{T \to \infty} \sum_{s' \in \Psi(s) \cap S^T} p(s')\left[x^h(s') - \omega^h(s')\right]. \quad (2.12)$$

Let

$$B^h(p) = \{(x,b) : (x,b) \text{ satisfy constraints } (2.10)\text{–}(2.12)\}. \quad (2.13)$$

We devote the next section to a thorough discussion of this condition. Notice that condition (2.12) is neither a short sales constraint as in Radner (1972) nor a borrowing constraint as in Hernández (1989) and Levine (1989). We must note, however, that the bankruptcy constraint (2.12) is not necessarily invariant to renormalizations of the financial market structure

(Assumption $F7$). Nevertheless, this does not limit our analysis any further. Assumption $C3$ will allow us to replace the budget correspondence (2.13) by an alternative form that we define in the next section that remains invariant to this type of normalizations.

As is to be expected, Assumption $F5$ and conditions (2.10)–(2.12) imply that $p \cdot \omega^h \geq p \cdot x$, for every $(x, b) \in B^h(p)$. The existence of incomplete markets does not enhance the consumption possibilities that a complete market structure offers.

2.7 Financial Equilibrium

Let $\mathscr{E} = ((\succcurlyeq_h, \omega^h), R)$ be a normalized economy that satisfies Assumptions $F1$–$F7$ and $C1$–$C3$. Then $((x^h)_h, (b^h)_h, p)$ *is a normalized financial equilibrium* if and only if

(i) $(x^h, b^h) \in B^h(p)$;
(ii) If $\hat{x}^h$ is strictly preferred to x^h, then there is no portfolio $\hat{b}^h$ such that $(\hat{x}^h, \hat{b}^h) \in B^h(p)$;
(iii) $\Sigma_h x^h = \Sigma_h \omega^h$;
(iv) $\Sigma_h b^h = 0$.

3. BANKRUPTCY CONDITION AND CONTINUITY OF THE BUDGET SET

In this section we discuss two issues concerning the definition of the budget set in an infinite-horizon setup. First, we study the so-called transversality condition, whose purpose is to rule out an indefinite state of indebtedness to finance consumption in the earlier periods. Second, we explore the lack of product continuity of two of these budget sets. It is shown that they feature some discontinuities not found in the complete markets framework. However, under certain assumptions on the wealth process, these sets are continuous in the standard sense.

3.1 The Bankruptcy Condition

The modelling strategy behind bankruptcy condition (2.12) from the previous section, for every $s \in S$,

$$\sum_{i \in \mathscr{I}_s} b_i^h(s) \geq \liminf_{T \to \infty} \sum_{s' \in \Psi(s) \cap S^T} p(s')\left[x^h(s') - \omega^h(s')\right], \qquad (3.1)$$

is to extend the terminal conditions of finite-horizon models to an infinite-horizon economy. In order to understand this condition, consider a finite-horizon economy that lives for L periods. The stochastic environment is described by the finite tree, (S^L, σ). The terminal conditions in this economy are

$$\sum_{i \in \mathscr{I}_s} b_i^h(s) \geq 0 \quad \text{for every } s \in S_L. \tag{3.2}$$

Since asset payoffs add up to one, by substituting this constraint into the budget constraints (2.12), it follows that for all $s \in S^L$

$$\sum_{i \in \mathscr{I}_s} b_i^h(s) \geq \sum_{s' \in \Psi(s) \cap S^L} p(s')\left[x^h(s') - \omega^h(s')\right],$$

which is the finite-horizon version of condition (3.1).

In principle, this is not the only way in which condition (3.2) can be generalized. Another formulation, which at first glance seems more appropriate is as follows. Let $\mathbf{s} = (s_0, s_1, s_2, \ldots)$, $s_0 = 0$, $s_T = \sigma(s_{T+1})$ be an infinite history. Then, require portfolio choices to satisfy

$$\limsup_{T \to \infty} \sum_{i \in \mathscr{I}_s} b_i^h(s_T) \geq 0 \qquad \text{for every infinite history } \mathbf{s}. \tag{3.3}$$

In other words, regardless of the path the stochastic process follows, some convergent subsequence of savings (along time periods) must converge to a nonnegative number.

However, a careful examination shows that this condition is devoid of content. Assumptions $F1$–$F7$ imply that for every date-event s, there is an asset i such that $r_i(s') < 1$ for all $s' \in \sigma^{-1}(s)$. Without loss of generality, assume that asset 1 has such a property. Furthermore, assume that there is $\gamma < 1$ such that, for all s and $s' \in \sigma^{-1}(s)$, $r_1(s') < \gamma$. We claim that consumers can arrange a portfolio plan that allows them to purchase arbitrarily large first period consumption without giving up any future resources, and satisfying condition (3.3). Let $\phi > 0$, and let $\hat{x}(0)$ be a consumption bundle at period zero with $p(0)\hat{x}(0) = \phi$. In order to purchase $\hat{x}(0)$, consumers sell short ϕ units of asset 1, $b_1^h(0) = -\phi$. Payments in the following period, $r_1(s)b_1^h(0)$, $s \in S_1$, can be covered by short selling once again asset 1, $b_1^h(s) = r_1(s)b_1^h(0) < -\gamma\phi$. Consumers can keep rolling their debts over in a similar fashion. In period 2, their debts equal $b_1^h(s') = r_1(s')b_1^h(s) < -\gamma^2\phi$. Repeating the argument, we can see that along any infinite history, the debts go to zero, satisfying condition (3.3). Since ϕ was chosen arbitrarily, any consumption bundle can be financed following a similar scheme, without committing any fraction of their wealth (see Figure 1 for a concrete illustration).

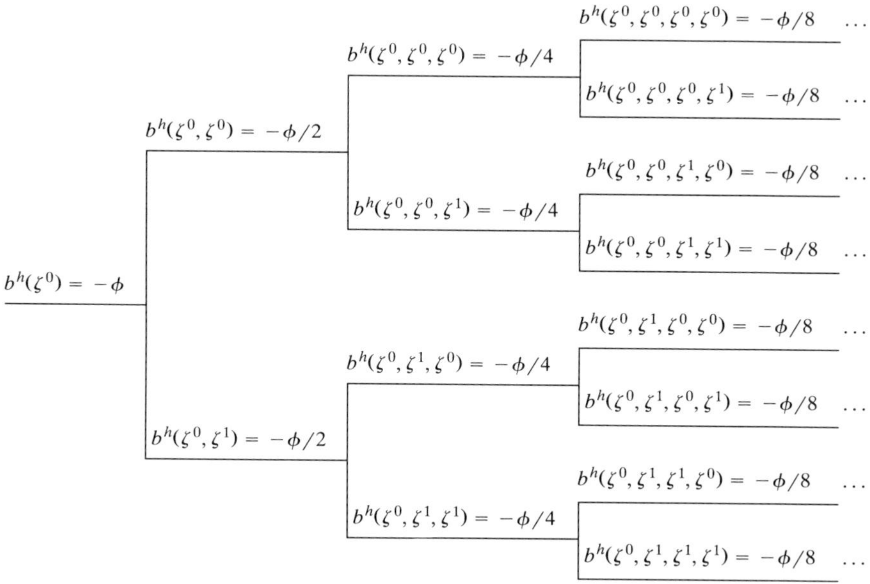

FIGURE 1 Let $N_s = 2$ and $I_s = 1$ for all s, with $r_s = (0.5, 0.5)$. A date-event s is represented as a partial history of realizations of a random variable $s = (\zeta_0, \zeta_1, \ldots, \zeta_{\tau(s)})$, with $\zeta_t \in \{\zeta^0, \zeta^1\}$ for all $t = 1, 2, \ldots,$ and with no loss of generality, $\zeta_0 = \zeta^0$. Notice that for every $\phi > 0$ condition (3.3) holds along any infinite history **s**; however, the consumer does not use any resources to pay back the initial debt.

In a way, it is due to the fact that the number of possible partial histories grows exponentially from one period to the next, that consumers can spread their debts out. In the limit, all debts go to zero. We can control for this effect by imposing, instead of (3.3), the condition that, as T goes to infinity, the sum of the debt over all nodes that occur in T goes to zero. Formally, let $A_T^h \subset S_T$ be the set of nodes at T where consumer h has negative savings.

$$A_T^h = \left\{ s \in S_T : \sum_i b_i^h(s) < 0 \right\}.$$

Then

$$\limsup_{T \to \infty} \sum_{s \in A_T^h} \sum_i b_i^h(s) \geq 0. \tag{3.4}$$

In the previous example, $\Sigma_{s \in A_t^h} b_1^h(s) = -\phi$ for all t, which violates condition (3.4). It is easy to prove that condition (3.4) implies our bankruptcy condition (3.1) [i.e., if (3.1) is not true, then (3.4) is not satisfied]. Also, if individual wealth is finite, condition (3.1) implies condition (3.4). Therefore, if individual wealth is finite, both conditions are equivalent. If consumers' wealth is infinite (see Section 4), we consider that (3.1) is a more natural condition. Using Assumption $F5$ we can see more transparently the main analytical difference between (3.1) and (3.4), since (3.1) can be written as follows, for every $s \in S$,

$$\limsup_{T\to\infty} \sum_{s' \in \Psi(s)\cap S_T} \sum_{i \in \mathscr{I}_{s'}} b_i^h(s') \geq 0.$$

Therefore, condition (3.4) is stronger than (3.1).

An alternative approach is to consider the budget set as the limit of budget sets for finite-horizon economies. For any price vector p, let $B_T^h(p)$ be the set of finite-horizon consumption and portfolio plans (x_T^h, b_T^h) such that

$$p(0)x_T^h(0) + \sum_{i\in\mathscr{I}_0} b_{iT}^h(0) \leq p(0)\omega^h(0); \tag{3.5}$$

$$p(s)x_T^h(s) + \sum_{i\in\mathscr{I}_s} b_{iT}^h(s) \leq p(s)\omega^h$$

$$+ r(s)b_T^h(s^-), \qquad s \in S^T \setminus S_0; \tag{3.6}$$

$$\sum_{i\in\mathscr{I}_s} b_{iT}^h(s) \geq 0, \qquad s \in S_T. \tag{3.7}$$

For the sake of notation, we shall use the expression x_T^h to refer to both the finite-horizon plan and its embedding in the original infinite-dimensional space.

We could define the consumer problem as follows. An infinite consumption and portfolio plan (x^h, b^h) is feasible if it is the limit of a convergent sequence of finite-horizon plans $\{(x_T^h, b_T^h)\}$, with $(x_T^h, b_T^h) \in B_T^h(p)$. Let $\hat{B}^h(p)$ denote the set of all such plans, i.e.,

$$\begin{aligned}\hat{B}^h(p) = \Big\{(x^h, b^h):\ & \text{there exists a sequence of periods } \mathscr{T},\\ & \text{and a sequence } \big\{\big(x_T^h, b_T^h\big)\big\}_{T\in\mathscr{T}},\\ & \text{with } \big(x_T^h, b_T^h\big) \in B_T^h(p), \text{ such that}\\ & \big(x_T^h, b_T^h\big) \to (x^h, b^h)\Big\}.\end{aligned} \tag{3.8}$$

This condition seems a reasonable extension of the finite-horizon terminal conditions (3.2), although it fails to capture the additional financial possibilities that an infinite horizon provides. In order to understand this limitation, consider the simplest stochastic environment with $N_s = 2$ for every $s \in S$. A date-event s is characterized by the partial history of realizations of a random variable ζ, $s = (\zeta_0, \zeta_1, \ldots, \zeta_{\tau(s)})$, with $\zeta_t \in \{\zeta^0, \zeta^1\}$, for every $t = 1, 2, \ldots$, and $\zeta_0 = \zeta^0$. Assume that all realizations are independent and identically distributed. At every date-event s there is a single asset with return structure $r_s = (0.5, 0.5)$, for all $s \in S$. Finally, assume that at prices p the value of consumer h's endowment is as follows:

$$p(s)\omega^h(s) = \begin{cases} 1/2^{\tau(s)-1} & \text{if } s = (\zeta^0, \zeta^0, \ldots, \zeta^0, \zeta^1) \\ 0 & \text{otherwise} \end{cases} \tag{3.9}$$

(see Figure 2).

Consider the truncated two-period economy ($T = 1$). Since

$$p(\zeta^0)\omega^h(\zeta^0) = 0,\; p(\zeta^0, \zeta^0)\omega^h(\zeta^0, \zeta^0) = 0,$$

and $p(\zeta^0, \zeta^1)\omega^h(\zeta^0, \zeta^1) = 1$, it follows that $(x_1, b_1) \in B_1^h(p)$, implies $b_1(\zeta^0) \geq 0$. A similar argument holds for any $T > 0$. $(x_T, b_T) \in B_T^h(p)$ implies $b_T(\zeta^0) \geq 0$. From the definition of $\hat{B}^h(p)$, it follows that $(x, b) \in \hat{B}^h(p)$ implies $b(\zeta^0) \geq 0$. Therefore, $x(\zeta^0) = 0$. The budget set $\hat{B}^h(p)$ precludes this agent from transferring any wealth to the initial period. Notice, however, that the budget set $B^h(p)$ in (2.13) gives more flexibility. Let x' be such that $p(\zeta^0)x'(\zeta^0) = 2$ and $x'(s) = 0$ for every $s \in S \setminus S_0$, and let b' be such that (x', b') satisfy the date-event budget constraints (2.10) and (2.11) with equality. We can show that condition (3.1) is also satisfied, which implies $(x', b') \in B^h(p)$.

An important (and convenient) property of the budget correspondence (3.8) is that the set of consumption allocations is invariant under the normalizations considered in Section 2.5. This requirement is not generally satisfied by condition (3.1). Further discussion of these constraints can be found in Hernández and Santos (1992) and Santos and Woodford (1992). Sometimes, both budget sets (2.13) and (3.8) are equivalent. However, they possess different continuity properties with respect to price approximations, which we now pass to explore.

3.2 Continuity Properties of Budget Sets

Although the budget set (3.8) is invariant under feasible normalizations of the return structure, we have shown, however, that this constraint builds a discontinuity of the feasible set with respect to truncations. (A similar discontinuity can arise with respect to more general approximations.) Also, budget set (2.13) gives rise to other kinds of discontinuous behavior.

Consider the economy of the previous example, where there is a single asset and two states of nature. The value of consumer h's endowment at

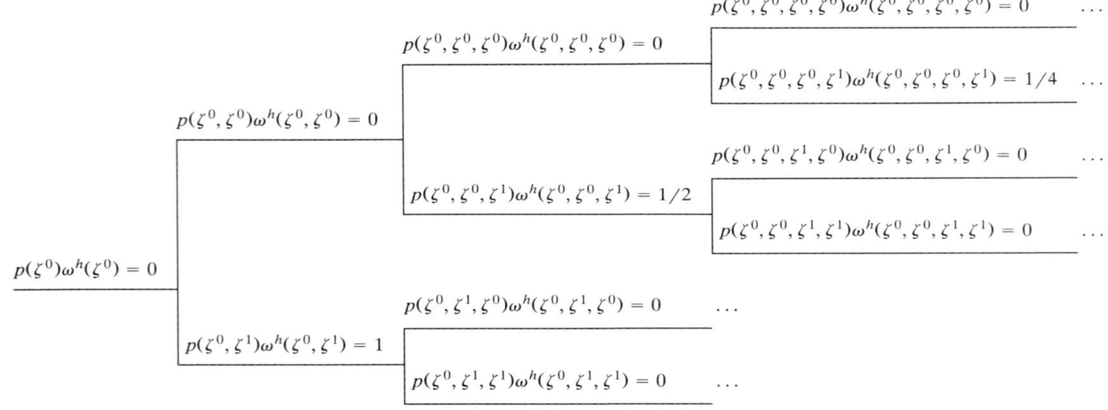

FIGURE 2 Let $N_s = 2$ and $I_s = 1$ for all s, with $r_s = (0.5, 0.5)$. A date-event s is represented as a partial history of realizations of a random variable $s = (\zeta_0, \zeta_1, \ldots, \zeta_{\tau(s)})$, with $\zeta_t \in \{\zeta^0, \zeta^1\}$ for all $t = 1, 2, \ldots,$ and with no loss of generality, $\zeta_0 = \zeta^0$. It is possible to construct $(\hat{x}, \hat{b}) \in B^h(p)$ with $\hat{b}^h(\zeta^0) = -2$. However, for any finite T, $(x_T, b_T) \in B_T^h(p)$ implies $b_T(\zeta^0) \geq 0$. Thus, $(\hat{x}, \hat{b}) \notin \hat{B}^h(p)$.

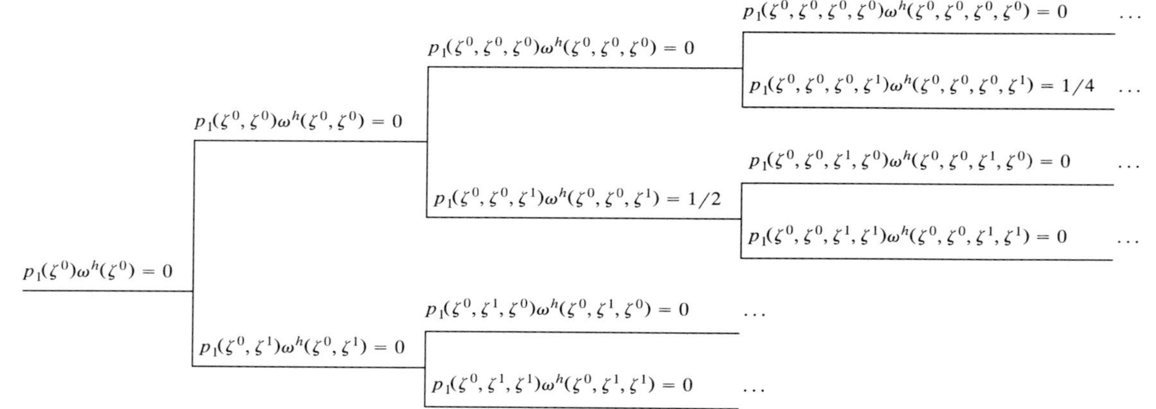

FIGURE 3 Let $N_s = 2$ and $I_s = 1$ for all s, with $r_s = (0.5, 0.5)$. A date-event s is represented as a partial history of realizations of a random variable $s = (\zeta_0, \zeta_1, \ldots, \zeta_{\tau(s)})$, with $\zeta_t \in \{\zeta^0, \zeta^1\}$ for all $t = 1, 2, \ldots,$ and with no loss of generality, $\zeta_0 = \zeta^0$. $(x, b) \in B^h(p_1)$ implies $b(\zeta^0) \geq 0$.

prices p is given by (3.9). Let p_ν be a price sequence such that

$$p_\nu(s)\omega^h(s) = \begin{cases} \dfrac{1}{2^{\tau(s)-1}} & \text{if } s = (\zeta^0, \zeta^0, \dots, \zeta^0, \zeta^1), \qquad \tau(s) \neq \nu, \\ 0 & \text{otherwise.} \end{cases}$$

In other words, $\omega^h(s)$ has the same value at prices p_ν and p at every node, except at $s = (\zeta^0, \zeta^0, \dots, \zeta^0, \zeta^1)$, $s \in S_\nu$, where $p_\nu(s)\omega^h(s) = 0$ (see Figure 3). Since $p_\nu(s)\omega^h(s) \to p(s)\omega^h(s)$, for all s, it is possible to define ω^h in such a way that $p_\nu \to p$ in the product topology. However, notice that $(x_\nu, b_\nu) \in B^h(p_\nu)$ implies $b_\nu(\zeta^0) = 0$. Hence, $B^h(p)$ is not lower semicontinuous. Moreover, we shall now illustrate that the upper semicontinuity of $B^h(p)$ holds under rather restrictive assumptions.

LEMMA 3.1. *Let $\{p^\gamma\}$ be a convergent sequence in the product topology, $p^\gamma \to p$, and $\{x^\gamma\}$ a convergent sequence in the product topology, $x^\gamma \to x \in X$. Let $p \cdot \omega^h < \infty$, and $p^\gamma \cdot \omega^h \to p \cdot \omega^h$, $p^\gamma \cdot x^\gamma \to p \cdot x$. Assume for each γ that there exists b^γ with $(x^\gamma, b^\gamma) \in B^h(p^\gamma)$. Then, $(x, b) \in B^h(p)$, for some b.*

Proof. In view of the assumptions of the lemma, there exists $k > 0$ such that $p^\gamma \cdot \omega^h < k$ for all γ large enough. Following Cass (1984, Lemma 2), we can find a constant $\eta(s) > 0$ such that $\|b^\gamma(s)\| < \eta(s)$, independently of γ. Therefore, a subsequence of $\{(x^\gamma, b^\gamma)\}$ must have a limit point (x, b) in the product topology. Without loss of generality, assume $(x^\gamma, b^\gamma) \to (x, b)$.

Since product convergence is equivalent to pointwise convergence, it follows that for every date-event s,

$$p^\gamma(s)x^\gamma(s) + \sum_{i \in \mathcal{I}_s} b_i^\gamma(s) \le p^\gamma(s)\omega^h + r(s)b^\gamma(s^-),$$

implies

$$p(s)x(s) + \sum_{i \in \mathcal{I}_s} b_i(s) \le p(s)\omega^h + r(s)b(s^-).$$

Moreover, by the assumptions of the lemma,

$$\sum_{i \in \mathcal{I}_s} b_i^\gamma(s) \ge \lim_{T \to \infty} \sum_{s' \in \Psi(s) \cap S^T} p^\gamma(s')\left[x^\gamma(s') - \omega^h(s')\right]$$

implies

$$\sum_{i \in \mathcal{I}_s} b_i(s) \ge \lim_{T \to \infty} \sum_{s' \in \Psi(s) \cap S^T} p(s')\left[x(s') - \omega^h(s')\right].$$

Therefore, (x, b) satisfies conditions (2.10)–(2.12), and so $(x, b) \in B^h(p)$. ■

The proof of Lemma 3.1 makes clear that in order to ensure the upper semicontinuity of $B^h(p)$, the bilinear convergence $p^\gamma \cdot \omega^h \to p \cdot \omega^h$ and $p^\gamma \cdot x^\gamma \to p \cdot x$ is generally required. [Note that without further qualifications, it is true only that $\lim_{\gamma \to \infty} p^\gamma \cdot \omega^h \geq p \cdot \omega^h$.]

In the complete markets case, the joint continuity of the maps $(p^\gamma, \omega^h) \mapsto p^\gamma \cdot \omega^h$ and $(p^\gamma, x^\gamma) \mapsto p^\gamma \cdot x^\gamma$ is automatically satisfied, since consumers are allowed to transfer wealth over time and across states of nature. Hence, by the product continuity of preferences $C3$, the value of endowments and consumptions in the distant future must always be relatively small, which implies such bilinear convergence.

In the incomplete markets setting, bilinear convergence is not generally guaranteed. Indeed, as illustrated in the following section, the endowment of a consumer may take on infinite values.

Using the previous example, consider instead the following approximation:

$$p_\nu(s)\omega^h(s) = \begin{cases} \dfrac{1}{2^{\tau(s)-1}} & \text{if } s = (\zeta^0, \zeta^0, \ldots, \zeta^0, \zeta^1), \\ \dfrac{1}{2^{\tau(s)-1}} & \text{if } s = (\zeta^0, \zeta^0, \ldots, \zeta^0, \zeta^0), \qquad \tau(s) = \nu, \\ 0 & \text{otherwise}. \end{cases}$$

We then immediately see that the budget set $\hat{B}^h(p)$ fails to be upper semicontinuous. Under certain assumptions this correspondence, however, is lower semicontinuous.

Lemma 3.2. *Let* $(x, b) \in \hat{B}^h(p)$ *with* $p \cdot \omega^h \leq k$ *and* $p \gg 0$. *Assume that the sequence* $\{p^\gamma\}$ *is such that* $p^\gamma \cdot \omega^h \leq k$ *and* $p^\gamma \to p$. *Then, there exists* $(x^\gamma, b^\gamma) \in \hat{B}^h(p^\gamma)$, *with* $(x^\gamma, b^\gamma) \to (x, b)$.

Proof. Let $\mathscr{T}$, and $\{(x_T, b_T)\}_{T \in \mathscr{T}}, (x_T, b_T) \in B_T^h(p)$, with $(x_T, b_T) \to (x, b)$, be the sequences in definition (3.8). Let $\{p^\gamma\}$ be an arbitrary price sequence converging to p with $p^\gamma \cdot \omega^h \leq k$. Assumption $C2$ implies that for every $p \gg 0$, every finite-horizon budget correspondence B_T^h is lower semicontinuous at p. Thus, for every T, there is a sequence $\{(x_T^\gamma, b_T^\gamma)\}, (x_T^\gamma, b_T^\gamma) \in B_T^h(p^\gamma)$, such that $(x_T^\gamma, b_T^\gamma) \to (x_T, b_T)$.

Fix γ, and consider the sequence $\{(x_T^\gamma, b_T^\gamma)\}_{T \in \mathscr{T}}$. By Assumption $C2$ and the fact that $p^\gamma \cdot x^\gamma \leq k$, consumptions and portfolios are pointwise bounded. Hence, there exists a subsequence $\mathscr{T}'$ along which (x_T^γ, b_T^γ) converges to a limit (x^γ, b^γ). By definition, this implies $(x^\gamma, b^\gamma) \in \hat{B}^h(p^\gamma)$.

It remains to be proved that $(x^\gamma, b^\gamma) \to (x, b)$. Since $(x_T^\gamma, b_T^\gamma) \to (x^\gamma, b^\gamma)$, along $\mathscr{T}'$; $(x_T^\gamma, b_T^\gamma) \to (x_T, b_T)$, along γ; and $(x_T, b_T) \to (x, b)$, along $\mathscr{T}$, it follows that for every $\epsilon > 0$ and $s \in S$, there exist $\gamma(\epsilon, s)$ and

$T(\epsilon, s) \in \mathscr{T}'$, such that

$$\left|(x_T(s), b_T(s)) - (x(s), b(s))\right| < \epsilon/3,$$

$$\left|(x_T^\gamma(s), b_T^\gamma(s)) - (x_T(s), b_T(s))\right| < \epsilon/3,$$

$$\left|(x_T^\gamma(s), b_T^\gamma(s)) - (x^\gamma(s), b^\gamma(s))\right| < \epsilon/3,$$

for every $\gamma \geq \gamma(\epsilon, s)$ and $T \geq T(\epsilon, s)$. Therefore,

$$\left|(x^\gamma(s), b^\gamma(s)) - (x(s), b(s))\right| < \epsilon,$$

which implies the pointwise convergence of $(x^\gamma(s), b^\gamma(s))$ to $(x(s), b(s))$. ■

LEMMA 3.3. *Under the conditions of bilinear convergence of prices, allocations and endowments of Lemma* 3.1, $\hat{B}^h(p) \subset B^h(p)$.

Proof. Let $(x, b) \in \hat{B}^h(p)$ and let $\mathscr{T}$, and $(x_T, b_T)_{T \in \mathscr{T}}, (x_T, b_T) \in B_T^h(p)$, with $(x_T, b_T) \to (x, b)$ be the sequences in definition (3.8).

Notice that $(x_T, b_T) \in B^h(p^T)$, where $p^T(s) = p(s)$ if $s \in S^T$, and $p^T(s) = 0$ otherwise.[4] Since $p^T \to p$ in the product topology, it follows from Lemma 3.1 that $(x, b) \in B^h(p)$. ■

We have, therefore, shown that under rather restrictive assumptions, the budget set $B^h(p)$ is upper semicontinuous—but fails to be lower semicontinuous—and the budget set $\hat{B}^h(p)$ is lower semicontinuous. Furthermore, $\hat{B}^h(p) \subset B^h(p)$. Our purpose now is to explore the sources of discontinuity of both correspondences.

Coming back to the example of Figure 2, one may notice that under Assumptions $C2$ and $C3$ the patterns of individual's wealth there illustrated would not be observed in a complete markets economy. Indeed, for every node $s = (\zeta^0, \zeta^0, \ldots, \zeta^0, \zeta^1)$ the wealth is $p(s)\omega^h(s) = 2^{-(\tau(s)-1)}$. Since all realizations are independent and identically distributed, the probability of occurrence of a node of the type $s = (\zeta^0, \zeta^0, \ldots, \zeta^0, \zeta^1)$ is $\pi(s) = 2^{-(\tau(s))} = p(s)\omega^h(s)/2$. Hence, this economy lacks discounting. In other words, the dynamic evolution of wealth is incompatible with consumers' impatience.

Although discounting plays a central role in equilibrium theory (see Araujo, 1985), our next example illustrates that an exponentially falling pattern of wealth is not enough to ensure the continuity of the correspondences $B^h(p)$ and $\hat{B}^h(p)$. The example is the same as in Figure 2 but returns at each date-event s for the one-period security are $r_s = (\frac{1}{3}, \frac{2}{3})$.

[4]As mentioned before (x_T, b_T) denotes either a finite-dimensional vector or, as in this case, its natural embedding in the original infinite-dimensional space, where $x_T(s) = 0$ and $b_T(s) = 0$ for every $s \notin S^T$.

Moreover, the wealth pattern is as follows:

$$p(s)\omega^h(s) = \begin{cases} 4\left(\frac{1}{3}\right)^{\tau(s)} & \text{if } s = (\zeta^0, \zeta^0, \dots, \zeta^0, \zeta^1), \\ 0 & \text{otherwise.} \end{cases}$$

The wealth in this example is constructed so that the consumer can "roll over" a debt of two units in period 0, and pay in every node of the form $s = (\zeta^0, \zeta^0, \dots, \zeta^0, \zeta^1)$. It follows then that the consumer can borrow two units, $b^h(0) = -2$, under $B^h(p)$ and no borrowing is allowed under $\hat{B}^h(p)$. Furthermore, by replicating the preceding arguments we can again show that $B^h(p)$ fails to be lower semicontinuous and $\hat{B}^h(p)$ fails to be upper semicontinuous. Observe that in this example $\beta^{\tau(s)}\pi(s) = (\beta/2)^{\tau(s)}$. Thus, for $0 < \beta < 1$ large enough we have that

$$\left(\frac{\beta}{2}\right)^{\tau(s)} > 4\left(\frac{1}{3}\right)^{\tau(s)} = p(s)\omega^h(s).$$

Hence, the pattern of wealth in this example could be generated by a complete markets framework. Nevertheless, the budget sets $B^h(p)$ and $\hat{B}^h(p)$ are discontinuous.

The discontinuity in the present example comes from a violation of Assumption $F7$. The conditional probability at each date-event s is $\pi_s = (0.5, 0.5)$, whereas the return structure at each date-event s is $r_s = (\frac{1}{3}, \frac{2}{3})$. Indeed, if in accordance with the normalizations performed in Section 2.5 we set at each date-event s the return structure to $r_s = (0.5, 0.5)$, we then obtain the same pattern of wealth as in Figure 2.

Under a complete markets structure, all equilibrium prices of the economy described in Section 2 belong to the following price space

$$\mathscr{P} = \left\{p\colon p_m(s) \leq k\beta^{\tau(s)}\pi(s), \quad \text{and } p_1(0) = 1\right\},$$

for every commodity m and some constant $k > 0$. It can be shown that in this price space, $B^h(p) \subset \hat{B}^h(p)$. Moreover, by Lemmas 3.1–3.3, $B^h(p) = \hat{B}^h(p)$, and both correspondences are continuous. In fact, the following more general result is available.

PROPOSITION 3.4. *Assume that for every* $\epsilon > 0$ *there is* T *such that for every* $s \in S_T$,

$$\pi(s)\epsilon \geq \sum_{s' \in \Psi(s)} p(s')\omega^h(s'). \tag{3.10}$$

Then $B^h(p) = \hat{B}^h(p)$ *under Assumptions* $C1$–$C2$ *and* $F1$–$F7$ *and the conditions of Lemma* 3.1. *Furthermore, if* $p \gg 0$, *the budget sets* $B^h(p)$ *and* $\hat{B}^h(p)$ *are continuous.*

The proof of this result is relatively long. The interested reader is referred to the companion paper, Hernández and Santos (1992).

To conclude this section, we would like to emphasize that in our incomplete markets framework, apart from bilinear convergence, the continuity of the budget sets $B^h(p)$ and $\hat{B}^h(p)$ is insured if the pattern of wealth satisfies condition (3.10) and the conditional probability distribution to abide by Assumption $F7$. Under mild assumptions, these requirements are always true in complete markets economies. Needless to say, the continuity of budget sets allows the use of standard finite-horizon approximations in proving the existence of an equilibrium.

4. PRICE SPACE

In economic models with a complete financial structure and a finite number of agents the value of the aggregate wealth is finite in every equilibrium. This is because agents face effectively a unique budget constraint, and with infinite wealth they would demand unbounded amounts of consumption. Under an incomplete markets structure, consumers cannot transfer income freely across states of nature. Hence, one cannot preclude, as equilibrium candidates, price vectors $\hat{p}$ such that $\hat{p} \cdot \omega = \infty$. At such prices, a consumer may want to incur an arbitrary large debt in the initial period to finance initial unbounded consumption. The bankruptcy conditions (2.12) and (3.8) seem to allow such a behavior. However, we must remember that these conditions must be met at every date-event. Therefore, a large initial debt could lead to bankruptcy in a future adverse state. As it stands, the definition of the consumer problem rules out these patterns of unlimited borrowing.

In this section we illustrate with an example the coexistence of equilibrium prices with finite and infinite wealth. The example draws inspiration from the indeterminacy results for finite economies of Cass (1985), Geanakoplos and Mas-Colell (1989), and Balasko and Cass (1989).

Consider a one good economy with a representative consumer. The stochastic environment and the market structure are as in the examples in Section 3. A date-event is characterized by the partial history of realizations of the stochastic endowment. Furthermore, $N_s = 2$ and $I_s = 1$, with $r_s = \pi_s = (0.5, 0.5)$, for all s. The realizations of the endowment are independent and identically distributed, with $\omega(s) \in \{\underline{\omega}, \overline{\omega}\}$, with $0 < \underline{\omega} < \overline{\omega}$. Without loss of generality, assume $\omega(0) = \overline{\omega}$. When necessary, we shall represent a date-event s as the finite sequence of realizations of the endowment.

Preferences are represented by a time-separable Von Neumann–Morgenstern utility function,

$$U(x) = \sum_{s \in S} \beta^{\tau(s)} \pi(s) u(x(s)),$$

where π is the probability distribution of S and $\pi(s) = 2^{-\tau(s)}$ for all s.

The assumption of a representative agent implies that at equilibrium consumption equals the endowment and portfolios are zero. For these economies, the equilibrium resource allocation is trivially unique. However, as we shall discuss in a moment, the market incompleteness generates a high degree of nominal indeterminacy. This indeterminacy allows us to construct equilibrium prices in which the wealth is not finite. Let p be a price vector such that

$$p(s) = \begin{cases} (\beta/2)^{\tau(s)} & \text{if } \omega(s) = \overline{\omega}, \\ (\beta/2)^{\tau(s)} u'(\underline{\omega})/u'(\overline{\omega}) & \text{if } \omega(s) = \underline{\omega}. \end{cases} \tag{4.1}$$

We first show that p is an equilibrium price vector. The necessary first-order conditions for utility maximization imply that for every s there is $\lambda(s) > 0$ such that

$$\beta^{\tau(s)} \pi(s) u'(x(s)) = \lambda(s) p(s) \tag{4.2}$$

and

$$\lambda(s) = \sum_{s' \in \sigma^{-1}(s)} r(s') \lambda(s'), \tag{4.3}$$

which implies

$$\frac{u'(x(s))}{p(s)} = \frac{\beta}{4}\left[\frac{u'(x(s,\overline{\omega}))}{p(s,\overline{\omega})} + \frac{u'(x(s,\underline{\omega}))}{p(s,\underline{\omega})}\right], \tag{4.4}$$

where $(s, \overline{\omega})$ and $(s, \underline{\omega})$ denote the immediate successors of s. We can easily verify that the allocation $x = \omega$ and $b = 0$ satisfies condition (4.4) at prices p. The bankruptcy conditions are trivially satisfied.

Notice that in this case the wealth of the economy is finite. We can show that p in (4.1) is an equilibrium price vector by considering a sequence of truncated economies and invoking the Kuhn–Tucker theorem for each element in the sequence. Moreover, the continuity of the budget constraint discussed in the previous section implies that the limit of finite horizon equilibria is an equilibrium for the infinite-horizon economy.

Since there is only one financial asset at every date-event, equation (4.4) is the only restriction on equilibrium prices at contiguous states. Thus, at every s, there is a single equation to determine $p(s)$ and $p(s')$, $s' \in \sigma^{-1}(s)$. This suggests that under regularity conditions, the degree of indeterminacy is positive. Naturally, this indeterminacy can only be nominal, since the equilibrium allocation is unique. We defer to the following section a discussion about the degree of real indeterminacy in economics with many consumers. In this section we simply exploit the nominal indeterminacy of equilibria to construct prices that generate infinite wealth.

Let $\hat{p}$ be a price vector, such that for all s of the form $(\overline{\omega}, \overline{\omega}, \ldots, \overline{\omega})$, $\hat{p}(s) = 1$. For all other nodes, $\hat{p}(s)$ is determined in a way that satisfies equation (4.4), while preserving the relative price structure defined by p for every subtree that originates from a node $(\overline{\omega}, \overline{\omega}, \dots, \overline{\omega}, \underline{\omega})$. Namely,

$$\hat{p}(s) = \begin{cases} 1 & \text{if } s = (\overline{\omega}, \overline{\omega}, \dots, \overline{\omega}), \\ \dfrac{4}{4-\beta}\left(\dfrac{\beta}{2}\right)^{-\overline{\omega}(s)} p(s) & \text{otherwise}, \end{cases} \tag{4.5}$$

where $\overline{\omega}(s)$ is the number of consecutive realizations $\overline{\omega}$ that occur before the first $\underline{\omega}$.

Let $\mathscr{S}_{\overline{\omega}}$ be the set of nodes $s = (\overline{\omega}, \overline{\omega}, \dots, \overline{\omega})$. Considering a sequence of truncated economies, it is easy to show that the new price vector $\hat{p}$ is an equilibrium. Moreover, this price vector $\hat{p}$ assigns infinite wealth, since the sum of its components is given by

$$\|\hat{p}\|_1 = \sum_{s \in \mathscr{S}_{\overline{\omega}}} \hat{p}(s) + \sum_{s \notin \mathscr{S}_{\overline{\omega}}} \hat{p}(s)$$

and the first term of the right-hand side is an infinite number.

The way $\hat{p}$ was defined was fairly general. We fixed a normalization (as defined in Section 2.5) and for such a given normalization we constructed equilibrium prices with finite wealth and equilibrium prices with infinite wealth. Our construction suggests that is possible to find many other equilibrium prices, some of them lying in and others out of l_1, the space of summable sequences. In fact, the equilibrium price set is a continuum.

At this stage, we can only conjecture about the extension of equilibria with infinite wealth to more complicated environments. The assumptions of a single commodity, a single asset and two states of nature are innocuous. The result can be extended with the corresponding notational cost. Also, the assumption of stationary endowments can be easily disposed. Care must be exercised when defining prices from equation (4.4) to guarantee that they are positive. However, the assumption of a single agent is crucial. It was precisely this assumption that allowed us to construct a new equilibrium solely by manipulating priccs according to the marginal utilities. In the presence of many agents, their marginal utilities are not necessarily colinear across states. Also, an equilibrium consumption and portfolio plan for consumer h does not necessarily remain feasible as prices change. In order to prove the general result, it is in general necessary to construct equilibria for the infinite economy.

THEOREM 4.1. *Every single-agent economy with incomplete markets has a financial equilibrium price vector with infinite wealth.*

Observe that under the normalizations performed in Section 2, the complete markets equilibrium of a representative consumer economy is also an equilibrium for the incomplete markets case [e.g., see (4.1)]. Therefore, in these simple economies we obtain coexistence of equilibria with both finite and infinite wealth. It becomes evident that the above example leaves open several important issues. For instance, as already pointed out, the coexistence of both types of equilibria may be a general feature of these models. Also, it is unknown whether these economies possess always an equilibrium of a certain type. In this respect, Hernández and Santos (1992) have shown that for an economy satisfying the assumptions of Section 2 there is always an equilibrium with finite wealth. As remarked above, the Arrow–Debreu model with a finite number of consumers contains only equilibria with finitely valued endowments. If in this model there are included an infinite number of consumers (e.g., an overlapping generations structure), it is possible to construct examples that simultaneously display equilibria with finite and infinite wealth. The same result may be obtained for some (trivially constructed) cases with borrowing constraints. However, some models with borrowing constraints, as standard monetary models, always exhibit equilibria with infinite wealth (Bewley, 1980; Santos, 1990).

5. INDETERMINACY

In this section we investigate some issues regarding the local uniqueness of financial equilibria in infinite-horizon economies. Primarily, we are interested in exploring the robustness of the indeterminacy of equilibria for finite economies (Cass, 1985; Balasko and Cass, 1989; Geanakoplos and Mas-Colell, 1989; Werner, 1990) when the terminal period is indefinite. The use of an infinite horizon has taught important lessons to economic theorists. For some economic problems, an infinite horizon may eliminate "bad" properties of finite-horizon equilibria. (For example, in monetary economies, if the horizon is finite, equilibria with a positive value of money do not exist.) It is also true that for other types of economic problems, an infinite horizon may remove an undesired property of the finite model only to introduce another unwanted property of a different sort. (For example, the only Nash equilibrium in finitely repeated games is the Nash equilibrium for the constituent game, but if the game is repeated indefinitely, any individually rational payoff can be sustained as an equilibrium.) In any case, an infinite horizon can change radically the qualitative nature of an economic equilibrium.

We have reasons to believe that the model with incomplete markets can be subject to some of these effects. The discontinuity of the feasible set with respect to truncations suggests that the equilibrium set for an infinite economy is different from that of any finite economy. In particular, the budget correspondence seems to be "larger," in the sense that the indefiniteness of the terminal period allows for more flexible portfolio sequences, making feasible consumption sequences that were not available in the finite economies. This discontinuity poses severe problems for the proof of existence, by making certain truncations inadequate.

A general study of the indeterminacy of the financial equilibrium set in infinite horizon economies may require techniques of differential topology in infinite-dimensional spaces. The few available results impose severe conditions on the topological structure of the model that lack economic significance (Santos and Bona, 1989).

For these reasons, we confine ourselves to a more limited analysis and investigate the dimensionality of a particular subset of the equilibrium manifold. For any given equilibrium e and any date T, we look at the set of equilibria that assign the same prices and resource allocation as e, at every date-event after T. Roughly speaking, what we are trying to determine is whether, given an initial equilibrium, it is possible to change finitely many prices, consumptions, and portfolios and obtain a new equilibrium. In our opinion, this question addresses the same issue of indeterminacy of finite equilibria that has been addressed by the authors mentioned above, but with a different twist. Instead of assuming that the world ends at period T, we recognize that the economy lives indefinitely. The "terminal" period should delimit not the life of the economy, but merely our period of analysis. What this implies is that instead of assuming that agents demand zero portfolios at any terminal node, we require them to hold portfolios that are consistent with the remaining and undisturbed tail of the equilibrium path.

For every $T = 1, 2, \dots$ and every infinite vector $z = (z(s))_{s \in S}$ let z_T be the initial segment of z and let z^T be the remaining part. In other words, z_T is the projection of z on the subspace generated by date-events that occur during or before T, $z_T = (z(s))_{s \in S^T}$, and z^T is the projection of z on the subspace generated by date-events that occur after T, $z^T = (z(s))_{s \in S \setminus S^T}$. Let $z = (z_T, z^T)$. Let $((x^h), (b^h), p)$ be a financial equilibrium for the incomplete markets economy with an infinite horizon. The problem we address is the following. Given $T > 0$, let us determine the degree of indeterminacy of equilibria $((\tilde{x}^h), (\tilde{b}^h), \tilde{p})$, such that $\tilde{x}^{hT} = x^{hT}$, $\tilde{b}^{hT} = b^{hT}$ and $\tilde{p}^T = p^T$.

We confine our exposition to an equilibrium where consumption vectors lie in the interior of the consumption set, so as to guarantee the regularity conditions of Debreu (1972) and Balasko and Cass (1989). Let

$$U_h(x) = \sum_{s \in S} \beta^{\tau(s)} \pi(s) u_h(x(s)) \tag{5.1}$$

be consumers h's utility function. For the remainder of the section, we fix an equilibrium $e = ((x^h), (b^h), p)$ for which we study its local uniqueness.

Given $T > 0$, let $\tilde{\mathscr{E}}^T$ be a T horizon economy, with a consumption space $\tilde{X}^T$ equal to the projection of the original space. Utility functions for $\tilde{\mathscr{E}}^T, U_{hT}$, are defined taking partial sums in equation (5.1). The financial structure for $\tilde{\mathscr{E}}^T$ is the same as the one in the original economy during the initial T periods.

We say that $((\tilde{x}_T^h), (\tilde{b}_T^h), \tilde{p}_T)$ is a *short-run equilibrium with respect to* e for the economy $\tilde{\mathscr{E}}^T$ if:

(i) For every $h, (\tilde{x}_T^h, \tilde{b}_T^h)$ maximizes U_{hT} over the set

$$\begin{aligned}
\tilde{B}_T^h(\tilde{p}_T; e) = \Big\{ \big(\hat{x}_T, \hat{b}_T\big) &: \tilde{p}_T(0)\hat{x}_T(0) \\
&+ \sum_{i \in \mathscr{I}_0} \hat{b}_{iT}(0) \le \tilde{p}_T(0)\omega_T^h(0); \\
&\tilde{p}_T(s)\hat{x}_T(s) + \sum_{i \in \mathscr{I}_s} \hat{b}_{iT}(s) \le \tilde{p}_T(s)\omega_T^h(s) \\
&+ \sum_{i \in \mathscr{I}_s} r_i(s)\hat{b}_{iT}(s^-), \qquad s \in S_j, j = 1, \dots, T-1; \\
&\tilde{p}_T(s)\hat{x}_T(s) + \sum_{i \in \mathscr{I}_s} b_i(s) \le \tilde{p}_T(s)\omega_T^h(s) \\
&+ \sum_{i \in \mathscr{I}_s} r_i(s)\hat{b}_{iT}(s^-), \qquad s \in S_T \Big\},
\end{aligned}$$

(ii) $\Sigma_h \tilde{x}_T^h = \Sigma_h \omega_T^h$,
(iii) $\Sigma_h \tilde{b}_T^h = 0$.

In other words, a short-run equilibrium with respect to e is a financial equilibrium for the finite economy $\tilde{\mathscr{E}}^T$ except for the terminal condition. Instead of requiring agents to hold zero assets in the terminal period, a short-run equilibrium requires agents to hold the portfolios that would be observed in the equilibrium e for the infinite economy. Naturally, if e is such that $b^h(s) = 0$ for all $s \in S_T$ and all h, a short-run equilibrium with respect to e corresponds to an equilibrium in the finite economy of Cass (1984), Werner (1985), and Duffie (1987).

Let $(\tilde{\lambda}_T^h)$ be the vector of marginal utilities of income along the short-run equilibrium $((\tilde{x}_T^h), (\tilde{b}_T^h), \tilde{p}_T)$. The incomplete markets assumption implies that, in general, $\tilde{\lambda}_T^h(s) \neq \tilde{\lambda}_T^h(s')$, $s \neq s'$, for any consumer h.

Let (λ^h) be the vector of marginal utilities of income along the infinite equilibrium e defined in equations (4.2) and (4.3).

The following lemma investigates the necessary and sufficient conditions for an allocation $((\hat{x}^h), (\hat{b}^h), \hat{p})$, where $\hat{x}^h = (\tilde{x}^h_T, x^{hT}) = (\tilde{b}^h_T, b^{hT})$ and $\hat{p} = (\tilde{p}_T, p^T)$, to be an equilibrium for the original economy.

LEMMA 5.1. *$((\hat{x}^h), (\hat{b}^h), \hat{p})$ is an equilibrium for the original economy if and only if, for every $s \in S_T$, every consumer $h = 1, \ldots, H$ and every financial asset $i = 1, \ldots, I_s$,*

$$\tilde{\lambda}^h_T(s) = \sum_{s' \in \sigma^{-1}(s)} r_i(s') \lambda^h(s').$$

Proof. Both $((\tilde{x}^h_T), (\tilde{b}^h_T), \tilde{p}_T)$ and e satisfy the same set of first-order conditions. We only need to check that both paths satisfy the same first-order conditions at date T, when they are appended to define the new infinite equilibrium $((\hat{x}^h), (\hat{b}^h), \hat{p})$. The hypothesis of the lemma guarantees precisely these first-order conditions. ■

We investigate the indeterminacy of the subset of short-run equilibria for the finite economy that satisfies the conditions of Lemma 5.1, which we denote E^e_T. Formally,

$$E^e_T = \Big\{ \big((\tilde{x}^h_T), (\tilde{b}^h_T), \tilde{p}_T \big) : \big((\tilde{x}^h_T), (\tilde{b}^h_T), \tilde{p}_T \big) \text{ is a short-run equilibrium with respect to } e \text{ and for every } s \in S_T \text{ and } i = 1, \ldots, I_s \;\; \tilde{\lambda}^h_T(s) = \sum_{s' \in \sigma^{-1}(s)} r_i(s') \lambda^h(s') \Big\}.$$

Notice that E^e_T is nonempty. By construction, $e \in E^e_T$.

THEOREM 5.2. *The short-run equilibrium with respect to e, $((\tilde{x}^h_T), (\tilde{b}^h_T), \tilde{p}_T)$, is locally unique in E^e_T.*

Proof. For the sake of notation, we sketch only the main steps of the proof. Suppose that e is such that for all $s \in S_T$, all $h = 1, \ldots, H$ and all $i = 1, \ldots, I$, $b^h_i(s) = 0$. Then, every short-run equilibrium with respect to e is an equilibrium for a finite economy that lives T periods. The indeterminacy of such an equilibrium (Werner, 1990), is at most

$$K_W = \sum_{s \in S^{T-1}} (N_s - I_s),$$

where N_s is the number of immediate successors from a nonterminal node s and I_s is the number of available assets at s. The previous formula follows from the fact that the indeterminacy at every market is at most $N_s - I_s$ (Balasko and Cass, 1989).

If the infinite equilibrium e is such that $b_i^h(s) \neq 0$ for some h, i and $s \in S_T$, the degree of indeterminacy of the short-run equilibrium with respect to e is $K_W + 1$, since the terminal conditions destroy the homogeneity of the demand for commodities with respect to prices and assets. Let $K = K_W + 1$.

However, we are not interested in the dimensionality of the short-run equilibrium set, but in that of the subset E_T^e of short-run equilibria that define an infinite equilibrium when appended to the tail of e. By Lemma 5.1, any such short-run equilibrium must satisfy the condition

$$\tilde{\lambda}_T^h(s) = \sum_{s' \in \sigma^{-1}(s)} r_i(s')\lambda^h(s') \tag{5.2}$$

for every $s \in S_T$ and every $i = 1, \ldots, I_s$.

Roughly speaking, every linearly independent restriction in the definition of E_T^e decreases in one the degree of indeterminacy. We need to determine the number of conditions (5.2) that are linearly independent. The set E_T^e imposes $\Sigma_{s \in S_T} I_s$ additional restrictions of the type (5.2) for each consumer. However, not all of them are linearly independent. For every consumer h, fix exogenously the marginal utility of income in period zero, $\tilde{\lambda}_T^h(0)$. The vector of marginal utilities of income at date one must be such that

$$\tilde{\lambda}_T^h(0) = \sum_{s \in \sigma^{-1}(0)} r_i(s)\lambda^h(s), \tag{5.3}$$

for every $i = 1, \ldots, I_0$. By $F2$, R_0 has rank I_0, therefore $N_0 - I_0$ marginal utilities of date 1 are left undetermined and can be set exogenously. The same procedure is applied for the following periods. As a result, for each consumer h, the set E_T^e imposes $1 + \Sigma_{s \in S^{T-1}}(N_s - I_s) = K$ linearly independent constraints. Thus, the set E_T^e imposes HK independent constraints. Recall that the indeterminacy of the set of short-run equilibria is K. Since the number of additional constraints is larger than the degree of indeterminacy of the unconstrained short-run equilibrium manifold, the degree of indeterminacy of E_T^e is zero. ■

In order to illustrate our discussion of the number of marginal utilities that are determined through equations such as (5.3), consider the complete markets case, $I_s = N_s$ for all $s \in S$. In this case $K = 1$, and $\tilde{\lambda}_T^h(s) = \tilde{\lambda}_T^h(s')$, for all $s \neq s'$. Therefore, E_T^e imposes a single constraint for each agent, namely, that the marginal utility of income at date zero, which was set exogenously, must be equal to the marginal utilities of income at dates after T.

Theorem 5.2 suggests that it is not possible to construct new equilibria by simply modifying an initial segment of another equilibrium. If infinite equilibria are not locally unique, two arbitrarily close equilibria must differ in infinitely many components. In a way, our result resembles those previously reported for overlapping generations economies (e.g., Balasko and Shell, 1981). In these economies, it is not generally possible to construct new equilibria by changing a finite number of consumptions and prices. However, these authors study infinite economies with complete markets and the equilibria for the finite-horizon models are locally unique. What is striking in our model is that the equilibria for finite economies are undetermined, and yet the same infinite number of modifications is required in order to construct new equilibria. Of course, this feature is characteristic not only of the infinite-horizon economy. For finite horizons, wherever commodity prices and allocations are predetermined in future dates, equilibria are locally unique.

In the previous exercise we assumed that security yields are exogenously given to the model. As already stressed, our analysis in previous sections does not depend on this rather stringent interpretation. It was necessary to assume only that at a given financial equilibrium consumers *view* commodity prices and security returns as given. Hence, we could alternatively inquire how the results of Theorem 5.2 would be modified if security yields are endogenously determined by the equilibrium conditions. Observe that in this case the degree of local indeterminacy of the short-run equilibrium is $\sum_{s \in S^{T-1}} N_s$ (cf. Werner, 1990). Consequently, in this case there are not in general enough independent constraints to assert the local uniqueness of equilibria. Hence, if security yields are endogenously formed, the model is still indeterminate under the rather strong criterion of fixing allocations and commodity prices at every date-event after time T.

6. CONCLUSIONS

In this paper we have studied some properties of equilibrium prices for dynamic economies with incomplete financial markets. In these economies, wealth cannot be transferred freely over time and across states of nature. Therefore, agents are subject to idiosyncratic risk, and may attach different valuations to certain assets or streams of wealth. In spite of this, this paper has analyzed several transversality conditions in an attempt to define the budget set of a consumer. These conditions entail an infinite number of effective constraints on future savings and produce certain types of discontinuities in the budget sets not found in the complete markets model. Continuity is, under mild conditions, obtained if the pattern of wealth evolves according to the probability distribution and the discount factor and the conditional probability belongs to the span of the financial structure.

Another feature of these economies is that they contain equilibria of finite wealth that may coexist with others in which the wealth is infinite. This may suggest that there is a large degree of indeterminacy in these economies. However, in Section 5 we have argued that the nature of the indeterminacy is different from the one that could be inferred from previous results on indeterminacy of equilibria in finite economies (Balasko and Cass, 1989; Geanakoplos and Mas-Colell, 1989; Werner, 1990).

Our analysis can be extended in several directions. First, one could consider production economies or exchange economies where the stochastic environment is defined in terms of continuous random variables. The lack of Arrow–Debreu securities makes it necessary to model the objectives of firms in a way that is consistent with the incomplete asset market structure (see Drèze, 1974). Our conjecture is that, provided the objectives of the firm are such that excess demand functions exhibit the usual properties, the introduction of a productive sector to the analysis should not present additional complications.

Another analytical result that remains to be studied is the degree of indeterminacy of the equilibrium set in the infinite economy. This line of research poses a challenge. To the best of our knowledge, no global methods for infinite-dimensional spaces have been reported that would allow the study of indeterminacy of equilibria in economies with imperfect capital markets and infinite-horizon consumers. [See Boldrin and Woodford (1990) for a discussion of partial results on this issue.]

With regard to applications of the theory, it may be interesting to explore the role of money and the nature of economic fluctuations. [See Magill and Quinzii (1989) for some results on the role of money in finite economies with incomplete markets.] Finally, the intertemporal structure of the model may furnish new insights for modeling the endogenous formation of securities and the behavior and organization of firms, along with an understanding of bankruptcy as an equilibrium outcome.

Acknowledgments

We are grateful to Elyès Jouini, David Levine, Andreu Mas-Colell, and Mike Woodford for helpful discussions.

References

Araujo, A. (1985). "Lack of equilibria in economies with infinitely many commodities: The need for impatience," *Econometrica* **53**, 455–462.

Arrow, K. (1964). "The role of securities in the optimal allocation of risk-bearing," *Rev. Econ. Studies* **31**, 91–96.

Balasko, Y., and D. Cass (1989). "The structure of financial equilibrium with exogenous yields: The case of incomplete markets," *Econometrica* **57**, 135–162.

Balasko, Y., and K. Shell (1981). "The overlapping generations model. III. The case of log-linear utility functions," *J. Econ. Theory* **24**, 143–152.

Bewley, T. (1980). "The optimum quantity of money," in *Models of Monetary Economics*, J. Kareken and N. Wallace (eds.) (Federal Reserve Bank of Minneapolis), pp. 169–210.

Boldrin, M., and M. Woodford (1990). "Equilibrium models displaying endogenous fluctuations and chaos," *J. Mon. Econ.* **25**, 189–222.

Cass, D. (1984). "Competitive equilibrium with incomplete financial markets," CARESS Working Paper No. 84-09, University of Pennsylvania.

Cass, D. (1985). "On the 'number' of equilibrium allocations with incomplete financial markets," CARESS Working Paper No. 85-16, University of Pennsylvania.

Debreu, G. (1972). "Smooth preferences," *Econometrica* **40**, 603–615.

Drèze, J. (1974). "Investment under private ownership: Optimality, equilibrium and stability," in *Allocation under Uncertainty: Equilibria and Optimality*, J. Drèze (ed.) (Wiley, New York), pp. 129–165.

Duffie, D. (1987). "Stochastic equilibrium with incomplete financial markets," *J. Econ. Theory* **41**, 405–416.

Duffie, D. (1990). "The nature of incomplete security markets," mimeograph, Stanford University, Stanford, Calif.

Duffie, D., J. Geanakoplos, A. Mas-Colell, and A. McLennan (1988). "Stationary Markov equilibria," mimeograph, Harvard University.

Duffie, D., and W. Shafer (1985). "Equilibrium in incomplete markets, I," *J. Math. Econ.* **14**, 285–300.

Duffie, D., and W. Shafer (1986). "Equilibrium in incomplete markets, II," *J. Math. Econ.* **15**, 199–216.

Geanakoplos, J., and A. Mas-Colell (1989). "Real indeterminacy with financial assets," *J. Econ. Theory* **47**, 22–38.

Geanakoplos, J., and H. Polemarchakis (1986). "Existence, regularity and constrained suboptimality of competitive allocations when markets are incomplete," in *Essays in Honor of Kenneth Arrow*, Vol. 3, W. Heller, R. Starr, and D. Starrett (eds.) (Cambridge University Press, Cambridge, U.K.), pp. 65–95.

Green, R., and S. Spear (1987). "Equilibria in large commodity spaces with incomplete financial markets," mimeograph.

Grossman, S., and R. Shiller (1981). "The determinants of the variability of stock market prices," *Am. Econ. Rev.* **71**, 222–227.

Hansen, L., and R. Jaganathan (1990). "Implications of security market data for models of dynamic economies," mimeograph, University of Chicago.

Hansen, L., and K. Singleton (1983). "Stochastic consumption, risk aversion and the temporal behavior of asset returns," *J. Polit. Econ.* **91**, 249–266.

Hart, O. (1975). "On the optimality of equilibrium when the market structure is incomplete," *J. Econ. Theory* **11**, 418–443.

Hayashi, F. (1985). "The effect of liquidity constraints on consumption: A cross-sectional analysis." *Quart. J. Econ.* **100**, 183–206.

Henández, A. (1989). "Existence of equilibrium with borrowing constraints: The deterministic case," CORE Discussion Paper No. 8916.

Hernández, A., and M. Santos (1992). "Competitive equilibria in infinite horizon economies with incomplete financial markets," mimeograph, Universidad Carlos III de Madrid.

Levine, D. (1989). "Infinite horizon equilibrium with incomplete markets," *J. Math. Econ.* **18**, 357–376.

Magill, M., and M. Quinzii (1989). "Real effects of money with nominal assets," mimeograph, University of Southern California.

Mas-Colell, A., and P. Monteiro (1991). "Self-fulfilling equilibria: An existence theorem for a general state space," mimeograph, Harvard University.

Radner, R. (1972). "Existence of equilibrium of plans, prices and price expectations in a sequence of markets," *Econometrica* **40**, 289–303.

Santos, M. (1990). "Existence of equilibria for monetary economies," *Int. Econ. Rev.* **31**, 783–797.

Santos, M. and J. Bona (1989). "On the structure of the equilibrium price set of overlapping generations economies," *J. Math. Econ.* **18**, 209–231.

Santos, M., and M. Woodford (1992). "Rational pricing bubbles," mimeograph, University of Chicago.

Schmachtenberg, W. (1989). "Stochastic overlapping generations models with incomplete financial markets," mimeograph, Universität Mannheim (Germany).

Werner, J. (1985). "Equilibrium in economies with incomplete financial markets," *J. Econ. Theory* **36**, 110–119.

Werner, J. (1990). "Structure of financial markets and real indeterminacy of equilibrium," *J. Math. Econ.* **19**, 217–232.

Zame, W. (1989). "Asymptotic behavior of asset markets: Asymptotic efficiency," mimeograph, University of California, Los Angeles.

Zeldes, S. (1989). "Consumption and liquidity constraints: An empirical investigation," *J. Polit. Econ.* **97**, 305–346.

COMMODITY PAIR DESIRABILITY AND THE CORE EQUIVALENCE THEOREM

Aldo Rustichini
Department of Economics
New York University
New York 10003

Nicholas C. Yannelis
Department of Economics
University of Illinois at Urbana-Champaign
Champaign, Illinois 61820

1. INTRODUCTION

The purpose of this paper is to study the core-Walras equivalence in economies with a continuum of agents and with an infinite-dimensional commodity space.

It may be useful to discuss briefly the general importance of infinite-dimensional commodity spaces in economics. As others have noted (e.g., Court, 1941; Debreu, 1954; Gabszewicz, 1991; Bewley, 1970; and Peleg-Yaari, 1970), infinite-dimensional commodity spaces arise quite naturally in economics. In particular, an infinite-dimensional commodity space may be desirable in problems involving an infinite time horizon, uncertainty about the possibly infinite number of states of nature of the world, or infinite varieties of commodity characteristics. For instance, the Lebesgue space L_∞ of bounded measurable functions on a measure space considered by Bewley (1970), Gabszewicz (1991), and Mertens (1991) is useful in modeling uncertainty or an infinite time horizon. The space L_2 of square-integrable functions on a measure space is useful in modeling the trading of long-lived securities over time. Finally, the space $M(\Omega)$ of measures on a compact metric space considered by Mas-Colell (1975) is useful in modeling differentiated commodities.

In this paper, we study core-Walras equivalence results for perfectly competitive economies with an infinite-dimensional commodity space that is sufficiently general to include all of the spaces that have been found most useful in equilibrium analysis. In particular, we cover all the Lebesgue

GENERAL EQUILIBRIUM, GROWTH, AND TRADE II

spaces L_p, $(1 \leq p \leq \infty)$, the space of measures $M(\Omega)$, and the space of continuous functions on a compact metric space $C(X)$.

It turns out that in infinite-dimensional commodity space whose positive cone has a nonempty (norm) interior one can obtain core-Walras equivalence results under quite mild assumptions. However, in infinite-dimensional commodity spaces whose positive cone has an empty (norm) interior, as Rustichini and Yannelis (1991a) showed, even under quite strong assumptions on preferences and endowments, core-Walras equivalence fails. In particular, those authors showed, that even when preferences are strictly convex, monotone, and weak* continuous and initial endowments are strictly positive, core-Walras equivalence fails to hold. It is important to note that this failure results despite the fact that these assumptions are much stronger than the standard assumptions that guarantee equivalence in the Aumann (1964) finite-dimensional commodity space setting.

Our main objective is to obtain core-Walras equivalence for infinite-dimensional commodity spaces (in particular, Banach lattices) whose positive cone may have an empty (norm) interior and are general enough to cover the space L_p $(1 \leq p \leq \infty)$ and $M(\Omega)$. In view of the Rustichini–Yannelis counterexample to the core-Walras equivalence in spaces whose positive cone has an empty interior, we introduce a new condition on preferences called *commodity pair desirability*. In essence, this assumption is a strengthening of the assumption of an extremely desirable commodity used in Yannelis and Zame (1986), which in turn is related to the condition of uniform properness in Mas-Colell (1986) (see also Chichilnisky and Kalman, 1980; and Chichilnisky, 1993). All of these assumptions are essentially bounds on the marginal rate of substitution, and in practice turn out to be quite weak. For example, all three of these assumptions are automatically satisfied whenever preferences are monotone and the positive cone of the commodity space has a nonempty (norm) interior. Hence, this assumption is implicit in the infinite dimensional work of Gabszewicz (1991), Mertens (1991), and Bewley (1973), and is automatically satisfied in the finite-dimensional work of Aumann (1964) and Schmeidler and Hildenbrand (Hildenbrand, 1972, 1974).[1] We also wish to note that in addition to the commodity pair desirability assumption, the lattice structure of the commodity space will play a crucial role in our analysis.

The remainder of the paper is organized as follows. Section 2 contains notation, definitions, and some results on Banach lattices and the integration of correspondences. The economic model is outlined in Section 3, where we also prove a core-Walras equivalence theorem for an ordered separable Banach space of commodities, whose positive cone has a

[1]Hildenbrand (1972, p. 85) attributes the proof to Schmeidler.

nonempty (norm) interior. The central assumption of the paper, commodity pair desirability, is introduced in Section 4. In Section 5 we prove a core-Walras equivalence result for a commodity space that can be any arbitrary separable Banach lattice, provided that the assumption of commodity pair desirability holds. Finally, some concluding remarks are given in Section 6.

2. PRELIMINARIES

2.1 Notation

R^l denotes the l-fold Cartesian product of the set of real numbers R.
int A denotes the interior of the set A.
2^A denotes the set of all nonempty subsets of the set A.
$\emptyset$ denotes the empty set.
/ denotes the set theoretic subtraction.
dist denotes distance.
If $A \subset X$, where X, is a Banach space, cl A denotes the norm closure of A.

If X is a Banach space, its dual is the space X^* of all continuous linear functionals on X.

If $q \in X^*$ and $y \in X$, the value of q at y is denoted by $q \cdot y$.

2.2 Definitions

We begin by collecting some useful notions on Banach lattices (a more detailed exposition may be found in Aliprantis and Burkinshaw (1978, 1985), which will be needed in the sequel.

A *normed vector square* is a real vector space E equipped with a norm $\|\cdot\|: E \to [0, \infty)$ satisfying

(i) $\|x\| \geq 0$ for all x in E, and $\|x\| = 0$ if and only if $x = 0$;
(ii) $\|\alpha x\| = |\alpha| \, \|x\|$ for all x in E and all α in R;
(iii) $\|x + y\| \leq \|x\| + \|y\|$ for all x, y in E.

A *Banach space* is a normed vector space for which the metric induced by the norm is complete.

If E is a Banach space, then its *dual space* E^* is the set of continuous linear functionals on E. The dual space E^* is itself a Banach space, when equipped with the norm

$$\|\phi\| = \sup\{|\phi(x)|: x \in E, \|x\| \leq 1\}.$$

A *Banach lattice* is a Banach space L endowed with a partial order $\leq$ (i.e., $\leq$ is a reflexive, antisymmetric, transitive relation) satisfying

1. $x \leq y$ implies $x + z \leq y + z$ (for all $x, y, z \in L$).
2. $x \leq y$ implies $tx \leq ty$ (for all $x, y \in L$, all real numbers $t \geq 0$).
3. Every pair of elements $x, y \in L$ has a supremum (least upper bound) $x \vee y$ and an infimum (greatest lower bound) $x \wedge y$.
4. $|x| \leq |y|$ implies $\|x\| \leq \|y\|$ (for all $x, y \in L$).

Here we have written, as $|x| = x^+ + x^-$ where $x^+ = x \vee 0$, $x^- = (-x) \vee 0$; we call x^+, x^- the *positive* and *negative parts* of x, respectively and $|x|$ the *absolute value* of x. Note that $x = x^+ - x^-$, and that $x^+ \wedge x^- = 0$. We say that $x \in L$ is *positive* if $x \geq 0$; we write L_+ (or L^+) for the set of all positive elements of L and refer to L_+ (or L^+) as the *positive cone* of L.

We will say that an element x of L is *strictly positive* (and write $x \gg 0$) if $\phi(x) > 0$ whenever ϕ is a positive nonzero element of L_+^*. Strictly positive elements are usually called *quasi-interior* to L_+. Note that if the positive cone L_+ of L has a nonempty (norm) interior, then the set of strictly positive elements coincides with the interior of L_+. However, many Banach lattices contain strictly positive elements even though the positive cone L_+ has an empty interior (see Aliprantis and Burkinshaw, 1985, p. 259). We will now give basic examples of separable Banach lattices:

(i) The Euclidean space R^N.
(ii) The space l_p $(1 \leq p < \infty)$ of real sequences (a_n) for which the norm $\|(a_n)\|_p = (\Sigma |a_n|^p)^{1/p}$ is finite.
(iii) The space $L_p(\Omega, \mathbf{R}, \mu)$ $(1 \leq p < \infty)$ of equivalence classes of measurable function f on the separable measure space $(\Omega, \mathbf{R}, \mu)$ for which the norm $\|f\|_p = (\int_\Omega |f|^p \, d\mu)^{1/p}$ is finite.
(iv) The space $C(K)$ of continuous, real-valued functions on the compact Hausdorff space K (with supremum norm).

A basic property of Banach lattices which will play a crucial role in the sequel, is the *Riesz decomposition property*. Let L be a Banach lattice, and let $x, y_1, \ldots, y_n$ be positive elements of L such that $0 \leq x \leq \Sigma_{i=1}^n y_i$. Then there are positive elements $x_1, \ldots, x_n$ in L such that $\Sigma_{i=1}^n x_i = x$ and $0 \leq x_i \leq y_i$ for each i.

We now define some measure-theoretic notions as well as the concepts of a Bochner integrable function and the integral of a correspondence.

Let X, Y be sets. The *graph* of the correspondence $\phi: X \to 2^Y$ is denoted by $G_\phi = \{(x, y) \in X \times Y\colon\ y \in \phi(x)\}$. Let (T, τ, μ) be a finite measure space [i.e., μ is a real-valued, nonnegative countably additive measure defined on a σ-field τ of subsets of T such that $\mu(T) < \infty$], and X be a Banach space. The correspondence ϕ: $T \to 2^X$ is said to have a *measurable graph* if $G_\phi \in \tau \otimes \mathscr{B}(x)$, where $\mathscr{B}(X)$ denotes the Borel σ-algebra on X and $\otimes$ denotes the product σ-algebra. A function $f\colon T \to X$ is called *simple* if there exist $x_1, x_2, \ldots, x_n$ in X and $a_1, a_2, \ldots, a_n$ in τ such that $f = \Sigma_{i=1}^n x_i \chi_{a_i}$, where $\chi_{a_i}(t) = 1$ if $t \in a_i$ and $\chi_{a_i}(t) = 0$ if $t \notin a_i$. A function $f\colon T \to X$ is said to be *μ-measurable* if there exists a sequence of simple functions $f_n\colon T \to X$ such that $\lim_{n\to\infty} \|f_n(t) - f(t)\| = 0$ μ-a.e. A μ-measurable function $f\colon T \to X$ is said to be *Bochner integrable* if there exists a sequence of simple functions $\{f_n\colon n = 1, 2, \ldots\}$ such that

$$\lim_{\mu\to\infty} \int_T \| f_n(t) - f(t) \| \, d\mu(t) = 0.$$

In this case we define for each $E \in \tau$ the integral to be $\int_E f(t)\, d\mu(t) = \lim_{n\to\infty} \int_E f_n(t)\, d\mu(t)$. It can be easily shown (see Diestel and Uhl, 1977, p. 45) that if $f\colon T \to X$ is a μ-measurable function, then f is Bochner integrable if and only if $\int_T \|f(t)\|\, d\mu(t) < \infty$. We denote by $L_1(\mu, X)$ the space of equivalence classes of X-valued Bochner integrable functions $x\colon T \to X$ normed by $\|x\| = \int_T \|x(t)\|\, d\mu(t)$. Note that one can easily show that if (T, τ, μ) is atomless, the subset of simple functions given by $B = \{x\colon T \to X,\ x = \Sigma_{i=1}^m x_i \chi_{T_i},\ \mu(T_i) = (1/m)\}$ is norm-dense in $L_1(\mu, X)$. Moreover, we denote by S_ϕ the *set of all X-valued Bochner integrable selections from the correspondence* $\phi\colon T \to 2^X$, i.e.,

$$S_\phi = \{x \in L_1(\mu, X)\colon x(t) \in \phi(t)\ \mu\text{-a.e.}\}.$$

The *integral of the correspondence* $\phi\colon T \to 2^X$ is defined as

$$\int_T \phi(t)\, d\mu(t) = \left\{ \int_T x(t)\, d\mu(t)\colon x \in S_\phi \right\}.$$

In the sequel we will denote the above integral by

$$\int \phi \quad \text{or} \quad \int_T \phi.$$

2.3 Lemmata

If (T, τ, μ) is atomless and $X = R^l$, it follows from Lyapunov's theorem that the integral of the correspondence $\phi\colon T \to 2^X$, i.e., $\int \phi$, is convex. However, this result is false in infinite-dimensional spaces (see, e.g., Yannelis, 1991). Nevertheless, it can be easily deduced (see, e.g., Hiai and Umegaki (1977), Khan 1985; or Yannelis (1991) from the approximate version of Lyapunov's theorem in infinite-dimensional spaces that the norm closure of $\int \phi$, i.e., cl $\int \phi$, is convex. More formally, the following Lemma is true.

LEMMA 2.1. *Let (T, τ, μ) be a finite atomles measure space, X be a Banach space, and $\phi: T \to 2^X$ be a correspondence. Then* cl $\int\phi$ *is convex.*

We will also need the following result whose proof follows from the measurable selection theorem and can be found in Hiai and Umegaki (1977, Theorem 2.2, p. 156).

LEMMA 2.2. *Let (T, τ, μ) be a finite measure space, X be a separable Banach space, and $\phi: T \to 2^X$ be a correspondence having a measurable graph. Suppose that $\int\phi \neq \emptyset$. Then for every $p \in X^*$ we have that*

$$\inf_{z \in \int\phi} p \cdot z = \int \inf_{y \in \phi(\cdot)} p \cdot y.$$

It should be noted that Lemma 2.2 has been proved in Hildenbrand (1974, Proposition 6, p. 63) for $X = R^l$. However, by recalling that the Aumann measurable selection theorem holds in separable metric spaces, one can easily see that Hildenbrand's argument remains true in separable Banach spaces. In fact, it is even true in arbitrary Hausdorff separable and metrizable linear topological spaces.

With all these preliminaries out of the way, we can now turn to our model.

3. THE MODEL AND A PRELIMINARY THEOREM

Denote by E the commodity space. Throughout this section the commodity space E will be an ordered Banach space.

An *economy* $\mathscr{E}$ is a quadruple $[(T, \tau, \mu), X, \succ_t, e]$, where

1. (T, τ, μ) is a *measure space of agents*.
2. $X: T \to 2^E$ is the *consumption correspondence*.
3. $\succ_t \subset X(t) \times X(t)$ is the *preference relation* of agent t.
4. $e: T \to E$ is the *initial endowment*, where e is Bochner integrable and $e(t) \in X(t)$ for all $t \in T$.

An *allocation* for the economy $\mathscr{E}$ is a Bochner integrable function $x: T \to E_+$. An allocation x is said to be *feasible* if $\int_T x(t)\, d\mu(t) = \int_T e(t)\, d\mu(t)$. A *coalition* S is an element of τ such that $\mu(S) > 0$. The coalition S can *improve on* the allocation x if there exists an allocation g such that

(i) $g(t) \succ_t x(t)$ μ-a.e. in S.
(ii) $\int_S g(t)\, d\mu(t) = \int_S e(t)\, d\mu(t)$.

The set of all feasible allocations for the economy $\mathscr{E}$ that no coalition can improve on is called the *core* of the economy $\mathscr{E}$ and is denoted by $\mathscr{C}(\mathscr{E})$.

An allocation x and a price $p \in E_+^*/\{0\}$ are said to be a *competitive equilibrium* (or a *Walras equilibrium*) for the economy $\mathscr{E}$, if

(i) $x(t)$ is a maximal element for $\succ_t$ in the budget set $\{y \in X(t): p \cdot y \leq p \cdot e(t)\}$ μ—a.e.
(ii) $\int_T x(t)\, d\mu(t) = \int_T e(t)\, d\mu(t)$.

We denote by $W(\mathscr{E})$ the set of all competitive equilibria for the economy $\mathscr{E}$.

We begin by stating some assumptions needed for the proof of our core-Walras equivalence result.

a0. E is an ordered separable Banach space whose positive cone E_+ has a nonempty norm interior, i.e., int $E_+ \neq \emptyset$.

a1. (*Perfect competition*): (T, τ, μ) is a finite atomless measure space.

a2. $X(t) = E_+$ for all $t \in T$.

a3. (*Resource availability*): The aggregate initial endowment $\int_T e(t)\, d\mu(t)$ is strictly positive, i.e., $\int e \gg 0$.

a4. (*Continuity*): For each $x \in E_+$ the set $\{y \in E_+ \colon y \succ_t x\}$ is norm open in E_+ for all $t \in T$,

a5. $\succ_t$ is irreflexive and transitive for all $t \in T$.

a6. (*Measurability*): The set $\{(t, y) \in T \times E_+ \colon y \succ_t x\}$ belongs to $\tau \otimes \mathscr{B}(E_+)$.

a7. (*Monotonicity*): If $x \in E_+$ and $v \in E_+/\{0\}$, then $x + v \succ_t x$ for all $t \in T$.

Theorem 3.1 (below) is taken from Rustichini and Yannelis (1991). Since the second part of the proof of Theorem 3.1 is the same as that of Theorem 5.1, we will provide the argument for the sake of completeness. It should be noted, that in view of Remark 3.1 (see below), Theorem 3.1 is more general than Theorem 4.1 of Rustichini and Yannelis (1991). In particular, E need not be separable.

THEOREM 3.1. *Under assumption* a0–a7, $\mathscr{C}(\mathscr{E}) = W(\mathscr{E})$.

Proof. The fact that $W(\mathscr{E}) \subset \mathscr{C}(\mathscr{E})$ is well known, and therefore its proof is not repeated here. We begin the proof by assuming that the allocation x is an element of the core of $\mathscr{E}$. We wish to show that for some price p, the pair (x, p) is a competitive equilibrium for $\mathscr{E}$.

To this end, define the correspondence $\phi\colon T \to 2^{E_+}$ by

$$\phi(t) = \{z \in E_+ \colon z \succ_t x(t)\} \cup \{e(t)\}. \tag{3.0}$$

We claim that

$$\operatorname{cl}\left(\int_T \phi - \int_T e\right) \cap \operatorname{int} E_- = \emptyset, \tag{3.1}$$

or equivalently,[2]

$$\left(\int_T \phi - \int_T e\right) \cap \operatorname{int} E_- = \varnothing. \tag{3.2}$$

Suppose otherwise, i.e.,

$$\left(\int_T \phi - \int_T e\right) \cap \operatorname{int} E_- \neq \varnothing$$

then there exists $v \in \operatorname{int} E_+$ such that

$$\int e - v \in \int \phi. \tag{3.3}$$

It follows from (3.3) that there exists a function y: $T \to E_+$ such that

$$\int_T y = \int_T e - v, \tag{3.4}$$

and $y(t) \in \phi(t)$ μ-a.e.

Let

$$S = \{t\colon y(t) \succ_t x(t)\};$$
$$S' = \{t\colon y(t) = e(t)\}.$$

Since $\int y \neq \int e$, we have that $\mu(S) > 0$. Define $\tilde{y}$: $S \to E_+$ by $\tilde{y}(t) = y(t) + [y/\mu(S)]$ for all $t \in S$. By monotonicity (assumption a7), $\tilde{y}(t) \succ_t y(t)$. Since $y(t) \succ_t x(t)$ for all $t \in S$, by transitivity (assumption a5) $\tilde{y}(t) \succ_t x(t)$ for all $t \in S$. Moreover, it can be easily seen that $\tilde{y}(\cdot)$ is feasible for the coalition S, i.e.,

$$\int_S \tilde{y} = \int_S y + v = \int_T y - \int_{S'} e + v$$
$$= \int_T e - \int_{S'} e = \int_S e \qquad \text{[recall (3.4)]}$$

Therefore, we have found an allocation $\tilde{y}(\cdot)$ that is feasible for the coalition S and is also preferred to the allocation x, which in turn was assumed to be in the core of $\mathscr{E}$, a blatant contradiction. The above contradiction establishes the validity of (3.1).

We are now in a position to separate the set $\operatorname{cl}(\int\phi - \int e) = \operatorname{cl}\int\phi - \int e$ from $\operatorname{int} E_-$. Clearly the set $\operatorname{int} E_+$ is convex and nonempty as well.

[2]This is so since $\operatorname{int} E_-$ is an open set. In particular if A and B are subsets of any topological space and B is open, then it can be easily seen that $A \cap B = \varnothing$ if and only if $\operatorname{cl} A \cap B = \varnothing$.

Observe first that by the definition of $\phi(\cdot)$, 0 is an element of $\int\phi - \int e$ and this shows that cl $\int\phi - \int e$ is nonempty. Since, (T, τ, μ) is atomless (assumption a1) by Lemma 2.1 cl $\int\phi$ is convex. Thus, by Theorem 9.10 in Aliprantis and Burkinshaw (1985, p. 136) there exists a continuous linear functional $p \in E^*/\{0\}$, $p \geq 0$ such that

$$p \cdot y \geq p \cdot \int e \quad \text{for all } y \in \int \phi. \tag{3.5}$$

Since by assumption a6, $\succ_t$ has a measurable graph, so does $\phi(\cdot)$, i.e., $G_\phi \in \tau \otimes \mathscr{B}(E_+)$. Therefore, it follows from Lemma 2.2 that

$$\inf_{y \in \int\phi} p \cdot y = \int \inf_{z \in \phi(\cdot)} p \cdot z \geq \int p \cdot e. \tag{3.6}$$

It follows from (3.6) that

$$\mu\text{—a.e. } p \cdot z \geq p \cdot e(t) \quad \text{for all } z \succ_t X(t). \tag{3.7}$$

To see this, suppose that for $z \in \phi(\cdot)$, $p \cdot z < p \cdot e(t)$ for all $t \in S$, $\mu(S) > 0$.

Define the function $\tilde{z}\colon T \to E_+$ by

$$\tilde{z}(t) = \begin{cases} z(t) & \text{if } t \in S, \\ e(t) & \text{if } t \notin S. \end{cases}$$

Obviously, $\tilde{z} \in \phi(\cdot)$. Moreover,

$$\begin{aligned} \int_T p \cdot \tilde{z} &= \int_S p \cdot z + \int_{T/S} p \cdot e \\ &< \int_S p \cdot e + \int_{T/S} p \cdot e = \int p \cdot e, \end{aligned}$$

a contradiction of (3.6).

We now show that μ—a.e. $p \cdot x(t) = p \cdot e(t)$. First note that it follows directly from (3.7) that $p \cdot x(t) \geq p \cdot e(t)$ μ—a.e. If now $p \cdot x(t) > p \cdot e(t)$ for all $t \in S$, $\mu(S) > 0$, then,

$$\begin{aligned} p \cdot \int_T x &= p \cdot \int_{T/S} x + p \cdot \int_S x \\ &> p \cdot \int_{T/S} e + p \cdot \int_S e = p \cdot \int_T e, \end{aligned}$$

contradicting $\int_T x = \int_T e$, since $p \geq 0$, $p \neq 0$.

To complete the proof we must show that $x(t)$ is maximal in the budget set $\{z \in E_+ : p \cdot e(t)\}$ μ—a.e. The argument is now routine. Since $\int_T e$ is strictly positive (assumption a3), it follows that $\mu(\{t: p \cdot e(t)\})\} > 0$, for if $p \cdot e(t) = 0$ μ—a.e., then $p \cdot \int e = 0$, contradicting the fact that $\int e$ is strictly positive since $p \geq 0$, $p \neq 0$.

Thus, we can safely pick an agent t with positive income, i.e., $p \cdot e(t) > 0$. Since $p \cdot e(t) > 0$, there exists an allocation x' such that $p \cdot x' < p \cdot e(t)$. Let y be such that $p \cdot y \leq p \cdot e(t)$, and let $y(\lambda) = \lambda x' + (1 - \lambda)y$ for $\lambda \in (0, 1)$. Then for any $\lambda \in (0, 1)$, $p \cdot y(\lambda) < p \cdot e(t)$, and by (3.7), $y(\lambda) \not\succ_t x(t)$, where $y \not\succ x$ denotes it is not the case that $y \succ x$. It follows from the norm continuity of $\succ_t$ (assumption a4) that $y \not\succ_t x(t)$. This proves that $x(t)$ is maximal in the budget set of agent t, i.e., $\{w: p \cdot w \leq p \cdot e(t)\}$. This, together with the monotonicity of preferences (assumption a7), implies that prices are strictly positive, i.e., $p \gg 0$. Indeed, if there exists $v \in E_+/\{0\}$ such that $p \cdot v = 0$, then $p \cdot (x(t) + v) = p \cdot e(t)$ and by monotonicity $x(t) + v \succ_t x(t)$, contradicting the maximality of $x(t)$ in the budget set.

Thus $p \gg 0$ and $x(t)$ is maximal in the budget set whenever $p \cdot e(t) > 0$. Consider now an agent t with zero income, i.e., $p \cdot e(t) = 0$. Since $p \gg 0$, that agent's budget set $\{z: p \cdot z = 0\}$ consists of zero only, and moreover, $p \cdot x(t) = p \cdot e(t) = 0$. Hence, $x(t) = 0$ for almost all $t \in T$, with $p \cdot e(t) = 0$; i.e., zero in this case is the maximal element in the budget set. Consequently, (p, x) is a competitive equilibrium for $\mathscr{E}$, and this completes the proof of Theorem 3.1.

Remark 3.1. It is possible to relax the assumption that E is separable. The argument (which is given to us by one of the referees) proceeds as follows. As before, we can obtain (3.5), i.e., there exists $p \in E^*/\{0\}$, $p \geq 0$ such that

$$p \cdot y \geq p \cdot \int e \quad \text{for all } y \in \int \phi.$$

We now show that $p \cdot x(t) = p \cdot e(t)$ μ—a.e. Let $S \subset T$, $\mu(S) > 0$, $\varepsilon > 0$, and $v \in E_{++}$. Define $x' : T \to E$ by

$$x'(t) = \begin{cases} x(t) + \varepsilon v & \text{if } t \in S, \\ e(t) & \text{if } t \notin S. \end{cases} \tag{3.8}$$

Then $x' \in S_\phi$ for all $S \subset T$. Hence,

$$p \cdot \left[\int_S x + \varepsilon v \mu(S) + \int_{T/S} e \right] > p \cdot e$$

and rearranging, we have that $\int_s p \cdot x \geq \int_s p \cdot e$ for any $S \subset T$ since $\varepsilon > 0$ is arbitrary. Thus, it follows (since S is arbitrary) that $p \cdot x(t) \geq p \cdot e(t)$ μ—a.e. Since x is feasible, i.e., $\int x = \int e$, we must have that $\int p \cdot x = \int p \cdot e$ and therefore $p \cdot x(t) = p \cdot e(t)$ μ—a.e. Now (3.7) follows by replacing in (3.8) $x + \varepsilon v$ by $z \in \phi(\cdot)$. We then have that $\int_s p \cdot z + \int_{t \in T/S} p \cdot e \geq \int p \cdot e$. Rearranging, we obtain $\int_s p \cdot z \geq \int p \cdot e,\ z \in S_\phi$, and we can conclude (since S is arbitrary) that μ—a.e. $p \cdot z \geq p \cdot e(t)$ for all $z \succ_t x(t)$. The rest of the proof is now identical with the one outlined above in the proof of Theorem 3.1.

Note that in the above step we avoided Lemma 2.2, which requires the use of the measurable selection theorem (recall that for Lemma 2.2, E needs to be separable), and as a consequence we do not need to assume that E is separable. In fact, one does not even need to assume that $\succ_t$ has a measurable graph (recall assumption a6).

It turns out that if one drops the assumption that the positive cone of the space E has a nonempty interior, then the preceding theorem fails. A counterexample to that effect can be found in Rustichini and Yannelis (1991a). In order to remedy this difficulty, we introduce the assumption of commodity pair desirability.

4. EXTREMELY DESIRABLE COMMODITIES AND COMMODITY PAIR DESIRABILITY

For notational convenience, in the following text we drop the subscript t on the preference relation $\succ$. We begin by defining the notion of an extremely desirable commodity. Let E be a Banach lattice and denote its positive cone (which may have an empty norm interior) by E_+. Let $v \in E_+$, $v \neq 0$, and U be an open neighborhood of zero. We say that $v \in E_+$ is an *extremely desirable commodity* if there exists U such that for each $x \in E_+$ we have that $x + \alpha v - z \succ x$ whenever $\alpha > 0$, $z \leq \alpha v$, and $z \in \alpha U$. In other words, v is extremely desirable if an agent would prefer to trade any commodity bundle z for an additional increment of the commodity bundle v, provided the size of z is sufficiently small compared to the increment of v. The above notion has a natural geometric interpretation. In particular, let $v \in E_+$, $v \neq 0, U$ be an open neighborhood and define the open cone C as follows:

$$C = \{\alpha v - z : \alpha > 0,\ z \in E,\ z \in \alpha U\}.$$

The bundle v is said to be an extremely desirable commodity, if for each $x \in E_+$, we have $y \succ x$ whenever y is an element of $(C + x) \cap E_+$. Note that this implies that v is an extremely desirable commodity if for each $x \in E_+$ we have that $((-C + x) \cap E_+) \cap \{y : y \succ x\} = \varnothing$, or equivalently

$-C \cap \{y - x \in E_+ \colon\ y \succ x\} = \varnothing$. The latter property is precisely the assumption we need for the core-Walras equivalence if we consider L_p as a commodity space $1 \leq p < \infty$ (see Rustichini and Yannelis, 1991a).

Recall that if the preference relation $\succ$ is monotone and int $E_+ \neq \varnothing$, then the assumption of an extremely desirable commodity is automatically satisfied (see, e.g., Yannelis and Zame, 1984).

We now turn to a strengthening of the preceding assumption. A pair $(x, y) \in E_+ \times E_+$ is said to be a *desirable commodity pair* if for every $z \in E_+$ we have $z + x - y \succ_t z$ whenever $y \leq x + z$ for each $t \in T$. The pair $(x, y) \in E \times E$ is said to have the *splitting property* if for any m-tuple $(s_1, \ldots, s_m) \in E \times \cdots \times E$ such that $\sum_{i=1}^m s_i = (x - y)^-$ there exists an m-tuple $(d_1, \ldots, d_m) \in E \times \cdots \times E$ such that $\sum_{i=1}^m d_i = (x - y)^+$ and the pair (d_i, s_i) is a desirable commodity pair.

We are now ready to define our key notion.

Definition 4.1. *Commodity pair desirability* obtains if there exists a $v \in E_+$, $v \neq 0$, and a neighborhood U of zero such that any commodity pair (w, u) of the form $w = \alpha v$, $\alpha > 0$, and $u \in \alpha U$ has the splitting property.

Let us discuss briefly the intuitive meaning of the commodity pair desirability condition. It may be considered as an extension to a multiperson setting of the idea of desirable commodity pair for the case of a single-agent decision. In this last case a pair (x, y) is desirable if the agent is always willing to trade the bundle y in exchange for a bundle x, that is, to accept the gain $(x - y)^+$ in exchange for the loss $(x - y)^-$. In the case of the splitting property we can imagine that the offer of exchanging $(x - y)^-$ for $(x - y)^+$ is presented to a group of m players. The splitting property that we introduce asks that no matter how the reduction in the consumption bundle [given by $(x - y)^-$] is allocated over the members of the group, they can always find a way of allocating the surplus [$(x - y)^+$] and make everyone better off.

Obviously this concept is a substitutability condition that roughly says that an agent would accept a sufficiently small amount of the commodity bundle s_i if he or she would be compensated by consuming more of the desirable commodity bundle d_i.[3]

A couple of comments are in order. First, notice that for $m = 1$ in the above definition we have that for any $z \in E_+$, $z + (w - u)^+ - (w - u)^- = z - w - u \succ z$ whenever $u \leq z + w$, $w = \alpha v$, $\alpha > 0$, and $u \in \alpha U$, i.e., for $m = 1$ we are reduced to the assumption of an extremely desirable commodity.

[3] Note that since we have allowed splitting for $(w - u)^-$ and $(w - u)^+$, we may think of i $(i = 1, 2, \ldots, m)$ as agents and the splitting property as a kind of redistribution. Hence, the notion of commodity pair desirability is a "coalitional type" of uniform properness.

Moreover, it is easy to show that if int $E_+ \neq \varnothing$ and the preference relation $\succ$ is monotone, then the condition of commodity pair desirability is automatically satisfied. Specifically, let $v \in \text{int } E_+$ and U be such that $v + U \subset E_+$, then for any pair (w, u) with $w = \alpha v$, $\alpha > 0$, $u \in \alpha U$ we have $(w - u) \in E_+$ so $(w - u)^- = 0$ and therefore by monotonicity for any $z \in E_+$, $z + w - u \succ z$.

5. CORE-WALRAS EQUIVALENCE IN BANACH LATTICES WHOSE POSITIVE CONE HAS AN EMPTY INTERIOR

In this section we state and prove our main result, i.e., a core-Walras equivalence theorem for a commodity space that can be any arbitrary separable Banach lattice whose positive cone may have an empty norm interior. We begin by stating the following assumptions:

a0′. E is any separable Banach lattice.

a8. (*Commodity pair desirability*): There exists $v \in E_+/\{0\}$ and an open neighborhood U of zero such that any commodity pair (w, u) of the form $w = \alpha v$, $\alpha > 0$, and $u \in \alpha U$, has the splitting property.

We are now ready to state and prove the following result.

THEOREM 5.1. *Under assumptions* a0′, a1–a8, $\mathscr{C}(\mathscr{E}) = W(\mathscr{E})$.

Proof. It can be easily shown that $W(\mathscr{E}) \subset \mathscr{C}(\mathscr{E})$. Hence, we will show that if $x \in \mathscr{C}(\mathscr{E})$, then for some price p, the pair (x, p) is a competitive equilibrium for $\mathscr{E}$. Define the correspondence ϕ: $T \to 2^{E_+}$ by

$$\phi(t) = \{z \in E_+ : z \succ_t x(t)\} \cup \{e(t)\}. \tag{5.1}$$

Let $C = \bigcup_{\alpha > 0} \alpha(v - U)$, where $v \in E_+/\{0\}$ and U given as in assumption a8. We claim that

$$\text{cl}\left(\int \phi - \int e\right) \cap -C = \varnothing \tag{5.2}$$

or equivalently

$$\left(\int \phi - \int e\right) \cap -C = \varnothing. \tag{5.3}$$

Since $-C$ is open, it suffices to show that for any $y \in S_\phi$ there exists a sequence $\{(\bar{y}^k, \bar{e}^k): k = 1, 2, \dots\}$ such that $\bar{y}^k$ converges in the $L_1(\mu, E)$

norm to y, $\int \bar{e}^k \to \int e$, and

$$\int_T \bar{y}^k - \int_T \bar{e}^k \notin -C. \tag{5.4}$$

Let $S = \{t\colon y(t) \succ_t x(t)\}$, $S' = T/S$. Without loss of generality we may assume that $\mu(S) > 0$. [For if $\mu(S) = 0$, then $y(t) = e(t)$ μ—a.e., which implies that $\int y - \int e = \notin -C$; consequently, (5.3) holds.] In the following argument y and e are restricted to S. Moreover, denote by μ_S the restriction of μ to S. Since $y\colon S \to E_+$ is Bochner integrable and $\succ_t$ is norm continuous (assumption a4), there exist $y_1^k, \ldots, y_{m_k}^k$ in E_+ and $T_1^k, T_2^k, \ldots, T_{m_k}^k$ in τ such that y^k converges in the $L_1(\mu_S, E)$ norm to y, and

$$y^k = \sum_{i=1}^{m_k} y_k^i \chi_{T_i^k} \tag{5.5}$$

$$y_i^k \succ_t X(t) \quad \text{for all } t \in T_i^k \text{ and all } i, i = 1, \ldots, m_k, \quad \text{and} \tag{5.6}$$

$$\mu_S(T_i^k) = \xi, \qquad i = 1, \ldots, m_k. \tag{5.7}$$

Let $e^k = \sum_{i=1}^{m_k}(\int_{T_i^k} e(t)\, d\mu(t))\chi_{T_i^k}$. In order to establish (5.4), we first show that

$$\int_S y^k - \int_S e^k \notin C. \tag{5.8}$$

Suppose that (5.8) is false; then

$$\sum_{i=1}^{m_k} y_i^k \xi - \sum_{i=1}^{m_k} e_i^k \xi e - \alpha(v + U);$$

and therefore

$$\sum_{i=1}^{m_k} y_i^k + w - u = \sum_{i=1}^{m_k} e_i^k, \tag{5.9}$$

where $x = (\alpha/\xi)v$, $u \in (\alpha/\xi)U$.

Since $\sum_{i=1}^{m_k} e_i^k \geq 0$, it follows from (5.9) that

$$(w - u)^- \leq \sum_{i=1}^{m_k} y_i^k. \tag{5.10}$$

Applying the Riesz decomposition property to (5.10), we can find $(s_1, \ldots, s_{m_k}) \in E_+ \times \cdots \times E_+$ such that

$$\sum_{i=1}^{m_k} s_i = (w - u)^- \; 0 \leq s_i \leq y_i^k \quad \text{for all } i. \tag{5.11}$$

It follows from the assumption of commodity pair desirability that there exists an m_k-tuple $(d_1, \dots, d_{m_k}) \in E_+ \times \cdots \times E_+$, such that $\sum_{i=1}^{m_k} d_i = (w - u)^+$ and

$$\tilde{y}_i^k = y_i^k + d_i - s_i \succ_t y_i^k \quad \text{for all } t \in T_i^k \text{ and for all } i. \tag{5.12}$$

Note that since $y_i^k \geq s_i$, it follows that $\tilde{y}_i^k \in E^+$. Moreover, since $y_i^k \succ_t x(t)$ for all $t \in T_i^k$ and all i, and $\tilde{y}_i^k \succ_t y_i^k$ for all $t \in T_i^k$ and all i, by transitivity of $\succ_t$ we have that $\tilde{y}_i^k \succ_t x(t)$ for all $t \in T_i^k$ and all i. Also,

$$\sum_{i=1}^{m} \bar{y}_i^k \xi = \sum_{i=1}^{m_k} e_i^k \xi = \int e.$$

Define $\tilde{y}^k = \sum_{i=1}^{m_k} \tilde{y}_i^k \chi_{T_i^k}$. Notice that $\int_S \tilde{y}^k = \int_S e$. Therefore, we have found an allocation $\tilde{y}^k(\cdot)$ feasible for the coalition S and preferred to $x(\cdot)$, which in turn was assumed to be in the core of $\mathscr{E}$, a contradiction. Hence, (5.8) holds.

We are now ready to construct the sequence $\{(\bar{y}^k, \bar{e}^k): k = 1, 2, \dots\}$. In particular, define $\bar{y}^k: T \to E_+$ by

$$\bar{y}^k(t) = \begin{cases} y^k(t) & \text{if } t \in S \\ y(t) & \text{if } t \notin S. \end{cases}$$

Similarly, define $\bar{e}^k: T \to E_+$ by

$$\bar{e}^k(t) = \begin{cases} e^k(t) & \text{if } t \in S \\ e(t) & \text{if } t \notin S. \end{cases}$$

Note that $\int_T \bar{y}^k - \int_T \bar{e}^k \notin -C$ and therefore (5.4) holds. We can now separate the convex nonempty set cl $\int \phi - \int e$ from the convex nonempty set $-C$. Proceeding as in the proof of Theorem 3.1, we can now complete the proof. ■

6. CONCLUDING REMARKS

Remark 6.1. Since in Banach lattices whose positive cone has a nonempty (norm) interior and preferences are monotone, assumption a8 is automatically satisfied, it follows that in such spaces Theorem 3.1 becomes a corollary of Theorem 5.1. However, since in Theorem 3.1 the commodity space is any arbitrary ordered Banach space (i.e., no lattice structure is required), we cannot derive Theorem 3.1 as a corollary of Theorem 5.1.

Remark 6.2. Notice that in Theorem 5.1 the commodity space was assumed to be a Banach lattice. However, in Theorem 3.1 we only needed the commodity space to be an ordered Banach space; i.e., no lattice structure was required. We needed the lattice structure in Theorem 5.1 to apply the Riesz decomposition property, which in turn has a natural economic meaning as was indicated in Yannelis and Zame (1986, p. 89). However, we do not know whether one can dispense with the lattice structure in Theorem 5.1. Aliprantis and Burkinshaw (1991) have shown that the lattice structure is a necessary and sufficient condition for the existence of Edgeworth equilibria in economies with finitely many agents.

Remark 6.3. Using the notion of commodity pair desirability, one can easily prove the second welfare economics theorem for economies with an atomless measure space of agents and with a commodity space that can be any arbitrary separable Banach lattice.

Remark 6.4. It is of interest to know whether under the assumption of Theorem 3.1 we have core-Walras existence as well. It is known, for instance, that this is not true if $X = R^n$ (see Aumann (1966, Section 8, p. 17)); this is also the case here. For instance, under a0–a7 a competitive equilibrium may not exist. However, by replacing a2 by

a2′. $X(t) = K$ for all $t \in T$, where K is a weakly compact convex nonempty subset of E_+,

and adding the assumption:

a11. for all $t \in T$, and for all $x(t) \in X(t)$ the set $\{y\colon y \succ_t x(t)\}$ is convex and the set $\{y\colon x(t) \succ_t y\}$ is norm open,

one can conclude, by virtue of the main theorem in Khan and Yannelis (1986) that both sets, i.e., $\mathscr{C}(\mathscr{E})$ and $W(\mathscr{E})$, are nonempty. Notice that in Khan and Yannelis it is assumed that preferences are convex (see also Bewley, 1991), an assumption which is dispensible in the finite-dimensional case. In fact, as Aumann (1964) showed, the Lyapunov convexity theorem convexifies the aggregate demand set. However, in infinite-dimensional spaces, the Lyapunov convexity result fails. It is also worth mentioning that in addition to the failure of Lyapunov's theorem, Fatou's lemma fails in infinite-dimensional spaces as well (see Yannelis, 1988 or Rustichini, 1989). Hence, there is no exact analog to Schmeidler's version of Fatou's lemma in infinite dimensions. However, approximate versions of Fatou's lemma have been obtained by Khan and Majumdar (1986) and Yannelis (1988). Moreover, with additional assumptions exact versions of Fatou's lemma in infinite-dimensional spaces can be obtained as well (see Rustichini, 1989; and Yannelis, 1988). Nevertheless, the latter versions of the Fatou lemma are not sufficient to prove the existence of Walrasian equilibrium. For more information on this problem see Rustichini and Yannelis (1991b), who have showed that in economies with "many more" agents than commodities, there is a nice convexifying effect on aggregation and the Fatou lemma still holds. As a consequence of this, the theorem on the existence of a Walrasian equilibrium is still true.

Acknowledgments

We would like to thank two anonymous referees for several useful comments. Tom Armstrong made several useful suggestions and special thanks are due to him. Of course, we are responsible for any remaining shortcomings.

References

Aliprantis, C. D., and O. Burkinshaw (1978), *Locally Solid Riesz Spaces* (Academic Press, New York).

Aliprantis, C. D., and O. Burkinshaw (1985), *Positive Operators* (Academic Press, New York).

Aliprantis, C. D., and O. Burkinshaw (1991), "When is the core equivalence theorem valid?" *Econ. Theory* **1**, 164–182.

Aumann, R. J. (1964), "Markets with a continuum of agents," *Econometrica* **22**, 265–290.

Aumann, R. J. (1966), "Existence of competitive equilibria in markets with a continuum of traders," *Econometrica* **34**, 1–17.

Bewley, T. (1970), "Equilibrium theory with an infinite dimensional commodity space," doctoral dissertation, University of California, Berkeley.

Bewley, T. (1973), "The equality of the core and the set of equilibria in economies with infinitely many commodities and a continuum of agents," *Int. Econ. Rev.* **14**, 383–393.

Bewley, T. (1991), "A very weak theorem on the existence of equilibrium in atomless economies with infinitely many commodities," in *Equilibrium Theory in Infinite Dimensional Spaces*, M. A. Khan and N. C. Yannelis (eds.) (Springer-Verlag, New York).

Chichilnisky, G. (1993), "The cone condition, properness, and extremely desirable commodities," *Econ. Theory* **3**, 177–182.

Chichilnisky, G., and P. J. Kalman (1980), "Application of functional analysis to models of efficient allocation of economic resources," *J. Optimization Theory Appl.* **30**, 19–32.

Court, L. (1941), "Entrepreneurial and consumer demand theories commodity spectra," *Econometrica* **9**, 135–162.

Debreu, G. (1954), "Valuation equilibrium and Pareto optimum," *Proc. Nat. Acad. Sci.* **40**, 588–592.

Diestel, J., and J. Uhl (1977), *Vector Measures*, (Mathematical Surveys, 15, American Mathematical Society, Providence, R.I.)

Gabszewicz, J. J. (1991), "A limit theorem on the core of an economy with a continuum of commodities," in *Equilibrium Theory in Infinite Dimensional Spaces*, M. A. Khan and N. C. Yannelis (eds.) (Springer-Verlag, New York).

Hiai, F., and H. Umegaki (1977), "Integrals, conditional expectations and Martingales of multivalued functions," *J. Multivariate Anal.* **7**, 149–182.

Hildenbrand, W. (1972), "Metric measure spaces of economic agents," in *Proceedings of the Sixth Berkeley Symposium on Mathematical Statistics and Probability*, L. LeCam *et. al* (eds.), (University of California Press, Berkeley), pp. 41–56.

Hildenbrand, W. (1974), *Core and Equilibria of a Large Economy* (Princeton University Press, Princeton, N.J.).

Khan, M. A. (1985), "On the integration of set-valued mappings in a non-reflexive Banach space, II," *Simon Stevin* **59**, 257–267.

Khan, M. A., and M. Majumdar (1986), "Weak sequential compactness in $L_1(\mu, X)$ and an approximate version of Fatou's lemma," *J. Math. Anal. Appl.* **114**, 569–573.

Khan, M. A., and N. C. Yannelis (1991), "Equilibria in markets with a continuum of agents and commodities," in *Equilibrium Theory in Infinite Dimensional Spaces*, M. A. Khan and N. C. Yannelis (eds.) (Springer-Verlag, New York).

Mas-Colell, A. (1975), "A model of equilibrium with differentiated commodities," *J. Math. Econ.* **2**, 263–293.

Mas-Colell, A. (1986), "The price equilibrium existence problem in topological vector lattices," *Econometrica* **54**, 1039–1053.

Mertens, F. J. (1991), "An equivalence theorem for the core of an economy with commodity space L_∞," in *Equilibrium Theory in Infinite Dimensional Spaces* M. A. Khan and N. C. Yannelis (eds.) (Springer-Verlag, New York).

Peleg, B., and M. Yaari (1970), "Markets with countably many commodities," *Int. Econ. Rev.* 369–377.

Rustichini, A. (1989), "A counterexample and an exact version of Fatou's lemma in infinite dimensions," *Archiv der Mathematik* **52**, 357–362.

Rustichini, A., and N. C. Yannelis (1991a), "Edgeworth's conjecture in economies with a continuum of agents and commodities," *J. Math. Econ.* **20**, 307–326.

Rustichini, A., and N. C. Yannelis (1991b), "What is perfect competition?" in *Equilibrium Theory in Infinite Dimensional Spaces* M. A. Khan and N. C. Yannelis (eds.) (Springer-Verlag, New York).

Yannelis, N. C. (1987), "Equilibria in non-cooperative models of competition," *J. Econ. Theory* **41**, 96–111.

Yannelis, N. C. (1988), "Fatou's lemma in infinite dimensional spaces," *Proc. Am. Math. Soc.* **102**, 303–310.

Yannelis, N. C. (1991), "Integration of Banach-valued correspondences," in *Equilibrium Theory in Infinite Dimensional Spaces*, M. A. Khan and N. C. Yannelis (eds.) (Springer-Verlag, New York).

Yannelis, N. C., and W. R. Zame (1984), "Equilibria in Banach lattices without ordered preferences," Institute for Mathematics and its Applications (University of Minnesota), Preprint No. 71. [A shortened version appeared in *J. Math. Econ.* **15**, 85–110 (1986).]

LUMP-SUM TAXATION: THE STATIC ECONOMY

Yves Balasko
Department of Econometrics
University of Geneva
CH-1211 Geneva 4
Switzerland

Karl Shell
Department of Economics
Cornell University
Ithaca, New York 14853-7601

1. INTRODUCTION

How does government fiscal policy affect the allocation of resources? This is a central question for the theory and practice of public finance. In a series of three papers (Balasko and Shell, 1981a, 1981b, 1986), we analyzed the effects of money lump-sum taxes and transfers in perfect-foresight, competitive, overlapping-generations economies. In the present chapter, we base our analysis on the finite (essentially static), pure-exchange, general-equilibrium, competitive model of Arrow, Debreu, and McKenzie. This should serve as a basis of comparison for similar analyses in more complicated economies. It also gives us the opportunity to present work in the tradition of Lionel McKenzie. In particular, we indicate that some of McKenzie's ideas for establishing the existence of nonmonetary equilibrium also turn out to play an important role in the analysis of monetary economies.

The government is assumed to be able to levy lump-sum taxes and distribute lump-sum transfers in terms of the monetary unit. The price of money (relative to commodities) is determined in the market.

The government's tax-transfer policy, or *fiscal policy*, is said to be *balanced* if the algebraic sum of taxes is zero. A fiscal policy is said to be *bonafide* (for a given economy) if it permits a competitive equilibrium in which the goods price of money is not zero; thus, if a fiscal policy is not

GENERAL EQUILIBRIUM, GROWTH, AND TRADE II

bonafide, it can have no effect on resource allocation. We establish for the static economy that a fiscal policy is bonafide if and only if it is balanced. (In finite, dynamic economies, balanced fiscal policies are those in which the public debt is retired at the final date. In dynamic economies with infinite time horizons, there can be bonafide policies that are not balanced, and balanced policies that are not bonafide.)

The government seeks to control the economy through its fiscal policy. We show that the government is able to move continuously from one bonafide fiscal policy to another without leaving the set of bonafide policies. Lump-sum taxes and transfers are fully potent in the following sense: (1) each competitive equilibrium allocation (with or without taxation) is Pareto-optimal; and (2) each Pareto-optimal allocation is achievable as a competitive equilibrium with an appropriately chosen fiscal policy, without reallocating endowments.

There is, however, a major obstacle that the government faces in its attempt to implement a given Pareto-optimal allocation through the imposition of tax policy. Competitive equilibrium is not unique. Indeed, for each bonafide fiscal policy, there is a continuum of competitive equilibria. The set of equilibrium money prices contains zero and a neighborhood of zero. For some economies, the set of equilibrium money prices is an interval. For other economies, the set of equilibrium money prices is not connected.

In the traditional model, taxes are levied in terms of accounting units (rather than in monetary units). For this case, we establish that the set of bonafide policies in the Arrow–Debreu–McKenzie economy is a bounded subset of the balanced policies. Sufficiently small balanced fiscal policies are contained in the set of bonafide policies. The government can move continuously from one bonafide policy to another without leaving the set of bonafide policies.

Costless lump-sum taxation is an idealization, representing the unrealistic case in which fiscal policy is fully potent. We hope that the present study will serve as a springboard for future research that reflects the fact that actual taxes are limited in scope (see, e.g., Mirrlees, 1986) or, more generally, that actual taxes are costly to administer (see, Heller and Shell, 1974), and that competition is imperfect (see Peck, Shell, and Spear, 1992).

The concept of bonafide policies was introduced and extensively analyzed for overlapping-generations economies by Balasko and Shell (1981a, 1981b, 1986). See also Balasko and Shell (1985). This chapter is based on the static model developed in our unpublished working papers, Balasko and Shell (1980, 1983).

Our model is presented in Section 2. Bonafide fiscal policies are analyzed in Section 3. Section 4 contains the analysis of the set of equilibrium money prices. In Section 5, we discuss the robustness of the results. For finite economies, only our implicit assumption of the irreducibility of the economy (see McKenzie, 1959)—or, alternatively, of resource-relatedness (see Arrow and Hahn, 1971)—is critical. Our basic results do not, however, extend to dynamic economies in which the time horizon is infinite.

2. PRELIMINARIES

There are l commodities and n consumers. The preferences of each consumer are defined on the strictly positive orthant; the consumer's consumption set is $\mathbb{R}^l_{++}$. We make the following assumptions to simplify the analysis. Preferences are strictly increasing and strictly convex. Each indifference set is a smooth surface. The closure of each indifference surface in $\mathbb{R}^l$ is contained in $\mathbb{R}^l_{++}$. (This last assumption allows us to avoid boundary problems involving free commodities.)

Let p^j denote the price of commodity j ($j = 1, \dots, l$), and let $p = (p^1, \dots, p^j, \dots, p^l)$ denote the vector of commodity prices. Choose commodity 1 as the numeraire and define the set of strictly positive, normalized commodity prices $\mathscr{P} = \{p \in \mathbb{R}^l_{++} | p^1 = 1\}$. We denote by $x_h = (x^1_h, \dots, x^j_h, \dots, x^l_h) \in \mathbb{R}^l_{++}$ the consumption plan for consumer h ($h = 1, \dots, n$) and define $x = (x_1, \dots, x_h, \dots, x_n) \in (\mathbb{R}^l_{++})^n$, the commodity allocation vector. Demand for commodities by consumer h is obtained by maximizing that individual's preferences on the budget set $\{x_h \in \mathbb{R}^l_{++} | p \cdot x_h \leqq w_h\}$, where w_h denotes the income of consumer h. For fixed $p \in \mathscr{P}$ and fixed $w_h \in \mathbb{R}_{++}$, this constrained maximization problem has a unique solution denoted by $f_h(p, w_h) \in \mathbb{R}^l_{++}$. Thus $f_h\colon \mathscr{P} \times \mathbb{R}_{++} \to \mathbb{R}^l_{++}$ is this consumer's demand function for the l commodities. Let $\omega_h = (\omega^1_h, \dots, \omega^j_h, \dots, \omega^l_h) \in \mathbb{R}^l_{++}$ denote the commodity endowments of consumer h, and define $\omega = (\omega_1, \dots, \omega_h, \dots, \omega_n) \in (\mathbb{R}^l_{++})^n$, the endowment allocation vector.

Next define the *fiscal policy* (or, a system of nominal (money) lump-sum taxes) by the vector $\tau = (\tau_1, \dots, \tau_h, \dots, \tau_n)$. The *set of feasible fiscal policies*, denoted by $\mathscr{F}$, is either $\mathbb{R}^n$ or a subset of $\mathbb{R}^n$. If τ_h is positive, consumer h is being taxed a positive amount, but if τ_h is negative, he is receiving a positive transfer (i.e., is "paying" a negative tax). If the government accepts only money in payment of taxes (i.e., it refuses to accept commodities of equal value), then the set of feasible fiscal policies $\mathscr{F}$ is given by $\{\tau \in \mathbb{R}^n | \Sigma^n_1 \tau_h \leqq 0\}$. That is, the government must distribute at least as much money as it collects. If, however, the government does accept commodities in lieu of money for payment of taxes, then τ_h ($h = 1, \dots, n$) can be any real number and $\mathscr{F} = \mathbb{R}^n$. The former description of $\mathscr{F}$ is obviously more realistic than the latter one, but our formal results apply equally well for either description; only the interpretations differ.

We next define balanced fiscal policies. These policies play a central role in the analysis of the finite economy with money taxes and transfers.

DEFINITION 2.1. A fiscal policy $\tau = (\tau_1, \ldots, \tau_h, \ldots, \tau_n) \in \mathscr{F}$ is said to be *balanced* if $\Sigma_1^n \tau_h = 0$. The *set of balanced fiscal policies* $\mathscr{F}_{\text{bal}}$ is defined by $\mathscr{F}_{\text{bal}} = \{\tau \in \mathscr{F} | \Sigma_1^n \tau_h = 0\}$.

If τ is balanced in the static economy, then the supply of outside money is zero. In the perfect-foresight *finite-horizon* dynamic economy, balanced fiscal policies also play a central role, even though they allow for nonzero outside money supplies (on a period-by-period basis) (see, Ricardo, 1817, Ch. 17; Lerner, 1947; Starr, 1974; Balasko and Shell, 1986). Neo-Ricardians such as Barro (1974) have incorrectly assigned the same central role to balanced fiscal policies in infinite-horizon models.

The price of money in terms of commodity 1 is p^m, a nonnegative scalar. We then have the income identities

$$w_h = p \cdot \omega_h - p^m \tau_h \tag{2.2}$$

for $h = 1, \ldots, n$. Income of consumer h is equal to the value of his commodity endowments minus the value of his tax obligation.

Let $q = (p, p^m)$ and $Q = \{q = (p, p^m) | p \in \mathscr{P} \text{ and } p^m \in \mathbb{R}_+\}$. We can now define competitive equilibrium.

DEFINITION 2.3. The price vector $q = (p, p^m) \in Q$ is said to be a *competitive equilibrium* associated with the endowments $\omega \in (\mathbb{R}_{++}^l)^n$ and the fiscal policy $\tau \in \mathscr{F}$ if it satisfies the equations

$$\sum_{h=1}^{n} f_h(p, w_h) = \sum_{h=1}^{n} \omega_h = r$$

and

$$w_h = p \cdot \omega_h - p^m \tau_h \qquad \text{for} \quad h = 1, \ldots, n,$$

where $r \in \mathbb{R}_{++}^l$ is the vector of aggregate resources. The competitive equilibrium $q = (p, p^m)$ is said to be *proper* if $p^m \neq 0$. The *set of competitive equilibria* associated with ω and τ is denoted by $Q(\omega, \tau) \subset Q = \mathscr{P} \times \mathbb{R}_+$.

The following proposition and its proof establish that there is always (at least the obvious) competitive equilibrium.

PROPOSITION 2.4. *The set $Q(\omega, \tau)$ is not empty. That is, there exists a competitive equilibrium.*

Proof. Set p^m equal to 0. Then $p^m \tau_h = 0$ and $w_h = p \cdot \omega_h$ for $h = 1, \dots, n$. The economy then reduces to a standard exchange economy without taxes and transfers. Equilibrium is thus assured (see, e.g., Arrow and Hahn, 1971, Chapter 5). That is, there is $p \in \mathscr{P}$ such that $q = (p, 0) \in Q(\omega, \tau)$. ■

If we change the monetary unit, then the set of competitive equilibria is changed in a simple way. The following proposition, which can be thought of as "absence of money illusion," spells this out.

PROPOSITION 2.5. *For each positive scalar λ, we have*

$$Q(\omega, \lambda\tau) = \{(p, (p^m/\lambda)) | (p, p^m) \in Q(\omega, \tau)\}.$$

Proof. From Definition 2.2, $w_h = p \cdot \omega_h - p^m \tau_h$ for $h = 1, \dots, n$. Since the only effect of τ or p^m on the demand function f_h is through w_h, the result follows immediately from Definition 2.3. ■

Proposition 2.5 is *not* a statement of the quantity theory of money. Doubling τ does double the outside money supply, but if τ is balanced,[1] the outside money supply is zero. Doubling τ is consistent with halving p^m, but that is not by any means the only possible outcome.

3. BONAFIDE FISCAL POLICIES

By Proposition 2.4, a competitive equilibrium always exists. However, for a given fiscal policy τ, all such equilibria might be trivial in the sense that the equilibrium price of money is zero. This reduces to the case without real taxes and transfers since then $p^m \tau = 0$ and $w_h = p \cdot \omega_h$ for $h = 1, \dots, n$. If for given endowments ω, the government were to choose a fiscal policy τ with the property that $Q(\omega, \tau)$ contains no *proper* competitive equilibrium, then the government could not have a "*good faith*" expectation that its fiscal policy would affect the allocation of resources. This idea is formalized in the following definition.

DEFINITION 3.1. Fix endowments ω and the preferences of the n consumers. The fiscal policy $\tau \in \mathscr{F}$ is said to be *bonafide* if there is a *proper* competitive equilibrium $q = (p, p^m) \in \mathscr{P} \times \mathbb{R}_{++}$ associated with τ. The fiscal policy is said to be *normalized bonafide* if $q = (p, 1)$ is a (proper) competitive equilibrium associated with τ. Let $\mathscr{F}_{\text{bon}}$ denote the *set of bonafide fiscal policies* and let $\mathscr{F}^{\text{n}}_{\text{bon}}$ denote the set of *normalized bonafide fiscal policies*; $\mathscr{F}^{\text{n}}_{\text{bon}} \subset \mathscr{F}_{\text{bon}} \subset \mathscr{F}$.

[1]We show in the next section that if τ is not balanced (i.e., the outside money supply is not zero), then the equilibrium price of money must be zero.

From Proposition 2.4, the so-called "absence of money illusion" theorem, we know that the set of bonafide fiscal policies $\mathcal{F}_{\mathrm{bon}}$ is the nonnegative cone in $\mathcal{F}$ generated by $\mathcal{F}^{\mathrm{n}}_{\mathrm{bon}}$, the set of normalized bonafide fiscal policies. The set $\mathcal{F}^{\mathrm{n}}_{\mathrm{bon}}$ is a "cross section" of the cone $\mathcal{F}_{\mathrm{bon}}$.

The following proposition begins our program of establishing the relationship between bonafide fiscal policies and balanced fiscal policies.

PROPOSITION 3.2. *If the fiscal policy $\tau \in \mathcal{F}$ is bonafide, then τ is balanced. That is, the set $\mathcal{F}_{bon}$ is included in the set $\mathcal{F}_{bal}$.*

Proof. Since preferences are unsatiated, we have $p \cdot f_h(p, w_h) = w_h = p \cdot \omega_h - p^m \tau_h$ for $h = 1, \dots, n$. Hence, using Definition 2.3 yields

$$p \cdot \sum_{h=1}^{n} f_h(p, w_h) = p \cdot \sum_{h=1}^{n} \omega_h - p^m \sum_{h=1}^{n} \tau_h = p \cdot \sum_{h=1}^{n} \omega_h,$$

and thus we have

$$p^m \sum_{h=1}^{n} \tau_h = 0.$$

We have shown that if the equilibrium (p, p^m) is proper, then the fiscal policy τ is balanced. ■

For any finite economy, Proposition 3.2 is a trivial consequence of Walras's law. In order to consider more interesting fiscal policies, one must go beyond the finite-horizon models to infinite economies such as the overlapping-generations model introduced by Samuelson (1958). That the balance of taxes and transfers permits a positive price of money in finite economies is neatly articulated in Starr (1974). Starr credits Lerner (1947) with the idea that the state through its taxing power can (at least temporarily) create fiat money that may bear a positive equilibrium price.

The next two propositions state that with lump-sum taxes as its only instrument the government's fiscal policy is fully potent, a well-known and important result in the public finance literature. We then use these propositions in analyzing the structure of the set of bonafide taxes.

PROPOSITION 3.3. *Fix resources $r \in \mathbb{R}^l_{++}$. Any Pareto-optimal allocation is a competitive equilibrium allocation associated with the fixed endowment vector $\omega = (\omega_1, \dots, \omega_h, \dots, \omega_n) \in (\mathbb{R}^l_{++})^n$ satisfying $\Sigma_1^n \omega_h = r$ and some fiscal policy $\tau = (\tau_1, \dots, \tau_h, \dots, \tau_n) \in \mathcal{F}$.*

Proof. We can restrict τ to the set $\mathcal{F}^{\mathrm{n}}_{\mathrm{bon}}$ and fix the value of p^m at 1.

A commodity price vector $p \in \mathcal{P}$ is said to *support* an allocation $x = (x_1, \dots, x_h, \dots, x_n)$ if for each consumer h ($h = 1, \dots, n$) there is an income $w_h \in \mathbb{R}_{++}$ such that that individual's preferences are maximized at x_h given that person's budget set defined by prices p and income w_h.

Let $\mathfrak{P} \subset (\mathbb{R}^l_{++})^n$ be the set of Pareto-optimal allocations $x = (x_1, \ldots, x_h, \ldots, x_n)$ defined by the given consumer preferences and the given resources r. Let $g\colon \mathfrak{P} \to \mathscr{P}$ be the mapping that associates the Pareto-optimal allocation x with the unique price vector $p \in \mathscr{P}$ that supports x (see, e.g., Arrow and Hahn, 1971, Chapters 4 and 5). Define $\phi(x)$ by $\phi(x) = (g(x) \cdot (\omega_1 - x_1), \ldots, g(x) \cdot (\omega_h - x_h), \ldots, g(x) \cdot (\omega_n - x_n))$. We have $\phi(x) \in \mathbb{R}^n$. We also have $\Sigma_1^n x_h = r = \Sigma_1^n \omega_h$ and hence $g(x) \cdot \Sigma_1^n(\omega_h - x_h) = 0$, i.e., $\phi(x) \in \mathscr{F}_{\text{bal}} \subset \mathscr{F}$.

Next observe that if $q = (p, 1) \in Q(\omega, \tau)$ is a competitive equilibrium price system, associated with the fiscal policy $\tau = (\tau_1, \ldots, \tau_h, \ldots, \tau_n)$, then the competitive equilibrium allocation vector is $(f_1(p, p \cdot \omega_1 - \tau_1), \ldots, f_h(p, p \cdot \omega_h - \tau_h), \ldots, f_n(p, p \cdot \omega_n - \tau_n))$. Then $\tau = \phi(x)$ is the unique normalized fiscal policy that decentralizes the Pareto-optimal allocation x. ■

Proposition 3.3 is the lump-sum taxation version of the second welfare theorem. In the next proposition, provided for completeness, we give the lump-sum taxation version of the first welfare theorem.

PROPOSITION 3.4. *Let x be the allocation associated with the competitive equilibrium $q = (p, p^m) \in Q(\omega, \tau)$. Then x is Pareto-optimal with respect to resources $r = \Sigma_1^n \omega_h$ and the given consumer preferences.*

Proof. From Definition 2.3 we have $\Sigma_1^n x_h = r$ and hence $p \cdot \Sigma_1^n x_h = p \cdot r$. Assume that the allocation $y = (y_1, \ldots, y_h, \ldots, y_n)$ is Pareto-superior to $x = (x_1, \ldots, x_h, \ldots, x_n)$. Then $p \cdot y_h \geqq p \cdot x_h$ for $h = 1, \ldots, n$ with strict inequality for at least one h. Hence, we have $p \cdot \Sigma_1^n y_h > p \cdot r$, which contradicts $\Sigma_1^n y_h \leqq r$. The allocation y is not feasible if resources are fixed at r. ■

The next proposition is our basic result of this section. In it, we describe the fundamental properties of the set of bonafide fiscal policies. We work with a "cross section" of that set, the set of normalized bonafide fiscal policies. Among other things, we establish a continuity property of the set of bonafide policies. Our formal continuity property is stated in terms of arc-connectedness, a generalization of the familiar notion of convexity. Before stating our results, we provide the definition of arc-connectedness (see, e.g., Arrow and Hahn, 1971, pp. 400–401).

DEFINITION 3.5. The set S is said to be *arc-connected* if for every $s^0 \in S$ and $s^1 \in S$, there is a continuous function, $s(t)$, defined for $t \in [0, 1]$, with the property $s(0) = s^0$ and $s(1) = s^1$, and $s(t) \in S$ for each $t \in [0, 1]$.

That is, any two points in an arc-connected set can be joined by a continuous path lying entirely in the set.

Proposition 3.6. *The set of normalized bonafide lump-sum taxes* $\mathscr{F}^{n}_{bon}$ *is bounded, arc-connected, and contains* 0 *in its relative interior.*

Proof.

(i) Boundedness. Let ϕ and g be the continuous mappings defined in the proof of Proposition 3.3. Let $\overline{\mathfrak{P}}$ be the closure of the set of Pareto-optimal allocations. The mappings g and ϕ have continuous extensions from $\mathfrak{P}$ to $\overline{\mathfrak{P}}$. The image $\phi(\overline{\mathfrak{P}})$ is compact, and hence bounded. Since we have $\phi(\mathfrak{P}) \subset \phi(\overline{\mathfrak{P}})$, $\phi(\overline{\mathfrak{P}})$ is bounded; i.e., $\mathscr{F}^{n}_{\text{bon}}$ is bounded.

(ii) Arc-connectedness. It is well known that the set of Pareto-optimal allocations, $\mathfrak{P}$, is arc-connected (see, e.g., Balasko, 1979, Appendix 3, pp. 378–379). Hence, the set $\mathscr{F}^{n}_{\text{bon}}$ is arc-connected as the image by the continuous mapping ϕ of the set $\mathfrak{P}$.

(iii) Interiority of zero. Restrict attention to the subspace $\{\tau \in \mathscr{F} | \Sigma_1^n \tau_h = 0\} = \mathscr{F}_{\text{bal}}$. Let $q = (p, 1) \in Q(\omega, \tau)$. It results from the numeraire assumption, $p^1 = 1$, and the restriction $p^m = 1$, that $q = (p, 1)$ also belongs to the set $Q(\omega', 0)$ where $\omega' = (\omega'_1, \ldots, \omega'_h, \ldots, \omega'_n)$ is given by

$$\left(\omega_h^k\right)' = \omega_h^k \qquad \text{for} \quad k = 2, \ldots, l, \quad h = 1, \ldots, n,$$

$$\left(\omega_h^1\right)' = \omega_h^1 - \tau_h \qquad \text{for} \quad h = 1, \ldots, n,$$

and

$$\omega'_h = \left(\left(\omega_h^1\right)', \ldots, \left(\omega_h^k\right)', \ldots, \left(\omega_h^l\right)'\right) \qquad \text{for} \quad h = 1, \ldots, n,$$

provided that $\omega_h^1 - \tau_h > 0$ for $h = 1, \ldots, n$. The set of vectors τ satisfying the above contains zero and is open in $\mathscr{F}_{\text{bal}}$. Since a (nonmonetary) competitive equilibrium obviously exists for these constructed no-taxation economies, the τ values thus constructed belong to $\mathscr{F}^{n}_{\text{bon}}$. ■

The following corollary states that set of bonafide fiscal policies is identical to the set of balanced fiscal policies.

Corollary 3.7. *The fiscal policy* $\tau \in \mathscr{F}$ *is bonafide if and only if it is balanced. That is, the set* $\mathscr{F}_{bon}$ *is identical to the set* $\mathscr{F}_{bal}$.

Proof. From Proposition 3.2, we have $\mathscr{F}_{\text{bon}} \subset \mathscr{F}_{\text{bal}}$. From Proposition 3.6, it follows that if τ belongs to $\mathscr{F}_{\text{bal}}$, then for each sufficiently large scalar θ, (τ/θ) belongs to $\mathscr{F}^{n}_{\text{bon}}$. Hence, from Proposition 2.5, we know that τ belongs to $\mathscr{F}_{\text{bon}}$. ■

The set of normalized bonafide fiscal policies has been useful in our analysis of bonafide policies (see, Corollary 3.7). It is also a useful construct for the analysis of equilibrium money prices (see, Section 4). But the set $\mathscr{F}^{n}_{\text{bon}}$ is interesting in its own right. In the traditional analysis of lump-sum fiscal policies, taxes and transfers are made in units of account rather than in monetary units. The traditional model is thus a special case of the present model, in which p^m is assumed to be identical to 1. Then the set of bonafide fiscal policies—policies consistent with equilibrium in which $p^m = p^1 = 1$—is the same as our set $\mathscr{F}^n_{\text{bon}}$ (Definition 3.1). If we accept the fiction of government taxes and transfers in accounting units (or in units of a given commodity), then we have from Proposition 3.6 that the set of bonafide fiscal policies is a bounded, arc-connected *subset* of the set balanced fiscal policies and that $\tau = 0$ lies in its relative interior. In the traditional model, not all balanced policies are bonafide, but sufficiently small balanced policies are bonafide (see Balasko and Shell, 1985).

We return in what follows to the case where taxes and transfers are denominated in money.

4. THE SET OF EQUILIBRIUM MONEY PRICES

Propositions 3.4 and 3.3 are respectively the lump-sum taxation versions of the first and second theorems of welfare economics. The second theorem (Proposition 3.3) is not quite as powerful as it might appear to be. It is true that each Pareto-optimal allocation is achievable as a competitive-equilibrium allocation for some properly chosen fiscal policy. If, however, the fiscal policy is bonafide, the competitive equilibrium allocation is not unique. This is easy to see. If τ is bonafide, there are at least two distinct equilibria: one with a zero money price (see, the proof of Proposition 2.4) and another with a positive price of money (see, Definition 3.1).

We shall establish that there is, in fact, at least a continuum of equilibria for each bonafide fiscal policy. (The vast multiplicity of equilibria is a common property of models with nominal assets.) The government imposes τ. The set of possible outcomes $Q(\omega, \tau)$ is infinite. A Pareto-optimal allocation will result, but it may very well not be the one the government is seeking.

Proposition 2.5 permits us to use Proposition 3.6 in analyzing the set of p^m consistent with competitive equilibrium for a given economy and a given fiscal policy. We begin with the basic definition.

Definition 4.1. The *set of equilibrium money prices* $\mathscr{P}^m(\omega, \tau) \subset \mathbb{R}_+$ for a given economy with fiscal policy $\tau \in \mathscr{F}$ is defined by

$$\mathscr{P}^m(\omega, \tau) = \{ p^m \mid (p, p^m) \in Q(\omega, \tau) \}.$$

Now we can derive some properties of the set $\mathscr{P}^m(\omega, \tau)$.

Proposition 4.2. *Let $\tau \neq 0$ be a nontrivial, (not necessarily normalized) balanced fiscal policy. Then the set $\mathscr{P}^m(\omega, \tau)$ is bounded. Furthermore, 0 belongs to $\mathscr{P}^m(\omega, \tau)$ and there is an interval of sufficiently small positive $p^m \in \mathscr{P}^m(\omega, \tau)$ so that 0 is not isolated.*

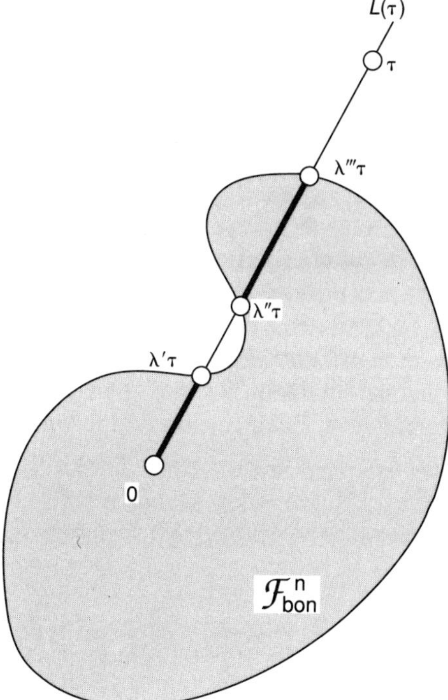

FIGURE 1

Proof. Let $L(\tau)$ be the nonnegative ray generated by $\tau \in \mathcal{F}_{\text{bal}}$, $L(\tau) = \{\lambda\tau | \lambda \in \mathbb{R}_+\}$. From the set $(\mathcal{F}^{\text{n}}_{\text{bon}} \cap L(\tau))$, the intersection of the set of normalized bonafide fiscal policies, and the nonnegative ray $L(\tau)$. Proposition 2.5 allows us to construct a one-to-one relationship between the set $\mathcal{P}^m(\omega, \tau)$ and the set $(\mathcal{F}^{\text{n}}_{\text{bon}} \cap L(\tau))$. Namely, map p^m in $\mathcal{P}^m(\omega, \tau)$ to $p^m\tau$ in $\mathcal{F}^{\text{n}}_{\text{bon}}$, where n is strictly larger than 2. The intersection of $\mathcal{F}^{\text{n}}_{\text{bon}}$ with $L(\tau)$ is shown in Figure 1; the ambient space (i.e., the space of the printed page) is $\mathcal{F}_{\text{bal}}$. The set $\mathcal{P}^m(\omega, \tau)$ is illustrated in Figure 2. Proposition 4.2 now can be shown to follow from Proposition 3.6. The boundedness of $\mathcal{F}^{\text{n}}_{\text{bon}}$ implies the boundedness of $\mathcal{P}^m(\omega, \tau)$. Since $\mathcal{F}^{\text{n}}_{\text{bon}}$ contains zero, $\mathcal{P}^m(\omega, \tau)$ contains zero. Since for p^m fixed at 1 there is a ball of $\tau \in \mathcal{F}_{\text{bal}}$ around the origin with the property that $\tau \in \mathcal{F}^{\text{n}}_{\text{bon}}$, we know that for fixed τ there is a positive scalar $\bar{p}^m$ such that $p^m \in \mathcal{P}^m(\omega, \tau)$ for each p^m in the interval $[0, \bar{p}^m)$. ■

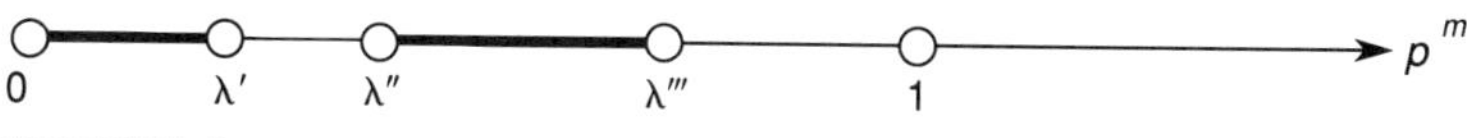

FIGURE 2

From Figures 1 and 2, we can see how the structure of the set $\mathscr{P}^m(\omega, \tau)$ is related to the structure of the set $\mathscr{F}^{\mathrm{n}}_{\mathrm{bon}}$. Figure 1 is an abstract representation. The space of the printed page is meant to represent the higher-dimensional object $\mathscr{F}^{\mathrm{n}}_{\mathrm{bal}} \subset \mathbb{R}^{n-1}$. The intersection of $\mathscr{F}^{\mathrm{n}}_{\mathrm{bon}}$ with the nonnegative ray generated by τ is indicated by two heavy line segments. The nonnegative ray intersects $\mathscr{F}^{\mathrm{n}}_{\mathrm{bon}}$ at $\lambda'\tau$, $\lambda''\tau$, and $\lambda'''\tau$. In Figure 2, $\mathscr{P}^m(\omega, \tau)$ is indicated by the two heavy line segments; $\mathscr{P}^m(\omega, \tau) = [0, \lambda') \cup (\lambda'', \lambda''')$.

If $\mathscr{F}^{\mathrm{n}}_{\mathrm{bon}}$ is convex (or merely star-shaped about the origin), then $\mathscr{P}^m(\omega, \tau)$ is a single interval. This is always the case in the two-consumer economy, $n = 2$, because $\mathscr{F}_{\mathrm{bal}} \subset \mathbb{R}^2$ is the (one-dimensional) line $\{\tau | \tau_1 + \tau_2 = 0\}$ and $\mathscr{F}^{\mathrm{n}}_{\mathrm{bon}}$ is a (one-dimensional) connected subset of that line. Furthermore, if there is only one commodity, $l = 1$, then $\mathscr{P}^m(\omega, \tau)$ is obviously a single interval. Examples have been constructed in which the set $\mathscr{P}^m(\omega, \tau)$ is not connected.[2]

5. EXTENSIONS

There are three nearly equivalent formulations of our central result about lump-sum taxes and transfers in the competitive economy: (1) a fiscal policy is bonafide if and only if it is balanced; (2) the trivial fiscal policy $\tau = (0, \ldots, 0)$ is in the interior (relative to the set of balanced policies) of the set of normalized bona fide fiscal policies; and (3) for each balanced fiscal policy, there is a positive scalar $\bar{p}^m$ with the property that the interval $[0, \bar{p}^m)$ is contained in the set of equilibrium money prices.

How robust is our result to relaxation of our maintained hypotheses?

The strong regularity assumptions about consumer preferences (i.e., *strict* convexity, *strict* monotonicity, smoothness, and closure of indifference surfaces within the consumption set) are made only for expository convenience; they are not necessary for our basic result. These regularity assumptions are somewhat relaxed by Balasko and Shell (1986, Section 3), in which the present analysis is extended to encompass the perfect-foresight, finite-horizon, overlapping-generations economy. In an informal seminar presentation, David Cass showed that, as one would expect, the results of the present analysis hold in an exchange economy satisfying only the (weaker) assumptions (such as irreducibility or resource-relatedness)

[2]Jim Peck (1987a) has constructed an example of an economy with two commodities and three consumers, satisfying the regularity hypotheses of Section 2, in which the set of equilibrium money prices is not connected.Strong income effects drive Peck's example. See also Peck (1987b). Rod Garratt (1992) shows by example that this connectedness property can depend on the numeraire choice.

required for the standard proofs of existence of (nonmonetary) competitive equilibrium. Adding production to the model would not be difficult, nor would we expect it to change anything substantial.

On the other hand, our implicit assumption of irreducibility or resource-relatedness (cf., e.g., Arrow and Hahn, 1971, Chapter 5) plays an essential role in the analysis. To see this, consider an example with two consumers ($n = 2$) and two goods ($l = 2$). Consumer 1 likes only the first good and is endowed with only the first good. Consumer 2 likes only the second good and is endowed with only the second good. Neither consumer has endowment of the good that the other consumer desires. Hence the consumers are not resource related and the economy is reducible.

The commodity price vector is $p = (p^1, p^2) \in \mathbb{R}^2_+$. Restrict attention to the set of normalized prices $\tilde{\mathscr{P}} = \{p \in \mathbb{R}^2_+ | p^1 + p^2 = 1\}$. Let $\tau = (\tau_1, \tau_2)$ be a balanced fiscal policy, so we have $\tau_1 + \tau_2 = 0$. Income of consumer h is given by $w_h = p^h \omega_h^h - p^m \tau_h$ for $h = 1, 2$, where p^m is the price of money. If $\tau_1 = \tau_2 = 0$, autarky is the unique competitive equilibrium allocation, i.e., $x_h^h = \omega_h^h$ for $h = 1, 2$. When $\tau \neq 0$, autarky (with $p^m = 0$) remains the unique competitive equilibrium allocation. The consumer with the subsidy (negative tax) desires to sell money in exchange for the commodity she desires, but the other consumer states that he cannot supply that commodity. Only the trivial fiscal policy $\tau = (0, 0)$ is bonafide. All other fiscal policies (balanced or not) are not bonafide.

Our basic result applies only to finite economies. That the number of commodities l and the number of consumers n are each finite is necessary to the linkage between bonafide and balanced policies. For the infinite-horizon overlapping-generations model, Samuelson (1958, esp. pp. 474–475) provides a nonpathological example in which bonafide policies are not necessarily balanced. See also Balasko and Shell (1981a). Balasko and Shell (1986) establish for the infinite-horizon overlapping-generations model that only *strongly* balanced fiscal policies, i.e., balanced policies with no more than a finite number of nonzero taxes, are necessarily bonafide. Balasko and Shell (1981a) provide a complete characterization of bonfide fiscal policies in the overlapping-generations economy.

Acknowledgments

We gratefully acknowledge the generous research support from a series of (Swiss and U.S.) National Science Foundation grants.

References

Arrow, K., and F. H. Hahn (1971). *General Competitive Analysis* (Holden-Day, San Francisco).

Balasko, Y. (1979). "Budget-constrained and Pareto-efficient allocations," *J. Econ. Theory* **21**, 359–379.

Balasko, Y. (1988). *Foundations of the Theory of General Equilibrium* (Academic Press, Boston).

Balasko, Y., and K. Shell (1980). "On taxation and competitive equilibria," CARESS Working Paper No. 80-18, Center for Analytic Research in Economics and the Social Sciences, University of Pennsylvania, Philadelphia.

Balasko, Y., and K. Shell (1981a). "The overlapping-generations model, II: The case of pure exchange with money," *J. Econ. Theory* **24**, 112–142.

Balasko, Y., and K. Shell (1981b). "The overlapping-generations model, III: The log-linear case," *J. Econ. Theory* **24**, 143–152.

Balasko, Y., and K. Shell (1983). "Lump-sum taxation: The static economy," CARESS Working Paper No. 83-08, Center for Analytic Research in Economics and the Social Sciences, University of Pennsylvania, Philadelphia.

Balasko, Y., and K. Shell (1985). "On taxation and competitive equilibria," in *Optimalité et Structures: Mélanges en Hommage à Edouard Rossier*, G. Ritschard and D. Royer (eds.) (Economica, Paris), 69–83.

Balasko, Y., and K. Shell (1986). "Lump-sum taxes and transfers: Public debt in the overlapping generations model," in *Essays in Honor of Kenneth J. Arrow, Volume II: Equilibrium Analysis*, Chapter 5, 121–153, W. Heller, R. Starr, and D. Starrett (eds.), (Cambridge University Press, New York).

Barro, R. J. (1974). "Are government bonds net wealth?" *J. Political Econ.* **82**, 1095–1117.

Garratt, R. J. (1992). "The connectedness of the set of equilibrium money prices depends on the choice of the numeraire," *J. Econ. Theory* **56**, 206–217.

Heller, W. P., and K. Shell (1974). "On optimal taxation with costly administration," *Am. Econ. Rev.* **64**, 338–345.

Lerner, A. P. (1947). "Money as a creature of the state," *Am. Econ. Rev.* **37**, 312–317.

McKenzie, L. W. (1959). "On the existence of general equilibrium for a competitive market," *Econometrica* **27**, 54–71, and (1961) "Some corrections," *Econometrica* **29**, 247–248.

Mirrlees, J. A. (1986). "The theory of optimal taxation," in *Handbook of Mathematical Economics*, Book 1, Vol. III, K. J. Arrow and M. Intriligator (eds.) (North Holland, Amsterdam).

Peck, J. (1987a). "Non-connectedness of the set of equilibrium money prices: The static economy," *J. Econ. Theory* **43**, 348–354.

Peck, J. (1987b). "Non-connectedness of the set of equilibrium money prices: The overlapping-generations economy," *J. Econ. Theory* **43**, 355–363.

Peck, J., Shell, K., and S. E. Spear (1992). "The market game: Existence and structure of equilibrium," *J. Math. Econ.* **21**, 271–299.

Ricardo, D. (1817). *The Principles of Political Economy and Taxation* (J. Murray, London).

Samuelson, P. A. (1958). "An exact consumption loan model of interest with or without the social contrivance of money," *J. Political Econ.* **66**, 467–482.

Starr, R. M. (1974). "The price of money in a pure exchange monetary economy with taxation," *Econometrica* **42**, 45–54.

EQUILIBRIUM, STABILITY, AND PRICE ADJUSTMENTS IN COMPETITIVE MARKETS

Edward Zabel
Department of Economics
University of Florida
Gainesville, Florida 32611

1. INTRODUCTION

In the theory of pure competition, as each agent is a price taker, price making is problematic. While the theory determines properties of an equilibrium, no mechanism exists to explain the attainment of equilibrium, except by appeal to some ad hoc price adjustment system. The objective in this paper is to introduce price-making agents explicitly into the theory of pure competition. To provide perspective on this objective we briefly outline early work on price adjustment mechanisms and also briefly outline more recent research on the price adjustment problem.

The early literature on price adjustments, developed by Hicks [12], Samuelson [18], Metzler [16], Arrow *et al.* [2], and others, considered Walrasian tâtonnement systems in which actual trading is suspended until equilibrium is attained, given that the system converges to an equilibrium. The emphasis in this literature is the specification of local and/or global stability conditions. As illustrated in the controversy between Jaffé and Morishima [15, 17], one way of viewing this process is in terms of dual time regimes, say, imaginary and real, with price adjustments occurring in imaginary time and transactions in real time so that in terms of real time it seems mandatory to conclude that price adjustments occur instantaneously.

Various extensions, referred to as *nontâtonnement processes*, have been proposed to modify the Walrasian mechanism to introduce elements

GENERAL EQUILIBRIUM, GROWTH, AND TRADE II

of rational adjustment among agents in the economy. Developments among authors in the 1960s and the 1970s of nontâtonnement processes are now referred to as the *Hahn process*. Some representative works are Hahn and Negishi [10], Arrow and Hahn [3], Fisher [5–7], and Hahn [11].[1] The essence of the Hahn process is to adapt the Walrasian analysis to permit trading in endowments and to allow modification of production plans prior to the attainment of equilibrium. With a number of more or less reasonable assumptions the Hahn process converges to an equilibrium. A major assumption is that, after trading has occurred at given prices out of equilibrium, for each commodity the sign of each agent's excess demand is the same as the sign of aggregate excess demand. An implication of this assumption is that all trading occurs out of equilibrium with a cessation of trade at the equilibrium position. That is, for each agent the excess demand for each commodity is nonpositive at equilibrium. As in the Walrasian process, actual consumption and production occur only at equilibrium so that, again, adjustments occur in imaginary time and consumption and production in real time.

The culmination of work in nontâtonnement processes is provided in Fisher [8]. Fisher extends the Hahn process in several directions. Trade, consumption and production occur out of equilibrium so that it is no longer necessary to distinguish imaginary and real time. Agents make point forecasts of prices over an indefinite horizon and, given prices, make optimal plans for the entire horizon. Plans need not be realized and, agents recognizing nonequilibrium positions, periodically adjust price forecasts and, hence, future plans, according to current experience. To consider convergence Fisher introduces an assumption called "no favorable surprise," which is a generalization of the assumption in the Hahn process that, after trade, an agent's excess demand for a commodity has the same sign as aggregate excess demand. "No favorable surprise," and other assumptions, assure convergence to an equilibrium that requires that individual price and other forecasts be correct so that in future periods trade occurs without further adjustments.

The Fisher analysis is very general and very elegant, but it does not explain how markets are made and how agents make and adjust price and other forecasts. Moreover, since all agents are price takers, no one explicitly makes current and future markets for the various commodities. "No favorable surprise," in conjunction with point estimates of prices, is the powerful assumption that permits Fisher to bypass explicit consideration of market making and forecasting.

[1] An alternative development in this period is the Edgeworth process, pioneered by Uzawa [22]. As Fisher [8] provides telling reservations about this process, it will not be considered further here.

Recent studies [1, 21] abandon the Walrasian tâtonnement or nontâtonnement approach by modifying the assumption that agents are passive price takers but, nevertheless, stop short of introducing explicit market-making agents. Allen and Hellwig [1] consider a single market for a single commodity with a given linear market demand function. Independently of each other, each firm chooses a price and the maximum quantity of the commodity available at that price. Consumers seek low prices and are subject to rationing. The major conclusion is that if each firm is small relative to the market, then, with high probability firms must charge prices close to a competitive equilibrium price and most transactions must occur at prices near a competitive price.

Simon [21] considers an exchange, monetary economy in which both buyers and sellers act strategically. Sellers announce prices and maximal quantity vectors, while buyers specify sums of money and alternative bundles of commodities they would accept for a given sum of money. Simon discusses at length reasons for the asymmetry of seller and buyer strategies. For this discussion it suffices to note that the asymmetry vanishes when the number of commodities is one: both sellers and buyers offer prices and maximal quantities for trade. Each agent has an endowment of commodities and money and a utility function defined on both commodities and money. A seller and a buyer trade at prices they announce if the buyer's bid price equals or exceeds the seller's ask price. Any surplus, which arises when bid prices exceed ask prices, leaks from the system as arbitrage profits, and trades are selected to maximize these arbitrage profits. Simon proves that Nash equilibria for this economy yield competitive allocations, provided that in every market at least two buyers and sellers are actively trading.

In this paper the focus is market-making agents. Some agents explicitly make markets by announcing prices at which they would honor buy and sell orders for commodities. This price making mechanism is derived from the operation of security markets such as the New York and the American Stock Exchanges. In these exchanges, which simulate purely competitive markets, a price-making agent, the specialist, assumes the responsibility of calling and supporting prices for a particular security. The specialist is an optimizing agent who makes a market in an asset by calling bid and ask prices periodically during the trading day. These prices are honored by the agent's own trading in shares to satisfy any excess demand.

In previous papers [4, 23] the author models the operation of this system, assuming randomness in the customer buy–sell ordering process. Among other outcomes, it is shown that, with some qualification, the price maker performs the competitive function of adjusting prices toward a position analogous to a competitive equilibrium, i.e., bid and ask prices at which expected excess demand equals zero. In my view these outcomes lend support to the intuition underlying the Walrasian tâtonnement process. In the Walrasian system the only obligation is the adjustment of prices according to the sign of current excess demand. The specialist system also operates with few restrictions. The major obligation is that the specialist satisfy excess demand at announced prices by adjustments in this agent's own position in the security. Rather than current excess demand, the specialist adjusts prices according to the sign of accumulated excess demand (this agent's current position in shares), reflecting an obligation to satisfy current orders. The major difference is that the specialist is an optimizing agent who incurs costs in holding either a long or a short position in shares of the security. The attempt to optimize returns, taking into account both costs and revenues, induces the specialist to simulate activities of the Walrasian auctioneer.

The Walrasian auctioneer succeeds in obtaining equilibrium when stability conditions are satisfied. In the author's security market studies it is assumed that the expected demand and supply functions and the expected excess demand function satisfy stability and uniqueness of equilibrium conditions for single markets. These assumptions facilitate the derivation of equilibrium and adjustment properties in the analysis of security markets.

The conjecture of this paper is that, even when stability and uniqueness conditions are violated, so that the Walrasian auctioneer fails to achieve equilibrium or to select a particular equilibrium, the optimizing activities of market-making agents may offset these obstacles. To test this conjecture, examples of nonstochastic, competitive exchange economies, characterized by instability or nonuniqueness of competitive equilibria, are reexamined in the presence of an optimizing price-making agent. This test is suggestive but certainly not conclusive.

Two well-known examples are reconsidered. While the known sufficient conditions that guarantee the global stability of the competitive economy are extreme, it was difficult to construct an example of an economy which is globally unstable under the Walrasian price adjustment mechanism. Scarf [19] succeeded in developing examples of unstable economies, and we examine the most extreme example. Gale [9] constructed another example of instability, involving a Giffen good, and an example of a globally stable economy with multiple competitive equilibria in which adjustments occur away from an equilibrium with positive prices. Here, only Gale's economy with multiple equilibria is considered.

The next section gives a brief exposition of these examples. Section 3 outlines the price-making system. Section 4 examines outcomes in the Scarf example when a price maker maximizes a single period objective function, subject to various constraints. Here, with favorable costs, price choices are not unique. Section 5 considers Scarf's example with a multiperiod objective function. Depending on inventory and backlog costs and other characteristics of the economy, outcomes vary from a choice of competitive (equilibrium) prices each period of any horizon to a choice of noncompetitive price vectors that vary cyclically throughout the horizon. Section 6 considers Gale's economy. In this example, if the price-maker incurs any positive inventory cost, the outcome is the choice of a particular competitive price vector. Section 7 provides concluding comments.

2. EXAMPLES OF COMPETITIVE ECONOMIES

Scarf considers an exchange economy of three individuals and three goods with each individual having a fixed coefficient utility function in two goods and an endowment of one unit of one of the goods. Individual 1 has the utility function $U^1(x_1^1, x_2^1, x_3^1) = \min(x_1^1, x_2^1)$ and endowment $(\bar{x}_1^1, \bar{x}_2^1, \bar{x}_3^1) = (1, 0, 0)$. Similarly, individuals 2 and 3 are described by the utility functions and endowments: $U^2 = \min(x_2^2, x_3^2), (0, 1, 0)$ and $U^3 = \min(x_1^3, x_3^3), (0, 0, 1)$. In this economy, of course, price changes cause income effects but no corresponding substitution effects. Maximizing utility subject to a budget constraint, all individuals divide their endowment incomes equally between two goods, so, for example, individual 1 has demands: $x_1^1 = x_2^1 = p_1/(p_1 + p_2)$ where $(p_1 + p_2) > 0$. Here it is implicitly assumed that if one price equals zero, demands that do not increase utility are constrained. For example, if $p_1 = 0$, so that individual 1 has zero income, then $x_1^1 = 0$ since $x_2^1 = 0$ and, similarly, $x_1^3 = 1$ since $x_3^3 = 1$. Letting market excess demands $E_i = x_i - \bar{x}_i = \Sigma_k x_i^k - \Sigma_k \bar{x}_i^k$, then

$$E_i = \frac{-p_j}{(p_i + p_j)} + \frac{p_k}{(p_i + p_k)} = \frac{p_i(p_k - p_j)}{(p_i + p_j)(p_i + p_k)}, \qquad i, j, k = 1, 2, 3, \tag{1}$$

where $i = 1 \Rightarrow j = 2,\ k = 3,\ i = 2 \Rightarrow j = 3,\ k = 1$ and $i = 3 \Rightarrow j = 1,\ k = 2$. Here, the denominator on the right is positive, or, equivalently, one price, at most, equals zero. If more than one price equals zero, the corresponding demands and excess demands are unbounded above. In this economy it easily follows that there exists a unique competitive equilibrium price ray with $p_1 = p_2 = p_3 \neq 0$. Now assuming the price adjustment rule satisfies

$$\dot{p}_i(t) = E_i(p_1, p_2, p_3), \qquad i = 1, 2, 3, \tag{2}$$

and invoking Walras' law, then $\Sigma p_i E_i = \Sigma p_i \dot{p}_i = 0$ so that $\Sigma p_i^2 =$

constant. Thus, the adjustment rule requires prices to be confined to the intersection of a sphere $\Sigma p_i^2 =$ constant, and $(p_1, p_2, p_3) \geq 0$. Now normalize prices so that $\Sigma p_i^2 = 3$ with $(1, 1, 1)$ specifying the competitive equilibrium prices.

To demonstrate that the economy is globally unstable, it suffices to show that $p_1 p_2 p_3 =$ constant for any solution of (2), which is seen as follows. First note that the equilibrium prices $(p_1, p_2, p_3) = (1, 1, 1)$ uniquely maximize $p_1 p_2 p_3$ subject to $\Sigma p_i^2 = 3$. Thus, if $p_1 p_2 p_3 =$ constant and the initial prices do not satisfy $(1, 1, 1)$, the system does not converge to the competitive equilibrium, and, as a consequence, the economy is globally unstable. To see that (2) implies $p_1 p_2 p_3 =$ constant, it only needs to be shown that $\dot{p}_1 p_2 p_3 + \dot{p}_2 p_1 p_3 + \dot{p}_3 p_1 p_2 = E_1 p_2 p_3 + E_2 p_1 p_3 + E_3 p_1 p_3 = 0$, but that result easily follows from (1).[2]

Gale's example consists of a two-person, two-good exchange economy, again, with each person having a fixed coefficient utility function. In his notation the goods are x and y with prices p and q. Individual 1 has utility function $\Phi_1(x, y) = \min(x, 2y)$ and endowment of one unit of good x, while individual 2 has utility function $\Phi_2(x, y) = \min(2x, y)$ and endowment of one unit of good y. In this example the excess demands for goods x and y are

$$E_x = \frac{q(p - q)}{\delta} \quad \text{and} \quad E_y = \frac{p(q - p)}{\delta} \tag{3}$$

where $\delta = 2p^2 + 5pq + 2q^2$ and $(p + q) > 0$. Again, it is implicitly assumed that if one price equals zero, demands do not exceed amounts that increase utility. If both prices are zero, excess demands are unbounded. From (3), for nonnegative prices, the requirements $E_x \leq 0$ and $E_y \leq 0$ yield as the competitive equilibria: $(p = q \neq 0)$, $(p > 0, q = 0)$ and $(p = 0, q > 0)$. Here, we could normalize prices so that $p^2 + q^2 = 2$ with competitive equilibria: $(1, 1)$, $(\sqrt{2}, 0)$ and $(0, \sqrt{2})$. Under the price adjustment mechanism (2) if the initial prices are unequal, prices will adjust away from the equilibrium $(1, 1)$ until one of the prices equals zero. For example, if $p > q \neq 0$, then $E_x > 0$ and $E_y < 0$ so that p will increase and q will decrease until q equals zero. Gale refers to the equilibrium $(1, 1)$ as being the "fair and natural" equilibrium since in this case each individual receives $\frac{2}{3}$ utils of satisfaction. The remaining equilibria are referred to as being "unfair" since in these cases one individual obtains 1 util and the other individual 0 utils of satisfaction.

[2] Hirota [13] has shown that instability is not inherent in the Scarf economy in that other initial endowments provide a globally stable competitive equilibrium. See also Scarf's comment [19] and Hirota's extension of his earlier work [14].

3. PRICE CHOICES WITH AN OPTIMIZING PRICE MAKER

In this section, to facilitate comparisons with the examples, only minimal changes in previous assumptions are made. Other modifications are discussed later. Here assumptions are altered only enough to introduce a trading process in which an optimizing price maker chooses prices.

The analysis is discrete time with each individual receiving an endowment of one unit of the appropriate good each period. Each period an individual exchanges the endowment for medium of exchange, say, dollars, provided to the price maker by a monetary authority. The dollar income is determined by current prices chosen by the price maker and, maximizing single period utility subject to current income, this entire income is paid to the price maker to place orders for commodities. The individual accepts and consumes whatever commodities are offered in response to the orders. Orders are not necessarily satisfied now since markets need not be cleared each period as the price maker may not have enough inventory on hand to honor all demands. However, unsatisfied orders are backlogged to be satisfied later. In this economy, individual demands are the same as in the examples and market excess demands are again given by (1) and (3) under the appropriate price restrictions, and the total amount of money provided by the monetary authority each period equals Σp_i, the value of endowments, where prices satisfy the condition: Σp_i^2 = constant.

Within this framework the price maker's activities are assumed to have properties analogous to the specialist system in securities exchanges. This system seems appropriate to introduce in the study of competitive markets since, even though the specialist is the single price maker in a security, this agent's noncompetitive advantage is severely limited. The specialist does not directly control the flow of buy and sell orders, as would a monopolist and/or a monopsonist, and has an obligation to satisfy incoming orders at announced prices. In particular, the specialist calls bid and ask prices and is required to satisfy any current excess demand from share holding or by going short. In this system the specialist does make a return on the spread between the bid and ask prices and may make a speculative return on the share position. Seemingly, this agent does act as a monopolist in choosing the spread between the bid and the ask, but even that advantage is restricted by the freedom of traders to arrange exchanges among themselves within the spread. In any event, since a spread would obscure a comparison with the examples in Section 2, which imply single prices for commodities, we assume that the price maker here also chooses single prices with only a prospect of a gain similar to the specialist's speculative return. Moreover, since consumers do not hold inventories, it is not possible for the price maker to take a short position by borrowing commodities, but it is possible to engage in a similar transaction involving the backlogging of unsatisfied demand. In this transaction, analogous to the situation in which the specialist goes short, the price maker incurs a debt by receiving payment for unsatisfied orders. This debt may be satisfied later by a delivery of commodities in the amount of the positive excess demand. Hence, as in the specialist system, we assume that the price maker is required to satisfy demands to the extent possible at announced prices with a backlog transaction in the event of positive excess demand. Thus, the current endowments and inventory are available to meet current demand plus any backlogged orders.

More specifically, in this economy the price maker acts as the agent of the monetary authority. Using currency provided by the monetary authority, this agent distributes income to consumers in exchange for their endowments and receives funds from consumers in payment for their demands. Part of the funds are returned to the monetary authority, and part is retained by the price maker as a debt to be repaid by a delivery of commodities to individuals. In particular, at current prices, the price maker retains as revenue the value of current positive excess demand and returns the remainder of the current fund to the monetary authority. The remainder of the fund equals the value of current goods delivered to individuals, or, equivalently, the value of current endowments for goods with positive excess demand plus the value of demand for goods in excess supply. The price maker also retains the amount of excess supply. The accumulation of excess supplies, the inventory, may be used to satisfy current or previous unsatisfied demands and, thus, to satisfy the debt. As in the case of the specialist, the price maker enjoys the opportunity of a gain by the prospect of using inventory to repay debt at a later time. However, the opportunity of gain may be diminished or offset by any cost of carrying inventory and any charge for unsatisfied demand. Inventory costs may arise in the operation of storage facilities, while backlog costs for positive excess demand may partially represent interest charges, payable to the monetary authority, for a debt incurred in accumulating unsatisfied demands, the debt being discharged only when demands are honored.

Finally, it is assumed that the price maker knows the properties of the excess demand functions and chooses prices to maximize the return, revenue minus costs, over some horizon, subject to the requirement of a constant price level each period, $\sum p_i^2$ = constant, and subject to the obligation of carrying inventory and backlogging unsatisfied demands. We leave unspecified the identify of the agent calling prices and the disposition of earnings.

As suggested earlier, this price-making mechanism represents only an initial step in attempting to resolve the question of price making in a competitive economy. While it is similar in some respects to price making in a real-world market, the specialist system in securities exchange markets, nevertheless, it is vulnerable to the charge of some degree of arbitrariness, as is the ad hoc price adjustment mechanism: $\dot{p}_i(t) = E_i$.

However, it represents a positive step in that it offers some advantages over an ad hoc mechanism. It does completely describe a viable trading mechanism in which exchanges occur each period of any horizon. It provides a motivation for the choice of prices and thus provides an opportunity to explore properties of the optimizing behavior of a price maker, in particular, in examining that agent's ingenuity in coping with unusual economies.

In analyzing the system the first, obvious observation is that the price maker's revenue each period is nonnegative for all nonnegative prices. That is, revenue $= \Sigma p_i \max(E_i, 0) \geq 0$. At a competitive equilibrium it clearly follows that revenue equals zero since then $E_i \leq 0$. In Scarf's example if any two prices are zero, revenue is also zero since the corresponding excess demands are unbounded above with the remaining excess demand being zero. Similarly, in Gale's example revenue is zero if one or both prices are zero. Thus, in searching for a positive return, the appropriate price set in Scarf's economy (the Scarf price set) consists of the collection of nonnegative price vectors in which not all prices are equal, not more than one price is zero and, normalizing, $\Sigma p_i^2 = 3$. In Gale's economy the appropriate price set consists of price vectors with unequal positive prices that satisfy $\Sigma p_i^2 = 2$.

4. SCARF'S ECONOMY: SINGLE-PERIOD HORIZON

In Scarf's economy we derive various propositions concerning price choices beginning with outcomes in two single-period problems whose solutions are informative in understanding multiperiod behavior. Hence, consider the choice of prices when the price maker maximizes single period revenue, the value of positive excess demand, subject to the Scarf price set. Here the solution is easily obtained and is relevant to multiperiod behavior.

PROPOSITION 1. *Suppose the price maker maximizes single-period revenue subject to the Scarf price set. Then the optimal choice of the prices* (p_1, p_2, p_3) *is not unique with outcomes* $(p^*, 0, p^*)$, $(p^*, p^*, 0)$, *and* $(0, p^*, p^*)$ *where* $p^* = (3/2)^{1/2}$.

Proof. Consider price vectors that, say, satisfy $p_1 \geq p_3 \geq p_2$ with $p_1 > p_2$ and $p_3 > 0$. In this case $E_1 \geq 0$, $E_2 \geq 0$, and $E_3 < 0$. Thus, revenue, the value of positive excess demand, equals

$$\frac{p_1^2(p_3 - p_2)}{(p_1 + p_2)(p_1 + p_3)} + \frac{p_2^2(p_1 - p_3)}{(p_1 + p_2)(p_2 + p_3)} = \frac{p_3^2(p_1 - p_2)}{(p_1 + p_3)(p_2 + p_3)}. \tag{4}$$

Solving the price level constraint for p_1, substituting the result into the maximand (4) and differentiating (4) with respect to p_2, gives a partial derivative that is negative for all prices satisfying the restrictions $p_1 \geq p_3 \geq p_2$, $p_1 > p_2$ and $p_3 > 0$. Thus, under these restrictions it is optimal to set $p_2 = 0$. It is then easy to verify that $p_1 = p_3 = (3/2)^{1/2}$ is also optimal with revenue $(3/2)^{1/2}/2$. A similar result applies in regard to the remaining vectors in the Scarf price set, a consequence of the cyclic and symmetric properties of the economy. For example, for price vectors satisfying $p_1 \geq p_2 \geq p_3$, $p_1 > p_3$ and $p_2 > 0$ it is optimal to set $p_1 = p_2 = (3/2)^{1/2}$ and $p_3 = 0$, again, with revenue $(3/2)^{1/2}/2$. Consequently, the choice of prices in not unique and, in the single period horizon, the price maker would make a selection arbitrarily among the price vectors $(p^*, 0, p^*)$, $(p^*, p^*, 0)$ and $(0, p^*, p^*)$ where $p^* = (3/2)^{1/2}$. ■

In the next problem we introduce inventories and the backlog. Here, we assume the price maker incurs a cost of h dollars per unit of inventory of each good per period and a cost of g dollars per unit per period of the backlog (the accumulated unsatisfied demand). In the single-period problem these costs are associated with current excess supply and positive excess demand. In this problem outcomes are more complex, depending on the magnitudes of the inventory and backlog costs.

PROPOSITION 2. *Suppose the price maker maximizes the single-period return, revenue minus costs, subject to the Scarf price set. Now, consider prices* $p^0 \geq p^{00}$ *which uniquely satisfy the conditions* $(p^{00})^3 - (p^0)^3 + 3|g - h| = 0$ *and* $(p^0)^2 + (p^{00})^2 = 3$.

Then, the price maker chooses the competitive prices $(1, 1, 1)$ with zero return under the following circumstances:

(a) If $h > g$, then $p^0 \leq h + g \cdot (p^0/p^{00})$.
(b) If $h < g$, then $p^0 \leq h \cdot (p^0/p^{00}) + g$.
(c) If $h = g$, then $(3/2)^{1/2} \leq g + h$.

Noncompetitive prices are chosen when conditions (a)–(c) are relaxed:

(d) If $h > g$ and $p^0 > h + g \cdot (p^0/p^{00})$, the price maker chooses arbitrarily among the price vectors $(p^{00}, 0, p^0)$, $(p^0, p^{00}, 0)$ and $(0, p^0, p^{00})$ with $p^0 > p^{00}$.
(e) If $h < g$ and $p^0 > h \cdot (p^0/p^{00}) + g$, the choice is among the set $(p^0, 0, p^{00})$, $(p^{00}, p^0, 0)$ and $(0, p^{00}, p^0)$, again, with $p^0 > p^{00}$.
(f) If $h = g$ and $(3/2)^{1/2} > g + h$, the price maker chooses arbitrarily among the price vectors $(p^*, 0, p^*)$, $(p^*, p^*, 0)$ and $(0, p^*, p^*)$ with $p^* = (3/2)^{1/2}$, as in Proposition 1. Here, $p^0 = p^{00} = p^*$.

Proof. (a) and (d): Suppose $h > g$. Again, consider price vectors that satisfy $p_1 \geq p_3 \geq p_2$, $p_1 > p_2$ and $p_3 > 0$ with $E_1 \geq 0$, $E_2 \geq 0$, and $E_3 <$

0. Thus, the return, revenue minus cost, equals $p_1E_1 + p_2E_2 - h(-E_3) - gE_1 - gE_2$ or

$$\frac{p_3^2(p_1 - p_2)}{(p_1 + p_3)(p_2 + p_3)} - \frac{hp_3(p_1 - p_2)}{(p_1 + p_3)(p_2 + p_3)} - \frac{gp_1(p_3 - p_2)}{(p_1 + p_2)(p_1 + p_3)}$$

$$- \frac{gp_2(p_1 - p_3)}{(p_1 + p_2)(p_2 + p_3)},$$

$$= \frac{\left[(p_3 - h)p_3(p_1 + p_2) - g\left(p_1p_2 + p_3^2\right)\right](p_1 - p_2)}{(p_1 + p_2)(p_1 + p_3)(p_2 + p_3)}. \tag{5}$$

Now, assume that the maximand in (5) is positive, which requires the existence of feasible prices such that the numerator is positive. As in the previous problem, eliminate p_1 by the price level constraint and differentiate (5) with respect to p_2. Again, it is possible to show that the derivative is negative for all feasible prices for which the maximand is positive. Setting $p_2 = 0$, the maximand becomes

$$\frac{p_1p_3 - (hp_1 + gp_3)}{(p_1 + p_3)}. \tag{6}$$

Now, eliminating p_3 by the price level constraint, where $p_2 = 0$, and differentiating (6) with respect to p_1, gives as the derivative

$$\frac{p_3^3 - p_1^3 + 3(g - h)}{p_3(p_1 + p_3)^2}. \tag{7}$$

If $h > g$, the derivative is negative for all $p_1 \geq p_3$. Hence, with the constraint $p_1 \geq p_3$, the price maker would choose $p_1 = p_3 = p^*$ and $p_2 = 0$.

This outcome is apparent from (6), in that, given $h > g$, the price maker wishes to reduce p_1 to economize on inventory cost, relative to backlog cost, but, in the given price sequence, that attempt is limited by the requirement $p_1 \geq p_3$. However, that barrier is relaxed by interchanging p_1 and p_3 to obtain the sequence: $p_3 \geq p_1 \geq p_2$, $p_3 > p_2$, and $p_1 > 0$. For this sequence, by an analogous argument, we again obtain (6) as the maximand and, differentiating with respect to p_3, the corresponding derivative

$$\frac{p_1^3 - p_3^3 + 3(h - g)}{p_1(p_1 + p_3)^2}. \tag{8}$$

If $h > g$, then from (8) the derivative is positive when $p_1 = p_3$, and as

$p_1 \to g$, it becomes negative. Thus, over the entire price set, an optimal price vector is attained when $p_2 = 0$ and p_1 and p_3 satisfy the conditions

$$p_1^3 - p_3^3 + 3(h - g) = 0, \qquad p_1^2 + p_2^3 = 3. \tag{9}$$

A solution, say, $(p_1 = p^{00},\ p_3 = p^0)$, is unique where the solution prices depend on the difference $(h - g)$ with $p^0 > p^{00}$. An optimal solution is then specified by the vector $(p^{00}, 0, p^0)$. Also when $h > g$, a consideration of other price sequences will verify that the price vectors $(p^0, p^{00}, 0)$ and $(0, p^0, p^{00})$ are also optimal in the single-period horizon.

Moreover, when $h > g$, it is now apparent from (6) that $p^0 p^{00} > (hp^{00} + gp^0)$, or, equivalently, that $p^0 > h + g \cdot (p^0/p^{00})$, is the necessary and sufficient condition for the optimality of noncompetitive prices, which proves (d). Hence, if this condition is violated, the price maker will choose the unique competitive prices $(1, 1, 1)$, markets will clear and the return will equal zero, which proves (a).

(b) and (e): Suppose $h < g$. Here, the price maker wishes to economize on backlog cost. Hence, once again consider the price sequence: $p_1 \geq p_3 \geq p_2$, $p_1 > p_2$ and $p_3 > 0$, which also gives the maximand (6) and derivative (7). This sequence is now relevant since it permits reduction of p_3 below p_1. In this case optimal prices satisfy $p_2 = 0$, and the conditions

$$p_3^3 - p_1^3 + 3(g - h) = 0, \qquad p_1^2 + p_3^2 = 3. \tag{10}$$

On comparing (9) and (10) it is seen that, in both cases, the optimal prices are the identical functions of the absolute difference $|g - h|$. That is, in both cases, optimal prices p^0 and p^{00} satisfy

$$(p^{00})^3 - (p^0)^3 + 3|g - h| = 0, \qquad (p^0)^2 + (p^{00})^2 = 3. \tag{11}$$

Thus, if $h < g$, an optimal solution is given by the vector $(p^0, 0, p^{00})$. Again, a consideration of other price sequences yields the optimality of the price vectors $(p^{00}, p^0, 0)$ and $(0, p^{00}, p^0)$ with the necessary and sufficient condition for the optimality of noncompetitive prices being $p^0 > h \cdot (p^0/p^{00}) + g$. Thus, (b) and (e) are verified.

(c) and (f): Suppose $h = g$. It now easily follows from (11), and earlier arguments, that $(3/2)^{1/2} > g + h$ is the necessary and sufficient condition for the optimality of price vectors with $p^0 = p^{00} = p^*$, which verifies (c) and (f). ∎

5. SCARF'S ECONOMY: MULTIPERIOD HORIZON

Proposition 2 does indicate that the price maker chooses prices to economize on costs but, nevertheless, in favorable cases outcomes are characterized by multiple solutions. But the outcomes are strikingly different in a long horizon. In multiperiod problems an added concern of the price maker is the management of the accumulation of the inventory and the backlog. Now a judicious choice of prices is needed to balance interperiod demand and supplies; otherwise, costs become excessive. In the solution of the multiperiod problem, price choices are unique (after an initial choice over several price vectors), price vectors are cyclic, and single-period prices may be modified to take into account balancing of demands and supplies. Before deriving outcomes, however, one more feature of the trading mechanism needs to be resolved to complete the characterization of the multiperiod problem, i.e., the opportune delivery time of available inventory to satisfy positive excess demand. The price maker will prefer immediate delivery to reduce cost, but the consumer may prefer delayed delivery since immediate delivery may not increase consumer utility. We examine consumer choice of delivery date in detail and comment briefly on price-maker delivery choice.

To illustrate the derivation of outcomes we first consider the special case where $h > 0$ and $g = 0$ and assume $(3/2)^{1/2} > h$.

PROPOSITION 3. *Suppose the price maker maximizes the multiperiod return, revenues minus costs, over a long horizon, subject to the Scarf price set. Suppose* $h > 0$, $g = 0$, *and* $(3/2)^{1/2} > h$. *Then, the following choice of prices is optimal where, as noted,* $p^* = (3/2)^{1/2}$. *In the first period, choose arbitrarily among price vectors in which two prices equal* p^* *and the remaining price equals zero, say,* $(p^*, 0, p^*)$. *In the next two periods, choose the price vectors:* $(0, p^*, p^*)$ *and* $(p^*, p^*, 0)$. *In subsequent periods repeat the three-period cycle of prices:* $(p^*, 0, p^*)$, $(0, p^*, p^*)$, *and* $(p^* p^*, 0)$.

Proof. To prove the proposition we calculate the multiperiod return with the three-period cycle of prices: $(p^*, 0, p^*)$, $(0, p^*, p^*)$, and $(p^*, p^*, 0)$ and then show that any other sequence of prices will reduce the return.

In this scheme, designating positive I_i as an inventory accumulation and negative I_i as a backlog accumulation, in each cycle the pattern becomes

$$\text{Period 1:} \quad (E_1, E_2, E_3) = \left(\tfrac{1}{2}, 0, -\tfrac{1}{2}\right), (I_1, I_2, I_3) = \left(-\tfrac{1}{2}, 0, \tfrac{1}{2}\right);$$

$$\text{Period 2:} \quad (E_1, E_2, E_3) = \left(0, -\tfrac{1}{2}, \tfrac{1}{2}\right), (I_1, I_2, I_3) = \left(-\tfrac{1}{2}, \tfrac{1}{2}, 0\right);$$

$$\text{Period 3:} \quad (E_1, E_2, E_3) = \left(-\tfrac{1}{2}, \tfrac{1}{2}, 0\right), (I_1, I_2, I_3) = \left(\left[\tfrac{1}{2}, -\tfrac{1}{2}\right], 0, 0\right). \tag{12}$$

The first element of inventory in period 3 indicates that consumers do not choose to have delivery of the backlog of the first good since, in this period, all current demands are satisfied by endowments and inventory so that a delivery of the first good will not increase their utility. Moreover, the availability of positive inventory of $\frac{1}{2}$ units of good 1 will satisfy their positive excess demand in the next period. Hence, the price maker carries both an inventory and a backlog of $\frac{1}{2}$ units of the first good in the third period. In the fourth and subsequent periods, all current demands are satisfied from the periodic endowments and the inventory and the positive excess demand of the initial period is never covered.

Nevertheless, the choice of prices balances demands and supplies in that the accumulated backlog never exceeds $\frac{1}{2}$ units of a good and the positive inventory in a period satisfies positive excess demand in the next period. The inventory cost each period becomes $\frac{1}{2}h$ dollars with a return per period of $[(3/2)^{1/2} - h]/2$ dollars.

To prove the optimality of the given price sequence note, first, that, apart from an arbitrary starting point among the three price vectors, any change in the sequence of these price vectors will reduce the return to the price maker since inventory, and inventory cost, will successively accumulate over the horizon.

Moreover, a little calculation will verify that any change in these prices in one or more periods such that more than one price is zero or all prices are positive will also reduce the return.

Finally, we need to consider price vectors in which one price is zero and the two positive prices are unequal. And, we need to select a sequence of these price vectors that balance demands and supplies; otherwise, the return will decrease. Hence, consider the prices $p^0 > p^{00}$ that satisfy (11) with $g = 0$ and the price vectors that solve the corresponding one-period problem: $(p^{00}, 0, p^0)$, $(p^0, p^{00}, 0)$ and $(0, p^0, p^{00})$. Now, introduce the price vectors specifying the remaining combinations in the three prices and consider the six-period cycle of prices: $(p^0, 0, p^{00})$, $(0, p^0, p^{00})$, $(p^{00}, p^0, 0)$, $(p^{00}, 0, p^0)$, $(0, p^{00}, p^0)$, and $(p^0, p^{00}, 0)$. Let $I^0 = p^0/(p^0 + p^{00})$ and $I^{00} = p^{00}/(p^0 + p^{00})$ so that $I^0 + I^{00} = 1$. Then, with I_i again specifying the inventory (backlog), in each cycle the result becomes

$$\text{Period 1:}\quad (E_1, E_2, E_3) = (I^{00}, 0, -I^0), (I_1, I_2, I_3) = (-I^{00}, 0, I^0);$$

$$\text{Period 2:}\quad (E_1, E_2, E_3) = (0, -I^{00}, I^0), (I_1, I_2, I_3) = (-I^{00}, I^{00}, 0);$$

$$\text{Period 3:}\quad (E_1, E_2, E_3) = (-I^0, I^{00}, 0), (I_1, I_2, I_3) = ([I^0, -I^{00}], 0, 0);$$

$$\text{Period 4:}\quad (E_1, E_2, E_3) = (I^0, 0, I^{00}), (I_1, I_2, I_3) = (-I^{00}, 0, I^{00});$$

Period 5: $(E_1, E_2, E_3) = (0, -I^0, I^{00}), (I_1, I_2, I_3) = (-I^{00}, I^0, 0);$

Period 6: $(E_1, E_2, E_3) = (-I^{00}, I^0, 0), (I_1, I_2, I_3) = ([I^{00}, -I^{00}], 0, 0).$

(13)

Over a six-period cycle the return equals $[6p^0p^{00}/(p^0 + p^{00})] - 3h$. Hence, the inventory cost becomes a fixed charge. In fact, any arbitrary prices p^0 and p^{00} that satisfy only $p^0 \geq p^{00}$, $(p^0)^2 + (p^{00})^2 = 3$ and the specified cyclical pattern of price vectors will give an analogous result with a fixed inventory cost. In particular, in the case $p^0 = p^{00} = p^*$, the six-period return becomes $3(3/2)^{1/2} - 3h$. It now easily follows that the solution to the problem, when $h > 0$, $g = 0$, is to choose prices $p^0 \geq p^{00}$, $(p^0)^2 + (p^{00})^2 = 3$ to maximize single-period revenue $p^0p^{00}/(p^0 + p^{00})$, when one price is zero, and, hence, that the optimal nonzero prices do satisfy $p^0 = p^{00} = p^* = (3/2)^{1/2}$. ■

Thus, prices that are optimal in a single-period horizon, when $h > 0$, $g = 0$, are no longer optimal in a long horizon since balancing of demands and supplies to reduce costs induces price adjustments. And, once an initial price vector is chosen, the choice of all subsequent price vectors is uniquely determined in a three-period cycle. Finally, the condition $(3/2)^{1/2} > h$ is now the necessary and sufficient condition for the optimality of noncompetitive prices.

Now, consider the outcome for consumers. Here, we need a distribution rule in the event of unsatisfied demand, but that rule is significant only in the first period of the horizon since in all subsequent periods all demands are satisfied by the endowments and the available inventory. In the first period, individual 2 receives 0 utils and, no matter what the distribution rule, individuals 1 and 3 share 1 util of satisfaction. The util distribution in the second and third periods of the first cycle are duplicated in all subsequent cycles. Thus, beginning in the second cycle, in successive periods, the util distribution becomes $(U^1, U^2, U^3) = (1, 0, \frac{1}{2})$, $(U^1, U^2, U^3) = (0, \frac{1}{2}, 1)$, and $(U^1, U^2, U^3) = (\frac{1}{2}, 1, 0)$. Relative to the competitive allocation of $\frac{1}{2}$ utils of satisfaction each period for each individual, some satisfaction is lost in the first cycle, but, subsequently, satisfactions are the same: under both schemes each individual receives $1\frac{1}{2}$ utils of satisfaction every cycle of three periods. Thus, starting in the second cycle, neither distribution dominates the other. Moreover, from (12), it is easy to verify that, if the price maker begins the horizon with an endowment of $\frac{1}{2}$ units of the first good, in fact, $\frac{1}{2}$ units of any good, all positive excess demands will be satisfied, with the backlog being zero in every period. In this event, each individual will receive $1\frac{1}{2}$ utils of satisfaction in each cycle beginning with the first cycle. Of course, these comparisons only refer to possible outcomes with the price maker since the Walrasian price adjustment mechanism fails to find prices at which trades are consummated.

When both h and g are positive, a three-period price cycle is no longer optimal since then the backlog cost depends on price choices. The need to balance the inventory and the backlog and to economize on costs induces a six-period cycle of prices. The outcome is specified in the next proposition.

PROPOSITION 4. *Suppose the price-maker maximizes the multi-period return, revenues minus costs, subject to the Scarf price set. Suppose* $h > 0$ *and* $g > 0$. *Consider the problem of choosing* $p^0 \geq p^{00}$ *to maximize*: $(p^0 p^{00} - gp^{00})/(p^0 + p^{00})$, *the single-period problem with one price zero and* $h = 0$, $g > 0$. *Moreover, for optimal prices* (p^0, p^{00}), *assume that* $2[(p^0 p^{00} - gp^{00})/(p^0 + p^{00})] > h$. *Then a six-period cycle of price vectors is optimal. The first price vector is any solution to the one-period problem. The subsequent price vectors are then uniquely determined. Choosing* $(p^0, 0, p^{00})$ *as the first price vector, the following six-period price cycle is then optimal*: $(p^0, 0, p^{00})$, $(0, p^0, p^{00})$, $(p^{00}, p^0, 0)$, $(p^{00}, 0, p^0)$, $(0, p^{00}, p^0)$, *and* $(p^0, p^{00}, 0)$.

Proof. The proof uses results already obtained in the proof of Proposition 3. In particular, the six-period price cycle above yields the excess demand and inventory allocation in (13). Here, the six-period return equals $6[(p^0 p^{00} - gp^{00})/(p^0 + p^{00})] - 3h$. The return reflects the inventory fixed cost and an effort to reduce the backlog cost. Adapting previous arguments the optimal solution is to choose $p^0 \geq p^{00}$ to maximize $(p^0 p^{00} - gp^{00})/(p^0 + p^{00})$ subject to $(p^0)^2 + (p^{00})^2 = 3$. Hence, optimal prices satisfy (11) when $h = 0$. Since $p^0 > p^{00}$, a six-period price cycle is required to balance demands and supplies. In the price cycle above the choice of the first, third, and fifth price vectors as the initial choice of prices yields the identical six-period return so that any of these price vectors may be chosen at the beginning of the horizon in which later price vectors are uniquely determined. The initial choice of the second, fourth, or sixth price vectors is not optimal, yielding the following return: $6[p^0 p^{00} - gp^0)/(p^0 + p^{00})] - 3h$. Here, the necessary and sufficient condition for the optimality of noncompetitive prices is $2[(p^0 p^{00} - gp^{00})/(p^0 + p^{00})] > h$. ■

As in the case with $h > 0$, $g = 0$, consumers now lose some satisfaction (I^{00} utils) in the first period of the first cycle, but, henceforth, satisfactions are the same as in the competitive allocation. Under both schemes consumers receive 3 utils of satisfaction every six periods. Moreover, if the price maker begins the horizon with an endowment of $\frac{1}{2}$ units of any single good, the solution will be the same as in the previous case with $g = 0$. The backlog will be zero in every period, all positive excess demands will be satisfied and a three-period cycle will be optimal with $p^0 = p^{00} = p^*$.

We now briefly consider cases in which the price maker chooses delivery dates in satisfying accumulated positive excess demand. As suggested, the price maker improves the return at the expense of consumers. Here, the inventory cost may not be a fixed charge, the choice of prices depends on the relative magnitude of g and h and, relative to the competitive allocation, consumers lose satisfaction in each price cycle. We illustrate these outcomes by examining the case where $g > h > 0$. Again, we consider the price cycle with $p^0 \geq p^{00}$, which yields the excess demands in (13). Here, the inventory needs to be modified to reflect the price maker's choice of delivery dates. In particular, in period 3 the inventory becomes $(I_1, I_2, I_3) = ([I^0 - I^{00}], 0, 0)$ and in period 6 $(I_1, I_2, I_3) = (0, 0, 0)$. Hence, all demands are eventually satisfied with the price maker having zero inventory and backlog in period 6. The return over six periods equals $[6p^0p^{00} - (4gp^{00} + 3hp^0 + hp^{00})]/(p^0 + p^{00})$. By previous analysis it is apparent that the six-period cycle of price vectors is optimal where p^0 and p^{00} maximize the return above subject to $p^0 \geq p^{00}$ and $(p^0)^2 + (p^{00})^2 = 3$ and that in an optimal solution $p^0 > p^{00}$. Moreover, while all demands are satisfied in each cycle, delivery occurs inopportunely in periods 3 and 6 and, as a consequence, relative to the competitive allocation consumers lose $2I^{00}$ utils of satisfaction in each six-period cycle. Analogous results occur in other cases. Again, it is easy to verify that, if the price maker begins the horizon with an endowment of $\frac{1}{2}$ units of any single good, a three-period cycle will be optimal with $p^0 = p^{00} = p^*$. Hence, whenever the price maker is endowed with $\frac{1}{2}$ units of a good, whether the consumer or the price maker chooses delivery dates for satisfying the backlog is irrelevant, and for all values of g and h, subject to the constraint $(3/2)^{1/2} > h$, the optimal price cycle has three periods with $p^0 = p^{00} = p^*$. In this situation the allocation to consumers and the competitive allocation each yield $1\frac{1}{2}$ utils of satisfaction in each cycle beginning with the first cycle.

6. GALE'S ECONOMY

In Gale's economy the outcomes are markedly different. In a long horizon, if the price maker incurs positive inventory cost, independently of the magnitude of a backlog cost, Gale's "fair and natural" competitive equilibrium always prevails. In a single-period horizon, with favorable costs the price maker chooses noncompetitive prices, but, as the horizon lengthens, due to an inability to balance demands and supplies, any choice of noncompetitive prices, or "unfair" competitive prices, eventually results in a negative multiperiod return. As a consequence, the best the price maker can do is to choose the market clearing competitive prices $(1, 1)$ that yield zero return in each period.

To verify these outcomes we first consider the single-period problem. Here, as in the Scarf economy, with favorable costs, price choices are not unique. In the next proposition, to illustrate the nonuniqueness but simplify the computation, we only consider the case with $h > 0$ and $g = 0$.

PROPOSITION 5. *Suppose the price maker maximizes the single-period return, revenue minus cost, subject to the Gale price set. Suppose $h > 0$ and $g = 0$. If $h > 1$, the optimal choice of prices (p, q) is the competitive solution* $(1, 1)$. *Otherwise, there exist unique, noncompetitive prices $p^h > p^l > 0$ that satisfy first-order optimality conditions such that both price vectors (p^h, p^l) and (p^l, p^h) are optimal.*

Proof. From (3), choosing $p > q > 0$, with $p^2 + q^2 = 2$, gives $E_x > 0$ and $E_y < 0$ with a return

$$\frac{pq(p-q)}{\delta} - \frac{hp(p-q)}{\delta} = \frac{p(p-q)(q-h)}{\delta}, \tag{14}$$

where, as earlier, $\delta = 2p^2 + 5pq + 2q^2$ and since $p^2 + q^2 = 2$, $\delta = 4 + 5pq$. Hence, from the price constraints and the right-hand side of (14), it follows that this return is negative if $h > 1$. The same result follows when $q > p > 0$. Thus, a competitive solution is to be chosen but only the solution $(1, 1)$ is optimal since the price vectors $(\sqrt{2}, 0)$ and $(0, \sqrt{2})$ yield zero revenue and inventory cost $h/2$.

Another examination of the price constraints and the right-hand side of (14) verifies that there exist feasible prices (p, q) such that the return is positive when $h < 1$. Differentiating the left-hand side of (14) with respect to p, subject to the constraint $p^2 + q^2 = 2$, gives

$$\frac{(p+q)}{q\delta^2}\left[5(pq)^2 + 12pq - 8\right] - \frac{2h}{q\delta^2}\left[2(p^2 - q^2) + 5p^2 + 4pq\right]. \tag{15}$$

Under the condition $h < 1$, this derivative becomes positive as $p \to q$ and negative as $q \to 0$ and, thus, optimal prices occur when (15) equals zero with $p > q$. Moreover, the solution is unique since the second derivative of the return (14) is negative when the first derivative (15) is zero. Call the solutions prices $p = p^h$ and $q = p^l$. Again, by symmetry, the two price vectors (p^h, p^l) and (p^l, p^h) are optimal for this problem when $h < 1$. ■

As shown in the final proposition, a peculiarity of the Gale model now ensures that the competitive solution $(1, 1)$ is optimal in every period of a long horizon for any $h > 0$, $g \geq 0$.

PROPOSITION 6. *Suppose the price maker maximizes the multiperiod return, revenues minus costs, over a long horizon, subject to the Gale price set. Suppose* $h > 0$, $g \geq 0$. *Then the competitive prices* $(1, 1)$ *are optimal in each period of the horizon.*

Proof. From (3) note that, whenever $p \neq q$,

$$E_x + E_y = \frac{(p - q)(q - p)}{\delta} < 0. \tag{16}$$

The meaning of (16) is that, given $p \neq q$, the number of units of excess supply of one good always exceeds the number of units of positive excess demand of the other good. The extreme cases here are the competitive solutions $(\sqrt{2}, 0)$ and $(0, \sqrt{2})$ in which one excess demand equals zero and one $(-\frac{1}{2})$. The importance of this result is that, unless the competitive solution $(1, 1)$ is chosen each period, excess supplies will dominate so that it is not possible to balance interperiod demands and supplies and per period holding cost will become successively larger, eventually leading to a negative multiperiod return. That is, to contain costs, it is necessary to choose price vectors in which the commodity with the high (low) price in one period has a low (high) price in the next period, but even that effort does not succeed because (16) implies that the inventory holding of both goods eventually becomes successively larger.

To verify this outcome we consider a case that is least favorable to the claim. Assume $h > 0$ but $g = 0$, which reduces cost. Now, suppose the price maker, rather than the consumer, chooses the delivery date to satisfy the backlog. This procedure reduces inventory cost relative to the alternative in which the consumer makes the choice.

Consider any prices $p^h > p^l > 0$ that satisfy $(p^h)^2 + (p^l)^2 = 2$. Beginning with (p^l, p^h), alternate the price vectors (p^l, p^h) and (p^h, p^l) in subsequent periods. In this scheme the commodity y (for which the price is p^h in the first period) always has a positive inventory that becomes successively larger. The commodity x has successively larger positive inventory in the even periods and inventory $(t - \frac{1}{2})I_h - (t + \frac{1}{2})I_l$ in the odd periods where t is odd, $I_h = p^h(p^h - p^l)/\delta$ and $I_l = p^l(p^h - p^l)/\delta$. Since $I_h > I_l$, this inventory eventually becomes positive. Nevertheless, in the least favorable case we suppose that this inventory is always negative, which reduces inventory cost and does not incur backlog cost since $g = 0$. Then, the return after t periods, where t is now even, becomes $t\{p^l I_h - (I_l/2)h - 3[(t + 2)/8]h(I_h - I_l)\}$. Clearly, this return is negative for an even t that is sufficiently large. An adjustment in the return when t is odd provides the same conclusion. And the same conclusion applies to any choice of high and low prices. The introduction of a positive backlog cost only reinforces this outcome. ■

What appears to be a peculiar property of Gale's economy accounts for the long-run optimality of the "fair and natural" competitive equilibrium. Surprisingly, perhaps, a similar property gives an analogous outcome in a Cobb–Douglas exchange economy, which, as is well known, has a unique, globally stable competitive equilibrium. Consider a two-person, two-good exchange economy where individual 1 has utility $U^1 = x_1^1 x_2^1$ with endowment $(\bar{x}_1^1, \bar{x}_2^1) = (1, 0)$ and individual 2 has utility $U^2 = x_1^2 x_2^2$ with endowment $(\bar{x}_1^2, \bar{x}_2^2) = (0, 1)$. Under the normalization $\Sigma p_i^2 = 2$, the competitive equilibrium is unique with prices (1, 1). In this economy it is easy to verify that, for positive noncompetitive prices, positive excess demands dominate. Hence, from the previous discussion it should be clear, without providing any of the details, that, if $g > 0$, independently of the magnitude of an inventory cost, the return eventually becomes negative as the horizon lengthens. Thus, the competitive equilibrium (1, 1) is optimal in a long horizon.

7. CONCLUDING COMMENTS

In extreme examples of nonstochastic, competitive exchange economies, we have illustrated that price making with optimization provides a motivation for the choice of prices and show that prices may depend on both characteristics of agents in the economy and characteristics of the trading process. As to consumers, with an optimizing price mechanism, they clearly benefit in the Scarf economy since; otherwise, trades are never consummated, and even when noncompetitive prices are chosen, they do not necessarily suffer relative to the choice of competitive prices. The outcomes for consumers tend to be favorable since, even though markets need not clear each period, all or most excess demands are eventually satisfied so that markets tend to clear, or nearly clear, on the average. This outcome is a consequence of the fact that nonzero market excess demands are undesirable to price makers in that such positions are associated with trading costs that induce efforts to manage the inventory and the backlog to reduce costs without unduly reducing revenue. In the Gale economy, even though competitive prices are selected in a long horizon, the price-making mechanism provides a unique choice among the several possible competitive price vectors. Again, trading costs are responsible for inducing a particular choice of prices.

The outcomes in this paper lend some support to the notion that the theory of pure competition should be augmented by the introduction of market-making agents. Moreover, in real-world competitive (and other) markets some agents do perform the task of organizing trading activities, making and honoring prices or otherwise act as intermediaries in arranging exchanges of commodities. The "specialist system" in organized securities markets provides an example in which agents directly call and honor prices and bear the risk of holding securities obtained as a consequence of trading activities. At the other extreme market makers may only serve as intermediaries, not directly calling prices and not bearing the risk of holding assets. In the housing market agents offer to arrange trades for a broker's fee (a spread) with the asset owner fixing a price and bearing the cost of holding the asset until it is sold. The fee charged by agents is limited by competing agents and the privilege the asset owner has of attempting to arrange an exchange without intermediation. Intermediate cases, which are more or less competitive, abound. For example, retailers usually carry inventories of goods to satisfy customer demands at a markup (a spread) over costs but limit risk by controlling inventory and by choosing whether to use a lost sales or backlogging method of sales. To develop a theory of pure competition in which consumers and suppliers of goods are price takers, a variety of more or less competitive price-making activities may plausibly be introduced to study the operation of a competitive economy. To develop analyses of real-world economies, a close study of real-world price-making activities, including adjustments to excess demands, seems needed.

To provide a final perspective on the present study we again compare the "specialist system" and Walrasian price adjustments. Earlier it was argued that the "specialist system" provides a competitive price adjustment process analogous to the Walrasian mechanism. The "specialist," who operates in a system in which the arrival of market orders is a random process, announces bid and ask prices prior to the actual arrival of market orders and then satisfies any revealed excess demand. The randomness in the system induces real-time price adjustment that emulates the Walrasian system. The Walrasian auctioneer chooses prices, observes excess demands, and adjusts prices according to the revealed excess demands. To support the intuition of the Walrasian mechanism also seems to demand some implicit notion of randomness in the excess demand process. Otherwise, if fully informed about excess demands, the auctioneer would at once choose competitive equilibrium prices and forestall any adjustment process.

The present study only considers nonstochastic systems and, hence, does not analyze any real-time adjustment processes induced by randomness in a system. The prices that are chosen in the examples are equilibrium prices, and these prices are chosen directly without the adjustments customary in stability analysis. An earlier version of this paper attempted to study real-time price adjustments in the Scarf economy by introducing randomness in periodic endowments. Some progress was made in analyzing price-maker and price-taker behavior in multiperiod horizons. That work suggests that price adjustments would occur in the direction of equilibrium price vectors in the nonstochastic economy, but computations of period by period price changes proved to be very difficult, so the actual outcome is still in doubt. Future work will reconsider price adjustments in the Scarf example and other competitive economies.

Acknowledgments

The author is indebted to Richard Romano for reading the manuscript carefully and offering useful comments. The author also benefitted from comments in seminars at the University of Florida and Tulane University and meetings of the Southern Economics Association.

References

1. B. Allen, and M. Hellwig, (1986). "Price-setting firms and the oligopolistic foundations of perfect competition," *Am. Econ. Rev.* **76**, 387–392.
2. K. Arrow, H. D. Block, and L. Hurwicz (1959). "On the stability of competitive equilibrium, II," *Econometrica* **25**, 82–109.
3. K. J. Arrow and F. H. Hahn (1971). *General Competitive Analysis* (Holden-Day, San Francisco).
4. J. Bradfield and E. Zabel (1979). "Price adjustment in a competitive market and the securities exchange specialist," *General Equilibrium, Growth and Trade* (in J. E. Green and J. A. Scheinkman (eds.), (Academic Press, New York).
5. F. M. Fisher (1972). "On price adjustment without an auctioneer," *Rev. Econ. Studies* **XXXIX**, 1–15.
6. F. M. Fisher (1974). "The Hahn process with firms but no production," *Econometrica* **42**, 471–486.
7. F. M. Fisher (1976). "A non-tâtonnement model with production and consumption," *Econometrica* **44**, 907–938.
8. F. M. Fisher (1983). *Disequilibrium Foundations of Equilibrium Economics* (Cambridge University Press, Cambridge, U.K.).
9. D. Gale (1963). "A note on global instability of competitive equilibrium," *Naval Res. Logistics Quart.* **10**, 81–87.
10. F. H. Hahn and T. Negishi (1962). "A theorem on non-tâtonnement stability," *Econometrica* **30**, 463–469.
11. F. H. Hahn (1978). "On non-Walrasian equilibria," *Rev. Econ. Studies* **XLV**, 1–18.
12. J. R. Hicks (1946). *Value and Capital*, 2nd ed. (Clarendon Press, Oxford, U.K.).
13. M. Hirota (1981). "On the stability of competitive equilibrium and the patterns of initial holdings: An example," *Int. Econ. Rev.* **22**, 461–470.
14. M. Hirota (1985). "Global stability in a class of markets with three commodities and three consumers," *J. Econ. Theory* **36**, 186–192.
15. W. Jaffé (1980). "Walras's economics as others see it," *J. Econ. Lit.* **XVIII**, 529–549.
16. L. Metzler (1945). "Stability of multiple markets: The Hicks conditions," *Econometrica* **10**, 277–292.
17. M. Morishima (1980). "W. Jaffé on Leon Walras: A comment," *J. Econ. Lit.* **XVIII**, 550–558.
18. P. Samuelson (1955). *Foundations of Economic Analysis* (Harvard University Press, Cambridge, Mass.).
19. H. Scarf (1960). "Some examples of global instability of the competitive equilibrium," *Int. Econ. Rev.* **1**, 157–172.
20. H. Scarf (1981). "Comment on: 'On the stability of competitive equilibrium and the patterns of initial holdings: An example'," *Int. Econ. Rev.* **22**, 469–470.
21. L. K. Simon (1984). "Bertrand, the Cournot paradigm and the theory of perfect competition," *Rev. Econ. Studies* **LI**, 209–230.
22. H. Uzawa (1962). "On the stability of Edgeworth's barter process," *Int. Econ. Rev.* **3**, 218–232.
23. E. Zabel (1981). "Competitive price adjustment without market clearing," *Econometrica* **49**, 1201–1221.

ASYMPTOTIC BEHAVIOR OF ASSET MARKETS: ASYMPTOTIC INEFFICIENCY

William R. Zame
Department of Economics
The Johns Hopkins University
Baltimore, Maryland 21208
and
Department of Economics
University of California at Los Angeles
Los Angeles, California 90024

1. INTRODUCTION

Underlying the Walrasian (Arrow–Debreu) model of economic activity are two assumptions: that agents act as price takers, and that there is a market for every commodity. When there is uncertainty about the future, the latter assumption entails a complete set of contingent claims; i.e., claims to consumption streams dependent on the future state of the world.

Arrow (1953, 1964) presents a different model, with trading in futures markets for securities (assets) whose payoffs depend on the state of the world, and in spot markets for physical commodities.[1] Although the Walrasian model and the security market model are formally different, Arrow shows that, if security markets are complete (i.e., if every wealth pattern can be obtained from a portfolio of available securities), the two models are equivalent: they support the same equilibrium allocations (of physical commodities). In particular, if security markets are complete, equilibrium allocations are efficient (Pareto-optimal).

If security markets are incomplete, however, the situation is quite different: the Walrasian model and the security market model are not

[1]Arrow considers only nominal securities; i.e., securities denominated in units of account. Radner (1972) considers a model with real securities (i.e., securities denominated in physical commodities).

GENERAL EQUILIBRIUM, GROWTH, AND TRADE II

equivalent. In particular, equilibrium allocations of security markets need not be Pareto-optimal.[2] Indeed, equilibrium allocations need not even be optimal within the set of allocations that can be obtained through trades in the given securities. [See Hart (1975), Grossman (1977), Newberry and Stiglitz (1982), Stiglitz (1982), and especially Geanakoplos and Polemarchakis (1987).]

Security markets equilibria will be efficient if assets span all the uncertainty; they may be inefficient if assets fail to span all the uncertainty. Intuition might suggest (and mine did) that security markets equilibria will be "nearly" optimal if assets span "most" of the uncertainty. The results of this paper suggest that this intuition may be wrong—badly wrong. In general, security markets equilibria may be inefficient, and remain inefficient (i.e., bounded away from Pareto-optimal allocations) even when the set of assets expands to a set that resolves all the uncertainty. Moreover, this "asymptotic inefficiency" is robust; in fact, "asymptotic inefficiency" is a generic property of asset sequences.

Our results suggest that, although a complete securities market is a perfect substitute for a Walrasian (complete contingent claims) market, a large securities market need not be a good approximation for a Walrasian market.

To establish these results, we construct a model of a securities market with a countably infinite number of states of nature.[3] When the number of assets is finite, we are able to prove (under appropriate assumptions about the returns on assets, and the preferences, endowments, and feasible trading sets of consumers) that such a securities market always has an equilibrium (Theorem 1). To study the behavior of equilibrium allocations when the assets span "most" of the uncertainty, we fix an infinite sequence (α_n) of assets, and consider, for each N, the corresponding securities market. We say that such a sequence is *asymptotically efficient* if, for all consumer preferences and endowments (in a well-behaved class), the equilibrium allocations of the security markets involving only the assets $(\alpha_n\colon 1 \leq n \leq N)$ converge to Pareto-optimal allocations of the underlying Walrasian markets. We identify a condition on an infinite sequence of assets that is necessary and sufficient that it be asymptotically efficient. Modulo a small technical caveat (that preferences be uniformly proper), sequences of assets that are asymptotically efficient are also *asymptotically complete*, in the sense that the equilibrium allocations of the security markets involving only the assets $(\alpha_n\colon 1 \leq n \leq N)$ converge to equilibrium

[2]Of course, they may be optimal in certain circumstances; the capital asset pricing model provides a notable example.

[3]It would be natural to allow for continuous uncertainty, but this would give rise to serious technical difficulties that we wish to avoid; see Section 7 for further discussion.

allocations of the underlying Walrasian market (Theorem 2).[4] The requisite condition for asymptotic efficiency (and asymptotic completeness) is that every Arrow security can be *uniformly* approximated by the returns from a *finite* portfolio. This condition is extremely strong: the sequences of assets that *fail* to satisfy this condition constitute a residual subset of the space of all asset sequences (Theorem 3).[5]

We find it convenient (for technical reasons) to work with *numeraire securities*; i.e., securities denominated in a single commodity. Numeraire securities constitute a convenient halfway station between the purely financial securities of Arrow and the general securities of Radner (1972). As shown by Geanakoplos and Polemarchakis (1987), the problems of existence identified by Hart (1975) for general security models do not arise in the case of numeraire securities.[6,7]

Our results do not depend on pathologies in securities structures, endowments, or preferences. We assume the existence of a riskless asset, and that the returns on other assets are bounded; we could, without loss, assume that all assets have strictly positive payoffs. We assume that endowments are bounded away from zero; we could also assume that endowments are bounded above. Finally, our negative results are obtained with preferences representable by separable, strictly concave utility functions (with bounded marginal rates of substitution); similar constructions could be carried out with preferences representable by homogeneous utility functions.

The crucial idea underlying our negative results is that the requirement that terminal consumption be nonnegative places severe constraints on the set of portfolios that can be traded. Terminal wealth constraints matter.

If consumption bundles are not required to be nonnegative (i.e., if we ignore terminal wealth constraints), the situation is quite different. On one hand, for a given set of assets an equilibrium need not exist; moreover, equilibrium allocations of security markets may become unbounded as the set of available assets expands. On the other hand, limits of equilibrium allocations of the finite securities markets will be equilibrium allocations

[4]This method of studying the assumption of complete markets seems analogous to the familiar method of studying the assumption of price-taking behavior by consumers; see Anderson (1986) for example.

[5]Recall that residual sets are large, and their complements are small, so "asymptotic inefficiency" is a generic property.

[6]This had already been established for models involving only purely financial securities by Cass (1984), Werner (1985) and Duffie (1985).

[7]There would be no particular difficulty in allowing for general real securities (i.e., securities denominated in arbitrary commodity bundles), provided we follow Radner (1972) and adopt appropriate lower bounds on asset trades.

of the underlying complete markets economy, *provided* that (i) the infinite sequence $\{\alpha_n\}$ of assets spans all the uncertainty, (ii) equilibria of the finite security markets exists, and (iii) these equilibrium allocations converge (Theorem 4).

The first research of which I am aware on the asymptotic behavior of security markets is due to Green and Spear (1987, 1989), and their thought-provoking work has provided some of the impetus for the present paper. However, the conclusions of the present paper are somewhat different from those reached by Green and Spear. For further discussion, see Section 7.

The remainder of the paper is organized in the following way. We describe the model in Section 2. Section 3 provides the basic existence theorem and its proof. Section 4 discusses asymptotic efficiency and asymptotic completeness, Section 5 presents the generic analysis, and Section 6 discusses the case of unconstrained consumption. Finally, Section 7 concludes the paper.

2. THE MODEL

We use a variant of the model of Geanakoplos and Polemarchakis (1987), adapted to accommodate an infinite number of possible states of the world.

Transactions occur (at date 0) in assets (or securities) before the state of nature is known, and then (at date 1) in real commodities, after the state of nature is known. (There would be no difficulty in allowing for consumption before the state of nature is known.) The state of nature is described by an atomic probability space (S, σ), where $S = \{1, 2, 3, \dots\}$ is the set of *states* of nature, and σ is a probability measure on S.[8] We assume that $\sigma(s) > 0$ for each $s \in S$. (This involves no loss of generality.)

At each state there are available for consumption l physical goods, $1, \dots, l$, of which the first is the *numeraire*. *Commodity bundles* (or consumption patterns) are elements of the *commodity space* $L_1(S, \sigma)^l$; i.e., functions $x : S \to \mathbb{R}^l$ for which the *norm*

$$\|x\| = \int |x(s)|\, d\sigma(s) = \int \sum_{i=1}^{l} |x_i(s)|\, d\sigma(s)$$

[8]The probability $\sigma(s)$ may be interpreted as the objective probability that state s will occur, or as the unanimous assessments of consumers, but neither of these interpretations is necessary. All that is necessary for our purposes is that assessments of consumers be consistent, in the minimal sense of allowing for the same consumption patterns.

is finite. Since σ is a probability measure, the norm of x is just the expectation of $|x| = \Sigma|x_i|$. We seldom distinguish between functions $x: S \to \mathbb{R}^l$ and l-tuples $(x_1, \ldots, x_l)$ of functions $x_i: S \to \mathbb{R}$. Since S is countable, a function $x_i: S \to \mathbb{R}$ may be identified with a sequence of real numbers, but it is convenient to use functional notation; we shall usually write $x(s,i)$ rather than $x_i(s)$. It is frequently convenient to identify a function $w \in L_1(S,\sigma)$ with the l-tuple $(w, 0, \ldots, 0) \in L_1(S,\sigma)^l$; w is a *numeraire pattern*. Given bundles $x, y \in L_1(S,\sigma)^l$, we write $x \leq y$ to mean $x(s,i) \leq y(s,i)$ for each i, s; $x < y$ to mean $x(s,i) \leq y(s,i)$ for each i, s and $x \neq y$; $x \ll y$ to mean $x(s,i) < y(s,i)$ for each i, s. We write χ_{si} for the consumption pattern that represents one unit of commodity i in state s and nothing in other states; i.e., $\chi_{si}(s,i) = 1$, $\chi_{si}(r,j) = 0$ if $(r,j) \neq (s,i)$.

An *asset* (or *security*) is a claim to a numeraire pattern at date 1. (Thus, securities are denominated in the numeraire commodity.) The *return* on asset α in state s is $\alpha(s)$, which may be positive, negative, or zero. We frequently use the same notation for an asset and for its returns; it should always be clear from context what is intended. We assume that asset returns are *bounded*; i.e., for each α, there is a constant c such that $|\alpha(s)| \leq c$ for each state s.[9] We assume that the first asset α_1 is *riskless*; i.e., $\alpha_1(s) = 1$ for each $s \in S$.[10] [We usually write 1 for this element of $L_1(S,\sigma)$.]

If there are N assets $\alpha_1, \ldots, \alpha_N$, a *portfolio* is a vector $y = (y_1, \ldots, y_N) \in \mathbb{R}^N$; y_k is the holding (number of shares) of the kth asset, and may be positive, negative, or zero. The *return* on the portfolio $y = (y_1, \ldots, y_N)$ is the numeraire pattern:

$$\text{return}(y) = \sum y_k \alpha_k \in L_1(S,\sigma).$$

We find it convenient to write δ_k for the portfolio consisting of one share of the kth asset and nothing else.

Asset prices are vectors $q \in \mathbb{R}^N$, where q_k is the price of the kth asset; if $y \in \mathbb{R}^N$ is a portfolio, then $q \cdot y = \Sigma q_k y_k$ is the *value* of the portfolio y at the prices q. The asset prices q *admit arbitrage* if there is a consumer h and a portfolio y such that $ty \in Y^h$ for every $t > 0$, return$(y) > 0$ and $q \cdot y \leq 0$.

Commodity prices are functions $p: S \to (\mathbb{R}^l)^+$; $p(s,i)$ is the price of commodity i in state s. We shall always normalize so that, for each state s, $\Sigma p(s,i) = 1$. [This is a free normalization, because there will be a different budget constraint in each state; see Geanakoplos and Polemarchakis

[9]The requirement that asset returns be bounded is likely unnecessary, but it is very convenient.

[10]This requirement too is likely unnecessary but very convenient.

(1987).] The *income pattern* $p \square x$ required to purchase a commodity bundle x at prices p is defined by

$$p \square x(s) = \sum p(s,i)x(s,i).$$

Consumers $h \in \{1, \ldots, H)$ are defined by *consumption sets*, *endowments* e^h, *preferences* $\preccurlyeq^h$, and *feasible trading sets* $Y^h \subset \mathbb{R}^N$. Except in Section 6, where we consider unconstrained consumption, we shall always assume that *consumption sets* for each consumer are the positive cone $[L_1(S,\sigma)^l]^+$; i.e., we require terminal consumption to be nonnegative. Henceforth, we suppress explicit reference to consumption sets. We assume that individual endowments are strictly positive in every state [i.e., $e^h(s) > 0$ for every h, s] and that numeraire endowments are bounded away from 0 [i.e., there is a $\delta > 0$ such that $e^h(s,1) \geq \delta$ for every h, s]. *Preferences* are (norm) continuous, convex, and strictly monotone; i.e., $x \prec^h y$ whenever $x < y$. [Such preferences are representable by continuous, quasiconcave, strictly monotonic utility functions $[L_1(S,\sigma)^l]^+ \to [0,\infty)$.] We assume that the numeraire is *desirable* in every state, in the sense that, for each commodity bundle $x \in [L^1(S,\sigma)^l]^+$ and state s, there is a $c > 0$ such that $x \prec^h c\chi_{s1}$. (Note that the right-hand side is the consumption pattern that yields c units of the numeraire in state s and nothing in other states.) The *trading set* $Y^h \subset \mathbb{R}^N$ defines the set of portfolios that consumer h is permitted to hold (and hence the set of asset trades that h is permitted to make). We assume throughout that Y^h is a closed, convex subset of $\mathbb{R}^N$, that 0 belongs to the interior of Y^h, and that $t\delta_1 \in Y^h$ for every $t \geq 0$. Thus, we may impose limits on short sales and on purchases, but some trading is always permitted, and arbitrarily long positions in the riskless asset are permitted.

A *securities* (or *asset*) *market* is a pair $\mathscr{E} = (\{\alpha_k\}, \{(e^h, \preccurlyeq^h, Y^h)\})$, where $\{\alpha_k\colon 1 \leq k \leq N\}$ is a finite set of assets and $\{(e^h, \preccurlyeq^h, Y^h)\colon 1 \leq h \leq H\}$ is a finite set of consumers. The assumptions above are understood to be in force at all times; in particular, α_1 is riskless.

Given securities prices q, commodity prices p, and endowments e^h, the *budget set* $B^h(q,p,e^h)$ for consumer h is the set of pairs (x^h, y^h) consisting of a commodity bundle $x^h \in [L_1(S,\sigma)^l]^+$ and a portfolio $y^h \in Y^h$ with the following properties:

(i) $q \cdot y^h \leq 0$ (y^h is affordable);

(ii) $p \square [x^h - e^h - \text{returns}(y^h)] \leq 0$ (y^h finances x^h).

[Note that (ii) is an infinite collection of budget constraints, one for each state, but that there is no overall budget constraint.]

A (*securities market*) *equilibrium* for the securities market $\mathscr{E}$ is a 4-tuple (q, p, x, y), where $q \in \mathbb{R}^N$ are asset prices, $p\colon S \to (\mathbb{R}^l)^+$ are commodity prices, $x = (x^1, \ldots, x^H)$ is the *equilibrium allocation* (so that x^h is consumer h's equilibrium consumption bundle), and $y = (y^1, \ldots, y^H)$ is the profile of portfolios, satisfying

(i) $\sum (x^h - e^h) = 0$ (commodity markets clear);

(ii) $\sum y^h = 0$ (assets are in zero net supply);

(iii) for all h, x^h is

$\preccurlyeq^h$-maximal in $B^h(q, p, e^h)$ (consumers optimize).

Notice that equilibrium asset prices cannot admit arbitrage.

Underlying every securities market $\mathscr{E}$ is a Walrasian (Arrow–Debreu) economy $\mathscr{E}^{\mathrm{CM}}$, with the same commodities and consumers, but with complete contingent claims to every state/commodity pair. *Commodity prices* for $\mathscr{E}^{\mathrm{CM}}$ are nonnegative linear functionals on the commodity space; i.e., elements of the space $[L_\infty(S, \sigma)^l]^+$ of nonnegative, bounded functions, $\pi \colon S \to (\mathbb{R}^l)^+$. A *Walrasian (competitive) equilibrium* for $\mathscr{E}^{\mathrm{CM}}$ is, as usual, a pair (π, x), where π are *commodity prices* and $x = (x^1, \ldots, x^H)$ is the *equilibrium allocation* (so that x^h is consumer h's equilibrium consumption bundle), satisfying

(i) $\sum (x^h - e^h) = 0$;

(ii) for each $h, \pi \cdot (x^h - e^h) \leq 0$;

(iii) for each h, if $x^h \prec^h y^h$, then $\pi \cdot (y^h - e^h) > 0$.

3. EXISTENCE OF SECURITIES MARKET EQUILIBRIUM

In this section, we show that securities market equilibria exist, provided that assets and trading sets satisfy appropriate assumptions. Our assumption on assets is that their returns are linearly independent; this is a rather innocuous assumption, and could likely be avoided altogether.[11] Our assumption on trading sets guarantees that liabilities on asset holdings can exceed endowments in only a finite number of states; this assumption is

[11]Geanakoplos and Polemarchakis (1987), for instance, allow for redundant assets. However, they assume that trading sets are equal to $\mathbb{R}^N$, in which case redundant assets can be priced by arbitrage, and every equilibrium has the same allocation of consumption goods as an equilibrium in which redundant assets are not traded. When trading sets are restricted, however, redundant assets cannot always be priced by arbitrage, and trading in redundant assets cannot always be eliminated.

not so innocuous. However, Mas-Colell and Zame (1991b) have shown that, without this assumption or one like it, equilibrium need not exist.[12] We refer the reader to that paper for discussion and a specific counterexample.

THEOREM 1. *Let* $\mathscr{E} = (\{\alpha_k\}, \{(e^h, \preccurlyeq^h, Y^h)\})$ *be a securities market. Assume that asset returns are linearly independent and that, for every h and every* $y^h \in Y^h$*, there is an index n such that* $[\mathrm{ret}(y^h) + e^h](s) \geq 0$ *for every* $s \geq n$*. Then* $\mathscr{E}$ *has an equilibrium.*

Proof. We construct a securities market equilibrium for $\mathscr{E}$ as the limit of securities market equilibria for finite-state securities markets that approximate $\mathscr{E}$.

The first step is to construct these finite-state markets and their equilibria. To this end, fix a positive integer n, and write $S_n = \{1, \ldots, n\}$, the first n states. Let L_n be the space of functions from S_n to $\mathbb{R}$, and let L_n^l be the space of functions from S_n to $\mathbb{R}^l$. We identify L_n (respectively L_n^l) with the subspace of $L_1(S, \sigma)$ [respectively $L_1(S, \sigma)^l$] consisting of functions that vanish off S_n. Let P_n: $L_1(S, \sigma) \to L_n$ and Q_n: $L_1(S, \sigma)^l \to L_n^l$ be the projections [so that $P_n(w)$ is the restriction of w to S_n, etc.].

For each n, we let $\mathscr{E}_n$ be the securities market with state space S_n, commodity space L_n^l, assets ${}_n\alpha_k = P_n(\alpha_k)$, endowments ${}_ne^h = Q_n(e^h)$, preferences the restrictions to L_n^l of the given preferences, and trading sets Y^h. By a result of Geanakoplos and Polemarchakis (1987), $\mathscr{E}_n$ has a securities market equilibrium $(q_n, p_n, {}_nx, {}_ny)$.[13] Without loss of generality, we may assume that the riskless asset α_1 has price 1; i.e., $q_n \cdot \delta_1 = 1$. This completes the first step.

The second step is to extract a convergent subsequence of the sequence $\{(q_n, p_n, {}_nx, {}_ny)\}$ of securities market equilibria. Note first that the equilibrium bundles ${}_nx^h$ are nonnegative and sum to the aggregate endowments Σe^h. Passing to a subsequence if necessary, we may (because S is countable) assume that the equilibrium bundles converge; i.e., there are bundles $x^h \in L_1(S, \sigma)^l$ such that ${}_nx^h(s, i) \to x^h(s, i)$ for each s, i. Note that ${}_nx^h \to x^h$ in the norm topology of $L_1(S, \sigma)$ (again because S is countable and because all the bundles ${}_nx^h$ are bounded by Σe^h). Write $x = (x^1, \ldots, x^H)$.

Since we have normalized the state prices to sum to 1, we may (again passing to a subsequence if necessary) also assume that the state prices $p_n(s, i)$ converge; say, $p_n(s, i) \to p(s, i)$. If $p(s, i) = 0$ for any state s and

[12] This fact was not realized in earlier versions of the present paper.

[13] Geanakoplos and Polemarchakis assume that trading sets are equal to $\mathbb{R}^N$, and that asset returns are linearly independent. However, their argument depends only on the existence of a suitable cone of no-arbitrage prices; our assumptions are sufficient for this purpose.

commodity i, then, for n sufficiently large, the demands in state s would be unbounded. Hence, $p(s,i) \neq 0$ for each s, i.

We assert that equilibrium security prices are bounded. To see this, fix an index k, and a consumer h. Since 0 belongs to the interior of $Y^h, t\delta_1 \in Y^h$ for each $t > 0$, and Y^h is closed, we can find a constant $r > 0$ such that $t\delta_1 - r\delta_k \in Y^h$ for each $t > 0$. Numeraire desirability implies that there is a constant $c > 0$ such that h prefers $c\chi_{11}$ to society's aggregate endowment. Since α_k is bounded and α_1 is riskless, there is a constant $c' > 0$ such that $\alpha_1 + c'\alpha_k \geq 0$ and $\alpha_1 - c'\alpha_k \geq 0$; hence ${}_n\alpha_1 + c'({}_n\alpha_k) \geq 0$ and $\alpha_1 - c'({}_n\alpha_k) \geq 0$ for each n. We have normalized so that $q_n \cdot \delta_1 = 1$; if $q_n \cdot \delta_k > c' + c/r$, then the portfolio $(c + c'r)\delta_1 - r\delta_k$ is affordable and yields a return of more than c units of the numeraire in state 1. Since h prefers $c\chi_{11}$ to society's aggregate endowment, this is incompatible with equilibrium. We conclude that $q_n \cdot \delta_k \leq c' + c/r$ for each k and n. Similarly, $q_n \cdot \delta_k \geq -c' - c/r$. In particular, the sequence $\{q_n\}$ of securities prices lies in a bounded subset of $\mathbb{R}^N$. Passing to a subsequence if necessary, we may assume that the securities prices q_n also converge to a limit, say, $q_n \to q$ for some $q \in \mathbb{R}^N$. Note that $q \cdot \delta_1 = 1$.

To show that the equilibrium portfolios ${}_ny$ lie in a bounded subset of $\mathbb{R}^N$, we show first that the price system q does not admit arbitrage for the securities $\{\alpha_k\}$. To see this, let γ be a portfolio of the securities $\{\alpha_k\}$, with returns $(\gamma) = g$; assume that $t\gamma \in Y^h$ for all $t > 0$ and that $g(s) \geq 0$ for every s, and that $g(r) > 0$ for some state r. Without loss, we may assume that $g(r) = 1$. For each $n \geq r$, γ may be viewed as a portfolio of the securities $\{{}_n\alpha_k\}$, with returns ${}_ng = P_n(g)$. In particular, ${}_ng(r) = g(r) = 1$. By assumption, $0 \in \text{int}\, Y^h$ and numeraire endowments are bounded away from 0, so there is a $\delta > 0$ such that $-\delta\alpha_1 \in Y^h$ and $e^h(1,s) > \delta > 0$ for each state s. Since $t\gamma \in Y^h$ for each $t > 0$, convexity implies that $(\frac{1}{2})t\gamma - (\frac{1}{2})\delta\alpha_1 \in Y^h$. If we choose t sufficiently large, numeraire desirability implies that the returns on this feasible portfolio, together with consumer h's endowment, are preferred to any feasible consumption bundle. Hence, this portfolio cannot be affordable at equilibrium. Thus, $q_n \cdot [(\frac{1}{2})t\gamma - (\frac{1}{2})\delta\alpha_1] > 0$ for each n, so that $q_n \cdot \delta > (\delta/t)$. Passing to the limit yields $q \cdot \gamma > (\delta/t)$; in particular, q does not admit arbitrage.

We can now show that, for each h, the equilibrium portfolios ${}_ny^h$ remain bounded (as $n \to \infty$). For, suppose not. Passing to a subsequence if necessary, we may assume that the portfolio directions ${}_ny^h/\|{}_ny^h\|$ have a limit $\tau \in \mathbb{R}^N$. Since τ is the limit of portfolios of norm 1, it, too, has norm 1; in particular, τ is not the 0 portfolio. Since $q_n \cdot {}_ny^h = 0$, it follows that $q_n \cdot ({}_ny^h/\|{}_ny^h\|) = 0$ and hence that $q \cdot \tau = 0$. Since the portfolios ${}_ny^h$ become unbounded (as $n \to \infty$), it follows that $t\tau \in Y^h$ for every $t > 0$. Since q does not admit arbitrage, it is impossible that τ has returns that are nonnegative, and strictly positive in some state. We have assumed that the returns $\alpha_1, \ldots, \alpha_N$ are linearly independent, so that, for some m, the returns $P_m(\alpha_1), \ldots, P_m(\alpha_N)$ are also linearly independent. This means that no nonzero portfolio of $\alpha_1, \ldots, \alpha_N$ can have 0 returns in the states $1, \ldots, m$; in particular, τ cannot have 0 returns (because $\tau \neq 0$). Hence τ must have negative returns in some state s. The portfolios ${}_n y^h$ are unbounded, and the state prices $p_n(s, i)$ converge to nonzero limits; hence, for n sufficiently large, the returns on the portfolios ${}_n y^h$ create liabilities in state s that cannot be satisfied. Since this contradicts the equilibrium conditions, we conclude that the portfolios ${}_n y^h$ remain bounded, as asserted.

Passing once again to a subsequence if necessary, we may assume that the portfolios ${}_n y^h$ also converge; say, ${}_n y^h \to y^h$ for each h. Write $y = (y^1, \ldots, y^H)$. This yields a limit 4-tuple (q, p, x, y), completing the second step.

The third step is to show that (q, p, x, y) is a securities market equilibrium for $\mathscr{E}$. It is routine to verify that assets are in zero net supply and that commodity markets clear, that all portfolios are feasible and affordable, and that a consumption bundle is in each consumer's budget set. It remains only to verify optimality of portfolios and consumption bundles.

To this end, suppose that consumer h's portfolio and consumption bundle are not optimal (in h's budget set). Then there is a consumption plan x such that $x \succ^h x^h$ and x is financed (at prices p) by a portfolio $y \in Y^h$ with $q \cdot y \leq 0$. We first construct a consumption plan x^* and a portfolio $y^* \in Y^h$ having the following properties:

(i) there is a k such $x^*(s) = 0$ for all $s \geq k$;
(ii) $x^* \succ^h {}_n x^h$ for all sufficiently large n;
(iii) $q \cdot y^* < 0$;
(iv) $p \,\square\, [x^* - \text{returns}(y^*) - e^h](s) < 0$ for each s.

To achieve this, write $\zeta = \text{returns}(y)$, and let t be a real number (to be chosen later), with $0 < t < 1$. Since y finances x, we have $p \,\square\, [x - \zeta - e^h] \leq 0$, so

$$p \,\square\, \left[tx - t\zeta - te^h\right] = t\left\{p \,\square\, \left[x - \zeta - e^h\right]\right\} \leq 0.$$

Note that $tx - t\zeta - te^h = tx + (1 - t)e^h - t\zeta - e^h$, so that the portfolio ty finances the consumption plan $x_1 = tx + (1 - t)e^h$. Write $\rho_1 = \text{returns}(\alpha_1)$; ρ_1 is the consumption plan that yields 1 unit of the numeraire in each state. Since $x \geq 0$ and numeraire endowments are bounded away from 0, $x_2 = x_1 - 2\varepsilon\rho_1 \geq 0$ for $\varepsilon > 0$ sufficiently small. Convexity of Y^h and the fact that $0 \in \operatorname{int} Y^h$ together imply that $y_2 = ty - 2\varepsilon\alpha_1$ belongs to Y^h (for $2\varepsilon < 1 - t$); evidently, y_2 finances x_2. If we choose t sufficiently close to 1 and ϵ sufficiently small, continuity of preferences yields $x_2 \succ^h x^h$. For k an index to be chosen, define the consumption plan x^* by

$x^*(s) = x_2(s)$ for $s \leq k$ and $x^*(s) = 0$ for $s > k$. Continuity of preferences implies that, for k sufficiently large, $x^* \succ^h x^h$, and hence that $x^* \succ^h{}_n x^h$ for n sufficiently large. Set $y^* = ty - \varepsilon \alpha_1$. The consumption plan x^* and the portfolio y^* satisfy all our requirements.

We claim that, for $n \geq k$ sufficiently large, y^* finances x^* at the prices p_n. To see this, note that our assumption about trading sets implies that there is an index m such that $[\text{returns}(y^*) + e^h](s) \geq 0$ for each $s \geq m$; without loss, choose $m \geq k$. Since $x^*(x) = 0$ for $s \geq k$, it follows that $p_n \square [x^* - \text{returns}(y^*) - e^h](s) \leq 0$ for each $s \geq m$ and every n. On the other hand, since $p \square [x^* - \text{returns}(y^*) - e^h](s) < 0$ for each s, and $p_n \to p$, it follows that, for n sufficiently large, $p_n \square [x^* - \text{returns}(y^*) - e^h](s) < 0$ for each $s \leq m$. Hence y^* finances x^* at prices p_n, for n sufficiently large. Since $q_n \to q$ and $q \cdot y^* < 0$, it follows that $q_n \cdot y^* < 0$ for n sufficiently large. If we keep in mind that $x^*(s) = 0$ for $s > n$, we may interpret these statements in the securities market $\mathscr{E}_n$ to conclude that y^* is a feasible and affordable (and security prices q_n) portfolio that finances (at commodity prices p_n) the consumption plan x^*, which is preferred to ${}_n x^h$. However, this contradicts the equilibrium conditions for the securities market $\mathscr{E}_n$. We conclude that portfolios and consumption bundles are optimal (given prices), so that (q, p, x, y) is an equilibrium for the securities market $\mathscr{E}$, as asserted. This completes the proof. ■

4. ASYMPTOTICS

The result of the previous section guarantees that securities market equilibria exist; in this section we study the asymptotic behavior of such equilibria as the set of securities grows. We ask: When do equilibrium allocations of the securities markets converge to Pareto-optimal allocations or to Walrasian (competitive equilibrium) allocations of the underlying Walrasian economy?

Before formalizing these questions, we address a small but important point. As Mas-Colell (1986) has pointed out, the usual assumptions on preferences and endowments that suffice to guarantee the existence of Walrasian equilibrium in the finite-dimensional setting do not suffice in infinite-dimensional settings such as ours. The difficulty is that the consumption sets of consumers are assumed to be the positive cone, which has an empty interior. This leaves open the possibility that individual preferred sets may not be supportable by prices; in such a case, competitive equilibria need not exist. To avoid this difficulty, Mas-Colell introduced a restriction on preferences that he called *uniform properness*; in essence, uniform properness bounds marginal rates of substitution. In conjunction with the usual assumptions on preferences and endowments, uniform properness suffices to guarantee the existence of competitive equilibria. If we hope to show that equilibrium allocations of securities markets converge to equilibrium allocations of the underlying Walrasian economy, we must surely make assumptions that are strong enough to guarantee the existence of Walrasian equilibria. The easiest way to do this is to assume the preferences are uniformly proper, and that is what we shall do.[14]

To formalize our questions about asymptotic behavior of securities market equilibria, fix consumer endowments and preferences $(e^h, \preccurlyeq^h)$, $h = 1, \ldots, H$, and an infinite sequence $\{\alpha_k\}$ of assets (of which the first is riskless). For each N, we consider a security market $\mathscr{E}_N = (\{\alpha_k: 1 \leq k \leq N\}, \{(e^h, \preccurlyeq^h, {}_NY^h)\})$ in which the first N assets are available for trade. (Note that trading sets ${}_NY^h$ depend on the assets available for trade. For the purposes of definition, we make no restrictions on the way trading sets change with the number of available assets.) We say that this sequence $\{\mathscr{E}_N\}$ of securities markets is *asymptotically efficient* if, for each $\varepsilon > 0$, there is an integer N_0 such that: for $N \geq N_0$, every equilibrium allocation of $\mathscr{E}_N$ is within ε (in norm) of a Pareto-optimal allocation of the underlying Walrasian economy $\mathscr{E}^{\mathrm{CM}}$. [Since the space of states of nature is countable, all these allocations lie in a norm compact subset of the commodity space $L_1(S, \sigma)$, so this requirement is equivalent to the requirement that equilibrium allocations of $\mathscr{E}_N$ converge, as N tends to ∞, to Pareto-optimal allocations of $\mathscr{E}^{\mathrm{CM}}$. Norm continuity of preferences implies that the utilities of equilibrium allocations of $\mathscr{E}_N$ also converge to the utilities of Pareto-optimal allocations.] We say that the sequence $\{\mathscr{E}_N\}$ is *asymptotically complete* if, for each $\varepsilon > 0$, there is an integer N_0 such that, for $N \geq N_0$, every equilibrium allocation of $\mathscr{E}_N$ is within ε of an equilibrium allocation of the underlying Walrasian economy $\mathscr{E}^{\mathrm{CM}}$. (Similarly, this is equivalent to the requirement that equilibrium allocations of $\mathscr{E}_N$ converge, as N tends to ∞, to equilibrium allocations of $\mathscr{E}^{\mathrm{CM}}$. Again, norm continuity of preferences implies that the utilities of equilibrium allocations of $\mathscr{E}_N$ also converge to the utilities of competitive equilibrium allocations of $\mathscr{E}^{\mathrm{CM}}$.) If the sequence $\{\mathscr{E}_N\}$ of securities markets is not asymptotically efficient (respectively not asymptotically complete), we say it is *asymptotically inefficient* (respectively *asymptotically incomplete*).

Such sequences of securities markets are the appropriate objects of study if we view assets, endowments, preferences, and trading sets as given. Alternatively, we may view assets as given (known), but endowments, preferences, and trading sets as variable (unknown).[15] Taking the latter point of view, we shall say that the sequence $\{\alpha_k\}$ of assets is *asymptotically efficient* (respectively *asymptotically complete*) if for all specifications $\{(e^h, \preccurlyeq^h)$ of endowments and (uniformly proper) preferences, there are trading sets ${}_NY^h$ for which the sequence $\{\mathscr{E}_N\}$ of securities

[14]For more on the meaning of uniform properness, see Richard and Zame (1986).

[15]Of course, many other points of view are also possible.

markets is asymptotically complete (respectively asymptotically efficient); otherwise $\{\alpha_k\}$ is *asymptotically incomplete* (respectively *asymptotically inefficient*).[16]

From this point of view, the basic questions are: When are asset sequences asymptotically efficient? When are they asymptotically complete? Theorem 2 provides complete answers to these questions (and its proof yields insights into various other questions). Before giving the formal statement, we collect some notation and terminology.

For $x, y \in L_1(S, \sigma)$, we define $d_\infty(x, y) = \sup_{s \in S}|x(s) - y(s)|$. Of course, this supremum will be infinite if $|x - y|$ is an unbounded function. Nevertheless, this "distance function" induces a well-defined (complete, metrizable) topology on $L_1(S, \sigma)$, which we call the *uniform topology*. If E is a subset of $L_1(S, \sigma)$, we denote its closure with respect to the uniform topology by $\mathrm{cl}_\infty(E)$; $x \in \mathrm{cl}_\infty(E)$ if and only if x can be *uniformly approximated* by elements of E. The distance from a point x to a set E is $d_\infty(x, E) = \inf\{d_\infty(x, y): y \in E\}$. Note that $d_\infty(x, E) = 0$ exactly when $x \in \mathrm{cl}_\infty(E)$. By an *Arrow security* (*for state* s) we mean the security χ_{s1} whose return is 1 in state s and 0 in every other state. (Note that this is in agreement with our previous usage.)

The following result completely characterizes asymptotic completeness and asymptotic efficiency for a sequence of assets.

THEOREM 2. *Let $\{\alpha_k\}$ be a sequence of assets, of which the first is riskless. The following statements are equivalent:*

(i) *the sequence $\{\alpha_k\}$ is asymptotically efficient;*
(ii) *the sequence $\{\alpha_k\}$ is asymptotically complete;*
(iii) *every Arrow security can be uniformly approximated by the returns on a finite portfolio of the securities α_k.*

The last condition may be formulated equivalently as follows: For every state s and every $\varepsilon > 0$, there is a finite portfolio of the assets $\{\alpha_k\}$ whose returns differ from χ_{s1} by at most ε in every state.

Proof. (iii) $\Rightarrow$ (i) and (ii). Consider a sequence $\{\alpha_k\}$ of assets (of which the first is riskless) having the property that every Arrow security can be uniformly approximated by the returns on a finite portfolio. Fix endowments and preferences $\{(e^h, \preccurlyeq^h)\}$. For each N and h, define the trading set ${}_NY^h$ as the set of portfolios $y \in \mathbb{R}^N$ such that $[\mathrm{returns}(y) + e^h](s) \geq 0$ for $s \geq N$. Assume we are given a subsequence $\mathscr{E}_{N(n)}$ of $\{\mathscr{E}_N\}$, and equilibrium allocations $x_n = ({}_nx^1, {}_nx^2, \ldots, {}_nx^H)$ for $\mathscr{E}_{N(n)}$, converging

[16]Because we only require convergence to Pareto-optimal allocations (or Walrasian allocations) for *some* sequence of trading sets, we have somewhat slanted these definitions in the direction of efficiency and completeness. This is consistent with our goal, which is to show that efficiency and completeness are difficult to obtain.

to $x = (x^1, x^2, \ldots, x^H)$; let q_n be the corresponding asset prices and let p_n be the corresponding state prices. We proceed by showing that x is in the core of the underlying Walrasian economy $\mathscr{E}^{\mathrm{CM}}$.

Suppose this were not so. Then there would be a set of consumers, which we may assume to be the consumers $M = \{1, 2, \ldots, M\}$, and an allocation $x^* = (x^{*1}, \ldots, x^{*M})$ that is a redistribution of the endowments $(e^1, \ldots, e^M)$ and is unanimously preferred to x by consumers in M. Continuity of preferences, together with the assumption that numeraire endowments are bounded away from zero, guarantees that we can find a state r, allocations $z = (z^1, \ldots, z^M)$ and $\tilde{z} = (\tilde{z}^1, \ldots, \tilde{z}^M)$, and a real number $\delta > 0$ such that $\tilde{z}$ is unanimously preferred to x by consumers in M and

$$\begin{aligned}
\tilde{z}^m(s,i) &= z^m(s,i) = 0 && \text{for } s > r,\ 1 \le i \le l;\\
\tilde{z}^m(s,i) &= z^m(s,i) && \text{for } s \le r,\ 2 \le i \le l;\\
\tilde{z}^m(s,1) &= z^m(s,1) - \delta && \text{for } s \le r;\\
e^m(s,1) &\ge \delta && \text{for all } s;\\
\sum_m z^m(s,i) &= \sum_m x^{*m}(s,i) = \sum_m e^m(s,i) && \text{for } s \le r,\ 1 \le i \le l.
\end{aligned}$$

Since we have normalized the state prices to sum to 1, we may (passing to a subsequence if necessary) assume that the state prices $p_n(s,i)$ converge; say, $p_n(s,i) \to p(s,i)$. As noted in the proof of Theorem 1, if $p(s,i) = 0$ for any state s and commodity i, then, for n sufficiently large, the state s demands in $\mathscr{E}_{N(n)}$ would exceed total endowments. Hence, $p(s,i) \neq 0$ for each s, i. (The limiting behavior of asset prices is irrelevant.)

For each price system p^* and each $m \in M$, define a numeraire pattern $w^m(p^*)$ by

$$\begin{aligned}
w^m(p^*, s) &= [1/p^*(s,1)][p^* \square (z^m - e^m)](s) && \text{for } s \le r;\\
w^m(p^*, s) &= 0 && \text{for } s > r.
\end{aligned}$$

For $s \le r$, $w^m(p^*, s)$ is the amount of numeraire that must be transferred into state s in order to make the net purchase $(z^m - e^m)(s)$, at prices p^*. Since z is a reallocation of endowments in states $s \le r$, and $w^m(p^*, s) = 0$ in states $s > r$, it follows that, for each price system p^* and each state s, $\Sigma w^m(p^*, s) = 0$ (summation over $m \in M$).

For each m, $w^m(p)$ is a finite linear combination of Arrow securities, so (iii) enables us to find finite portfolios $y^1, \ldots, y^{M-1}$, such that d_∞(returns$(y^m), w^m(p)) < \delta/M$ for $1 \le m \le M - 1$. The definition of the trading sets ${}_NY^h$ implies that these portfolios are feasible if N is sufficiently large. Set

$$y^M = -\sum_{m=1}^{M-1} y^m$$

so that y^M is a finite portfolio, and $d_\infty(\text{returns}(y^M), w^M(p)) < \delta$. Since the state prices $p_n(s,i)$ converge to $p(s,i)$ for each s, i and $w^m(p^*, s) = 0$ for states $s > r$, we conclude that $d_\infty(\text{returns}(y^m), w^m(p_n)) < \delta$. For each $m \in M$, provided that n is sufficiently large.

Our construction guarantees that, at all prices p_n sufficiently close to p, the portfolio y^m is feasible for consumer m (i.e., it does not impose unsatisfiable liabilities). Since we have constructed y^M so that $\Sigma y^m = 0$, at least one of the portfolios y^m must have a nonpositive price (at asset prices q_n). However, at prices p_n sufficiently close to p, the returns ζ^m on the portfolio y^m will finance purchase of the commodity bundle $\tilde{z}^m$. Since ${}_nx^m \to x^m$ and $x^m \prec^m \tilde{z}^m$, continuity of preferences implies that ${}_nx^m \prec^m \tilde{z}^m$ for n sufficiently large. Since $\tilde{z}^m$ belongs to the budget set of consumer m, this contradicts the equilibrium conditions in $\mathscr{E}_{N(N)}$. It follows that x is in the core of the underlying complete markets economy, as desired.

We have just proved that (iii) implies that every limit of equilibrium allocations of the finite securities markets is in the core of the underlying Walrasian economy. Since allocations in the core are Pareto-optimal, this certainly yields asymptotic efficiency, and we obtain the implication (iii) $\Rightarrow$ (i).

If we replicate the economy, and note that a securities market equilibrium for the original economy is necessarily a securities market equilibrium for the replicated economy, we conclude that every limit of equilibrium allocations of the finite securities markets is in the core of every replication of the underlying complete markets economy. We can now apply a result of Aliprantis *et al.* (1987), which is the infinite-dimensional version of the Debreu and Scarf (1963) core convergence theorem; assuming that preferences are uniformly proper, equilibrium allocations are precisely those in the core of every replication. This yields asymptotic completeness, and we obtain the implication (iii) $\Rightarrow$ (ii).

(i) $\Rightarrow$ (iii) and (ii) $\Rightarrow$ (iii). We establish the contrapositives. Suppose that some Arrow security, say χ_{11} (without loss), cannot be uniformly approximated by returns on a finite portfolio. Note that the set of returns on finite portfolios constitutes a linear subspace of $L_1(S, \sigma)$ coinciding with the linear span span$\{\alpha_k\}$ of the securities. Set $4\rho = d_\infty(\chi_{11}, \text{span}\{\alpha_k\}) > 0$. We find two consumers so that the equilibrium allocations of the corresponding securities markets are bounded away from Pareto-optimal allocations of the underlying Walrasian economy, independently of the choice of trading sets. It is convenient to give the construction first for the case of one commodity (the numeraire) in each state; the general case requires only a simple adaptation.

For the one commodity case, let u: $[0, \infty) \to [0, \infty)$ be any continuously differentiable, strictly concave function such that $u'(0) < \infty$ and $u'(\infty) > 0$. The two consumers will have identical utility functions $U^1 = U^2 = U$, where $U(x) = \Sigma a_k u(x(k))\sigma(k)$, and $\{a_k\}$ is a bounded sequence of strictly positive numbers, to be chosen later.[17] Endowments are $e^1 = (3, \rho, \rho, \rho, \ldots), e^2 = (1, 3\rho, \rho, \rho, \ldots)$. Write $e = e^1 + e^2$ for the aggregate endowment. Since consumers have identical, separable, strictly concave utility functions, it is easy to see that every Pareto-optimal allocation is of the form $(\lambda e, (1 - \lambda)e)$ for some real number λ with $0 \leq \lambda \leq 1$. To obtain the Pareto-optimal allocation $(\lambda e, (1 - a)\lambda)$ requires the net trade (for consumer 1):

$$\lambda e - e^1 = (4\lambda - 3, (4\lambda - 1)\rho, (2\lambda - 1)\rho, (2\lambda - 1)\rho, \ldots).$$

Equilibrium allocations of securities markets (and hence their limits) are individually rational, so any Pareto-optimal allocation that is the limit of equilibrium allocations of the securities markets must also satisfy the individual rationality requirements $U(\lambda e) \geq U(e^1)$ and $U((1 - \lambda)e) \geq U(e^2)$. By choosing the coefficient sequence $\{a_k\}$ appropriately, we can guarantee that these inequalities are satisfiable only if λ is very close to $\frac{1}{2}$. (We leave the details to the reader.)

Now consider a securities market $\mathscr{E}_N = (\{\alpha_k: 1 \leq k \leq N), \{(e^h, \preccurlyeq^h)\})$, and an equilibrium allocation (x^1, x^2) of $\mathscr{E}_N$; suppose that (x^1, x^2) is close (in the L_1 norm) to a Pareto-optimal allocation. If we choose $\{a_k\}$ so that λ is close to $\frac{1}{2}$, then x^1 must be close (in the L_1 norm) to λe, for some λ close to $\frac{1}{2}$, and the net trade of consumer 1, which is $x^1 - e^1$, must be close (in the L_1 norm) to $\lambda e - e^1$. If λ is close to $\frac{1}{2}$, the net trade of consumer 1 must be close to 1 in the first state, be close to ρ in the second state, and be bounded by ρ in every other state (since neither consumer 1 nor consumer 2 can incur liabilities greater than endowments). Hence, we can obtain [by choosing $\{a_k\}$ so that λ is sufficiently close to $\frac{1}{2}$] that $d_\infty(x^1 - e^1, \chi_{11}) \leq 2\rho$. Since there is only one commodity in each state, equilibrium trades in the securities market $\mathscr{E}_N$ must be effected entirely through transactions in available securities. In particular, we can find a finite portfolio whose returns are precisely $x^1 - e^1$, and hence differ from χ_{11} by at most 2ρ. This contradicts our supposition that $d_\infty(\chi_{11}, \text{span}\{\alpha_k\}) = 4\rho$. We conclude that (for appropriately chosen $\{a_k\}$), no equilibrium allocation of the securities market

$$\mathscr{E}_N = (\{\alpha_k: 1 \leq k \leq N\}, \{(e^h, \preccurlyeq^h)\})$$

[17]Any choice of the sequence $\{a_k\}$ will lead to a well-defined utility function U on $L_1(S, \sigma)$; U will be uniformly proper if we choose the sequence $\{a_k\}$ bounded away from 0.

can be close to a Pareto-optimal allocation of the underlying Walrasian economy; since Walrasian allocations are Pareto-optimal, it follows a fortiori that no equilibrium allocation of the securities market $\mathscr{E}_N = (\{\alpha_k: 1 \le k \le N\}, \{(e^h, \preccurlyeq^h)\})$ can be close to a Walrasian allocation of the underlying Walrasian economy. This completes the proofs of (iii) $\Rightarrow$ (i) and (ii) for the case of one commodity in each state.

To obtain the case of l commodities from the case of one commodity, we simply choose utility functions so that, in each state, all l commodities are perfect substitutes. (Of course, this is incompatible with strict concavity of utility functions, but strict concavity can be restored by making a tiny perturbation. Again, we leave the details to the reader.) ■

The argument of Theorem 2 actually proves a bit more. The argument that equilibrium allocations of $\mathscr{E}_N$ converge to a core allocation (and in particular, to a Pareto-optimal allocation) of the underlying Walrasian economy requires only that for every numeraire pattern x that is nonzero in only a finite number of states, every $\varepsilon > 0$, every state s_0, every consumer h, and all sufficiently large indices N_0, there is portfolio $y \in_N Y^h$ whose returns differ from x by at most ε in states $s \le s_0$, and are bounded (in absolute value) in every other state by numeraire endowments divided by the number of consumers. Informally: If the assets span a norm dense subspace of $L_1(S, \sigma)$, endowments are "large enough," and sufficiently large shorts sales are permissible, then securities markets equilibria will converge to equilibria of the underlying complete markets economy (and a fortiori to Pareto-optimal allocations). However, these are stringent requirements; see Example 4 below and Section 5, particularly the concluding discussion.

We now give a number of examples. [See also Green and Spear (1989) and Zame (1990).] It is convenient to describe an asset sequence by an infinite matrix, the jth column of which represents returns on the jth asset (so that the entry in the ith row and jth column is the return paid by the jth asset in the ith state, etc.).

Example 1.

$$\mathbf{A} = \begin{bmatrix} 1 & 1 & 0 & 0 & 0 & 0 & \cdot & \cdot & \cdot \\ 1 & 0 & 1 & 0 & 0 & 0 & \cdot & \cdot & \cdot \\ 1 & 0 & 0 & 1 & 0 & 0 & \cdot & \cdot & \cdot \\ 1 & 0 & 0 & 0 & 1 & 0 & \cdot & \cdot & \cdot \\ \cdot & \cdot & \cdot & \cdot & \cdot & \cdot & \cdot & \cdot & \cdot \\ \cdot & \cdot & \cdot & \cdot & \cdot & \cdot & \cdot & \cdot & \cdot \\ \cdot & \cdot & \cdot & \cdot & \cdot & \cdot & \cdot & \cdot & \cdot \end{bmatrix}$$

$\mathbf{A}$ is asymptotically efficient; of course, it is simply a riskless security, together with a complete set of Arrow securities.

EXAMPLE 2.

$$\mathbf{B} = \begin{bmatrix} 1 & 0 & 0 & 0 & 0 & \cdot & \cdot & \cdot \\ 1 & 1 & 0 & 0 & 0 & \cdot & \cdot & \cdot \\ 1 & 1 & 1 & 0 & 0 & \cdot & \cdot & \cdot \\ \cdot & \cdot & \cdot & \cdot & \cdot & \cdot & \cdot & \cdot \\ \cdot & \cdot & \cdot & \cdot & \cdot & \cdot & \cdot & \cdot \\ \cdot & \cdot & \cdot & \cdot & \cdot & \cdot & \cdot & \cdot \\ \cdot & \cdot & \cdot & \cdot & \cdot & \cdot & \cdot & \cdot \end{bmatrix}$$

B is asymptotically efficient. This is merely to illustrate the point that asymptotic efficiency depends only on the space spanned by the assets; note that the space spanned by the first n columns of **B** is precisely the same as that spanned by the first n columns of **A**.

EXAMPLE 3.

$$\mathbf{C} = \begin{bmatrix} 1 & 0 & 0 & 0 & 0 & \cdot & \cdot & \cdot \\ 1 & 1 & 0 & 0 & 0 & \cdot & \cdot & \cdot \\ 1 & 0 & 1 & 0 & 0 & \cdot & \cdot & \cdot \\ 1 & 0 & 0 & 1 & 0 & \cdot & \cdot & \cdot \\ \cdot & \cdot & \cdot & \cdot & \cdot & \cdot & \cdot & \cdot \\ \cdot & \cdot & \cdot & \cdot & \cdot & \cdot & \cdot & \cdot \\ \cdot & \cdot & \cdot & \cdot & \cdot & \cdot & \cdot & \cdot \end{bmatrix}$$

C is asymptotically inefficient. Indeed, the distance from χ_{11} to the span of the columns of **C** is $\frac{1}{2}$.

EXAMPLE 4.

$$\mathbf{D} = \begin{bmatrix} 1 & 0 & 0 & & 0 & \cdot & \cdot & \cdot \\ 1 & 1 & 0 & 0 & 0 & \cdot & \cdot & \cdot \\ 1 & -1 & 1 & 0 & 0 & \cdot & \cdot & \cdot \\ 1 & 0 & -1 & 1 & 0 & \cdot & \cdot & \cdot \\ \cdot & 0 & 0 & -1 & 1 & \cdot & \cdot & \cdot \\ \cdot & \cdot & \cdot & \cdot & \cdot & \cdot & \cdot & \cdot \\ \cdot & \cdot & \cdot & \cdot & \cdot & \cdot & \cdot & \cdot \\ \cdot & \cdot & \cdot & \cdot & \cdot & \cdot & \cdot & \cdot \end{bmatrix}$$

D is asymptotically inefficient; as in Example 3, the distance from χ_{11} to the span of the columns of **D** is $\frac{1}{2}$. Note that any sequence in the span of the columns of **D** that converges to χ_{11} in the $L_1(S, \sigma)$ norm is necessarily unbounded. (See the comments following the proof of Theorem 2 above.)

We have required that endowments be bounded away from 0; the final example shows the kind of difficulties that could arise if we did not make this restriction.

EXAMPLE 5. Consider the sequence of assets $\{\alpha_k\}$ whose returns are $\alpha_k(s) = k^{-s}$. If endowments are $e^h(s) = \exp(-s)$, then *no finite nonzero portfolio* (except for the 0 portfolio) is dominated by endowments. Hence *no finite portfolio can be traded*. We surely cannot expect to say much about asymptotic efficiency for such sequences of assets.

5. GENERICITY

In Section 4 we presented a characterization of asymptotic efficiency and examples of sequences that are or are not asymptotically efficient. The purpose of this section is to show that it is the asymptotically inefficient examples that are typical: "most" asset sequences are asymptotically *inefficient*. To make this assertion precise, we need to identify the family of asset sequences under consideration and a topology on it.

Since all of our results are invariant to change of scale, there is no loss of generality in restricting our attention to assets satisfying $\|\alpha\| \leq 1$. (Recall that $\|\alpha\|$ is the expectation with respect to σ of $|\alpha(s)|$.) Since we have required that the returns on assets be bounded, we should take account of this. The simplest way to do this is to restrict our attention to asset sequences for which the kth asset is bounded by a preassigned number. To this end, fix, once and for all, a sequence $\{B_k\}$ of positive numbers; let $\mathscr{A}$ be the set of asset sequences $\alpha = \{\alpha_k\}$ such that $\alpha_1 = 1$ is riskless, and $\|\alpha_k\| \leq 1$ and $|\alpha_k(s)| \leq B_k$ for each s, k.

$\mathscr{A}$ carries several natural topologies. The simplest corresponds to the distance function defined on pairs of asset sequences α, β by

$$d^1(\alpha, \beta) = \sum \sigma(s) |\alpha_k(s) - \beta_k(s)|$$

the sum extending over all indices k and all states s. (Strictly speaking, this is not a metric, since it might be infinite; nonetheless, it induces a well-defined topology.)

An alternative topology may be defined on $\mathscr{A}$ by noting that every element $\alpha \in \mathscr{A}$ gives rise to a bounded operator (continuous linear transformation) R^α from l_1 (the space of all summable real sequences) into $L_1(S, \sigma)$ defined by

$$R^\alpha(c) = \sum c_k \alpha_k$$

for $c = (c_1, c_2, \dots) \in l_1$. If we identify asset sequences with the operators they induce, it seems natural to define the *operator distance* between asset sequences α, β as

$$d^{\text{op}}(\alpha, \beta) = \|R^\alpha - R^\beta\|_{\text{op}} = \sup\left\{ \sum \sigma(s) \left| R^\alpha(c)(s) - R^\beta(c)(s) \right| \right\},$$

where the sum extends over all states s, and the supremum extends over all sequences $c \in l_1$ with $\|c\|_{l_1} = \Sigma|c_i| \leq 1$. In the topology induced by this distance function, two asset sequences α, β are close together if the same portfolios yield nearly the same (expected) returns, uniformly over all portfolios representing total trades of at most 1 share [see Dunford and Schwartz (1958) for further discussion].[18]

It is not hard to see that the topology on $\mathscr{A}$ induced by d^1 is stronger than that induced by d^{op}, and that they are both complete, metric topologies.

Recall that a subset of a complete metric space is *residual* if it contains the countable intersection of dense, open sets. (Recall that residual sets are large and that their complements are small. In particular, the Baire category theorem implies that a residual subset of a complete metric space is dense.) Since we have identified two different complete metric topologies on $\mathscr{A}$, we have two possible interpretations of "residual" for subsets of $\mathscr{A}$. As it happens, the "bad set" is residual in *both* these topologies.

At this point, we need to address two issues. The first is that we have established the existence of equilibrium only when asset returns are linearly independent. It therefore seems reasonable to incorporate the requirement of linear independence into the definition of the "bad set." This poses no difficulties. The second issue is more substantive. As a consequence of the infinite dimensionality of $L^1(S, \sigma)$, there are linearly independent sequences of assets that do not span $L^1(S, \sigma)$ or any dense subspace. Consider for example the sequence $\alpha = \{\alpha_k\}$ for which α_1 is riskless, and $\alpha_k = \chi_{1,2k}$ is the Arrow security yielding 1 unit of the numeraire in state $2k$ and nothing in other states. This sequence is linearly independent and asymptotically inefficient. On the other hand, it fails—in every reasonable sense—to "span all the uncertainty." In particular, the Arrow security χ_{11}, which yields 1 unit of the numeraire in state 1 and nothing in other states, does not lie in the closure of the space spanned by the sequence α. It seems clear that α is not a "complete sequence of assets" in any reasonable sense, but it is not entirely clear should constitute a "complete sequence of assets."

Two natural notions of completeness come to mind. In the finite-dimensional setting, completeness of a set of assets means that every prescribed numeraire pattern can be obtained as the returns of a suitable finite portfolio. Since the set of states and available assets is infinite, we

[18] If we identify asset sequences with the operators they induce, then d^1 is the distance function corresponding to the *trace norm*; again, we refer to Dunford and Schwartz (1958) for further details. One point to note: if $d^1(\alpha, \beta)$ is finite, then the difference $R^\alpha - R^\beta$ is a compact operator from l_1 to $L_1(S, \sigma)$; i.e., it maps bounded subsets of l_1 to relatively compact subsets of $L_1(S, \sigma)$.

should allow for approximations or for infinite portfolios. The identification of asset sequences as operators $l_1 \to L_1(S, \sigma)$ provides an easy way to express these conditions. If R^α has dense range, then every numeraire pattern can be approximated (in expectation) by the returns on a finite portfolio. If R^α is onto, then every numeraire pattern can be obtained as the returns on a suitable (infinite) portfolio.[19] Because S is countable, the set of invertible operators $l_1 \to L_1(S, \sigma)$ is not empty; moreover, this set is open in the topology induced by d^{op}, and a fortiori in the topology induced by d^1 (since it is stronger). Hence, whichever definition we take for completeness of a set of asset sequences, we conclude that the set of complete asset sequences certainly contains a nonempty, open subset of $\mathscr{A}$. In particular, the set of complete asset sequences is quite large.

Having addressed these issues, we now turn to the main result of this section, which establishes that the set of linearly independent, asymptotically independent asset sequences is residual, and therefore large.

THEOREM 3. *The set of asymptotically inefficient, linearly independent asset sequences is a residual subset of $\mathscr{A}$ in both the d^1 and d^{op} topologies.*

To motivate the proof, write $C_0(S)$ for the set of functions $v \in L_1(S, \sigma)$ with the property that $|v(s)| \to 0$ as $s \to \infty$. Note that $C_0(S)$ is exactly the uniform closure of the subspace of $L_1(S, \sigma)$ spanned by Arrow securities. Theorem 2 tells us that the asset sequence $\{\alpha_k\}$ is asymptotically efficient exactly when every Arrow security, and hence every numeraire pattern in $C_0(S)$, lies in the d_∞ closure of span$\{\alpha_k\}$. Equivalently, for every vector $v \in C_0(S)$, we have $d_\infty(v, \text{span}\{\alpha_k\}) = 0$. Of course, 0 is the closest a numeraire pattern can be to span$\{\alpha_k\}$; since $\alpha_1 = 1$, the furthest a numeraire pattern can be from span$\{\alpha_k\}$ is its distance from the one-dimensional subspace spanned by the asset 1. We show that, for a residual set of asset sequences, all vectors in $C_0(S)$ are at least half as far from span$\{\alpha_k\}$ as they could possibly be.

Before beginning the proof proper, it is convenient to isolate the most technical part in a lemma.

LEMMA. *For each $v \in L_1(S, \sigma)$, the set $\mathbf{Q}(v)$ of linearly independent asset sequences $\{\alpha_k\}$ with the property*

$$d_\infty(v, \text{span}\{\alpha_k\}) \geq \left(\tfrac{1}{2}\right) d_\infty(v, \text{span}\{1\})$$

is a residual subset of $\mathscr{A}$ in both the d^1 and d^∞ topologies.

Proof. For each $s \in S$, and $w \in L_1(S, \sigma)$, write $w^{(s)}$ for the numeraire pattern that coincides with w in states $1, 2, \ldots, s$ and is 0 else-

[19]It is not clear which infinite portfolios we should allow. However, if $\theta \in l_1$, then the series $\Sigma \theta_j \alpha_j$ converges absolutely (in expectation), so we should certainly allow portfolios in l_1.

where. Fix positive integers m, n; write $\rho = (\frac{1}{2}) - 2^{-m}$, and let $\mathbf{Q}(v, m, n)$ be the set of asset sequences $\{\alpha_k\}$ in $\mathscr{A}$ such that

(i) $\alpha_1^{(n)}, \ldots, \alpha_n^{(n)}$ are linearly independent;
(ii) $d_\infty(v, \text{span}\{\alpha_1, \ldots, \alpha_n\}) > \rho d_\infty(v, \text{span}\{1\})$.

It is easily seen that $\mathbf{Q}(v)$ contains the intersection (taken over all integers n, m) of the sets $\mathbf{Q}(v, m, n)$, so it suffices to show that each $\mathbf{Q}(v, m, n)$ is an open subset of $\mathscr{A}$ with respect to d^{op} and is dense with respect to d^1.

To see that $\mathbf{Q}(v, m, n)$ is an open subset of $\mathscr{A}$ with respect to d^{op}, note first that the linear independence of $\alpha_1^{(n)}, \ldots, \alpha_n^{(n)}$ is certainly preserved by any perturbation of the sequence $\{\alpha_k\}$ that is small in the first n states and for the first n terms of the sequence. Hence the set of sequences $\{\alpha_k\}$ satisfying the linear independence condition (i) is open. Note too that, if

$$d_\infty\big(v, \text{span}\{\alpha_1, \ldots, \alpha_n\}\big) > \rho d_\infty\big(v, \text{span}\{1\}\big),$$

then there is a state s such that

$$d_\infty\Big(v^{(s)}, \text{span}\big(\alpha_1^{(s)}, \ldots, \alpha_n^{(s)}\big)\Big) > \rho d_\infty\big(v, \text{span}\{1\}\big).$$

Since the vectors $v^{(s)}, \alpha_1^{(s)}, \ldots, \alpha_n^{(s)}$ all lie in the finite-dimensional space $\mathbb{R}^s$, a simple continuity argument shows that the last inequality is also satisfied by any perturbation of $\{\alpha_k\}$ that is sufficiently small in the first s states and for the first n terms of the sequence. Hence, the set of sequences $\{\alpha_k\}$ satisfying the span condition (ii) is open, as desired.

To see that $\mathbf{Q}(v, m, n)$ is a dense subset of $\mathscr{A}$ with respect to d^1, fix a sequence $\beta = \{\beta_k\} \in \mathscr{A}$; we construct a perturbed sequence $\tilde{\beta} = \{\tilde{\beta}_k\} \in \mathbf{Q}(v, m, n)$ such that $\Sigma\sigma(r)|\tilde{\beta}_k(r) - \beta_k(r)|$ is arbitrarily small (the sum extending over all states r, and all indices $k \leq n$). Since $\|\beta_i - \beta_i^{(s)}\| \to 0$ as s tends to ∞, we may (choosing s sufficiently large), assume that $\beta_j^{(s)} = \beta_i$ for $i = 2, \ldots, n$. Moreover, since linear independence of $\beta_1^{(n)}, \ldots, \beta_n^{(n)}$ is equivalent to the vanishing of an $n \times n$ determinant, this condition can be achieved by an arbitrarily small perturbation, which we assume to have been already carried out.

To achieve the span condition, it is convenient to work with the linear transformation $R^\beta: \mathbb{R}^n \to L_1(S, \sigma)$. If the span condition (ii) is not satisfied, let C be the set of vectors $c \in \mathbb{R}^n$ such that

$$\|R^\beta(c) - v\|_\infty \leq \rho d_\infty\big(v, \text{span}\{1\}\big).$$

Since $\{\beta_1^{n)}, \ldots, \beta_n^{(n)}\}$ is a linearly independent set, the linear transformation R^β is an isomorphism of $\mathbb{R}^n$ with a finite-dimensional subspace of $L_1(S, \sigma)$, so that C is compact. For each $c \in C$, the above inequality, the triangle inequality, and the facts that $\beta_1 = 1$ and that $\rho < \frac{1}{2}$ imply that

$$\sum_{i=2}^{n} |c_i| \, \|\beta_i\|_\infty \geq \left\| R^\beta(c) - c_1 1 \right\|_\infty > \rho d_\infty(v, \mathrm{span}\{1\}).$$

Choose *any* state $r > s$. For $1 = 2, \ldots, n$, define δ_i in the following way: if $c_i = 0$, then $\delta_i = 0$; if $c_i \neq 0$ but $v(r) = 0$, then $\delta_i = \mathrm{sign}(c_i)$; otherwise, $\delta_i = \mathrm{sign}(v(r)/c_i)$. Define $\tilde{\beta}_i$ and β_i^* by

$$\tilde{\beta}_i(t) = \beta_i(t) \quad \text{for } t \neq r,$$

$$\tilde{\beta}_i(r) = \delta_i \|\beta_i\|_\infty,$$

$$\beta_i^* = \tilde{\beta}_i / \|\tilde{\beta}_i\|.$$

This yields a perturbation $\{\beta_i^*\}$ of $\{\beta_i\}$ such that

$$\left\| R^{\beta^*}(c) - v \right\|_\infty > \rho d_\infty(v, \mathrm{span}\{1\}).$$

Since R^{β^*} is continuous, we conclude that

$$\left\| R^{\beta^*}(c') - v \right\|_\infty > \rho d_\infty(v, \mathrm{span}\{1\})$$

for all c' in some neighborhood W_c of c. Since C is compact, we can cover C with a finite number of these neighborhoods. Since we can make these perturbations in different states r, we conclude that there is a single perturbation $\{\tilde{\beta}_i\}$ such that $\|R^{\tilde{\beta}}(c) - v\|_\infty > \rho d_\infty(v, \mathrm{span}\{1\})$ for every $c \in C$. Since we have made these perturbations in states where the β_i vanished, we conclude that $\|R^{\tilde{\beta}}(c'') - v\|_\infty > \rho d_\infty(v, \mathrm{span}\{1\})$ for every $c'' \in \mathbb{R}^n \setminus C$. Finally, since we can make these perturbations only in states of arbitrarily low probability, we can guarantee that $d^1(\beta, \tilde{\beta})$ is as small as we like. Hence the perturbation $\tilde{\beta}$ has all the required properties. We conclude that $\mathbf{Q}(v, m, n)$ is dense with respect to d^1, as desired. This completes the proof. ■

With this technical result in hand, we turn to the proof of Theorem 3.

Proof of Theorem 3. Write $\mathbf{Q}$ for the set of linearly independent asset sequences $\{\alpha_k\} \in \mathscr{A}$ having the property that, for each $v \in C_0(S)$,

$$d_\infty(v, \mathrm{span}\{\alpha_k\}) \geq (\tfrac{1}{2}) d_\infty(v, \mathrm{span}\{1\}).$$

We claim that $\mathbf{Q}$ is a residual subset of $\mathscr{A}$ in both the topologies d^1 and d^∞. To see this, note that for each $v \in C_0(S, \sigma)$, the lemma provides a residual set $\mathbf{Q}(v)$ of asset sequences $\{\alpha_k\}$ such that

$$d_\infty(v, \operatorname{span}\{\alpha_k\}) \geq (\tfrac{1}{2}) d_\infty(v, \operatorname{span}\{1\}).$$

If $\{\alpha_k\} \in \mathbf{Q}(v)$ and $d_\infty(v, v') < (\frac{1}{4}) d_\infty(v, \operatorname{span}\{1\})$, the triangle inequality implies that

$$d_\infty(v', \operatorname{span}\{\alpha_k\}) \geq (\tfrac{1}{4}) d_\infty(v', \operatorname{span}\{1\}).$$

Since $C_0(S, \sigma)$ is d_∞-separable, we may choose a countable dense subset $\{v_i\}$. Set $\mathbf{Q} = \bigcap \mathbf{Q}(v_i)$; as the countable intersection of residual sets, $\mathbf{Q}$ is also a residual set. For each nonzero vector $w \in C_0(S)$, we can find a v_i such that

$$d_\infty(w, v_i) < (\tfrac{1}{2}) d_\infty(w, \operatorname{span}\{1\}).$$

It follows that $d_\infty(w, \operatorname{span}\{\alpha_k\}) > (\frac{1}{2}) d_\infty(w, \operatorname{span}\{1\})$ for all $\{\alpha_k\} \in \mathbf{Q}(v_i)$, and a fortiori for all $\{\alpha_k\} \in \mathbf{Q}$. Thus, $\mathbf{Q}$ has the properties required.

In view of Theorem 2, each asset sequence in $\mathbf{Q}$ is asymptotically inefficient; this completes the proof of Theorem 3. ■

An observation about $\mathbf{Q}$ may serve to explicate further the sense in which "large trades" are important. Consider any two consumers $(e^1, \preccurlyeq^1)$, $(e^2, \preccurlyeq^2)$, for whom

(i) there is an s^* such that $e^1(s) + e^2(s) \leq 1$ for $s \geq s^*$;
(ii) if z is an individually rational, Pareto-optimal net trade (for consumer 1), then $z(1) \geq +4$ and $z(2) \leq -4$.

Fix an asset sequence $\alpha \in \mathbf{Q}$. For any N, consider a securities market $\mathscr{E} = (\{\alpha_k: 1 \leq k \leq N\}, \{(e^h, \preccurlyeq^h, Y^h)\})$, and let w be an equilibrium net trade in $\mathscr{E}$. Feasibility of w implies that $|w(s)| \leq 1$ for $s \geq s^*$. On the other hand, if z is an individually rational, Pareto-optimal net trade then (ii) entails $d_\infty(z^{(s^*)}, \operatorname{span}\{1\}) > 4$, and the definition of $\mathbf{Q}$ therefore entails $d_\infty(z^{(s^*)}, \operatorname{span}\{\alpha_k\}) > 2$. In particular, $d_\infty(z^{(s^*)}, w) > 2$. Since $|w(s)| \leq 1$ for $s \geq s^*$, we conclude that $d_\infty(z^{(s^*)}, w^{(s^*)}) > 1$, and hence that

$$\|z - w\| > \sum_{s \leq s^*} \sigma(s).$$

That is, no security market equilibrium net trade is close to any Pareto-optimal net trade. In particular, no security market equilibrium allocation is close to a Pareto-optimal allocation.

We can obtain similar genericity results if we restrict ourselves to sequences of assets with positive returns; all that is required is a small change in the proof of the Lemma. For details, and for discussion of genericity in assets *and* endowments, see Zame (1990).

6. UNCONSTRAINED CONSUMPTION

As we noted earlier, the asymptotic inefficiency we have demonstrated may be traced directly to the requirement that consumption bundles be nonnegative in each state. In this section, we ask what happens when we drop this requirement; i.e., *we assume in what follows that the consumption set of each consumer is the entire commodity space* $L_1(S, \sigma)^l$. (Allowing for negative consumption may be natural when the commodities are themselves assets, and the discussion that follows might be viewed in the light of asset pricing models.) The other assumptions of Section 2 are understood to remain in force. In particular, preferences are monotone, norm continuous, and convex, and endowments are positive.

The first comment that needs to be made is that, in the absence of consumption constraints, the set of feasible consumption bundles is not compact; as a consequence, equilibria need not exist. This can, of course, be the case even for complete market economies with one commodity and two states of nature. [See Werner (1987) and Nielsen (1986) for elegant treatments of the existence problem in the finite-dimensional case.] Unboundedness of feasible consumption bundles also opens the possibility that the securities markets corresponding to each finite set of assets might have equilibria, but that equilibrium allocations might not converge (or have a convergent subsequence) as the set of assets expands. In short, without consumption constraints, existence and convergence of equilibria are problematic; as we shall see, however, *efficiency* of limits of equilibria is not problematic. If assets span a dense subspace of the set of all wealth streams (a condition that seems like a natural formalization of the idea that assets span all the uncertainty), if trading sets are sufficiently large, if the securities markets corresponding to a sequence of assets have equilibria, and if the equilibrium allocations converge, then the limit is an equilibrium allocation of the underlying complete markets economy (and in particular is Pareto-optimal).

A small point should be addressed here. Positivity constraints imply that all feasible allocations (and thus all equilibrium allocations of finite securities markets) lie in a norm compact set, so norm convergence of equilibrium allocations of finite securities markets is the relevant notion. Moreover, since preferences are norm continuous, norm convergence of allocations implies convergence of the corresponding utilities. The absence of positivity constraints raises the possibility that equilibrium allocations lie in a set that is weakly compact but not norm compact, so it seems useful to consider *weak* convergence of equilibrium allocations. However, since utility functions need not be weakly continuous, weak convergence of arbitrary allocations does not imply convergence of the corresponding utilities. As we show, however, weak convergence of *equilibrium* allocations does imply convergence of the corresponding utilities.

A final issue concerns trading sets. It is intuitively clear that equilibrium allocations cannot be nearly efficient if trading sets are very small. To rule out this possibility, consider a sequence $\{{}_N Y\}$ of trading sets, ${}_N Y \subset \mathbb{R}^N$. For $N < N'$, we regard $\mathbb{R}^N$ as the subset of $\mathbb{R}^{N'}$ consisting of vectors whose last $N' - N$ coordinates are 0. Say that $\{{}_N Y\}$ *expands unboundedly* if for each N and each compact set $K \subset \mathbb{R}^N$ there is an N_0 such that, if $N < N'$, then $K \subset {}_{N'}Y$.

THEOREM 4. *Fix consumers $\{(e^h, \preccurlyeq^h)\}$, and norm continuous, quasiconcave utility functions $u^h \colon L_1(S, \sigma)^l \to \mathbb{R}$ representing the preference relations $\preccurlyeq^h$. Let $\{\alpha_k\}$ be a linearly independent sequence of assets that spans a weakly dense subspace of $L_1(S, \sigma)$; assume that α_1 is riskless. For each N, consider the securities market $\mathscr{E}_N = (\{\alpha_k \colon 1 \leq k \leq N\}, \{(e^h, \preccurlyeq^h, {}_N Y^h)\})$ in which the first N assets are available for trade, and let $(q_N, p_{N,N}x, {}_N y)$ be an equilibrium for $\mathscr{E}_N$. Assume that the equilibrium allocations $\{{}_N x\}$ converge weakly to an allocation x, and that the trading sets $\{{}_N Y^h\}$ expand unboundedly. Then x is an equilibrium allocation for the underlying complete markets economy, and $u^h({}_n x^h) \to u^h(x^h)$ for every consumer h.*[20]

Proof. The argument is very similar to the argument of Theorem 2. We first establish the following:

Claim. There does not exist a set C of consumers and an allocation X that is feasible for consumers in C (i.e., the restriction of X to C is a reallocation of the endowments of consumers in C), such that

$$u^c(X^c) > \limsup u^c({}_n x^c) \quad \text{for every } c \in C.$$

If this is not so, then there is a set of consumers, which we may assume to be the consumers $M = (1, 2, \ldots, M)$, and an allocation $X = (X^1, \ldots, X^M)$ that is a redistribution of the endowments $(e^1, \ldots, e^M)$ and has the property that $u^m(X^m) > \limsup u^m({}_n x^m)$ for $m \in M$. Continuity of preferences, together with the assumption that numeraire endowments are bounded away from zero, guarantees that we can find a state r, allocations $z = (z^1, \ldots, z^M)$ and $\tilde{z} = (\tilde{z}^1, \ldots, \tilde{z}^M)$, and a real number $\delta > 0$ such that $u^m(\tilde{z}^m) > \limsup u^m({}_n x^m)$ for $m \in M$ and

$$\begin{aligned}
\tilde{z}^m(s,i) &= z^m(s,i) = 0 && \text{for } s > r,\ 1 \leq i \leq l; \\
\tilde{z}^m(s,i) &= z^m(s,i) && \text{for } s \leq r,\ 2 \leq i \leq l; \\
\tilde{z}^m(s,1) &= z^m(s,1) - \delta e^m(s,1) && \text{for } s \leq r; \\
\sum_m z^m(s,i) &= \sum_m X^m(s,i) = \sum_m e^m(s,i) && \text{for } s \leq r,\ 1 \leq i \leq l.
\end{aligned}$$

[20] Note that the latter property is independent of the choice of utility functions representing the given preferences.

Since we have normalized the state prices to sum to 1, we may (passing to a subsequence if necessary) assume that the state prices $p_n(s,i)$ converge; say, $p_n(s,i) \to p(s,i)$. If $p(s,i) = 0$ for any state s and commodity i, then, for n sufficiently large, the demands in state s would be unbounded. Hence, $p(s,i) \neq 0$ for each s, i. (The limiting behavior of asset prices is irrelevant.)

For each price system p^* and each $m \in M$, define a numeraire pattern $w^m(p^*)$ by

$$w^m(p^*, s) = [1/p^*(s,1)][p^* \square (z^m - e^m)](s) \quad \text{for } s \leq r;$$

$$w^m(p^*, s) = 0 \quad \text{for } s > r.$$

For $s \leq r$, $w^m(p^*, s)$ is the amount of numeraire that must be transferred into state s in order to make the net purchase $(z^m - e^m)(s)$, at prices p^*. Since z is a reallocation of endowments in states $s \leq r$, and $w^m(p^*, s) = 0$ in states $s > r$, if it follows that, for each price system p^* and each state s, $\Sigma w^m(p^*, s) = 0$ (summation over $m \in M$).

We now use the density of span$\{\alpha_k\}$ in $L_1(S, \sigma)$ to find portfolios $\theta^1, \ldots, \theta^{M-1}$ whose returns $\zeta^1, \ldots, \zeta^{M-1}$ are within δ/M of $w^m(p)$ in the L_1 norm; i.e., $\|\zeta^m - w^m(p)\| < \delta/M$ for $1 \leq m \leq M-1$. If we set

$$\theta^M = -\sum_{m=1}^{M-1} \theta^m$$

we obtain a portfolio whose returns ζ^M are also within δ of $w^M(p)$ in the L_1 norm; i.e., $\|\zeta^M - w^M(p)\| < \delta$. Since the state prices $p_n(s,i)$ converge to $p(s,i)$ for each s, i and $w^m(p^*, s) = 0$ for states $s > r$, we conclude that $\|\zeta^m - w^m(p_n)\| < \delta$ for each $m \in M$, provided that n is sufficiently large.

Since the trading sets expand unboundedly, our construction guarantees that, if n is sufficiently large then the portfolio $\theta^m \in {}_nY^m$. Since we have constructed θ^M so that $\Sigma\theta^m = 0$, at least one of the portfolios θ^m must have a nonpositive price (at asset prices q_n). However, if n is sufficiently large, so that prices p_n are sufficiently close to p, then the returns ζ^m on the portfolio θ^m will finance purchase of the commodity bundle $\tilde{z}^m$. By construction, $u^m(\tilde{z}^m) > \limsup u^m({}_nx^m)$ for each m. Since $\tilde{z}^m$ belongs to the budget set of consumer m, this contradicts the equilibrium conditions in $\mathscr{E}_{N(n)}$. This establishes the claim.

If x is not in the core of the underlying complete markets economy, there is a set C of consumers and an allocation y that is feasible for consumers in C such that $u^c(y^c) > u^c(x^c)$ for $c \in C$. However, norm continuity and quasiconcavity of utility functions imply that $\limsup u^h({}_nx^h) \leq u^h(x^h)$ for every h (i.e., utility functions are weakly upper semicontinuous), so this would contradict the claim. We conclude that x is in the core of the underlying complete markets economy; that it is a competitive equilibrium allocation follows, as before, by replication.

It remains only to establish that utilities converge. If not there would be a consumer, say, consumer 1, for whom $\{u^1({}_nx^1)\}$ does not converge to $u^1(x^1)$. Passing to a subsequence if necessary, and keeping in mind that utility functions are weakly upper semicontinuous, we obtain $\limsup u^1({}_nx^1) < u^1(x^1)$. Continuity allows us to choose a number $r < 1$, sufficiently close to 1 so that $\limsup u^1({}_nx^1) < u^1(rx^1)$. Write $y^1 = rx^1$ and $y^h = x^h + (1/H)(1 - r)x^1$ for $h \neq 1$. Then $y = (y^1, \ldots, y^H)$ is a redistribution of endowments, and $u^j(y^j) > \limsup u^j({}_nx^j)$ for every j, so this again contradicts the claim. This completes the proof. ■

7. CONCLUDING REMARKS

There is an old intuition that opening new markets should lead to a Pareto improvement (of the equilibrium allocation). Hart (1975) has shown that this intuition is not always correct: opening new markets may, in fact, lead to a Pareto worsening (of the equilibrium allocation). Despite Hart's examples, the intuition may persist that opening more and more markets should eventually be an improvement, and indeed that, as markets come closer and closer to being complete, equilibrium allocations should become closer and closer to Pareto-optimal allocations.

In this paper, we have examined this intuition by studying the asymptotic behavior of securities markets as the number of securities grows. Our results show that equilibrium allocations of the securities markets need not converge to Pareto-optimal allocations, and that such behavior is not at all pathological. Thus a large—but incomplete—security market may not be a good approximation to a Walrasian market.

Green and Spear (1987, 1989) consider similar questions, and isolate a condition on asset returns and endowments that guarantees asymptotic efficiency. Roughly speaking, their requirement (Assumption A′) is that endowments are eventually large in comparison to asset returns. This condition is very strong; indeed, if endowments are fixed, the set of asset sequences *failing* this condition is a residual set. Their result is thus not at variance with the results here (although they interpret their results slightly differently than I interpret the results in the present paper).

An alternative way to examine the intuition that, as markets come closer and closer to being complete, equilibrium allocations should become closer and closer to Pareto-optimal allocations, is to consider a framework in which a complete set of securities is available for trade, but participation is restricted, so that some fraction of consumers are constrained from trading in some markets. Letting this fraction converge to zero is another way of letting the market converge to completeness. Such an analysis has been carried out by Cass (1990) in a model with a finite number of states. Cass shows that, as the fraction of consumers whose participation is restricted converges to zero, equilibrium allocations converge to Pareto-optimal allocations (indeed, to Walrasian allocations of the complete markets economy).[21]

We have found it convenient to work in the commodity space $L_1(S, \sigma)$, but other choices could be made. For instance, so long as the set of states of nature is countable, all of our work could be carried out in any of the spaces $L_p(S, \sigma)$, $1 \leq p \leq \infty$, with suitable adjustments.[22]

As noted earlier, it would be natural to model the set of states of nature by a continuum (rather than by a countable set, as we have done). However, the existence proof given here does not generalize to this setting; the difficulty is that the wealth mapping $(p, x) \to p \square x$ need not be jointly continuous in the relevant topologies. In the complete markets setting, Bewley (1972) cleverly finesses a similar issue [for a general discussion of this point, see Mas-Colell and Zame (1991a)], but it seems that Bewley's method does not work when markets are incomplete, and the existence of equilibrium in this setting is problematical. For the case of separable preferences, see Hellwig (1991), Mas-Colell and Monteiro (1991), Mas-Colell and Zame (1991b), and Monteiro (1991).

The methods employed here could easily be adapted to the context of multiple trading dates, but they do not seem easily adaptable to continuous time models of trading (for precisely the reason above); see Duffie and Huang (1985), Duffie and Zame (1989) for example.

As we have shown, asymptotic inefficiency arises because some portfolios create liabilities that are unsatisfiable, given endowments and the constraints that terminal consumption be positive. Relaxing these terminal consumption constraints to allow for unboundedly negative terminal consumption restores asymptotic efficiency. However, when consumption goods are physical commodities (rather than assets), consumption of negative quantities does not seem to have a clear interpretation. A more attractive method of addressing this problem would be to insist that terminal consumption be nonnegative, but allow for the possibility that some liabilities are not met; i.e., to allow for the possibility of default. For such a model, see Zame (1990).

Acknowledgments

My interest in this area was stimulated by the 1988 Bonn Workshop on Incomplete Markets; I am indebted to Werner Hildenbrand for his invitation to participate. I have benefited from comments by Marcus Berliant, Darrell Duffie, Jerry Green, Andreu Mas-Colell, Herakles

[21]I am grateful to a referee for pointing out this work.

[22]For $1 \leq p < \infty$, virtually no changes are required, save for altering the definitions in the appropriate way. The case $p = \infty$ is a little more complicated; see Zame (1990).

Polemarchakis, Steven Spear, Yu Jian, and a referee, and from access to the unpublished work of Richard Green and Steven Spear. I am grateful for financial support from the National Science Foundation through Grants SES-8720966 and SES-9012853, from the Deutscheforschungsgemeinschaft, Gottfried Wilhelm Leibniz Forder preis during BoWo 1988 and 1989, and from the Danish National Research Council.

References

Aliprantis, C. D., D. J. Brown, and O. Burkinshaw (1987). "Edgeworth equilibria," *Econometrica* **55**, 1109–1138.

Anderson, R. M. (1986). "Notions of core convergence," in *Contributions to Mathematical Economics*, W. Hildenbrand and A. Mas-Colell (eds.), (North-Holland, Amsterdam).

Arrow, K. J. (1953). "Le role des valeurs boursieres pour la repartition la meilleure des risques," *Econometrie* (Calloques Internationaux du C.N.R.S.) **11**, 41–47.

Arrow, K. J. (1964). "The role of securities in the optimal allocation of risk-bearing," *Rev. Econ. Studies* **31**, 91–96.

Bewley, T. (1972). "Existence of equilibria in economies with infinitely many commodities," *J. Econ. Theory* **4**, 514–540.

Cass, D. (1984). "Competitive equilibrium with incomplete financial markets," CARESS Working Paper, University of Pennsylvania.

Cass, D. (1990). "Real indeterminacy from imperfect financial markets: Two addenda," CARESS Working Paper, University of Pennsylvania.

Debreu, G., and H. Scarf (1963). " A limit theorem on the core of an economy," *Int. Econ. Rev.* **4**, 235–246.

Duffie, D. (1985). "Stochastic equilibria with incomplete financial markets," *J. Econ. Theory* **41**, 405–416.

Duffie, D., and C. F. Huang (1985). "Implementing Arrow–Debreu equilibria by continuous trading of few long-lived securities," *Econometrica* **53**, 1337–1365.

Duffie, D., and W. R. Zame (1989). "The consumption-based capital asset pricing model," *Econometrica* **54** 1279–1317.

Dunford, N., and J. T. Schwartz (1958). *Linear Operators* Part I [Interscience (Wiley), New York].

Geanakoplos, J., and H. Polemarchakis (1987). "Existence, regularity and constrained suboptimality of competitive portfolio allocations when the asset market is incomplete," in *Uncertainty, Information and Communication: Essays in Honor of Kenneth J. Arrow*, Vol. 3 W. Heller *et al.* (ed.) (Cambridge University Press, Cambridge, U.K.).

Green, R., and S. Spear (1987; revised 1989). "Equilibria in large commodity spaces with incomplete financial markets," Working Paper, Carnegie-Mellon University, Pittsburgh, Pa.

Grossmand, S. (1977). "A characterization of the optimality of equilibrium with incomplete markets," *J. Econ. Theory* **15**, 1–15.

Hart, O. (1975). "On the optimality of equilibrium when the market structure is incomplete," *J. Econ. Theory* **11**, 418–443.

Hellwig, M. (1991). "Rational expectations equilibria in sequence economies with symmetric information: The two-period case," Working Paper, University of Basel, *J. Math. Econ.* (in press).

Mas-Colell, A. (1986). "The price equilibrium existence problem in topological vector lattices," *Econometrica* **54**, 1039–1054.

Mas-Colell, A., and P. Monteiro (1991). "Self-fulfilling equilibria: An existence theorem for a general state space," Working Paper, Harvard University, *J. Math. Econ.* (in press).

Mas-Colell, A., and W. R. Zame (1991a). "Equilibrium theory in infinite dimensional spaces," in *Handbook of Mathematical Economics*, Vol. IV, W. Hildenbrand and H. Sonnenschein (eds.), (North Holland, Amsterdam).

Mas-Colell, A., and W. R. Zame (1991b). "Existence of security market equilibrium with a non-atomic state space," Working Paper, Harvard University, *J. Math. Econ.* (in press).

Monteiro, P. (1991). "A new proof of the existence of equilibrium in incomplete markets economies," Working Paper, Harvard University, *J. Math. Econ.* (in press).

Newberry, D. M. G., and J. Stiglitz (1982). "The choice of technique and the optimality of equilibrium with rational expectations," *J. Political Econ.*, **90**, 223–246.

Nielsen, L. T. (1986). "Existence of equilibrium in the classical CAPM," Working Paper, University of Texas.

Radner, R. (1972). "Existence of equilibrium of plans, prices and price expectations in a sequence of markets," *Econometrica* **40**, 289–303.

Richard, S., and W. Zame (1986). "Proper preferences and quasi-concave utility functions," *J. Math. Econ.*, **15**, 231–247.

Stiglitz, J. (1982). "The inefficiency of stock market equilibrium," *Rev. Econ. Studies* **49**, 241–261.

Werner, J. (1985). "Equilibrium in economies with incomplete financial markets," *J. Econ. Theory* **36**, 110–119.

Werner, J. (1987). "Arbitrage and the existence of competitive equilibrium," *Econometrica*, **44**, 1403–1418.

Zame, W. (1990). "Efficiency and the role of default when security markets are incomplete," Working Paper, UCLA (Univ. Calif. at Los Angeles), *Amer. Econ. Review* (in press).

PART II

GROWTH

ENDOGENOUS FERTILITY AND GROWTH

Jess Benhabib
Department of Economics
New York University
New York, New York 10003

Kazuo Nishimura
Institute of Economic Research
Kyoto University
Yoshidahonmachi, Sakyoku
Kyoto 606, Japan

1. INTRODUCTION

Traditional approaches to growth theory have modeled the process of growth as arising from decisions to invest in physical capital and from technological progress (see McKenzie, 1986). A recent model by Barro and Becker (1989) has incorporated fertility decisions, or decisions about the number of children to have, into a growth theoretic context. The welfare of children (through their per capita consumption) is incorporated into the utility of their parents (also see Kemp and Kondo, 1986, 1989); Benhabib and Nishimura (1989). Since consumption must be sacrificed to educate children, the investment decisions become more complex in such a setting. The model can further be enriched by allowing parents to invest in the human capital of their children so as to raise their productivity. We propose to study the implications of introducing technological progress and human capital into the Barro–Becker model of endogenous fertility.

Harrod-neutral technical progress, apart from human capital, is incorporated into our analysis. One of the implications of technical progress is that steady states are no longer in levels; they represent growth paths of per capita variables like output, consumption on capital. The next section spells out the model. We then show that the dynamic behavior of physical capital will be monotonic or oscillatory, depending on the elasticity of a certain "altruism" function that may also be viewed as the elasticity of an inverse demand curve for children. This elasticity, which is always equal to unity in the Barro–Becker model, also plays a major role in determining the existence of multiple steady states. From an empirical perspective multiple steady states may be useful to explain persistent differentials in wealth between some poor and rich countries.

Another important issue is the characterization of the correlation between wealth and fertility. In Section 3, we give conditions, again in terms of preference elasticities, for wealth and fertility to be positively correlated. In Theorem 4 we show that when these conditions fail, wealth and fertility can be negatively correlated. Empirically, while studies using short-run data indicate a positive relation between income and fertility, long-run data show a negative relationship, possibly because of the correlation of income with education and the costs of raising children, both of which have a negative impact on fertility (see Easterlin, 1973, 1987; Simon, 1977, Chapters 14–16). Our model also incorporates the increasing opportunity cost of raising children in terms of forgone output.

Finally in Section 4, we explicitly introduce investment decisions in the schooling of children. Higher investment in schooling makes children more productive in adulthood. To keep the analysis manageable, we abstract from physical capital, which simplifies the portfolio decisions of parents. We show that the results of the previous section that apply to physical capital, that is, to the properties of monotonicity or oscillation, multiplicity of steady states, and positive or negative correlation with wealth, also apply to investments in schooling.

2. THE MODEL AND ASSUMPTIONS

Becker and Barro (1988) consider a model where parents derive utility from their own consumption as well as from the utility of their children. Given the utility attained by each child V^{t+1}, the utility of each adult is

$$V^t = U(c_t) + \alpha(n_t)n_t V^{t+1}, \tag{1}$$

where c_t is the consumption of parents and n_t is one plus the endogenous population growth rate. By substituting out for V^{t+1} and V^{t+2}, etc., in equation (1), we get the dynastic utility function

$$V^0 = U(c_0) + \sum_{t=1}^{\infty} \prod_{w=1}^{t} \alpha(n_w)n_w U(c_t). \tag{2}$$

We introduce the production function with Harrod-neutral technical process.

$$Y_t = F\left(K_t, \lambda^t L_t\right), \tag{3}$$

where Y_t is output of goods, K_t is capital stock, L_t is labor, and λ is exogenous factor of technological progress and $\lambda > 1$. The production function satisfies the following assumptions.

Assumption 1. F is differentiable on $\mathbb{R}^2_+ = \{x \in \mathbb{R}^2 | x_1 \geq 0,\ x_2 \geq 0\}$ with $F_K > 0$ and $F_L > 0$.

Assumption 2. F is concave and linearly homogenous.

Each adult earns the wage w_t, has a capital stock $(1 - \delta)k_t$ that yields a rent $r_t k_t$, where r_t is the interest rate and δ is the depreciation rate. Each adult's wealth is $w_t + (1 - \delta + r_t)k_t$, which the person spends on personal consumption c_t, on bequests to children $n_t k_{t+1}$, and on costs of raising and educating children $n_t B_t$, where $B_t = \lambda^t \beta$. Here we assume that the cost of raising children increases with technological progress that is confined to the goods sector. Otherwise the cost of raising and educating children would eventually be negligible in terms of output. The budget constraint for each adult is

$$w_t + (1 - \delta + r_t)k_t = c_t + n_t(B_t + k_{t+1}). \tag{4}$$

Total capital stocks K_t and K_{t+1} satisfy

$$K_t = L_t k_t, \qquad K_{t+1} = L_{t+1} k_{t+1}. \tag{5}$$

The production function may be rewritten as the following:

$$Y_t = \lambda^t F(\lambda^{-t} K_t, L_t). \tag{6}$$

Using per capita variables $y_t = Y_t/L_t$ and $k_t = K_t/L_t$, we obtain

$$y_t = \lambda^t F(\lambda^{-t} k_t, 1). \tag{7}$$

Set $x_t = \lambda^{-t} k_t$ and $h(x) = F(x, 1)$. Then the profit maximizing conditions imply

$$r_t = F_k(K_t, \lambda^t L_t) = h'(x_t), \tag{8}$$

$$w_t = \lambda^t F_L(K_t, \lambda^t L_t) = \lambda^t[h(x_t) - x_t h'(x_t)]. \tag{9}$$

By substituting (8) and (9) and $B_t = \lambda^t \beta$ into the budget constraint (4), we get

$$h(x_t) + (1 - \delta)x_t = \lambda^{-t} c_t + n_t(\beta + \lambda x_{t+1}). \tag{10}$$

Given x_0, each adult maximizes the dynastic utility function (2) subject to the constraints (10) for $t \geq 0$. We specify the utility function and assume the following.

Assumption 3. $U(c) = c^{\sigma}, \quad 0 < \sigma \leq 1.$

If $\sigma = 1$, then utility is linear and if $0 < \sigma < 1$, it is strictly concave. Then using $V(k_0)$ of the dynastic utility (2), we can rewrite the maximizing problem into the following:

$$V(x_0) = \max_{c_0, n_0, x_1} (U(c_0) + a(n_0)V(x_1)),$$

$$\text{s.t. } f(x_0) = c_0 + n_0(\lambda x_1 + \beta), \quad c_0 \geq 0, \quad n_p \geq 0, \quad x_1 \geq 0, \tag{11}$$

where $a(n_0) = \lambda^{\sigma}\alpha(n_0)n_0$ and $f(x) = h(x_0) + (1 - \delta)x_0$. Here $a(n_0)$ is assumed to be increasing and strictly concave, which assumes that the utility of the parents is increasing at a diminishing rate with the number of children, for a given level of well-being $V(x_1)$ per child.

Assumption 4. $a(n)$ is defined on $[0, \bar{n}]$ with $a(0) = 0$ and $a(\bar{n}) = 1$.

Assumption 5. $a(n)$ is differentiable on $(0, \bar{n}]$ with $a'(n) > 0$ and $a''(n) < 0$.

In order to interpret the conditions that characterize the solutions, we confine our analysis to the restricted nonempty convex domain $D \times (0, \bar{n}) \subset \mathbb{R}^3_+$ on which

$$W(k_0, k_1, n) \equiv U(f(x) - n_0(\lambda x_1 + \beta)) + a(n_0)V(x_1) \tag{12}$$

is differentiable.

After choosing n_0 optimally as a function of (x_0, x_1), equation (11) can also be written as

$$V(x_0) = \max_{x_1} W(x_0, x_1, n(x_0, x_1)). \tag{13}$$

Define $\overline{W}(x_0, x_1) \equiv W(x_0, x_1, n(x_0, x_1))$ and $\overline{W}_1 = \partial\overline{W}/\partial k_0$. Let x^* be a steady state satisfying $V(x^*) = \overline{W}(x^*, x^*) = \max_{x_1} \overline{W}(x^*, x_1)$. We assume that a nontrivial steady state $x^* > 0$ exists, and we let E be the set of nontrivial steady states.

Assumption 6. $E \neq \phi$ and $E \subset D$.

Then the nontrivial steady-state value x^* and $n(x^*, x^*)$ are the solutions of the following equations:

$$W_n = -(\lambda x + \beta)U'(c) + a'(n)V(x) = 0; \tag{14}$$

$$W_{x_1} = -\lambda n U'(c) + a(n)V'(x) = 0. \tag{15}$$

In addition, by the envelope theorem we have

$$V'(x) = U'(c)f'(x). \tag{16}$$

Hence from (15) and (16)

$$f'(x) = \frac{\lambda n}{a(n)} \tag{17}$$

must be satisfied at steady states.

3. CHARACTERIZATION OF FERTILITY RATE CHANGES

We will use the following lemma, which holds on the relevant domain D.

LEMMA 1.

(*i*) *If* $\overline{W}_{12}(x_0, x_1) > 0$, *then an optimal path* $\{x_t\}$ *from any* $x_0 > 0$, $x_0 \notin E$, *is strictly monotone, i.e.,* $(\hat{x}_{t+1} - \hat{x}_t)(\hat{x}_t - \hat{x}_{t-1}) > 0$, *as long as it remains in D.*

(*ii*) *If* $\overline{W}_{12}(x_0, x_1) = 0$, *the capital stock jumps to its steady state value in one period, i.e.,* $\hat{x}_2 = \hat{x}^*$.

(*iii*) *If* $\overline{W}_{12}(x_0, x_1) < 0$, *then an optimal path from any* $x_0 > 0$, $k_0 \notin E$, *fluctuates, i.e.,* $(\hat{x}_{t+1} - \hat{x}_t)(\hat{x}_t - \hat{x}_{t-1}) < 0$, *as long as it remains in D.*

Proof of Lemma 1.

(i) Consider optimal paths $(\hat{x}_t), (\hat{x}'_t)$ from $\hat{x}_0, \hat{x}'_0$ respectively, where $\hat{x}'_0 > \hat{x}_0$, $(\hat{x}_0, \hat{x}_1) \in D$, and $(\hat{x}'_0, \hat{x}'_1) \in D$. Then

$$\overline{W}(\hat{x}_0, \hat{x}_1) \geq \overline{W}(\hat{x}_0, \hat{x}'_1); \tag{18}$$

$$\overline{W}(\hat{x}'_0, \hat{x}'_1) \geq \overline{W}(\hat{x}'_0, \hat{x}_1). \tag{19}$$

Hence

$$W(\hat{x}'_0, \hat{x}'_1) - \overline{W}(\hat{x}_0, \hat{x}'_1) + \overline{W}(\hat{x}_0, \hat{x}_1) - \overline{W}(\hat{x}'_0, \hat{x}_1) \geq 0. \tag{20}$$

This implies

$$\int_{\hat{x}_0}^{\hat{x}'_0} \left[\overline{W}_1(s, \hat{x}'_1) - \overline{W}(s, \hat{x}_1) \right] ds \geq 0,$$

$$\int_{\hat{x}_1}^{\hat{x}'_1} \int_{\hat{x}_0}^{\hat{x}'_0} [\overline{W}_{12}(s, t)\, ds\, dt \geq 0. \tag{21}$$

Since $\overline{W}_{12} > 0$ and $\hat{x}'_0 > \hat{x}_0$, $\hat{x}'_1 \geq \hat{x}_1$ must hold. We note that along the optimal paths,

$$\overline{W}_2(\hat{x}_0, \hat{x}_1) = W_{x_1} + W_n(\partial n / \partial x_1) = 0. \tag{22}$$

The relationship $\overline{W}_{12} > 0$ implies

$$0 = \overline{W}_2(\hat{x}_0, \hat{x}_1) < \overline{W}_2(\hat{x}'_0, \hat{x}_1) \tag{23}$$

for $\hat{x}'_0 > \hat{x}_0$. Hence $(\hat{x}'_0, \hat{x}_1, \ldots)$ cannot be an optimal path, and $\hat{x}'_1$ must differ from $\hat{x}_1$. We have shown that $\hat{x}'_0 > \hat{x}_0$ implies $\hat{x}'_1 > \hat{x}_1$. Therefore $\hat{x}_0 (\gtrless) \hat{x}$ implies $\hat{x}_t (\gtrless) \hat{x}$.

(ii) Let x^* be a steady state. It satisfies

$$\overline{W}_2(x^*, x^*) = 0. \tag{24}$$

Since $\overline{W}_{12} = 0$, $\overline{W}_{12}$ is independent of the value of $\hat{x}_0$. Hence $(\hat{x}_0, x^*)$ for any $\hat{x}_0 > 0$ satisfies

$$\overline{W}_2(\hat{x}_0, x^*) = 0. \tag{25}$$

Therefore $(\hat{x}_0, x^*, x^*, \ldots)$ is an optimal path from any $\hat{x}_0 > 0$.

(iii) The inequality (17) and $\overline{W}_{12}$ are used to get $\hat{x}'_0 > \hat{x}_0 \to \hat{x}'_0 \leq \hat{x}_1$. The relationship $\hat{x}'_1 = \hat{x}_1$ is excluded by the same argument as in the proof of (i). ■

At this stage we consider, the marginal evaluation of children's utility by each adult, that is,

$$p(n) = \frac{a'(n_0)V(x_1)}{a(n_0)V(x_1)} = \frac{a'(n_0)}{a}(n_0) \tag{26}$$

This gives a kind of inverse demand function for children. We introduce the elasticity of this inverse demand curve:

$$e = -\frac{n}{a'/a} \cdot \frac{d(a'/a)}{dn} = \frac{n}{a/a'} \cdot \frac{d(a/a')}{dn}. \tag{27}$$

If $e < 1$ (> 1), then the inverse demand is inelastic (elastic) with respect to the number of children. This corresponds to the case where the demand for children is elastic (inelastic) in the usual sense. Note that Barro and Becker (1989) use a Cobb–Douglas form for $a(n)$ that forces e to be equal to unity. The next theorem shows that the elasticity determines the behavior of the optimum paths of capital stocks within the set D.

THEOREM 1. *If $e < 1$ (> 1) and $0 < \sigma < 1$, then the capital stock oscillates (is monotonic). If $e = 1$ (or $\sigma = 1$), the capital stock jumps to its steady-state value in the first period.*

Proof. The theorem follows from Lemma 1 if we can establish that the sign of $\overline{W}_{12}$ is the same as that of $e - 1$. We set

$$W(x_0, x_1, n_0) = U(f(x_0)) - n(\lambda x_1 + \beta)) + a(n_0)V(x_1). \tag{28}$$

Maximizing $W(x_0, x_1, n_0)$ with respect to n and x_1 yields

$$W_n = (\lambda x_1 + \beta)U'(c_0) + a'(n_0)V(x_1) = 0 \tag{29}$$

and

$$W_{x_1} = -\lambda n_0 U'(c_0) + a(n_0)V'(x_1) = 0. \tag{30}$$

Using (29), we can obtain the optimal value of n_0 as $n(x_0, x_1)$ with the following derivatives:

$$\frac{\partial n}{\partial x_0} = \frac{(\lambda x_1 + \beta)U''(c_0)f'(x_0)}{a''(n_0)V(x_1) + (\lambda x_1 + \beta)^2 U''(c_0)} > 0 \tag{31}$$

$$\frac{\partial n}{\partial x_1} = \frac{\lambda U'(c_0) - a'(n_0)V'(x_1) - \lambda(\lambda x_1 + \beta)n_0 U''(c_0)}{a''(n_0)V(x_1) + (\lambda x_1 + \beta)^2 U''(c_0)}. \tag{32}$$

Using (28) and (29), we can evaluate $\overline{W}_{12}$ as follows:

$$\begin{aligned} \overline{W}_{12} = W_{x_0 x_1} &+ W_{x_0 n_0}\left(\frac{\partial n_0}{\partial x_1}\right) + W_{n_0 x_1}\left(\frac{\partial n_0}{\partial x_0}\right) \\ &+ W_{n_0 n_0}\left(\frac{\partial n_0}{\partial x_1}\right) \cdot \left(\frac{\partial n_0}{\partial x_0}\right), \end{aligned} \tag{33}$$

where

$$W_{x_0 x_1} = -\lambda n_0 f'(x_0)U''(c_0), \quad W_{x_0 n_1} = -(\lambda x + \beta)U''(c_0)f'(x_0),$$

$$W_{n_0 n_0} = (\lambda x_1 + \beta)^2 U''(c_0) + a''(n_0)V(x_1),$$

$$W_{x_1 n_0} = \lambda U'(c_0) + \lambda n_0(\lambda x_1 + \beta)U''(c_0) + a'(n_0)V'(k_1).$$

Substituting into (33) and canceling, we obtain

$$\begin{aligned} \overline{W}_{12} = &\frac{f'(x_0)U''(c_0)}{a''(n_0)V(x_1) + (\lambda x_1 + \beta)^2 U''(c_0)} \\ &\times\big((\lambda x_1 + \beta)\big(a'(n_0)V'(x_1) - \lambda U''(c_n)\big) - \lambda n_0 a''(n_0)V(x_1)\big). \end{aligned}$$

Solving for $V(x_1)$ and $V'(x_1)$ from (29) and (30) and substituting, we obtain

$$\begin{aligned} \overline{W}_{12} = &\frac{f'(x_0)U''(c_0)}{a'(n_0)V(x_1) + (\lambda x_1 + \beta)^2 U''(c_0)} \\ &\times\left((\lambda x_1 + \beta)\left(\frac{\lambda n_0 a'(n_0)U'(c_0)}{a(n_0)} - \lambda U'(c_0)\right)\right. \\ &\left.\qquad - \frac{\lambda n_0 a''(n_0)(\lambda x_1 + \beta)U'(c_0)}{a'(n_0)}\right), \end{aligned}$$

which reduces to

$$\overline{W}_{12} = \frac{\lambda f'(x_0)U''(c_0)(\lambda x_1 + \beta)U'(c_0)}{a''(n_0)V(x_1) + (\lambda x_1 + \beta)^2 U''(c_0)} \left(\frac{n_0 a'(n_0)}{a(n_0)} - 1 - \frac{n_0 a''(n_0)}{a'} \right). \tag{34}$$

If $1 > \sigma > 0$, then the first square bracket on the right is positive by strict concavity. The second can be further simplified so that it equals

$$\left(\left(\frac{n_0 a'}{a} \right) \frac{(a'(n_0))^2 - a(n_0)a''(n_0)}{(a'(n_0))^2} - 1 \right) = \left(\frac{n_0 a'}{a} \right) \frac{d(a/a')}{dn} - 1 = e - 1. \tag{35}$$

Therefore, the sign of $\overline{W}_{12}$ is the same as that of $e - 1$. If $\sigma = 0$, then $U''(c_0) = 0$ and $\overline{W}_{12}$ is always equal to 0. ■

Theorem 1 gives conditions under which the capital stock is oscillatory or monotonic. We now turn to the analysis of how the fertility rate n changes with the capital stock.

THEOREM 2.

(i) If $e < 1$ and $1 > \sigma > 0$, the fertility rate n oscillates in phase with the per capita stock k, that is, $dn_0/dx_0 > 0$.

(ii) If $e = 1$ or $\sigma = 1$, then the fertility rate n jumps to its steady-state value in one period.

Proof.

(i) We have $dn_0/dx_0 = \partial n_0/\partial x_0 + (\partial n_0/\partial x_1)\, dx_1/dx_0$. From the proof of Lemma 1, we know that $e < 1$ implies $dx_1/dx_0 < 0$. From (30), (31), and (32) we can compute how the optimal value of n_0 changes with x_0:

$$\frac{dn_0}{dx_0} = \frac{\lambda U'(c_0)\left(1 - \dfrac{n_0 a'}{a}\right)\dfrac{dx_1}{dx_0} + \lambda(\lambda x_1 + \beta)U''(c_0)\left(f'(x_0) - \lambda n_0 \dfrac{dx_1}{dx_0}\right)}{a''(n_0)V(x_1) + (\lambda x_1 + \beta)^2 U''(c_0)} \tag{36}$$

However, we also have

$$1 - \frac{n_0 a'}{a} = \frac{a - n_0 a'}{a} > 0 \tag{37}$$

by Assumption 4. Thus, $dn_0/dx_0 > 0$ follows under our concavity assumptions and $e < 1$. Since the capital stock oscillates when $e < 1$, so does n.

(ii) In this case $dx_1/dx_0 = 0$. Hence $dn_0/dx_0 = \partial n_0/\partial x_0 > 0$. ■

We will show how previous results are related to the uniqueness of the steady state.

THEOREM 3. *If* $0 < e \leq 1$ *or* $\sigma = 0$, *then the steady state is unique.*

Proof. From (17) the steady-state condition is

$$f'(x) = \frac{\lambda n}{a(n)}, \tag{38}$$

where $n = n(x, x)$. The left-hand side of the equation is decreasing in x as $f''(x) < 0$. The derivative of the right-hand side of the equation is

$$\frac{\lambda[a - a'n]}{a^2} \frac{dn}{dx}. \tag{39}$$

This is increasing in x by the strict concavity of $a(n)$ and $dn/dx > 0$ for the cases of $e \leq 1$ or $\sigma = 0$. Hence the solution of (38) must be unique. ∎

Remark 1. When $e > 1$, the relationship between fertility and wealth may become negative, since the sign of (36) becomes indeterminate. This seems to be supported by long-run data (see Easterlin, 1973, 1987), while a positive relation seems to be observed with short-run data (see Simon, 1977, Chapters 14–17). If we choose an altruism function of the form $a(n) = \delta(n + z)^{\mathrm{A}}$ (for $n + z \geq 0$), then $e = n/(n + z)$. Note that $e > 1$ (< 1) if $z < 0$ $(z > 0)$ and that e may vary positively with n. Barro and Becker (1988, 1989) use a Cobb–Douglas altruism function for which $e = 1$.

Remark 2. When $e > 1$ there may also be multiple steady states. Note that Theorem 3, which guarantees the uniqueness of the steady state, assumes $e < 1$. Therefore, the multiplicity of steady states arises when the inverse demand function for children is elastic. This may be useful to explain persistent wealth differentials between certain rich and poor countries (see Figure 1).

When there are multiple steady states, we can compare the values of the fertility rate at the different steady-state levels of the capital stocks.

THEOREM 4. *Let* x_j^* *and* $n_j^* = n(x_j^*, x_j^*)$ *be steady-state values for* $j = 1, 2$. *If* $x_1^* < x_2^*$, *then* $n_1^* > n_2^*$.

Proof. From the left-hand side of (38), $f'(x_1^*) > f'(x_2^4)$. But the right-hand side of (38) is an increasing function of n. This means that $n_1^* > n_2^*$. ∎

Remark 3. If multiple steady states can explain the persistent wealth differentials between some rich and poor countries, Theorem 4 then can

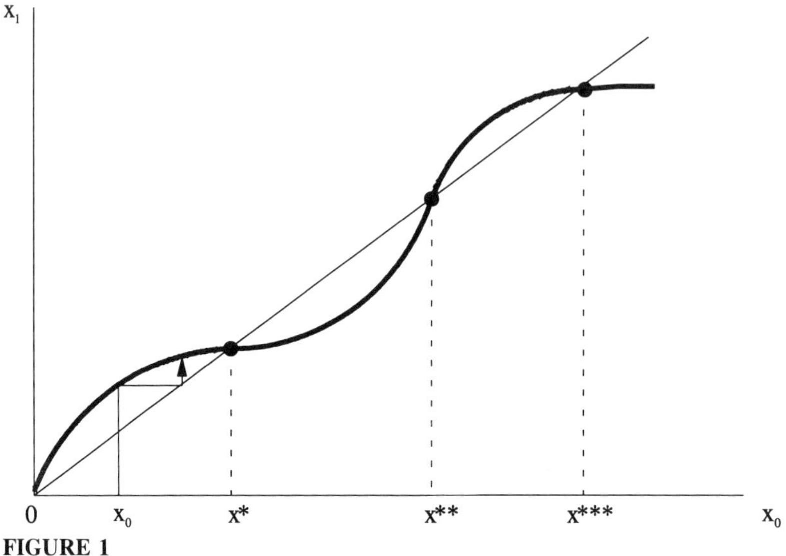

FIGURE 1

also account for the observed inverse relationship between wealth and fertility rates.

4. THE MODEL WITH SCHOOLING

We can incorporate the decision of a parent to invest in the human capital of her children with a simple modification. We denote the cost of raising children by $B_t = s_t \lambda^t \beta$ where s_t is a choice variable. The productivity of labor in period $t + 1$ is affected by the choice of s_t, so that output becomes $Y_{t+1} = F(K_{t+1}, s_t \lambda^{t+1} L_t)$. Defining $x_t = s_{t-1} \lambda^{-t} k_t$, we obtain a budget constraint

$$s_{t-1}\big(h(x_t) + (1-\delta)x_t\big) = \lambda^{-t} c_t + n_t s_t(\beta + \lambda x_{t+1}). \qquad (10)'$$

This constraint generates a model with two state variables, human and physical capital, that is difficult to analyze and can involve complex dynamics. We may substantially simplify the analysis by eliminating physical capital and adopting a technology linear in labor. Let output be denoted by $aL\lambda^t s_{t-1}$. Then the budget constraint for the parent is

$$as_{t-1}\lambda^t = c_t + n_t\big(\beta_0 \lambda^t s_t\big)$$

or, defining $x_t \equiv s_{t-1}\lambda^t$,

$$ax_t = c_t + n_t((\beta_0/\lambda)x_{t+1}).$$

In the terminology of the previous section, if we now let $f(x) = ax$, set $\delta = 1$, and redefine λ as β_0/λ, we have the problem described in equation (11). Therefore, the results of the previous section immediately apply. In particular, the dynamic behavior of x_t and therefore of s_t is determined by e, as described in Theorems 1 and 2. All this implies that investment in children's schooling may be monotonic or oscillatory, depending on the sign of $1 - e$, that there may be multiple steady states if $e > 1$, and that investment in human capital may be positively or negatively correlated with wealth.

Acknowledgments

Kazuo Nishimura's research was supported by grants from The Murata Science Foundation and the Ministry of Education in Japan. The authors also acknowledge the technical support of the C. V. Starr Center for Applied Economics at New York University.

References

Barro, R., and C. Becker (1989). "Fertility choice in a model of economic growth," *Econometrica* **57**, 481–501.

Becker, C. (1981). *A Treatise on the Family* (Harvard University Press, Cambridge, Mass.).

Becker, C. (1988). "A family economic and macro behavior," *Am. Econ. Rev.* **78** 1–13.

Becker, C., and R. Barro (1988). "A reformulation of the economic theory of fertility," *Quart. J. Econ.* **103**, 1–25.

Benhabib, J., and K. Nishimura (1985). "Competitive equilibrium cycles," *J. Econ. Theory* **35**, 284–307.

Benhabib, J., and K. Nishimura (1989). "Endogenous fluctuations in the Barro–Becker theory of fertility," in *Demographic Change and Economic Development*, Alois Wening and Klaus Zimmermann (eds.) (Springer-Verlag, New York), pp. 29–41.

Easterlin, R. (1973). "Relative economic status and the American fertility swing," in *Family Economic Behavior: Problems and Prospects*, E. B. Sheldon, (ed.) (Lippincott, Philadelphia), pp. 170–223.

Easterlin, R. (1987). *Birth and Fortune*, 2nd ed. (University of Chicago Press, Chicago, Ill.).

Kemp, M., and H. Kondo (1986). "Overlapping generations, competitive efficiency and optimal population," *J. Public Econ.* **30**, 237–247.

Kemp, M., and H. Kondo (1989). "Analysis of international migration: The unilateral case," in *Economic Theory and Optimal Population*, K. Zimmerman (ed.) (Springer-Verlag, New York), pp. 153–165.

McKenzie, L. (1986). "Optimal economic growth and turnpike theorems," in *Handbook of Mathematical Economics*, vol. 1, K. Arrow and M. Intrilligator (eds.) (North-Holland, Amsterdam), pp. 1281–1355.

Simon, J. (1977). *The Economics Population Growth* (Princeton University Press, Princeton, N.J.).

A VINTAGE CAPITAL MODEL OF INVESTMENT AND GROWTH: THEORY AND EVIDENCE

Jess Benhabib
Aldo Rustichini
Department of Economics
New York University
New York, New York 10003

1. INTRODUCTION

Does a model of vintage capital contribute to our understanding of growth and of investment expenditures? In this paper we provide a model that combines a vintage capital structure with elements of the "naive accelerator" in an infinitely lived representative agent framework. We then conduct empirical tests of our model and find convincing evidence to support the vintage structure framework.

The so-called "naive" accelerator theory was motivated by empirical observations and sought to explain the strong volatility of investment expenditures. According to the naive accelerator, increases in demand, which necessitate a higher productive capacity, initiate sudden investment expenditures. These expenditures may then suddenly stop if the growth of demand subsides, giving rise to amplified swings in investment. The accelerator theory in this naive form was criticized for its treatment of expectations, its lack of an explicit equilibrium framework, and its neglect of issues concerning dynamic adjustment. The "flexible accelerator" and adjustment cost theories of investment that were subsequently developed addressed these criticisms by explicitly introducing a microeconomic decision-making framework. The dynamic elements in these theories arose from the specification which discourages productive capacity to be adjusted to its desired level all at once, but required investment to proceed slowly in order to avoid the costs of rapid adjustments.

GENERAL EQUILIBRIUM, GROWTH, AND TRADE II

In our paper we adopt a vintage capital version of the optimal growth model, and for the most part we postulate a linear utility function. This linearity, or the lack of any sort of adjustment costs, in a model without vintages would lead to investment patterns that result in the instantaneous adjustment of capital to its desired steady-state level. However, the introduction of vintages produces a different dynamic mechanism that we describe below, as well as in the later sections in more detail. (We should note at this point that the results of our paper are robust to the introduction of strict curvature into the utility function, provided it is not too large, as is discussed in Sections 4 and 6.)

In the 1960s and 1970s a number of papers were written on vintage capital models (see, e.g., Solow, 1960; Phelps, 1962; Bliss, 1968; Levhari and Sheshinski, 1967; Bardhan, 1969; Denison, 1964)). This literature was mainly concerned with the role of investment in technological change, or with the "embodiment" hypothesis. In particular, the effects of the composition of embodied and disembodied technical change on the growth rates, and the effect of the savings rate on the steady-state age distribution of capital were extensively debated. There was limited discussion of the dynamic properties of these models and the analyses were mostly confined to balanced growth paths. [Among the exceptions, as far as we are aware, are the articles by Solow et al. (1966) and Sheshinski (1967).] The dynamics of investment in a vintage capital model however, is of particular interest. Unlike the standard growth models, in a vintage model the returns to investment depend on the distribution of previous vintages that are expected to remain in use in the subsequent periods. The source of this dependence is the limited amount of labor (or land) that has to be allocated across the vintages. The level of labor available to the vintages necessarily affects their productivity. A large amount of existing capital, if it remains in use, draws a large amount of the available labor, thereby reducing the productivity of new investment and depressing its level. When the large quantity of old capital is retired due to economic obsolescence, existing levels of capital will be low, in turn leading to higher levels of investment. In a stochastic economy subject to aggregate shocks, a positive technological shock will induce high levels of economy-wide investments as all sectors find themselves undercapitalized, especially if interindustry linkages are strong. In subsequent times, as this large stock of aging investments draws large amounts of labor, the amount of new investment will be depressed as the economy "lives off" its past investments.[1] In fact, investment in a new vintage will be negatively related to the older vintages that are expected to survive into the next period. These types of fluctuations and volatility in the composition of vintages and in

[1]Note how such an economy would be vulnerable to sudden foreign competition from countries that undertake investments in new and more efficient vintages.

the levels of investment cannot be captured by the standard adjustment cost or optimal growth models. In such models savings and gross investment levels are monotonically increasing functions of the aggregate capital stock. Vintage models therefore offer a particularly suitable framework in which to study the volatile behavior of investment and growth. We will formally address the issues raised above first in a deterministic framework, then in Section 8 in a stochastic model, before we present some empirical findings in Section 9.

One final remark. Although our analysis of a vintage model is developed in the setup of optimal growth with a representative agent, we believe that the fundamental result (that a high level of past investments tends to reduce the present level) would hold even in different formulations (e.g., an overlapping-generations model, or the investment decision of a firm) as long as the investment depends on the rates of return of past investments.

The idea that investment may take place in lumps in a particular industry goes back to Marx (in the second volume, part 2, Chapter 9 of *The Capital*). It subsequently was discussed by Robertson (1915), among others, in a loose macroeconomic context and came to be known as the "echo" principle. Recently Mitra and Wan (1985), (1986), Mitra et al. (1988), and Wan (1988) studied a vintage model of intertemporal equilibrium in the context of forestry, which incorporates the "echo" principle. A simpler model that is similar to ours was given by Ferri (1986). Rustichini (1989) constructed a model with delayed depreciation, giving rise to oscillations in the capital stock. A recent paper by Chari and Hoppenhayn (1987) studied a vintage model of human capital. Kydland and Prescott (1982) were the first to propose "time to build" or gestation lags, in a representative agent model of equilibrium growth to account for the observed volatility of investment relative to other economic time series. Finally, in an "industrial organization" context, vintage models are used in Holmes and Schmitz (1988).

Our paper is organized as follows. Section 2 describes the model. Section 3 contains a few technical results, with most of the proofs relegated to the appendix (Section 9). There is also in this section a discussion of alternative technological assumptions to those made in Section 2 and of the properties of the value function for our model. Section 4 provides general results on the non-monotonicity of investment paths for our model. Section 5 discusses comparative static properties of steady states. Section 6 derives the properties of the linear policy function and discusses its dynamic implications. The behavior of wages and output along an equilibrium path is analyzed in this section and a number of examples are provided. Section 7 establishes properties of the stochastic version of our model when technology is subject to stochastic shocks. Finally, in Section 8 we estimate the model using maximum likelihood methods and provide empirical results. We note that the lemmas in the text are numbered according to their order in the appendix and that some lemmas are omitted from the main text to ease the flow of exposition.

2. THE MODEL: DESCRIPTION AND GENERAL PROPERTIES

At each point in time, the productive factors available in the economy are the (possibly infinite) string of investments in previous periods and a (constant) amount of labor. In the rest of the paper we refer to these investments as capital stocks, and we index them to reflect their vintage. A formal definition is given below.

2.1 Capital

Formally, the state space for the capital stock is the positive cone of l_∞ (the space of bounded sequences) denoted l_∞^+. We shall use the convention of indexing an element of l_∞^+ over the negative integers: an element $k \in l_\infty^+$ is $(k_s)_{s=0,\ldots,-\infty}$.

Any such element will be referred to as the *capital string*.

2.2 Labor

At the beginning of each period there is a finite amount of labor to be allocated over the capital string k. We normalize this constant and finite amount to 1 and we denote

$$L \equiv \left\{ l \in l_1^+ : \sum_{s=-\infty}^{0} l_s \leq 1 \right\}. \tag{1.1}$$

Notice that (by Fatou's lemma) L is (identified with) a closed subset of the unit ball of l_∞^+, where this last space is endowed with the topology of pointwise convergence.

(We note that an exponentially growing labor force can be incorporated into our analysis since later on we introduce Harrod-neutral technical change and measure factors in efficiency units anyway. See Section 7.)

2.3 Production

One of our intermediate tasks ahead is the characterization of the efficient allocation of labor across vintages and of the total output that results from this allocation. In particular, we would like to assure that the age of the oldest capital to which labor is allocated is finite. We assume that the output of each vintage of capital is described by a production function that combines the vintage capital with labor, and that total output is the sum of outputs across vintages. We denote $\mathbf{R}^m_+ = \{x \in \mathbf{R}^m\colon x_i \geq 0 \ i = 1, \dots, m\}$. Also for any extended real valued function f we denote $f(0+) \equiv \lim_{x \downarrow 0} f(x)$, $f(+\infty) = \lim_{x \to +\infty} f(x)$, whenever such limits exist.

We also implicitly assume that at each time only new and most efficient machines are produced. This of course is not entirely realistic since some investment in the construction and maintenance of old machines is undoubtedly undertaken. Explicitly allowing for radioactive depreciation and treating new machines as net investment would to some extent accommodate such considerations. (We should note, however, that this kind of radioactive depreciation, although widely used for accounting purposes, does not do justice to reality either.) Technically, introducing radioactive depreciation would simply require us to redefine some constants in our model without making substantive changes in results. We will discuss this issue further in Section 7 and in relation to empirical results in Section 8.

For this section we will use a production technology described by the assumptions below (in later sections we will discuss alternative technologies).

Assumption 1. (i) $f\colon \mathbf{R}^2_+ \to \mathbf{R}_+$ is concave, C^2 in the interior of the region of definition and continuous in it; is homogeneous of degree 1.

Assumption 2. (ii) $f(k,0) = 0$ for every $k \geq 0$, $f_{kl}(k,l) \geq 0$ for every k, l.

Assumption 3. f is strictly concave: if $(k_1, l_1) \neq (k_2, l_2)$ then for any $\theta \in (0,1)$ one has

$$f(\theta k_1 + (1-\theta)k_2, \theta l_1 + (1-\theta)l_2) > \theta f(k_1, l_1) + (1-\theta) f(k_2, l_2).$$

Assumption 4. For some continuous real function $m\colon \mathbf{R}_+ \to \mathbf{R}_+$,

$$f_l(k, 0+) \leq m(k), \quad \text{for every } k \geq 0.$$

Remark 1. Assumptions 1–4, together with embodied technological change, described below, will assure that sufficiently old capital stock will not be allocated any labor. In early vintage models this type of economic obsolescence was obtained by assuming fixed coefficient production functions which in the constant elasticity of substitution (CES) class imply that $\rho \to -\infty$, whereas our assumptions only imply that $\rho < 0$.

Embodied technological change, which improves the efficiency of the production process of each successive vintage, will be described below.

Remark 2. From Assumptions 1 and 4 one derives:

$$f(k,l) \leq m(k)l \quad \text{for every } (k,l) \in R^2_+. \tag{1.2}$$

Remark 3. A well-known example of a function satisfying Assumptions 1–4 is the CES, which we write in the form

$$f(k,l) = (ak^{\rho} + bl^{\rho})^{1/\rho} \quad \text{for } k \geq 0, \quad l \geq 0.$$

Here a and b are two positive real numbers, and ρ is a constant that we require to be negative. In this case it is easy to check that $f_l(k, 0+) = b^{1/\rho}$ for every $k \geq 0$ (so Assumption 4 is satisfied), and $f_{kl}(k,l) \geq 0$ for any k, l as would be true of any constant returns-to-scale production function. The other conditions are also easily checked.

Before we proceed, we pause to remark that the embodied technical change makes the problem nonstationary, because the technology is time-dependent. In fact the same capital string at two different points in time will meet labor with different productivity. This nonstationarity is, anyway, of a very mild nature, since the embodied technical change has a constant rate of growth, and there is (see Lemma 1.1 in Section 9) a very simple relationship between the production possibility from a given capital string at different points in time.

2.4 Efficient Production

Into our vintage model of production we introduce embodied technical change of the Harrod-neutral type. While an analysis in terms of Hicks or Solow neutral technical change is possible, the Harrod-neutral technical change is the only one that allows the existence of a balanced growth path (see Bliss, 1968). More importantly, empirical observation suggest that over the long-run the capital/output ratio is roughly constant while factor shares also remain unchanged. This is possible along a balance growth path for each vintage, and therefore in the aggregate, for Harrod-neutral technical change but fails in cases like the Hicks-neutral case, unless the elasticity of substitution in production is identically equal to 1 [for further discussion see Burmeister and Dobell (1970), Chapter 3].

We shall find convenient the use of the notation

$$F(k,l) \equiv \sum_{s=-\infty}^{0} f(k_s, l^s\beta^s) \quad \text{for every } k \in l_{\infty}^{+}, l \in L \text{ and for } \beta > 1.$$

Let the map $\Phi\colon l_{\infty}^{+} \to R_{+}$, giving the maximum production from a capital string k at time zero be defined by

$$\Phi(k) \equiv \sup_{l \in L} F(k,l). \tag{1.3}$$

For times different from zero we define the map

$$G(t,k,l) \equiv \sum_{s=-\infty}^{0} f(k_s, l_s\beta^{t+s}), \quad \text{for every } k \in l_\infty^+, l \in L, t \in N,$$

where $N = \{0, 1, 2, \dots\}$ and

$$\Psi(k,t) \equiv \sup_{i \in L} G(t,k,l). \tag{1.4}$$

The function defined in (1.3) above gives total production over the vintages under the assumption that the age of the vintage diminishes the efficiency of labor allocated to it. (Thus $\beta > 1$.) Note that while the efficiency of labor depends only on the age of the vintage to which it is allocated, it is independent of actual time. This may be viewed as a case where capital simply depreciates or deteriorates with age. By contrast, (1.4) represents embodied technical change. In this case the productivity of labor depends on both the age of the vintage it uses and the time at which the vintage was built. This is because we assume that a vintage that is built later in time makes labor more effective, that is, it augments labor by a factor of β.

Although we are mainly interested in the case of Harrod-neutral embodied technical change, the case given by (1.4), we find it convenient to carry out technical arguments and proofs in terms of (1.3). We then use the sample relationships (see Lemma 1.2 in Section 9) given by

$$G(t,k,l) = \beta^t F(\beta^{-t}k, l), \qquad \Psi(t,k) = \beta^t \Phi(\beta^{-t}k)$$

to reformulate the results in terms of the quantities of the model of embodied technical change. Let $s(t,k)$ denote, for $\Psi(t,k)$, the lowest integer for which $\hat{l}_s(t,k)$ is positive; $s(t,k)$ represents the oldest vintage of capital to which a positive amount of labor is allocated. Since under Assumption 1, $f(k,0) = 0$ for $k \geq 0$, we call $s(t,k)$ the truncation time. For $\Phi(k)$, which is independent of t, we denote the truncation time as $s(k)$.

LEMMA 1.7. *For every $k \in l_\infty^+$ there exists a finite truncation time $s(t,k)$ for $\Psi(t,k)$, and $s(k)$ for $\Phi(k)$.*

COROLLARY 1.11(A). (This is abridged from Corollary 1.11 in Section 9): *Let l_∞^+, l_1^+ be endowed with the norm topology. Then*

(*i*) *The truncation times $s(t,k)$ and $s(k)$ are upper semicontinuous.*
(*ii*) *The optimal allocations of labor $\hat{l}(t,k)$ and $\hat{l}(k)$ are continuous,*

2.5 Preferences

The consumer is described by the following assumption.

Assumption 5. The preferences of the representative consumer are described by a linear utility function for consumption in every period, and a discount factor $\delta < 1$.

Remark. The assumption that the utility function is linear can be relaxed. In Sections 4 and 6 we show that the main results derived below are preserved with a strictly concave and increasing utility function, provided the curvature of the utility function remains small. In those sections the utility function will be denoted by $U: R_+ \to R$.

We now turn to the properties of the reduced utility function (or consumption, since the one-period utility is assumed to be linear). If we denote consumption by c we have $c = \Phi(k) - x$ in the time-independent "depreciation" case and $c = \Psi(t, k) - x$ in the case of embodied technical change. Let $V: l_\infty^+ \times R_+ \to R_+$ be defined as

$$V(k, x) \equiv \Phi(x) - x = \sum_{s=-\infty}^{0} f\left(k_s, \hat{l}_s(k)\beta^s\right) - x$$

for the time independent case and

$$V(t, k, x) \equiv \Psi(t; k) - x = \sum_{s=-\infty}^{0} f\left(k_s, \hat{l}_s(k, t)\beta^{t+s}\right) - x$$

in the time-dependent case. We seek to establish the cross partial derivatives of V that we will need in Section 4 in order to establish the nonmonotonicity properties of the optimal investment path.

2.6 The Growth Problem

We can now define, for $\beta > 1$, the intertemporal optimization problem for a planner or a representative agent as follows:

$$\max_{\{k_t, \{l^t\}\}} \sum_{t=0}^{\infty} \left(\sum_{s=-\infty}^{0} f\left(k_s^t, l_s^t \beta^{t+s}\right) - k_{t+1} \right) \delta^t, \qquad (P_a)$$

subject to

$$f\left(k_s^t, l_s^t \beta^{t+s}\right) - k_{t+1} \geq 0$$

$$k^0 = \left\{k_0^0, k_{-1}^0, \dots\right\} \text{ given}$$

$$l^t \in L \quad \text{for every } t;$$

where k_t represents investment at time t, k^t and l^t represent the capital string and labor allocations at time t, $k_s^t \equiv k_{t+s}$ is the investment made at s with the superscript denoting the time at which it is being used, and l_s^t is the allocation of labor to vintage s at time t.

Given Lemma 1.2, and setting $x_t \equiv k_t \beta^{-t}$, we can redefine problem (P_a) as a standard stationary problem with discount rate $\delta\beta$ as follows:

$$\max_{\{k_t, \{l^t\}\}} \sum_{t=0}^{\infty} \left(\sum_{s=-\infty}^{0} f(x_s^t, \beta^s l_s^t) - x_{t+1} \right) (\delta\beta)^t, \qquad (P_a^*)$$

subject to

$$\sum_{s=-\infty}^{0} f(x_s^t, \beta^s l_s^t) - x_{t+1} \geq 0,$$

$$x^0 = \{x_0^0, x_{-1}^0, \dots\} \quad \text{given}$$

$$l^t \in L \quad \text{for every } t.$$

In the rest of the paper we will refer to x_t values as "detrended" investments.

In the following sections we analyze the properties of the solution to the problem posed above. Section 7 extends the model to a stochastic framework to implement testing. Empirical results are given in Section 8.

Remark. With a simple modification, we could interpret our model as that of a firm maximizing discounted cash flow. The only substantive change required would be to replace the fixity of labor by allowing the firm to choose the total amount of labor used. For the problem to remain meaningful the firm would have to face an upward sloping supply curve of labor. Given the optimal amount of labor the allocation problem would be the same. Such a specification would allow us to conduct the empirical work in Section 8 at the level of the firm or industry. Note also that in a similar vein, in the context of the growth problem that we are studying, we could replace the assumption of fixed labor by introducing leisure into the utility function (for simplicity in a separable way) to determine the labor supply at each point in time.

3. SOME TECHNICAL RESULTS

In this section we provide some technical results concerning the efficient allocation of labor and the properties of the output functions that allow us to reduce the problem to finite-dimensional one. While the proofs and most of the lemmas are relegated to the appendix, a few of the lemmas that are integral to the arguments in the subsequent section are also given below.

LEMMA 1.1.

(*i*) *If f satisfies, the Assumptions* 1 *and* 3, *the suprema in the definition of* $\Phi(k)$ *and* $\Psi(t,k)$ *are achieved.*

(*ii*) *If f satisfies Assumption* 2, *the optimal labor allocations, denoted* $\hat{l}(k)$ *for* $\Phi(k)$, *and* $\hat{l}(t,k)$ *for* $\Psi(t,k)$, *are unique, and the entire labor is used; i.e.* $\Sigma_s \hat{l}(k) \equiv 1$ *and* $\Sigma_s \hat{l}(t,k) \equiv 1$ *for every* k.

The functions V: $l_\infty^+ \times R_+ \to R_+$, and the time-dependent V: $N \times l_\infty^+ \times R_+ \to R_+$ are defined as

$$V(k,x) \equiv \Phi(k) - x = \sum_{s=-\infty}^{0} f\left(k_s, \hat{l}(k)_s \beta^s\right) - x$$

$$V(t,k,x) \equiv \Psi(t;k) - x = \sum_{s=-\infty}^{0} f\left(k_s, \hat{l}(k,t)\beta^{t+s}\right) - x.$$

LEMMA 1.12.

(*i*) *The partial derivatives* $(\partial V/\partial k_i)(k,x), (\partial^2 V/\partial k_i\, \partial k_j)(k,x)$ *exist for every pair* (k,x). *In addition, one has*

(*ii*) $(\partial V/\partial k_i)(k,x) = f_k(k_i, \hat{l}(k)_i \beta^i) \equiv V_i(k,x) \geq 0,$

$$\frac{\partial^2 V}{\partial k_i} \partial k_j(k,x) = f_{kl}\left(k_i, l(k)_i \beta^i\right) \frac{\partial \hat{l}(k)_i}{\partial k_j} \beta^i$$

$$\equiv V_{ij}(k,x) \leq 0 \text{ for every pair } (i,j), i \neq j.$$

(*iii*) $\partial V/\partial k_i(t,k,x) = f_k(k_i, \hat{l}(k,t)_i \beta^{t+i}) \equiv V_i(t;k,x),$

$$\frac{\partial V}{\partial k_i\, \partial k_j}(t,k,x) = f_{xl}\left(k_i, \hat{l}(k,t)_i \beta^{t+i}\right) \frac{\partial \hat{l}(k,t)_i}{\partial k_j} \beta^{t+i}$$

$$\equiv V_{ij}(t,k,x) \leq 0 \text{ for every pair } (i,j), i \neq j.$$

3.1 An Alternative Description of the Technology: The One Hoss-Shay model

For this model the vintage production function satisfies Assumptions 1–3 as above. Assumption 4 is now replaced by the following.

Assumption 4′.

$$f(k, 0+) = +\infty \quad \text{for every } k \geq 0.$$

Assumption 4′ would imply that every vintage, no matter how old, would be activated where labor is allocated optimally. To avoid this unrealistic situation we require that, for some finite integer T, only vintages T units of time old or less were actually available; that is the aggregate production from $(k, l) \in l_\infty^+ \times l_1^+$ is $F(k, l) = \sum_{s=-T}^{0} f(k_s, l_s)$.

The problem of optimal allocation of labor is now finite-dimensional. Therefore, existence and characterization of such optimum are entirely standard. Notice that from Assumption 4′ it now follows that the truncation time is always equal to T.

Remark. Examples of functions satisfying the above assumptions are of course the Cobb–Douglas, which we formulate as $f(k, l) = (1-\alpha)^{-1} k^{1-\alpha} l^{\alpha}$, and the CES production function when the parameter ρ is in the interval $(0, 1)$.

3.2 The Value Function

It is well known that in a standard model of technical progress sufficient discounting ensures that the value of the optimal program is bounded and standard arguments yield the value function. The situation is similar for vintage models that can be transformed into the form presented by problem (P_a^*) in Section 2, although some technical details have to be addressed to assure that the output stream remains finite. In particular, if truncation times are unbounded or if capital can produce output without labor when truncation times are finite (as with CES production functions) problems may arise. Below we show for Cobb–Douglas and a class of CES production functions compatible with our Assumptions (1)–(4) that our problem is well defined.

LEMMA 1.13. *If any of the following conditions holds, then the value of the optimal program is finite*:

(*i*) *The vintage production function is Cobb–Douglas* (*given by* $(1-\alpha)k^{\alpha}l^{1-\alpha}$) *and* $\delta\beta^{1/\alpha} < 1$.

(*ii*) *The vintage production function is CES* (*given by* $(ak^{\rho} + bl^{\rho})^{1/\rho}$), $\rho < 0$, *the maximal truncation time is T and* $\max\{a^{1/\delta}T, \beta\}\delta < 1$.

(*iii*) *The vintage production function is CES*, $\rho < 0$, *the truncation time is endogenous and* $\max\{a^{1/\delta}, 1^{\delta}\}\delta < 1$.

For any capital string k the set of *admissible paths starting at* k is the set of elements of which satisfy

(i) $k^0 = k$,

(ii) $\Phi(k^t) - k_{t+1} \geq 0$ for every $t \geq 0$.

We denote such set by $A(k)$. Analogously, we define $A'(k)$ when (ii) above is replaced by (ii)′

$$\Psi(t, k^t) - k_{t+1} \geq 0, \quad \text{for every } t \geq 0.$$

We can now define the value function $W\colon l_\infty^+ \times R_+$ by the map

$$W(k,t) = \sup_{y \in A(k)} \sum_{t=0}^{\infty} \delta^t U(\Psi(t, y^t) - y^{t+1})$$

or, in the time-independent case, $W\colon l_\infty^+ \times R$ by

$$W(k) = \sup_{y \in A(k)} \sum_{t=0}^{\infty} \delta^t U(\Phi(y^t) - y_{t+1}).$$

Note that the suprema will be achieved at unique elements $\hat{y}(k) \in A'(k)$ or $\hat{y}(k) \in A(k)$, the optimal admissible paths. Further properties of the value function are given in the lemma below.

LEMMA 1.14.

(*i*) *$W(k)$ and $W(\cdot, k)$ are concave.*
(*ii*) *For any fixed $k \in l_\infty^+$ and integer m, the function $W(k, \cdot)\colon R \to R_+$ defined by $x \to W(k,x)$ is C^1.*

4. NONMONOTONICITY PROPERTIES OF THE OPTIMAL PATH

Let a segment of length T of an optimal trajectory for problem P_a^* starting at t be denoted $\{\hat{x}_s\}_t^{t+T}$. Note that for problem (P_a^*) of Section 2, x values denote "detrended" optimal stocks. We will say that a segment of a trajectory is interior if none of its elements lie on the boundary of its feasible set. We will also say that a segment of a trajectory is weakly decreasing (increasing) if $x_t \geq x_{t+1}$ $(x_t \leq x_{t+1})$ for all t along the segment, with at least one strict inequality on this segment. In Lemma 3.1 we state a nonmonotonicity property of an optimal trajectory for the case where a maximal truncation time T exists. The corollary generalizes this result.

LEMMA 4.1. *Consider an interior optimal trajectory along which the maximal truncation time is T. If a segment $\{\hat{x}_s\}_t^{t+2T-2}$ of this trajectory is weakly decreasing (increasing), then $\hat{x}_{t+2T-1} > \hat{x}_{t+2T-2}(\hat{x}_{t+2T-1} < \hat{x}_{t+2T-2})$.*

Lemma 4.1 applies to cases where there is a fixed truncation time. A more general result is given in the corollary below.

COROLLARY. *Consider an interior segment of the optimal trajectory $\{\hat{x}_s\}_{T+t}^{2T-1+t}$ of length T, and let the truncation times along this segment be less than or equal to T. If the segment $\{\hat{x}_s\}_t^{2T-2+t}$ is weakly decreasing (increasing), then $\hat{x}_{2T-2+t} < \hat{x}_{2T-1+t}(\hat{x}_{2T-2+t} > \hat{x}_{2T-1+t})$.*

The proof of this corollary follows immediately from the proof of Lemma 4.1.

When the utility function is strictly concave, the nonmonotonicity properties will be preserved if the curvature of the utility function is sufficiently small. This will be discussed in Section 6.

Remark. It can be shown that the nonmonotonicity results above will hold with a strictly concave utility function provided its second derivative is sufficiently small. To sketch the argument, we first note that the proof uses the cross-partial derivatives of the reduced utility function given in Lemma 1.12 to establish certain inequalities. These inequalities will still hold if the second derivative of the utility function is sufficiently small. If $\beta = 1$, this would conclude the proof. However, the proof also uses the fact that the optimal choice of investment in any period is independent of time. This is justified with a linear utility function because then the problem can be transformed into a stationary problem, as shown at the end of Section 2. When the utility function is nonlinear, instantaneous utility at time t is given by

$$\delta^t U\left(\beta^t \sum_{s=-\infty}^{0} f\left(x_s^t, \beta^s l_s^t\right) - x_{t+1}\right)$$

so that it no longer is possible to interpret $\delta\beta$ as the discount factor, as was done for problem (P_a^*) at the end of Section 2. Nevertheless, if truncation times remain finite and bounded over relevant segments, the maximum theorem implies that the optimal choice will be continuous with respect to parameters of the utility function. Optimal choices from a given history will remain close for linear and close to linear utility functions over a finite history. Therefore, the strict inequalities established with a linear utility can be preserved for slight perturbations of the utility function, and the nonmonotonicity results continue to hold. In Section 6.5 a rigorous argument establishing the continuity of the policy function with respect to parameters of the utility function will be provided.

5. THE STEADY STATE

For any $\delta > 0$, a steady state is defined, as usual, to be the special optimal path of the form $k_t = k(\delta)\beta^t$, for every t, for some constant $k(\delta)$. The real number $k(\delta)$ is referred to as the *steady-state capital stock*.

We proceed to characterize the steady state. The value of the steady-state solution is given by the series

$$\left(\Psi(0, k^0) - k_1\right) + \delta\left(\Psi(1, k^1) - k_2\right) + \cdots + \delta^i\left(\Psi(i, k^i) - k_{i+1}\right) + \cdots .$$

Differentiating with respect to the term k_j, we get

$$-1 + \delta\Psi_1(j, k^j) + \delta^2\Psi_2(j+1, k^{j+1}) + \cdots = 0, \tag{5.1}$$

but since

$$\Psi(j, k^j) = \sum_{s=-\infty}^{0} f\big(k_s^j, \hat{l}(k^j, j)_s \beta^{j+s}\big),$$

one has

$$\Psi_n(j, k^j) = f_k\big(k_j, \hat{l}(k^j, j)_{-n} \beta^{j-n}\big), \quad \text{for } n = 0, -1, \ldots .$$

Then (5.1) becomes

$$-1 + \sum_{i=0} \delta^i f_k\big(k_j, \hat{l}(k^{j+i}, j+i)_{-i} \beta^j\big) = 0 \quad \text{for every } j \geq 1.$$

If we consider $k_j = k\beta^j$, we have equivalently

$$-1 + \sum_{i=0} \delta^i f_k\big(k, \hat{l}(k^{j+i}, j+i)_{-i}\big) = 0 \quad \text{for every } j \geq 1 \tag{5.2}$$

from the homogeneity property of f.

Now we consider the allocation of labor in the steady state. For the string

$$k^j = (\ldots, k\beta^{j-1}, k\beta^j),$$

we have the first-order conditions:

$$f_l\big(k_s^j, \hat{l}(k^j, j)_s \beta^{j+s}\big)\beta^{j+s} = w(k^j, j), \qquad s \in (s(k), \ldots, 0)$$

But since

$$k_s^j = k_{j+s} = k\beta^{j+s},$$

the above system becomes

$$f_l\big(k\beta^{j+s}, \hat{l}(k^j, j)_s \beta^{j+s}\big)\beta^{j+s} = w(k^j, j)$$

or

$$f_l\big(k, \hat{l}(k^j, j)_s\big)\beta^s = w(k^j, j)\beta^{-j}, \qquad s \in (s(k, j), \ldots, 0). \tag{5.3}$$

Now (5.3), together with $\sum_{s=-\infty}^{0} \hat{l}(k^j, j)_s = 1$, gives that

$$\hat{l}(k^j, j)_s = \hat{l}(k)_s, \quad \text{a constant over } j, \tag{5.4}$$

$$s(k, j) = s(k) \quad \text{for every } j. \tag{5.5}$$

Note, however, that $\hat{l}(k)_s$ and $s(k)$ still depend on β.

Equations (5.4) and (5.5) imply that

$$\Psi_i(k^j, j) = f_k\big(k, \hat{l}(k)_{-i+1}\big), \qquad i = 1, 2, \ldots \tag{5.6}$$

Now (5.2), (5.5), and (5.6) give

$$1 = \delta f_k\big(k, \hat{l}(k)_0\big) + \delta^2 f_k\big(k, \hat{l}(k)_{-1}\big) + \cdots + \delta^{-s(k)} f_k\big(k, \hat{l}(k)_{s(k)}\big) \tag{5.7}$$

as the equation that characterizes the steady-state capital stock k.

Let $k(\delta)$ be the set of k values that satisfy (5.7), that is the set of steady-state stocks. Also, for two sets A_i, $i = 1, 2$, $A_i \subset \mathbb{R}$, we say $A_1 \geq A_2$ iff $a_i \geq a_2$ for every pair (a_1, a_2), $a_i \in A_i$; and a correspondence ϕ: $R \to R$ is increasing if $x \geq y$ implies $\sup \phi(x) \geq \sup \phi(y), \inf \phi(x) \geq \inf \phi(y)$.

LEMMA 5.2

(*i*) *$k(\delta)$ is an increasing correspondence.*
(*ii*) *If f_k is strictly decreasing, then the steady state is unique.*

In other words, as impatience grows (δ falls), the steady-state capital falls and the period of production falls.

6. THE POLICY FUNCTION

6.1 Linearity of the Policy Function

Recall that the functions f_l, f_k are homogeneous of degree zero, and can therefore be written as functions of the ratio $(k/l) \equiv x$. With a slight abuse of notation, we will denote this function by f_l and f_k. We now introduce one additional assumption, of the Inada type:

$$-1 + \delta f_k(+\infty) + \cdots + \delta^{T+1} f_k(+\infty) < 1 \tag{Ii}$$

$$f_l(+\infty) = +\infty. \tag{Iii}$$

Remark. Examples of pairs (δ, f) that satisfy (Ii) and (Iii) are easily found. A Cobb–Douglas production function always does, and a CES with $\rho \in (0, 1)$ will also satisfy them for δ small enough.

THEOREM 6.1. *Assume Assumptions* 1–3 *and* 4′ *and I, and a finite truncation time T. Then the optimal investment policy is linear with constant coefficients of the form*

$$\hat{x}_t = a_0 - \sum_{j=-T}^{-1} a_j x_{t+j},$$

where

$$k_j = x_j \beta^j$$

and

$$a_0 > 0,$$

$$0 < a_{-T} \leq a_{-T+1} \cdots \leq a_{-1} < 1,$$

with strict inequalities if $\beta > 1$ *and* $a_j = 1$ *for* $j = -T$ *to* -1 *if* $\beta = 1$.

Remark. Note that Theorem 6.1 states that the weighted sum of detrended investments remains constant; we may consider this constant as a measure of aggregate capital. Nevertheless, the detrended yearly investments, which are the variables of concern here, continually fluctuate. Also note that our aggregation holds along the optimal path and is different from the capital aggregation results obtained in earlier literature (see, e.g., Gorman, 1968). In this literature general results on aggregation are shown to hold only if the technical progress is of the capital augmenting type.

Proof. Recall that the problem is to determine

$$\sup_{\{k_t\}_{t \geq 1}} \sum_{t=0}^{\infty} \delta^t \left\{ \sum_{s=-T}^{0} f\left(k_s^t, l_s^t \beta^{t+s}\right) - k_{t+1} \right\}$$

over the sequences of investment that satisfy

$$k^0 = k,$$

$$\Psi(t, k^t) - k_{t+1} = c_t \geq 0,$$

and where $l_s^t \equiv \hat{l}(k^t, t)_s$. The Euler equations are

$$-1 + \delta f_k\left(k_t, l_0^t \beta^t\right) + \delta^2 f_k\left(k_t, l_{-1}^{t+1} \beta^t\right) + \cdots + \delta^{T+1} f_k\left(k_t, \hat{l}_{-T}^{t+t} \beta^t\right) = 0$$

$$f_l\left(k_t, l_0^t \beta^t\right) \beta^T = f_l\left(k_{t-1}, l_{-1}^t \beta^{t-1}\right) \beta^{T-1} = f_l\left(k_{t-T}, l_{-T}^t \beta^{t-T}\right)$$

for $t = 1, 2, \ldots$.

We now introduce the notation

$$x_t \equiv k_t \beta^{-t} \quad \text{at} = 0, 1,$$

$$R_j^t \equiv \frac{x_t}{l_{-j}^{t+j}} t = 0, 1, \ldots; \qquad j = 0, 1, \ldots, T.$$

We can now rewrite the (infinite) system of equations above as

$$-1 + \delta f_k(R_0^t) + \delta^2 f_k(R_{-1}^t) + \cdots + \delta^{T+1} f_k(R_{-T}^t) = 0, \qquad (\text{IE})_t$$

$$f_l(R_{-T}^{t-T}) = \beta f_l(R_{-T+1}^{t-T+1}) = \cdots = \beta^T f_l(R_0^t) \qquad (\text{LME})_t$$

for $t = 1, 2, \ldots,$ where IE stands for investment equilibrium and LME for labor market equilibrium.

It is clearly sufficient to prove that the following system of $T + 1$ equations in the $T + 1$ variables $R_0, R_{-1}, \ldots, R_{-T}$ has a solution

$$-1 + \delta f_k(R_0) + \delta^2 f_k(R_{-1}) + \cdots + \delta^{T+1} f_k(R_{-T}) = 0, \qquad (\text{IE})$$

$$f_l(R_{-T}) = \beta f_l(R_{-T+1}) = \cdots = \beta^T f_l(R_0). \qquad (\text{LME})$$

Recall that f_l is a continuous nonnegative increasing (because $f_{kl} > 0$) function; therefore $f_l(0+)$ exists and is nonnegative. We first determine a one-parameter family of solutions of the equations (LME).

Set $R_0 = t$ and define G: $\overline{R}_+ \to \overline{R}_+^T$, ($\overline{R}_+ = R_+ \cup \{+\infty\}$), as follows:

$$\beta^{T-i} f_l(t) = f_l(G(t)_{-T+i}), \qquad i = 0, \ldots, T.$$

Note that for any $t > 0$, $f_l(t) < \beta^{T-i} f_l(t) \in \{x\colon x = f_l(t')t' > 0\}$ because f_l is increasing, so G is well defined. Also

$$G(t)_0 = t < G(t)_{-1} \cdots < G(t)_{-T}, \quad \text{for every } t > 0,$$

$$G(0+) = (0, R_{-1}, \ldots, R_{-T}), \quad \text{for some } 0 < R_{-1} < \cdots < R_{-T},$$

$$G(+\infty) = (+\infty, \ldots, +\infty).$$

Consider now the extended real-valued, continuous function H defined over $\overline{R}_+$:

$$H(t) \equiv -1 + \delta f_k(G(t)_s) + \cdots + \delta^{T+1} f_k(G(t)_{-T}).$$

Clearly

$$H(0+) = -1 + \delta f_k(0+) + \cdots = +\infty$$

and also

$$H(+\infty) = -1 + \delta f_k(+\infty) + \cdots + \delta^{T+1} f_k(+\infty) < 0$$

by assumption (Iii); so $H(t_0) = 0$ for some positive t_0.

We have proved that a solution to the Euler equations exist, and is $(R_0, R_{-1}, \ldots, R_{-T}) = (G(t_0)_0, G(t_0)_{-1}, \ldots, G(t_0)_{-T})$.

Now recall that $\Sigma_{j=-T}^0 l_j^t = 1$ and $(x_{t+j}/l_j^t) = R_j$, $j = 0, \ldots, -T$. Therefore, if we denote by $\hat{x}_t$ the optimal detrended investment

$(x_t = k_t \beta^{-t})$ at time t, given a string $(x_{t-1}, \ldots, x_{t-T})$, we have

$$\hat{x}_t = R_0 - \sum_{j=-T}^{-1} \frac{R_0}{R_j} x_{t+j},$$

or, in terms of the original quantities

$$\hat{k}_t = R_0 \beta^t - \sum_{j=-T}^{-1} \beta^{-j} \frac{R_0}{R_j} k_{t+j},$$

as claimed. Identifying (R_0/R_j) with a_j and a_0 with R_0 concludes the proof of the theorem. ■

Remark. It is easy to see that the solution $(R_0, \ldots, R_{-T})$ of the Euler equations is (componentwise) increasing in β, where $R_s \equiv (x_{t+s}/l_s^t)$, $s = -T, \ldots, 0$, for every t. We note that the constancy of $(R_0, R_{-1}, \ldots, R_{-T})$ along the optimal path implies that the ratio of "detrended" capital to the labor that is allocated to it depends only on the age of the capital. Furthermore, since $R_0 < R_{-1} < \cdots < R_T$ when $\beta > 1$, the "detrended" capital to labor ratio is smallest for the most recent vintage.

Remark. Consider the case $T = 1$. Then $\hat{x}_t = R_0 - (R_0/R_{-1})x_{t-1}$, where $0 < (R_0/R_{-1}) < 1$. It is now easy to see how the path of (detrended) investments is determined. The parameters of the problem (f, δ, β) determine the quantity R_0 and the slope R_0/R_{-1}. The initial condition x_0 determines the future path.

The difference equation describing the motion of x_t is clearly stable, and converging to $\bar{x}$, as long as $\beta > 1$. For example, in the case where the production function is Cobb–Douglas, it can easily be shown that $R_0 R_{-i}^{-1} = (\beta^{1/(\alpha-1)})^i$ where α is the exponent of labor. For the case of $T = 2$ we have $x_{t+1} = R_0 - R_0 R_{-1}^{-1} x_t - R_0 R_{-2}^{-1} x_{t-1}$, we can see that the roots of the characteristic equation are

$$\lambda_{\pm} = \frac{\beta^{1/(\alpha-1)}}{2}\{-1 \pm i\sqrt{3}\}, \qquad |\lambda_{\pm}| = \beta^{1/(\alpha-1)}.$$

For the general case of vintage production functions homogeneous of degree 1, we have seen that the detrended investment is the solution of the difference equation

$$x_t = R_0 - a_{-1} x_{t-1} \quad - a_{-T} x_{t-T},$$

where

$$0 < a_{-T} < a_{-T-1} < \cdots < \quad a_{-1} < 1$$

for any production function, if $\beta > 1$. When $\beta = 1$ then $a_i = 1$, $i = -1, \ldots, -T$. If $\beta > 1$, the characteristic equation

$$\lambda^T + a_{-1}\lambda^{T-1} + \cdots + a_{-T} = 0$$

has (complex) roots of absolute value strictly less than 1 (say, $\delta < 1$ at most). Therefore, we can construct the following corollary.

COROLLARY. *If the vintage production function is homogeneous of degree one, and $\beta > 1$, the optimal investment converges exponentially to the steady state, i.e., for some $\delta \in (0,1)$ and $A > 0$*

$$|\hat{x}_t - x_{ss}| < A\delta^t, \qquad t \geq 0$$

where x_{ss} is the steady-state value of x_t.

6.2 Effect of β on the Labor Allocation

We can also compute the change in the allocation of labor over the vintages in response to a change in β, the rate of technical progress. The allocation of labor over the vintages for those $\hat{l}(k)_s > 0$ is determined by

$$f_L^s \equiv \beta^s f_L(k_s, l(k)_s) = f_L\left(k_0, 1 - \sum_{s=-T}^{-1} l(k)_s\right) \equiv f_L^0 = w(k),$$

$$s = -T, \ldots, -1,$$

where $w(k)$ is defined in Lemma 1.3 and corresponds to the marginal product of labor, equalized across vintages using positive labor, and the k's are "detrended" as usual for simplicity.

Differentiating with respect to β the above equations, denoting $f_{LL}^s \equiv f_{LL}(k_s, l(k)_s)$, and noting that $\beta^T f_L^{-T} = w(k)$, we obtain

$$\left[\begin{bmatrix} \beta^{-T} & f_{LL}^{-T} & & 0 \\ 0 & \beta^{-T+1} & f_{LL}^{-T+1} & \\ 0 & & \beta^{-1} & f_{LL}^{-1} \end{bmatrix} + \begin{bmatrix} f_{LL}^0 & \cdots & f_{LL}^0 \\ \cdot & & \cdot \\ \cdot & & \cdot \\ \cdot & & \cdot \\ \cdot & & \cdot \\ f_{LL}^0 & \cdots & f_{LL}^0 \end{bmatrix}\right] \begin{bmatrix} dl_{-T} \\ dl_{-T+1} \\ dl_{-1} \end{bmatrix}$$

$$= \begin{bmatrix} \beta^{-1} w(k) T \\ \beta^{-1} w(k)(T-1) \\ \beta^{-1} w(k)(T-2) \\ \beta^{-1} w(k) \end{bmatrix} \tag{6.1}$$

Tedious simplifications and Cramer's rule yield

$$\frac{dl_{-m}}{d\beta} = -\frac{\left(\prod_{s\neq m-T}^{-1}(\beta^s f_{LL}^s)\right)\cdot\left[mw(k)\beta^{-1} - w(k)\beta^{-1}f_{LL}^0\left(\sum_{s\neq -m-T}^{-1}(-s-m)(\beta^s f_{ll}^s)^{-1}\right)\right]}{\left(\prod_{s=-(T-1)}^{-1}(\beta^s f_{LL}^s)\right)\left[f_{LL}^0 + \beta^{-T}f_{LL}^{-T} + \beta^{-T}f_{LL}^{-T}f_{LL}^0\left(\sum_{s=-(T-1)}^{-1}(\beta^s f_{LL}^s)^{-1}\right)\right]}.$$

Inspection of the above expression shows that $(dl_{-T}/d\beta) < 0$; that is, the labor allocated to the oldest vintage declines with β. It also follows from the proof of Lemma 1.7 that the truncation time is finite and that for any $s < 0$ and sufficiently high β, $\beta^s f_L(k_s, 0) < w(k) \leq f_L(k_0, 1)$, so that vintage s will not be allocated any labor. Note also that since $R_0 < R_{-1} < \cdots R_{-T}$, as shown above, if $l_s > 0$ then $l_n > 0$ for $0 \geq n > s$.

It follows from the above discussion that the truncation time $s(k)$ is nonincreasing in β, and that for a sufficiently high β only the newest vintage is actually used. We formally state these results as follows.

LEMMA 6.1. *The truncation time $s(k)$ is nonincreasing in β and for any $n \leq -1$, there exists a β sufficiently high so that $s(k) \geq n$.*

We can also inquire about the effect of a change in β on the steady-state capital stock and the steady-state value of the labor allocated to the oldest vintage in use. The problem can be tackled, in principle, by differentiating the steady-state equation (5.2) up to the oldest vintage in use and then expanding (6.1) to include the appropriate derivatives with respect to k. The response of the steady-state capital to changes in β will be ambiguous, and will depend on the signs of $\beta^i f_{KL}^i - f_{KL}^0$, $-T \leq i \leq -1$, where $-T$ is the index of the oldest vintage in use. This can be seen by computing the simple case where $-i = T = 1$. However, in this case steady-state l_{-1} still diminishes with β, as can also be readily computed. When more than two vintages are used ($T > 1$), the labor allocated to the oldest vintage probably still diminishes with β, implying that the steady-state "string length" of vintages in use in nonincreasing in β, although we have not been able to formally establish this result because of the messy linear algebra (see also Chari and Hoppenhayn, 1991).

6.3 The Behavior over Time of Wages and Output

If the rate of technical change β is greater than one, there is a growing trend in the economy. For this reason we shall again concentrate our attention on "detrended" variables: if $\{y_t\}_{t\geq 1}$ is the sequence we are considering, the detrended sequence is $\{y_t\beta^{-t}\}_{t\geq 1}$.

We can now determine what the output will be.

COROLLARY. *Let the assumptions in Theorem* 6.1 *hold. Then*

1. *The sequence of detrended outputs is a linear combination, with constant coefficients, of detrended investments.*
2. *The sequence of detrended equilibrium wages is a constant, equal to* $f_l(R_0)$.

Proof.

1. As usual we shorten $\hat{l}(k^t, t)_s = l_s^t$. Then the output Y_t is

$$
\begin{aligned}
Y_t &= \sum_{s=-T}^{0} f\left(k_s^t, l_s^t\beta^{t+s}\right),\\
&= \sum_{s=-T}^{0} f\left(x_{t+s}, l_s^t\right)\beta^{t+s},\\
&= \sum_{s=-T}^{0} l_s^t f(R_s)\beta^{t+s},
\end{aligned}
$$

where we have used the fact that $R_s^t = R_s$, and the usual abuse of notation appears. Now recalling that $R_s^{t+s} = (x_{t+s}/l_s^t)$, one has

$$Y_t = \sum_{s=-T}^{0} x_{t+s}\frac{f(R_s)\beta^{t+s}}{R_s}, \text{ or for the detrended output,}$$

$$y_t = \sum_{s=-T}^{0} x_{l+s}\frac{f(R_s)\beta^{s}}{R_s}, \text{ where } \quad y_t = Y_t\beta^{-t},$$

as claimed. Notice that each coefficient $[f(R_s)\beta^s/R_s]$ is positive.

2. The equilibrium wages are determined by

$$
\begin{aligned}
w_t = w(k^t, t) &= f_l\left(k_t, \hat{l}(k^t, t)_0\beta^t\right)\beta^t = f_l\left(x_t, \hat{l}(k^t, t)_0\right)\beta^t\\
&= f_l(R_0)\beta^t,
\end{aligned}
$$

and so our claim follows.

Remark. Using the equation

$$x_t = R - \frac{R_0}{R_{-1}}x_{t-1} \cdots - \frac{R_0}{R_{-T}}x_{t-T},$$

one can rewrite the equation for detrended output as

$$y_t = f(R_0) + \sum_{s=-T}^{-1} \left(\frac{f(R_s)\beta^s}{R_s} - \frac{f(R_0)}{R_s} \right) x_{t+s}. \qquad (6.2)$$

6.4 Examples

If $T = 1$, we obtain, using the equation (6.2) above and the linear policy $x_t = R_0 - (R_0/R_{-1})x_{t-1}$,

$$Y_t = \beta^t\{A + mx_{t-1}\}, \quad \text{where } A \equiv f(R_0), \qquad m = \frac{f(R_{-1})}{\beta R_{-1}} - \frac{f(R_0)}{R_{-1}}.$$

Recall that (R_0, R_{-1}) satisfies the equation $f_l(R_{-1}) - \beta f_l(R_0) = 0$; or if f is CES,

$$aR_{-1}^{\rho} + b = \beta^{\rho/1-\rho}(aR_0^{\rho} + b). \qquad (6.3)$$

Now $m = 0$ is equivalent to $f(R_{-1}) = \beta f(R_0)$, or, if f is CES,

$$aR_{-1}^{\rho} + b = \beta^{\rho}(aR_0^{\rho} + b). \qquad (6.4)$$

Therefore, $m = 0$ with (R_0, R_{-1}) satisfying equation (6.2) if and only if $\rho = 0$; that is if and only if the production function is Cobb–Douglas.

For all other cases ($\rho \in (0, 1)$) the oscillations of investment will be reflected in the oscillation of output.

We remark that for a CES function with $\rho > 0$ the constant term m is positive, if $\beta > 1$. Consider in fact a fixed R_0, and denote by $R_{-1,L}$ (respectively, $R_{-1,m}$) the values of R_{-1} such that the equation (6.3) [respectively (6.4)] is satisfied. Since $\beta^{[\rho/(1-\rho)]} > \beta^{\rho}$, $R_{-1,L} > R_{-1,m}$. Since f is an increasing function, at the pair $(R_0, R_{-1,L})$, which is the solution of the Euler equations, one has $f(R_{-1,L}) - \beta f(R_0) > 0$, and therefore $m > 0$ as claimed.

The equation for the detrended output as a function of the detrended one-period lagged investment $y_t = mx_{t-1} + A$ bears an interesting similarity with the multiplier equation, with marginal propensity to consume $1 - m^{-1}$ and autonomous expenditure $f(R_0)$.

Recalling that f_k is a decreasing function, it is easy to see that the equilibrium vector $(R_0, R_{-1}, \ldots, R_{-T})$ is increasing (componentwise) in the discount factor δ. In the simple case examined above the A term is therefore increasing in the discount factor. The rate of technical progress β has no effect on A; it does anyway affect the term m; note that $m = 0$ where $\beta = 1$. The effect of δ on m is of a less definite nature.

We may conclude this discussion noting: $y_t = m(\delta, \beta)x_{t-1} + A(\delta)$, where A is increasing in δ and $m(\delta, 1+) = 0$.

As a further example, let the production function for every vintage be a Cobb–Douglas function of the form $f(k,l) = (1-\alpha)^{-1}k^{1-\alpha}l^{\alpha}$, and assume a fixed truncation time T, so that

$$G(k^t, l, t) = \sum_{s=-T}^{0} f\left(k_s^t, l_s \beta^{t+s}\right).$$

Denote the following:

$$\tilde{\beta} = \beta^{\alpha/\alpha-1} \quad \text{and note that } \left(\tilde{\beta}\beta^{-1}\right)^{\alpha} = \tilde{\beta}.$$

$$\bar{\beta} = \beta^{1/\alpha-1} \quad \text{and note that } \bar{\beta} \text{ and } \tilde{\beta} \text{ are less than 1.}$$

Then

$$\sum(k^t) = k_t + \tilde{\beta}k_{t-1} + \cdots + \tilde{\beta}^T k_{t-T},$$

$$C \equiv \left(\delta + \delta^2\tilde{\beta} + \cdots + \delta^{T+1}\tilde{\beta}^T\right)^{1/\alpha}.$$

Then we can easily compute the following:

$$\hat{l}(k^t, t) = \left(\frac{\tilde{\beta}^T k_{t-T}}{\sum(k^t)}, \ldots, \frac{k_t}{\sum(k^t)}\right)$$

$$k_t = C\beta^t - \tilde{\beta}k_{t-1} - \cdots - \tilde{\beta}^T k_{t-T}$$

$$R_0 = C, \qquad R_{-i} = R_0\bar{\beta}^{-i}$$

$$x_t = C - \bar{\beta}x_{t-1} - \cdots - \bar{\beta}^T x_{t-T}$$

$$Y_t = \frac{C^{1-\alpha}}{1-\alpha}\beta^t$$

$$w_t = \frac{C^{1-\alpha}\alpha}{1-\alpha}\beta^t = \alpha Y_t.$$

Note that in this special Cobb–Douglas case $Y_t\beta^{-t}$ and $w_t\beta^{-t}$ are constants. In particular, fluctuations in investments completely smoothes output around trend.

6.5 Nonlinear Utility Functions

So far we have restricted the one period utility function to be linear. Such a simple form has allowed us to derive exact characterizations of the policy function, but the reader may wonder how robust such results are to perturbations of the utility function. In this section we show that they are indeed robust for small perturbations of the utility function. Before we proceed, we introduce a topology on the space of utility functions:

$$|U_1 - U_2|_C = \sup_{C \in R_+} |U_1(C) - U_2(C)|.$$

In the following we shall find useful to reformulate our problem. The state space will be the product of the capital string space (infinite sequences, with the product topology) and time. The action space will be the proportion of the total production that is reinvested. The one period reward function, r, will be defined on the product space of states and actions:

$$S \times A = (R_+^\infty \times N) \times A, \qquad A \equiv [0,1];$$

$$r: S \times A \to R^+, \quad \text{wherefore } s = (k, t)$$

$$r(s, a) = U(\Psi(S)(1 - a)) = U(c).$$

The topology of uniform convergence on the space of utility functions induces a natural topology on the space of reward functions:

$$|r_1 - r_2|_C = \sup_{S \times A} |r_1(s, 2) - r_2(s, a)|$$

Remark. $r_n \to r$ in the τ_c-topology if and only if, for the associated sequence of utility functions $\{U_n, U\}_{n \geq 0}$, one has $U_n \to U$.

The transition function is now defined by

$$T: S \times A \to S,$$

$$T(s, a) = T(k, t; a) \equiv (\sigma(k), \Psi(k, t)a; t + 1),$$

where σ is the shift operator, defined by $\sigma(k)_i \equiv k_{i+1}$, for $i = 1, \ldots.$

The value function is now naturally defined on the state space S; and satisfies the equation

$$W(s) = W(k, t) = \max_{a \in [0,1]} \{r(s, a) + \delta W(T(s, a))\}.$$

The (unique) maximer of the right-hand side is denoted $h_r(s)$, where the subscript r denotes the dependence on r. Similarly, we will denote the value function by $W_r(s)$ to indicate its dependence on the reward function r. Let C be the space of continuous functions on R_+. We shall denote

$$F: A \times S \times C \to R_+$$

$$F(a, s; r) \equiv r(s, a) + \delta W(T(s, a)).$$

One can now prove the following lemmas.

LEMMA 6.1. *$W: r \to W_r$ is a Lipschitz continuous function, with Lipschitz constant* $(1-\delta)^{-1}$.

LEMMA 6.2. *Suppose that $r_n \to r$ in τ_c. Then*

1. *$h_{r_n}(s) \to h_r(s)$ for every $s \in S$*
2. *$h_r(\cdot)$ is a continuous function.*

We shall now examine the continuity property of the map that gives the optimal policy as depending on the reward function r. We shall endow the space of policy functions with the topology of uniform convergence on compact subsets of S; and we shall use τ_k to denote this topology.

LEMMA 6.3. *Suppose that F is a continuous function. Then $H: r \to h_r$ is a continuous function, when the space of policy functions is endowed with τ_k.*

THEOREM 6.4. *As a map from C, with the τ_c topology, to the space of policy functions with the τ_k topology, H is continuous.*

Proof. Obvious from Lemmas 6.1–6.3. ■

Remark. If $r_\nu \to r$ uniformly on $S \times A$ (for instance, if $U_\nu \to U$ uniformly on R), then the corresponding policy function h_{r_ν} converges to h_r uniformly on compact subsets of S.

7. THE STOCHASTIC MODEL

We define a stochastic process by

$$Z_{t+1} = Z_t^\theta \varepsilon_t,$$

where $\theta \in (0,1)$ and $\{\varepsilon_t\}_{t \geq 0}$ is a sequence of i.i.d random variables, which are $\varepsilon_t > 0$ a.s. for every t, and $\ln \varepsilon_t \sim N(0, \sigma^2)$.

We assume that the random shocks affect directly the total amount produced: the production from a pair (k, l) at time t is the random variable $F(t, k, l)Z_t$.

We also assume in this section, that the vintage production function is Cobb–Douglas of the form $f(k, l) = (1-\alpha)^{-1}k^{1-\alpha}l^\alpha$.

Notice that since the random shocks affect only the aggregate production (overvintages), the optimal allocation of labour is identical to the deterministic case. Therefore, the stochastic optimization problem we are considering is

$$\sup_{\{k_t\}_{t\geq 1}} E_0 \sum \delta^t \{\Psi(k^t, t)Z_t - k_{t+1}\},$$

where as usual the sequence $\{k_t\}_{t\geq 1}$ is constrained to

$$\Psi(k^t, t)z_t - k_{t+1} \geq 0; \qquad k^0 = k.$$

We denote the realization of a random variable Z_t by the lowercase z_t.

LEMMA 7.1. *Assume $\theta < 1$, $\delta\beta > 1$. Then the supremum of the stochastic program is finite.*

We can now derive the explicit form of the optimal investment policy.

THEOREM 7.1. *The optimal policy function for the stochastic optimization problem (S) is given by*

$$\hat{k}(k_{t-1}, \dots, k_{t-T}, z_t) = \Gamma(z_t)\beta^t - \tilde{\beta}k_{t-1} \cdots - \tilde{\beta}^T k_{t-T} \qquad \text{(OP)}$$

where

$$\Gamma(x) = C^{-1/\alpha}x^{\theta/\alpha}, \qquad C \equiv \left(\delta + \delta^2\tilde{\beta} + \cdots + \delta^T\tilde{\beta}^{T-1}\right)^{-1}.$$

Remark. Substituting the optimal investment into the aggregate production function, one can now determine the form of the stochastic "output" process. We have

$$k_t = CZ_t^{\theta/\alpha}\beta^t - \tilde{\beta}k_{t-1} \cdots - \tilde{\beta}^T k_{t-T},$$

$$Y_t = \frac{C^{1-\alpha}}{1-\alpha}\beta^t Z_t Z_{t-1}^{\theta/\alpha}, \quad \text{where } \tilde{\beta} = \beta^{\alpha/(\alpha-1)}.$$

Because of the Cobb–Douglas assumption output is independent of capital stocks, which are in fact used to smooth the output path. In this stochastic case detrended output is a simple stochastic process rather than a deterministic trend. With a more general production function, we would expect output fluctuations to depend on fluctuations in stocks, as in the deterministic case with a CES production function.

For simplicity of exposition we have so far ignored the possibility that the amount of labor available in each period may be growing over time. We have also ignored the possibility that the capital good over its active life period, may depreciate. The above analysis can be easily extended to account for both of these facts.

More formally, we may assume that the set of feasible labor allocations is

$$L_t \equiv \left\{l\colon l_s \geq 0,\ \sum_s l_s \leq L(t)\right\}, \quad \text{where } L(t+1) = L(t)(1+g),$$

for some $g > 0$. The capital stock depreciates at a rate $(1-\lambda)$, $\lambda \in (0, 1)$, at each period. To summarize, at period t the vintage that is s units old produces with the amount l_s^+ of labor the quantity $f(k_s^t\lambda^{-s}, l_s^t\beta^{t+s})$ of goods. The efficient production problem is now

$$\Psi(k^t, t) = \max\left\{\sum_{s=-\infty}^{0} l_s \leq L(t)\right\} \sum_{s=-\infty}^{0} f\left(k_s^t\lambda^{-s}, l_s^t\beta^{t+s}\right).$$

Substituting this new efficient production function in the stochastic problem (S) above, we may now consider the new stochastic optimization problem (S′); the following characterization of the optimal policy is then easily proved: (here $f(k,l) = (1-\alpha)^{-1}k^{1-\alpha}l^{\alpha}$).

Corollary 7.1. *The optimal policy function for the stochastic optimization problem* (*S′*) (*with capital depreciation rate* $1-\lambda$ *and labor growth rate* g) *is given by*

$$\hat{k}_t = \Gamma'(z_t)[\beta(1+g)]^t - (\tilde{\beta}\lambda)k_{t-1} - \cdots - (\tilde{\beta}\lambda)^T k_{t-T},$$

where

$$\Gamma'(x) \equiv C'^{-1/\alpha}x^{\theta/\alpha}; \qquad C' \equiv \left(\delta + \delta^2\tilde{\beta}\lambda + \cdots + \delta^T(\tilde{\beta}\lambda)^{T-1}\right)$$

$$\tilde{\beta} = \beta^{\alpha/(a-1)}.$$

8. EMPIRICAL RESULTS

In this section we suggest and undertake a test of the stochastic model presented in the previous section. To use maximum-likelihood estimation, we take logarithms of the policy function given in Theorem 7.1 and proceed to take first differences after multiplying the lagged value by θ, the autoregressive coefficient of the stochastic process. We also redefine the stochastic process by adding two moving average terms so that $z_{t+1} = z_t^{\theta}\varepsilon_t\varepsilon_{t-1}^{\rho_1}\varepsilon_{t-2}^{\rho_2}$. The result, for a fixed truncation T, is

$$\ln\varepsilon_t = (\alpha/\theta)\left[\ln\left(k_t + \tilde{\beta}k_{t-1} + \cdots\right) - \theta\ln\left(k_{t-1} + \tilde{\beta}k_{t-2} + \cdots\right)\right.$$
$$\left. -(1-\theta)\ln C + (t - \theta(t-1)\ln\beta\right] - \rho_1\ln\varepsilon_{t-1} - \rho_2\ln\varepsilon_{t-2}$$

[we recall $\tilde{\beta} \equiv \beta^{\alpha/(\alpha-1)}$; $C \equiv (\delta + \delta^2\tilde{\beta} + \cdots + \delta^T\tilde{\beta}^{T-1})^{-1}$], where $\ln x$ denotes the natural logarithm of x. Since ε_t is assumed to be iid and log-normally distributed, standard maximum-likelihood methods will apply. Our procedure will be to fix α at 0.67, as suggested by factor shares, and δ, the annual discount factor, at 0.96. (The results will not be sensitive

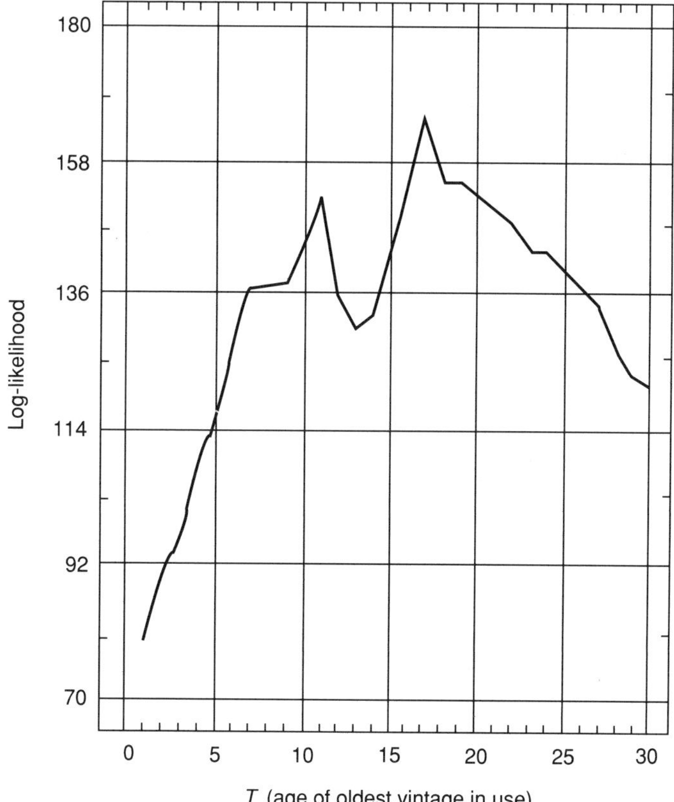

FIGURE 1 Nonresidential fixed investment.

to small changes in the values of α and δ.) We use two annual investment series, from 1929 to 1988 that we obtained from Data Resources, Incorporated (DRI; (U.S. Central Data): fixed nonresidential gross investment and gross investment in producer durable equipment.

We estimate, for various values of T, the parameters β, θ, ρ_1, and ρ_2. To show the existence of vintage effects we would like to estimate the "correct" value of T. Although some error must necessarily enter the estimation of T because of aggregation, we would at least want to show that T is significantly higher than zero and also that it is unlikely to be excessively high. Here we can suggestively use likelihood ratio tests to determine the best T, although T is a discrete variable, and the distributional assumptions for the likelihood ratio tests may be violated. On the other hand, the improvement in the likelihood function is sufficiently dramatic for the best T-values against very small or large values of T, that we feel justified in drawing some tentative conclusions that support our

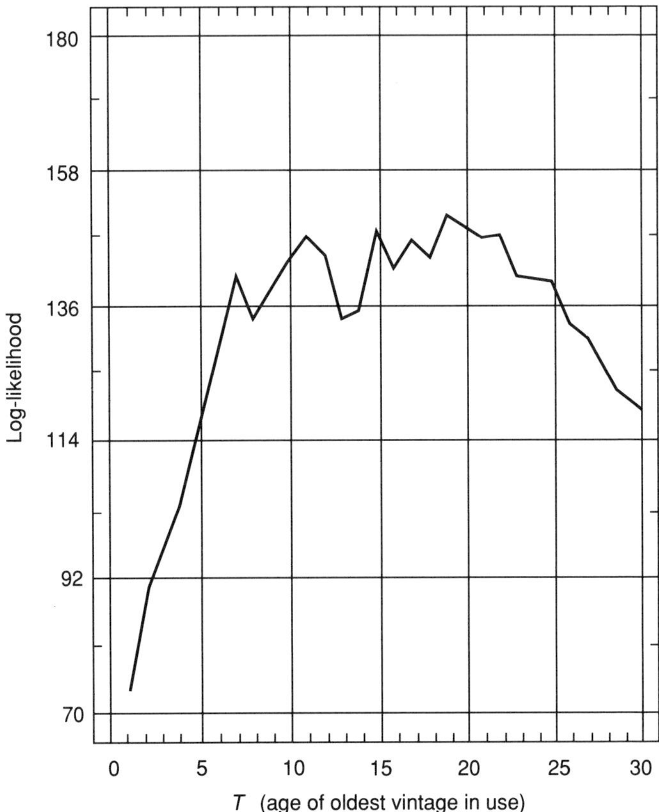

FIGURE 2 Producer durable equipment.

model. Note of course that changing T does not change the number of parameters to be estimated. Otherwise if the number of parameters were to increase with the string length T (as would be the case in an ARMA model) the number of available observations would make the estimation meaningless for large values of T, in the range of 17–20, which provide the best estimates.

Before presenting the results, we will briefly discuss the values that we can reasonably expect for β, θ, and T.

Corollary 7.1 presents results for the reinterpretation of β to include a fixed rate of labor growth. Under the assumption that the "residual" depreciation rate $(1 - \lambda)$ is balanced by the rate of population growth, that is, $(1 + g)\lambda^{(1-\alpha)/\alpha} \cong 1$, our estimates of β can be revised so that $\beta = \beta^*(1 + g)$, where β^* represents pure technical progress and g is the rate of population growth. We note again that we interpret "residual

TABLE 1 Estimation Results for Various Values of T; for Nonresidential Gross Fixed Investment, 1929–1988 (DRI, U.S. Central Data)[a]

T	β	θ	ρ_1	ρ_2	Likelihood
1	1.1017	0.9527	1.2498	0.4338	
	(0.0183)	(0.0191)	(0.1160)	(0.1214)	79.2401
	1.0983	0.9450	1.1559	0.7047	
	(0.0144)	(0.0182)	(0.1171)	(0.1033)	89.7651
3	1.0889	0.9605	0.9505	0.5685	
	(0.0187)	(0.0201)	(0.1201)	(0.1230)	96.0939
4	1.0872	0.9628	1.1561	0.6074	
	(0.0156)	(0.0170)	(0.1461)	(0.1255)	108.3291
5	1.0635	0.9895	0.8078	−0.0040	
	(0.0286)	(0.0146)	(0.1492)	(0.1322)	115.1470
6	1.0436	0.9974	0.8435	0.4543	
	(0.0023)	(0.0083)	(0.1350)	(0.0939)	129.2096
7	1.0412	0.9990	1.0517	0.6770	
	(0.0146)	(0.0051)	(0.1091)	(0.1456)	137.3950
8	1.0395	0.9970	1.1851	0.7248	
	(0.0175)	(0.0067)	(0.1275)	(0.1306)	137.4856
9	1.0293	1.0028	0.8599	0.1430	
	(0.0151)	(0.0043)	(0.1404)	(0.1264)	137.8719
10	1.0188	1.0056	0.8614	0.4418	
	(0.0107)	(0.0026)	(0.1447)	(0.1115)	143.0805
11	1.0165	1.0063	1.2849	0.6983	
	(0.0071)	(0.0018)	(0.1042)	(0.0956)	152.9096
12	1.0269	1.0024	1.0432	0.5812	
	(0.0150)	(0.0044)	(0.1143)	(0.1343)	136.4188
13	1.0167	1.0050	0.9793	0.4740	
	(0.1424)	(0.0036)	(0.1409)	(0.1191)	130.6798
14	1.0261	1.0039	0.8865	0.3232	
	(0.0128)	(0.0034)	(0.1360)	(0.1687)	132.8884
15	1.0273	1.0039	0.9893	0.5408	
	(0.1000)	(0.0028)	(0.1346)	(0.1369)	142.2054
16	1.0207	1.0063	1.0981	0.5008	
	(0.0060)	(0.0015)	(0.1250)	(0.1310)	151.9141
17					166.0000[b]
18	1.0025	1.0097	1.1669	0.6430	
	(0.0054)	(0.0010)	(0.1652)	(0.1401)	154.6727
19	1.0211	1.0056	1.0870	0.4618	
	(0.0126)	(0.0018)	(0.1626)	(0.1901)	154.6664
20	1.0158	1.0068	1.1939	0.5680	
	(0.0038)	(0.0006)	(0.1523)	(0.1403)	152.4141
21	1.0122	1.0075	1.1125	0.6003	
	(0.0058)	(0.0012)	(0.1383)	(0.1337)	150.2931
22	1.0148	1.0066	1.2238	0.5832	
	(0.0058)	(0.0012)	(0.1590)	(0.1453)	148.1011
23	1.0130	1.0073	1.1002	0.4320	
	(0.0056)	(0.0012)	(0.1385)	(0.1756)	143.6745
24	1.0127	1.0070	1.1527	0.5192	
	(0.0059)	(0.0013)	(0.1380)	(0.1581)	144.0494

(continues)

TABLE 1 (*continued*)

T	β	θ	ρ_1	ρ_2	Likelihood
25	1.0131	1.0071	1.1685	0.2966	
	(0.0074)	(0.0014)	(0.1445)	(0.3221)	141.4732
26	1.0145	1.0065	1.1992	0.3334	
	(0.0053)	(0.0012)	(0.1643)	(0.1538)	138.0188
27	1.0037	1.0089	1.2789	0.5998	
	(0.0047)	(0.0008)	(0.1682)	(0.9835)	135.3407
28	1.0142	1.0060	1.1462	0.3244	
	(0.0055)	(0.0013)	(0.1737)	(0.1437)	128.0440
29	1.0119	1.0066	1.1522	0.4795	
	(0.0015)	(0.0006)	(0.0734)	(0.0676)	123.5194
30	1.0128	1.0065	1.3957	0.5111	
	(0.0018)	(0.0006)	(0.1535)	(0.1292	122.3927

[a]Standard errors are in parentheses.
[b]See footnote 2 in Section 8 of this chapter.

depreciation" as the loss of efficiency and the increased maintenance costs of capital equipment associated with the wear and tear due to age, so that it excludes the imputation of economic or physical obsolescence. The latter is already incorporated into our model. Therefore assuming that residual depreciation is in the order of 3.5% is not unreasonable. (Note that standard accounting assumptions on depreciation, including wear and tear and obsolescence is around 10%.)

Estimates of θ in the literature, computed from ARMA models on GNP (gross national product), are in the close vicinity of unity. [See, for example Nelson and Plosser (1982) and Campbell and Mankiw (1987); they also find that one of their best fit comes from ARMA $(2, 2)$] In our model we expect some competition between β and θ to explain growth, so that (in retrospect) a θ that is very slightly above one is not very surprising.

Finally, as noted above, the degree of aggregation makes it improbable that we will obtain a sharp estimate of T. We would expect "producers durable equipment" to last at least 10 years, and a similar lower bound to hold for nonresidential fixed investments. At the higher end we expect investments to be scrapped after about 25 or at most 30 years, with the possible exception of buildings. (Note that producer's durable equipment does not include buildings and our fixed investment series excludes residential buildings).

Figures 1 and 2 present the log-likelihoods against values of T that we have obtained from our estimation. Both series are essentially inverse U-shaped, with a first local maximum at $T = 11$ for both series, a global maximum at $T = 17$ for "nonresidential fixed investment" and at $T = 19$

TABLE 2 Estimation Results for Various Values of T for Gross Investment in Producer Durable Equipment, 1929–1988 (DRI, U.S. Central Data)[a]

T	β	θ	ρ_1	ρ_2	Likelihood
1	0.9850	1.0088	1.2549	0.5220	
	(0.0782)	(0.0160)	(0.1194)	(0.1232)	73.4110
2	0.8761	1.0175	1.2513	0.9195	
	(0.0296)	(0.0038)	(0.1122)	(0.0848)	89.6576
3	0.9481	1.0146	1.0269	0.5395	
	(0.0323)	(0.0046)	(0.1161)	(0.1440)	96.5971
4	0.9813	1.0117	1.0889	0.5665	
	(0.0435)	(0.0067)	(0.1856)	(0.1933)	104.1207
5	1.0272	1.0062	0.8082	0.0006	
	(0.0237)	(0.0066)	(0.1367)	(0.1679)	116.7467
6	1.0171	1.0088	0.8018	0.4650	
	(0.0163)	(0.0040)	(0.1214)	(0.1103)	129.6748
7	1.0085	1.0601	1.3311	0.8651	
	(0.0086)	(0.0029)	(0.0815)	(0.0741)	140.7975
8	1.0138	1.0083	1.0768	0.5538	
	(0.0149)	(0.0040)	(0.1217)	(0.1135)	133.5231
9	1.0224	1.0074	0.9866	0.0251	
	(0.0134)	(0.0041)	(0.1292)	(0.1264)	138.8236
10	1.0069	1.0112	0.7958	0.3950	
	(0.0098)	(0.0022)	(0.1542)	(0.1026)	143.7060
11	1.0007	1.0128	1.1740	0.5205	
	(0.0081)	(0.0018)	(0.1082)	(0.1167)	147.4816
12					≈ 144[b]
13	1.0052	1.0106	1.0953	0.3520	
	(0.0114)	(0.0027)	(0.1423)	(0.1267)	133.8612
14	1.0084	1.0110	0.7923	0.6874	
	(0.0103)	(0.0024)	(0.1102)	(0.1337)	135.5841
15	1.0050	1.0121	1.3825	0.6276	
	(0.0072)	(0.0017)	(0.1063)	(0.1350)	148.5816
16	1.0104	1.0110	1.0757	0.4652	
	(0.0081)	(0.0019)	(0.1302)	(0.1235)	142.0025
17	0.9979	1.0137	1.2120	0.4371	
	(0.0058)	(0.0012)	(0.1329)	(0.1200)	146.8496
18	0.9965	1.0139	0.9115	0.5003	
	(0.0090)	(0.0016)	(0.2518)	(0.1257)	144.0164
19	1.0101	1.0109	1.0921	0.6042	
	(0.0060)	(0.0013)	(0.1349)	(0.1729)	151.1572
20	1.0040	1.0122	1.2051	0.6531	
	(0.0075)	(0.0015)	(0.2441)	(0.2170)	149.2578
21	1.0062	1.0117	0.9581	0.5459	
	(0.0054)	(0.0012)	(0.1575)	(0.1119)	147.5030
22	1.0044	1.0119	1.3344	1.0599	
	(0.0052)	(0.0010)	(0.0451)	(0.0483)	147.6594
23	1.0042	1.0119	1.0749	0.5274	
	(0.0058)	(0.0012)	(0.1791)	(0.1735)	140.8007
24	1.0046	1.0114	0.9689	0.5078	
	(0.0048)	(0.0011)	(0.1379)	(0.1610)	140.9295
25	1.0024	1.0118	1.0552	0.5199	
	(0.0048)	(0.0010)	(0.1585)	(0.1855)	140.3583

(continues)

TABLE 2 (*continued*)

T	β	θ	ρ_1	ρ_2	Likelihood
26	1.0052	1.0112	0.9577	0.2608	
	(0.0051)	(0.0011)	(0.1700)	(0.1636)	133.6141
27	1.0009	1.0122	1.0477	0.4568	
	(0.0051)	(0.0010)	(0.1674)	(0.1895)	131.3965
28	1.0011	1.0114	1.0049	0.4811	
	(0.0013)	(0.0014)	(0.1060)	(0.2331)	126.8890
29	1.0039	1.0112	1.0399	0.4407	
	(0.0052)	(0.0011)	(0.1615)	(0.1425)	121.6472
30	0.9999	1.0118	1.2116	0.7833	
	(0.0054)	(0.0016)	(0.0978)	(0.1894)	119.6136

[a]Standard errors are in parentheses.
[b]See footnote 2 in Section 8 of this chapter.

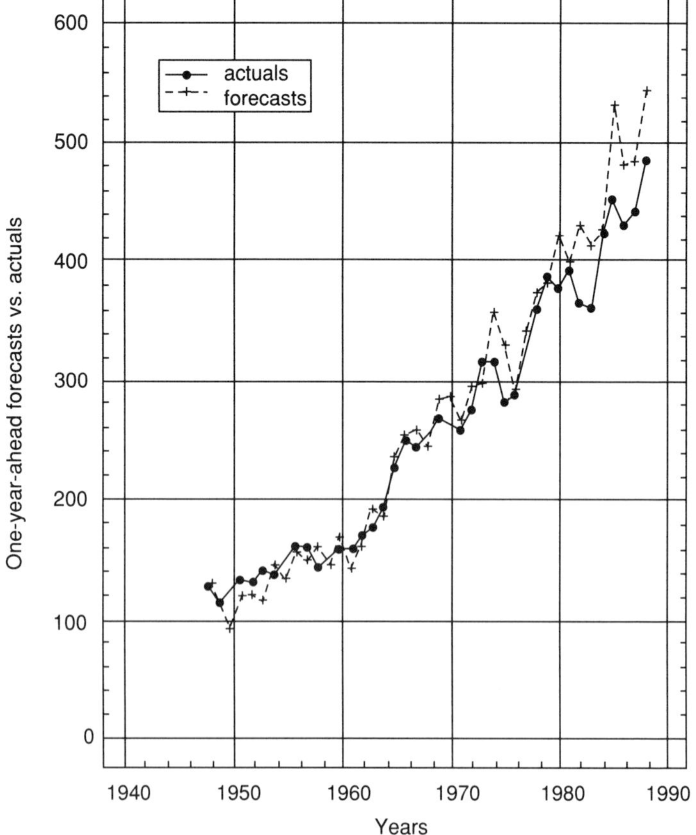

FIGURE 3 Nonresidential fixed investment in 1982 prices (T = 18).

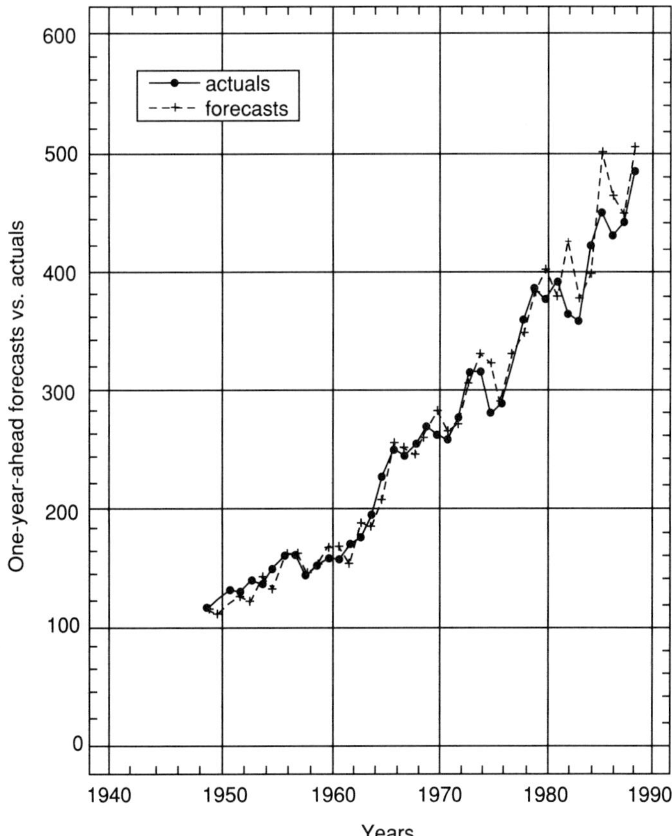

FIGURE 4 Nonresidential fixed investment in 1982 prices ($T = 19$).

for "producers durable equipment."[2] Tables 1 and 2 present the estimates of $\beta, \theta, \rho_1, \rho_2$ corresponding to various T-values and the associated likelihoods. It is clear that likelihood ratio tests would dramatically reject small or large values of T. The standard errors of the estimates for β and θ are also quite small. The values of β range from 1.0025 to 1.041 (not monotonically in T) for the fixed investment series and from 0.87 (at $T = 2$) to 1.022 for the producer durable series. The estimates for θ range from 0.94 to 1.008 for the fixed investment series and from 1.007 to 1.017 for "producers durables." Notice also that the roots of the moving average

[2]We had a numerical problem with estimating the parameters β, θ, ρ_1 and ρ_2 for $T = 17$ in the fixed investment series. While the log-likelihood hovered at values slightly above those for $T = 16$ and $T = 18$, the parameter estimates oscillated, without converging, between the values of the corresponding estimates for $T = 16$ and $T = 18$. We used the Gauss software for maximum likelihood estimation. A similar problem arises for $T = 12$ in the gross investment series.

processes are all less than 1 in modulo with the only exception of $T = 22$ for producers durable equipment, for which the modulo is 1.06.

An analysis of the serial correlation of the error terms at various lags for both investment series and various T-values shows that, they are reasonably small for a nonlinear model. In Tables 3 and 4, we report the sample autocorrelations of up to 19 lags for the T-values corresponding to the three highest likelihood values for both investment series. Standard errors are in parentheses.

For the producer durables, at the best T-values of 19, 20 and 21, the autocorrelations are all below 0.23, and all except two are below 0.2. For the fixed investment series, the best T-values are 18, 19, and 11 (we cannot use 17; see footnote 2). For $T = 11$ and 19, autocorrelations are all below 0.25, and except for three values, they are all below 0.20. For $T = 18$, the estimate of β is quite low, and this may be responsible for autocorrela-

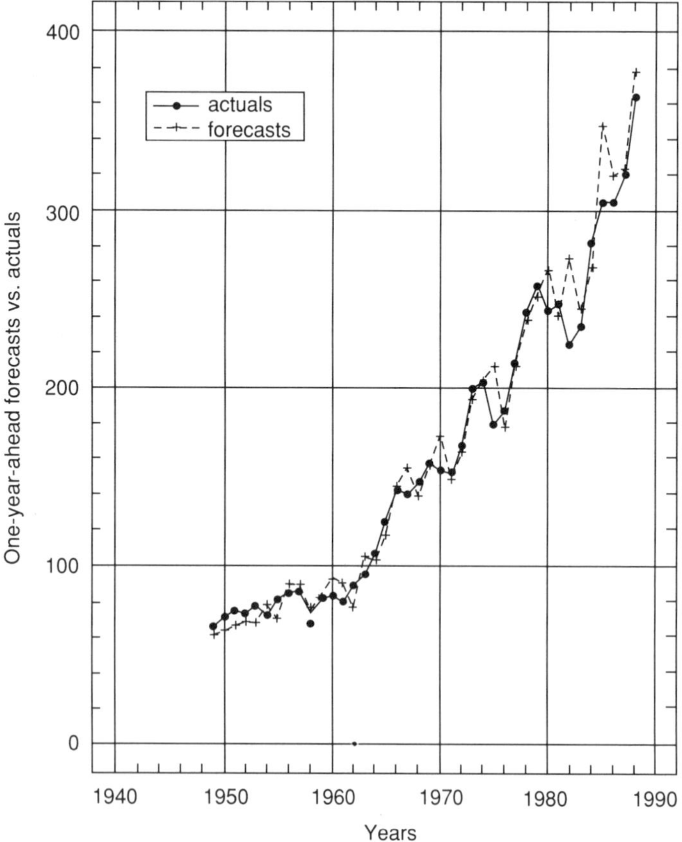

FIGURE 5 Producer durable equipment in 1982 prices ($T = 19$).

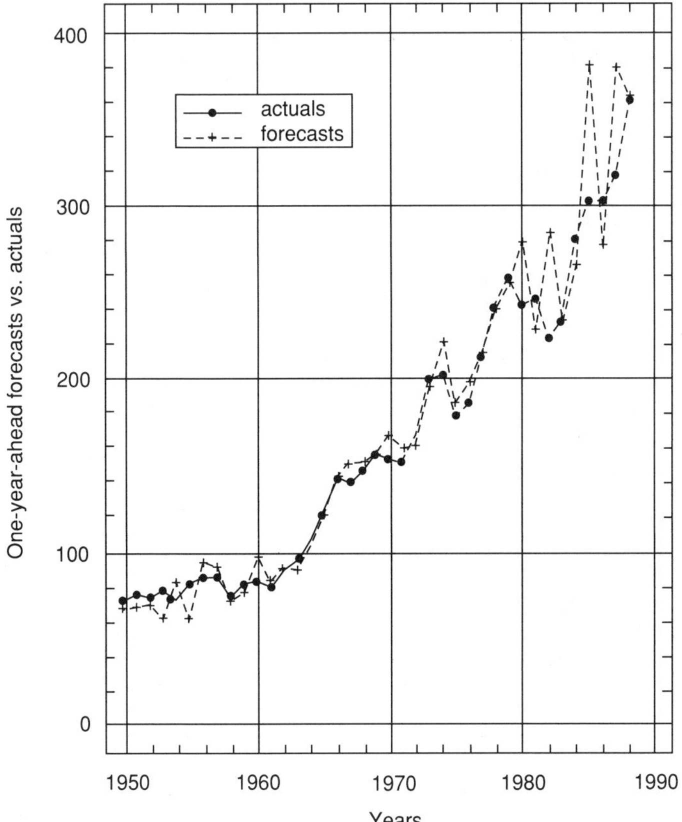

FIGURE 6 Producer durable equipment in 1982 prices ($T = 20$).

tions in the errors of 0.36, 0.34, and 0.27 at the second, third, and fifth lags. In any case these autocorrelations are all within two standard errors of zero, with the exception of the second lag for $T = 18$ in the fixed investment series, which is within 2.25 standard errors of zero. We conclude that for a nonlinear model the autocorrelations in the error structure are relatively small and in line with expectations.

In Figures 3–6 we present one-year-ahead forecasts for the producer durable equipment goods data as well as for the nonresidential fixed investments data; the parameters are estimated using data up to 1980, and the best time T.

Given the volatility of investments, the estimates in the post-1980 period look reasonable; the pre-1980 forecast also seem to fit well.

TABLE 3 Estimated Autocorrelations IPP19.var1

Lag	Estimate	Standard error	Lag	Estimate	Standard error
1	.03071	.15811	2	.10231	.15826
3	.23911	.15991	4	.06877	.16861
5	−.00270	.16931	6	−.06149	.16931
7	.10444	.16987	8	−.19758	.17147
9	−.06849	.17707	10	.01970	.17773
11	−.02122	.17778	12	.03958	.17785
13	.04110	.17807	14	−.00639	.17830
15	.10654	.17831	16	.02572	.17989
17	−.12607	.17998	18	−.04286	.18218
19	.09348	.18243			

IPP20.var1

Lag	Estimate	Standard error	Lag	Estimate	Standard error
1	−.02066	.16013	2	.18216	.16020
3	.18122	.16542	4	.08221	.17044
5	−.07747	.17145	6	.09696	.17235
7	−.05919	.17374	8	−.05543	.17426
9	.01563	.17471	10	.00559	.17474
11	.09989	.17475	12	.03558	.17621
13	.05305	.17639	14	.16952	.17680
15	−.04641	.18092	16	−.09602	.18122
17	−.02041	.18190	18	−.07483	.18195
19	−.04752	.18274			

IPP21.var1

Lag	Estimate	Standard error	Lag	Estimate	Standard error
1	.12537	.16222	2	.15104	.16475
3	.08277	.16836	4	−.04809	.16942
5	.04848	.16978	6	−.03741	.17015
7	−.14302	.17036	8	.02153	.17349
9	.07558	.17356	10	−.13201	.17443
11	.22380	.17704	12	.15382	.18433
13	.14392	.18768	14	.09371	.19056
15	−.09771	.19177	16	−.12315	.19308
17	.01963	.19513	18	−.10813	.19518
19	−.02446	.19675			

We finally report that we have also tested our model using gross investment data, which includes inventory fluctuations and may be inappropriate for our model. Nevertheless, the results are very much in line with what we find for the other series, as presented in Tables 3 and 4.

We conclude from all this that the estimation results lend support to the hypothesis that vintage effects play a role in the determination of investment expenditures.

TABLE 4 Estimated Autocorrelations IFIX11.var1

Lag	Estimate	Standard error	Lag	Estimate	Standard error
1	.19062	.14434	2	.20755	.14949
3	.08171	.15538	4	−.14199	.15627
5	−.01025	.15894	6	−.08334	.15895
7	.02852	.15986	8	−.05225	.15996
9	−.03265	.16032	10	−.01432	.16046
11	−.02601	.16048	12	−.18707	.16057
13	−.14851	.16505	14	−.12268	.16781
15	−.04939	.16967	16	.04767	.16997
17	.01815	.17025	18	.09375	.17029
19	.10205	.17136	20	.06787	.17262
21	−.00165	.17317	22	.06716	.17317
23	.00880	.17372	24	−.06283	.17373

IFIX18.var1

Lag	Estimate	Standard error	Lag	Estimate	Standard error
1	.20096	.15617	2	.36420	.16236
3	.34040	.18119	4	.13809	.19617
5	.27452	.19853	6	.14645	.20758
7	.11114	.21008	8	.05958	.21151
9	.13055	.21192	10	−.03648	.21387
11	.24624	.21403	12	.09589	.22083
13	−.00931	.22184	14	.01408	.22185
15	−.00562	.22187	16	.02718	.22188
17	−.04250	.22196	18	−.00644	.22216
19	−.15538	.22216	20	−.05290	.22480

IFIX19.var1

Lag	Estimate	Standard error	Lag	Estimate	Standard error
1	.10576	.15811	2	.21657	.15987
3	.25536	.16705	4	.07319	.17654
5	.13151	.17729	6	−.03855	.17971
7	.08692	.17992	8	−.09911	.18097
9	.06468	.18232	10	−.02087	.18289
11	.10063	.18295	12	.16944	.18433
13	.01235	.18818	14	.13161	.18820
15	.03639	.19049	16	.04909	.19067
17	−.06095	.19098	18	−.08861	.19147
19	.02261	.19249	20	−.22493	.19256

APPENDIX

LEMMA 1.1

(*i*) *If f satisfies Assumptions* 1 *and* 3, *the suprema in the definition of* Φ *and* Ψ *are achieved.*

(*ii*) *If f satisfies Assumption* 2, *the optimal labor allocation* $\hat{l}(k)$ *is unique, and the entire labor is used*; *i.e.*, $\sum_s \hat{l}(k) \equiv 1$ *for every* k.

Proof

(i) From Assumption 3 and Fatou's lemma the function

$$l \to \sum_{s=-\infty}^{0} f(k_s, l_s \beta^s)$$

is upper semicontinuous, when L is endowed with the topology of pointwise convergence. Hence the sup in the definition of Φ is achieved. The same argument holds for Ψ.

(ii) The proof follows immediately from f being strictly concave and everywhere strictly increasing in l. ■

Also one has the following simple relationship.

LEMMA 1.2

$$G(t, k, l) = \beta^t F(\beta^{-t} k, l); \qquad \Psi(t, k) = \beta^t \Phi(\beta^{-t} k).$$

Proof. By homogeneity,

$$\sum_{s=-\infty}^{0} f(k_s, l_s \beta^s \beta^t) = \beta^t \sum_{s=-\infty}^{0} f(\beta^{-t} k_s, l_s \beta^s) = \beta^t F(\beta^{-t} k). \qquad ■$$

We now proceed to prove some basic properties of the optimal production maps Φ and Ψ.

LEMMA 1.3. *A necessary condition for $\hat{l}(k)$ to be optimal is*

(i) $f_l(k_s, \hat{l}(k)_s \beta^s)\beta^s \le w(k)$ *a for every* $s \le 0$; (T)
(ii) $(f_l, k_s, \hat{l}(k_s \beta^s)\beta^s - w(k))\hat{l}(k)_s = 0$ *for every* $s \le 0$;
(iii) $\Sigma_s \hat{l}(k)_s = 1$,

where w(k) is a real positive number.

Proof. Let $\{\hat{l}(k)_s\}_{s \le 0}$ be the optimal labor allocation, and let **s** be *the first* (maximum) integer for which $\hat{l}(k)_s \neq 0$. For any $s_0 \le \mathbf{s}$, consider now the program $P_{s_0}(k)$:

$$P_{s_0}(k) = \max \left\{ \sum_{s=-s_0}^{0} f(k_s, l_s \beta^s) | l_s \ge 0 \sum_{s=-s_0}^{0} l_s = \sum_{s=-s_0}^{0} \hat{l}(k)_s \right\}.$$

Clearly the solution to $P_{s_0}(k)$ must be $\hat{l}(k)_s$ for every $s \in \{s_0, \ldots, 0\}$, and for every problem $P_{s_0}(k)$ the (KT) conditions must hold for every $s \in \{s_0, \ldots, 0\}$, with a constant $w(k; s_0)$, by the classical Kuhn–Tucker conditions. Finally note that $w(k, s_0)$ is constant over s_0. ■

For the time-dependent problem an analogous result holds, with virtually the same proof.

LEMMA 1.4. *A necessary condition for* $\hat{l}(k,t)$ *to be optimal is*

(*i*) $f_l(k_s, \hat{l}(k,t)_s\beta^{s+t})\beta^{s+t} \le w(k,t)$ (KT)

(*ii*) $(f_l(k_s, \hat{l}(k,t)_s\beta^{s+t})\beta^{s+t} - w(k,t))\hat{l}(k,t)_s = 0$ *for every* $s \ge 0$.

LEMMA 1.6

(*i*) Φ *is concave, increasing* (*strictly concave, if f is strictly concave*).

(*ii*) Φ *is continuous over the set* $\{k \in l_\infty^+ : |k| \le M\}$ *is the topology of pointwise convergence.*

(*iii*) *The same statements hold for the function* $\Psi(t, \cdot)$, *for every* $t \ge 0$.

Proof

(i) Let $k^i \in l_\infty^+$, $i = 1, 2; \theta \in (0,1)$;

$$\theta\Phi(k^1) + (1-\theta)\Phi(k^2)$$

$$= \sum_{s=-\infty}^{0} \left\{\theta f\left(k_s^1, \hat{l}(k^1)_s\beta^s\right) + (1-\theta) f\left(k_s^2, \hat{l}(k^2)_s\beta^s\right)\right\}$$

$$\le \sum_s f\left(\left[\theta k^1 + (1-\theta)k^2\right]_s, \hat{l}(k_\theta)_s\beta^s\right)$$

$$\equiv \Phi\left(\theta k^1 + (1-\theta)k^2\right).$$

(ii) Let $k^\nu \to k$ pointwise. We prove

(a) $\liminf_\nu \Phi(k^\nu) \ge \Phi(k)$. Denote, for any $k \in l_\infty^+$ and integer s, $k1|_s = (\ldots, 0, \ldots, 0, k_s, k_{s+1}, \ldots, k_0)$. Then $\Phi(k^\nu) \ge \Phi(k^\nu 1|_{s(k)})$. Also

$$\lim_\nu \max_{l \in L} F\left(k^\nu 1|_{s(k)} l\right) = \max_{i \in L} F\left(k, l1|_{s(k)}\right) = \Phi(k).$$

(b) $\limsup_\nu \Phi(k^\nu) \le \Phi(k)$. For an arbitrary $\varepsilon > 0$ find an integer s_ε such that $\sum_{s=-\infty}^{s_\varepsilon} f(M, \beta^s) < \varepsilon$. Then

$$\Phi(k^\nu) \le \Phi\left(k^\nu 1|_{s_\varepsilon}\right) + \varepsilon \to \Phi(k) + \varepsilon.$$

(iii) Clear from i, ii above and Lemma 1.1. ∎

LEMMA 1.7. *For every* $k \in l_\infty^+$ *there exists a finite transition time.*

Proof. From the necessary condition (Lemma 1.3) we have that $w(k) = f_l(k_{s_0}, \hat{l}(k)_{s_0}\beta^{s_0})\beta^{s_0}$ for some finite s_0, with $w(k) > 0$. But $f_l(k_s, \hat{l}(k)_s\beta^s)\beta^s \le f_l(|k|, 0)\beta^s$ for every s, and the last quantity is less than $w(k)$ for some finite s. Note that $\mathbf{s} = \mathbf{s}(k)$, which is continuous if $w(k)$ is, *mk* with the norm topology $\hat{l}(k)_s = 0$ for every $s \le \mathbf{s}$; i.e., a finite function time exists. An analogous argument shows that $s(k,t)$ is finite for every k and t. ■

COROLLARY 1.8. *If f satisfies Assumption 4, then*

$$s(k) \geq \frac{\log w(k)/m(|k|)}{\log \beta} - 1 \equiv s(k)$$

where $m(k)$ is defined in Assumption 4.

Proof. Obvious. ■

We now study the continuity properties of the map w, from l_∞^+ endowed with the norm topology.

LEMMA 1.9. *Both w and $w(t,\cdot)$ are lower semicontinuous functions for every $t \geq 0$, when l_∞^+ is endowed with the norm topology.*

Proof. We consider the function w; the case of $w(t,\cdot)$ is analogous. Consider first the case $k^0 \neq 0$, and assume without loss of generality that $|k_i| \leq |k^0| + 1$ for every i. It is clearly enough to prove that $\liminf_i s(k^i) > -\infty$. In fact, denoting by m such a finite-limit inferior, we can reformulate the original problem $P(k)$ as an equivalent m-dimensional problem, for which the statement holds.

Assume therefore, arguing by contradiction; that $\liminf s(k^i) = -\infty$. By definition of $s(k^i)$ there exists a sequence of integers $\{s_i\}$ such that $s_i \to -\infty$, $\hat{l}(k^i)_{s_i} \neq 0$. Therefore, since $w(k^i) = f_l(k^i, l(k^i)_{s_i}\beta^{s_i})\beta^{s_i} \leq f_l(|k^0| + 1, 0)\beta^{s_i}$, we conclude

$$\lim w(k^i) = 0. \tag{1.4}$$

Choose now s^* such that $k_s^0 \neq 0$. Then

$$f_l\left(k_{s^*}^i, \hat{l}(k^i)_{s^*}\beta^{s^*}\right)\beta^{s^*} \geq f_l\left(k_{s^*}^i, 1\right) \to f_l\left(k_{s^*}^0, 1\right)\beta^{s^*} \equiv \alpha > 0 \tag{1.5}$$

Since $f_l(k_{s^*}^i, \hat{l}(k^i)_{s^*}\beta^{s^*})\beta^{s^*}$ is bounded below, and $\lim w(k^i) = 0$, we have $\hat{l}(k^i)_{s^*} = 0$ for every i large enough, and so

$$f_l\left(k_{s^*}^i, 0\right)\beta^{s^*} \leq w(k^i). \tag{1.6}$$

We conclude

$$\alpha_{s^*}/2 < f_l\left(k_{s^*}^i, 1\right) \leq f_l\left(k_{s^*}^i, 0\right) \leq w(k^i) < \alpha_{s^*}/2$$

for i sufficiently large enough, which is a contradiction.

Consider now the case $k^0 = 0$. Note $w(k^0) = 0$, because $f_l(0, l) = 0$. Also $w(k^i) = f_l(k^i_s, \hat{l}(k^i)_s \beta^s) \leq f_l(|k^i|, 0) \to 0$. ∎

LEMMA 1.10. *Both w and $w(t, \cdot\,)$ are upper semicontinuous functions, for every $t \geq 0$, and l^+_∞ endowed with the norm topology.*

Proof. Let $\{k^i\}$ be a sequence in l^+_∞; we claim

$$\limsup_i w(k^i) \leq w(k^0).$$

Fix first an integer $\mathbf{s}$ such that

$$f_l(|k^0| + 1, 0)\beta^s < w(k^0).$$

Now if for some integer $s < \mathbf{s}$ we have $\hat{l}(k^i)_s \neq 0$; then $w(k^i) < w(k^0)$. In fact $w(k^i) = f_l(k^i_s, l(k^i)_s \beta^s)\beta^s \leq f_l(|k^0| + 1, 0) < w(k^0)$. Our claim follows. The proof for $w(t, \cdot\,)$ is analogous. ∎

We can now conclude with some very useful properties of the two maps s (truncation time) and $\hat{l}$ (optimal labor allocation).

COROLLARY 1.11. *Let l^+_∞, l^+_1 be endowed with the norm topology. Then*

(*i*) *The function* $\mathbf{s}$ *is continuous.*
(*ii*) *The truncation time s is upper semicontinuous.*
(*iii*) *The optimal allocation of labour $\hat{l}$ is continuous.*
(*iv*) *analogous statements for* $\mathbf{s}(t, \cdot\,)$, $s(t, \cdot\,)$, $\hat{l}(t, \cdot\,)$.

Proof

(i) From the continuity of w it follows that the function $\mathbf{s}$ is also continuous in k.

(ii, iii) Now in a neighborhood of $k_0 N(k_0) = \{k \in l^+_\infty : |k - k_0| < \varepsilon\}$ we can consider the finite-dimensional problem

$$P_E(k) \quad \max_{l=(l_0,\ldots,l_s)} \left\{ \sum_s f(k_s, l_s \beta^s) \,\middle|\, \sum_{s=0}^{\mathbf{s}} l_s = 1 \right\},$$

where $\mathbf{s} = \mathbf{s}(k^0) + 1$.

The optimal l^* for such a problem is (once extended to an element of l^+_1 in the natural way) the same as the optimal $\hat{l}(k)$, for every $k \in N(k_0)$. We have reduced the problem to a finite-dimensional one, where statements (ii) and (iii) are obvious. ∎

LEMMA 1.12

(i) The partial derivatives $\dfrac{\partial V(k,x)}{\partial k_i}, \dfrac{\partial^2 V(k,x)}{\partial k_i \partial k_J}$ *exist for every pair* (k, x). *In addition, one has*

(ii) $\dfrac{\partial V(k,x)}{\partial k_i} = f_k(k_i, \hat{l}(k)_i \beta^i) \equiv V_i(k,x) \geq 0$

$\dfrac{\partial^2 V(k,x)}{\partial k_i \partial k_j} = k_{kl}(k_i, \hat{l}(k)_i \beta^i) \dfrac{\partial \hat{l}(k)_i}{\partial k_j} \beta^i \equiv V_{ij}(k,x) \leq 0$ *for every pair* (i, j), $i \neq j$.

(iii) $\dfrac{\partial V(t,k,x)}{\partial k_i} = f_k(k_i, \hat{l}(k,t)_i / \beta^{t+1}) \equiv V_i(t,k,x)$

$\dfrac{\partial^w V(t,k,x)}{\partial k_i \partial k_j} = f_{kl}(k_i, \hat{l}(k_i,t)_i / \beta^{t+i}) \dfrac{\partial \hat{l}(k,t)_i}{\partial k_j} \beta^{t+i} = V_{ij}(t,k,x) \leq 0$

for every pair (i, j), $i \neq j$.

Proof. Note that in some (norm) neighborhood of (k, x) we may write (see Corollary 1.7 above):

$$V(k,x) = \sum_{s=\mathbf{s}(k)}^{0} f\left(k_s, \hat{l}(k)_s \beta^s\right) - x$$

so that in such neighborhood the maximization problem defining the functions Φ and V can be reduced in fact to a finite $(-\mathbf{s}(k)$-dimensional) one. Now the result follows as in Benhabib and Nishimura (1979), Appendix A1.

$$\frac{\partial V}{\partial k_i}(k,x) = f_k\left(k_i, \hat{l}(k)_i \beta^i\right) + \sum_{s=-\infty}^{0} f_l\left(k_s, \hat{l}(k)_s \beta^s\right) \beta^s \frac{\partial \hat{l}(k)_s}{\partial k_i}$$

$$= f_k\left(k_i, \hat{l}(k)_i \beta^i\right) + w(k) \sum_{s=-\infty}^{0} \frac{\partial \hat{l}(k)}{\partial k_i} = f_k\left(k_i, \hat{l}(k)_i, \beta^i\right) \tag{ii}$$

because $\Sigma_s \hat{l}(k)_s \equiv 1$. Note that if $[\partial \hat{l}(k)_s / \partial k_i] \neq 0$, then the equality $f_l(k_s, \hat{l}(k)_s \beta^s) \beta^s = w(k)$ holds, because $\hat{l}(k + h_n e_i) \neq 0$ for a sequence $h_n \to 0$, and $\hat{l}$ and w are continuous functions (see Lemma 1.10 and Corollary 1.11). Then a simple computation establishes that $[\partial \hat{l}(k_s) / \partial k_i] < 0$ for $i \neq s$. This concludes the proof. The proof of (iii) is identical to that of (ii). ■

Proof of Lemma 1.13. Consider a production function that depends on time, and where capital is the only input, so that the quantity produced is $f(k,t)$. We denote

$$f^0(k) = f(k,0), \qquad f^t(k) = f(f^{t-1}(k),t), \qquad t \geq 0,$$

and we shall refer to the sequence $\{f^t(k)\}_{t\geq 0}$ as the *maximal accumulation path*.

We first consider, for simplicity of exposition, the case of a fixed exogenous truncation.

(i) Since the utility function U is concave and $\delta < 1$, it is enough to show that the path of maximal accumulation has a finite discounted value. Clearly for an initial capital string k, it is enough to show our claim for the function $f(t,x) = Tx^{1-\alpha}\beta^t$ and the capital stock $x = |k|$. But one has $f^t(x) \leq T^{1/\alpha}\beta^{t/\alpha}\max\{1, x^{1-\alpha}\}$, and our claim follows.

(ii) As for (i) above it is enough to prove our statement for the single-vintage time-dependent production function $f(t,x) = T(ax^\rho + b\beta^{\rho t})^{1/\rho}$. By redefining, if necessary, the two constants a and b we may assume w.l.o.g. that $T = 1$. Now $f^t(k) = (a^t x^\rho + c_t)^{1/\rho}$ where c_t is the solution of $c_{t+1} = ac_t + b\beta^{\rho t}$, $c_1 = b\beta^\rho$. Since

$$c_t = Aa^t + b(\beta^\rho - a)^{-1}\beta^{\rho t}, \qquad A \equiv \frac{b\beta^\rho}{a}\left\{1 - (\beta^\rho - a)^{-1}\right\},$$

our claim follows.

(iii) We now turn to the case where the truncation is determined endogenously. Again it is enough to prove that the path of maximal accumulation has a finite discounted value. To this end, if $\{\tilde{k}_t\}$ is such path, it will be enough to show our statement for the path defined by $k_t \equiv \max_{s\leq t}\tilde{k}_s$, an increasing path for which $k_t \geq \tilde{k}_t$ for every t.

Now if for some $M < +\infty$:

1. $\limsup_{t\geq 0}|k^t|\beta^{-t} < M$, then our claim follows. Recall, in fact, $\Psi(k^t,t) = \beta^t\Phi(k^t\beta^{-1}) \leq \beta^t\Phi((\ldots,M,\ldots,M)) < +\infty$ (this last inequality because Φ is continuous in the pointwise topology). Now the inequality $\delta\beta < 1$ concludes the proof and condition 1 holds. Therefore, we are reduced to the case where $\limsup_{t\geq 0}|k^t|\beta^{-t} = +\infty$. Now we assume without loss of generality that the sequence $\{k_t\beta^{-t}\}$ is increasing. For this last step we first prove that there exists a t_0 such that

2. if $t \geq t_0$, then $\hat{l}(k^t,t)_s = 0$ for $s = -1, -2, \ldots$. In fact, in this case we can repeat the proof presented for the case of an exogenous truncation time T, with $T = 1$. Notice that will suffice to prove our

statement if for any time t we replace k_{t+s} with $|k^t|_{l_\infty}$, for every $s \leq 0$, because it is an increasing function. Notice

3. $f_l(|k^t|\beta^{-t}, 0+)\beta^s \leq f_l(|k^t|\beta^{-t}, 0+)\beta^{-1} = b^{1/\rho}\beta^{-1}$ for every $s \leq 0$;
4. $\lim_x \to +\infty f_l(x, 1) = b^{1/\rho}$.

Now choose t_0 such that $f_l(|k^{t_0}|\beta^{-t_0}, 1) > b^{1/\rho}\beta^{-1}$ (such t_0 exists because $\limsup_{t \geq 0} |k^t|\beta^{-t} = +\infty$). We claim that for such t_0 condition 2 above holds. Consider, in fact, any $t \geq t_0$. By homogeneity $\bar{l}(k^t, t)$ is the optimal allocation of labor for $\max_{l \in L} \Sigma_s f(k_{t+s}\beta^{-t}, l_s\beta^s)$. Clearly

$$f_l\big(k_t\beta^{-1}, 1\big) > f_l\big(k_t\beta^{-t}, 0+\big)\beta^{-1} > f_l\big(k_{t+s}\beta^{-t}, 0+\big)$$

(recall that $\{k_t\beta^{-t}\}$ is increasing). ■

LEMMA 1.14

(i) $W(k)$ and $W(\cdot, x)$ are concave.

(ii) For any fixed $k \in l_\infty^+$ and integer m, the function $W(k, \cdot)$: $R^n \to R_+$ defined by $x \to W(k, x)$ is C^1.

Proof

(i) Condition (i) in Lemma 1.14 is clear from the concavity of U and Φ.

(ii) Let $m = s(k, x)$, and consider the function

$$\tilde{W}(k) = \sup_{x \in A(k)} \sum_{t=0}^{\infty} \delta^t U\big(\Phi^m(y^t) - y_{t+1}\big),$$

$$\text{with} \quad \Phi^m(k) \equiv \max_{i \in L} \sum_{s=-m}^{-1} f(k_s, l_s\beta^s).$$

$\tilde{W}$ is a concave C^1 function, and $\tilde{W}(k, x) = W(k, x)$. Now use Lemma 1 in Benveniste and Scheinkman (1979). ■

LEMMA 4.1. *Consider an interior optimal trajectory along which the maximal truncation time is T. If a segment $\{\hat{x}_s\}_t^{2T+t-2}$ of this trajectory is weakly decreasing (increasing), then $\hat{x}_{t+2T-1} > \hat{x}_{t+2T-2}(\hat{x}_{t+2T-1} < \hat{x}_{t+2T-2})$.*

Proof. The proof generalizes the one given in Benhabib and Nishimura (1985, 1988), in which further details can be found. Since the truncation time is always less than or equal to T, we can consider the functions V and W as defined on R^T; for simplicity we leave the notation unchanged. We consider two sets of initial conditions:

$$(k_{t-T}, \ldots, k_t), \qquad (k'_{t-T}, \ldots, k'_t)$$

and define V independently of time. This is justified for the time-dependent, embodied technical change case if we use detrended capital stocks, as shown in Section 1 in the transformation of problem (P_a) to problem (P_a^*).

The following equalities must hold:

$$\begin{aligned} & V(k_{t-T}, \ldots, k_t; k_{t+1}) + \delta V(k_{t-T+1}, \ldots, k_{t+1}, k_{t+2}) \\ & \qquad + \cdots + \delta^{T+1} W(k_{t+1}, \ldots, k_{t+T}) \\ & \quad \geq V(k_{t-T}, \ldots, k_t, t'_{k+1}) + \delta V(k_{t-T+1}, \ldots, k'_{t+1}, k'_{t+2}) \\ & \qquad + \cdots + \delta^{T+1} W(k'_{t+1}, \ldots, k'_{t+T}) \end{aligned} \tag{4.1}$$

$$\begin{aligned} & V(k'_{t-T}, \ldots, k'_t, k'_{t+1}) + \delta V(k'_{t-T+1}, \ldots, k'_{t+1}, k'_{t+2}) \\ & \qquad + \cdots + \delta^{T+1} W(k'_{t+1}, \ldots, k'_{t+T}) \\ & \quad \geq V(k'_{t-T}, \ldots, t'_t, k_{t+1}) + \delta V(k'_{t-T+1}, \ldots, k_{t+1}, k_{t+2}) \\ & \qquad + \cdots + \delta^{T+1} W(k_{t+1}, \ldots, k_{t+T}) \end{aligned} \tag{4.2}$$

[where, for problem (P_a^*), δ should be replaced with $\beta\delta$ above, as well as for the remainder of the proof].

Adding the two inequalities gives

$$\begin{aligned} & V(k_{t-T}, \ldots, k_t, k_{t+1}) - V(k_{t-T}, \ldots, k_t, k'_{t+1}) \\ & \quad + V(k'_{t-T}, \ldots, k'_t, k'_{t+1}) - V(k'_{t-T}, \ldots, k'_t, k_{t+1}) \\ & \quad + \delta\{V(k_{t-T+1}, \ldots, k_{t+1}, k_{t+2}) - V(k_{t-T+1}, \ldots, k'_{t+1}, k'_{t+2}) \\ & \quad + V(k'_{t-T+1}, \ldots, k'_{t+1}, k'_{t+2}) - V(k'_{t-T+1}, \ldots, k_{t+1}, k_{t+2}) \\ & \quad + \cdots \\ & \quad + \delta^T\{V(k_t, \ldots, k_{t+T}, k_{t+T+1}) - V(k_t, k'_{t+1}, \ldots, k'_{t+T}, k'_{t+T+1}) \\ & \quad + V(k'_t, \ldots, k'_{t+T}, k'_{t+T+1}) - V(k'_t, k_{t+1}, \ldots, k_{t+T}, k_{t+T+1}) \\ & \quad \geq 0. \end{aligned}$$

which we rewrite as

$$
\begin{aligned}
&V(k_{t-T},\ldots,k_t,k_{t+1}) - V(k_{t-T},\ldots,k_t,k'_{t+1}) \\
&\quad + V\big(k^{t-T'},\ldots,k'_t,k'_{t+1}\big) - V(k'_{t-T},\ldots,k'_t,k_{t+1}) \\
&\quad + \delta\{V(k_{t-T+1},\ldots,k_{t+1},k_{t+2}) - V(k'_{t-T+1},\ldots,k'_t,k_{t+1},k_{t+2}) \\
&\qquad + V(k'_{t-T+1},\ldots,k'_{t+1},k'_{t+2}) - V(k_{t-T+1},\ldots,k'_t,k'_{t+1},k'_{t+2})\} \\
&\quad + \cdots \\
&\quad + \delta^i\big\{V(k_{t-T+i},\ldots,k_{t+i},k_{t+i+1}) \\
&\qquad - V\big(k^{t-T+i'},\ldots,k'_t,k_{t+1},\ldots,k_{t+1},k_{t+i+1}\big) \\
&\qquad + V(k'_{t-T+i},\ldots,k'_{t+i},k'_{t+i+1}) \\
&\qquad - V(k_{t-T+i},\ldots,k_t,k'_{t+1},k'_{t+i},k'_{t+i+1})\big\} \\
&\quad + \cdots \\
&\quad \delta^T\{V(k_t,\ldots,k_{t+T},k_{t+T+1}) - V(k'_t,k_{t+1},\ldots,k_{t+T},k_{t+T+1}) \\
&\qquad + V(k'_t,\ldots,k'_{t+T},k'_{t+T+1}) - V(k_t,k'_{t+1},\ldots,k'_{t+T+1})\} \\
&\quad \geq 0.
\end{aligned}
\tag{4.4}
$$

The first term of the above summation can be rewritten as

$$
\sum_x \int_{k_{t+1}}^{k_{t+1}} \int_{k'_{t-T+k}}^{k_{t-T+k}} V_{T+2,\,t-T+k}(k'_{t-T},\ldots,k'_{t-T+k-1},u,
$$

$$
k_{t-T+k+1},\ldots,k_t,S)\,ds\,du \equiv A.
$$

All the other terms have the general form

$$
\begin{aligned}
&V(k_1,\ldots,k_m) - V(k_1,\ldots,k_i,k'_{i+1},\ldots,k'_m) \\
&\qquad + V(k'_1,\ldots,k'_m) - V(k'_1,\ldots,k'_i,k_{i+1},\ldots,k_m) \\
&\quad = V(k_1,k_2,\ldots,k_i,k_{i+1},\ldots,k_m) - V(k'_1,k_2,\ldots,k_i,k_{i+1},\ldots,k_m) \\
&\qquad + V(k'_1,\ldots,k'_m) - V(k'_1,\ldots,k'_{i-1},k_i,k'_{i+1},\ldots,k'_m) \\
&\qquad + \cdots \\
&\quad V(k'_1,\ldots,k'_{i-j-1},k_{i-j},\ldots,y_m) - V(k'_1,\ldots,k'_{i-j},k_{i-j+1},\ldots,k_m) \\
&\quad V(k'_i,\ldots,k'_{i-j},k_{i-j+1},k_i,k'_{i+1},\ldots,k'_m) \\
&\qquad - V(k'_1,\ldots,k'_{i-j-1},k_{i-j},\ldots,k_i,k'_{i+1},\ldots,k'_m) \\
&\qquad + \cdots \\
&\quad V(k'_1,\ldots,k'_{i-1},k_i,k_{i+1},\ldots,k_m) - V(k'_1,\ldots,k'_i,k_{i+1},\ldots,k_m) \\
&\quad V(k'_1,k_2,\ldots,k_i,k'_{i+1},\ldots,k'_m) - V(k_1,\ldots,k_i,k'_{i+1},\ldots,k'_m);
\end{aligned}
$$

for $\rho = 0, \ldots, i-1$, $j = i-1, \ldots, 0$. This term is equal to

$$\int_{k_i'}^{k_i} V_1(s, k_2, \ldots, k_i, k_{i+1}, \ldots, k_m) - V_1(s, k_2, \ldots, k_i, k_{i+1}', \ldots, k_m')\, ds$$

$$+ \int_{k_{ij}'}^{k_{i-j}} V_{i-j}(k_1', \ldots, k_{i-j-1}', s, k_{i-j+1}, \ldots, k_m)$$

$$- V_{i-j}(k_1', \ldots, k_{i-j-1}', s, k_{i-j+1}, \ldots, k_i, k_{i+1}', \ldots, k_m')\, ds$$

$$+ \int_{k_i'}^{k_i} V_i(k_1', \ldots, k_{i-1}', s, k_{i+1}, \ldots, k_m)$$

$$- V_i(k_1', \ldots, k_{i-1}', s, k_{i+1}', \ldots, k_m)\, ds$$

$$= \int_{k_i'}^{k_i} V_1(s, k_2, \ldots, k_i, k_{i+1}, \ldots, k_m) - V_1(s, k_2, \ldots, k_i, k_{i+1}', \ldots, k_m')\, ds$$

$$+ \int_{k_{i-j}}^{k_{i-j}} V_{i-j}(k_1', \ldots, k_{i-j-1}', s, k_{i-j+1}, \ldots, k_m)$$

$$- V_{i-j}(k_1', \ldots, k_{i-j-1}, s, k_{i-j+1}, \ldots, k_{m-1}, k_m')$$

$$V_{i-j}(k_1', \ldots, k_{i-j-1}', s, k_{i-j+1}, \ldots, k_{i+k}, k_{i+k+1}', \ldots, k_m')$$

$$- V_{i-j}(k_1', \ldots, k_{i-j-1}', s, k_{i-j+1}, \ldots, k_{i+k-1}, k_{i+k}', k_{i+k+1}', \ldots, k_m')$$

$$V_{i-j}(k_1', \ldots, k_{i-j-1}', s, k_{i-j+1}, \ldots, k_i, k_{i+1}, k_{i+2}', \ldots, k_m')$$

$$- V_{i-j}(k_1', \ldots, k_{i-j-1}', s, k_{i-j+1}, \ldots, k_i, k_{i+1}', \ldots, k_m')$$

$$(k = 1, \ldots, m-1)$$

$$+ \cdots$$

$$\times \sum \int_{k_{i-j}}^{k_{i-j}} \int_{k_{i+k}}^{k_{i+k}} V_{i-j,i+k}(k_1', \ldots, k_{i-j-1}', s, k_{i-j+1}, \ldots,$$

$$k_{i+k-1}, u, k_{i+k+1}', \ldots, k_m')\, ds\, du \equiv B.$$

Consider a monotonic T-history of an optimal trajectory $k_{t-T} \leq k_{t-T+1}, \ldots, k_t$. Without loss of generality, as long as we have a stationary problem like (P_a^*) where V is independent of time, we can set $k_{t+1} = k_i'$ and construct a $2T-1$ monotonic trajectory with the implication that $k_i < k_i'$. We now note that if, as implied for our model by Lemma 1.12, all the cross-partials $V_{ij} \leq 0$ (with some $V_{ij} < 0$, and if either $k_i < k_i'$ for $i = t-T$ to $t+T-1$ or if $k_i > k_i'$ for $i = t-T$ to $t+T-1$, then the sum $A + B$ derived above must be negative, contradicting the inequality

(4.4). We conclude that an optimal path cannot remain strictly monotonic for $2T - 1$ steps.

So far we have established that $\hat{x}_{t+2T-1} \geq \hat{x}_{t+2T-2}$. We can establish the strictness of the inequality from the first order conditions given by

$$V_{T+2}(k_{t-T}, \ldots, k_t, k_{t+1}) + \delta V_{T+1}(k_{t-T+1}, \ldots, k_{t+1}, k_{t+2}) \cdots$$
$$+ \delta^{T+1} V_1(k_{t+1}, \ldots, k_{t+T}, k_{t+T+1}) = 0, \qquad \text{all } l.$$

After one iteration along a weakly decreasing path, k_s is replaced with k_{s+1} which is less than or equal to k_s, for $t - T \leq s \leq t + T$. Since the cross-partials of V that do not include the last argument are negative, and at least one k_s is replaced by a k_{s+1} that is strictly less than k_s by the definition of a weakly decreasing path, k_{2T+t-1} must strictly exceed k_{2T+t-2} if the first-order condition continues to hold. The situation is analogous for a weakly increasing path. ■

LEMMA 5.1. *Let the function on the right side of* (5.7) *be denoted as* $Z(\delta, k)$.

(*i*) *For every* δ, $Z(\delta, \cdot)$ *is continuous and decreasing.*
(*ii*) *For every* k, $Z(\cdot, k)$ *is continuous and increasing.*

Proof

(i) From Corollary 1.7 we know that the integer-valued map s (truncation time) is upper semicontinuous. Fix k and denote

$$S \equiv \{x \in R_+ : s(x) < s(k)\}, \qquad E \equiv \{x \in R_+ : s(x) = s(k)\}.$$

We obviously need to consider only the case where $k \in \bar{S}$. In this case

$$\lim_{\substack{x \to k \\ x \in S}} Z(\delta, k) = \lim_{\substack{x \to k \\ x \in S}} \left\{ \delta^{-s(x)} f_k\left(x, \hat{l}_{s(x)}\right) + \cdots \right\}$$
$$= \delta^{+s(x)+1} f_k(k, 0) + \cdots$$
$$= \delta^{s(k)} f_k\left(k, l_{s(k)} \beta^{s(k)+1}\right) + \cdots = Z(\delta, k).$$

$Z(\delta, \cdot)$ is decreasing because the function $k \to \Sigma_{i=s(k)}^{-1} f(k, \hat{l}(k)_i \beta^{i+1})$ is concave.

(ii) Condition (ii) is obvious. ■

LEMMA 5.2

(*i*) $k(\delta)$ *is an increasing correspondence.*
(*ii*) *If* f_k *is strictly decreasing, then the steady state is unique.*

Proof. Condition (i) follows from properties of Z in Lemma 5.1, and condition (ii) follows from (i) and properties of s. ■

Proof of Lemma 6.1. For a given state s, we define the set of admissible capital string and consumption paths.

$$E(s) \equiv \{(s_i, c_i)_{i \geq 1}: s_{i+1} = T(s_i, a_i), c_i = \Psi(s_i)(1 - a_i)\}.$$

Then, for an arbitrary $s \in S$:

$$\begin{aligned} &|W_{r_1}(s) - W_{r_2}(s)| \\ &= \left| \sup_{\{(s_t, a_t)\}_{t \geq 0} \in E(s)} \sum \delta^t r_1(s_t, a_t) - \sup_{\{(s_t, a_t)\}_{t \geq 0} \in E(s)} \sum \delta^t r_2(s_t, a_t) \right| \\ &\leq \sup_{\{(s_t, a_t)\}_{t \geq 0} \in E(s)} \sum \delta^t |r_1(s_t, a_t) - r_2(s_t, a_t)| \\ &\leq \sup_{\{(s_t, a_t)\}_{t \geq 0} \in E(s)} \sum \delta^t \sup_{(s, a) \in S \times A} |r_1(s_t, a_t) - r_2(s_t, a_t)| \\ &= \frac{1}{1 - \delta} |r_1 - r_2|_C. \end{aligned}$$

Therefore

$$|W_{r_1} - W_{r_2}|_C \equiv \sup_{s \in S} |W_{r_1} - W_{r_2}|_R \leq \frac{1}{1 - \delta} |r_1 - r_2|_C. \qquad \blacksquare$$

Lemma 6.2 follows easily from Lemma 6.1 and the maximum theorem.

Proof of Lemma 6.3. We argue by contradiction, and we suppose that for some compact subset K of S the sequence $\{h_{r_n}\}$ does not converge uniformly to h_r. Therefore there exists an $\varepsilon > 0$ and a (sub) sequence $\{s_n\}$ converging to $s \in K$ such that (d_A is the Euclidean distance in A):

$$d_A(h_{r_n}(s_n), h(s_n)) > \varepsilon. \tag{1}$$

Since h is uniformly continuous in k, there exists an n_1 such that

$$d_A(h(s_n), h(s)) < \varepsilon/2 \quad \text{for } n \geq n_1, \tag{2}$$

and since

$$d_A(h_{r_n}(s_n), h(s_n)) \leq d_A(h_{r_n})(s_n), h(s)) + d_A(h(s), h(s_n)),$$

one has

$$d_A(h_{r_n}(s_n), h(s)) \geq \varepsilon/2 \qquad \text{for } n \geq n. \tag{3}$$

Let now (again on a subsequence if necessary) $\lim_n h_{r_0}(s_n) = a$; from inequality (3) we have

$$d_A(a, h(s)) \geq \varepsilon/2. \tag{4}$$

We now claim that $F(a, s, r) \geq F(h_r(s), s, r)$. Note that this implies that $a = h(s)$ (by uniqueness of the maximizer), and we have a contradiction to (4) above. From the definition of h_{r_n} we have in fact

$$F\left(h_{r_n}(s_n), s_n, r_n\right) \geq F(a, s_n, r_n) \quad \text{for every } a \in A;$$

so in particular choosing $a \equiv h(s)$, one has

$$F\left(h_{r_n}(s_n), s_n, r_n\right) \geq F\left(h(s), s_n, r_n\right) \tag{5}$$

and

$$\lim_n F\left(h_{r_n}(s_n), s_n, r_n\right) = F(a, s, r);$$

$$\lim_n F\left(h(s), s_n, r_n\right) = F\left(h(s), s, r\right), \tag{6}$$

so that $F(a, s, r) \geq F(h(s), s, r)$ as claimed. ∎

LEMMA 8.1. *Assume $\theta < 1$, $\delta\beta < 1$. Then the supremum of the stochastic program is finite.*

Proof. We consider, as for the deterministic case, the path of maximal accumulation. Now the element t of the sequence is a random variable given by

$$\begin{aligned} f^t(k) &= k^{(1-\alpha)^{t+1}} \quad \beta^{\alpha t + (t-1)\alpha(1-\alpha) + \cdots + \alpha(1-\alpha)^{t-1}} \quad T^{1+(1-\alpha)+\cdots+(1-\alpha)^t} \\ &\quad Z_t Z_{t-1}^{1-\alpha} \cdots Z_0^{(1-\alpha)^t} \\ &\leq \max\{1, k^{(1-\alpha)}\}\beta^t T^{1/\alpha} Z_t Z_{t-1}^{1-\alpha} \cdots Z_0^{(1-\alpha)^t}. \end{aligned}$$

Now if $W_t = Z_t Z_{t-1}^{(1-\alpha)} \cdots Z_0^{(1-\alpha)^t}$, from the equation for Z_t and recalling that if $\ln \varepsilon \sim N(0, \sigma^2)$ then $E(\varepsilon^r) = \exp \mathbf{r}^{12}\sigma^2/2$ for any $r > 0$ one has:

$$E_0(W_t) = \exp\left\{\frac{\sigma^2}{2}\left(1 + (\theta + (1-\alpha))^2 + \left(\theta^2 + (1-\alpha)\theta + (1-\alpha)^2\right)^2 + \cdots\right)\right\}.$$

Denoting $r \equiv \max\{\theta, (1-\alpha)\}$, the preceding series is dominated by a series with general term $t^2 r^{2t}$, where $r < 1$. This is a convergent series, from which we derive $E_0(W_t) \leq M < +\infty$, for every t. This completes the proof of the lemmas. ∎

THEOREM 7.1. *The optimal policy function for the stochastic optimization problem* (S) *is given*

$$\hat{k}(k_{t+1},\ldots,k_{t-T},z_t) = \Gamma(z_t)\beta^t - \tilde{\beta}k_t + \cdots - \tilde{\beta}k_{t-T} \qquad \text{(OP)}$$

$$\Gamma(x) = C^{1/\alpha}x^{\theta/\alpha}; \qquad C \equiv \left(\delta + \delta^2\tilde{\beta} + \cdots + \delta^T\tilde{\beta}^{T-1}\right)^{-1}.$$

Proof. We begin by solving the problem of maximizing output in each period. The optimal allocation of labor is described by a map $\hat{l}$: $R^T_+ \times N \to R^T_+$, $\hat{l}(k^t,t) = (\hat{l}(k^t,t)_{-T+1,\ldots,}\hat{l}(k^t,t)_0)$. In our special case one computes easily

$$\hat{l}(k^t,t)_i = k_i^t\tilde{\beta}^{-i}c(k^t), \qquad c(k^t) \equiv \left(\sum_{i=-T+1}^{0} k_i^t\tilde{\beta}^{-i}\right)^{-1}. \qquad (7.1)$$

When there is no confusion over which k^t we are considering, we use $\hat{l}(k^t,t) = l^t$.

We now consider the Euler equation. Differentiation with respect to k_t yields

$$1 + \delta E_t\left\{f_k\left(\frac{k_t}{l^t\beta^t}\right)Z_{t+1}|Z_t = t_t\right\} + \cdots + \delta^{j+1}E_t\left\{f_k\left(\frac{k_t}{l^{t+j}_{-j}\beta^t}\right)Z_{t+j}|Z_t = z_t\right\}$$

$$= 0. \qquad \text{(E)}$$

Recall that the marginal product of the investment k_t at times after t is a random variable because the amount of labor allocated to k_t, l^{t+j}_{-j} depends on future investments, which in turn depend on future realizations of the random variables $Z_{t'}$, $t' > t$.

The final step is to substitute in the equation (E) the optimal labor allocation and the optimal policy function stated, and verify that the equation is indeed satisfied.

Substituting 8.1 into (E), we find that (E) is equivalent to

$$-1 + \delta E_t\left\{\left(k_{t-T+1}\tilde{\beta}^{T-1} + \cdots + k_t\right)^{-\alpha}\beta^{\alpha t}Z_{t+1}|Z_t = t_t\right\}$$

$$+ \delta^{j+1}E_t\left\{\left(k_{t-T+1+j}\tilde{\beta}^{T-1} + \cdots + k_{t-j}\right)^{-\alpha}\tilde{\beta}^{\alpha j}\beta^{\alpha t}Z_{t+j+1}|Z_t = t_t\right\}$$

$$+ \cdots = 0 \qquad (7.2)$$

for every $t \geq 1$.

Substituting now (OP) into the above equations one derives the equivalent

$$1 + \delta E_t\left\{\Gamma(Z_t)^{-\alpha} Z_{t+1} | Z_t = t_t\right\}$$
$$+ \cdots + \delta^{j+1} E_t\left\{\Gamma(Z_{t+j})^{-\alpha} \beta^{-\alpha j} Z_{t+j} | Z_t = t_t\right\}$$
$$+ \cdots = 0. \tag{7.3}$$

From the equation describing the stochastic process $\{Z_t\}_{t \geq 0}$ one derives, for a given realization z_t of Z_t

$$Z_{t+k} = z_t^{\theta^k} \varepsilon_t^{\theta^{k-1}} \varepsilon_{t+k-1} \quad \text{for every } k \geq 0.$$

Substitution of (7.4) into (7.3) finally proves that equation (IE) is indeed satisfied for any $t \geq 1$, when the labor allocation is the optimal one and investment follows the optimal policy. This concludes the proof of the theorem. ■

Acknowledgments

We thank Buzz Brock, Prajit Dutta, Chris Flinn, Roman Frydman, Dermott Gately, Bojan Jovanovic, Ned Nadiri, Salih Neftci, James Ramsey, and Charles Wilson for valuable conversation; Francesco Goletti for technical assistance; and the C. V. Starr Center for research facilities and technical assistance. We also thank participants at the seminars in Northwestern, Boston, Brown, and New York Universities for stimulating discussions.

References

Bardhan, P. K. (1969). "Equilibrium growth in a model with economic obsolescence of machines," *Quart. J. Econ.*, **83**, 312–323.

Benhabib, J., and K. Nishimura (1979). "The Hopf bifurcation and the existence and stability of closed orbits in multisection models of optimal economic growth," *J. Econ. Theory* **21**, 421–444.

Benhabib, J., and K. Nishimura (1985). "Competitive equilibrium cycles," *J. Econ. Theory*, 35, 284–306.

Benhabib, J., and K. Nishimura (1988). "Endogenous fluctuations in discrete time optimal growth models," in *Optimal Control Theory and Economic Analysis*, Gustav Feichtinger (ed.) Vol. 3, [Elsevier Science Publishers B. V. (North-Holland), New York] pp. 3–20.

Benveniste, L., and J. Scheinkman, (1979). "Differentiable value functions in concave dynamic optimization problems," *Econometrica* **47** (3), 727–732.

Bliss, C. J. (1968). "On putty-clay," *Rev. Econ. Studies* **35**, 105–132.

Burmeister, E., and A. R. Dobell (1970). *Mathematical Theories of Economic Growth* (Macmillan, London.

Campbell, J. V., and N. O. Mankiw (1987). "Are output fluctuations transistory?" *Quart. J. Econ.* **102**, 857–880.

Chari, V. V., and H. Hoppenhayn (1991). "Vintage human capital, growth and the difference of new technology," *J. Pol. Econ.* **99**, 1142–1165.

Denison, E. F. (1964). "The unimportance of the embodiment question," *Am. Econ. Rev.* **54**, 90–94.

Ferri, G. (1986). "Essays in economic dynamics," Ph.D. thesis, New York University (NYU), Chapter 2.

Gorman, W. M. (1968). "Measuring the quantities of fixed factors," in *Value, Capital and Growth, Papers in Honor of Sir John Hicks*, J. N. Wolfe, (ed.) (Edinburgh Univ. Press, U.K.), pp. 141–173.

Holmes, T. J., and J. A. Schmitz (Dec. 1988). "A theory of entrepreneurship and its application to the study of business transfers, Stony Brook Univ. Research Paper 314.

Kydland, F. E., and E. C. Prescott (1982). "Time to build and aggregate fluctuations," *Econometrica* **50** 1345–1370.

Levhari, D., and E. Sheshinski (1967). "On the sensitivity of the level of output to savings," *Quart. J. Econ.* **81**, 524–528.

Marx, K. (1967). *Capital: A Critique of Political Economy* (International Publishers, New York).

Mitra, T., D., Ray, and R. Roy (1988). "The economics of orchards: an exercise in point input, flow output capital theory," Conselho National de Desenuoluimento Cientifico e Tecnologico, IMPA, Serie B-048-OUT.188.

Mitra, T., and H. Wan, Jr. (1985). "Some theoretic results on the economics of forestry," *Rev. Econ. Studies* **52**, 263–282.

Mitra, T., and H. Wan, Jr. (1986). "On the Faustmann solution to the forest management problem," *J. Econ. Theory* **40**, 229–249.

Nelson, C. R., and C. I. Plosser (1982). "Trends and random walks in macroeconomic time series: Some evidence and implications," *J. Monetary Econ.* **10**, 139–162.

Phelps, E. S. (1962). "The new view of investment: A neoclassical analysis," *Quart. J. Econ.* **76**, 548–567.

Robertson, D. H. (1915). *A Study of Industrial Fluctuations* (P. S. King and Sons, London).

Rustichini, A. (1989). "Hopf bifurcation for functional differential equations of mixed type," *J. Dynamics and Differential Equations* **1** (2), 145–177.

Sheshinski, E. (1967). "Balanced growth and stability in the Johansen vintage capital model," *Rev. Econ. Studies* **34**, 239–248.

Solow, R. M. (1960). "Investment and technical progress," in *Mathematical Methods in the Social Sciences*, K. J. Arrow, S. Karlin, and P. Suppes (eds.) (Stanford University Press, Stanford, Calif.), pp. 89–104.

Solow, R. M., J. Tobin, C. von Weizsäcker, and M. Yaari (1966). "Neoclassical growth with fixed factor proportions," *Rev. Econ. Studies* **33**, 79–115.

Wan, H. Jr., (1988). "Optimal paths without GAS at any discount rates; new examples from forest management," CAE Working Paper, Cornell University, Ithaca, N.Y.

Wan, H., Jr. (1989). "Durable assets and replacement cycles," Working Paper No. 419, Cornell University, Ithaca, N.Y.

THOUGHTS ON VOLATILITY TESTS OF THE INTERTEMPORAL ASSET PRICING MODEL

Truman F. Bewley
Department of Economics and Cowles Foundation
Yale University
New Haven, Connecticut 06520

1. INTRODUCTION

In this paper, I suggest that a solution to the puzzle posed by the apparent excessive volatility of asset prices may be found by considering models that include a borrowing constraint and uninsured risk. Until now, general equilibrium models of asset prices have been Arrow–Debreu models or models with one consumer. These models exclude phenomena that may be important and may explain the volatility of asset prices. Thus, it is premature to reject rational expectations or the basic structure of intertemporal asset pricing models.

The volatility tests were discovered by Shiller (1979) and Leroy and Porter (1981). Their work has led to a fairly large literature, which is reviewed very briefly below. Mehra and Prescott (1982), in their contribution to this literature, suggest that the excessive risk premia on assets may be explained by the presence of uninsurable risk. This paper follows up on their suggestion.

The main point I wish to make is that when consumers cannot borrow and when they face uninsurable risk, their investment behavior can be understood only by considering their indirect utility for wealth, where by "wealth" I mean the value of currently held liquid assets. The indirect utility for wealth may have a variable coefficient of relative risk aversion, even when the relative risk aversion of utility for consumption is constant. It follows, for instance, that the prices of assets could depend very much on the distribution of wealth in society.

GENERAL EQUILIBRIUM, GROWTH, AND TRADE II

The importance of the indirect utility for wealth seems to have been overlooked in the literature on finance. The reason for this oversight has probably been that in the Arrow–Debreu and one-consumer models popular in finance, no insight is gained by considering this indirect utility.

Consideration of the indirect utility for wealth leads quickly to a possible explanation of volatility. It seems reasonable to suppose that relative risk aversion decreases with wealth, at least for large levels of wealth. Also, it seems reasonable to suppose that risky assets would tend to be concentrated in the hands of the wealthy. If all this is true, then the effect of changes in expected dividends on asset prices would be reinforced by changes in investors' relative risk aversion and hence in risk premia.

The organization of the paper is as follows. In the next section, I try to make the topic of discussion more precise by defining the notion of market efficiency being tested in studies of volatility. In this section, I also suggest that market efficiency might be tested by comparing returns in the reinsurance market with returns elsewhere. In Section 3, I survey briefly the empirical literature on volatility tests. In Section 4, I describe my model. In Sections 5 and 6, I discuss properties of equilibria and investor behavior in the model. Most of the discussion is in terms of examples. In Section 6, I demonstrate that the indirect utility for wealth may have a variable coefficient of relative risk aversion, even when the utility for consumption has constant relative risk aversion. In Section 7, I elaborate the explanation of volatility mentioned above. Townsend (1982) has given a related explanation of volatility. I discuss it in Section 7.

2. DEFINITION OF MARKET EFFICIENCY

There is literature on the subject of the definition of market efficiency, which includes Fama (1970, 1976), Leroy (1976), Rubinstein (1974), Easley and Jarrow (1981), and Verrecchia (1980). Possible definitions of efficiency include those listed below. [Others exist; see, for instance, Rubinstein (1975).]

1. The true probability distribution of returns on an asset conditional on all information available to any trader is the same as the true probability distribution conditional on the current price of the asset and all other publicly available information.

2. The true probability distribution of future returns conditional on all information available to any trader is the same as the probability distribution believed to be valid by any trader.

3. It is not possible to make economic profits by trading on the basis of publicly available information. [This definition is copied almost word for word from Jensen (1978).]

The first and second definitions seem to be the ones prevailing in the literature on markets in which prices reveal information. [See Jordan (1983) and Easley and Jarrow (1981).] Fama seems to have had the second and third definitions in mind. (Fama, 1970, 1976). In this paper, I discuss tests of the third definition.

The third definition remains ambiguous until "economic profits" are defined. The meaning of "economic profits" can be made precise only in terms of a model with at least one good besides the asset in question, for the simple reason that if there is no second good, investors have no alternative but to hold the asset forever. It follows that one cannot determine whether opportunities for profit exist by looking at the history of returns on one asset alone.

If there are many goods or assets, then market efficiency implies that no trader can gain by switching assets. In order to proceed further, "gain" must be defined. Suppose that gain is defined to be the expected value of next period's wealth and suppose that there are two assets, a one-period bond and a stock. Then, investors cannot gain by switching between the bond and the stock if

$$q_t = (1 + r_t)^{-1} E_t[q_{t+1} + d_{t+1}], \tag{2.1}$$

where q_t is the price of the stock in period t, r_t is the yield from period t to $t + 1$ on the bond, d_{t+1} is the dividend in period $t + 1$, and E_t is expected value conditional on information available in period t. Similarly, if an indexed bond were also available, which paid interest at a real rate of r, one would be led to

$$q_t p_t^{-1} = (1 + r)^{-1} E_t\left[(q_{t+1} + d_{t+1}) p_{t+1}^{-1}\right], \tag{2.2}$$

where p_t is the level of the price index in period t.

Equations (2.1) and (2.2) look like the conditions for a martingale with drift, but the notion of martingale seems to be a distraction. One might believe that the returns $R_t = (q_{t+1} + d_{t+1} - q_t)q_t^{-1}$ on the stock should obey a martingale. That is, one might believe that $R_{t-1} = E_t[R_t]$. This equation implies that

$$q_t = (1 + R_{t-1})^{-1} E_t[q_{t+1} + d_{t+1}].$$

This would be a condition for efficiency based on the returns from one asset alone, but I see no economic justification for this equation.[1]

[1]Fama (1970) attempted a definition of market efficiency that also used a condition on the returns of a single asset. His condition was that $q_t(1 + E_t r_t) = E_t[q_{t+1} + d_{t+1}]$, where $r_t + (q_{t+1} + d_{t+1})q_t^{-1}$. As Leroy (1976) has pointed out, this equation is an identity.

A disadvantage of equations (2.1) and (2.2) is that they make no allowance for risk. One might add a constant risk adjustment ϕ to equation (2.1), obtaining

$$q_t = (1 + r_t + \phi)^{-1} E_t[q_{t+1} + d_{t+1}]. \tag{2.3}$$

Equations (2.1)–(2.3) all have a respectable tradition. In fact, Shiller (1981b) and Leroy and Porter (1981) test equation (2.2) in their volatility tests for stock market efficiency, and Shiller (1979, 1981a) tests equation (2.3) in his volatility tests for the efficiency of the market for long-term bonds.

Equation (2.3) leaves unexplained the risk premium ϕ. One can make ϕ endogenous by including consumption as an alternative to the asset. The trade-off between consumption and asset holding leads to the equation

$$q_t p_t^{-1} u'(x_t) = (1 + \rho)^{-1} E_t\left[u'(x_{t+1})(q_{t+1} + d_{t+1}) p_{t+1}^{-1}\right], \tag{2.4}$$

where u' is the derivative of the utility function, x_t is consumption at time t of a single composite consumption good, ϕ is a pure rate of time preference, and p_t is an index of the level of consumption good prices at time t. This equation appears in Lucas' (1978) paper on asset prices and is the basis for Breeden's (1979) "consumption beta" theory of asset prices. Much effort has gone into empirical tests of this equation. This work is reviewed in the next section.

By considering new trade-offs between various assets, it should be possible to construct new and interesting tests of market efficiency. It might be helpful to think of an analogy with Savage's theory of personal probabilities. In that theory, one can measure personal probabilities only by having an individual choose between lotteries with known probabilities and lotteries with only subjectively assessed probabilities. Similarly, one might compare investors' evaluation of ordinary securities with their evaluation of investments with a known payoff distribution. Such investments should exist in the reinsurance market, for actuarial risks are no doubt calculated accurately and published. One could measure the return on such risks and compare it with the return on other securities whose risks (as measured by the history of returns) was of the same magnitude.

3. A QUICK REVIEW OF TESTS OF MARKET EFFICIENCY

I here review briefly tests that have been made of equations (2.2)–(2.4).

Striking evidence was found against the validity of equations (2.2) and (2.3) by Leroy and Porter (1981), Shiller (1979, 1981a, 1981b, 1981c), and Singleton (1980). The basic idea of these tests is that since the current price is a discounted sum of future dividends (or coupon payments), the variance of the price should be less than that of the discounted value of the future dividends. For instance, equation (2.2) leads to the equation

$$Q_t = E_t\left[\sum_{s=0}^{T-t} (1+r)^{-s} D_{t+s} + (1+r)^{-T+t} Q_T\right],$$

where T is the last date for which observations are available and where $Q_t = q_t p_t^{-1}$ and $D_t = d_t p_t^{-1}$. Let $Q_t^* = \Sigma_{s=0}^{T-t}(1+r)^{-s}D_{t+s} + (1+r)^{-T+t}Q_t$. Since $Q_t = E_t p_t^*$, it follows that $\operatorname{var} Q_t < \operatorname{var} Q_t^*$. The tests, roughly speaking, involve comparing the observed variation of Q_t and Q_t^*. That of Q_t is found to be much larger. [These tests have been criticized by Kleidon (1986). West (1988) surveys the literature.]

In reaction to these results, there has been an attempt to determine whether volatility in the prices of securities has resulted from fluctuations in the real discount factor, $(1+\rho)^{-1}u'(x_{t+1})[u'(x_t)]^{-1}$, coming from equation (2.4). The goal of all this work is to detect a relation between predicted movements in returns and the discount factor. Roughly speaking, investigators look for a relation between $E_t[u'(x_{t+1})[u'(x_t)]^{-1}$ and $E_t[(q_{t+1} + d_{t+1})q_t^{-1}p_t p_{t+1}^{-1}]$.[2] This work includes that of Grossman and Shiller (1981) and Hall (1981). The results have been mixed. One cannot say that the model has been decisively rejected or accepted. The main difficulty is that since World War II, there has been very little variability in consumption in the United States, whereas stock prices have varied a great deal. Hall simply concludes that the elasticity of intertemporal substitution in the consumption of nondurables is very low.

It should be noticed that this work is closely related to earlier work on whether aggregate personal savings are sensitive to interest rates. That literature too never found persuasive evidence that interest rates have a significant effect on savings (see Howrey and Hymans, 1978).

Mehra and Prescott (1985) have made another test of the model represented by equation (2.4). They construct a simple model of the American economy with one asset that yields a stochastic dividend. The dividend is the economy's entire national product. There is a single consumer with utility function of the form $\Sigma_{t=0}^{\infty}(1+\rho)^{-1}u(x_t)$, where u has constant relative risk aversion. The growth rate of the asset's dividend forms a two-state Markov process. The parameters of this process are chosen so that the rate of growth, variance, and intertemporal covariance of the dividend are comparable to those of the American gross national product. They compute the equilibrium price of the asset of the model and compare its average rate of return with the average rate of return on a

[2]It would be more accurate to say that they have looked for a relation between $E_t[\ln(u'(x_{t+1})(u'(x_t))^{-1}]$ and $E_t[\ln(u'(q_{t+1} + d_{t+1})q_t^{-1}p_t p_{t+1}^{-1})]$.

hypothetical risk free asset (or indexed bond). They find that for all reasonable values of the parameters of the consumer's utility function, the difference is much smaller than the differences between the actual average rate of return on stocks and on short-term government securities. (The average interest rate on the latter is assumed to approximate the rate on an indexed bond.) Mehra and Prescott conclude that risk premia on stocks are too high to be consistent with the intertemporal asset pricing model.

No one to my knowledge has asked whether the actual covariation of stock returns and aggregate consumption is large enough to explain the differences between the average rate of return on stocks and that on a low-risk asset. The studies referred to above looked for a relation between the conditional means $E_t[u'(x_{t+1})[u'(x_t)^{-1}]$ and $E_t[(q_{t+1} + d_{t+1})q_t^{-1}p_t p_{t+1}^{-1}]$. They did not estimate the average value of

$$\mathrm{cov}_t\left(u'(x_{t+1})\left[u'(x_t)\right]^{-1}, (q_{t+1} + d_{t+1})q_t^{-1}p_t p_{t+1}^{-1}\right),$$

where cov_t is covariance conditional on information available at time t. Theoretically, this covariance could be positive even if there were no covariation of the expected values presented above. It is the preceding covariance that would determine risk premia on stocks in a single-consumer economy.

4. THE MODEL

I now describe the model I use to discuss issues raised by the literature just reviewed. The model is designed to include a no-borrowing constraint, uninsurable risk and money in as simple a way as possible. Otherwise, the model is like the general equilibrium models currently fashionable in finance. I follow current fashion by assuming that consumers live forever and that they maximize a discounted sum of future utilities. I imitate Lucas (1978) in assuming that assets are claims on an endowment stream. If one includes production, one must deal with the fact that in a world with uninsurable risk, stockholders may not agree on the objective of their firm. There are two sources of uncertainty in the model, private and public. Private uncertainty is never insurable. Public uncertainty may or may not be insurable. Private uncertainty affects an individual's endowments and utility function. It washes out in the aggregate, for there are a continuum of consumers, and the private uncertainty experienced by each is independent of that of others.

The novel properties of equilibria in the model result from three things taken together, the heterogeneity of consumers and the restrictions that they cannot borrow and cannot buy insurance against private risk. These imply, for instance, that stationary equilibria may have rates of return much less than any consumer's pure rate of time preference. In a model with one consumer or with heterogeneous consumers and borrowing, stationary equilibrium is possible, roughly speaking, only if rates of return equal consumers' pure rate of time preferences. In the model used here, consumers may hold assets as a buffer against private risk and so may even accept negative rates of return. It is also true that consumers may not always hold assets. Consumers may randomly fluctuate between bad times when they have no assets and good times when they have lots of assets. This behavior is discussed in Schechtman (1976) and Schechtman and Escudero (1977).

I now turn to a formal description of the model.

4.1 The Underlying Stochastic Processes

All agents in the economy observe a stochastic process $\{s_t\}_{t=0}^{\infty}$. This process may be thought of as generating public uncertainty. Each consumer i also observes a stochastic process $\{a_{it}\}_{t=0}^{\infty}$. This process is observed only by consumer i and so represents private, uninsurable uncertainty. I assume that each consumer i knows the true probability distribution of s_t and a_{it}. That is, I assume rational expectations. Assumptions 4.1 and 4.2 are made.

Assumption 4.1. The processes $\{a_{it}\}_{t=0}^{\infty}$ are mutually independent and identically distributed as i varies and are independent of the process $\{s_t\}$.

Assumption 4.2. All the s_t belong to a finite set S and all the a_{it} belong to a finite set A.

4.2 Commodities and Assets

There is one consumption good and there are J assets. Asset j yields a random dividend at time t of $d_{ji}(s_t)$ units of consumption good.

4.3 Consumers

There are a continuum of consumers, indexed by $i \in [0, 1]$. I denote by $u_i(x, a_{it})$ the utility experienced by consumer i at time t if this individual consumes x units of consumption good. Consumer i discounts future utility at rate ρ_i. A consumption program is of the form $\mathbf{x} = (x_0, x_1, \ldots)$, where

$$x_t = x_t(a_{i0}, \ldots, a_{it}; s_0, \ldots, s_t).$$

Consumer i acts so as to maximize this expected discounted utility

$$U_i(x) = E\sum_{t=0}^{\infty}(1+\rho_i)^{-t}u_i(x_t(a_{i0},\dots,a_{it};s_0,\dots,s_t),a_{it}).$$

Consumer i also has an endowment at time t of $\omega_{it}(a_{it})$ units of consumption good.

The following assumptions are made.

Assumption 4.3. For each i, t and a, $u_{it}(x,a)$ is a continuously differentiable, strictly concave and strictly increasing function of x.

Assumption 4.4. For each x and t, the function of i, $\omega_{it}(a):[0,1]\to[0,\infty]$ is integrable.

Assumption 4.5. For each a and t, the function of i and x,

$$\frac{d}{dx}u_i(x,a):[0,1]\times[0,\infty]\to[0,\infty]$$

is measurable.

4.4 Government Bonds or Money

The unit of account is interest bearing money or government debt. Each period, this money earns interest at a market-determined rate. The interest payments are financed by a lump-sum tax on consumers. All consumers pay the same tax. The tax paid by each consumer in period t is $\tau_t(s_0,\dots,s_t)$. The interest earned on money held from period t to period $t+1$ is $r_t(s_0,\dots,s_t)$. The term $\underset{\sim}{r}$ denotes the vector $(r_t(s_0,\dots,s_t))$, where $t=0,1,\dots$ and $(s_0,\dots,s_t)$ varies over all sequences occurring with positive probability.

4.5 Prices

The price of the consumption good in period t is $p_t(s_0,\dots,s_t)$. The price of asset j in period t is $q_{jt}(s_0,\dots,s_t)$. $\underset{\sim}{p}$ and $\underset{\sim}{q}$ denote the vectors of all goods and asset prices, respectively. The full-price system is $(\underset{\sim}{p},\underset{\sim}{r},\underset{\sim}{q})$. The components of $\underset{\sim}{p}$ and $\underset{\sim}{q}$ are required to be positive. Those of $\underset{\sim}{r}$ are required to be nonnegative.

4.6 Consumer Demand

Consumer i's holdings of money and of asset j at the end of period t are denoted by $M_{it}(a_{i0},\dots,a_{it};s_0,\dots,s_t)$ and $\theta_{ijt}(a_{i0},\dots,a_{it};s_0,\dots,s_t)$, respectively. The holdings at the end of period -1 are part of the givens of the model. The following is assumed.

Assumption 4.6. $M_{i,-1}$ and $\theta_{ij,-1}$ are integrable, nonnegative functions of i and $\int_0^1 \theta_{ij,-1}\, di = 1$, for all j.

A program consists of $(\underset{\sim}{x}_i, \underset{\sim}{M}_i, \underset{\sim}{\theta}_i)$, where $\underset{\sim}{x}_i$ is a consumption program, $\underset{\sim}{M}_i = (M_{it}(a_{i0}, \ldots, a_{it}; s_0, \ldots, s_t))$ and $\underset{\sim}{\theta}_i = \theta_{ijt}(a_{i0}, \ldots, a_{it}; s_0, \ldots, s_t))$. This program is said to be financially feasible (given $\underset{\sim}{p}$ and $\underset{\sim}{q}$) if

(i)

$$\begin{aligned} M_{i,t+1}&(a_{i0}, \ldots, a_{i,t+1}; s_0, \ldots, s_{t+1}) \\ &= (1 + r_t(s_0, \ldots, s_t))M_{it}(a_{i0}, \ldots, a_{it}; s_0, \ldots, s_t) \\ &\quad + p_t(s_0, \ldots, s_t)(\omega_{it}(a_{it}) - x_{it}(a_{i0}, \ldots, a_{it}; s_0, \ldots, s_t)) \\ &\quad - \sum_j q_{jt}(s_0, \ldots, s_t)\theta_{ijt}(a_{i0}, \ldots, a_{it}; s_0, \ldots, s_t) \end{aligned}$$

almost surely, for all t, and

(ii)

$$M_{it}(a_{i0}, \ldots, a_{it}; s_0, \ldots, s_t) \geq 0 \quad \text{and}$$
$$\theta_{ijt}(a_{i0}, \ldots, a_{it}; s_0, \ldots, s_t) \geq 0$$

almost surely for all i, t and t. The second condition forbids short sales and borrowing.

The budget set of consumer i is

$$\beta_i(\underset{\sim}{p}, \underset{\sim}{r}, \underset{\sim}{q}) = \{(\underset{\sim}{x}_i, \underset{\sim}{M}_i, \underset{\sim}{\theta}_i) | (\underset{\sim}{x}_i, \underset{\sim}{M}_i, \underset{\sim}{\theta}_i) \text{ is a financially feasible program}\}.$$

Consumer i's demand correspondence is

$$\begin{aligned} \beta_i(\underset{\sim}{p}, \underset{\sim}{r}, \underset{\sim}{q}) = \Big\{ &(\underset{\sim}{x}_i, \underset{\sim}{M}_i, \underset{\sim}{\theta}_i) \in \beta_i(\underset{\sim}{p}, \underset{\sim}{r}, \underset{\sim}{q}) | U_i(\underset{\sim}{x}_i) \geq U_i(\underset{\sim}{\bar{x}}_i), \quad \text{for all } \underset{\sim}{\bar{x}}_i \\ &\text{such that } \left(\underset{\sim}{\bar{x}}_i, \underset{\sim}{\overline{M}}_i, \underset{\sim}{\bar{\theta}}_i\right) \in \beta_i(\underset{\sim}{p}, \underset{\sim}{r}, \underset{\sim}{q}), \quad \text{for some } \underset{\sim}{\overline{M}}_i \text{ and } \underset{\sim}{\bar{\theta}}_i \Big\}. \end{aligned}$$

4.7 Allocations

An allocation consists of $((\underset{\sim}{x}_i, \underset{\sim}{\theta}_i))_{i\varepsilon[0,1]}$ satisfying

(i) For each i, $\underset{\sim}{x}_i$ is a consumption program and $\underset{\sim}{\theta}_i$ is an investment program for consumer i.

(ii) $x_{it}(a_{i0}, \ldots, a_{it}; s_0, \ldots, s_t)$ and $\theta_{it}(a_{i0}, \ldots, a_{it}; s_0, \ldots, s_t)$ are integrable functions of i, for each t and $a_{i0}, \ldots, a_{it}$ and $s_0, \ldots, s_t$.

The allocation is said to be feasible if

$$\int_0^t E[x_{it}|s_0, \ldots, s_t]\,di = \int_0^t E\omega_{it}\,di + \sum_{j=1}^{J} d_{jt}(s_0, \ldots, s_t) \quad \text{and}$$
$$\int_0^t E\left[\theta_{ijt}|s_0, \ldots, s_t\right] di = 1 \quad \text{almost surely, for all } t. \tag{4.8}$$

Notice that aggregates are defined using the integral of conditional expectations. This procedure is justified in Bewley (1986). It corresponds to the idea that individual fluctuations average out.

4.8 Equilibrium without Insurance

An equilibrium without insurance consists of $((\underset{\sim}{x}_i, \underset{\sim}{M}_i, \underset{\sim}{\theta}_i), (\underset{\sim}{p}, \underset{\sim}{r}, \underset{\sim}{q}))$, where

(i) $(\underset{\sim}{x}_i, \underset{\sim}{M}_i, \underset{\sim}{\theta}_i)$ is a feasible allocation,
(ii) $(\underset{\sim}{p}, \underset{\sim}{r}, \underset{\sim}{q})$ is a price system, and
(iii) $(\underset{\sim}{x}_i, \underset{\sim}{M}_i, \underset{\sim}{\theta}_i) \in \xi_i(\underset{\sim}{p}, \underset{\sim}{r}, \underset{\sim}{q})$, for almost every i.

4.9 Insurance

Insurance can be bought only on events associated with the process $\{s_t\}$. Insurance for period $t+1$ is arranged forward during period t. That is, transactions are arranged in period t, but payments are made in period $t+1$. An insurance contract on state s in period $t+1$ gives that holder the right to receive one unit of money in period $t+1$ if $s_{t+1} = s$. Contracts on a particular state $\bar{s} \in S$ are used as means of payment. I assume that

$$\text{Prob}\left[s_{t+1} = \bar{s}|s_0, \ldots, s_t\right] > 0, \quad \text{almost surely, for all } t. \tag{4.9}$$

The price of a contract on state s in period $t+1$ is denoted by $\pi_t(s_0, \ldots, s_t; s)$. It is the number of units of money that must be paid in period $t+1$ if $\bar{s}$ occurs in order to receive one unit of money in the same period if s occurs. Thus $\pi_t(s_0, \ldots, s_t; \bar{s}) = 1$. A price system now consists of $(\underset{\sim}{p}, \underset{\sim}{r}, \underset{\sim}{q}, \underset{\sim}{\pi})$, where $\underset{\sim}{\pi} = (\pi_t(s_0, \ldots, s_t; s_{t+1}))$.

An insurance program for consumer i consists of

$$\underset{\sim}{c}_i = \left(c_{it}(a_{i0}, \ldots, a_{it}; s_0, \ldots, s_t, s_{t+1})\right),$$

where $c_{it}(a_{i0}, \ldots, a_{it}; s_0, \ldots, s_t, s_{t+1})$ is the quantity of money to be received in period $t+1$ if s_{t+1} occurs.

The initial contracts $c_{i,-1}$ are part of the givens of the model. It is assumed that

$$c_{i,-1} \text{ is an integrable function of } i \text{ and } \int_0^1 c_{i,-1}\,di = 0. \qquad (4.10)$$

A program for consumer i consists of $(\underset{\sim}{x}_i, \underset{\sim}{M}_i, \underset{\sim}{\theta}_i, \underset{\sim}{c}_i)$. It is financially feasible, given $(\underset{\sim}{p}, \underset{\sim}{r}, \underset{\sim}{q}, \underset{\sim}{\pi})$, if

(i) $M_{i,t+1} = (1 + r_t)M_{it} + p_t(\omega_{it} - x_{it}) - \sum_j q_{jt}\theta_{ijt} + c_{it}$ almost surely for all t;
(ii) $M_{it} \geq 0$ and $\theta_{ijt} \geq 0$ almost surely, for all i, j, and t; and
(iii) $\sum_{s_{t+1}} \pi_t(s_0, \ldots, s_t; s_{t+1}) c_{it}(a_{i0}, \ldots, a_{it}; s_0, \ldots, s_t; s_{t+1}) = 0.$

The budget set of consumer i is

$$\beta_i(\underset{\sim}{p}, \underset{\sim}{r}, \underset{\sim}{q}, \underset{\sim}{\pi}) = \{(\underset{\sim}{x}_i, \underset{\sim}{M}_i, \underset{\sim}{\theta}_i, \underset{\sim}{c}_i) | (\underset{\sim}{x}_i, \underset{\sim}{M}_i, \underset{\sim}{\theta}_i, \underset{\sim}{c}_i) \text{ is a financially feasible program}\}.$$

This consumer's demand correspondence is $\xi_i(\underset{\sim}{p}, \underset{\sim}{r}, \underset{\sim}{q}, \underset{\sim}{\pi}) = \{(\underset{\sim}{x}_i, \underset{\sim}{M}_i, \underset{\sim}{\theta}_i, \underset{\sim}{c}_i) \in \beta_i(\underset{\sim}{p}, \underset{\sim}{r}, \underset{\sim}{q}, \underset{\sim}{\pi}) | U_i(\underset{\sim}{x}_i) \geq U_i(\underset{\sim}{\bar{x}}_i)$, for all $\underset{\sim}{\bar{x}}_i$ such that $(\underset{\sim}{\bar{x}}_i, \underset{\sim}{\bar{M}}_i, \underset{\sim}{\bar{\theta}}_i, \underset{\sim}{\bar{c}}_i) \in \beta_i(\underset{\sim}{p}, \underset{\sim}{r}, \underset{\sim}{q}, \underset{\sim}{\pi})$, for some $\underset{\sim}{\bar{M}}_i$, $\underset{\sim}{\bar{\theta}}_i$ and $\underset{\sim}{\bar{c}}_i\}$.

A feasible allocation consists of $((\underset{\sim}{x}_i, \underset{\sim}{\theta}_i, \underset{\sim}{c}_i))$ such that $((\underset{\sim}{x}_i, \underset{\sim}{\theta}_i))$ is a feasible allocation in the sense of (4.8) and $\int_0^1 E[c_{it}(\cdot; s_{t+1}) | s_0, \ldots, s_t]\,di = 0$ almost surely, for all t.

An equilibrium with insurance consists of $((\underset{\sim}{x}_i, \underset{\sim}{M}_i, \underset{\sim}{\theta}_i, \underset{\sim}{c}_i), (\underset{\sim}{p}, \underset{\sim}{r}, \underset{\sim}{q}, \underset{\sim}{\pi}))$, where

(i) $(\underset{\sim}{x}_i, \underset{\sim}{\theta}_i, \underset{\sim}{c}_i)$ is a feasible allocation,
(ii) $(\underset{\sim}{p}, \underset{\sim}{r}, \underset{\sim}{q}, \underset{\sim}{\pi})$ is a price system, and
(iii) $(\underset{\sim}{x}_i, \underset{\sim}{M}_i, \underset{\sim}{\theta}_i, \underset{\sim}{c}_i) \in \xi_i(\underset{\sim}{p}, \underset{\sim}{r}, \underset{\sim}{q}, \underset{\sim}{\pi})$ for almost every i.

With the addition of special assumptions, it is possible to prove that equilibria exist with or without insurance. Since these existence results are tangential to the main thrust of the paper, they are not included.

5. ASSET PRICES WITH INSURANCE

If the insurance just defined exists and the prices π_t are observable, then it is possible to devise a good test of the model using an arbitrage equation for asset prices. This test does not test for rational expectations. If the prices π_t are not observable, then the knowledge that consumers were perfectly insured could be helpful. However, it does not help if the risks associated with asset holding affect investors' consumption and if one has data only on aggregate consumption. An example is given to illustrate why.

The following equation holds in an equilibrium $((\underset{\sim}{x}_i, \underset{\sim}{M}_i, \underset{\sim}{\theta}_i, \underset{\sim}{c}_i), (p, \underset{\sim}{r}, q, \underset{\sim}{\pi}))$, provided there is a positive amount of money in the economy at time t and in event $[s_0, \ldots, s_t]$.

$$\sum_{s_{t+1}} \pi_t(s_0, \ldots, s_t; s_{t+1}) q_{jt}(s_0, \ldots, s_t)(1 + r_t(s_0, \ldots, s_t))$$

$$= \sum_{s_{t+1}} \pi_t(s_0, \ldots, s_t; s_{t+1}) \big(q_{j,t+1}(s_0, \ldots, s_{t+1}) + d_{j,t+1}(s_0, \ldots, s_{t+1})\big). \qquad (5.1)$$

This is an arbitrage equation. It is not hard to see that if, for instance, the left-hand side exceeds the right-hand side, then consumers who held the jth asset could increase their wealth for sure in period $t + 1$ by selling the asset, holding the proceeds as money and making suitable forward transactions in the insurance market. Thus, no one would hold the jth asset and the economy would not be in equilibrium. Similarly, if the right-hand side exceeded the left-hand side, no one would hold money. Thus, equation (5.1) is completely in the spirit of Stephen Ross' (1978) arbitrage theory of pricing.

Notice that the expectation operator does not appear in (5.1). Thus, empirical tests of this equation would not be tests of rational expectations.

Of course, equation (5.1) could be tested empirically, provided the states s_t could be identified and the prices π_t observed or inferred.

It might be possible to infer the prices π_t from the prices of other assets. As is well known, insurance can be arranged, at least to some extent, by transactions in options on assets or in the assets themselves (see Ross, 1976). If options span in the sense of Ross, then the prices π_t can be calculated from the price of options. [Friesen (1979) shows how to calculate prices of Arrow–Debreu state-contingent securities from option prices.]

It might be that the returns in assets themselves span.[3] [Ekern and Wilson (1974) have used such a spanning condition as a condition for stockholder unanimity.] If the returns on the assets span, then the prices π_t can be calculated uniquely from equation (5.1) and the condition $\pi_t(s_0, \ldots, s_t; \underline{s}) = 1$. Hence, equation (5.1) becomes a tautology and cannot be tested at all.

Suppose now that for some reason the prices π_t cannot be observed or inferred at all, even though consumers are fully insured. Knowledge that consumers are insured should still be helpful. However, if one

[3]In order to take full advantage of assets as a means of insurance, consumers would have to sell short, which they are forbidden to do in the model. But equation (5.1) still applies if the model is changed so as to allow short selling.

pursues the theory, one is led to the conclusion that the data would probably reject the assumption that all public risk is insurable.

In order to discuss these matters more precisely, let us turn to the first order conditions of a consumer's maximization problem. Let $\lambda_{it}(a_{i0}, \ldots, a_{it}; s_0, \ldots, s_t)$ be the marginal utility of money for consumer i at time t. It is not hard to show that λ_{it} exists. The first-order conditions are (5.2)–(5.5), as follows.

$$\lambda_{it} \geq (1+\rho)^{-1}(1+r_t)E_{it}\lambda_{i,t+1} \tag{5.2}$$

almost surely, for all t, with equality when $M_{it} > 0$, where E_{it} is the expectation conditional on $a_{i0}, \ldots, a_{it}$ and $s_0, \ldots, s_t$.

$$\lambda_{it}q_{jt} \geq (1+\rho_i)^{-1}E_{it}\left[\lambda_{i,t+1}(q_{j,t+1}+d_{j,t+1})\right] \tag{5.3}$$

almost surely, for all t, with equality when $\theta_{ijt} > 0$.

For each t,

$$\begin{aligned}\lambda_{i,t+1}(a_{i0}, \ldots, a_{i,t+1}; s_0, \ldots, s_t, s)&\mathrm{Prob}[s_{t+1} = s | s_0, \ldots, s_t] \\ &= \lambda_{i,t+1}(a_{i0}, \ldots, a_{i,t+1}; s_0, \ldots, s_t, \underline{s}) \\ &\quad \times \mathrm{Prob}[s_{t+1} = \underline{s} | s_0, \ldots, s_t]\pi_t(s_0, \ldots, s_t; s)\end{aligned} \tag{5.4}$$

almost surely for all s, provided

$$\begin{aligned}p_{t+1}(s_0, \ldots, s_{t+1})&x_{i,t+1}(a_{i0}, \ldots, a_{i,t+1}; s_0, \ldots, s_{t+1}) \\ &+ M_{i,t+1}(a_{i0}, \ldots, a_{i,t+1}; s_0, \ldots, s_{t+1}) \\ &+ \sum_j q_{j,t+1}(s_0, \ldots, s_{t+1})\theta_{ijt}(a_{i0}, \ldots, a_{i,t+1}; s_0, \ldots, s_{t+1}) > 0,\end{aligned}$$

for $s_{t+1} = s$ and $\underline{s}$.

The qualifying phrase is needed in (5.4) because the inability to borrow may prevent consumers from taking full advantage of insurance. The final first-order condition is

$$u_i'(x_{it}, \cdot) \leq \lambda_{it}p_t \tag{5.5}$$

almost surely, for all t, with equality when $x_{it} > 0$. If inequalities (5.2) and (5.3) hold with equality, then

$$q_{jt}E_{it}\lambda_{i,t+1} = (1+r_t)^{-1}E_{it}\left[\lambda_{i,t+1}(q_{j,t+1}+d_{j,t+1})\right]. \tag{5.6}$$

Let us consider only those consumers i for whom (5.4) and (5.6) apply. By (5.4), there is a vector $\Lambda_t(s_0, \ldots, s_t)$ such that for each i, $\lambda_{it}(s_0, \ldots, s_t) =$

$\alpha_i \Lambda_t(s_0, \ldots, s_t)$, for some $\alpha_i > 0$. Then, (5.6) becomes

$$q_{jt} E_t \Lambda_{t+1} = (1 + r_t)^{-1} E_t\left[\Lambda_{t+1}(q_{j,t+1} + d_{j,t+1})\right], \tag{5.7}$$

where E_t is expectation conditional on $s_0, \ldots, s_t$.

U.S. postwar data seem to indicate that consumption varies very little away from an exponential growth path. Using this fact, we can surmise that Λ_t should be nearly proportional to p_t^{-1}. [In the absence of insurance, it would not be correct to conclude that the λ_{it} of equation (5.6) were proportional to p_t^{-1}, for the consumption of many consumers might not be much affected by changes in asset returns. However, if markets are complete, then everyone's consumption should move in sympathy with asset returns, and aggregate consumption should do so as well.] If the Λ_t are proportional to p_t^{-1}, then (5.7) becomes

$$q_{jt} E_t p_{t+1}^{-1} = (1 + r_t)^{-1} E_t\left[p_{t+1}^{-1}(q_{j,t+1} + d_{j,t+1})\right] \quad \text{or}$$

$$q_{jt} = (1 + r_t)^{-1}\Big[E_t(q_{j,t+1} + d_{j,t+1})$$

$$+ \operatorname{cov}_t\Big(p_{t+1}^{-1}\big(E_t p_{t+1}^{-1}\big)^{-1}, q_{j,t+1} + d_{j,t+1}\Big)\Big].$$

(For simplicity, I ignore the growth factor in consumption.) Thus, we are led to a kind of "inflation beta" theory of nominal asset prices. Note, however, that if asset prices are measured in real terms, then there should be no risk premia, since

$$q_{jt} p_t^{-1} = (1 + \bar{r}_t)^{-1} E_t\left[p_{t+1}^{-1}(q_{j,t+1} + d_{j,t+1})\right],$$

where $\bar{r}_t = (1 + r_t) p_t E p_{t+1}^{-1} - 1$ is the real interest rate. Since the risk premia associated with real asset prices are observed to be positive, it seems doubtful that any serious empirical study would uphold the assumption that consumers insure themselves against the risk in the returns on all assets.

It is, of course, possible that fluctuations in the returns on particular assets could be fully insurable. In this case, equations (5.1) and (5.7) apply to these assets, when suitably modified so as to make the π_t and Λ_t measurable only with respect to the field generated by the return of the asset in question.

If investors' consumption is significantly affected by asset returns, then equation (5.7) is of no interest. In order to include consumption, one must assume that inequality (5.5) holds with equality. One then obtains

$$u_i'(x_{it}, \cdot) q_{jt} p_t^{-1} = (1 + \rho_i)^{-1} E_{it}\left[u_i'(x_{i,t+1}, \cdot) p_{t+1}^{-1}(q_{j,t+1} + d_{j,t+1})\right]. \tag{5.8}$$

This equation applies whether consumers are fully insured or not. There is literature associated with variants of this equation, including Grossman and Shiller (1982), Leroy (1982), Leroy and LaCivita (1981), and Lucas (1978).

In Section 3, I mentioned that a great deal of effort has gone into testing this equation using aggregate consumption data. I now point out that even if public risk is fully insurable, equation (5.8) may not hold even approximately when aggregate consumption is substituted for x_{it}. Aggregate consumption in the model of this paper is $\bar{x}_t(s_0, \ldots, s_t) = \int_0^1 E[x_{it} | s_0, \ldots, s_t]\, di$. Assume that $u_i = u$ and $\rho_i = \rho$, for all i. The empirical work referred to tests the equation

$$u'(\bar{x}_t) q_{jt} p_t^{-1} = (1 + \rho)^{-1} E_t\left[u'(\bar{x}_{t+1}) p_{t+1}^{-1}(q_{j,t+1} + d_{j,t+1})\right]. \qquad (5.9)$$

It is not correct to infer (5.9) from (5.8), even if u' happens to be linear because some consumers could have no asset holdings. For these consumers, the left-hand side of (5.8) could exceed the right-hand side. It is at this point that the presence of uninsured risk and the heterogeneity of consumers becomes important. If there were complete markets or if there were only one consumer, (5.8) would always apply. The problem is illustrated by the following example.

EXAMPLE 5.1. For every consumer, $u_i(x) = \log x$ and $\rho_i = \rho > 0$. There is only one asset and the dividend d is nonstochastic and constant over time. For simplicity, suppose that the tax is zero, that there is no money, and that the consumption good is the unit of account. (The inclusion of money does not change the conclusions.) Finally, assume that the a_{it} are independently and identically distributed, as i and t vary, and that $\omega_{it}(a_{it})$ equals one with probability $\frac{1}{2}$ and two with probability $\frac{1}{2}$, for all i and t. Notice that there is no public uncertainty at all, so that insurance of this uncertainty is automatic.

For the purposes of this example, I modify the definition of equilibrium and allocation, so that the allocation to consumer i depends on the infinite history of the process $\{a_{it}\}$. That is, $x_{it} = x_{it}(\ldots, a_{i,t-1}, a_{it})$ and $\theta_{it} = \theta_{it}(\ldots, a_{i,t-1}, a_{it})$.

I now sketch how a stationary equilibrium may be defined. Proofs are contained in another, as yet unfinished paper. Let the price of the consumption good be one and let the price of one share of the asset be q in every period. The implied real rate of return is $R = dq^{-1}$. It can be proved that for each R there is a unique stationary program $(\underset{\sim}{x}_i, \underset{\sim}{\theta}_i)$ optimal for consumer i, where $x_{it} = x(\ldots, a_{i,t-1}, a_{it})$ and $\theta_{it} = \theta(\ldots, a_{i,t-1}, a_{it})$. Since the a_{it} are independently and identically distributed, it follows that the aggregate asset holdings at any time are

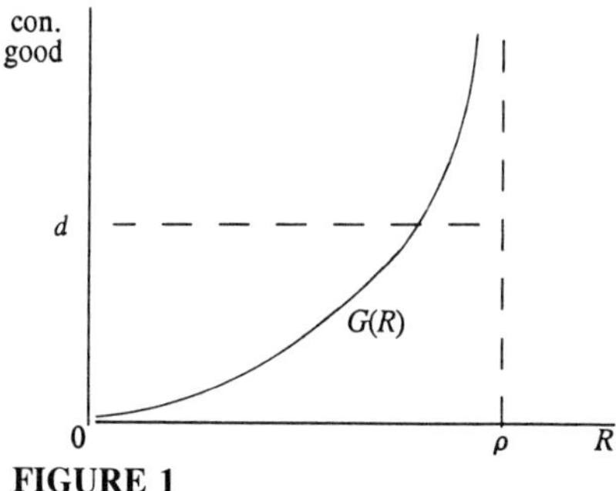

FIGURE 1

$\int_0^1 E\theta_{it}\, di = E\theta_{it}$. It can be proved that this number is of the form $G(R)d^{-1}$, where G is a continuous function of R, for $0 < R < \rho$. It can also be proved that $\lim_{R \to 0} G(R) = 0$ and $\lim_{R \to \rho} G(R) = \infty$. Since equilibrium occurs where $G(R) = d$, it follows that there exists at least one equilibrium. It also follows that R can be any number between 0 and ρ, depending on the size of d. The situation is depicted in Figure 1.

If equation (5.9) applied, then the price of a share of the asset would be $\rho^{-1}d$, whereas it in fact equals $R^{-1}d$, where $R < \rho$. Thus equation (5.9) never holds in this simple example, and the degree to which it does not hold depends in a complicated way on individual uninsurable risk and the amount of asset to be held by consumers.

One might hope to test equation (5.8) by looking at the consumption of luxury goods as an indicator of the consumption by wealthy consumers. Example 5.1 shows that this might be a faulty procedure. In the example, one gains no more information by looking at the aggregate consumption of those who are temporarily wealthy than by looking at the aggregate consumption of all consumers. Both are constant. In order to estimate and test the model, it would be necessary to watch one consumer as he fluctuates between rags and riches.

6. ASSET PRICES WITHOUT INSURANCE

The model becomes much more interesting if one assumes that consumers cannot insure themselves against variation in s_t. I discuss below various topics relating to this case. Points are made by means of a series of examples. I apologize for the crude nature of the examples. They were computed on a hand calculator. More interesting and elegant examples could be calculated on a computer.

6.1 The Distribution of Asset Holdings

It is often assumed in the literature on finance that the utility for consumption has constant relative risk aversion. That is, it is assumed that $u(x) = \ln x$ or $u(x) = x^{1-a}/1 - a$, for $a > 0$ and $a \neq 1$. The chief advantage of this assumption is that the relative quantities of various assets demanded by consumers do not depend on their wealth, where wealth is defined to be the value of current holdings plus the present value of all future income. This statement is true only if the consumers can borrow against all future income. If their future incomes are random, they must in addition be able to insure their future income completely. That is, they must be able to sell contingent claims on all of their future incomes.

If all consumers have the same constant coefficient of relative risk aversion, one can model the demand of all investors as that of a single investor (see Rubenstein, 1974). That is, an Arrow–Debreu model with many consumers can be reduced to one with a single consumer.[4]

This reduction fails when one drops the assumption that there are complete markets for contingent claims. If investors cannot sell contingent claims on their future incomes, then their behavior is guided by their indirect utility for wealth next period, and this utility function may have a highly variable coefficient of relative risk aversion, even if the relative risk aversion of the utility for consumption is constant. For this reason, the prices of risky assets may depend very much on the distribution of wealth among consumers.

The next example shows that the relative risk aversion of the indirect utility for wealth may be variable.

EXAMPLE 6.1. A single consumer has utility for consumption equal to $\ln x$ and discounts future utility at rate $\rho > 0$. In every period, this consumer receives an income of one. The price of the consumption good is always one. The only asset the consumer can hold is money. Money earns no interest. The consumer cannot borrow.

The consumer's indirect utility for money held at the end of period zero is

$$V(M) = \max\left\{ \left| \sum_{t=1}^{\infty} (1+\rho)^{-1} \ln(M_t + 1) \right| \sum_{t=1}^{\infty} M_t = M,\ M_t \geq 0, \text{ all } t \right\}.$$

[4]As Constantinides (1981) has pointed out, in any general equilibrium model with complete markets, an equilibrium may be viewed as that of an economy with a single composite consumer. Thus the assumption of constant relative risk aversion in a sense buys very little in the way of aggregation.

The solution to this problem is

$$V(M) = \sum_{k=1}^{n} (1+\rho)^{-k} \log\left[(1+\rho)^{n-k}(M+n)\left(1+(1+\rho) + \cdots + (1+\rho)^{n-1}\right)\right],$$

if $C_{n-1} \le M \le C_n$, for $n = 1, 2, \ldots,$ where

$$C_n = \rho\left[n + (n-1)(1+\rho) + (n-2)(1+\rho)^2 + \cdots + (1+\rho)^{n-1}\right].$$

The relative risk aversion of V is $R(M) = M(M+n)^{-1}$, when $C_{n-1} \le M \le C_n$, for $n = 1, 2, \ldots$

If $C_{n-1} \le M \le C_n$, then $M_t > 0$ for $t \le n$ and $M_t = 0$ for $t > n$. That is, the consumer distributes expenditure of M over n periods. As M increases, the consumer distributes this expenditure over more and more periods.

Notice that $R(0) = 0$, that $R(M) > 0$, for $M > 0$, and that $\lim_{M\to\infty} R(M) = 0$. That is, $R(M)$ is small for very small M and for very large M. This property seems to be true for many indirect utility functions for wealth. When wealth is small, future consumption is nearly independent of wealth since it is determined by future income. For this reason, the marginal utility of future consumption depends proportionately very little on current wealth and relative risk aversion is small. When wealth is large, the consumer distributes additional amounts of wealth over many periods, so that the marginal utility of future consumption again depends proportionately very little on current wealth.

Roughly speaking, the proportion of an investor's wealth held in risky assets increases as the relative risk aversion of his indirect utility for wealth decreases. For this reason, one might expect that the poorest and the richest investors (in terms of wealth, not income) would be the most inclined to invest in risky assets. The following two examples show that either the poorer or richer consumers could be inclined to bear more risk.

EXAMPLE 6.2. All consumers are identical. Their utility for consumption is $u(x) = \ln x$ and they discount future utility at rate $\rho = 1$. The random variables s_t are independently and identically distributed and equal 0 or 1 with equal probability. The random variables $\{a_{it}\}_{t=-\infty}^{\infty}$ form a Markov chain with states P, M, and R (poor, middle class, and rich). The transition matrix is as shown below:

	P	M	R
P	0.5	0.25	0.25
M	1	0	0
R	1	0	0

The endowment function of each consumer is as follows.

$$\omega_{it}(P) = 1.0098$$

$$\omega_{it}(M) = 4.5553$$

$$\omega_{it}(R) = 8.1007$$

There is one asset. Its dividend, $d_t(s_t)$, is defined to be $d_t(0) = 0$ and $d_t(1) = 0.0098$. There is money. The tax paid by each consumer each period is $\tau = 0.0201$ units of consumption good.

The equilibrium is stationary. In every period, the price of the consumption good is $p = 1$, the interest rate on money is $r = 0.1$ and the price of the asset is $q = 0.4015$. A consumer's program may be written as

$$x_t = x(a_{t-1}, a_t, s_t),$$

$$M_t = M(a_{t-1}, a_t, s_t),$$

$$\theta(a_{t-1}, a_t, s_t).$$

These are as follows:

$$x(P,P,s) = 1 \quad \text{and} \quad \theta(P,P,s) = M(P,P,s) = 0, \quad \text{for } s = 0,1$$

$$x(P,M,s) = 3.6364, \theta(P,M,s) = 2.2641, \quad \text{and}$$

$$M(P,P,s) = 0, \quad \text{for } s = 0,1$$

$$x(P,R,s) = 6, \theta(P,R,s) = 3.7358, \quad \text{and}$$

$$M(P,P,s) = 0.5909, \quad \text{for } s = 0,1$$

$$x(M,P,0) = 1.909 \quad \text{and} \quad x(M,P,1) = 2.1$$

$$x(R,P,0) = 3.15 \quad \text{and} \quad x(R,P,1) = 3.465$$

$$\theta(M,P,s) = \theta(R,M,s) = M(M,P,s) = M(R,P,s) = 0,$$

$$\text{for } s = 0,1$$

Since $M(P,M,s) = \theta(P,M,s) = 0 < M(P,R,s)/\theta(R,P,s) = 0.1582$, for $s = 0,1$, it follows that the relatively poorer investors invest relatively more in the risky asset.

The preceding equilibrium is just like the equilibrium of an overlapping-generations model. Consumers with $a_{it} = M$ or R are like young consumers. Those with $a_{i,t-1} = M$ or R and $a_{it} = P$ are like old consumers. Consumers with $a_{i,t-1} = a_{it} = P$ just consume their endowment. Because of the high rate of time preference, consumers never save anything during a period in which $a_{it} = 0$.

EXAMPLE 6.3. There are four types of consumers. One-fourth of the population is of each type. All consumers have utility for consumption $u(x) = \ln x$. Types 1 and 2 discount future utility at rate $\rho = 0.1$. Types 3 and 4 discount utility at rate $\rho = 0.5$. There are no random variables a_{it}. Consumers of type 1 have endowments defined by $\omega_{1,3t} = 1.1984$ and $\omega_{1,3t+1} = \omega_{1,3t+2} = 1$, for all t. Consumers of type 2 have endowments $\omega_{2,3t} = 1.1578$ and $\omega_{2,3t+1} = \omega_{2,3t+2} = 1$. Consumers of type 3 have endowments $\omega_{3,3t+1} = 1.8033$ and $\omega_{3,3t} = \omega_{3,3t+2} = 1$. Consumers of type 4 have endowments $\omega_{4,3t+2} = 1.7937$ and $\omega_{4,3t} = \omega_{4,3t+1} = 1$.

A new asset is created during every period that is a multiple of 3. In such periods, the asset is the property of agents of type 4. That is, each agent of type 4 holds four units of asset at the beginning of period $3t$. The asset pays a dividend in period $3t + 1$ with probability $\frac{1}{2}$. If it pays a dividend, it is $d = 0.00396$. The asset ceases to exist after period $3t + 1$.

Agents of type 4 pay a tax in periods $3t$. The tax is 0.0532 if the asset paid a dividend in period $3t - 2$. The tax is 0.0543 if no dividend was paid in period $3t - 2$. No other taxes are paid.

It is awkward to have such a random tax, but if no adjustment were made, it would be impossible to have a cyclic equilibrium and so it would be impossible to describe an equilibrium fully.

I now describe a cyclic equilibrium. The price of the consumption good is one in every period. The price of the asset is $q = 0.0018$ (in periods $3t$). Interest rates are as follows:

$$r_{3t} = r_{3t+1} = 0.1 \qquad r'_{3t+1} = 0.095 \qquad r_{3t+2} = 0.1006 \qquad r'_{3t+1} = 0.1,$$

where the prime indicates that a dividend was paid during the period or during the previous period. Consumption is as follows:

$$\begin{array}{lll}
x_{1,3t} = 1.1027 & x_{1,3t+1} = 1.0959 & x'_{1,3t+1} = 1.1038 \\
x_{2,3t} = 1.0827 & x_{2,3t+1} = 1.08 & x'_{2,3t+1} = 1.1085 \\
x_{3,3t} = 1 & x_{3,3t+1} = 1.6274 & x'_{3,3t+1} = 1.6299 \\
x_{4,3t} = 1.1708 & x_{4,3t+1} = 1 & x'_{4,3t+1} = 1 \\
x_{1,3t+2} = 1.0045 & & x'_{1,3t+2} = 1.007 \\
x_{2,3t+2} = 1 & & x'_{2,3t+1} = 1 \\
x_{3,3t+2} = 1.1934 & & x'_{3,3t+1} = 1.1898 \\
x_{4,3t+2} = 1.5957 & & x'_{4,3t+1} = 1.5966,
\end{array}$$

where x_{it} is the consumption of a type i consumer during period t and a prime again indicates that a dividend was paid during the period or during the previous period. The shares of stock held at the end of periods $3t$ is as follows:

$$\theta_{1,3t} = 2.6415, \qquad \theta_{2,3t} = 1.3585, \qquad \theta_{3,3t} = \theta_{4,3t} = 0,$$

where the subscripts have the same meaning as above.

In this example, consumers of type 1 have slightly more income in periods $3t$ than do consumers of type 2, but otherwise the two types are the same. The higher income induces consumers of type 1 to save for two periods, whereas consumers of type 2 save for only one period. The extra period of saving makes consumers of type 1 less relatively risk-averse, and they in fact invest a higher proportion of their assets in the risky asset. At the end of periods $3t$, type 1 consumers hold $M_{1,3t} = 0.0909$ units of money and type 2 agents hold $M_{2,3t} = 0.0727$ units of money. Hence

$$\theta_{1,3t} M_{1,3t}^{-1} = 29.05613 > 18.6798 = \theta_{2,3t} M_{2,3t}^{-1}.$$

Thus, the wealthier agent has a greater tendency to hold the risky asset.

6.2 Who Bears Risk?

An interesting aspect of the previous example is that consumers of type 1 do not bear all the risk arising from the assets they hold. Some of the risk is transferred to consumers of type 3. When dividends are paid, consumers of type 1 receive $\theta_{1,3t} d = 0.0105$. However, when the dividends are paid, their consumption goes up by only $x'_{1,3t+1} - x_{1,3t+1} = 0.080$. The rest of the increase in supply is absorbed by consumers of type 3. That is,

$$\theta_{1,3t} d - (x'_{1,3t+1} - x_{1,3t+1}) = 0.0025 = x'_{3,3t+1} - x_{3,3t+1}.$$

(Consumers of type 2 consume all of their dividend, and the period $3t + 1$ consumption of consumers of type 4 is not affected by the dividend.) Thus, about one-fourth of the risk associated with the asset is transferred from consumers of type 1 to consumers of type 4.

The mechanism of transfer is extremely simple. When consumers of type 1 receive a dividend, they save more. This saving drives down the interest rate (from 0.1 to 0.095) and induces consumers of type 3 to save less and consumer more.

This sort of risk transfer can occur very easily. There is, so to speak, a fixed amount of undiversifiable risk in the economy arising from fluctuations in dividends. The people who bear this risk are those whose consumption varies in sympathy with the dividends. These people are not necessarily the owners of the assets.

The existence of risk transfer among holders of the same asset may be seen by considering equation (5.6), which implies that

$$\begin{aligned} q_t &= (1+\rho_i)^{-1} E_{it}\left[u_i'(x_{i,t+1})(u_i'(x_{it}))^{-1}(q_{j,t+1}+d_{j,t+1})\right] \\ &= (1+\rho_i)^{-1}\operatorname{cov}_{it}\left(u_i'(x_{i,t+1})(u_i'(x_{it}))^{-1}, q_{j,t+1}+d_{j,t+1}\right) \\ &\quad +(1+\rho_i)^{-1}E_{it}\left(u_i'(x_{i,t+1})(u_i'(x_{it}))^{-1}E_t(q_{j,t+1}+d_{j,t+1}\right), \end{aligned}$$

where cov_{it} stands for covariance conditional on information available to consumer i at time t. If inequalities (5.2) and (5.5) hold with equality, then

$$E_{it}\left[u_i'(x_{i,t+1})(u_i'(x_{it}))^{-1}\right] = (1+\rho_i)(1+r_t)^{-1},$$

so that $E_{it}[u_i'(x_{i,t+1})(u_i'(x_{it}))^{-1}]$ is independent of the wealth of a consumer. Hence, by the previous equation

$$R_{it} \equiv \operatorname{cov}_{it}\left(u_i'(x_{i,t+1})(u_i'(x_{it}))^{-1}, q_{j,t+1}+d_{j,t+1}\right)$$

is independent of the wealth of the consumer and even of the shape of the function u_i. But R_{it} is a measure of the risk borne by the investor. Thus, the risk borne by the investor is independent of that person's wealth, even though the proportion of that wealth invested in risky assets may change as that person's wealth changes. This is a way of saying that the distribution of risk bearing in society is not necessarily the same as the distribution of holdings of risky assets.

6.3 Prices and the Distribution of Wealth

It should be clear that the prices of assets can depend on the distribution of wealth among consumers, even if consumers have identical utility functions and endowment functions. It should also be clear that the random dividends on assets affect the distribution of wealth and hence asset prices. These effects occur to a slight extent in the previous example. Because of the interaction between dividends, the distribution of wealth and asset prices, equilibria are very unlikely to be stationary in any sense. In fact, I doubt that stochastically stationary equilibria exist, except in very special cases. One can, of course, achieve a stationary equilibrium by arranging taxes, as I did in the previous example, so as to make the equilibrium cyclic. These taxes must depend on the name of the taxpayer.

6.4 The Results of Mehra and Prescott

As mentioned in Section 3, Mehra and Prescott observe that the difference between the rate of return on equity and that on a risk free asset is too great to be explained by fluctuations in aggregate consumption. They suggest that the discrepancy might be due to uninsured individual risk. The following examples show that when such risk is included, the difference between the returns on equity and on a risk-free asset could be either higher or lower than the difference predicted by a model using aggregate data. Thus, one cannot say that individual uninsured risk would necessarily work in the direction that would account for Mehra and Prescott's results. (I do not mean to imply that Mehra and Prescott asserted that uninsured risk would always work in the right direction. They did not do so.)

EXAMPLE 6.4. The utility for consumption of each consumer is $\ln x$. Consumers discount future utility at rate $\rho = 0.0864$. There are two types of consumers, types 1 and 2. Half of all consumers are of each type. Consumers of type 1 have an endowment of 4.1 in odd periods and zero in even periods. Consumers of type 2 have an endowment of 4.1 in even periods and zero in odd periods. There are two assets, asset 1, which is risk-free, and asset 2, which is risky. The dividends are defined by $d_{1t} = 0.02$, all t, and d_{2t} equals zero with probability $\frac{1}{2}$ and 0.04 with probability $\frac{1}{2}$. There is no money.

I now describe a stationary equilibrium. x_1 denotes the consumption of a consumer who has an endowment of 4.1. x_0 denotes the consumption of a consumer who has endowment zero and when $d_{2t} = 0$. x_0' denotes the consumption of a consumer who has endowment zero and when $d_{2t} = 0.04$. The price of the consumption good is always 1. q_1 and q_2 are the prices of assets 1 and 2, respectively. The following values describe an equilibrium: $x_1 = 2.1349$, $x_0 = 2.0051$, $x_0' = 2.1251$, $q_1 = 0.4$, and $q_2 = 0.5826$.

The rate of return on the risk-free asset is $r_1 = 0.02q_1^{-1} = 0.05$; that on the risky asset is $r_2 = 0.06(2q_2)^{-1} = 0.0515$.

Suppose that one observed only aggregate data. The average consumption per period would be either $x \equiv 2^{-1}(x_0 + x_2) = 2.07$ or $x' \equiv 2^{-1}(x_0' + x_2) = 2.13$. If one knew that the utility function was $\ln x$ and one knew ρ, then one could compute theoretical prices for the assets. Let q_1 and q_2 be these prices for assets 1 and 2, respectively, when asset 2 pays no dividend. Let q_1' and q_2' be the prices when a dividend is paid. The first order conditions give four simultaneous equations for these prices. For instance, one such equation is

$$q_1 x^{-1} = 2^{-1}(1+\rho)^{-1}\left[x^{-1}(q_1 + 0.02) + (x')^{-1}(q_1' + 0.02)\right].$$

Solving these equations, one obtains

$$q_1 = 0.2283,\ q_1' = 0.0235,\ q_2' = 0.03376 \quad \text{and} \quad q_2' = 0.3473.$$

The average rate of return on the risk free asset is,

$$\bar{r}_1 = 0.02\left[(2q_1)^{-1} + (2q_1')^{-1}\right] = \rho = 0.0864.$$

That on the risky asset is

$$\bar{r}_2 = 0.06\left[(4q_2)^{-1} + (4q_2')^{-1}\right] = 0.0876.$$

Proceeding as Mehra and Prescott did, one would predict that the difference in rates of return would be $\bar{r}_2 = \bar{r}_1 = 0.0012$. However, the observed difference would be $r_2 = r_1 = 0.0015$, which exceeds the predicted one, as Mehra and Prescott found to be the case.

EXAMPLE 6.5. This example is the same as the previous one, except for the following changes of parameters. Consumers discount future utility at rate $\rho = 1.7617$. The endowment of consumers when they have an endowment is 5.4484. The dividend on the risky asset is $d_2 = 0.3$, when a dividend is paid.

The equilibrium is as follows:

$$x_1 = 4, \qquad x_0 = 1.4884, \qquad x_0' = 2.0884, \qquad q_1 = 0.1, \qquad q_2 = 0.6241.$$

The returns on the assets are $r_1 = 0.2$ and $r_2 = 0.2403$. Considering the aggregated model, as before, one obtains $\bar{r}_1 = \rho = 1.7617$ and $\bar{r}_2 = 1.8580$. Since $\bar{r}_2 - \bar{r}_1 = 0.0963 > 0.0403 = r_2 - r_1$, the aggregated model would predict a higher difference in rates of return than would be observed.

6.5 The Risk-Free Asset

In the literature on asset prices, frequent mention is made of risk-free assets. Such an asset usually corresponds to a bond whose return is indexed to the consumer price level. In a one-commodity world, the coupon payment of such a bond would be a constant amount of the commodity. It may be perfectly sensible to call such a bond risk-free, but it should not be believed that the bond would have the lowest rate of return of all asset returns. If prices went up in good times and down in bad times, then the short-term nonindexed bonds would be more valuable than indexed bonds, for the real value of a nonindexed bond would increase during bad times, precisely when wealth would be most needed. That is, the nonindexed bond would be less risky and earn a lower rate of return than would the indexed bond.

Nonindexed bonds correspond to what I have called money in the model of Section 4. The next example illustrates that money would earn a lower rate of return than a risk-free asset.

Remark. The following example differs from the model of Section 4 in that consumers' endowments depend on the publicly observed random variable s_t. A similar but more complicated example could be constructed by including an asset with a dividend that was correlated with the price level.

EXAMPLE 6.6. The random variables s_t are independently and identically distributed over time. Each s_t takes on either of the two values 0 or 1 with equal probability. There are no random variables a_t. There are two types of consumers, 0 and 1, and half of all consumers are of each type. The endowment of each type depends on s_t. The endowment of type 0 is defined by

$$\omega_{2t}^{0}(s_{2t}) = \begin{cases} 3, & \text{if } s_{2t} = 0 \\ 2.8, & \text{if } s_{2t} = 1 \end{cases}$$

and

$$\omega_{2t+1}^{0}(s_{2t+1}) = \begin{cases} 0, & \text{if } s_{2t+1} = 0 \\ 1.2, & \text{if } s_{2t+1} = 1. \end{cases}$$

The endowment of type 1 is defined by $\omega_t^1(s_t) = \omega_{t+1}^0(s_t)$. The utility function of every consumer is $u(x) = \ln x$. All consumers discount future utility at rate $\rho = 1$. The tax function is $\tau_t(s_t)$, and is defined by

$$\tau_t(s_2) = \begin{cases} 0.2, & \text{if } s_t = 0 \\ 0, & \text{if } s_t = 1 \end{cases}$$

There are no assets other than money.

I describe an equilibrium for this economy that is stationary in the sense that all variables depend only on s_t. I use the following notation:

$x_t^i(s_t)$ is the consumption of type i in period t.
$p_t(s_t)$ is the price of the consumption good in period t.
$r_t(s_t)$ is the interest rate on money held from period t to $t + 1$.
$M_t(s_t)$ is the money supply at the end of period t.

The following defines an equilibrium:

$$x_{2t}^{0}(0) = x_{2t}^{0}(1) = x_{2t+1}^{1}(0) = x_{2t+t}^{1}(1) = x_{2t+1}^{0}(1) = x_{2t}^{1}(1) = 2,$$

$$x_{2t+1}^{0}(0) = x_{2t}^{1}(0) = 1, \qquad p_t(0) = 1, \qquad p_t(1) = \tfrac{3}{2},$$

$$r_t(0) = \tfrac{1}{2}, \qquad r_t(1) = 0, \qquad M_t(0) = \tfrac{4}{5}, \qquad M_t(1) = \tfrac{6}{5}.$$

There is no risk-free asset in the model, but one can calculate what rate of return it would earn if an infinitesimal amount of it were included. Suppose that a unit of the asset paid a dividend of one unit of consumption good in every period. Let $q(s_t)$ be the price of the asset. Then the numbers $q(0)$ and $q(1)$ satisfy the equations

$$q(s_{2t})\left(x_{2t}^0(s_{2t})\right)^{-1} = 4^{-1}E\left[\left(x_{2t+1}^0(s_{2t+1})\right)^{-1}\left(q(s_{2t}) + p_{2t+1}(s_{2t+1})\right)\right],$$

for $s_t = 0, 1$. The solution of these equations is $q(0) = 3$ and $q(1) = 4.5$. The implied rates of return, $R_t(s_t)$, are $R_t(0) = \frac{2}{3}$ and $R_t(1) = \frac{1}{9}$. Since the rates of return on money are $r_t(0) = \frac{1}{2}$ and $r_t(1) = 0$, they are less than the rates of return on the risk free asset in both states of the world. The risk-free asset is more risky than money. This is so because the price level is positively correlated with endowments during the period in which consumers spend their savings.

7. A POSSIBLE EXPLANATION OF VOLATILITY

Recall that the work of Grossman and Shiller (1981), Hall (1988), and Hansen and Singleton (1983) studied

$$\operatorname{cov}\left(E_t\left[u'(x_{t+1})(u'(x_t))^{-1}\right], E_t\left[(q_{t+1} + d_{t+1})q_t^{-1}p_t p_{t+1}^{-1}\right]\right). \qquad (7.1)$$

The general conclusion to be drawn from this work seems to be that there is not enough covariation between expected consumption and expected asset returns to explain the volatility of asset prices.

I propose that an explanation for volatility be sought by looking for fluctuations in

$$\operatorname{cov}_t\left(u'(x_{t+1})(u'(x_t))^{-1}, (q_{t+1} + d_{t+1})q_t^{-1}p_t p_{t+1}^{-1}\right). \qquad (7.2)$$

Observe that this covariance could fluctuate even if the covariance (7.1) were zero. Positivity of (7.1) would imply simultaneous fluctuations of returns on all assets. Fluctuations in (7.2) would correspond to fluctuations in risk premia only. The returns on riskless assets might not fluctuate at all.

It is easy to see how the covariance in (7.2) could vary and vary in sympathy with asset prices. Suppose that the relative risk aversion of investors' indirect utility for wealth decreases as wealth increases, at least for sufficiently high levels of wealth. Example (6.1) indicates that this might be a reasonable assumption. One could imagine that the wealthy use their assets in order to insure themselves against fluctuations in consumption. The assumption implies that the wealthier consumers would tend to invest a higher proportion of their wealth in risky assets than would poorer consumers. Now suppose that there is bad news and that dividends from risky assets are expected to decline. This news would lead to a decline in the price of risky assets and hence to a decline in the wealth of the wealthy. The decline in wealth would in turn increase the relative risk aversion of their indirect utility for wealth and so would make them less inclined to hold risky assets. The resulting decrease in demand for risky assets could lead to a further decrease in their price. The increase in the relative risk aversion of the wealthy would correspond to an increase in the perceived value of the covariance (7.2).

Shiller (1982) finds that real returns on long-term bonds, on land, and on housing have historically not moved in sympathy with each other and with real returns on stocks. He interprets this as evidence against the intertemporal pricing model represented by equation (2.4) or (5.8). He does so because he thinks of the model as implying that the covariance (7.1) should be positive. However, the model is also consistent with fluctuations in the covariance (7.2). If it is these fluctuations that are responsible for excess volatility, then it need not be the case that all asset prices move together. For instance, the real rate of return on long-term bonds increased during the great depression, whereas that on stocks decreased dramatically. The increase in long-term bond returns may have occurred because the effects of deflation overcame the effect of increased risk premia. Of course, it may be that the real coupon payments on long-term bonds have fluctuated very little historically, just as real dividends have fluctuated little (Shiller, 1981b). If this is the case, then any single explanation of volatility would require that real returns on stocks and bonds move more or less together.

When one says that an investor's risk aversion increases, one means that the investor perceives an increase in the covariance between next period's asset returns and consumption. One might imagine that if individuals suffered a covariance between asset returns and consumption, then the same covariation should be observed in the aggregate. As I mentioned in Section 3, no one has tested whether such a covariation exists. However, the absence of covariation would not be sufficient reason to reject the above explanation of volatility. Many consumers may be saturated with risky assets because of wide variation in risk aversion (as measured from the indirect utility for wealth). That is, many may hold essentially nothing but risky assets. They may hold low return, low risk assets and money only for making transactions. Also, many other consumers may hold no financial assets at all, except for money for making transactions. Only a small proportion of all consumers might be at the margin where they would hold both high- and low-risk assets. It is only to these consumers that equation (5.8) applies. The covariation between the consumption and asset returns of the few marginal investors might not be apparent in aggregate data.

Townsend (1987) has proposed an explanation of volatility that is related to but distinct from that given above. He considers a model with a Clower payments constraint that requires that purchases be paid for with money. He points out that in such a model, money enjoys a liquidity premium, so that equilibrium real returns on money could be less than those on other assets. Fluctuations in this premium could lead to anomalous asset price behavior.

It should be clear that Townsend's explanation is distinct from that given here. I have pointed to the possibility of fluctuations in risk premia, not liquidity premia. In Townsend's model, consumers could be very wealthy in the sense of this paper and yet suddenly and temporarily be short of cash for making transactions.

It should be possible to test the explanation I have given of excess volatility. A really good test would require panel data on the asset holdings, income, and consumption of individuals. Such data are, no doubt, unavailable. However, one could make a crude test similar to the variance bound tests of Leroy and Porter (1981) and Shiller. This test would test the hypothesis that the discount rate on future real dividends or coupon payments is a constant plus a multiple of some measure of investors' aggregate wealth. The multiple would have to be estimated. In order for this test to make any sense, it should be applied to the prices and returns of individual assets, and the measure of investors' aggregate wealth should include all privately held liquid assets.

Acknowledgment

The research reported here was done with the support of National Science Foundation Grant No. SES-79-06672.

References

Bewley, T. (1986). "Stationary monetary equilibrium with a continuum of independently fluctuating consumers," Chapter 5 in *Contributions to Mathematical Economics in Honor of Gerard Debreu* (North Holland, Amsterdam), pp. 79–102.

Breeden, D. (1979). "On intertemporal asset pricing model with stochastic consumption and investment opportunities," *J. Financial Econ.* **7**, 265–296.

Brock, W. (1982). "Asset prices in a production economy," in *The Economics of Information and Uncertainty* J. J. McCall (ed.), (University of Chicago Press).

Constantinides, G. M. (1982). "Intertemporal asset pricing with heterogeneous consumers and without demand aggregation," *J. Business* **55**, 253–267.

Easley, D. and R. Jarrow (1981). "Security market efficiency: A definition and clarification," Cornell University Discussion Paper.

Ekern, S., and R. Wilson (1974). "On the theory of the firm in an economy with incomplete markets," *Bell J. Econ. Management Sci.* **5**, 171–180.

Fama, E. (1970). "Efficient capital markets: A review of theory and empirical work," *J. Finance* **25**, 383–417.

Fama, E. (1976). "Reply," *J. Finance* **31**, 143–145.

Friesen, P. (1979). "The Arrow–Debreu model extended to financial markets," *Econometrica* **47**, 689–707.
Grossman, S., and R. Shiller (1981). "The determinants of the variability of stock prices," *Am. Econ. Rev.*, **71**, 222–227.
Grossman, S., and R. Shiller (1982). "Consumption correlation and risk measurement in economies with non-traded assets and heterogeneous information," *J. Financial Econ.* **10**, 195–210.
Hall, R. (1988). "Intertemporal substitution in consumption," *J. Political Econ.* **96**, 339–357.
Hanson, L. P., and K. Singleton (1983). "Stochastic consumption, risk aversion and the temporal behavior of asset returns," *J. Political Econ.* **91**, 249–265.
Howrey, E. P., and S. Hymans (1978). "The measurement and determination of loanable-funds saving," *Brookings Papers in Economic Activity*, 655–705.
Jensen, M. (1978). "Some anomalous evidence regarding market efficiency," *J. Financial Econ.* **6**, 95–101.
Jordan, J. (1983). "On the efficient markets hypothesis," *Econometrica* **51**, 1325–1343.
Kleidon, A. (1986). "Variance bounds tests and stock price valuation models," *J. Political Econ.* **94**, 953–1001.
Leroy, S. (1976). "Efficient capital markets: Comment," *J. Finance* **31**, 139–141.
Leroy, S. (1982). "Expectations models of asset prices: A survey of theory," *J. Finance* **37**, 185–217.
Leroy, S., and C. J. LaCivita (1981). "Risk aversion and the dispersion of asset prices," *J. Business* **54**, 535–547.
Leroy, S., and R. Porter (1981). "The present-value relation: Tests based on implied variance bounds," *Econometrica* **49**, 555–574.
Lucas, R. (1978). "Asset prices in an exchange economy," *Econometrica* **46**, 1429–1445.
Mehra, R., and E. C. Prescott (1985). "The equity premium: A puzzle," *J. Monetary Econ.* **15**, 145–161.
Ross, S. (1976). "Options and efficiency," *Quart. J. Econ.* **90**, 75–89.
Ross, S. (1978). "A simple approach to the variation of risky streams," *J. Business* **51**, 453–475.
Rubenstein, M. (1974). "A aggregation theorem for securities markets," *J. Financial Econ.* **1**, 225–244.
Rubenstein, M. (1975). "Securities market efficiency in an Arrow–Debreu economy," *Am. Econ. Rev.* **65**, 812–824.
Schechtman, J. (1976). "An income fluctuation problem," *J. Econ. Theory* **12**, 218–241.
Schechtman, J., and V. Escudero (1977). "Some results on 'an income fluctuation problem'," *J. Econ. Theory* **16**, 151–166.
Shiller, R. (1979). "The volatility of long-term interest rates and expectations models of the term structure," *J. Political Econ.* **87**, 1190–1219.
Shiller, R. (1981a). "Alternative tests of rational expectations models: The case of the term structure," *J. Econometrics* **16**, 71–87.
Shiller, R. (1981b). "Do stock prices move too much to be justified by subsequent changes in dividends?" *Am. Econ. Rev.* **71**, 421–436.
Shiller, R. (1981c). "The use of volatility measures in assessing market efficiency," *J. Finance* **36**, 291–304.
Shiller, R. (1982). "Consumption, asset markets and macroeconomic fluctuations," *Senses on Public Policy* **17**, 203–238.
Singleton, K. (1980). "Expectations models of the term structure and implied variance bounds," *J. Political Econ.* **88**, 1159–1176.
Townsend, R. (1987). "Asset return anomalies in a monetary economy," *J. Econ. Theory* **41**, 219–247.
Verrecchia, R. E. (1980). "Consensus beliefs, information acquisition, and information efficiency," *Am. Econ. Rev.* **70**, 874–884.
West, K. (1988). "Bubbles, fads and stock price volatility tests: A partial evaluation," *J. Finance* **43**, 639–656.

STATIONARY MARKOVIAN STRATEGIES IN DYNAMIC GAMES

Rose-Anne Dana
Laboratoire de Mathematiques Fondamentals
Université Pierre et Marie Curie
Paris 75252, France

Luigi Montrucchio
Instituto di Matematica Finanziaria
Universita' di Torino
Turin 10122, Italy

1. INTRODUCTION

In the last 15 years, infinite-horizon discrete time dynamic games where agents discount the future have been used in a variety of economic models. Several authors have considered the problem of stationary Markovian strategies. While it is very well known that the one-agent optimal growth model and the intertemporal equilibrium model are strongly related, it is less emphasized that dynamic games with stationary strategies are at the junction of two lines of research, namely, optimal growth and dynamic game theory. The main difficulty with the analysis arises from the fact that nonconvexities are inherent to such problems.

The purpose of this paper is to study a number of models that have appeared in the literature by stressing the analogies between the dynamic game models and the dynamic programming framework. We review some known results, give new proofs of others, and present some new results. While we have tried to stress the difficulty of the existence problems and the lack of generality in the results obtained, we have also emphasized the link between these models and the infinite-horizon dynamic programming. In fact, this link enables us to give a general method in the spirit of Boldrin and Montrucchio's (1986) method. In particular, we show that their method to construct chaotic examples can be extended to most models described here.

The first model we present is the closest one to the one-sector growth model. It is a model of strategic intertemporal resource allocation where

GENERAL EQUILIBRIUM, GROWTH, AND TRADE II

players maximize the discounted utilities sum of their own consumptions. The symmetric n-agent case has been discussed by Sundaram (1989a, 1989b). The method he uses is based on two different sets of techniques. The first one, initiated by Dechert and Nishimura (1983), relates to optimal growth with increasing marginal returns. The second one, started with Bernheim and Ray (1987) and Leininger (1986), is used for growth models with intergenerational altruism.

We shall present here a simplified version of the proof of existence of equilibrium given by Sundaram. It remains an open question as to whether it can be generalized to the nonsymmetric case or to higher dimensions.

Section 3 is devoted to the study of Markov perfect equilibria in Maskin and Tirole's (1988) duopoly game. The two agents move alternately, and it is assumed that the choice of each agent depends only on the last choice of the opponent agent. Although it is difficult to state general theorems on the existence of Markov perfect equilibria, we calculate the equilibria for the quadratic case. Moreover, we give a couple of examples that show the existence of chaotic perfect equilibria.

Finally, in Section 4 we analyze the same duopoly game but with simultaneous moves for the two agents and construct several examples as well.

2. A DYNAMIC GAME MODEL OF RESOURCE EXPLOITATION

This section is concerned with the model of infinite-horizon duopoly game stemming from the exploitation of common property resources. It is described by Sundaram (1989a, 1989b).

Time is discrete, and the horizon is infinite. Periods are indexed by $t(t = 0, 1, 2, \dots)$. The environment is stationary. At each date there is a single good that can be either consumed or used as input for production.

The two agents' preferences are identical and described by the additively separable utility functions U: $\mathbb{R}_+^\infty \to \mathbb{R}$ defined by $U(c) = \sum_{t=0}^{\infty} u(c_t)\delta^t$, and where $c = (c_t)_0^\infty$ and $0 < \delta < 1$ is the common discount factor of two agents.

The one-period felicity function $u(c)$ is assumed to be strictly increasing and strictly concave.

The technology is invariant through time and is described by a production function f: $\mathbb{R}_+ \to \mathbb{R}_+$. It will be assumed that f is continuous and strictly increasing on $\mathbb{R}_+$, $f(0) = 0$ and there exists a level $x^* > 0$ such that $f(x) \leq x$ for all $x \geq x^*$. In the context of resource games $f(x)$ can be interpreted as the natural one-period growth rate of the resource.

The dynamics of common-property capital is governed by $x_{t+1} = f(x_t - c_t^1 - c_t^2)$, with $0 \leq c_t^1 + c_t^2 \leq x_t$ and where c_t^1, c_t^2 are the consumptions by the two agents at stage t.

Given an initial stock $x_0 > 0$, we define $s_0 = \max(x_0, x^*)$ and $S = [0, s_0]$. The interval S that is invariant under f will be the state space.

Let us assume that the two agents are identical and consider dynamic strategies of consumption that depend only on the current state of the capital stock. Whenever agent i expects agent j to use a stationary (time-invariant) dynamic strategy $c = \gamma(x)$, he or she must solve the following problem:

$$V_\gamma(x_0) = \sup \sum_{t=0}^{\infty} u(c_t)\delta^t \qquad \text{s.t.}$$

$0 \leq c_t \leq x_t - \gamma(x_t)$, $x_{t+1} = f(x_t - \gamma(x_t) - c_t)$ for all $t \geq 0$ and x_0 given.

Since the constraints are not convex, this is a nonconcave optimization problem. The method we shall next develop is very close to that used by Dechert and Nishimura (1983).

It follows from standard dynamic programming arguments [see, for instance, Theorems 4.2 and 4.3 Stokey and Lucas (1989)] that $V_\gamma(x)$ is the unique bounded solution to Bellman's equation:

$$V_\gamma(x) = \sup_c\left[u(c) + \delta V_\gamma(f(x - \gamma(x) - c))\right]$$

$$\text{s.t.} \qquad 0 \leq c \leq x - \gamma(x). \tag{2.1}$$

We shall say that the map γ is a (*symmetric*) *stationary equilibrium* if $c = \gamma(x)$ solves (2.1), i.e., if

$$\gamma(x) \in \operatorname{argmax}_c\left[u(c) + \delta V_\gamma(f(x - \gamma(x) - c))\right]$$

$$\text{s.t.} \qquad 0 \leq c \leq x - \gamma(x).$$

In other words, the pair $c^1 = \gamma(x)$, $c^2 = \gamma(x)$ is a Nash equilibrium where both players employ the same dynamic strategy. Of course this Nash equilibrium satisfies subgame perfection concept [see Sundaram (1989a) for details].

However, without some assumption of regularity for γ, there may exist no best response to γ. More importantly, the best response, whenever it exists, may fail to be unique since the problem is not concave.

We shall prove that the best-response function exists and it can be selected univocally if γ belongs to the functional space Γ described below;

$\gamma \in \Gamma$ iff

(i) γ maps S into itself;
(ii) γ is lower semicontinuous on S;
(iii) $[\gamma(x) - \gamma(x')]/(x - x') \leq \frac{1}{2}$ for all x, x' in S;
(iv) $\gamma(0) = 0$.

It should be noted that (ii) and (iii) imply that any function $\gamma \in \Gamma$ is right continuous, while from (iii), (iv) it follows that $0 \leq \gamma(x) \leq x/2$, i.e., dynamic constraints $0 \leq c_t^1 + c_t^2 \leq x_t$ are fulfilled in equilibrium at each date.

Now define the new space of functions Ψ, with elements $\psi(x) = x - 2\gamma(x)$, for $\gamma \in \Gamma$. It is not difficult to check that all functions ψ satisfy:

(i) $\psi: S \to S$.
(ii) ψ is upper semicontinuous.
(iii) $0 \leq \psi(x) \leq x$ and ψ is nondecreasing.

If we replace in (2.1) c and $\gamma(x)$ with $a = x - \gamma(x) - c$ and $\psi(x) = x - 2\gamma(x)$ respectively, Bellman's equation becomes

$$V_\psi(x) = \sup_a\big(u[(x + \psi(x))/2 - a] + \delta V_\psi(f(a))\big)$$
$$\text{s.t.} \qquad 0 \leq a \leq (x + \psi(x))/2 \tag{2.2}$$

Suppose that $a = \psi(x)$ solves (2.2). Coming back to the old variables, we have $x - \gamma(x) - c = x - 2\gamma(x)$, i.e., $c = \gamma(x)$. It follows that $\gamma(x)$ solves (2.1), i.e., $\gamma(x)$ is a stationary equilibrium. Note that $a = \psi(x) = x - 2\gamma(x)$ has an obvious interpretation as saving function: a is the amount of good assigned to accumulation, when both players use the same consumption policy $c = \gamma(x)$.

If we define the correspondence

$$F_\psi(x) = \operatorname{argmax}_a\big(u[(x + \psi(x))/2 - a] + \delta V_\psi(f(a))\big)$$
$$0 \leq a \leq (x + \psi(x))/2 \tag{2.3}$$

then we can say that γ is a stationary equilibrium iff $\psi = Id - 2\gamma$ satisfies $\psi(x) \in F_\psi(x)$ for every x in S.

The following results justifies the choice of the functional class Ψ. They rest on dynamic programming methods.

Proposition 2.1. *Assume $\psi \in \Psi$. Then*

(*i*) *The value function $V_\psi(\cdot)$ is upper semicontinuous and nondecreasing. If $\psi_1 \leq \psi_2$, then $V_{\psi_1} \leq V_{\psi_2}$. In particular:*

$$V_0 \leq V_\psi \leq V_{id} \text{ holds for all } \psi \in \Psi.$$

(*ii*) *The correspondence* $F_\psi(\cdot)$: $S \to S$ *is nondecreasing.*

(*iii*) *There exists a unique* $\psi^* \in \Psi$ *such that* $\psi^*(x) \in F_\psi(x)$, *i.e., there is one and only one best response to* γ *within the functional class* Γ. *Moreover,* $\psi^*(x) = \max(y; y \in F_\psi(x))$.

The proofs of these statements are given in the Appendix.

We can now state the main theorem of this section [see also Theorem 4.1 in Sundaram (1989a)].

THEOREM 2.2. *There exists a symmetric stationary equilibrium within the class of lower-semicontinuous consumption policies* $c = \gamma(x)$ *with slopes bounded above on* S *by* $\frac{1}{2}$. *The corresponding saving function* $\psi(x) = x - 2\gamma(x)$ *turns out to be nondecreasing and right continuous.*

The method of proving Theorem 2.2 will be based on showing that the map $\psi \to \psi^*$ has a fixed point. Up to now we have taken a purely algebraic point of view. However, in order to prove the existence of a fixed point, we need to endow the set Ψ with a weak topology.

Let $\mathscr{BV}(S)$ denote the Banach space of right-continuous functions on S that are zero at zero and have bounded variation, endowed with the variation norm. It is well known that $\mathscr{BV}(S)$ is the dual of the space of continuous functions on S. Therefore $\mathscr{BV}(S)$ can be endowed with the weak-star topology.

As it has been remarked in the proof of Proposition 2.1, the functions $\psi \in \Psi$ are right continuous, thus the space Ψ, which is clearly convex, is a subset of $\mathscr{BV}(S)$. Furthermore, the space Ψ, endowed with the topology of weak convergence (w), will also be compact since it is weakly closed and contained into a ball of radius s_0.

Let us recall that a sequence ψ_n weakly (w) converges to ψ iff $\psi_n(s) \to \psi(s)$ for all $s \in [0, s_0)$ such that ψ is continuous at s and $\psi_n(s_0) \to \psi(s_0)$ (see Billingsley, 1968).

Analogously, we endow the set of value functions with the topology of weak convergence. Clearly $V_\psi(x) \leq u(s_0)/(1-\delta)$ holds for all $x \in S$, and thus they are contained in a ball, too.

We need now some technical lemmas. Throughout the rest of the paper we shall denote with $g(x^-)$ the left limit of the function g at the point x.

LEMMA 2.3. *Assume* $g_n \overset{w}{\to} g$, *with* $g_n \in \mathscr{BV}(S)$ *and* g_n *nondecreasing. Then for every sequence* $x_n \to x$, *limsup* $g_n(x_n) \leq g(x)$ *and liminf* $g_n(x_n) \geq g(x^-)$, *as* $n \to \infty$. *In particular, lim* $g_n(x_n) = g(x)$, *if* x *is a continuity point for* g.

LEMMA 2.4. *Assume* $\psi_n \overset{w}{\to} \psi$. *Let* V_n *and* V *be the associated value functions. Let* ψ *be continuous at* x. *If* $a \in [0, (x + \psi(x))/2)$, *then there exists a subsequence* n_k *and a sequence* $a_k \to a$ (*from the right*) *such that*

(*i*) $a_k \in [0, (x + \psi_{n_k}(x))/2]$ *for any* k.
(*ii*) $\lim V_{n_k}(f(a_k)) = V(f(a))$ *as* $k \to \infty$.

Lemma 2.3 will be discussed in Section 6. Lemma 2.4 comes from Sundaram (1989b).

We can now proceed to the proof of Theorem 2.2, by showing that the map $\psi \to \psi^*$ is continuous whenever Ψ is endowed with the weak topology. As Ψ is metrisable we may make use of sequential properties.

Let $\psi_n \to \psi$, weakly, and let ψ_n^* and V_n denote the associated best replies and value functions, respectively. Then some subsequence of (ψ_n^*, V_n) will weakly converge to some (ψ^*, V). Let us show that ψ^* is the best reply to ψ and V is its value function.

Let A denote the subset of $[0, s_0)$ of common continuity points of ψ, ψ^* and V. The set A^c turns out to be countable.

Fix now a point $x \in A$. In view of (2.2), for every n we have

$$\begin{aligned} V_n(x) &= u\big((\tfrac{1}{2})(x + \psi_n(x)) - \psi_n^*(x)\big) + \delta V_n\big(f(\psi_n^*(x))\big) \\ &\geq u\big((\tfrac{1}{2})(x + \psi_n(x)) - a\big) + \delta V_n(f(a)) \end{aligned}$$

for all $0 \leq a \leq (\frac{1}{2})(x + \psi_n(x))$.

Since $\psi_n^*(x) \to \psi^*(x)$, $f(\psi_n^*(x)) \to f(\psi^*(x))$, and $\psi_n(x) \to \psi(x)$, it follows from Lemma 2.3 that

$$V(x) = \lim_n V_n(x) \leq u\big((\tfrac{1}{2})(x + \psi(x)) - \psi^*(x)\big) + \delta V\big(f(\psi^*(x))\big) \tag{2.4}$$

From Lemma 2.4 we know that for every $a \in [0, (x + \psi(x))/2)$, it is possible to choose an adequate subsequence n_k such that for the associated sequence a_k one has

$$V_{n_k}(x) \geq u\big((x + \psi_{n_k}(x))/2 - a_k\big) + \delta V_{n_k}(f(a_k)).$$

Taking the limit as k goes to infinity, we get

$$V(x) \geq u((x + \psi(x))/2 - a) + \delta V(f(a)) \tag{2.5}$$

for all $0 \leq a < (x + \psi(x))/2$.

Let us now prove that (2.5) holds also for the final point $a = (x + \psi(x))/2$.

In fact, $V_n(x) \geq u(0) + \delta V_n(f(x + \psi_n(x))/2))$ holds for any n and x in A. Let y be any $y > x$ and $y \in A$. Since

$$V_n(y) \geq u(0) + \delta V_n\big(f(y + \psi_n(y))/2)\big)$$

it follows from Lemma 2.3 that

$$\liminf V_n(y) = \lim V_n(y) = V(y) \geq u(0) + \delta V(f(y + \psi(y))/2)^{-}).$$

On the other hand, $V(x) = \inf(V(y); y > x \text{ and } y \in A)$, thus

$$V(x) \geq u(0) + \delta \inf V(f(y + \psi(y))/2)^{-}).$$

Since $V(f(y + \psi(y))/2)^{-}) \geq V(f(x + \psi(x))/2))$ for any $y > x$, we have

$$V(x) \geq u(0) + \delta V(f(x + \psi(x))/2))$$

and thus (2.5) is valid for any $a \in [0, (x + \psi(x))/2]$.

It should be noted that the last argument requires that there exist points $y > x$, and therefore it fails for the end point $x = s_0$.

Equations (2.4) and (2.5) imply that ψ^* is the best reply to ψ and V is its value function whenever $x \in A$. Now let ψ' denote the optimal response to ψ. Since $\psi^* = \psi'$ over A and ψ^*, ψ' are both right continuous and nondecreasing, then they must agree everywhere on $[0, s_0)$. To complete the proof of the continuity, we need to prove that $\psi^*(s_0) = \psi'(s_0)$. If this is true, then the map $\psi \to \psi^*$ is continuous. From Schauder and Tychonoff's theorem it follows the existence of a fixed point and thus Theorem 2.2 is proven.

To check that $\psi^*(s_0) = \psi'(s_0)$ we enlarge the state space by an amount η. Thus the new space is now $S^\wedge = [0, s_0 + \eta]$. As S is invariant, whenever $\psi_1 = \psi_2$ over S, it follows that $V_{\psi_1} = V_{\psi_2}$ and $\psi_1^* = \psi_2^*$ over S.

Given an element $\psi \in \Psi$, its extension $\psi^\wedge$ on $S^\wedge$ is defined as $\psi^\wedge(x) = \psi(x)$ for all $x \in S$ and $\psi^\wedge(x) = \psi(s_0)$ for $0 \leq x \leq s_0 + \eta$. Of course, if $\psi_n \to \psi$, weakly on S, then $\psi_n^\wedge \to \psi^\wedge$, weakly on $S^\wedge$. Now let ψ_n weakly converge to ψ on S such that $\psi_n^* \to \psi^*$, weakly on S. By taking subsequence we can guarantee that

(i) $\psi_n^\wedge \to \psi^\wedge$, weakly on $S^\wedge$;
(ii) $(\psi_n^\wedge)^* \to \rho$, weakly on $S^\wedge$;
(iii) $(\psi_n^\wedge)^* \to \rho$, weakly on S.

As $(\psi_n^\wedge)^*$ agree with ψ_n^* over S, it follows from (iii) that ρ agrees with ψ^* over S. On the other hand, from the previous proof it follows that ρ agrees with the best response $(\psi^\wedge)'$ over $[0, s_0 + \eta)$. Thus we have $\psi^*(s_0) = \rho(s_0) = (\psi^\wedge)'(s_0) = \psi'(s_0)$, which completes our proof.

2.1 Nonsymmetric Stationary Equilibria: Some Examples

There is no solution yet to the nonsymmetric case, which is much more difficult since one does not have an invariant space as in the symmetric case. Let us, however, conclude this section by directly computing the stationary equilibria for a couple of examples taken from Levhari and Mirman (1980).

In the first example $u_i(c) = \log c$ for $i = 1, 2$ and $f(x) = x^\alpha$, $0 < \alpha < 1$. Given agent 2's strategy γ_2, agent 1 solves the following dynamic programming problem:

$$\max \sum_{t=0}^{\infty} \log\left[x_t - \gamma_2(x_t) - x_{t+1}^{1/\alpha}\right] \delta_1^t$$

subject to constraints

$$0 \leq x_{t+1} \leq \left(x_t - \gamma_2(x_t)\right)^\alpha, \qquad t = 0, 1, 2, \ldots$$

and symmetrically for agent 2.

We show the following.

PROPOSITION 2.5. *For any pair of discount factors (δ_1, δ_2) there exists a unique stationary linear equilibrium that is dynamically stable.*

Of course, this does not imply that there exists a unique equilibrium.

Let us assume that $\gamma_i(x) = l_i x$ for some $0 < l_i < 1$, $i = 1, 2$. Since the utility and production function satisfy an infinite boundary condition, the optimal solution to agent 1's problem is interior and satisfies the Euler equation:

$$\frac{\delta_1(1 - l_2)}{x_t(1 - l_2) - x_{t+1}^{1/\alpha}} = \frac{(1/\alpha)\, x_t^{(1/\alpha)-1}}{x_{t-1}(1 - l_2) - x_t^{1/\alpha}}$$

and symmetrically for player 2.

Setting $z_t = x_{t-1}^{-1} x_t^{1/\alpha}$ and solving for the stationary solution in z, we get the following solution to Euler's equation:

$$x_t = \left((1 - l_2)\alpha\delta_1 x_{t-1}\right)^\alpha,$$

which converges to $x^* = ((1 - l_2)\alpha\delta_1)^{\alpha/(1-\alpha)}$. Thus it is optimal since it satisfies the transversality condition (see Stokey and Lucas, 1989).

The associated consumptions turn out to be

$$c_t^1 = (1 - l_2)(1 - \alpha\delta_1)x_t \quad \text{and} \quad c_t^2 = (1 - l_1)(1 - \alpha\delta_2)x_t.$$

Therefore, we easily get

$$l_1 = \alpha\delta_2(1 - \alpha\delta_1)/\left[1 - (1 - \alpha\delta_1)(1 - \alpha\delta_2)\right]$$

$$l_2 = \alpha\delta_1(1 - \alpha\delta_2)/\left[1 - (1 - \alpha\delta_1)(1 - \alpha\delta_2)\right]$$

Levhari and Mirman also consider the case where $f(x) = rx$, $0 < r < 1$, and $u_i(c) = \log c$, for $i = 1, 2$.

The same method adopted above leads to Euler's equation:

$$x_{t+1} - r(1 - l_2)(1 + \delta_1)x_t + r^2\delta_1^2(1 - l_2)x_{t-1} = 0$$

for agent 1.

The solution to this dynamic equation that satisfies the transversality condition is $x_t = [r(1 - l_2)\delta_1]^t x_0$. With some algebra we get

$$l_1 = (1 - \delta_1)\delta_2[1 - (1 - \delta_1)(1 - \delta_2)],$$
$$l_2 = (1 - \delta_2)\delta_1[1 - (1 - \delta_1)(1 - \delta_2)].$$

3. CYERT–DEGROOT–MASKIN–TIROLE DUOPOLY GAMES

This section is concerned with the model of infinite-horizon duopoly game with agents moving alternatingly. It is described extensively by Maskin and Tirole in several papers (1987, 1988a, 1988b) and can be seen as a generalization of the finite-horizon quantity setting model discussed by Cyert and deGroot (1970).

Time is discrete and horizon is infinite. Periods are indexed by $t(t = 0, 1, \dots)$. The environment is stationary, and we shall assume that agents' strategy sets X and Y and instantaneous profit functions U^1, U^2 satisfy the following hypotheses: X and Y are compact and convex subsets of Euclidean spaces, while the continuous scalar functions $U^1(\cdot, y)$ and $U^2(x, \cdot)$ are concave.

Both agents are assumed to discount future utilities with the same interest rate. Thus their intertemporal return can be written as $U_i^* = \sum_{t=1}^{\infty} U^i(x_t, y_t)\delta^{t-1}$, $i = 1, 2$, where $0 < \delta < 1$ is their discount factor. The two agents move sequentially. In odd-numbered periods $(t = 1, 3, \dots)$ agent 1 chooses an action that is maintained for two periods. That is, $x_{2k+2} = x_{2k+1}$ for all $k \geq 0$. Similarly, agent 2 moves in even-numbered periods $(t = 0, 2, \dots)$, i.e., $y_{2k+1} = y_{2k}$.

Let us consider dynamic strategies that depend *only* on the previous physical state of the world. Agent 1 expects agent 2 to use such a stationary stratgegy $r_2(x)$, and then solves the following problem:

$$\begin{aligned} V^1(y; r_2) = \max U^1(x_1, y) &+ \delta U^1(x_1, r_2(x_1)) \\ &+ \cdots + \delta^{2n} U^1(x_{2n+1}, r_2(x_{2n-1})) \\ &+ \delta^{2n+1} U^1(x_{2n+1}, r_2(x_{2n+1})) + \cdots \end{aligned}$$

where the maximization is made over the sequences $(x_1, x_3, x_5, \dots)$. The value function $V^1(y; r_2)$ is the maximal discounted profit that agent 1 can obtain just before moving, the other is committed to the action y and henceforth agent 2 will play according to r_2. The value $V^2(x; r_1)$ of agent 2 is defined similarly.

It follows from Bellman's principle that

$$V^1(y; r_2) = \max_{x \in X} \left[U^1(x, y) + \delta U^1(x, r_2(x)) + \delta^2 V^1(r_2(x); r_2) \right].$$

Therefore, $V^1(y; r_2)$ turns out to be a fixed point of the operator $P(r_2)$, acting from $C^0(Y)$ into itself, defined by

$$(P(r_2)f)(y) = \max_{x \in X} \left[U^1(x, y) + \delta U^1(x, r_2(x)) + \delta^2 f(r_2(x)) \right].$$

The operator $P(r_2)$ turns out to be a contraction of modulus δ^2, and therefore $V^1(y; r_2)$ exists and is unique, for any fixed r_2. This statement can be proved by using Blackwell's standard method (see Dana and Montrucchio, 1987).

The same argument holds for the value function $V^2(x; r_1)$. Note, however, that the value functions are not generally concave and thus there may exist several functions r_1^* that are "best response" to r_2.

We shall say that a pair of reaction functions (r_1, r_2) are a *Markov perfect equilibrium* (MPE) if r_2 belongs to the set of agent 2's optimal policies given that henceforth agent 1 will move according to r_1 and the analogous condition holds for agent 2. More formally, a pair (r_1, r_2) is a MPE iff

$$r_1(y) \in \operatorname*{argmax}_{x \in X} \left[U^1(x, y) + \delta U^1(x, r_2(x)) + \delta^2 V^1(r_2(x); r_2) \right]$$

$$r_2(x) \in \operatorname*{argmax}_{y \in Y} \left[U^2(x, y) + \delta U^2(r_1(y), y) + \delta^2 V^2(r_1(y); r_1) \right]$$

There is no general theorem on the existence of MPE for the model described above. An existence result will be given for the linear–quadratic case. We, however, provide a method to construct models with MPE. Actually, we show that any pair of continuous maps can be viewed as a MPE of some duopoly game for a fixed discount factor δ, if it is small enough.

The next proposition provides a characterization of the reaction functions that can be regarded as a MPE.

PROPOSITION 3.1. *A pair (r_1, r_2) of maps is a MPE for some Maskin–Tirole model and for a fixed value of the discount factor δ iff the* *following two conditions are met:*

(*i*) *There exist two real functions* $G_1(x, y)$ *and* $G_2(x, y)$ *on* $X \times Y$ *such that*

$$\max[G_1(x, y), x \in X] = G_1(r_1(y), y)$$

$$\max[G_2(x, y), y \in Y] = G_2(x, r_2(x))$$

(*ii*) *Setting* $G_1(r_1(y), y) = V^1(y)$ *and* $G_2(x, r_2(x)) = V^2(x)$, *the two return functions* U^1, U^2 *defined as follows:*

$$U^1(x, y) = G_1(x, y) - [\delta/(1+\delta)]G_1(x, r_2(x)) - [\delta^2/(1+\delta)]V^1(r_2(x))$$

$$U^2(x, y) = G_2(x, y) - [\delta/(1+\delta)]G_2(r_1(y), y) - [\delta^2/(1+\delta)]V^2(r_1(y))$$

satisfy the assumptions made on the model; i.e., the former is concave in x *and the latter is concave in* y.

Theorem 3.1 and the following, which is its trivial consequence, may be found in Dana and Montrucchio (1986).

THEOREM 3.2. *Let* $r_1: Y \to X$ *and* $r_2: X \to Y$ *be any pair of continuous functions. Let* δ *be fixed in* $(0, 1)$. *There exist continuous payoffs* U^1, U^2 *such that* (r_1, r_2) *is a MPE for the associated Maskin–Tirole duopoly game whenever the discount factor equals* δ. *Moreover, if* r_1 *and* r_2 *are twice continuously differentiable,* $U^1(\cdot, y)$ *and* $U^2(x, \cdot)$ *can be chosen strictly concave for* δ *small enough.*

The method behind the proof of this theorem makes use of the characterization of MPE given in Proposition 3.1. Take any pair of maps (r_1, r_2) and set

$$G_1(x, y) = -(\tfrac{1}{2})\|x - r_1(y)\|^2 + L_1(y)$$

$$G_2(x, y) = -(\tfrac{1}{2})\|y - r_2(x)\|^2 + L_2(x)$$

where $L_1(y)$ and $L_2(x)$ are two unspecified continuous functions.

The functions G_1 and G_2 satisfy condition (i) of Proposition 3.1 and $V^1(y) = L_1(y), V^2(x) = L_2(x)$. Therefore, the return functions U^1 and U^2, defined as in conditions (ii), exhibit reaction maps (r_1, r_2) as a MPE. In general, $U^1(\cdot, y)$ and $U^2(x, \cdot)$ are not concave. However, whenever r_1, r_2 are chosen of class C^2, U^1 and U^2 turn out to be concave for δ small enough.

Theorem 3.2 can be seen as an analog of the "indeterminacy theorem" stated for one-person model (see Boldrin and Montrucchio, 1986; Dana and Montrucchio, 1986). Contrary to the model with one decision maker, however, no "turnpike" property seems to be true and small discount factors are no longer necessary. The next proposition makes this statement precise (see Dana and Montrucchio, 1987).

Let us recall that a twice-differentiable function $f(x)$ is strongly convex over $X \subset \mathbb{R}^n$ if there exists some positive number α such that $h' \cdot D^2 f(x) \cdot h \geq a|h|^2$ for all x in X and all h in $\mathbb{R}^n$.

PROPOSITION 3.3. *Let (r_1, r_2) be C^2 functions, and let us assume that there exist two C^2 functions: L_1: $Y \to \mathbb{R}$ and L_2: $X \to \mathbb{R}$ such that $L_1(r_2(x))$ and $L_2(r_1(y))$ are strongly convex. Under these assumptions, the statement of Theorem 3.2 holds for any fixed discount factor δ in $(0, 1)$.*

Let us conclude this section by giving some applications derived from the preceding theory.

3.1 The Linear–Quadratic Case

Assume that $X = Y = [0, 1]$ and $U^1(x, y) = x(1 - x - y), U^2(x, y) = y(1 - x - y)$. Of course, this symmetric game can be seen as a quantity setting model of duopoly with two identical zero-cost duopolists that face a linear demand for the good. Maskin and Tirole (1987) provide two methods to show existence of a MPE. Here we use the characterization given in Proposition 3.1 and look for symmetric linear MPEs of the kind: $r_1(y) = a - by, r_2(x) = a - bx$, with $0 \leq b \leq a \leq 1$. This assumption assures that the reaction functions belong to the unit square. Using quadratic functions for $G_1(x, y)$ of Proposition 3.1, it is not difficult to check that condition (i) implies

$$G_1(x, y) = -(1/2b)x^2 - xy + (a/b)x + c,$$

where c is a constant to be determined. So $V^1(y) = G_1(r_1(y), y)$ becomes

$$V^1(y) = (b/2)y^2 - ay + (a^2/2b) + c.$$

In view of condition (ii) in Proposition 3.1, one gets that a, b, c must satisfy

$$\delta^2 b^4 + 2\delta b^2 - 2(1 + \delta)b + 1 = 0, \tag{3.1}$$

$$\delta^2 ab^2(1 - b) + b\delta(1 - a) + b - a = 0, \tag{3.2}$$

$$c = \delta a\left[2 - 2b + \delta a(1 - b)^2\right] \Big/ \left[2b(1 - \delta^2)\right]. \tag{3.3}$$

Of course, to any pair (a, b) that satisfies (3.1)–(3.3) there will correspond a linear MPE. On the other hand, equation (3.1) has one and only one solution $b(\delta)$ in the unit interval $[0, 1]$ for any fixed discount factor δ. This can be easily proved since the function $\phi(b) = \delta^2 b^4 + 2\delta b^2 - 2(1 + \delta)b + 1$ is convex on the real axis.

Moreover, one finds that the slope b satisfies

$$\tfrac{1}{4} \le 1/[2(1+\delta)] \le b(\delta) \le \tfrac{1}{2}. \tag{3.4}$$

The intercept a can be found by (3.2). In fact, from (3.2), it follows that $a = b(1 + \delta)/[1 + b\delta - b^2\delta^2 + b^3\delta^2]$. From (3.1) and (3.2) it follows that $a = (1 + b)/(3 - \delta b)$.

From estimate (3.4), one gets $(3 + 2\delta)/(6 + 5\delta) \le a(\delta) \le 3/(6 - \delta)$. Thus $\frac{5}{11} \le a(\delta) \le \frac{3}{5}$.

Furthermore, again from (3.2), one has $a - b = \delta^2 ab^2(1 - b) + b\delta(1 - a) \ge 0$. Thus all the assumptions made on a and b are met, and we can establish the existence of a pair of stable symmetric linear MPE: $r_1(y) = a(\delta) - b(\delta)y$, $r_2(x) = a(\delta) - b(\delta)x$.

It should be noted that $a(\delta) \to \frac{1}{2}$, $b(\delta) \to \frac{1}{2}$ as $\delta \to 0^+$. This confirms the fact, established in Dana and Montrucchio (1986), that MPE reaction curves converge to Cournot–Nash best response as the discount factor δ goes to zero. In fact, the reaction curve $r_1(y) = \frac{1}{2} - (\frac{1}{2})y$ is the Cournot best response, which can be interpreted as a MPE for agents with infinite rate of impatience.

3.2 Example of a Chaotic MPE

Let us use Proposition 3.3 to construct a chaotic MPE. Take reaction functions $r_1(y) = y$ and $r_2(x) = 4x(1 - x)$, with x and y belonging to $[0, 1]$. Fix δ and take $L^1(y) = -y$, $L^2(x) = x^2$ and

$$G_1(x, y) = -(\tfrac{1}{2})(x - y)^2 - m_1 y,$$

$$G_2(x, y) = -(\tfrac{1}{2})(y - 4x(1 - x))^2 + m_2 x^2.$$

Using conditions (ii) on Proposition 3.1, we get

$$U^1(x, y) = -(\tfrac{1}{2})(x - y)^2 - m_1 y + (\tfrac{1}{2})(\delta/1 + \delta)x^2(4x - 3)^2 + 4m_1\delta x(1 - x),$$

$$U^2(x, y) = -(\tfrac{1}{2})(y - 4x(1 - x))^2 + m_2 x^2 + (\tfrac{1}{2})(\delta/1 + \delta)y^2(4y - 3)^2 - \delta m_2 y^2.$$

The pair (U^1, U^2) fulfills the hypotheses of the model for

$$m_1 > (32\delta - 1)/(8\delta(1+\delta)) \quad \text{and} \quad m_2 > (32\delta - 1)/(2\delta(1+\delta)).$$

Thus it is possible to choose m_1 and m_2 as claimed in Proposition 3.3. For example, one may pick $m_1 > 4$ and $m_2 > 16$, independently of δ.

It is easily seen that the sequences of moves of each agent are $y_{2k} = r_2^k(y_0)$, $x_{2k+1} = r_2^k(y_0)$, where y_0 denotes the first move of agent 2. Therefore, the moves of both agents are the iterates of the chaotic logistic map r_2.

3.3 An Example of Nonuniqueness

Proposition 3.1 can be profitably used for finding equilibrium reactions in games with finite strategies. Of course we drop continuity and concavity in such a case. Take the one-shot symmetric game, like "prisoner's dilemma," depicted below.

	NC	*C*
NC	(0, 0)	(2, −10)
C	(−10, 2)	(1, 1)

The one-shot best replies are: $r_1(NC) = NC, r_1(C) = NC$, r_2 is the same. Proposition 3.1 provides a straightforward method to find all MPE. Tedious calculations lead to the following result.

All the equilibria are symmetric. The one-shot reactions $r_1(NC) = NC, r_1(C) = NC$ are MPE for all discount factors. For discount factors: $\frac{1}{2} \leq \delta \leq \frac{10}{11}$, another MPE arises: $r_1(C) = C, r_1(NC) = NC$. It is the "tit-for-tat" strategy.

4. REACTION FUNCTION EQUILIBRIA

Friedman (1977) has developed models of infinite-horizon duopoly games with simultaneous moves and a Markovian assumption on dynamic strategies. He called them *reaction functions* (RF). They can be represented by two maps $r_1: X \times Y \to X$, $r_2: X \times Y \to Y$.

Let $x_t = r_1(x_{t-1}, y_{t-1})$ represent the move of player 1 at time t as a function of the moves of both players chosen previously at time $t - 1$. In supergame notation (r_1, r_2) are *closed-loop stationary strategies* that depend only on last moves instead of all past history (see Friedman, 1986).

Methods similar to those used in Section 3 may be applied.

Let $V_{r_2}^1(x, y)$ be the maximal value of the discounted sum of profits one may get given that in the last period the strategic variables were x and y and that player 2 will use the stationary Markovian continuous strategy

r_2: $X \times Y \to Y$. Then $V_{r_2}^1(x, y)$ is the unique fixed point of the following operator defined on $C^0(X, Y)$:

$$(Pf)(x, y) = \max_{x_1 \in X} \left[U^1(x_1, r_2(x, y)) + \delta f(x_1, r_2(x, y)) \right].$$

The value function $V_{r_1}^2(x, y)$ is defined symmetrically.

As in the alternating-moves case, in general there does not exist a unique best reply to a given expectation r_2.

A pair (r_1, r_2), with r_1: $X \times Y \to X$ and r_2: $X \times Y \to Y$, will be a *reaction function equilibrium* (RFE) iff

$$r_1(x, y) \in \operatorname{argmax}_{x_1 \in X} \left[U^1(x_1, r_2(x, y)) + \delta V_{r_2}^1(x_1, r_2(x, y)) \right]. \quad (4.1)$$

$$r_2(x, y) \in \operatorname{argmax}_{y_1 \in Y} \left[U^2(r_1(x, y), y_1) + \delta V_{r_1}^2(r_1(x, y), y_1) \right]. \quad (4.2)$$

Equations (4.1) and (4.2) imply that (r_1, r_2) is a Nash equilibrium for the supergame. Moreover, the stationarity of strategies implies their subgame perfection.

Contrary to the alternating-moves case, a trivial solution always exists for any δ. It is sufficient to take $r_1(x, y) = x_0$ and $r_2(x, y) = y_0$, where (x_0, y_0) is a Cournot–Nash solution to the one-shot game. This can easily be verified by setting $V^1(x, y) = U^1(x_0, y_0)/(1 - \delta)$ and $V^2(x, y) = U^2(x_0, y_0)/(1 - \delta)$ in (4.1) and (4.2).

It can also be shown [see, e.g., Cyert and DeGroot, 1970] that if agents have a finite horizon, the only sequences of reaction functions that can be optimal against each other are functions equal to a Nash equilibrium of the one-shot game in each period.

The issue we want to address is whether some model with nontrivial RFE exists. We first characterize RFE in a way similar to Proposition 3.1.

PROPOSITION 4.1. *A pair (r_1, r_2) is a RFE for a fixed discount factor δ iff the following two conditions are met*:

(*i*) *There exist two real functions G^1 and G^2 defined on $X \times Y$ such that*

$$\max_{x_1} G^1(x_1, r_2(x, y)) = G^1(r_1(x, y), r_2(x, y)) = V^1(x, y),$$

$$\max_{y_1} G^2(r_1(x, y), y_1) = G^2(r_1(x, y), r_2(x, y)) = V^2(x, y).$$

(*ii*) $U^1(x, y) = G^1(x, y) - \delta V^1(x, y)$ *is concave in x and* $U^2(x, y) = G^2(x, y) - \delta V^2(x, y)$ *is concave in y.*

The proof of Proposition 4.1 is similar to that of Proposition 3.1 for alternate moves. Details can be found in Dana and Montrucchio (1987).

Using Proposition 4.1, we can get examples of games that exhibit nontrivial RFE. The next two propositions are motivated by this problem.

PROPOSITION 4.2. *Let r_1 and r_2 be two C^2 functions. Let us suppose that there exists a C^2 diffeomorphism m from Y into X such that $r_1(x, y) = m(r_2(x, y))$. Then a discount factor δ^* exists such that for every $\delta \in (0, \delta^*)$ there exist payoffs U^1, U^2 that exhibit (r_1, r_2) as RFE for that value δ.*

PROPOSITION 4.3. *Suppose that there exist functions $s_1: X \to \mathbb{R}$ and $s_2: Y \to \mathbb{R}$ such that $s_2(r_2(x, y))$ is strictly convex in x and $s_1(r_1(x, y))$ is strictly convex in y. For any δ, there exist functions $U^1(x, y)$ and $U^2(x, y)$ exhibiting (r_1, r_2) as a RFE for that value δ.*

Proofs of Proposition 4.2 and 4.3 can be found in Dana and Montrucchio (1987).

Let us conclude this section by giving a proposition that illustrates what happens when the discount factors goes to zero. The proof is given in Dana and Montrucchio (1986). The assumption of compactness for strategy spaces X and Y is essential. A counterexample is given later.

PROPOSITION 4.4. *Suppose that the one-shot game has a unique Nash equilibrium (x_0, y_0). Let $(r_{1\delta}, r_{2\delta})$ be a family of RFE for the infinite-horizon game with simultaneous moves for $\delta \in (0, \delta^*)$, and let the associated value functions (V_δ^1, V_δ^2) be upper semicontinuous. Then $\lim r_{1\delta}(x, y) = x_0$ and $\lim r_{2\delta}(x, y) = y_0$ as δ goes to zero.*

Let us now give a few examples which make use of the theory developed above.

A plethora of RFE. Take the symmetric quadratic duopoly with returns $U^1 = U^2 = -(x + y - 1)^2$ defined on the unit square $[0, 1] \times [0, 1]$. The static equilibria are all the points $(s, 1 - s)$ in the unit square. Thus $r_1(x, y) = s$, $r_2(x, y) = 1 - s$ are RFE for any discount factor. Let us show that there are many more RFE, including chaotic ones, independently of the discount factor. Use Proposition 4.2 as follows. Take any function $y' = \phi(y)$ from $[0, 1]$ into itself and look at this function as the reaction function of player 2, i.e., $r_2(x, y) = \phi(y)$. Now take $r_1(x, y) = 1 - \phi(y)$. Following the notation of Proposition 4.2: $r_1(x, y) = m(r_2(x, y))$, where $m(\phi) = 1 - \phi$.

If we set $G^1(x, y) = -(x + y - 1)^2$, we have

$$U^1(x, y) = -(x + y - 1)^2 - \delta(1 - \phi(y) + \phi(y) - 1)^2$$
$$= -(x + y - 1)^2.$$

The same holds for $U^2(x, y)$, and therefore the pair $r_1(x, y) = 1 - \phi(y)$, $r_2(x, y) = \phi(y)$ is a RFE for any δ. As one can note, the trajectory starting at (x, y) is contained in the set $(s, 1-s)$ of static equilibria of the game. Clearly, if ϕ is chaotic [e.g., $\phi = 4y(1-y)$], the moves wander randomly in this set.

A one-parameter family of chaotic RFE.[1] The symmetric game on unit square with payoffs $U^1(x, y) = -y + 10^{-1}x(1-x), U^2(x, y) = -x + 10^{-1}y(1-y)$ has the unique static equilibrium: $x = y = \frac{1}{2}$. Therefore, $r_1(x, y) = r_2(x, y) = \frac{1}{2}$ is a RFE, for all discount factors. Let us show that there is another equilibrium: $r_{1\delta}(x, y) = (10\delta)^{-1}y(1-y), r_{2\delta}(x, y) = (10\delta)^{-1}x(1-x)$ for discount factors $\frac{1}{40} \le \delta \le 1$. As δ decreases the dynamical complexity increases. When δ assumes the value $\frac{1}{40}$, the dynamic strategies become $x_{t+1} = 4y_t(1-y_t), y_{t+1} = 4x_t(1-x_t)$.

All this can be easily derived from Proposition 4.3. In fact, take $r_1 = (10\delta)^{-1}y(1-y), r_2 = (10\delta)^{-1}x(1-x), s_1 = -x, s_2 = -y$. So $U^1 = -y + (10)^{-1}x(1-x)$, and similarly for U^2.

Note that the value functions associated to this equilibrium are $V^1(x, y) = (10\delta)^{-1}x(1-x), V^2(x, y) = (10\delta)^{-1}y(1-y)$, whereas the maximal utility associated to the equilibrium $r_1 = r_2 = \frac{1}{2}$ is equal to $-19[40\delta(1-\delta)]^{-1}$. Thus the chaotic equilibrium Pareto-dominates the constant equilibrium.

It should be noted that if one drops the constraint $X = Y = [0, 1]$ for choice variables and one adopts $X = Y = \mathbb{R}_+$, the equilibrium $r_{1\delta}(x, y) = (10\delta)^{-1}y(1-y), r_{2\delta}(x, y) = (10\delta)^{-1}x(1-x)$ holds for any $\delta > 0$. This contradicts Proposition 4.4 since $r_{i\delta}$ do not converge to $\frac{1}{2}$ as δ goes to zero. Thus the compactness condition in Proposition 4.4 is necessary.

Henon's attractor as a RFE (Dana and Montrucchio, 1987). A game with quadratic payoffs may display the Henon's attractor as a RFE. Let

$$r_1(x, y) = \left(\tfrac{1}{2}\right)\left[1 + (b+1)x + (b-1)y - a(x+y)^2\right],$$

$$r_2(x, y) = \left(\tfrac{1}{2}\right)\left[1 + (1-b)x - (b+1)y - a(x+y)^2\right],$$

where a and b are positive parameters.

Proposition 4.3 applies by taking $s_1(x) = -x$ and $s_2(y) = -y$. This leads to the quadratic functions $U^1(x, y) = -y + \delta r_2(x, y), U^2(x, y) = -x + \delta r_1(x, y)$.

By the linear change of variables $X = x + y, Y = x - y$, the first-order difference system $x_{t+1} = r_1(x_t, y_t), y_{t+1} = r_2(x_t, y_t)$ becomes $X_{t+1} = 1 + Y_t - aX_t^2$ and $Y_{t+1} = bX_t$.

This is the well-known two-dimensional dynamic system studied by Henon (1976). For example, for $a = 1.4$ and $b = 0.3$, it displays a "strange attractor," which appears to be the product of a one-dimensional manifold by a Cantor set.

[1]This example is due to N. Persico (1991).

Pseudo-trigger strategies. Friedman (1986) has used the so-called "trigger strategies" for sustaining cooperative equilibria by noncooperative strategies. They are non-Markovian since they depend on all the past history. Let us define Markovian strategies that are strictly related to such strategies.

Let (U^1, U^2) be a static game and (x_0, y_0) be a Nash equilibrium. Suppose that $(x^*, y^*) \in X \times Y$ is a pair of static strategies that Pareto-dominates (x_0, y_0), i.e., such that

$$U^1(x^*, y^*) > U^1(x_0, y_0) \qquad \text{and} \qquad U^2(x^*, y^*) > U^2(x_0, y_0).$$

Given a pair $(x, y) \in X \times Y$, $\Phi_1(x, y) = \max_{x_1} U^1(x_1, y)$ is named the *best-reply payoff* for player 1. $\Phi_2(x, y)$ is defined similarly.

A *pseudo-trigger strategy* for player 1 is defined as (see Persico, 1991): $r_1(x, y) = x^*$ if $(x, y) = (x^*, y^*)$ and $r_1(x, y) = x_0$ otherwise. A similar definition holds for player 2.

Although discontinuous, pseudo-trigger strategies are Markovian. Let us prove that pseudo-trigger strategies are RFE whenever the discounting is not too high.

Define the map $R\colon X \times Y \to X \times Y$ as $R(x, y) = (x^*, y^*)$, if $(x, y) = (x^*, y^*)$, and $R(x, y) = (x_0, y_0)$ otherwise.

PROPOSITION 4.5. *A pair (r_1, r_2) of pseudo-trigger strategies is a RFE if the discount factor*

$$\delta \geq \max_{i=1,2} \left[\Phi_i(x^*, y^*) - U^i(x^*, y^*)\right] \Big/ \left[\Phi_i(x^*, y^*) - U^i(x_0, y_0)\right].$$

The value functions associated to (r_1, r_2) are

$$V^1_{r_2}(x, y) = U^1(R(x, y))/(1 - \delta) \quad \text{and}$$

$$V^2_{r_1}(x, y) = U^2(R(x, y))/(1 - \delta).$$

This can be proved by checking that the functions $V^1_{r_2}(x, y)$ and $V^2_{r_1}(x, y)$ defined above are fixed points for the two operators $(P_{r_2} f)(x, y), (P_{r_1} f)(x, y)$.

In fact, let us compute

$$\max_{x_1} \left[U^1(x_1, r_2(x, y)) + (\delta/1 - \delta) U^1(R(x_1, r_2(x, y)))\right]. \tag{4.3}$$

If (x, y) is different from (x^*, y^*), then (4.3) becomes

$$\max_{x_1} \left[U^1(x_1, y_0) + (\delta/1 - \delta) U^1(x_0, y_0)\right] = (1/1 - \delta) U^1(x_0, y_0)$$

$$= (1/1 - \delta) U^1(R(x, y)).$$

If $(x, y) = (x^*, y^*)$, then (4.3) is

$$\max_{x_1}\left[U^1(x_1, y^*) + (\delta/1-\delta)U^1(R(x_1, y^*))\right]$$

$$= \max\Bigl((1/1-\delta)U^1(x^*, y^*);$$

$$\max_{x_1 \neq x^*}\left[U^1(x_1, y^*) + (\delta/1-\delta)U^1(x_0, y_0)\right]\Bigr).$$

It is not difficult to verify that if

$$\delta \geq \left[\Phi_1(x^*, y^*) - U^1(x^*, y^*)\right]/\left[\Phi_1(x^*, y^*) - U^1(x_0, y_0)\right],$$

then

$$(1/1-\delta)U^1(x^*, y^*) \geq \max_{x_1 \neq x^*}\left[U^1(x_1, y^*) + (\delta/1-\delta)U^1(x_0, y_0)\right],$$

and thus (4.3) is equal to $(1/1-\delta)U^1(x^*, y^*) = (1/1-\delta)U^1(R(x, y))$. Therefore, $V^1_{r_2}(x, y)$ is the unique fixed point of P_{r_2} and the pseudo-trigger strategies (r_1, r_2) are a RFE.

5. CONCLUDING REMARKS

In this paper we compared a certain number of dynamic games to optimal growth by means of infinite-horizon dynamic programming technique. Although general-existence results are very hard to obtain, we were able to characterize the stationary Markovian equilibria in most models and also to construct several examples by using Bellman's equation.

APPENDIX

Proof of Proposition 2.1

(i) Define the operator P_ψ as

$$P_\psi \phi(x) = \sup_a \left(u[(x + \psi(x))/2 - a] + \delta\phi(f(a))\right)$$

$$\text{s.t.} \qquad 0 \leq a \leq (x + \psi(x))/2$$

It follows from the maximum theorem that if ϕ is upper semicontinuous, then $P_\psi\phi(x)$ is also upper semicontinuous. Further, if $\psi \in \Psi$, then $P_\psi\phi(x)$ is nondecreasing. Therefore, P_ψ defines an operator on the space of upper semicontinuous and nondecreasing functions defined over S. By Blackwell's theorem, we know that V_ψ is the unique fixed point of the operator P_ψ. Therefore V_ψ turns out to be an upper semicontinuous and nondecreasing function.

If $\psi_1 \le \psi_2$, then $P_{\psi_1}\phi \le P_{\psi_2}\phi$ holds for every ϕ. Moreover, from $\phi \le \phi'$ it follows $P_\psi\phi \le P_\psi\phi'$ for any ψ. Let us assume by induction that $P^n_{\psi_1}(\phi) \le P^n_{\psi_2}(\phi)$ for every upper semicontinuous and nondecreasing ϕ. Then $P^{n+1}_{\psi_1}(\phi) \le P_{\psi_1}(P^n_{\phi_2}(\phi)) \le P_{\psi_2}(P^n_{\psi_2}(\phi)) = P^{n+1}_{\psi_2}(\phi)$. Thus $P^n_{\psi_1}(\phi) \le P^n_{\psi_2}(\phi)$ holds for any n. Taking the limit as $n \to \infty$ and using the fact that $V_\psi = \lim_n P^n_\psi(\phi)$, we get $V_{\psi_1} \le V_{\psi_2}$.

(ii) This property has been argued by Dechert and Nishimura (1983) and Benhabib and Nishimura (1985).

(iii) Let us first remark that a nondecreasing function is upper semicontinuous iff it is right continuous. Thus all $\psi \in \Psi$ are right continuous. It then follows from a right-continuity version of the maximum theorem that the correspondence $F_\psi(\cdot)$ defined in (2.3) is right continuous. Thus if we define:

$$\psi^*(x) = \max\left[y \quad \text{such that} \quad y \in F_\psi(x)\right],$$

then $\psi^*(x)$ turns out to be nondecreasing and right continuous. Assume that there exists another best-response $\psi'(x) \in F_\psi(x)$ that is nondecreasing and upper semicontinuous. Assume that for some $y \in S$ one has $\psi^*(y) > \psi'(y)$. Take any sequence $y_n \to y$ from the right, i.e., with $y_n > y$. As $\psi'(y)$ is right continuous, for n large enough $\psi^*(y) > \psi'(y_n)$, and this contradicts (ii).

The other properties of $\psi^*(x)$, such as $0 \le \psi^*(x) \le x$, are obviously fulfilled, and thus $\psi^* \in \Psi$. We can conclude that the best response is unique within our class of functions. ■

Proof of Lemma 2.3. Choose any δ such that $x + \delta$ is a continuity point of V. Then $\exists N$ such that $x - \delta \le x_n \le x + \delta$ for any $n > N$. By monotonicity, $g_n(x - \delta) \le g_n(x_n) \le g_n(x + \delta)$. It follows that $\limsup_n g_n(x_n) \le \lim_n g_n(x + \delta) = g(x + \delta)$. On the other hand, since g is right continuous at x, then $\forall\varepsilon, \exists\delta$ such that $g(x) \le g(x + \delta) < g(x) + \varepsilon$. Therefore, $\limsup_n g_n(x_n) < g(x) + \varepsilon$. Since ε is arbitrary small, we get: $\limsup_n g_n(x_n) \le g(x)$, and the first part of the lemma is proved.

Choose now δ so that $x - \delta$ is a continuity point for g. The same reasoning leads to $g(x - \delta) \le \liminf_n g_n(x_n)$. This leads to $g(x^-) \le \liminf_n g_n(x_n)$. ■

Acknowledgments

Luigi Montrucchio was partially supported by Italian MURST, National Group "Nonlinear Dynamics in Economics and Social Sciences." We are grateful to R. Amir for helpful comments.

References

Benhabib, J., and K. Nishimura (1985). "Competitive equilibrium cycles," *J. Econ. Theory* **35**, 284–306.

Bernheim, B. D., and D. Ray (1987). "Economic growth with intergenerational altruism," *Rev. Econ. Studies* **54**, 227–242.

Billingsley, P. (1968). *Convergence of Probability Measures* (Wiley, New York).

Boldrin, M., and L. Montrucchio (1986). "On the indeterminacy of capital accumulation paths," *J. Econ. Theory* **40**, 26–39.

Cyert, R. M., and M. H. DeGroot (1970). "Multiperiod decision models with alternating choice as a solution to the duopoly problem," *Quart. J. Econ. Theory* **84**, 410–429.

Dana, R. A., and L. Montrucchio (1986). "Dynamic complexity in duopoly games," *J. Econ. Theory* **40**, 40–56.

Dana, R. A., and L. Montrucchio (1987). "On rational dynamic strategies in infinite horizon models where agents discount the future," *J. Econ. Behavior and Organization* **8**, 497–511.

Dechert, D., and K. Nishimura (1983). "A complete characterization of optimal growth paths in an aggregated model with a non-concave production function," *J. Econ. Theory* **31**, 322–354.

Friedman, J. W. (1977). *Oligopoly and the Theory of Games* (North-Holland, Amsterdam).

Friedman, J. W. (1986). *Game Theory with Applications to Economics*, (Oxford University Press, Oxford).

Henon, M. (1976). A two-dimensional mapping with a strange attractor, *Comm. Math. Phys.* **50**, 69–77.

Leininger, W. (1986). "The existence of perfect equilibria in a model of growth with altruism between generations," *Rev. Econ. Studies* **53**, 349–367.

Levhari, D., and J. J. Mirman (1980). "The great fish war. An example using a dynamic Cournot Nash Solution," *Bell. J. Econ.* **11**, 322–344.

Maskin, E., and J. Tirole (1988a). "A theory of dynamic oligopoly, I: Overview and quantity competition with large fixed costs," *Econometrica* **56**, 549–569.

Maskin, E., and J. Tirole (1988b). "A theory of dynamic oligopoly, II: Price competition, kinked demand curves, and Edgeworth cycles," *Econometrica* **56**, 571–599 (1988).

Maskin, E., and J. Tirole (1987). "A theory of dynamic oligopoly, III: Cournot competition," *Eur. Econ. Rev.* **31**, 947–968.

Montrucchio, L. (1986). "Optimal decisions over time and strange attractors: An analysis by the Bellman principle," *Math. Model.* **7**, 341–352.

Persico, N. (1991). *Caos in Giuochi Dinamici dove Importa l'Impazienza* (Tesi di Laurea, Univesità Bocconi).

Stokey, N. L., and R. E. Lucas (1989). *Recursive Methods in Economic Dynamics* (Harvard University Press, Cambridge, Mass.).

Sundaram, R. K. (1989a). "Perfect equilibrium in non-randomized strategies in a class of symmetric dynamic games," *J. Econ. Theory* **47**, 153–177.

Sundaram, R. K. (1989b). "Perfect equilibrium in non-randomized strategies in a class of symmetric dynamic games, Corrigendum," *J. Econ. Theory* **49**, 385–387.

TURNPIKE PROPERTIES AND COMPARATIVE DYNAMICS OF GENERAL CAPITAL ACCUMULATION GAMES

Engelbert J. Dockner
Institute of Economic Theory and Policy
Vienna University of Economics and Business Administration
Vienna A-1090, Austria

Harutaka Takahashi
Department of Economics
Meiji Gakuin University
Tokyo 108, Japan

1. INTRODUCTION

A challenging topic in the theory of market structures is the study of the behavior of firms over time. A recent approach to this topic is to explain market dynamics through game theoretic models of investment. Fershtman and Muller (1984) introduced a class of differential games in which two players in the game accumulate capital. Each firm's payoff is assumed to depend on its own capital stock as well as on the capital stock of its rival. Changes in the capital stock cannot be achieved instantaneously but can be brought about by an investment strategy. Capital stocks depreciate at a constant rate. Using open-loop strategy spaces Fershtman and Muller (1986a) (see also Fershtman and Muller, 1984, 1986b) show the global convergence of the long-run capital stocks of the firms. Convergence of the long-run capital stocks implies that firms tend to behave similarly in the long run even if they start off with different capital equipments initially.

In this paper we introduce a discrete time N-player generalization of the Fershtman–Muller (1984) game and state a sufficient condition for the global convergence of the capital stocks that relates to theirs and has a nice economic interpretation. Global convergence results are extensively studied in the turnpike literature in optimal economic growth. For review articles on that topic, see McKenzie (1976, 1986, 1987). Traditionally

GENERAL EQUILIBRIUM, GROWTH, AND TRADE II

turnpike results in the optimal growth or adjustment cost literature[1] deal with single decision makers (a central planner, a representative agent or a single (competitive) firm) and are results for small discount rates only, i.e., the discount rate ρ being near one in a discrete time framework or close to zero in a continuous time framework.

In an important paper Araujo and Scheinkman (1977) introduce a new sufficient condition for the turnpike property that is independent of the discount rate.[2] Assuming differentiability of the indirect utility function in the intertemporal objective function and a dominant diagonal block condition for the appropriate Jacobian matrix allows them to derive their results. The differentiability assumption also facilitates comparative statics and dynamics for the model. Dasgupta and McKenzie (1985) use a related technique to show global asymptotic stability of the stationary state and to derive comparative dynamics and statics results. Their proofs are based on a symmetry assumption, however, that is not very likely met in optimal growth models.

Infinite-horizon dynamic games are extensively discussed in Friedman (1977). He too, is concerned with global stability properties in noncooperative equilibrium solutions. His approach is based on a contraction mapping property and is related to the one introduced by Araujo and Scheinkman (1977), as we will point out later.

The focus of this paper is on the application of techniques developed by Araujo and Scheinkman (1977), Dasgupta and McKenzie (1985), and Friedman (1977) to a general class of capital accumulation games and characterize its noncooperative equilibrium solutions. The key assumption for stability in our paper is a dominant diagonal for the "Hessian" matrix of the profit functions of the firms in the industry. This assumption can be given a straightforward economic interpretation. The dominant diagonal assumption is the weakest possible assumption we can impose to ensure the global asymptotic stability.

The critical assumption in our game is our selection of the strategy spaces. We consider only the case of open-loop strategies, i.e., time paths of equilibrium capital stocks as compared to decision rules. Open-loop strategy spaces are rather restrictive because they require precommitment on behalf of all the players of the game. In choosing open-loop investment sequences each firm decides to announce its equilibrium strategy at the beginning of the game and commits itself to stick to that strategy over the entire infinite-horizon game. Moreover, open-loop equilibrium strategies

[1] For an application of turnpike theory to adjustment cost models, see Brock and Scheinkman (1977) or recently Sorger (1989).

[2] They apply the implicit function theorem generalized to infinite dimensional spaces to their dynamic optimization problem.

are in general not subgame-perfect.[3] For an economic justification of the use of open-loop strategies in dynamic games, we refer to Flaherty (1980b).

A more desirable choice of strategies would be to employ Markov strategies. In this case firms use decision rules dependent on the current states (capital stocks in the industry) and stick to a given rule over the infinite horizon. Markov strategy equilibria derived through backward induction methods are subgame-perfect but are in general difficult to analyze. In particular, the existence of a perfect Nash equilibrium in (stationary) pure Markov strategies is not a straightforward task owing to a peculiarity inherent to dynamic games (time-dependent supergames). This is that in general strategies and their best responses will not belong to the same class of functions. For example, if we restrict the analysis to the class of continuous strategies best responses will belong only to the larger class of semicontinuous functions. Hence, the standard Debreu–Nash argument of obtaining the equilibrium as a fixed point of a continuous mapping defined from a compact set into itself fails to hold. There are, however, classes of dynamic games for which the existence of Markov-perfect equilibria can be established and corresponding equilibrium behavior be studied. Those include the widely used class of linear quadratic games that allow for globally and asymptotically stable linear Markov-perfect strategies (Reynolds, 1987), or games with specific utility and transition functions (see Levhari and Mirman, 1980). Recently, Sundaram (1989) (see also Dutta and Sundaram, 1989) was able to prove existence of a symmetric Markov-perfect equilibrium for a game with general utility and transition functions but with only a single state variable. His result, however, critically depends on the imposed symmetry and cannot be carried over to the asymmetric case (Dutta and Sundaram, 1990). All these existence results apply for games in which players move simultaneously (i.e., games with imperfect information). For games of perfect information, existence of Markov-perfect Nash equilibria is demonstrated by Bernheim and Ray (1987), Leininger (1986), and Hellwig and Leininger (1988). Finally, it should be pointed out that Fudenberg and Tirole (1983) analyze a capital accumulation game very similar to ours. They are able to show existence of subgame-perfect equilibria, but assumed linear investment cost functions as well as no discounting.

The remainder of our paper is organized as follows. In the next section we introduce the formulation and the notation of our game. In Section 3 we show the existence of an open-loop Nash equilibrium as well as the existence and uniqueness of a stationary state. Section 4 is devoted

[3]For a class of dynamic games for which open-loop equilibrium strategies also qualify as feedback strategies and hence are subgame-perfect we refer to Dockner *et al.* (1985).

to a discussion of comparative statics and dynamics of our model, and Section 5 concludes the paper.

2. FORMULATION AND NOTATION

Consider an oligopolistic market consisting of $N \geq 2$ firms in which each firm accumulates capital according to the accumulation equations

$$k_i(t+1) - k_i(t) = I_i(t) - \delta_i k_i(t), \qquad i = 1, \ldots, N, \tag{1}$$

$$k_i(0) = k_{i0}, \tag{2}$$

where $k_i(t)$ is the capital stock of firm i at time period t, $I_i(t)$ is its gross investment and $\delta_i > 0$ is a constant rate of depreciation. Instantaneous profits $\pi^i(k_1(t), \ldots, k_N(t))$ of the ith firm do depend on its own capital stock as well as on the capital stocks of its rivals. Investment is costly. Investment costs are described by the cost functions $C_i(I_i(t))$. The objective of each firm is to choose a sequence of investments to maximize the discounted stream of profits over an infinite time period subject to the accumulation equations (1), the initial conditions (2) and the reaction patterns of the rivals. Thus the problem becomes

$$\max_{\{I_i(t)\}_{t=0}^{\infty}} \sum_{t=0}^{\infty} \rho^t \left[\pi^i(k(t)) - C_i(I_i(t))\right], \qquad i = 1, \ldots, N$$

$$\text{subject to (1) and (2)}, \tag{3}$$

where ρ is a constant discount rate and $k(t) = (k_1(t), \ldots, k_N(t))$. We will assume the following.

Assumption 1. Profits earned today are strictly preferred to those earned tomorrow, i.e., $0 < \rho < 1$.

Assumption 2. $C_i(I_i)$ is C^2 on the interval $(0, \bar{I}_i)$ and strictly convex, where $\bar{I}_i$ is the upper bound of investment. Moreover, $\lim_{I_i \to \bar{I}_i} C_i(I_i) = \lim_{I_s \to \bar{I}_s} C_i'(I_i) = \infty$ and $C_i'(0) = 0$.

Assumption 3. $\pi^i(k)$ is C^2 defined on $K = \prod_{i=1}^N K_i$ where $K_i = (0, \bar{I}_i/\delta_i)$, and strictly concave with respect to k_i. Additionally $(\partial \pi^i / \partial k_i) > 0$ and $(\partial \pi^i / \partial k_j) < 0$, $(i \neq j)$, holds.

Assumption 1 is obvious by noting that $\rho = [1/(1+r)]$ where r is a unique interest rate. Assumption 2 states that as investment of firm i reaches an upper bound $\bar{I}_i$ marginal and total costs of investment go to infinity. Assumption 3 implies that there are diminishing marginal profits for firm i to increasing capacity k_i; moreover, increasing capacity of a firm's rivals lowers its profit.

Let us denote $k_{(i)}(t) = (k_1(t), \ldots, k_{i-1}(t), k_{i+1}(t), \ldots, k_N(t))$. Using the above formulation and notation, (1)–(3) can be transformed into a general dynamic optimization problem in state space; i.e., the capital stocks. Denoting

$$V^i(k_i(t), k_i(t+1), k_{(i)}(t)) \equiv \pi^i(k_i(t), k_{(i)}(t)) - C_i(k_i(t+1) - (1-\delta_i)k_i(t)),$$

where $V^i : K_i \times K_i \times (\prod_{i=1, i\neq j}^N K_i) \to \mathbb{R}_+$, leads us to the following general optimization problem:

$$\max_{\{k_i(t)\}_{t=0}^\infty} J_i \equiv \sum_{t=0}^\infty \rho^t V^i(k_i(t), k_i(t+1), k_{(i)}(t)), \qquad i = 1, \ldots, N$$

$$\text{subject to } k_0 = (k_{10}, \ldots, k_{N0}). \qquad (4)$$

The formulation (4) is standard in discrete time optimal growth models (see McKenzie, 1986) but can be applied to any difference game as well.

For the purposes in this paper, we have to restrict our discussion to sequences of investment and, hence, capital stocks that are bounded from above and below by uniform bounds not equal to zero.

Definition 1. A sequence $\tilde{k}_i = \{k_i(t)\}_{t=0}^\infty$ of capital stocks of firm i is called a regular path if there exist $\bar{\kappa}_i \geq \underline{\kappa}_i > 0$ such that

$$0 < \underline{\kappa}_i \leq k_i(t) \leq \bar{\kappa}_i \quad \text{for all } t \geq 0,\ i = 1, \ldots, N,$$

and the second-order partial derivatives of V^i are bounded on $[\underline{\kappa}_i, \bar{\kappa}_i] \times \prod_{i=1}^N [\underline{\kappa}_i, \bar{\kappa}_i]$.

Regularity of a path is a rather strong assumption, but it can be guaranteed if one requires $\pi^i(k)$ to satisfy generalized Inada-type conditions. Generalized Inada-type conditions were introduced by Brock and Scheinkman (1977) for a single firm adjustment cost model but can be adopted easily to our case.

In order to characterize a noncooperative equilibrium for the game, we have to specify the equilibrium concept employed as well as the strategy spaces available to the firms. As far as the latter is concerned we assume that firms choose their investment strategies as time paths (sequences), i.e., they use open-loop strategy spaces.

Denote by $\mathcal{F}_i \equiv [\underline{\kappa}_i, \bar{\kappa}_i]$ the compact interval introduced with the regularity assumption of a path $\tilde{k}_i = \{k_i(t)\}_{t=0}^\infty$.

Definition 2. The open-loop strategy space S_i of firm i is

$$S_i \equiv \{\tilde{k}_i \in l^\infty : k_i(t) \in \mathcal{F}_i \text{ for all } t \geq 0\}. \qquad (5)$$

It is obvious that the sets S_i are convex subsets of the set of bounded real valued sequences, l^∞. Based on the topology generated by the norm $\|\tilde{k}_i\| = \sum_{t=0}^{\infty}\rho^t\|k_i(t)\|$ the sets S_i are compact.

In this paper our attention is centered around regular open-loop Nash equilibrium solutions, which are defined as follows.

Definition 3. A N-tuple of sequences $\tilde{k}^* = (\tilde{k}_1^*, \ldots, \tilde{k}_N^*)$, $\tilde{k}_j^* \in S_j$ $(j = 1, \ldots, N)$, constitutes a regular open-loop Nash equilibrium[4] if and only if

$$J_i(\tilde{k}^*) \geq J_i\left(\tilde{k}_1^*, \ldots, \tilde{k}_{i-1}^*, \tilde{k}_i, \tilde{k}_{i+1}^*, \ldots, k_N^*\right)$$

holds for all $i = 1, \ldots, N$ and for all $\tilde{k}_i \in S_i$ $(i \neq j)$.

Candidates for Nash equilibria can be found by applying the first-order necessary conditions given by the following set of Euler-like difference equations.

$$\rho V_1^i\big(k_i(t), k_i(t+1), k_{(i)}(t)\big) + V_2^i\big(k_i(t-1), k_i(t), k_{(i)}(t-1)\big) = 0, \qquad i = 1, \ldots, N, \tag{6}$$

where numerical subscripts on the functions V^i mean partial derivatives with respect to the corresponding arguments, i.e., $V_1^i = [\partial V^i(x, y, z)/\partial x]$ and $V_{11}^i = [\partial^2 V^i(x, y, z)/\partial x^2]$, etc. In vector notation we can rewrite equation (6) as

$$\rho V_1(k(t), k(t+1)) + V_2(k(t-1), k(t)) = 0, \tag{7}$$

with $V_i = (V_i^1, \ldots, V_i^N)$, $i = 1, 2$.

In the case of regular paths and given strict concavity of $\pi^i(\cdot)$ with respect to its own capital stock the necessary conditions (7) are sufficient as well (see Scheinkman, 1976, Lemma 16). Hence a noncooperative equilibrium is completely characterized by equations (7). This enables us to define a regular stationary Nash equilibrium as follows.

Definition 4. A N-tuple of sequences $k^\rho = (k_1^\rho, \ldots, k_N^\rho)$ is said to be a regular stationary Nash equilibrium if and only if

$$\rho V_1(k^\rho, k^\rho) + V_2(k^\rho, k^\rho) = 0. \tag{8}$$

A regular stationary Nash equilibrium represents a set of capital stocks of the firms in the industry that can be maintained forever with constant replacement investment.

[4]Starting from now we refer to a regular open-loop Nash equilibrium simply as a Nash equilibrium.

In the next section we are examining the existence of a Nash equilibrium, the existence and uniqueness of a stationary Nash equilibrium, and the stability properties of the stationary state.

3. EXISTENCE AND STABILITY PROPERTIES

The major aim of our paper is to characterize industry equilibrium paths for the model defined above. This amounts to demonstrating (i) the existence of an industry equilibrium path of firms' mutually consistent sequences of capital stocks, (ii) the existence and (possibly) uniqueness of a stationary equilibrium; (iii) the stability properties of a stationary equilibrium, as well as (iv) comparative statics and dynamics of an equilibrium path.

Existence and stability results for capital accumulation games are derived also in Fershtman and Muller (1984, 1986a) for the two-player continuous-time case and in Flaherty (1980a) for a general discrete-time symmetric N-player game.

THEOREM 1. *Given Assumptions* (1)–(3), *there exists a Nash equilibrium path.*

Proof. This follows from Theorem 4.6 in Flaherty (1980a), which is based on Theorem 9.6 in Friedman (1977). ∎

Theorem 1 provides us with the existence of a Nash equilibrium. Before we study the stability properties of our game, we examine the existence and uniqueness of a stationary Nash equilibrium. This requires the following additional concepts and assumptions.

DEFINITION 5. A matrix $F = (f_{ij})_{i=1,\dots,N;\, j=1,\dots,N}$ is said to have a column dominant diagonal if there exist positive scalars d_j $(j = 1,\dots,N)$ such that

$$d_j|f_{jj}| > \sum_{i=1,\, i\neq j}^{N} d_i|f_{ij}|, \qquad j = 1,\dots,N.$$

The concept of a dominant diagonal matrix as used in Definition 5 was introduced by McKenzie (1960). Here we state it by referring to a column-dominant diagonal. We could have introduced a row-dominant diagonal as well.

Assumption 4. Let $(\pi^i_{ij})_{i=1,\dots,N;\, j=1,\dots,N}$ be the matrix of second-order partial derivatives of the instantaneous profit functions π^i, i.e.,

$\pi^i_{ij} = [\partial^2 \pi^i / \partial k_i \partial k_j]$. It holds that (i) $|\pi^i_{ii}| > C''_i/\rho^2$ and (ii) that the matrix

$$\begin{pmatrix} \pi^1_{11} + C''_1/\rho^2 & \pi^1_{12} & \cdots & \pi^1_{1N} \\ \vdots & \vdots & \vdots & \vdots \\ \pi^N_{N1} & \pi^N_{N2} & \cdots & \pi^N_{NN} + C''_N/\rho^2 \end{pmatrix}$$

has row- and column-dominant diagonal.

Assumption 4 can be given a nice economic interpretation. The first part means that the marginal instantaneous profit function of each firm is steeper than its marginal adjustment cost function. In the case of a row-dominant diagonal, the second part means that the effect of an action taken by firm i on its own marginal profit dominates the effects of actions taken by its rivals. For a column-dominant diagonal, we get that the effect of an action taken by firm i on its own marginal profit dominates the effects of the same action on the marginal profits of the rivals.[5]

In what follows we will make use of the following matrices.

$$V_{11} = \begin{pmatrix} \pi^1_{11} & \cdots & \pi^1_{1N} \\ \vdots & \vdots & \vdots \\ \pi^N_{N1} & \cdots & \pi^N_{NN} \end{pmatrix} + \begin{pmatrix} (1-\delta_1)^2 & \cdots & 0 \\ 0 & \ddots & 0 \\ 0 & \cdots & (1-\delta_N)^2 \end{pmatrix} \times \begin{pmatrix} -C''_1 & \cdots & 0 \\ 0 & \ddots & 0 \\ 0 & \cdots & -C''_N \end{pmatrix}$$

and

$$V_{22} = \begin{pmatrix} -C''_1 & \cdots & 0 \\ 0 & \ddots & 0 \\ 0 & \cdots & -C''_N \end{pmatrix}$$

$$V_{12} = V_{21} = \begin{pmatrix} C''_1(1-\delta_1) & \cdots & 0 \\ 0 & \ddots & 0 \\ 0 & \cdots & C''_N(1-\delta_N) \end{pmatrix}.$$

[5]The dominant diagonal condition in Assumption 4 does depend on the discount rate ρ. Hence, our stability condition does as well. This observation clearly distinguishes the discrete-time model from the continuous time framework of Fershtman and Muller (1984, 1986). In their model the stability condition is independent of the discount rate. In that respect their result is weaker than ours. It is, however, a well documented fact (see, e.g., Dasgupta, 1985) that conditions sufficient for stability in a continuous-time model do not imply the turnpike property in a corresponding discrete-time version.

Note that from Assumption 4 it follows that $\rho V_{11} + V_{22}$ has a dominant diagonal and therefore is nonsingular. The fact that $\rho V_{11} + V_{22}$ is nonsingular enables us to apply the implicit function theorem to equation (7). Thus, there exists a vector valued C^1 function $\phi = (\phi_1, \ldots, \phi_N)$ such that

$$k(t) = \phi(k(t-1), k(t+1)), \qquad t \geq 1. \tag{9}$$

Any Nash equilibrium established in Theorem 1 can be represented by ϕ. If we are able to show that ϕ satisfies an appropriate Lipschitz condition (contraction mapping), existence and uniqueness of a steady state follows as a logical consequence (cf. Theorem 9.4 in Friedman, 1977). To establish this let us apply the mean value theorem to the function ϕ to get the following.

LEMMA 1. *Suppose the points $a = (k'(t-1), k'(t+1))$, and $b = (k''(t-1), k''(t+1))$ as well as the line joining them are in $\prod_{i=1}^N \mathcal{F}_i \times \prod_{i=1}^N \mathcal{F}_i$. There exists a point c on the line segment S joining a and b such that*

$$\begin{aligned} &\|\phi(k'(t-1), k'(t+1)) - \phi(k''(t-1), k''(t+1))\| \\ &\quad \leq \left\| \frac{\partial \phi(c)}{\partial k(t-1)} \right\| \|k'(t-1) - k''(t-1)\| \\ &\qquad + \left\| \frac{\partial \phi(c)}{\partial k(t+1)} \right\| \|k'(t+1) - k''(t+1)\|, \end{aligned}$$

where $\|\cdot\|$ is an appropriate operator norm.[6]

Proof. See Bartle (1976, p. 366). ■

Notice that $(\partial\phi(c)/\partial k(t-1))$ and $(\partial\phi(c)/\partial k(t+1))$ are $N \times N$ matrices given by

$$\left(\frac{\partial \phi(c)}{\partial k(t-1)}\right) = -(\rho V_{11} + V_{22})^{-1} V_{21}$$

$$\left(\frac{\partial \phi(c)}{\partial k(t+1)}\right) = -\rho(\rho V_{11} + V_{22})^{-1} V_{12},$$

and evaluated at c. Given regularity as well as boundedness of the second-order derivatives, it follows that there exist uniform bounds on

[6]Let M be the set of all $N \times N$ matrices with real entries. Any norm $\|\cdot\|$ in $\mathbb{R}^N$ induces a norm $\|\cdot\|$ in M given by $\|A\| = \sup_{\|x\|=1} \|Ax\|$. If for a given $k = (k_1, \ldots, k_N) \in \prod_{i=1}^N \mathcal{F}_i$ we use $\|k\| = (\Sigma_{i=1}^N k_i^2)^{1/2}$, then $\|A\| = \tilde{\rho}(A^T A)$, where $\tilde{\rho}(A^T A)$ denotes the square root of the modulus of the eigenvalues of $A^T A$ of highest modulus.

$(\partial\phi(c)/\partial k(t-1))$ as well as $(\partial\phi(c)/\partial k(t+1))$. Thus, we get

$$\begin{aligned}
&\|\phi(k'(t-1), k'(t+1)) - \phi(k''(t-1), k''(t+1))\| \\
&\quad\leq \left\|(\rho V_{11} + V_{22})^{-1} V_{21}\right\| \|k'(t-1) - k''(t-1)\| \\
&\quad+\rho\left\|(\rho V_{11} + V_{22})^{-1} V_{12}\right\| \|k'(t+1) - k''(t+1)\|, \qquad (10)
\end{aligned}$$

where the matrix $(\rho V_{11} + V_{22})^{-1}V_{12}$ is evaluated at a point $\tilde{c}$, giving the uniform bounds.

A dominant diagonal of a matrix has to be distinguished from dominant diagonal blocks of a matrix. The latter concept was introduced by Araujo and Scheinkman (1977), and in our case it can be defined as follows.[7]

Definition 6. The matrix of second-order derivatives of the value functions $V(k(t), k(t+1))$ is said to have dominant diagonal blocks if and only if

$$\left\|(\rho V_{11} + V_{22})^{-1} V_{12}\right\| + \rho\left\|(\rho V_{11} + V_{22})^{-1} V_{21}\right\| < 1$$

for all $(k(t), k(t+1)) \in \Pi_{i=1}^{N}\mathcal{F}_i \times \Pi_{i=1}^{N}\mathcal{F}_i$. Given the definition of a matrix with dominant diagonal blocks, we are able to establish the stability properties of the game.

Lemma 2. *Given Assumptions* 1–4, *the Hessian of the value function V has dominant diagonal blocks.*

Proof. See Appendix. ■

Lemma 2 establishes the function ϕ as a contraction mapping. Exactly this property drives all the stability arguments in the remaining parts of the paper. We are now in a position to state the following.

Theorem 2. *Given Assumptions* 1–4, *there exists a unique regular stationary Nash equilibrium.*

Proof. Making use of the result established in Lemma 2 (contraction mapping property of ϕ), we immediately recognize that all the conditions of Theorem 9.4 in Friedman (1977) are satisfied. ■

Lemma 2 also implies that the diagonal block condition introduced by Araujo and Scheinkman is satisfied. This enables us to apply their method to establish the global convergence of a Nash equilibrium to a steady state.

[7]The concept of dominant diagonal blocks was introduced for an infinite matrix by Araujo and Scheinkman (1977, Definition 2.4). We use a definition that is adopted to our problem.

Instead, however, we apply Friedman's (1977) technique to establish the result since his Assumption S6 (p. 195) is satisfied and the equilibrium is fully characterized by the equilibrium function ϕ.

THEOREM 3. *If* $\{k^{\rho}(t)\}_{t=0}^{\infty}$ *is a Nash equilibrium, then*

$$\lim_{t\to\infty} k^{\rho}(t) = k^{\rho}.$$

Proof. See Theorem 9.5 of Friedman (1977). ■

The last theorem establishes the global asymptotic stability property of our game. Independent of the initial conditions every Nash equilibrium path converges to the unique stationary equilibrium.

4. COMPARATIVE STATICS AND DYNAMICS

The block diagonal structure introduced in the preceeding section is the result which enables us to readily conduct comparative statics or dynamics analyses of a Nash equilibrium. Araujo and Scheinkman (1977) have shown that this condition implies the differentiability of a regular path with respect to the parameters of the model. In our case the parameters are the discount rate and the initial conditions. We concern ourselves with the comparative statics and dynamics with respect to the discount rate. The following derivations are related to Dasgupta and McKenzie (1985) and Araujo and Scheinkman (1979). For a general optimal growth model they show comparative statics and dynamics results with respect to the discount rate. Their key assumptions are that V_{12} is symmetric and that system (7) possesses the saddlepoint property, i.e., N characteristic roots of the system are less than one. In our game V_{12} is a diagonal matrix so their first condition is satisfied trivially. We need to show only that the linearized system (7) possesses the saddlepoint property. The characteristic equation of the linearized system (7) is given as

$$\left|\rho V_{12}\lambda^2 + (V_{22} + \rho V_{11})\lambda + V_{21}\right| = 0. \tag{11}$$

LEMMA 3. *If* λ *is a root of* (11), *then* $|\lambda| \neq 1$.

Proof. In Dockner and Takahashi (1990) we show that if λ is a root of (11), then $1/\rho\lambda$ is a root as well. Since Theorem 2 establishes that the game possesses the global asymptotic stability property, we know that it is locally and asymptotically stable. Therefore, there exist N roots of the system (11) that are less than 1. Since $|\lambda_i| < 1$ for $i = 1, \ldots, N$ we know that $|\lambda_j| = 1/\rho|\lambda_i| > 1$ for $j = N, \ldots, 2N$. ■

We are now in a position to state the next result.

THEOREM 4

(*a*) *The aggregated value of the stationary Nash equilibrium capital stocks evaluated at initial prices and measured in terms of marginal profits* $V_1(k^\rho, k^\rho)$, *increases with increasing* ρ.

(*b*) *The aggregated value of the Nash equilibrium capital stocks at every period in time, evaluated at present value prices and measured in terms of marginal profits* $\rho^t V_1(k(t), k(t+1))$, *increases with increasing* ρ *in a sufficient small neighbourhood of the stationary Nash equilibrium.*

Proof. See Dasgupta and McKenzie (1985), Theorem 1 and Theorem 3. ■

The last theorem provides two interesting results. First, it identifies the response of the unique stationary Nash equilibrium to a change in the discount rate; specifically the aggregated value of the stationary equilibrium increases with a decrease in the interest rate. Second, it identifies the response of the entire industry equilibrium path to a change in the discount rate. The value of the stocks increases with the discount rate.

5. CONCLUSIONS

This paper deals with stability properties of Nash equilibrium solutions for a general class of capital accumulation games. Emphasis is put on the application of turnpike theory to dynamic games. It is shown that the turnpike results known from the theory of optimal economic growth can be used to derive a general convergence result. They also yield comparative statics and dynamics properties. Our key result is the global convergence of the Nash trajectories to a unique steady state provided that the matrix of second order derivatives of the profit functions has a dominant diagonal. This result implies that the block diagonal assumption introduced by Araujo and Scheinkman (1977) is satisfied. Thus, comparative statics and dynamics analyses are possible.

The model introduced here is very general in nature and can be applied to various market situations. In Dockner and Takahashi (1988b), we use it to show quasicompetitive behavior for dynamic Cournot competition, while in Dockner and Takahashi (1988a), we prove two additional turnpike theorems. We investigate the relationship between the equilibrium path of the finite and infinite-horizon games and show that the finite horizon eqilibrium path stays within a closed neighborhood of the stationary equilibrium.

Finally, we want to lay stress on the point that all the results obtained in this paper can easily be generalized to the case of $m \geq 1$ capital goods for each individual firm in the industry.

APPENDIX

Proof of Lemma 2. We have to show that the following inequality holds.

$$\left\|(\rho V_{11} + V_{22})^{-1} V_{12}\right\| < \frac{1}{1+\rho}.$$

Let us define $B = \rho V_{11} + V_{22}$ and $A = V_{12}$ and note that A is a diagonal matrix. Moreover, we define $\overline{V}_{11} = \frac{1}{2}(V_{11} + V_{11}^T)$ and note by Assumption 4 that $\overline{V}_{11}$ is a negative definite matrix (cf. Namatame and Tse, 1981). Given that V_{22} is a diagonal matrix with negative diagonal elements, it follows that $\overline{B} = \rho\overline{V}_{11} + V_{22}$ is negative definite. With this and the fact that A is diagonal we are able to apply Lemma 12.1 of McKenzie (1986). We need to prove two lemmas to achieve this.

LEMMA A.1. *If A is nonsingular and symmetric and $-\overline{B}$ positive definite, the characteristic roots of $\overline{B}^{-1}A$ are less than $1/(1+\rho)$ in absolute value, if and only if there are N roots of the equation*

$$\left|\rho A \lambda^2 + \overline{B}\lambda + A\right| = 0 \tag{A.1}$$

with absolute value less than 1.

Proof. See Lemma 12.1 on page 1339 in McKenzie (1986). ■

Next we establish the result that (A.1) has N roots with absolute value less than 1.

LEMMA A.2. *Equation* (*A*.1) *possesses N roots with absolute value less than one.*

Proof. Note that if λ is a root of (A.1), then $1/\rho\lambda$ is also a root with the same multiplicity. Suppose that $1 \leq |\lambda| \leq 1/\rho$. As the matrix in (A.1) is singular there is a nontrivial solution to the equation system

$$\left(\rho A \lambda^2 + \overline{B}\lambda + A\right)(x + iy) = 0.$$

Multiplying on the left side with $\overline{\lambda}(x - iy)^T$ where $\overline{\lambda}$ is the conjugate to λ and using $\lambda\overline{\lambda} = |\lambda|^2$, we find

$$(x - iy)^T\left[\rho|\lambda|^2 V_{21}\lambda + |\lambda|^2\left(\rho\overline{V}_{11} + V_{22}\right) + V_{12}\overline{\lambda}\right](x + iy) = 0.$$

Let us now look at the following form:

$$\left(\overline{\lambda}(x - iy)^T, (x - iy)^T\right)\begin{pmatrix} \rho\overline{V}_{11} & V_{12} \\ \rho|\lambda|^2 V_{21} & |\lambda|^2 V_{22} \end{pmatrix}\begin{pmatrix} \lambda(x + iy) \\ (x + iy) \end{pmatrix}$$
$$= (x - iy)^T\left[\rho|\lambda|^2 V_{21}\lambda + |\lambda|^2\left(\rho\overline{V}_{11} + V_{22}\right) + V_{12}\overline{\lambda}\right](x + iy) = 0.$$

However, the first matrix has row- and column-dominant diagonal for $1 \leq |\lambda| \leq 1/\rho$ and is quasinegative definite. So the last value must be negative, a contradiction. Hence, we can conclude that it is impossible for all roots to lie outside the unit circle. Given that the roots come in pairs $(\lambda, 1/\rho\lambda)$ there are N roots with absolute value less than one. ■

This implies that the matrix $\overline{B}^{-1}A = (\rho\overline{V}_{11} + V_{22})^{-1}V_{12}$ has characteristic roots less than $1/(1+\rho)$. Thus, we get

$$\left|x^T V_{12} x / x^T \overline{B} x\right| = \left|x^T V_{12} x / x^T (\rho V_{11} + V_{22}) x\right| < \frac{1}{1+\rho}$$

where $x^T x = 1$. From Theorem 2 of Wielandt (1973) we know, however, that if μ is a characteristic root of $(\rho V_{11} + V_{22})^{-1} V_{12}$ then it belongs to the set of the ratio of quadratic form given by $x^T V_{12} x / x^T (\rho V_{11} + V_{22}) x$ with $x^T x = 1$. Hence, $|\mu| < 1/(1+\rho)$, which implies

$$\left\|(\rho V_{11} + V_{22})^{-1} V_{12}\right\| < \frac{1}{1+\rho}.$$

This completes the proof of Lemma 2.

Acknowledgments

An earlier draft of this paper was presented at the Conference on General Equilibrium and Growth: The Legacy of Lionel McKenzie (May 1989), the Far Eastern Meeting of the Econometric Society in Kyoto (June 1989), the University of Saskatchewan and the Technical University of Vienna. The authors are particularly grateful for the comments and criticism of J. Scheinkman, G. Schwann and H. Wan as well as two anonymous referees. The research of the second author was supported by the Nomura Foundation for Social Sciences.

References

Araujo, A., and J. A. Scheinkman (1977). "Smoothness, comparative dynamics, and the turnpike property," *Econometrica* **45**, 601–620.

Araujo, A., and J. A. Scheinkman (1979). "Notes on comparative dynamics," in *General Equilibrium, Growth and Trade*, J. R. Green and J. A. Scheinkman (eds.) (Academic Press, New York).

Bartle, R. (1976). *The Elements of Real Analysis* (Wiley, New York).

Bernmeim, D., and D. Ray (1977). "Economic growth with intergenerational altruism," *Rev. Econ. Studies* **54**, 227–242.

Brock, W., and J. A. Scheinkman (1987). "On the long-run behaviour of a competitive firm," in *Equilibrium and Disequilibrium in Economic Theory*, G. Schwödiauer (ed.) (Reidel, Dordrecht).

Dasgupta, S. (1985). "A local analysis of stability and regularity of stationary states in discrete symmetric optimal capital accumulation models," *J. Econ. Theory* **36**, 302–318.

Dasgupta, S., and L. W. McKenzie (1985). "A note on comparative statics and dynamics of stationary states," *Econ. Lett.* **18**, 333–338.

Dockner, E. J., G. Feichtinger, and S. Jorgensen (1985). "Tractable classes of nonzero-sum open-loop Nash differential games: Theory and examples," *J. Opt. Theory Appl.* **45**, 179–197.

Dockner, E. J., and H. Takahashi (1988a). "Further turnpike properties for general capital accumulation games," *Econ. Lett.* **28**, 321–325.

Dockner, E. J., and H. Takahashi (1988b). "Stability and entry in a dynamic Cournot market," Working Paper, University of Saskatchewan.

Dockner, E. J., and H. Takahashi (1990). "On the saddle-point stability for a class of dynamic games," *J. Opt. Theory Appl.* **67**, 247–258.

Dutta, P. K., and R. K. Sundaram (1989). "The tragedy of the commons? A complete characterization of stationary equilibria of dynamic resource games," Working Paper, University of Rochester.

Dutta, P. D., and R. K. Sundaram (1990). "How different can strategic models be? Non-existence, chaos and underconsumption in Markov-perfect equilibria," Working Paper, University of Rochester.

Fershtman, C., and E. Muller (1984). "Capital accumulation games of infinite duration," *J. Econ. Theory* **33**, 322–339.

Fershtman, C., and E. Muller (1986a). "Turnpike properties of capital accumulation games," *J. Econ. Theory* **38**, 167–177.

Fershtman, C., and E. Muller (1986b). "Capital investment and price agreements in semicollusive markets," *Rand J. Econ.* **17**, 214–226.

Flaherty, M. T. (1980a). "Industry structure and cost-reducing investment," *Econometrica* **48**, 1187–1209.

Flaherty, M. T. (1980b). "Dynamic limit pricing, barriers to entry, and rational firms," *J. Econ. Theory* **23**, 160–182.

Friedman, J. W. (1977). *Oligopoly and the Theory of Games* (North-Holland, Amsterdam/New York).

Fudenberg, D., and J. Tirole (1983). "Capital as a commitment: Strategic investment to deter mobility," *J. Econ. Theory* **31**, 227–250.

Hellwig, M., and W. Leininger (1988). "Markov-perfect equilibrium in games of perfect information," Working Paper, University of Basel.

Leininger, W. (1986). "The existence of perfect equilibria in a model of growth with altruism between generations," *Rev. Econ. Studies* **53**, 349–367.

Levhari, D., and L. Mirman (1980). "The great fish war: An example using dynamic Cournot-Nash solution," *Bell J. Econ.* **11**, 322–334.

McKenzie, L. W. (1960). "Matrices with dominant diagonals and economic theory," in *Mathematical Methods in the Social Sciences*, 1959, K. J. Arrow, S. Karlin, and P. Suppes (eds.) (Stanford Univ. Press, Stanford, Calif.).

McKenzie, L. W. (1986). "Optimal economic growth, turnpike theorems and comparative dynamics," in *Handbook of Mathematical Economics*, K. J. Arrow and M. Intriligator (eds.) (North Holland, Amsterdam).

McKenzie, L. W. (1976). "Turnpike theory," *Econometrica* **44**, 841–865.

McKenzie, L. W. (1987). "Turnpike theory," in *The New Palgrave, a Dictionary of Economics*, J. Eatwell, M. Milgate, and P. Newman (eds.) (Macmillan, New York).

Namatame, A., and E. Tse (1981). "Adaptive expectations and dynamic adjustment in noncooperative games with incomplete information," *J. Opt. Theory Appl.* **34**, 243–261.

Reynolds, S. S. (1987). "Capacity investment, preemption, and commitment in an infinite horizon model," *Int. Econ. Rev.* **28**, 69–88.

Scheinkman, J. A. (1976). "An optimal steady states of n-sector growth models when utility is discounted," *J. Econ. Theory* **12**, 11–30.

Sorger, G. (1989). "On the optimality and stability of competitive paths in continuous time growth models," *J. Econ. Theory* **48**, 526–547.

Sundaram, R. K. (1989). "Perfect equilibrium in non-randomized strategies in a class of symmetric dynamic games," *J. Econ. Theory* **47**, 153–177.

Wielandt, H. (1973). "On the eigenvalues of $A + B$ and AB," *J. Res. Nat. Bur. Standards*, **77B**, 61–63.

EXPERIMENTAL CONSUMPTION FOR A GENERAL CLASS OF DISTURBANCE DENSITIES

Jerry M. Fusselman
Poly Systems
Chicago, Illinois 60602

Leonard J. Mirman
Department of Economics
University of Virginia
Charlottesville, Virginia 22901

1. INTRODUCTION

In a world of incomplete information, economic agents make inferences about the structure of the economy by observing economic variables, such as prices and quantities. They use the information contained in these observations to update their beliefs about the structural parameters. In fact, this type of learning and updating of beliefs, based on endogenous information, plays an important role in economic decision making. However, there is another activity—not easily observed and not normally modeled—that also plays an important role in economic decision making. This phenomenon is known as experimentation. An experimenting consumer, desiring to obtain information about structural variables affecting his decisions, *actively* generates information in order to make more informed decisions in the future.

This distinguishes the experimenting consumer from the learning consumer. A learning consumer is one who does not take into account the effect of his actions on the flow of information and hence, *passively* accepts the existing information contained in the economic variables. By actively generating information by his actions the consumer can vary the accuracy of the information that is observed. In particular, the experimenting consumer may change his myopically optimal decision to increase the information flow in order to make better or more informed decisions in the future, while the learning consumer, by not taking account of his decisions on the flow of information, makes myoptically optimal decisions.

GENERAL EQUILIBRIUM, GROWTH, AND TRADE II

In this paper we study the effect of experimental consumption on the decision of the consumer. In particular, we compare the optimal decision of the learning consumer with the optimal decision of the experimenting consumer.

The use of endogenous data as the basis for updating subjective beliefs about an unknown structural parameter has been explored in papers by Prescott and by Grossman, Kihlstrom, and Mirman (GKM). Prescott deals with a macroeconomic model in which a controller tries to obtain information about an unobservable structural parameter governing the macroeconomic system. GKM deals with two applications; the first is a consumer who purchases a commodity having an unknown effect on his utility. Endogenous data is then used to update the consumer's subjective beliefs about the effect that the commodity has on his utility. Secondly a model of a monopolist is presented. The monopolist varies either price or output in order to obtain profits while trying to learn about an unknown structural parameter of the market demand curve. These examples illustrate the importance of the use of information obtained from endogenous data.[1]

In Prescott and GKM, it is assumed that the structural parameters cannot be directly observed or inferred from observations, since there is a noise term that obscures the relationship between the unknown structural parameter and the observed variable. In these models observations yield statistical information about the structural parameters and the choice of decision variables affects the distribution of the observations. Each possible decision yields different statistical information, and involves different costs; i.e., each level of the choice variable yields a different degree of information, which is valuable for future decisions. This problem is analogous to the experimental design problem in the theory of statistics. Both Prescott and GKM study the effect of this information on the choice of a consumer. Their work may be interpreted as the choice of an optimal statistical design by the experimenting consumer. In the following discussion the results obtained by Prescott and GKM are discussed. However, the discussion is in terms of the notation, model and proof of GKM.

The major result of GKM is that experimental consumption does not decrease consumption; i.e., myopic consumption is always less than or equal to experimental consumption. This is striking since endogenous data are the most frequent and important observation that economic agents can use to adjust their subjective beliefs about the structure of the economy.

[1]There is another strand of the literature dealing with experimental consumption. Among these are the papers of Easley and Kiefer (1988), Kihlstrom *et al.* (1984), McLennan (1984), and Rothschild (1974). These papers deal with the question of whether the economic agent eventually learns the true value of the unknown parameter. Since this question is not raised in this paper, this strand of the literature will not be discussed.

However the results of both papers, although suggestive, are derived for a very special case. Both Prescott and GKM assume that the noise term is normally distributed (actually Prescott assumes that the a priori distribution of the unknown structural parameter is also normal while GKM assume a discrete set of possible values with an arbitrary a priori distribution). Indeed, the distribution of the noise term plays a crucial role in the way signals (or observations on the outcomes) are interpreted.

In this paper we extend the result of GKM to a large class of density functions, although only two possible values for the unknown parameter are allowed. (It is clear that some structure on the distribution of the noise term is necessary to derive a general result consistent with the results of Prescott and GKM.) The class of density functions of the noise term for which the proof is valid include those satisfying the monotone likelihood ratio property (MLRP). MLRP density functions have the property that higher observed values of the signal imply a higher probability of the larger value of the unknown parameter.

The proof in this paper is quite different from the corresponding proof of GKM. There the notion of "sufficiency" is used, while our proof depends on the notion of "more informative." This, in turn, depends on the work of Rothschild and Stiglitz (1970) (RS), where the term "riskier" is used. In our context "more informative" makes more sense, since while RS concentrate on concave "utility" functions, we deal with convex "value" functions. Hence the notion of "more informative" is similar to the notion of "riskier," except that these ideas are used in a slightly different context.

The basic idea of the GKM proof is that each level of consumption yields a different distribution of possible signals; i.e., each consumption level is associated with a different statistical "experiment." These experiments are then ordered by the notion of sufficiency in the sense of Blackwell; i.e., higher levels of consumption yield experiments that are sufficient for experiments based on a lower level of consumption. It is then shown that a sufficient experiment increases the expected future returns. In other words, sufficient experiments are "more informative" experiments since they yield information that increases expected future utility. This, in turn, implies that optimal experimental consumption is greater than myopic consumption; with myopic consumption only passive learning takes place. Our proof is essentially along the same lines, with the exception that we look at the distribution of posterior beliefs rather than the distribution of possible signals (or experiments) as the basis of the proof. In particular, the relationship between the consumption decision and the corresponding random variable of posterior beliefs is studied. It is shown that higher consumption levels imply more informative, in the sense of Rothschild and Stiglitz, distributions. Hence as in GKM higher levels of consumption yield higher expected future utilities. The result of GKM is then used to show that experimental consumption is greater than myopic consumption.

This paper is organized as follows. In Section 2 the model is presented. The main results are presented in Section 3. It is shown in Theorem 2 that higher levels of consumption imply a more informative distribution of posteriors. Theorem 3 shows that the experimenting consumer never buys less of the commodity with the unknown effect when the MLRP holds. In Section 4, these results are extended by Theorem 4 to cover a larger class of density functions; for instance, density functions with bounded support are now covered. Section 5 includes several examples. Among these is an example in which experimentation does not change the myopically optimal decision. An example is given in which the disturbance density does not satisfy the assumptions of Theorem 4, yet experimentation still increases consumption. Finally, we give an example in which experimentation decreases consumption.

2. THE MODEL

A consumer allocates his income, $I > 0$, in each period between two goods, x and y. The amounts of the goods consumed at time t are denoted by x_t and y_t. Prices are normalized so that the price per unit of good x is 1. The price of good y is $p > 0$. The budget constraint in each period is given by

$$x_t + py_t = I, \qquad x_t \geq 0 \quad \text{and} \quad y_t \geq 0. \tag{1}$$

There is no uncertainty about the services that x provides; one unit of x provides one unit of service. This is not true of y. Let z_t denote the quantity, at time t, of services provided by y_t units of good y, where z_t is assumed to be related to y_t by the linear equation

$$z_t = z_t(y_t) = \beta y_t + \xi_t. \tag{2}$$

Here ξ_t is a random variable. Thus z_t is also a random variable.

The consumer's preferences for x_t and z_t are represented by the von Neumann–Morganstern utility function $u(x_t, z_t)$, which is assumed to be strictly monotonic in both arguments. It is also assumed that u is continuous and defined for all feasible realizations of (x_t, z_t).

The random variables $\xi_t, t = T, T-1, \dots, 1, 0$, are independently and identically distributed with known density function h, which is continuous almost everywhere (i.e., except possibly on a set of Lebesgue measure 0). The value of t represents the number of periods before the last period—as is standard in dynamic programming. From the consumer's point of view,

β is also a random variable, independent of all the ξ_t's. The consumer knows that the true value of β is either $\bar{\beta}$ or $\underline{\beta}$, where $\bar{\beta} > \underline{\beta}$. Before observing any of the z_t's, the consumer has a (subjective) prior probability that $\beta = \bar{\beta}$. In general, this probability will be updated from period to period as z_t's are observed.

More formally, for every $\rho \in [0, 1]$, there exist (by Billingsley, 1986, Theorem 20.4) on some probability space $(\Omega, \mathscr{F}, P_\rho)$, independent random variables $\beta, \xi_T, \xi_{T-1}, \ldots \xi_0$, such that each ξ_t has density h with respect to P_ρ, $P_\rho[\beta = \bar{\beta}] = \rho$, and $P_\rho[\beta = \underline{\beta}] = 1 - \rho$.[2] For a consumer whose prior is ρ, P_ρ summarizes his knowledge before observations are made. For any random variable X, define $E_\rho[X] = \int_\Omega X\, dP_\rho$. For any $A \in \mathscr{F}$, let $I_A(\omega) = \begin{cases} 1 & \omega \in A \\ 0 & \omega \notin A \end{cases}$ for $\omega \in \Omega$. (I_A is the indicator, or characteristic, function of the set A.)

LEMMA 1. *A random variable Y is measurable $\sigma(z_T, \ldots, z_0)$ if and only if there exists some real measurable function f: $\mathbf{R}^{T+1} \to \mathbf{R}$ such that $Y = f(z_T, \ldots, z_0)$ for all $\omega \in \Omega$. If Y is measurable $\sigma(z_T, \ldots, z_0)$ and $E_\rho[Y]$ exists and is finite, then*

$$E_\rho[Y] = \rho E_1[Y] + (1 - \rho) E_0[Y]. \tag{3}$$

Proof. The necessary and sufficient condition for the existence of f is a well-known result in measure theory—see, for example, Billingsley (1986), Theorem 20.1. Since $Y = I_{[\beta = \bar{\beta}]}Y + I_{[\beta = \underline{\beta}]}Y$ with probability 1, $z_t = \beta y + \xi_t$, and β is independent of

$$\xi_T, \ldots, \xi_0, E_\rho[Y] = E_\rho\left[I_{[\beta = \bar{\beta}]}\right] E_\rho\left[f\left(\bar{\beta} y + \xi_T, \ldots, \bar{\beta} y + \xi_0\right)\right] + E_\rho\left[I_{[\beta = \underline{\beta}]}\right] E_\rho\left[f\left(\underline{\beta} y + \xi_T, \ldots, \underline{\beta} y + \xi_0\right)\right].$$

Since

$$E_\rho[I_A] = P_\rho[A]$$

for any set $A \in \mathscr{F}$, this implies

$$E_\rho[Y] = \rho E_\rho\left[f\left(\bar{\beta} y + \xi_T, \ldots, \bar{\beta} y + \xi_0\right)\right] + (1 - \rho) E_\rho\left[f\left(\underline{\beta} y + \xi_T, \ldots, \underline{\beta} y + \xi_0\right)\right]. \tag{4}$$

[2] In Billingsley's proof, the σ-field $\mathscr{F}$ is the class of Borel subsets of $\Omega = (0, 1]$. The probability measure P_ρ varies with ρ. The random variables also depend on ρ, but there is no need to write $\beta_\rho, \xi_{0,\rho}$, etc., because they enter into the argument only by way of their distributions.

In particular, $E_1[Y] = E_1[f(\bar{\beta}y + \xi_T, \ldots, \bar{\beta}y + \xi_0)]$. Since the distribution of $\xi_T, \ldots, \xi_0$ is unaffected by ρ, $E_1[f(\bar{\beta}y + \xi_T, \ldots, \bar{\beta}_y + \xi_0)] = E_\rho[f(\bar{\beta}y + \xi_T, \ldots, \bar{\beta}y + \xi_0)]$. Similarly,

$$E_0[Y] = E_\rho\left[f\left(\underline{\beta}y + \xi_T, \ldots, \underline{\beta}y + \xi_0\right)\right].$$

Combining these yields (3). ■

Remark. If f does not vary with ρ, then $E_\rho[f(z_T, \ldots, z_0)]$ is linear in ρ.

COROLLARY 1. *If $c \in \mathbf{R}$ and ϕ is a real, measurable function, then*

$$P_\rho[\phi(z_T) \le c] = \rho P_\rho\left[\phi\left(\bar{\beta}y + \xi_T\right) \le c\right] + (1-\rho)P_\rho\left[\phi\left(\underline{\beta}y + \xi_T\right) \le c\right].$$

To show this, set

$$f(z) = \begin{cases} 1 & \text{if } \phi(z) \le c \\ 0 & \text{if } \phi(z) > c \end{cases} \quad \text{and} \quad Y = f(z_T).$$

Substitute these expressions into (4) and use the fact that $E_\rho[I_A] = P_\rho[A]$ for any $A \in \mathcal{F}$.

COROLLARY 2. *If H is a (measurable) subset of $\mathbf{R}$, then*

$$P_\rho[z_T \in H] = \rho P_\rho\left[\bar{\beta}y + \xi_T \in H\right] + (1-\rho)P_\rho\left[\underline{\beta}y + \xi_T \in H\right].$$

Let $g(y, \rho)$ be the current period expected utility if y is chosen and the prior is ρ, that is,

$$g(y,\rho) = E_\rho\left[u(I - py, z_T(y))\right], \qquad y \in \left[0, \frac{I}{p}\right]. \tag{5}$$

The budget constraint, equation (1), has been used to substitute x_T out of the utility function. The function $g(y, \rho)$ represents the expected utility in period T for a consumer whose prior is ρ, if $y_T = y$ is selected and all remaining period T income is spent on good x. Finally, it is assumed that the expectation in (5) is well defined and finite for every feasible y and every prior $\rho \in [0, 1]$.

The consumers' problem is to find controls $y_T, \ldots, y_0$ that maximize the sum of expected discounted utilities. Let $V_T(\rho)$ be the maximum of this sum, i.e.,

$$V_T(\rho) = \max_{y_T, \ldots, y_0} E_\rho\left[\sum_{t=0}^{T} \delta^t u(I - py_{T-t}, z_{T-t}(y_{T-t}))\right], \tag{6}$$

where $\delta \in (0, 1]$ is the consumer's discount factor. Solving the maximization problem in (6) requires the simulation selection of a number, $y_T \in [0, (I/p)]$, and strategies $y_{T-1}, \dots, y_0$ that are inside $[0, (I/p)]$ for all outcomes ω. Each of these strategies is allowed to be a function of all earlier realizations of z. In measure-theoretic language, y_{T-1} must be measurable with respect to $\sigma(z_T)$, y_{T-2} must be measurable with respect to $\sigma(z_T, z_{T-1})$, etc.[3] In Theorem 1 below, $V_T(\rho)$ is shown to exist and be finite.

Given any prior $\rho \in [0, 1]$, it is convenient to define

$$X_\rho(y) = P_\rho\big[\beta = \bar{\beta} \| z_T(y)\big], \qquad y \in \left[0, \frac{I}{p}\right]. \tag{7}$$

The random variable $X_\rho(y)$ is the posterior probability that $\beta = \bar{\beta}$ after $y_T = y$ is chosen and z_T is observed. (For example, suppose that a consumer with prior ρ selects $y_T = y$ and observes z_T. $P_\rho[X_\rho(y) > \frac{1}{2}]$ is the probability that this consumer's posterior is greater than $\frac{1}{2}$.) By Bayes' rule,

$$X_\rho(y) = \frac{\rho h\big(z_T(y) - \bar{\beta} y\big)}{\rho h\big(z_T(y) - \bar{\beta} y\big) + (1 - \rho) h\big(z_T(y) - \underline{\beta} y\big)} \tag{8}$$

with probability 1 (w.r.t. p_ρ).[4] Note that

$$P_\rho\big[\rho h(z_T - \bar{\beta} y) + (1 - \rho) h(z_T - \underline{\beta} y) = 0\big] \le \rho P_1\big[h(z_T - \bar{\beta} y) = 0\big]$$
$$+ (1 - \rho) P_0\big[h(z_T - \underline{\beta} y) = 0\big] = P_\rho[h(\xi_T) = 0] = \int I_{[h(\xi_T) = 0]} h(\xi_T)\, dP_\rho = 0,$$

by Lemma 1, so the denominator is nonzero with probability 1.

Recall that $V_T(\rho)$ in (6) equals the highest utility level attainable for the consumer with prior ρ who is facing the $(T + 1)$-period problem. The optimal y_T for this problem is not random, but depends on T and ρ, so denote this number, if it exists, by $y_T(\rho)$. By the optimality principle of

[3]Thus y_{T-1} may depend on y_T (as well as $\rho, \delta, I, \dots$), since y_T is also measurable $\sigma(z_T)$, y_{T-2} may depend on y_{T-1} and y_T, because both are measurable $\sigma(z_T, z_{T-1})$. By Lemma 1, the realizations of y_{T-1} must be equal (for all ω) to some (real) measurable function of the realizations of z_T; the realizations of y_{T-2} must be equal to some measurable function of the realizations of z_T and z_{T-1}, etc.

[4]This may also be verified using Theorem 33.1 of Billingsley (1986): Clearly, $X_\rho(y)$ is measurable $\sigma(z_T)$, so we need only verify (33.15) for $G = [z_T \le c]$ where c is a constant. By a change of variable, $\int_{[z_T \le c]} X_\rho(y) P_\rho(d\omega) = \int_{-\infty}^{c} \rho h(x - \bar{\beta} y)/[\rho h(x - \bar{\beta} y) + (1 - \rho) h(x - \underline{\beta} y)] P_\rho z_T^{-1}(dx)$. By Corollary 1 to Lemma 1, $P_\rho z_T^{-1}((-\infty, x]) \equiv P_\rho[z_T \le x] = \rho \int_{-\infty}^{x - \bar{\beta} y} h(s)\, ds + (1 - \rho) \int_{-\infty}^{x - \underline{\beta} y} h(s)\, ds$, so the measure $P_\rho z_T^{-1}$ has density $\rho h(x - \bar{\beta} y) + (1 - \rho) h(x - \underline{\beta} y)$. Hence $\int_{[z_T \le c]} X_\rho(y) P_\rho(d\omega) = \int_{-\infty}^{c} \rho h(x - \bar{\beta} y)\, dx = P_\rho[\beta = \bar{\beta}] P_\rho[\xi_T \le c - \bar{\beta} y] = P_\rho[\beta = \bar{\beta}, z_T \le c]$. This is (33.15) in Billingsley. Setting $c = \infty$ gives an immediate proof for Lemma 3.

dynamic programming and Bayes' rule,

$$y_T(\rho) \in \operatorname*{Argmax}_{y} E_\rho\Big[u(I - py, z_T(y)) + \delta V_{T-1}\big(P_\rho[\beta = \bar{\beta} \| z_T(y)]\big)\Big].$$

The posterior probability that $\beta = \bar{\beta}$, after $z_T(y)$ is observed, becomes the prior for the next period. Using (5) and (7), we have

$$y_T(\rho) \in \operatorname*{Argmax}_{y \in \left[0, \frac{I}{p}\right]} \Big\{g(y, \rho) + \delta E_\rho\big[V_{T-1}(X_\rho(y))\big]\Big\}, T \geq 1, \quad (9)$$

$$V_T(\rho) = g(y_T(\rho), \rho) + \delta E_\rho\big[V_{T-1}(X_\rho(y_T(\rho)))\big], T \geq 1. \quad (10)$$

and

$$V_0(\rho) = g(y_0(\rho), \rho), \quad \text{where } y_0(\rho) \in \operatorname*{Argmax}_{y \in \left[0, \frac{I}{p}\right]} g(y, \rho). \quad (11)$$

Note that the controls $y_T, \ldots, y_0$ in (6) are random variables, while $y_T(\rho), \ldots, y_0(\rho)$ in (9) and (11) are deterministic functions of the current prior, ρ. The precise relationship between these is given at the end of the proof of Theorem 1.

2.1 Existence

The following theorem establishes that a solution to the consumer's problem in (6) exists. Note that the solution need not be unique. Moreover, examples of corner solutions are easy to construct—e.g., Example 1 (p. 386) with

$$|\bar{\xi}| = \frac{IE_\rho[\beta]}{p}.$$

THEOREM 1. *A solution to the maximization problem* (6) *exists, and* $V_T(\rho)$ *is continuous in* ρ.

Proof. We have already assumed that $g(y, \rho)$ in (5) is a finite, well-defined function of y. By (2), both arguments of u in (5) are continuous in y, so $g(y, \rho)$ is continuous in y. By Weierstrass' theorem, since $y \in [0, (I/p)]$, a solution to (11) exists. Furthermore, g is continuous in ρ by the remark to Lemma 1, so by Berge's maximum theorem, $V_0(\rho)$ is continuous.

Assume now that $y_{T-1}(\rho)$ exists and $V_{T-1}(\rho)$ is continuous. Fix $y' \in [0, (I/p)]$. Since h is continuous except on a set of Lebesgue measure zero, by (8), $X_\rho(y)$ is with probability 1 (relative to P_ρ) continuous in y at

y'. Hence $V_{T-1}(X_\rho(y))$ is almost everywhere continuous in y at y'. By Theorem 16.8 in Billingsley (1986), $E_\rho[V_{T-1}(X_\rho(y))]$ is continuous in y. By Lemma 1, $E_\rho[V_{T-1}(X_\rho(y))]$ is also continuous in ρ. Again by Weierstrass' theorem, $y_T(\rho)$ in (9) exists, and by Berge's maximum theorem, $V_T(\rho)$ in (10) is continuous. Consequently, $y_T(\rho)$ exists for all T and ρ, and V_T is continuous for all T.

By Bellman's maximum principle, a solution $\hat{y}_T, \ldots, \hat{y}_0$ to (6), which satisfies

$$\hat{y}_T = y_T(\rho), \qquad \hat{y}_{T-1} = y_{T-1}\big(P_\rho\big[\beta = \bar{\beta} \| z_T(\hat{y}_T)\big]\big), \qquad \ldots,$$

$$\hat{y}_0 = y_0\big(P_\rho\big[\beta = \bar{\beta} \| z_T(\hat{y}_T), \ldots, z_1(\hat{y}_1)\big]\big),$$

exists. ■

3. MAIN RESULTS

Although u need not be concave, $V_T(\rho)$ is convex.

LEMMA 2. *$V_T(\rho)$ is convex for $T = 0, 1, \ldots$.*

Proof. Suppose $\rho_1, \rho_2 \in [0,1]$, and $\hat{\rho} = \alpha\rho_1 + (1-\alpha)\rho_2$ where $\alpha \in [0,1]$. Let $\hat{y}_T, \ldots, \hat{y}_0$ be feasible controls yielding $V_T(\hat{\rho})$ in (4), and set $Q = \sum_{t=0}^{T} \delta^t u(I - p\hat{y}_{T-t}, z_{T-t}(\hat{y}_{T-t}))$. By definition, $V_T(\hat{\rho}) = E_{\hat{\rho}}[Q]$. Since $\hat{y}_T, \ldots, \hat{y}_0$ are feasible controls for all priors ρ, $V_T(\rho) \geq E_\rho[Q]$. By the remark to Lemma 1, $E_\rho[Q]$ is linear in ρ. Hence $V_T(\hat{\rho}) = E_{\hat{\rho}}[Q] = \alpha E_{\rho_1}[Q] + (1-\alpha)E_{\rho_2}[Q] \leq \alpha V_T(\rho_1) + (1-\alpha)V_T(\rho_2)$, so V_T is convex. ■

The idea of the proof of Lemma 2 is illustrated in Figure 1 for a given $\hat{\rho}$.

LEMMA 3. *For every $\rho \in [0,1]$ and $y \in [0, (I/p)]$, $E_\rho[X_\rho(y)] = \rho$.*

Proof. With probability 1, $X_\rho(y) = E_\rho[I_{[\beta=\bar{\beta}]} \| z_T]$, so by the law of iterated expectations, $E_\rho[X_\rho(y)] = E_\rho[E_\rho[I_{[\beta=\bar{\beta}]} \| z_T]] = E_\rho[I_{[\beta=\bar{\beta}]}] = P_\rho[\beta = \bar{\beta}] = \rho$. ■

LEMMA 4. *Suppose X and $\bar{X}$ are arbitrary real random variables and $P_\rho[X \in [0,1]] = P_\rho[\bar{X} \in [0,1]] = 1$. Let $F(c) = P_\rho[X \leq c]$, $G(c) = P_\rho[\bar{X} \leq c]$, and $S(c) = G(c) - F(c)$. The following two conditions are equivalent:*

(*a*) *$E_\rho[V(X)] \leq E_\rho[V(\bar{X})]$ for all bounded, convex functions $V\colon [0,1] \to R$.*

(*b*) *$\int_0^1 S(x)\,dx = 0$ and* (12.1)

$\int_0^c S(x)\,dx \geq 0$, $c \in (0,1)$. (12.2)

We say that $\bar{X}$ is more informative than X (with respect to P_ρ) when either of these conditions is satisfied. For a proof, see RS, Theorem 2.

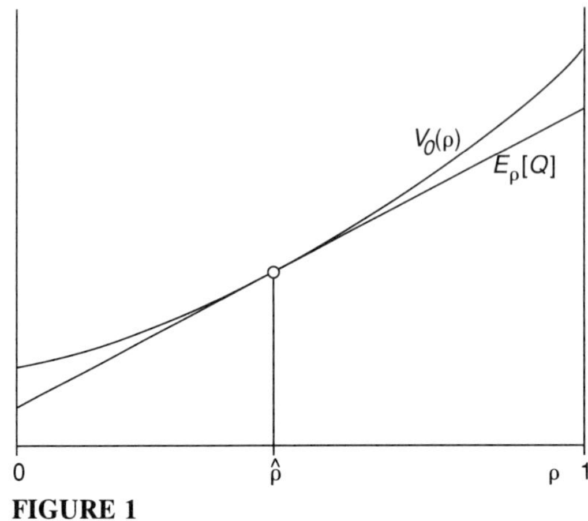

FIGURE 1

This way of stating the lemma is slightly different from (but equivalent to) the RS version. In RS, the inequality in (a) is reversed, and in place of convex functions V, they use *concave* utility functions.[5] They say that $\bar{X}$ is "riskier" than X largely because their version of (a) implies that all risk averters prefer lottery $\bar{X}$ to X. In this paper, X and $\bar{X}$ are not lotteries. Instead, X and $\bar{X}$ represent information (i.e. posterior probabilities) generated by experiments. Since *information*, not risk, is involved, we substitute "more informative" for "riskier".[6]

THEOREM 2. *Assume that $\bar{y} > y$ implies that $X_\rho(\bar{y})$ is more informative (with respect to P_ρ) than $X_\rho(y)$. Assume also that u is strictly quasiconcave. Then $y_0(\rho)$ is unique, and for all $T > 0$ and all selections of $y_T(\rho)$ that solve* (9), $y_T(\rho) \geq y_0(\rho)$.

Proof. V_{T-1} is convex by Lemma 2 and bounded by Theorem 1, so Lemma 4 implies that $E_\rho[V_{T-1}(X_\rho(y))] \leq E_\rho[V_{T-1}(X_\rho(\bar{y}))]$ whenever $\bar{y} \geq$

[5]A second difference is that RS implicitly assumes that $P_\rho[X = 0] = P_\rho[\bar{X} = 0] = 0$. The equivalent of (a) and (b) in our version can be established by applying Theorem 2 in RS to $(X + 1)/2$. (Since the version of (a) for $(X + 1)/2$ implies the version of (b) for $(X + 1)/2$, (a) for X implies (b) for X. Since (b) implies (a) for $(X + 1)/2$, (b) for X implies that $E_\rho[V(X)] \leq E_\rho[V(\bar{X})]$ for all *continuous*, convex V. By the bounded convergence theorem, this implies (a). We have used the fact that a function that is convex on an interval is continuous on the interior of the interval.)

[6]An intuitive justification for this term can probably be developed more or less paralleling the justification of "riskier" (in terms of mean-preserving spreads) in RS. For a brief example, first note that X and $\bar{X}$ satisfy $E_\rho[X] = E_\rho[\bar{X}] = c$ for some constant c by (a), because both $V(x) = x$ and $V(x) = x$ are convex. If $X = c$ with probability one, it seems correct to call X less informative than any other experiment $\bar{X}$ that has mean c. In this case, (a) holds by Jensen's inequality.

y. Hence $E_\rho[V_{T-1}(X_\rho(y))]$ is increasing (not necessarily strictly) in y.

To get a contradiction, assume that $y_T(\rho) < y_0(\rho)$. Since u is strictly quasiconcave, (5) and (1) imply that $g(y, \rho)$ is strictly concave in y. By (11), $y_0(\rho)$ is unique, so $g(y_T(\rho), \rho) < g(y_0(\rho), \rho)$. We have by (10) and (9) that $\delta E_\rho[V_{T-1}(X_\rho(y_T(\rho)))] = V_T(\rho) - g(y_T(\rho), \rho) \geq g(y_0(\rho), \rho) + \delta E_\rho[V_{T-1}(X_\rho(y_0(\rho)))] - g(y_T(\rho), \rho) > \delta E_\rho[V_{T-1}(X_\rho(y_0(\rho)))]$ where the first inequality follows from the fact that $y_0(\rho)$ might not solve (9), but this contradicts the fact that $\delta E_\rho[V_{T-1}(X_\rho(y))]$ is increasing. ■

Henceforth, it is assumed that u is strictly quasiconcave. We now use Theorem 2 to prove Theorem 3, which is a generalization of GKM. The generalization consists of replacing GKM's assumption of the normality (of the noise term ξ_t) with a variant of the *monotone likelihood ratio property* (MLRP). For our purposes, MLRP will be interpreted as follows. Let

$$L(x) \equiv \frac{h'(x)}{h(x)}.$$

The density function h has MLRP if $L(x)$ is continuous and strictly decreasing on $\mathbf{R}$.

The strategy of the proof of Theorem 3 is to show that $X_\rho(\bar{y})$ is more informative than $X_\rho(y)$ by showing that their distributions satisfy condition (b) of Lemma 4. This is accomplished by showing that their distributions are piecewise differentiable and cross exactly once, as is illustrated in Figure 2.

THEOREM 3. *Assume that $h(x)$ satisfies MLRP. Then $y_T(\rho) \geq y_0(\rho)$.*

Proof. Let $\rho \in [0, 1]$, and $\bar{y} > y$, where $y, \bar{y} \in [0, (I/p)]$. If we can show that $X_\rho(\bar{y})$ is more informative than $X_\rho(y)$, then, by Theorem 2, we are done.

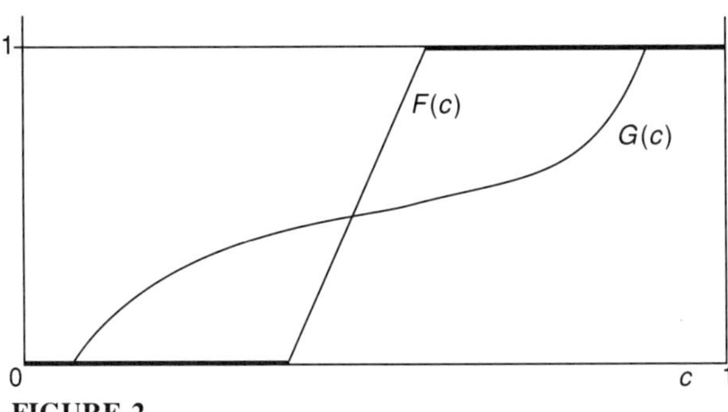

FIGURE 2

By Lemma 3, $E_\rho[X_\rho(\bar{y})] = \rho$. By (8), $X_\rho(0) = \rho$ with probability 1, and $X_\rho(\bar{y})$ is more informative than $X_\rho(0)$ by Jensen's inequality. This disposes of the $y = 0$ case. Henceforth assume that $y > 0$.

By (8), if $\rho = 0$ or $\rho = 1$, then $X_\rho(y) = X_\rho(\bar{y})$ with probability 1, hence $X_\rho(\bar{y})$ is trivially more informative than $X_\rho(y)$. This disposes of the $\rho = 0$ and $\rho = 1$ cases. Henceforth assume that $\rho \in (0, 1)$.

For $c \in [0, 1]$, let

$$F(c) = P_\rho\big[X_\rho(y) \leq c\big],$$

$$G(c) = P_\rho\big[X_\rho(\bar{y}) \leq c\big].$$

The following facts are crucial—the proof is deferred.

LEMMA 5

(*a*) $P_\rho[X_\rho(y) \in (0, 1)] = P_\rho[X_\rho(\bar{y}) \in (0, 1)] = 1$
(*b*) $F(0) = G(0) = 0$, $F(1) = G(1) = 1$.
(*c*) *F and G are continuous on* $[0, 1]$.
(*d*) *F and G are differentiable everywhere except on a finite set.*
(*e*) *If $c' \in (0, 1)$ and $0 < F(c') = G(c') < 1$, then $F'(c') > G'(c')$.*

Set $S(c) = G(c) - F(c)$. By Lemma 5, $S(0) = S(1) = 0$, and S is continuous on $[0, 1]$. In order to show that $X_\rho(\bar{y})$ is more informative than $X_\rho(y)$, it is sufficient to establish (12.1) and (12.2). Integrating by parts using Lemma 5, $\int_0^1 S(x)\,dx = xS(x)|_0^1 - \int_0^1 x(G'(x) - F'(x))\,dx = E_\rho[X_\rho(y) - X_\rho(\bar{y})] = 0$ by Lemma 3, so (12.1) holds.

Let $c' \in (0, 1)$ have the property $0 < F(c') = G(c') < 1$. If there were no such number, then since F and G are continuous, we would have either $F \geq G$ and $E_\rho[X_\rho(y)] > E_\rho[X_\rho(\bar{y})]$, or $F \leq G$ and $E_\rho[X_\rho(y)] < E_\rho[X_\rho(\bar{y})]$. But this contradicts Lemma 3; hence c' exists. By Lemma 5(e), $S'(c') < 0$.

Now let $N = \{x \in (0, c'): S(x) < 0\}$, and $c = \sup N$. Assume that $N \neq \phi$, so $c > 0$. Since $S(c') = 0$ and $S'(c') < 0$, S is positive on some interval $(\bar{x}, c')$; hence $c < c'$. By the continuity of S, $S(c) = 0$. Now $F(c) \leq F(c') < 1$. Also, by the definition of c, $S(x) < 0$ for some $x < c$, so $0 \leq G(x) < F(x) \leq F(c)$. Hence, $0 < F(c) < 1$ and $F(c) = G(c)$, so $S'(c) < 0$ by Lemma 5(e). But $S(c) = 0$, so this implies that S is negative on some interval $(c, \bar{x})$, which contradicts the definition of c. Thus, $N = \phi$. Similarly, $\{x \in (c', 1): S(x) > 0\} = \phi$. Hence $S(x) \gtreqless 0$ as $x \lessgtr c'$.

If $c \in (0, c']$, then $\int_0^c S(x)\,dx \geq 0$. If $c \in (c', 1)$, then $\int_0^c S(x)\,dx = -\int_c^1 S(x)\,dx \geq 0$. Thus (12.2) holds and $X_\rho(\bar{y})$ is more informative than $X_\rho(y)$. ∎

Proof of Lemma 5. By (8) and the facts that $\rho \in (0, 1)$ and h is positive, $X_\rho(y) \in (0, 1)$ with probability 1. Similarly for $X_\rho(\bar{y})$, hence (a) is true, and (b) follows immediately.

Note that by (8) and Corollary 1 to Lemma 1, $F(c) =$

$$(1-\rho)P_\rho\left[\frac{\rho h\left(\xi_T+\left(\underline{\beta}-\overline{\beta}\right)y\right)}{\rho h\left(\xi_T+\left(\underline{\beta}-\overline{\beta}\right)y\right)+(1-\rho)h(\xi_T)}\le c\right]$$

$$+\rho P_\rho\left[\frac{\rho h(\xi_T)}{\rho h(\xi_T)+(1-\rho)h\left(\xi_T+\left(\overline{\beta}-\underline{\beta}\right)y\right)}\le c\right]$$

and hence for $c > 0$,

$$F(c)=(1-\rho)P_\rho\left[\Psi(\xi_T)\ge\left(\frac{\rho}{1-\rho}\right)\left(\frac{1-c}{c}\right)\right]$$

$$+\rho P_\rho\left[\Psi\left(\xi_T+\left(\overline{\beta}-\underline{\beta}\right)y\right)\ge\left(\frac{\rho}{1-\rho}\right)\left(\frac{1-c}{c}\right)\right]\qquad(13)$$

where $\Psi(b) = [h(b)/h(b-(\overline{\beta}-\underline{\beta})y)]$. Note that for all $b \in \mathbf{R}$, $\Psi(b) > 0$ and $\Psi'(b) = \Psi(b)(L(b) - L(b-(\overline{\beta}-\underline{\beta})y)) < 0$ by MLRP.

Assume that the distribution function F is *not* continuous, so there exists some number c such that $P_\rho[X_\rho(y) = c] > 0$. By (a), $c \in (0,1)$. But by (13),

$$P_\rho\left[X_\rho(y)=c\right]=(1-\rho)P_\rho\left[\Psi(\xi_T)=\left(\frac{\rho}{1-\rho}\right)\left(\frac{1-c}{c}\right)\right]$$

$$+\rho P_\rho\left[\Psi\left(\xi_T+\left(\overline{\beta}-\underline{\beta}\right)y\right)=\left(\frac{\rho}{1-\rho}\right)\left(\frac{1-c}{c}\right)\right].$$

The first term here equals

$$(1-\rho)P_\rho\left[\xi_T\in\Psi^{-1}\left\{\left(\frac{\rho}{1-\rho}\right)\left(\frac{1-c}{c}\right)\right\}\right].$$

Because Ψ^{-1} of any singleton set contains at most one number, and ξ_T has a density, this term vanishes. The second term also vanishes, so F is continuous, and similarly G is continuous, which establishes (c).

Let $b(c) = \Psi^{-1}(((1-c)/c)(\rho/(1-\rho)))$, so if $b(c)$ exists, it satisfies

$$\frac{h(b(c))}{h\left(b(c)-\left(\overline{\beta}-\underline{\beta}\right)y\right)}=\left(\frac{1-c}{c}\right)\left(\frac{\rho}{1-\rho}\right).\qquad(14)$$

Again, since $\Psi' < 0$, if $b(c)$ exists, it must be unique. Since Ψ is continuous, if $b(c)$ does not exist, then by (13) $F(c) = 0$ or $F(c) = 1$. Hence, for all c, $F(c) \in (0,1)$ implies that $b(c)$ exists and is unique. Moreover, by (13) and the fact that $\Psi' < 0$, if $F(c) \in (0,1)$ then $F(c) = (1-\rho)P_\rho[\xi_T \leq b(c)] + \rho P_\rho[\xi_T + (\bar{\beta} - \underline{\beta})y \leq b(c)]$. Hence

$$F(c) = (1-\rho)\int_{-\infty}^{b(c)} h(x)\,dx + \rho\int_{-\infty}^{b(c)-(\bar{\beta}-\underline{\beta})y} h(x)\,dx, \tag{15}$$

provided $F(c) \in (0,1)$. Since $\Psi'(b) < 0$ and $b(c)$ is unique, by the implicit function theorem, $b(c)$ is continuously differentiable for all c for which $F(c) \in (0,1)$.[7] Hence F is differentiable on $F^{-1}((0,1))$. Since F is continuous, $F^{-1}((0,1))$ is open. Since F is monotonic, $F^{-1}((0,1))$ is an open interval. Since F is constant outside $F^{-1}((0,1))$, F is differentiable everywhere except possible at the two endpoints of $F^{-1}((0,1))$. Similarly, G fails to be differentiable at at most two points, so part (d) is true.

As with F in (15), if $G(c) \in (0,1)$, then

$$G(c) = (1-\rho)\int_{-\infty}^{\bar{b}(c)} h(x)\,dx + \rho\int_{-\infty}^{\bar{b}(c)-(\bar{\beta}-\underline{\beta})\bar{y}} h(x)\,dx$$

where $\bar{b}(c)$ uniquely satisfies

$$\frac{\bar{h}(\bar{b}(c))}{h\left(\bar{b}(c) - \left(\bar{\beta}-\underline{\beta}\right)\bar{y}\right)} = \left(\frac{1-c}{c}\right)\left(\frac{\rho}{1-\rho}\right). \tag{16}$$

If $F(c) \in (0,1)$ and $G(c) \in (0,1)$, then

$$F(c) - G(c) = (1-\rho)\int_{\bar{b}(c)}^{b(c)} h(x)\,dx + \rho\int_{\bar{b}(c)-(\bar{\beta}-\underline{\beta})\bar{y}}^{b(c)-(\bar{\beta}-\underline{\beta})y} h(x)\,dx. \tag{17}$$

Assume that $c' \in (0,1)$ where $F(c') = G(c') \in (0,1)$. To simplify notation, set $b' = b(c')$ and $\bar{b}' = \bar{b}(c')$, so at $c = c'$, we have

$$(1-\rho)\int_{b'}^{\bar{b}'} h(x)\,dx = -\rho\int_{b'-(\bar{\beta}-\underline{\beta})y}^{\bar{b}'-(\bar{\beta}-\underline{\beta})\bar{y}} h(x)\,dx. \tag{18}$$

We shall now establish the inequalities:

$$\bar{b}' > b' > b' - \left(\bar{\beta}-\underline{\beta}\right)y > \bar{b}' - \left(\bar{\beta}-\underline{\beta}\right)\bar{y}. \tag{19}$$

In order to do so, assume that both sides of (18) are nonpositive. This implies that $\bar{b}' \leq b'$ and $b' - (\bar{\beta}-\underline{\beta})y \leq \bar{b}' - (\bar{\beta}-\underline{\beta})\bar{y}$, so $\bar{b}' \leq b' \leq$

[7]Specifically, fix $\bar{c}$ such that $F(\bar{c}) \in (0,1)$ and let $H(b,c) = \Psi(b) - ((1-c)/c)(\rho/(1-\rho))$. The implicit function theorem guarantees the existence of a C^1 function γ that satisfies $H(\gamma(c), c) = 0$ for c in some neighborhood of $\bar{c}$. Since $b(c)$ uniquely solves $H(b(c), c) = 0$, $b(c)$ is C^1 at $\bar{c}$.

$\bar{b}' + (\bar{\beta} - \underline{\beta})(y - \bar{y})$ which, since $y < \bar{y}$ by assumption, is impossible. Hence both sides of (18) are positive, establishing (19). Note that $y > 0$ implies the middle inequality.

By (14), $h'(b(c))b'(c) = (-1/c^2)(\rho/(1-\rho))h(b(c) - (\bar{\beta} - \underline{\beta})y) + ((1-c)/c)(\rho/(1-\rho))h'(b(c) - (\bar{\beta} - \underline{\beta})y)b'(c)$. Hence

$$b'(c) = \frac{-(1/c^2)(\rho/1-\rho)h\left(b(c) - \left(\bar{\beta} - \underline{\beta}\right)y\right)}{h'(b(c)) - (1-c/c)(\rho/1-\rho)h'\left(b(c) - \left(\bar{\beta} - \underline{\beta}\right)y\right)}.$$

Moreover, by (14) and the definition of L,

$$b'(c) = \frac{1}{c(1-c)\left\{L\left(b(c) - \left(\bar{\beta} - \underline{\beta}\right)y\right) - L(b(c))\right\}}.$$

Similarly,

$$\bar{b}'(c) = \frac{1}{c(1-c)\left\{L\left(\bar{b}(c) - \left(\bar{\beta} - \underline{\beta}\right)\bar{y}\right) - L(\bar{b}(c))\right\}}.$$

By (19) and MLRP, we have

$$b'(c') > \bar{b}'(c') > 0. \tag{20}$$

By MLRP, $\log h(x)$ is strictly concave. Since e^x is strictly increasing, $e^{\log h(x)} = h(x)$ is strictly quasiconcave. Hence, if $x \in (\bar{b}' - (\bar{\beta} - \underline{\beta})\bar{y}, \bar{b}')$, then $h(x) > \min\{h(\bar{b}' - (\bar{\beta} - \underline{\beta})\bar{y}), h(\bar{b}')\}$. Since both b' and $b' - (\bar{\beta} - \underline{\beta})y$ are, by (19), elements of this interval,

$$h(b') > h(\bar{b}') \quad \text{or} \quad h\left(b' - \left(\bar{\beta} - \underline{\beta}\right)y\right) > h\left(\bar{b}' - \left(\bar{\beta} - \underline{\beta}\right)\bar{y}\right). \tag{21}$$

Equating (14) and (16) when $c = c'$ yields

$$\frac{h(b')}{h\left(b' - \left(\bar{\beta} - \underline{\beta}\right)y\right)} = \frac{h(\bar{b}')}{h\left(\bar{b}' - \left(\bar{\beta} - \underline{\beta}\right)\bar{y}\right)}.$$

Consequently, either inequality in (21) implies the other, hence

$$h(b') > h(\bar{b}') \quad \text{and} \quad h\left(b' - \left(\bar{\beta} - \underline{\beta}\right)y\right)\Big) > h\left(\bar{b}' - \left(\bar{\beta} - \underline{\beta}\right)\bar{y}\right)\Big). \tag{22}$$

Differentiating (17) at $c = c'$, we find that

$$F'(c') - G'(c') = (1-\rho)\{h(b')b'(c') - h(\bar{b}')\bar{b}'(c')\} + \rho\Big\{h\Big(b' - \big(\bar{\beta} - \underline{\beta}\big)y\Big)b'(c') - h\Big(\bar{b}' - \big(\bar{\beta} - \underline{\beta}\big)\bar{y}\Big)\bar{b}'(c')\Big\}.$$

Equations (20) and (22) imply that $F'(c') - G'(c') > 0$, so part (e) is true. ∎

4. AN EXTENSION

In this section, the results are extended to include distributions of ξ_t whose densities do not satisfy MLRP as defined above. In Theorem 4 we allow the support of the distribution of ξ_t to be any interval. The likelihood ratio must be decreasing (not necessarily strictly) on the interior of the interval. In Theorem 3, the support was $\mathbf{R}$, and the likelihood ratio was *strictly* decreasing on $\mathbf{R}$. Distributions of ξ_t that are now covered include the uniform, the exponential, and truncated-normal distributions.

LEMMA 6. *Suppose $K \subset \mathbf{R}$ is compact. Let $\{a_n\}$ and $\{b_n\}$ be a sequence of continuous functions on K that converge uniformly to the continuous functions a and b respectively. If there exists a $\lambda > 0$ for which $b_n(z) \geq \lambda$, for $z \in K$ and all n, then $a_n/b_n \to a/b$ uniformly and $\{a_n/b_n\}$ is equicontinuous on K.*

Proof. Clearly, $b(z) \geq \lambda$ for $z \in K$. By Theorem 7.9 in Rudin (1964),

$$A_n \equiv \sup_{z \in K} |a_n(z) - a(z)| \to 0$$

$$\text{and} \quad B_n \equiv \sup_{z \in K} |b_n(z) - b(z)| \to 0 \quad \text{as } n \to \infty.$$

Since K is compact and $|a_n(z)| \leq |a(z)| + A_n$, there is some M such that $|a_n(z)| \leq M$ for all n and all $z \in K$. Hence, for $n > n_0$,

$$\sup_{z \in K} \left| \frac{a_n(z)}{b_n(z)} - \frac{a(z)}{b(z)} \right| \leq \sup_{z \in K} |a_n(z)| \left| \frac{b(z) - b_n(z)}{b_n(z) b(z)} \right| + \left| \frac{a_n(z) - a(z)}{b(z)} \right|$$

$$\leq \frac{MB_n}{\lambda^2} + \frac{A_n}{\lambda} \to 0$$

as $n \to \infty$. By Rudin's Theorem 7.9 again, $(a_n/b_n) \to a/b$ uniformly. By his Theorem 7.24, the a_n/b_n are equicontinuous on K.

LEMMA 7. *Let* $\{h_n\}_{n=n_0}^{\infty}$ *be a sequence of density functions. For every* $n \geq n_0$, *let* ξ_T^n *have density* h_n *with respect to* P_ρ. *Let* $y > 0$, $z_T^n = \xi_T^n + \beta y$, $X_\rho^n(y) = P_\rho[\beta = \bar{\beta} \| z_T^n]$, $F_n(c) = P_\rho[X_\rho^n(y) \leq c]$, $F(c) = P_\rho[X_\rho(y) \leq c]$. *Suppose* $D \subset \mathbf{R}$ *is a finite set that contains all the discontinuities of* h *and the* h_n. *Also suppose that* $\{x\colon h(x) = 0\}$ *is closed.*

If $h_n(x) \to h(x)$ *locally uniformly for all* $x \in D^c$, *then* $F_n(c) \to F(c)$ *at all* c *where* F *is continuous.*

Proof. By definition, $P_\rho \xi_T^{-1}$ and $P_\rho \xi_T^{n^{-1}}$ are probability measures with densities (with respect to Lebesgue measure) h and h_n, respectively. Since $h_n(x) \to h(x)$ almost everywhere, Scheffe's theorem implies that $P_\rho[\xi_T^n \in H] \to P_\rho[\xi_T \in H]$ for all Borel sets H. Hence $P_\rho(\xi_T^n)^{-1} \Rightarrow P_\rho \xi_T^{-1}$. By Theorem 3.2 in Billingsley (1968), $P_\rho(\xi_T^n, \beta)^{-1} \Rightarrow P_\rho(\xi_T, \beta)^{-1}$, because $\mathbf{R} \times \{\underline{\beta}, \bar{\beta}\}$ with Euclidean distance is separable. By (4.5) there, $(\xi_T^n, \beta) \xrightarrow{D} (\xi_T, \beta)$, hence by his Theorem 7.7, $z_T^n \xrightarrow{D} z_T$. Let

$$\phi_n(z) = \frac{\rho h_n(z - \bar{\beta} y)}{\rho h_n(z - \bar{\beta} y) + (1 - \rho) h_n(z - \beta y)}$$

$$\phi(z) = \frac{\rho h(z - \bar{\beta} y)}{\rho h(z - \bar{\beta} y) + (1 - \rho) h(z - \underline{\beta} y)}$$

and define ϕ_n and ϕ to be equal to zero for values of z that make their respective denominators zero. Let

$$E = \left\{z\colon \rho h(z - \bar{\beta} y) + (1 - \rho) h(z - \underline{\beta} y) = 0\right\}$$
$$\cup \left\{z\colon z - \bar{\beta} y \in D\right\} \cup \left\{z\colon z - \underline{\beta} y \in D\right\}.$$

Since D is finite and z_T has a density, $P_\rho[z_T - \bar{\beta} y \in D] = P_\rho[z_T - \underline{\beta} y \in D] = 0$. Now $P_\rho[h(\xi_T) = 0] = 0$, so $\rho P_\rho[\rho h(\xi_T) = 0] = (1 - \rho) P_{\underline{\rho}}[(1 - \rho) h(\xi_T) = 0] = 0$. Thus $P_\rho[z_T \in E] \leq \rho P_\rho[\rho h(z_T - \bar{\beta} y) = 0, \beta = \bar{\beta}] + (1 - \rho) P_\rho[(1 - \rho) h(z_T - \underline{\beta} y) = 0, \beta = \underline{\beta}] = 0$, hence $P_\rho[z_T \in E] = 0$.

Assume $z' \in E^c$ and $\{z_n\}$ is a sequence of numbers approaching z'. In order to show that $\phi_n(z_n) \to \phi(z')$, let $\xi > 0$. Since E is the union of three closed sets, E^c is open. Since $h_n \to h$ locally uniformly at $z' - \bar{\beta} y$ and $z' - \underline{\beta} y$, there exists some $\eta > 0$ such that $K \equiv [z' - \eta, z' + \eta] \subset E^c$, and that $h_n(z - \bar{\beta} y) \to h(z - \bar{\beta} y)$ and $h_n(z - \underline{\beta} y) \to h(z - \underline{\beta} y)$ uniformly on $z \in K$.

Since $K \subset E^c$, $b(z) \equiv \rho h(z - \bar{\beta} y) + (1 - \rho) h(z - \beta y) > 0$ and $\phi(z)$ is continuous on $z \in K$. Thus there exists a $\lambda > 0$ such that $b(z) \geq 2\lambda$ for $z \in K$. Since $b_n(z) \equiv \rho h_n(z - \bar{\beta} y) + (1 - \rho) h_n(z - \underline{\beta} y) \to b(z)$, uniformly on $z \in K$, there exists an $n_1 \geq n_0$ for which $b_n(z) \geq \lambda$, for all $n \geq n_1$ and all $z \in K$. By Lemma 6, $\phi_n \to \phi$ uniformly on K and $\{\phi_n, n \geq n_1\}$ is equicontinuous on K. Hence there exists a $\delta \in (0, \eta)$ such that if $n > n_1$ and $|z - z'| < \delta$, then $|\phi_n(z) - \phi_n(z')| \leq \xi/2$.

Since $z_n \to z'$, there exists an $n_2 \geq n_1$ such that $|z_n - z'| < \delta$ for $n > n_2$. Since $\phi_n(z') \to \phi(z')$, there exists an $n_3 \geq n_2$ such that $|\phi_n(z') - \phi(z')| \leq \xi/2$ for $n > n_3$. Now if $n > n_3$, then $|\phi_n(z_n) - \phi(z')| \leq |\phi_n(z_n) - \phi_n(z')| + |\phi_n(z') - \phi(z')| \leq \xi$. Hence $\phi_n(z_n) \to \phi(z')$.

To summarize, E contains the set of z such that $\phi(z_n) \to \phi(z)$ fails to hold for some sequence $\{z_n\}$ approaching z. Furthermore, $P_\rho(z_T^n)^{-1} \to P_\rho z_T^{-1}$ and $(P_\rho z_T^{-1})(E) = 0$. Theorem 5.5 in Billingsley (1968) establishes that $(P_\rho z_T^{n^{-1}})\phi_n^{-1} \to (P_\rho z_T^{-1})\phi^{-1}$. Since $\phi(z_T) = X_\rho(y)$ by (8) and similarly $\phi_n(z_T^n) = X_\rho^n(y)$, this implies that $F_n \to F$.

THEOREM 4. *Assume that $h(x)$ is positive only on an interval (and zero elsewhere) and that $L(x) = [h'(x)/h(x)]$ is continuously (not necessarily strictly) decreasing on the interior of this interval. Then $y_T(\rho) \geq y_0(\rho)$.*

Proof. Let $\rho \in [0, 1]$ and $0 \leq y < \bar{y} \leq I/p$. If we can show that $X_\rho(\bar{y})$ is more informative than $X_\rho(y)$, then, by Theorem 2, we are done. To do this, we construct a sequence of density functions and apply Lemma 7 to show that (12.1) and (12.2) are satisfied for $X = X_\rho(y)$ and $\bar{X} = X_\rho(\bar{y})$. As in the proof of Theorem 3, we may assume $y > 0$.

Since changing the values of h on a finite number of points does not affect the distribution of ξ_T, we may assume that $h(x) > 0$ on some *open* interval (a, b) and $h(x) = 0$ elsewhere ($a = -\infty$ or $b = \infty$ is allowed).

Fix $n_0 > 2/(b - a)$, and for $n \geq n_0$, define

$$g_n(x) =$$

$$\begin{cases} h\left(a + \dfrac{1}{n}\right)\exp\left\{\dfrac{-x^2}{2n} + \left(x - a - \dfrac{1}{n}\right)L\left(a - \dfrac{1}{n}\right) - 2^n\left(x - a - \dfrac{1}{n}\right)^2\right\}, & x \leq a + \dfrac{1}{n} \\ h(x)\exp\left(\dfrac{-x^2}{2n}\right), \quad x \in \left(a + \dfrac{1}{n}, b - \dfrac{1}{n}\right) & \\ h\left(b - \dfrac{1}{n}\right)\exp\left\{\dfrac{-x^2}{2n} + \left(x - b + \dfrac{1}{n}\right)L\left(b - \dfrac{1}{n}\right) - 2^n\left(x - b + \dfrac{1}{n}\right)^2\right\}, & x \geq b - \dfrac{1}{n}. \end{cases}$$

For $n \geq n_0$, g_n is positive and continuous on $\mathbf{R}$. Assume $x' \in (a, b)$. For n sufficiently large and for x is some neighborhood of x', $g_n(x) = h(x)\exp(-x^2/2n)$, so $g_n(x') \to h(x')$ locally uniformly by Theorem 7.13 in Rudin (1976). Hence $g_n \to h$ locally uniformly on (a, b).

Now assume $x' < a$ and let $\eta = (a - x')/2$ and $n_1 = \max(1/\eta, n_0)$. For $x \in [x' - \eta, x' + \eta]$ and $n \geq n_1$, $-4\eta \leq x - a - (1/n) \leq -\eta$, and $(x - a - (1/n))L(a + (1/n)) \leq (x - a - (1/n))L(a + (1/n_1)) \leq 4\eta|L(a + (1/n_1))|$, so $0 < g_n(x) \leq h(a + (1/n))\exp\{4\eta|L(a + (1/n_1))|$

$-2^n\eta^2\} \to 0$ as $n \to \infty$. Hence $g_n(x') \to h(x')$ locally uniformly for $x' < a$, and similarly for $x' > b$. Hence $g_n \to h$ locally uniformly on the complement of the finite set $D \equiv \{a, b\}$. By the bounded convergence theorem, $a_n \equiv \int_{-\infty}^{\infty} g_n(x)\,dx \to \int_{-\infty}^{\infty} h(x)\,dx = 1$ and $0 < a_n < \infty$ for each n. Let ξ_T^n be a random variable with density $h_n(x) \equiv 1/a_n g_n(x)$ for each n. Use the definitions in Lemma 7 for z_T^n, $X_\rho^n(y)$, $F_n(c)$ and $F(c)$. By Lemma 7, $F_n(c) \to F(c)$ for almost all c. Similarly, if we let $G_n(c) = P_\rho[X_\rho^n(\bar{y}) \le c]$ and $G(c) = P_\rho[X_\rho(\bar{y}) \le c]$, then $G_n(c) \to G(c)$ for almost all c.

Let $S_n(c) = F_n(c) - G_n(c)$ and $S(c) = F(c) - G(c)$. By the bounded convergence theorem, $\int_0^c S_n(x)\,dx \to \int_0^c S(x)\,dx$ for all $c \in [0, 1]$. Since $h_n = (1/a_n g_n)$,

$$\frac{h_n'(x)}{h_n(x)} = \begin{cases} L\left(a + \dfrac{1}{n}\right) - \dfrac{x}{n} - 2^{n+1}\left(x - a - \dfrac{1}{n}\right) & x \le a + \dfrac{1}{n} \\ L(x) - \dfrac{x}{n} & x \in \left(a + \dfrac{1}{n}, b - \dfrac{1}{n}\right) \\ L\left(b - \dfrac{1}{n}\right) - \dfrac{x}{n} - 2^{n+1}\left(x - b + \dfrac{1}{n}\right) & x \ge b - \dfrac{1}{n}. \end{cases}$$

Since $L(x)$ is decreasing on (a, b), $h_n'(x)/h_n(x)$ is continuously and strictly decreasing in x on $\mathbf{R}$. By Theorem 3, S_n satisfies (15) and (16) for all n. Hence S satisfies (15) and (16), so $X_\rho(\bar{y})$ is more informative than $X_\rho(y)$. ■

5. EXAMPLES

The result that $y_T(\rho) \ge y_0(\rho)$, which means that the experimenting consumer buys no less of good y than the myopically learning consumer, was established in Theorem 3 for disturbances that satisfy MLRP. This naturally raises the following issue: Under what conditions will $y_T(\rho) > y_0(\rho)$? Although we do not study this problem, two examples are given to shed some light on it. In the first example $y_T(\rho) > y_0(\rho)$ for all $\rho \in (0, 1)$, while in the second example, $y_T(\rho) = y_0(\rho)$ even if $\rho \in (0, 1)$ and $y_0(\rho)$ is an interior solution.

However, there are several outstanding issues related to densities not covered by Theorem 4. The remaining examples explore these issues. It is shown in Example 2 that there are disturbance densities for which $y_T(\rho) \le y_0(\rho)$. In Theorem 2 we established that if higher values of y generate more informative signals, then the experimenting consumer does not choose lower values of y. Theorem 3 adds the fact that for any MLRP density, higher y values generate more informative signals. In contrast with Theorem 3, higher y values can generate *less* information for the density function of Example 2. The logic of Theorem 2 is then used to show that in this case, the experimenting consumer selects lower values of y than the learning consumer.

Example 3 exhibits a situation in which higher y values yield neither more, nor less informative signals. This lack of ordering by informativeness seems to preclude using any variant of Theorem 2 to determine the sign of $y_T(\rho) - y_0(\rho)$.

Finally, note that any density function that satisfies the conditions of Theorem 4 is also quasiconcave. However, the density functions in Examples 2 and 3 are not quasiconcave. This leads to the conjecture that the quasiconcavity of h is necessary for $y_T(\rho) \geq y_0(\rho)$ when $y_0(\rho)$ is an interior optimum. Example 4 shows that this is not the case. An unsolved problem is whether or not the quasiconcavity of h is sufficient for $y_T(\rho) \geq y_0(\rho)$.

EXAMPLE 1.[8] Let $u(x, z) = xz$ and $T = 1$. Suppose $\underline{\beta} > 0$, so $E_\rho[\beta] > 0$ for all ρ. Assume that ξ_t is uniformly distributed on $[\bar{\xi} - \frac{1}{2}, \bar{\xi} + \frac{1}{2}]$. Also assume that $(I/p) < [1/(\bar{\beta} - \underline{\beta})]$. [This implies that for $y \leq (I/p)$, $z_0(y)$ will not perfectly reveal β.] By (5) and (2),

$$g(y, \rho) = (I - py)\left(E_\rho[\beta]y + \bar{\xi}\right) \tag{23}$$

is the expected current period utility.

By (11), since $\partial g/\partial y = IE_\rho[\beta] - 2E_\rho[\beta]py - p\bar{\xi}$,

$$y_0(\rho) = \frac{IE_\rho[\beta] - p\bar{\xi}}{2pE_\rho[\beta]} \tag{24}$$

unless $y_0(\rho)$ is 0 or I/p. To guarantee an interior solution for all ρ, we assume that $|\bar{\xi}| < I\underline{\beta}/p$. By (11) again,

$$\begin{aligned} V_0(\rho) &= \left(I - \frac{IE_\rho[\beta] - p\bar{\xi}}{2E_\rho[\beta]}\right)\left(\frac{IE_\rho[\beta] - p\bar{\xi}}{2p} + \bar{\xi}\right) \\ &= \frac{\left(IE_\rho[\beta] + p\bar{\xi}\right)^2}{4pE_\rho[\beta]}, \end{aligned}$$

so

$$V_0(\rho) = \frac{I^2}{4p}E_\rho[\beta] + \frac{I\bar{\xi}}{2} + \frac{p\bar{\xi}^2}{4}\left(\frac{1}{E_\rho[\beta]}\right). \tag{25}$$

[8]We would like to thank Edward Schlee for pointing out this example to us.

By the Remark to Lemma 1, $E_\rho[\beta]$ is linear in ρ, so $(1/E_\rho[\beta])$ is strictly convex in ρ. Hence $V_0(\rho)$ is strictly convex when $\bar{\xi} \neq 0$, and linear when $\bar{\xi} = 0$.

Since $h(x) = 1$ only for $x \in [\bar{\xi} - \frac{1}{2}, \bar{\xi} + \frac{1}{2}]$, by (8), with probability 1,

$$X_\rho(y) = \begin{cases} 0 & \text{if } z_1 < \bar{\beta}y + \bar{\xi} - \frac{1}{2} \\ 1 & \text{if } z_1 > \underline{\beta}y + \bar{\xi} + \frac{1}{2} \\ \rho & \text{otherwise.} \end{cases} \tag{26}$$

Assume $0 \leq y \leq (I/p)$ and set $q = P_1[z_1 > \underline{\beta}y + \bar{\xi} + \frac{1}{2}]$. Now $q = P_1[\xi_1 > (\beta - \bar{\beta})y + \bar{\xi} + \frac{1}{2}] = P_1[\xi_1 \in ((\underline{\beta} - \bar{\beta})y + \bar{\xi} + \frac{1}{2}, \bar{\xi} + \frac{1}{2})]$. Since $y \leq (I/p) < [1/(\bar{\beta} - \underline{\beta})]$ by assumption, $(\underline{\beta} - \bar{\beta})y + \bar{\xi} + \frac{1}{2} > \bar{\xi} - \frac{1}{2}$, so $q = (\bar{\beta} - \underline{\beta})y < 1$.

Similarly, $P_0[z_1 > \underline{\beta}y + \bar{\xi} + \frac{1}{2}] = 0$, $P_0[z_1 < \bar{\beta}y + \bar{\xi} - \frac{1}{2}] = P_0[\xi_1 < (\bar{\beta} - \underline{\beta})y + \bar{\xi} - \frac{1}{2}] = q$ and $P_1[z_1 < \bar{\beta}y + \bar{\xi} - \frac{1}{2}] = 0$. By Lemma 1 and equation (26), $P_\rho[X_\rho(y) = 0] = \rho P_1[X_\rho(y) = 0] + (1 - \rho)P_0[X_\rho(y) = 0] = (1 - \rho)q$. Similarly, $P_\rho[X_\rho(y) = 1] = \rho q$, so $P_\rho[X_\rho(y) = \rho] = 1 - q$. Thus $E_\rho[V_0(X_\rho(y))] = (1 - \rho)qV_0(0) + \rho q V_0(1) + (1 - q)V_0(\rho)$. Hence,

$$\frac{dE_\rho\left[V_0\left(X_\rho(y)\right)\right]}{dy} = \left[(1 - \rho)V_0(0) + \rho V_0(1) - V_0(\rho)\right]\left(\bar{\beta} - \underline{\beta}\right), \tag{27}$$

provided $0 \leq y \leq (I/p)$.

Case A: $\bar{\xi} = 0$. Here, by (25), V_0 is linear, so

$$E_\rho\left[V_0\left(X_\rho(y)\right)\right] = V_0\left(E_\rho\left[X_\rho(y)\right]\right) = V_0(\rho)$$

for all y. In this case, by (9) and (11), $y_1(\rho) = y_0(\rho)$.

Case B: $\bar{\xi} \neq 0$. Assume $\rho \in (0, 1)$. Since V_0 is strictly convex,

$$V_0(\rho) < \rho V_0(1) + (1 - \rho)V_0(0),$$

by Jensen's inequality. By (27), $(d/dy)E_\rho[V_0(X_\rho(y))] > 0$, so by (9) and (11), $y_1(\rho) \neq y_0(\rho)$. By Theorem 4, $y_1(\rho) > y_0(\rho)$.

From (24), we can derive the following comparative static results: $(\partial y_0/\partial p) < 0$, $(\partial y_0/\partial I) > 0$, and $\text{sgn}(\partial y_0/\partial \rho) = \text{sgn}(\bar{\xi})$.

However, more interesting comparative statics involve the amount of experimentation, $y_1(\rho) - y_0(\rho)$. As we have seen, this is zero when $\bar{\xi} = 0$, so henceforth we assume that $\bar{\xi} \neq 0$. For $\rho = 0$ and $\rho = 1$, by (27), (9), and (11), $y_1(\rho) - y_0(\rho) = 0$. We have already established, in Case B, that $y_1(\rho) - y_0(\rho) > 0$ for $\rho \in (0, 1)$. We now show that $y_1(\rho) - y_0(\rho)$ is strictly quasiconcave in ρ, i.e., there exists some $\hat{\rho} \in (0, 1)$ such that experimentation increases in ρ for $\rho < \hat{\rho}$ and decreases for $\rho > \hat{\rho}$.

Just as (11) and (23) imply (24), (9) implies

$$y_1(\rho) = \frac{IE_\rho[\beta] - p\bar{\xi} + \delta\left\{dE_\rho\left[V_\rho\left(X_\rho(y)\right)\right]/dy\right\}}{2pE_\rho[\beta]},$$

provided $y_1(\rho) < (I/p)$. By (27), if $y_1(\rho) < (I/p)$, then

$$y_1(\rho) - y_0(\rho) = \frac{\delta\left(\bar{\beta} - \underline{\beta}\right)[(1-\rho)V_0(0) + \rho V_0(1) - V_0(\rho)]}{2pE_\rho[\beta]}.^9 \tag{28}$$

We have already established the existence of a $\hat{\rho} \in (0,1)$ such that $(d/dy)(y_1(\hat{\rho}) - y_0(\hat{\rho})) = 0$ (because an interior maximum exists). To show that $y_1 - y_0$ is strictly quasiconcave, it suffices to show that $\hat{\rho}$ is unique. Note that

$$\operatorname{sgn}\left\{\frac{d}{dy}(y_1(\rho) - y_0(\rho))\right\}$$
$$= \operatorname{sgn}\left\{\psi(\rho) - \left(\bar{\beta} - \underline{\beta}\right)((1-\rho)V_0(0) + \rho V_0(1) - V_0(\rho))\right\}, \tag{29}$$

where $\psi(\rho) = (V_0(1) - V_0(0) - V_0'(\rho))E_\rho[\beta]$. By the definition of $\hat{\rho}$, (29), and (28), $\psi(\hat{\rho}) = (2pE_{\hat{\rho}}[\beta]/\delta)(y_1(\hat{\rho}) - y_0(\hat{\rho})) > 0$. By the strict convexity of $V_0(\rho)$, $V_0(1) - V_0(0) - V_0'(\rho) \geq \psi(\hat{\rho})/E_{\hat{\rho}}[\beta] > 0$ for $0 \leq \rho \leq \hat{\rho}$. Hence $(\bar{\beta} - \underline{\beta})((1-\rho)V_0(0) + \rho V_0(1) - V_0(\rho))$ is strictly increasing on $[0, \hat{\rho}]$. Now $\psi'(\rho) = -V_0''(\rho)E_\rho[\beta] - (\bar{\beta} - \underline{\beta})(V_0(1) - V_0(0) - V_0'(\rho)) < 0$ for $0 \leq \rho \leq \hat{\rho}$, because both terms are negative for these values of ρ. Hence both terms on the right side of (29) are strictly decreasing on $[0, \hat{\rho}]$. Since $\hat{\rho}$ is an arbitrary zero of (29), $\hat{\rho}$ is unique. Hence $y_1 - y_0$ is quasiconcave.

The next result is used in Examples 2 (where $a = 0$), 3 ($0 < a < \frac{1}{5}$) and 4 ($a \geq \frac{1}{5}$). Notice that the $a = \frac{1}{3}$ and $a = 1$ cases yield uniform disturbance densities, so they are already covered by Theorem 4.

LEMMA 8. *Suppose*

$$\bar{\beta} = 1, \quad \underline{\beta} = 0, \quad a \in [0,1], \quad \textit{and}$$

$$h(x) = \begin{cases} \dfrac{1-a}{2} & x \in [0,1] \cup [2,3] \\ a & x \in (1,2), \\ 0 & \textit{otherwise}. \end{cases}$$

[9]It is clear from (28) that increasing δ will increase the amount of experimentation.

If $y \in [1,2]$, *then*

$$X_\rho(y) = \begin{cases} 1 & \text{with probability } \rho\left(a(y-1) + \dfrac{1-a}{2}\right) \\ 0 & \text{with probability } (1-\rho)\left(a(y-1) + \dfrac{1-a}{2}\right) \\ \rho & \text{with probability } (y-1)\left(\dfrac{1-a}{2}\right) \\ x_1 & \text{with probability } (2-y)\left((1-\rho)\dfrac{1-a}{2} + \rho a\right) \\ x_2 & \text{with probability } (2-y)\left(\rho\dfrac{1-a}{2} + (1-\rho)a\right), \end{cases} \tag{30}$$

where

$$x_1 = \frac{\rho a}{\rho a + (1-\rho)(1-a/2)},$$

$$x_2 = \frac{\rho(1-a/2)}{\rho(1-a/2) + (1-\rho)a}.^{10}$$

$$\begin{aligned} &\text{If } \rho \in (0,1) \quad \text{and} \quad 0 < a < \tfrac{1}{3}, \quad \text{then } 0 < x_1 < \rho < x_2 < 1. \\ &\text{If } \rho \in (0,1) \quad \text{and} \quad \tfrac{1}{3} < a < 1, \quad \text{then } 0 < x_2 < \rho < x_1 < 1. \end{aligned} \tag{31}$$

Proof. Let $q = P_\rho[h(z_T - y) = (1-a)/2$ and $h(z_T) = a]$. Assume that $\rho \in (0,1)$, $a \in (0,1)$ and $a \neq \frac{1}{3}$, so x_1, x_2, ρ, 0, and 1 are all distinct. Hence by (8), $P_\rho[X_\rho(y) = x_2] = q$. By the definition of h, $q = P_\rho[z_T - y \in [0,1]$ and $z_T \in (1,2)]$, so by Corollary 2 to Lemma 1,

$$q = \rho P_\rho[\xi_T \in [0,1] \cap (1-y, 2-y)]$$
$$+(1-\rho)P_\rho[\xi_T \in [y, y+1] \cap (1,2)] = \rho P_\rho[\xi_T \in [0, 2-y)]$$
$$+(1-\rho)P_\rho[\xi_T \in [y,2)] = (\rho((1-a)/2) + (1-\rho)a)(2-y).$$

[10]Note that there is a difficulty in interpreting (30) and (32) when 1, 0, ρ, x_1, and x_2 are not all distinct. This is a problem when a is either 0, $\frac{1}{3}$, or 1, and also when ρ equals 0 or 1. In any of these cases, the probability that the value of $X_\rho(y)$ equals a number with multiple representations equal to the sum of the corresponding probabilities.

This establishes the fifth line of (30). The other facts in (30) follow by similar arguments. Thus (30) is true assuming $\rho \in (0,1)$, $a \in (0,1)$ and $a \neq \frac{1}{3}$.

If $\rho = 0$ or $\rho = 1$, then by (8), (30) is true as long as it is interpreted as indicated in footnote 10. Similarly, (30) is easily established for the difficult cases where $a = 0$, $\frac{1}{3}$, or 1, since for $a_n \to a$ with $a_n \in (0, \frac{1}{3}) \cup (\frac{1}{3}, 1)$, $X_\rho(y)|_{a_n} \xrightarrow{D} X_\rho(y)|_a$ as $n \to \infty$ by (30).

Now assume $\rho \in (0,1)$ and $0 < a < \frac{1}{3}$. Since $a < [(1-a)/2]$, $\rho((1-a)/2) + (1-\rho)a < [(1-a)/2]$, so $\rho < x_2 < 1$. Similar arguments establish the other inequalities in (31). ■

Let $1 \le y < \bar{y} \le 2$ and $\Delta y = \bar{y} - y$. By Lemma 8,

$$\begin{aligned} \Delta P_\rho\big[X_\rho(y) = 0\big] &= (1-\rho)a\,\Delta y, \\ \Delta P_\rho\big[X_\rho(y) = x_1\big] &= -\left(\rho a + (1-\rho)\frac{1-a}{2}\right)\Delta y, \\ \Delta P_\rho\big[X_\rho(y) = 1\big] &= \rho a\,\Delta y. \end{aligned} \tag{32}$$

Set $F(c) = P_\rho[X_\rho(y) \le c]$, $G(c) = P_\rho[X_\rho(\bar{y}) \le c]$, and $S(c) = G(c) - F(c)$. By Lemma 3, (12.1) holds.[11] Now the support of $X_\rho(y)$ and $X_\rho(\bar{y})$ is $\{0, 1, \rho, x_1, x_2\}$, so $\int_0^c S(x)\,dx$ is piecewise linear in c on $[0,1]$. Since $\int_0^c S(x)\,dx$ is also continuous, its sign for c equal to x_1, x_2, and ρ determines its sign for $c \in (0,1)$. This fact is crucial to Examples 2, 3, and 4.

EXAMPLE 2. Assume $\rho \in (0,1)$ and let $a = 0$ in Lemma 8, so $x_1 = 0$ and $x_2 = 1$. As mentioned above, $\int_0^c S(x)\,dx$ is linear for $c \in [0,\rho]$, and for $c \in [\rho, 1]$. By (32),

$$\int_0^\rho S(x)\,dx = \int_0^\rho \Delta P_\rho\big[X_\rho(y) = x_1\big]\,dx = -\rho\left(\frac{1-\rho}{2}\right)\Delta y < 0.$$

Hence $\int_0^c S(x)\,dx < 0$ for $c \in (0,1)$, and by (12), $X_\rho(y)$ is more informative than $X_\rho(\bar{y})$. Assuming now that $p = 1$ and $I = 2$, so $y > 2$ is not feasible, and assuming that $y_0(\rho) \in [1,2)$ (inspection of (11), (5), and (2) reveals that this is no difficulty), it follows that $y_1(\rho) \le y_0(\rho)$. The proof of this fact exactly parallels the proof of Theorem 2.[12]

[11] Let $x_3 = 0$, $x_4 = 1$, $x_5 = \rho$, so $\int_0^1 F(c)\,dc = \int_0^1 \Sigma_{n=1}^5 P_\rho[X_\rho(y) = x_n \le c]\,dc = \Sigma_{n=1}^5 \int_{x_n}^1 P_\rho[X_\rho(y) = x_n]\,dc = 1 - E_\rho[X_\rho(y)]$. Similarly, $\int_0^1 G(c)\,dc = 1 - E_\rho[X_\rho(\bar{y})]$, so $\int_0^1 S(c)\,dc = 0$.

[12] $E_\rho[V_{T-1}(X_\rho(y))]$ is now decreasing for $y \in [1,2]$, so assuming $y_T(\rho) > y_0(\rho)$ results in a contradiction.

EXAMPLE 3. Assume $\rho \in (0,1)$ and let $0 < a < \frac{1}{5}$ in Lemma 8. By (32) and (31),

$$\int_0^{x_1} S(x)\,dx = \int_0^{x_1} \Delta P_\rho\big[X_\rho(y) = 0\big]\,dx = x_1(1-\rho)a\,\Delta y > 0.$$

On the other hand,

$$\begin{aligned}
\int_0^{\rho} S(x)\,dx &= \int_0^{\rho} \Delta P_\rho\big[X_\rho(y) \le x\big]\,dx \\
&= \int_0^{\rho} \Delta P_\rho\big[X_\rho(y) = 0 \le x\big]\,dx + \int_0^{\rho} \Delta P_\rho\big[X_\rho(y) = x_1 \le x\big]\,dx \\
&= \rho(1-\rho)a\,\Delta y - \int_{x_1}^{\rho}\left(\rho a + (1-\rho)\frac{1-a}{2}\right)\Delta y\,dx \\
&= \rho(1-\rho)a\,\Delta y + \left(-\rho^2 a - \rho(1-\rho)\left(\frac{1-a}{2}\right) + \rho a\right)\Delta y \\
&= \rho(1-\rho)\frac{5a-1}{2}\,\Delta y < 0.
\end{aligned}$$

By (12), $X_\rho(\bar{y})$ is neither more nor less informative than $X_\rho(y)$; i.e., $X_\rho(y)$ cannot be ordered by informativeness. By Lemma 4, $E_\rho[V(X_\rho(\bar{y}))] - E_\rho[V(X_\rho(y))]$ is positive for some bounded, convex functions V, and negative for others. Hence we can say nothing about the sign of $y_T(\rho) - y_0(\rho)$.

EXAMPLE 4. Assume $\rho \in (0,1)$ and let $\frac{1}{5} \le a \le 1$ in Lemma 8. To simplify the exposition, let $\frac{1}{5} \le a < \frac{1}{3}$, so by (31), $0 < x_1 < \rho < x_2 < 1$. Since $\int_0^c S(x)\,dx$ is piecewise linear, its values for c equal to x_1, ρ, and x_2 suffice to completely describe its behavior for $c \in [0,1]$. The calculations from Example 3 that $\int_0^{x_1} S(x)\,dx = x_1(1-\rho)a\,\Delta y$ and $\int_0^{\rho} S(x)\,dx = \rho(1-\rho)[(5a-1)/2]\,\Delta y$ still hold, except that since $a \ge \frac{1}{5}$, both integrals are now nonnegative. Furthermore, by (32),

$$\begin{aligned}
\int_0^{x_2} S(x)\,dx &= -\int_{x_2}^{1} S(x)\,dx \\
&= \int_{x_2}^{1} -\Delta P_\rho\big[X_\rho(y) < 1\big]\,dx \\
&= \int_{x_2}^{1} \Delta P_\rho\big[X_\rho(y) = 1\big]\,dx = (1-x_2)\rho a\,\Delta y > 0.
\end{aligned}$$

Hence (12.2) holds, so $X_\rho(\bar{y})$ is more informative than $X_\rho(y)$.

Similar reasoning can be applied to the case $\frac{1}{3} < a < 1$, where by (31), $0 < x_2 < \rho < x_1 < 1$. Furthermore, this can be generalized to the case in which $0 \leq y < \bar{y} \leq (I/p)$. Hence by Theorem 2, $y_T(\rho) \geq y_0(\rho)$. As in Example 1, Case B, where $u(x, z) = xz$, this inequality can be made strict.

Acknowledgment

Support through grant SES-8177265 from the National Science Foundation is greatly appreciated.

References

Billingsley, P. (1968). *Convergence of Probability Measures*, (Wiley, New York).

Billingsley, P. (1986). *Probability and Measure*, 2nd ed. (Wiley, New York).

Blackwell, D. (1951). "The comparison of experiments," *Proceedings of the Second Berkeley Symposium on Mathematical Statistics and Probability*, (Univ. California Press, Berkeley), pp. 93–102.

Easley, D., and N. M. Kiefer (1988). "Controlling a stochastic process with unknown parameters," *Econometrica* **56**, 1045–1064.

Grossman, S. J., R. E. Kihlstrom, and L. J. Mirman (1977). "A Bayesian approach to the production of information and learning by doing," *Rev. Econ. Studies* **44** (3), 533–547.

Kihlstrom, R., L. J. Mirman, and A. Postlewaite (1984). "Experimental consumption and the 'Rothschild Effect'," in *Bayesian Models of Economic Theory*, M. Boyer and R. E. Kihlstrom (eds.) (Elsevier, Amsterdam).

McLennan, A. (1984). "Price dispersion and incomplete learning in the long run," *J. Econ. Dyn. Contr.*, **7**, 331–347.

Prescott, E. C. (1972). "The multi-period control problem under uncertainty," *Econometrica* **40**, 1043–1058.

Rothschild, M. (1974). "A two-armed bandit theory of market pricing," *J. Econ. Theory* **9**, 185–202.

Rothschild, M., and J. E. Stiglitz (1970). "Increasing risk: I, A definition," *J. Econ. Theory* **2**, 225–243.

Rudin, W. (1976). *Principles of Mathematical Analysis*, 3rd ed. (McGraw-Hill, New York).

THE FIRM AND THE PLANT IN GENERAL EQUILIBRIUM THEORY*

Andreas Hornstein
Department of Economics
University of Western Ontario
London, Ontario N6A 5C2
Canada

Edward C. Prescott
Research Department
Federal Reserve Bank of Minneapolis
Minneapolis, Minnesota 55480
and
Department of Economics
University of Minnesota
Minneapolis, Minnesota 55455

1. INTRODUCTION

In this paper we introduce the firm and the plant into classical general equilibrium theory. Our approach follows McKenzie's in having a convex cone aggregate technology. McKenzie (1959) shows this formulation is equivalent to the one of Arrow and Debreu (1954), who assume a finite set of technologies and an ownership distribution. The nature of McKenzie's argument is that a distinct entrepreneurial factor can be introduced for each firm. In the Arrow–Debreu setup, the quantities of these factors are normalized to one and distributed proportionally to ownership shares. Both the McKenzie and the Arrow–Debreu formulations are equivalent mathematically. They are not, however, equivalent from the perspective of economics. The approach of identifying each firm with a distinct technology set is not at all useful for developing a theory of industrial organizations. As McKenzie (1959) points out, when nonconvexities are small

*The views expressed herein are those of the authors and not necessarily those of the Federal Reserve Bank of Minneapolis or the Federal Reserve System.

relative to the size of the economy and access to the underlying technologies is free, the aggregate production possibility set is approximately a convex cone. In this paper, we adopt this approach and formally develop the theory of the aggregate production possibility set for two economies.

In Section 2, we represent the Lucas (1978) managerial span-of-control theory of the firm in the McKenzie-type general equilibrium language. With this representation the proof of existence and optimality of equilibrium is a simple application of standard theorems in general equilibrium theory. One element of this environment is a nonconvexity in the household consumption possibility set: An agent can either be a manager or be managed by someone else but cannot be one-third manager and two-thirds worker. This nonconvexity disappears with the introduction of lotteries: An agent can be a manager with probability one-third and a worker with probability two-thirds. This is the approach that Prescott and Townsend (1984) use to extend competitive theory to a class of economies with private information. For the span-of-control economy, as well as for the Prescott–Townsend private information economies, the production possibility set is a convex cone.

In Section 3, we consider an environment in which both the length of time a plant can be operated and the number of workers operating it can be varied. This introduces what appears to be a nonconvexity in the production possibility set because a plant's output increases proportionally to hours of operation, given the number of workers operating it and the capital stock used by the workers. Until now, this feature has not been introduced into quantitative general equilibrium analyses. Here, using the abstract language of general equilibrium theory, we develop a simple, tractable way to introduce this feature. The important result is that in this world of identical individuals, some people work and some do not, even though preferences are convex. This result provides theoretical justification for the labor indivisibility constraint of Rogerson (1988) and Hansen (1985). Again, the production possibility set is a convex cone.

In Section 4 we use a theorem of McKenzie (1959) to establish the existence of a competitive equilibrium for the managerial span-of-control economy.

Throughout this paper, we use the McKenzie-type representation of an economy. A commodity point x is an element of a linear commodity space L. There is a finite number of agent types, $i \in I$, and a continuum of each type. The measure of type i is λ^i, and the total measure of agents in the economy is $\lambda = \sum_{i \in I} \lambda^i$. The consumption set X^i of a type i agent is a subset of the commodity space L. Preferences over consumption bundles in X^i are represented by the utility functions u^i: $X^i \to \mathbb{R}$. Production is described by some aggregate production possibility set Y, which is a convex cone in L. An allocation $[(x^i)_{i \in I}, y]$ is feasible if $x^i \in X^i$ for all

$i \in I$, $y \in Y$, and $\Sigma_{i \in I} \lambda^i x^i = y$. Endowments are subsumed in X^i. An economy is thus completely described by $E = \{(u^i, X^i, \lambda^i)_{i \in I}, Y\}$.[1]

2. THE FIRM IN GENERAL EQUILIBRIUM THEORY

In a paper on the distribution of firm size, Lucas (1978) describes a static model of entry and exit with competition in which firms arise endogenously.[2] His model is a general equilibrium model, but his representation of the environment is such that its relationship to the standard general equilibrium formulation is not apparent. We show that by defining the commodity points in terms of contracts with lotteries, we can represent his environment as an economy whose production set is a convex cone. This formulation makes transparent the role of entrepreneurial ability as a production factor. It allows us to use standard existence results from general equilibrium theory, and it provides an example for McKenzie's interpretation of the aggregate production set.

We describe the environment of this economy as follows. There is a continuum of agents. Each agent is characterized by managerial ability, $m \in M$, and by endowment of the homogeneous capital good, $k \in K$. There is a finite number of agent types, $i \in I$. Each type is characterized by the pair (k^i, m^i). The measure of agent type i is λ^i and $\Sigma_i \lambda^i = 1$. A homogeneous consumption good is produced using managerial ability, labor, and capital. The technology is such that if one agent of ability $m \in M$ manages $n \in N$ workers and $k \in K$ units of capital, then $mg[f(k,n)]$ units of the consumption good can be produced by this firm. The function f displays constant returns to scale. Function g is increasing, differentiable, and strictly concave with $g'(\infty) = 0$ and $g'(0) = \infty$. The vector $a = (k, m, n) \in A = K \times M \times N$ denotes a particular productive activity.

Preferences with respect to random consumption allocations with support $C \subset \mathbb{R}_+$ are represented by their expected utility $E[U(c)]$. The function U is increasing and has a strictly concave extension on $\mathbb{R}_+$. An agent can act as either a manager or a worker, but not as both simultaneously.

Let the sets C, K, M, and N be finite subsets of $\mathbb{R}$, and let q be the cardinality of $S = C \times K \times (M \cup \{0\})$. For this environment the commod-

[1]The fact that we restrict allocations to ones that treat agents of the same type in the same way is discussed in Section 3.

[2]In his study of executive compensation, Tuck (1954) deals with managerial span-of-control in an informal but general equilibrium way. We thank Lionel McKenzie for bringing this work to our attention.

ity space L is $\mathbb{R}^q$. We restrict our attention to finite sets for ease of exposition. This does not imply any loss of generality, and we will relax this assumption when appropriate.

For an agent, the feasible consumption bundle is interpreted as a contract that specifies the probabilities x_s of the events $s = (c, k, m) \in S$.[3] If the realization of the lottery is s, the agent receives c units of the consumption good and provides k units of capital services; if $m = 0$, provides one unit of labor services; or if $m \neq 0$, provides one unit of managerial services of type m. Let

$$S^i = \{s \in S\colon k \leq k^i, m = 0 \quad \text{or} \quad m = m^i\}.$$

Given that the agent's endowment of managerial ability and capital is assumed to be verifiable, the consumption possibility set of a type i agent is

$$X^i = \{x \in L_+\colon \Sigma_s x_s = 1, x_s = 0 \quad \text{if} \quad s \notin S^i\}. \tag{1}$$

Note that an agent's consumption possibility set is a lower-dimensional subspace of the commodity space. This is a nonstandard feature that our economy has in common with McKenzie's general equilibrium approach. Preferences with respect to elements of this set are represented by the utility function

$$u(x) = \Sigma_{c,k,m} U(c) x_{ckm} = \Sigma_s U(c) x_s. \tag{2}$$

An allocation $(x^i)_{i \in I}$ is resource feasible if there exists a $z \in \mathbb{R}^l_+$, where l is the cardinality of A, such that the following constraints are met:

$$\Sigma_i \lambda^i \Sigma_s c x^i_s - \Sigma_a m g[f(k,n)] z_a \leq 0, \tag{3}$$

$$- \Sigma_i \lambda^i \Sigma_s k x^i_s + \Sigma_a k z_a \leq 0, \tag{4}$$

$$- \Sigma_i \lambda^i \Sigma_{c,k} x^i_{ck0} + \Sigma_a n z_a \leq 0, \tag{5}$$

$$- \Sigma_i \lambda^i \Sigma_{c,k} x^i_{ckm} + \Sigma_{k,n} z_{kmn} \leq 0, \quad \text{for each} \quad m \in M. \tag{6}$$

We assume that a law of large numbers holds such that the realized distribution on outcomes s for an agent type i coincides with that agent type's probability measure x^i (see, e.g., Uhlig, 1988). The vector z is a measure on the set of feasible activities $a \in A$. The measure z specifies the activities internal to the production set.

Constraint (3) says the total quantity of the consumption good distributed is less than or equal to the total amount produced. Constraint

[3]Although it is possible to define a lower-dimensional commodity space for this example, it is not desirable. By considering the more general space, results such as the convexity of Y are transparent.

(4) says the total quantity of capital provided by the agents is at least as great as the quantity used in production. Constraints (5) and (6) state the same about the production factors, labor ($m = 0$) and managerial abilities ($m \in M$).

The system of linear constraints (3)–(6) can be expressed in the following compact form

$$r\left(\Sigma_i \lambda^i x^i, z\right) \leq 0, \tag{7}$$

where r is a linear function.

We now define the technology for this economy. The production set is

$$Y = \left\{y \in L_+ : \exists z \in \mathbb{R}_+^l \quad \text{s.t. } r(y, z) \leq 0\right\}, \tag{8}$$

where r represents a finite number of linear constraints. As defined, the production set is McKenzie's convex cone. This general equilibrium formulation seems to provide no information about the industrial structure of the economy because the structure has been subsumed in the production set Y. We can—and do—interpret a firm to be some combination of a manager, capital, and workers, and in equilibrium there will be some distribution z over firms. The formation of firms thus becomes part of the economy's production possibility set, not something that exists independently of it.

3. THE PLANT IN GENERAL EQUILIBRIUM THEORY

Rogerson (1988) and Hansen (1985) have done important work on modeling employment in quantitative general equilibrium theory. They introduce a labor indivisibility constraint in the environments considered. In those environments, in which all individuals are identical, equilibrium is characterized by some people working and some not. We consider an environment in which the same employment pattern is observed, although hours of employment is not constrained to two values. In our environment both the time a plant can be operated and the number of workers operating a plant can be varied. This introduces what appears to be a nonconvexity in the production possibility set, since the output of a plant is $hf(k, n)$, where h is hours the plant is operated, f is a neoclassical production function with constant returns to scale, k is capital input, and n is the number of workers operating a plant. For this technology, we no longer assume that production uses two distinct inputs, managerial services and labor services, as in Section 2.

We now consider an economy of ex ante identical individuals, where the measure of agents is one. Preferences with respect to random consumption work pairs (c, h) are represented by their expected utility

$E[U(c, h)]$, where $c \geq 0$ is consumption, $0 \leq h \leq 1$ is the fraction of time allocated to market activities, and $1 - h$ is the fraction of time allocated to nonmarket activities. Each agent is endowed with $\bar{k} > 0$ units of capital. The function U is increasing in c and decreasing in h.

The problem is to represent this economy in our McKenzie-type general equilibrium language. Let C, H, and K be finite sets, and let S be $C \times H \times K$ with generic element $s = (c, h, k)$. The commodity space L is the Euclidean space with dimension equal to the cardinality of the set S. For an agent, the consumption bundle is interpreted as a contract that obliges the agent to provide k units of capital and h units of time, for which the agent receives c units of the consumption good. The probability of an event $s = (c, h, k)$ is x_s. There is only one type of agent with the consumption possibility set

$$X = \left\{x \in L_+ : \Sigma_{s \in S} x_s = 1, \text{ and } x_{chk} = 0 \text{ if } k > \bar{k}\right\} \tag{9}$$

and the utility function

$$u(x) = \Sigma_{c,h,k} U(c, h) x_{chk} = \Sigma_s U(c, h) x_s. \tag{10}$$

Let N be a finite set, and let $A = H \times K \times N$ with generic element $a = (h, k, n)$ and cardinality l. We let z_a be the number of plants operated h hours using k units of capital and n workers. An allocation is resource feasible if there exists some $z \in \mathbb{R}_+^l$ such that

$$\Sigma_s c x_s - \Sigma_a h f(k, n) z_a \leq 0 \tag{11}$$

$$-\Sigma_s k x_s + \Sigma_a k z_a \leq 0, \tag{12}$$

$$-\Sigma_{c,k} x_{chk} + \Sigma_{k,n} n z_{hkn} \leq 0, \qquad \forall h \in H. \tag{13}$$

Constraint (11) says the amount of the consumption good distributed is less than or equal to the quantity produced. Constraint (12) says the quantity of capital obtained is at least as great as the quantity of capital used in the production. Finally, constraints (13) state that the numbers of people working h hours are the numbers of people working in plants that are operated h hours.

Constraints (11)–(13) can be expressed in the compact form

$$r(x, z) \leq 0,$$

and the technology set is

$$Y = \left\{y \in L_+ : \exists z \in \mathbb{R}_+^l \quad \text{s.t. } r(y, z) \leq 0\right\}. \tag{14}$$

The constraints defining Y are jointly linear in y and z. It is immediate that Y is a convex cone. The set X is convex, and the utility function $u(x)$ is concave and continuous. Both sets are closed, and the set X is compact.

In this economy with one agent type, the anonymous Pareto-optimal allocation is the one that maximizes $u(x)$ subject to $x \in X \cap Y$. An optimum exists, given that u is continuous and $X \cap Y$ is compact. For economies with only one agent type, the anonymous competitive equilibrium and the anonymous Pareto-optimal allocations coincide.

The characteristics of an anonymous Pareto-optimal allocation are derived by analyzing a simpler equivalent problem. For this version, we no longer distinguish between the organization of consumption (x) and the organization of production (z). The event $s = (c, h, k) \in S$ is now interpreted as an agent receiving c units of the consumption good, providing h units of time, and working in a plant that uses k units of capital per worker. The Pareto-optimal allocation then solves the following linear program:

$$\max_{x \geq 0} \Sigma_s U(c, h) x_s \tag{15}$$

subject to the constraints

$$\Sigma_s x_s = 1, \tag{16}$$

$$\Sigma_s [c - f(k, 1)h] x_s \leq 0, \tag{17}$$

$$\Sigma_s k x_s \leq \bar{k}. \tag{18}$$

Given that f displays constant returns to scale, the solution to this problem has the same measure of agents consuming c units and working h hours in plants with k units of capital per worker as does the solution to the original problem.

For the rest of this section, we choose standard functional forms for the utility and production function. The utility function is

$$U(c, h) = \frac{\left[c^{\gamma}(1 - h)^{(1-\gamma)}\right]^{(1-\sigma)} - 1}{(1 - \sigma)}$$

where $\gamma \in (0, 1)$ and $\sigma \geq 0$. The production function is Cobb–Douglas,

$$f(k, n) = k^{\alpha} n^{(1-\alpha)}$$

with $\alpha \in (0, 1)$.

We now show that for the case in which the economy is parameterized in this way and S is a rectangular subset of $\mathbb{R}^3_+$, there are two types of equilibria, depending on the parameter values. For type 1, the equilibrium consumption vector places mass one on some point $s_1 = (c_1, h_1, k_1)$ that has $h_1 > 0$. Consequently, all agents work the same number of hours. For type 2, the equilibrium consumption vector places mass on two points, s_0 and s_1. For s_0 the value of h_0 is zero. Thus, some fraction of the agents work $h_1 > 0$ hours and receive consumption c_1, while the remaining agents do not work (i.e., $h_0 = 0$) and receive consumption c_0.

We start by describing the properties of solutions for the problem when S is finite. We solve such finite-dimensional linear programs by using the simplex algorithm, which searches for optimal basic solutions. A basic solution is a feasible x that puts mass on a number of points equal to the number of constraints. Let $B \subseteq S$ be the set of these points and $a(s) = [1, c - f(k,1)h, k]'$ be the column vector defined by s. A basic solution also requires that the set of the column vectors defined by the basic solution, $\{a(s)\colon s \in B\}$, be linearly independent. A basic solution is degenerate if the number of points with strictly positive mass is less than the number of constraints.

When the constraint set is closed, bounded, and nonempty, a solution exists. The dual constraints or first-order conditions with respect to x_s of the finite-dimensional linear program are

$$U(c,h) - \mu_0 - \mu_1[c - f(k,1)h] - \mu_2 k \leq 0, \qquad \forall s = (c,h,k) \in S \tag{19}$$

where μ_0, μ_1, and μ_2 are the Lagrange multipliers associated with the constraints (16)–(18). Equation (19) must hold with equality if x_s is strictly positive.

Numerical calculations deliver basic solutions for the finite-dimensional linear programs that are nondegenerate; that is, three points receive strictly positive mass. We, however, observe clusters: two or all three of the three points are close. If we choose progressively finer grids on S, we observe that the points in a cluster converge. The basic solutions remain nondegenerate.

The convergence associated with the grid refinement is a convergence toward the solution of the linear programming problem where S is no longer a finite set but a rectangular subset of $\mathbb{R}^3$. For this case, the summation is replaced by integration over a positive measure x. The number of constraints remains finite. Consequently, we are dealing with a semiinfinite linear program.

Basic solutions for linear programs of this type are similar to solutions of finite-dimensional programs. An optimal measure x is atomic and assigns positive mass to no more points than there are constraints. All points in S continue to satisfy equation (19), and if a point receives positive mass, (19) holds with equality. This equality implies that any point $s_i = (c_i, h_i, k_i)$ that receives positive mass must maximize the left side of (19) with respect to s. For an introduction to semiinfinite linear programming see Glashoff and Gustafson (1983).

We now show that there can be, at most, two points which receive positive mass; that is, the solution to the infinite-dimensional program is degenerate. We first note that, conditional on k, the left side of (19) is a strictly concave function in c and h:

$$V(c,h,k) \equiv \mu_1 f(k,1)h + U(c,h) - \mu_1 c - \mu_2 k.$$

The solution to the problem of maximizing $V(c,h,k)$ by choice of c and h is

$$h^*(k) = \begin{cases} 1 - \left[\dfrac{\mu_1}{\gamma}\right]^{-1/\sigma}\left[\dfrac{\gamma}{(1-\gamma)}k^{\alpha}\right]^{-(\gamma\sigma+1-\gamma)/\sigma} & k \geq \underline{k} \\ 0 & k < \underline{k} \end{cases} \tag{20}$$

and

$$c^*(k) = \begin{cases} \left[\dfrac{\mu_1}{\gamma}\right]^{-1/\sigma}\left[\dfrac{\gamma}{(1-\gamma)}k^{\alpha}\right]^{-(1-\gamma)(1/\sigma-1)} & k \geq \underline{k} \\ \left[\dfrac{\mu_1}{\gamma}\right]^{-1/(\gamma\sigma+1-\gamma)} & k < \underline{k} \end{cases} \tag{21}$$

where $\underline{k} > 0$ depends on μ_1, γ, and σ.

From the definition of the function V, it is immediate that $(c_0, h_0, k_0) = (c^*(0), 0, 0)$ is a local maximum of V, given μ_1 and μ_2. Now let

$$W(k) = V[c^*(k), h^*(k), k].$$

The first and second derivatives of W with respect to k, for $k > \underline{k}$, are

$$\frac{\partial W}{\partial k} = \alpha\mu_1 k^{(\alpha-1)}h^*(k) - \mu_2, \tag{22}$$

$$\frac{\partial^2 W}{\partial k^2} = \alpha\mu_1 k^{(\alpha-2)}\left\{\alpha\left[\gamma + \frac{(1-\gamma)}{\sigma}\right][1 - h^*(k)] - (1-\alpha)h^*(k)\right\}. \tag{23}$$

Since h^* is a monotone increasing function of k, the second derivative of W changes sign only once: it starts out positive for $k = \underline{k}$ ($h^* = 0$) and then becomes negative. Thus, the first derivative of W, which is negative at $\underline{k}$, first increases and then decreases. There are then, at most, two values for which the first derivative is zero. If there are two, then only the larger is a local maximum. We do know that a global maximum exists at some $k_1 > 0$, since any solution involves some production of the consumption good. Therefore, at most, the function W has two local maxima, $k_0 = 0$ and $k_1 > 0$. To illustrate, we include a graph of the function W, shown in

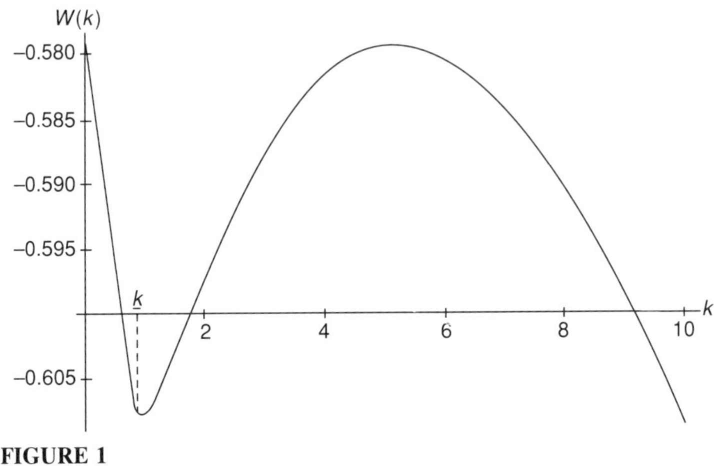

FIGURE 1

Figure 1. The plot is for the parameter values $\alpha = 0.3$, $\gamma = 0.3$, $\sigma = 0.8$, and $\bar{k} = 2.0$.

We now develop a sufficient condition that ensures the solution has positive mass on two points. The nature of the argument is to show that under this condition, a solution which puts mass on a single point leads to a contradiction.

PROPOSITION. *If*

$$\alpha\left[\gamma + \frac{(1-\gamma)}{\sigma}\right](1-\gamma) - (1-\alpha)\gamma > 0, \tag{24}$$

then the equilibrium places positive mass on two points.

Proof. Under the conjecture of all the mass being placed on a single point $s_1 = (c_1, h_1, k_1)$, $x_{s1} = 1$, the value of k_1 must be $\bar{k}$. After solving for μ_1, (23) implies that the second derivative of W is positive at $k = \bar{k}$, if and only if (24) is satisfied. The second derivative of W, being positive at k_1, contradicts k_1 maximizing W. But we have already shown that points receiving positive mass must maximize W. This establishes the result. ∎

The result implies that for parameter values commonly used in real business cycle theory (e.g., Hansen, 1985), or public finance (e.g., Auerbach and Kotlikoff, 1987), we will have a type 2 solution, where not all agents will be working. If $\gamma \leq 2 - 1/\alpha$, then inequality (24) holds for all σ. If $\gamma > 2 - 1/\alpha$, inequality (24) is satisfied for a sufficiently small σ. The intuition for the existence of type 2 solutions is that the gains in production, generated by splitting the population into two groups, more than compensate for the corresponding loss in expected utility due to the implied randomness in the agents' consumption. A sufficiently small risk aversion σ ensures that this loss is not too large.

4. EXISTENCE OF COMPETITIVE EQUILIBRIUM

The economies discussed so far share the following structure: On the consumption side, there is a finite set S with cardinality q. There is a finite number of agent types $i \in I$, and each agent type i has preferences on S represented by U^i: $S \to \mathbb{R}$. There is a continuum of measure λ^i of each agent type i. The commodity space L is the space of signed measures defined on the Borel σ-algebra of S. The consumption set of a type i agent is defined as

$$X^i = \left\{x \in L_+ : \Sigma_{s \in S} x_s = 1,\ g^i(x) \leq 0\right\},$$

where g^i is a finite-dimensional linear mapping defined on L. Preferences on consumption bundles are represented by the linear functional u^i: $X^i \to \mathbb{R}$ of the form $u^i(x) = \Sigma_s U^i(s) x_s$. The production set is

$$Y = \left\{y \in L_+ : \exists z \in \mathbb{R}^l_+ \quad \text{s.t. } r(x, z) \leq 0\right\},$$

where r is also a finite-dimensional linear mapping defined on $\mathbb{R}^{q+l}$.

For the economy E, a competitive equilibrium is a price system (linear functional) v: $L \to \mathbb{R}$ and a feasible allocation $[(x^{i*})_{i \in I}, y^*]$ such that

(i) for all i, $v(x^{i*}) \leq 0$, and for all $x \in X^i$ with $u^i(x) > u^i(x^{i*})$, $v(x) > 0$;
(ii) $y \in Y$ implies $v(y) \leq v(y^*)$.

We consider competitive equilibrium allocations that are anonymous. For these allocations an agent's consumption bundle or contract depends only on that agent's type. A more general formulation would allow for the possibility that agents of the same type receive different contracts. Below we first argue that theory imposes restrictions only on the realized distribution of consumption allocations. We then show that given any possible competitive equilibrium allocation, there will be an anonymous competitive equilibrium with the same realized distribution of consumption allocations. Thus the restriction to anonymous competitive equilibrium allocations is not binding with respect to the realized distribution of consumption allocations, and it is this distribution that is to be explained.

When we confront our model economies with empirical observations, we treat lottery contracts in the same way we treat the Walrasian auctioneer in competitive economic theory. There, we do not expect to have observations of the auctioneer's actions in clearing markets; rather, the auctioneer is used as an "as-if" construct. The observed consumption allocations, however, are interpreted as the equilibrium outcomes of an economy in which an auctioneer clears all markets. Here, we treat contracts analogously. We do not expect to make observations on actual contracts, but we do expect to make observations on realized distributions of consumption allocations for different agent types. To evaluate the model, we are then limited to its implications for these distributions. Our point is that, given this interpretation, the two formulations are observationally equivalent.

Let each agent be indexed by a name $e \in E = [0, \lambda]$, and let μ be the Lebesgue measure. [This approach follows Hildenbrand (1974).] Let h: $E \to I$ be some Borel-measurable function that assigns each agent to some type. The function h is such that for the set of agents of each type i, expressed as

$$E^i = \{e \in E: h(e) = i\},$$

the measure of E^i is λ^i.

Let $\phi(v, i)$ be the demand correspondence of a type i agent. Since agent e is of type $h(e)$, the demand correspondence of this agent is $\phi(v, h(e))$. Using this notation, we define a competitive equilibrium allocation as a price v^*; an integrable function x^*: $E \to I$ satisfying $x^* \in \phi(v^*, h(e))$, $\forall e \in E$; and a profit-maximizing production plan $y^* \in Y$ such that $\int_E x^*(e)\mu(de) = y^*$.

Given a competitive equilibrium, we construct an anonymous competitive equilibrium with the same realized distribution on consumption allocations for each agent type as follows. Let

$$\bar{x}^i \equiv \int_{E^i} x^*(e)\mu(de)/\lambda^i.$$

The measure $\bar{x}^i$ defined above is a probability measure on consumption allocations. It is not the measure for a particular agent e, but it is a probability measure conditional on the fact that we have an agent e of type i holding an equilibrium contract $x^*(e)$.

Since the demand correspondence is convex valued, then $\bar{x}^i$, which is a convex combination of elements belonging to $\phi(v^*, i)$, also belongs to that set. That is, $\bar{x}^i$ is optimal given v^*. Point y^* is profit maximizing, given v^*.

We still need to show that the anonymous allocation $[(\bar{x}^i), y^*]$ is market clearing. Given the definition of $\bar{x}^i$,

$$\Sigma_i \lambda^i \bar{x}^i = \Sigma_i \int_{E^i} x^*(e)\mu(de) = y^*.$$

This establishes that the anonymous allocation $[(\bar{x}^i), y^*]$ and the price system v^* are an anonymous competitive equilibrium.

What we have just defined is a mapping from the set of competitive equilibria into the set of anonymous competitive equilibria. Given this mapping, we can group competitive equilibrium allocations into equivalence classes indexed by their implied anonymous competitive equilibrium allocation.

Since we assume that a law of large numbers holds, the realized distribution on consumption allocations for an agent type i coincides with the probability measure $\bar{x}^i$. This holds for all competitive allocations. Therefore, all competitive equilibrium allocations within an equivalence class and their corresponding anonymous competitive equilibrium allocation do, in this sense, have these same observational implications. The two equilibrium formulations are observationally equivalent, if we have data on the realized outcomes and not the contracts themselves. Typically, we deduce the nature of the equilibrium contract from the realized distributions of actual consumption allocations.

To prove existence of a competitive equilibrium, we slightly modify McKenzie's (1959, 1981) proof. The first modification is a matter of interpretation. McKenzie assumes a finite number of agents, but we interpret his agent i as the agent *type* i. For our problems we show that all of McKenzie's assumptions that guarantee existence of an equilibrium are satisfied, except for Assumption 4. We also show that for our problems Assumption 4 can be dispensed with.

Assumption 1. X^i is convex, closed, and bounded from below.

From the definition of the consumption possibility set, it follows that X^i is a closed convex subset of the unit simplex. Thus, X^i not only satisfies Assumption 1 but is also compact.

Assumption 2. X^i is completely ordered by a convex and closed preference relation.

In the span-of-control economy, preference relations are represented by linear functions on X^i and, therefore, are continuous and convex.

Assumption 3. $Y \subseteq \mathbb{R}^q_+$ is a closed convex cone.

The assumption follows from the definition of Y.

Assumption 4. $Y \cap \mathbb{R}^q_+ = \{0\}$.

This assumption states that null is the only joint element of the production set and the positive orthant. For our economy, however, the production set is actually a subset of the positive orthant. We can still use McKenzie's proof since Assumption 4 is used only to prove compactness of the set of feasible allocations. For our application, the compactness of this set follows trivially from our additional assumption that the consumption possibility set for each agent type is compact, together with Assumption 3.

The appropriate assumptions concerning the relation between the production and consumption sides are also satisfied. Let $X = \Sigma_i \lambda^i X^i$, and let I', I'' be nonempty subsets of I such that $I' \cap I'' = \phi$ and $I' \cup I'' = I$. Then define $X^{I'} = \Sigma_{i \in I'} \lambda^i X^i$ and $X^{I''} = \Sigma_{i \in I''} \lambda^i X^i$.

Assumption 5. $X^i \cap Y \neq \phi$ for all i. Moreover, there is a common point $\bar{x}$ in the relative interiors of X and Y.

The commodity point x, which puts unit mass on the event $s = (0, k^i, m^i)$, is a joint element of X^i and Y. A point $\bar{x}$ that is in the relative interior of X and in the relative interior of Y can be constructed as follows. For each agent type i, choose a point x^i that puts equal mass on each set $S^i_{km} = \{s' = (c', k', m') \in S^i \colon k' = k, m' = m\}$, where $k \in K$ and $k \leq k^i$ and $m \in \{0, m^i\}$. This implies that certain quantities of labor, capital, and managers of each type are available for production. Now distribute labor and capital equally among all available managers. This distribution implies that a certain quantity of the consumption good will be produced. So far, only the marginal distribution of x on S with respect to h and m has been determined. Within each set S^i_{km}, assign equal mass to each point. There is then a unique value for that mass such that total production and total consumption of the consumption good are equal. We now have a point $\bar{x} \in X \cap Y$ such that $\bar{x}_s > 0$ for all $s \in \cup_{i \in I} S^i$.

Let $H_y = \{x \in \mathbb{R}^q \colon x_s = 0 \text{ if } s \notin \cup_{i \in I} S^i\}$. Point $\bar{x}$ is in the nonempty interior of Y relative to H_y. Let $H_x = \{x \in H_y \colon \Sigma_s x_s = 1\}$. Point $\bar{x}$ is in the nonempty interior of X relative to H_x.

Assumption 6. However I' and I'' may be selected, if $x^{I'} \in Y - X^{I''}$, then there is also $w \in Y - X^{I''}$ such that $w = \bar{x}^{I'} - x^{I'}$ and $u(\bar{x}^i) \geq u(x^i)$ for all $i \in I'$, and $u(\bar{x}^i) > u(x^i)$ for some $i \in I'$.

This assumption is satisfied if C contains an element $c_{\max}$ that cannot be produced, given the endowment of capital and labor. In this case, preferences satisfy local and global nonsatiation with respect to feasible allocations.

Given that these five assumptions are satisfied, by Theorem 1 of McKenzie (1959) a competitive equilibrium exists for the economy E.

We can relax the restriction that S is a finite set and allow it to be a compact subset of a finite-dimensional Euclidean space. Then the commodity space L becomes the space of signed measures on the Borel σ-algebra of these sets, $M(S)$. The subset of feasible allocations is compact with respect to the weak* topology since these allocations are probability measures and therefore uniformly bounded.

To show that a competitive equilibrium for such an economy exists, we study competitive equilibria for a sequence of economies. We show that the competitive equilibrium allocations and prices converge to an allocation and price system that is a competitive equilibrium for the economy with commodity space $M(S)$. The proof follows Mas-Colell (1975) and Prescott and Townsend (1984), and proceeds in three steps. First, we construct a sequence of economies and show that their competitive equilibrium allocations converge to a limit allocation that is feasible for the economy with commodity space $M(S)$. Second, we prove the existence of a continuous price function υ and a cheaper point at prices υ for each agent type in the limit economy. In the third and last step we use the results from the second step to establish that the limit allocation is optimal at the limit price system υ.

We consider sequences of economies where, for the jth economy, we restrict the commodity space $L_j = M(S_j)$ to a set of atomic signed measures that have mass only on a finite number of points, $S_j \subseteq S$. Let D be a countable, everywhere dense subset of S and let S_j contain the first j elements of D and the set $\{(c_{\max}, k^i, m^i)\colon i \in I\}$. Then $S_j \to S$ in closed convergence. Similarly, for the production possibility set we restrict the space of activity measures to atomic signed measures that have mass only on a finite number of points, $A_j \subseteq A$, and $A_j \to A$ in closed convergence.

For each of the economies E_j, there exist a competitive equilibrium allocation and price system, $[(\bar{x}_j^i)_{i \in I}, \bar{y}_j]$ and υ_j, as already shown. Since the sequence of equilibrium allocations is a subset of a weak* compact set, the sequence has a convergent subsequence. And again, the limit of this subsequence of competitive equilibrium allocations, $[(\bar{x}^i)_{i \in I}, \bar{y}]$, is a feasible allocation for the economy with an unrestricted commodity space L. This completes the first step of the proof.

The second step of the argument is specific to our economy and concerns the existence of a continuous price function υ and the existence of a cheaper point at prices υ for each agent type in the limit economy.

LEMMA 1. *There exists a subsequence of equilibrium prices υ_j that converges uniformly to a continuous function υ on S.*

Proof. We first show that we can define equilibrium prices υ_j as a linear function on S_j. This property is then used to prove the existence of a limit price function υ that is continuous on S.

The equilibrium price function for the jth economy is constructed from the firm's optimality conditions. These conditions are

$$\upsilon_{sj} - \mu_{1j}c + \mu_{2j}k + \mu_{3mj} \leq 0, \qquad \forall s = (c, k, m) \in S_j, \tag{25}$$

$$\mu_{1j}mg[f(k, n)] - \mu_{2j}k - \mu_{3mj} - \mu_{30j}n \leq 0, \qquad \forall a = (k, m, n) \in A_j, \tag{26}$$

where μ_1, μ_2, and μ_{3m} are the Lagrange multipliers associated with constraints (3)–(6).

For each economy j there is a competitive equilibrium with a price system v_j such that (25) is binding for all $s \in S_j$. To see that such an equilibrium exists, take any competitive equilibrium for the jth economy. If for this equilibrium (25) is not binding for some $s' \in S_j$, then s' is not produced and its price is below the supply reservation price. In this case the price for s' can be raised until (25) is binding. The competitive equilibrium allocation continues to be optimal at the higher price. The firm's optimality conditions are satisfied, and since agents did not consume s' at the original price they will not consume s' now at higher prices.

The sequence of competitive equilibria associated with the sequence of economies is chosen from the class of equilibria with (25) binding. Equation (25) thereby defines the price system v_j as a linear function on S. Given this representation of the price system v_j, there is a subsequence of equilibrium prices that converges uniformly to a continuous function v on S, if there exists a converging subsequence for the Lagrange multipliers μ_j.

We first show that $\mu_{1j} > 0$. Suppose $\mu_{1j} = 0$. Then from the definition of prices, it follows that $v_{sj} \leq 0$ for all $s \in S_j$. Now an agent of type i solves the following problem in the jth economy:

$$\max_{x \geq 0} \Sigma_{s \in S_j^i} U(c) x_s$$

subject to constraints

$$\Sigma_{s \in S_j^i} v_{sj} x_s \leq 0, \qquad \Sigma_{s \in S_j^i} x_s = 1.$$

If $v_{sj} \leq 0$ for all s in S_j^i, then each agent will put mass only on points s with $c = c_{\max}$ as U is monotone increasing in c. But $c_{\max}$ cannot be produced for all agents of any type; thus, the allocation cannot be feasible. Therefore, $\mu_{1j} > 0$.

Prices of a competitive equilibrium can be normalized arbitrarily. Since equations (25) and (26) are jointly linear in prices v_j and multipliers μ_j, multipliers can be normalized arbitrarily. The Lagrange multipliers are nonnegative and we have shown that for the jth economy $\mu_{1j} > 0$. Therefore, it is possible to normalize μ_j so that $|\mu_j| = 1$. This, in turn, ensures the existence of a converging subsequence $\mu_j \to \mu$. Given our definition of the price system in equation (25), the limit price function v is continuous on S and the subsequence of price systems converges uniformly. This completes the proof. ■

To show that the limit allocation is utility maximizing at the limit prices, we now prove the existence of a cheaper point for each type.

LEMMA 2. *For each agent type i, there is a feasible choice $x_0 \in X^i$ such that $v(x_0) < 0$.*

Proof. We show that for the converging subsequence of Lagrange multipliers, $\mu_j \to \mu$ (developed in Lemma 1), the limit of μ_{1j} is strictly positive. This implies that $\mu_{3m} > 0$ for all $m \in M$, which guarantees the existence of a cheaper point.

Suppose that $\mu_{1j} \to 0$. If, in addition, $\mu_{2j} \to 0$, then there is at least one m such that $\mu_{3mj} \to \mu_{3m}$ and $\mu_{3m} > 0$, since $|\mu_j| = 1$. But then the measure $x_{\max}$, which puts unit mass on the point $(c_{\max}, k^i, m^i)$, will be in the budget set for agents with the ability $m^i = m$ for some economy j. The agents of this type will choose this measure, but the choice is not feasible. Therefore, $\mu_2 > 0$ if $\mu_1 = 0$. But if $\mu_2 > 0$, the same $x_{\max}$ is again in the budget set for some agent type in some economy j. Thus, μ_1 must be strictly positive.

It follows from (26) that $\mu_{3m} > 0$ for all $m \in M$ if $\mu_1 > 0$. To see this, rewrite (26) as follows:

$$\mu_{3m} \geq \mu_1 mg[f(k,n)] - \mu_2 k - \mu_{30} n, \qquad \forall a \in A. \tag{27}$$

The maximum of the right side of (27) is greater than or equal to zero. Since by assumption $g'(0) = \infty$ and since $\mu_1 > 0$, the maximum of the right side attains a value strictly greater than zero. Therefore, $\mu_{3m} > 0$ for all $m \in M$.

Each agent type is endowed with some managerial ability $m \in M$. Therefore, the measure x_0 that puts unit mass on the point $s = (0, 0, m)$ is feasible for that agent. But since $\mu_{3m} > 0$, the value of this bundle is negative; that is, $v(x_0) < 0$. This completes the proof of Lemam 2. ∎

For the third and final part of the argument we now use Lemmas 1 and 2, to establish that the limit allocation is optimal at the limit price system. We first discuss the problems facing the households. Since the analysis applies to all agent types, we simplify the notation by dropping the agent-type superscript.

Suppose that the consumption point $\bar{x}$ is not optimal at the price system v; that is, suppose there exists an x such that $x \in X$, $u(x) > u(\bar{x})$, and $v(x) \leq v(\bar{x}) = 0$. We distinguish two cases, $v(x) < v(\bar{x})$ and $v(x) = v(\bar{x})$. We establish that the first case leads to a contradiction. We then show that the second case implies that there is some $x' \in X$ such that $u(x') > u(\bar{x})$ and $v(x') < v(\bar{x})$. But the existence of such a point leads to a contradiction, as already established for the first case.

Suppose that the first case is true; that is, suppose $v(x) < v(\bar{x})$. As $S_j \to S$ in closed convergence and S is compact, we can find a sequence of allocations $\{x_j\}$ such that $x_j \in X_j$ and $x_j \to x$. [See Fact 6 of Mas-Colell (1975), p. 274.] But then $v_j(x_j) \to v(x)$ and $v_j(\bar{x}_j) \to v(\bar{x})$, since the measures x are bounded and v_j converges uniformly. In addition, $u(x_j) \to u(x)$ and $u(\bar{x}_j) \to u(\bar{x})$. This means that there is some economy E_j for which $v_j(x_j) < v_j(\bar{x}_j)$ and $u(x_j) > u(\bar{x}_j)$. This contradicts $\bar{x}_j$ being optimal at the price system v_j.

Alternatively, suppose that the second case is true; that is, suppose $v(x) = v(\bar{x})$. We have already shown that there is a cheaper point for each agent type. Let $x_0 \in X$ with $v(x_0) < 0$ be such a point. Define points $x^t = (1 - t)x + tx_0$ with $t \in [0, 1]$. Then $x^t \in X$, $v(x^t) < v(\bar{x})$ for $t > 0$ and $u(x^t) > u(\bar{x})$ for t sufficiently small. But this means that x^t satisfies the conditions of the first case, and we have already established that this leads to a contradiction.

The argument proving that the limit allocation is optimal for the firm is similar. Suppose $\bar{y}$ is not optimal for the firm; that is, suppose there exists some $y \in Y$ such that $v(y) > v(\bar{y})$. We can find a sequence $\{y_j\}$ such that $y_j \in Y_j$ and $y_j \to y$. But then $v_j(y_j) \to v(y)$ and $v(\bar{y}_j) \to v(\bar{y})$. This implies that there is some economy E_j such that $v_j(y_j) > v_j(\bar{y}_j)$, which contradicts $\bar{y}_j$ being optimal at the price system v_j.

Acknowledgment

This paper was presented at the Conference on General Equilibrium and Growth: The Legacy of Lionel McKenzie, held May 5–7, 1989, at the University of Rochester. We would like especially to thank Lionel McKenzie and an anonymous referee for helpful comments.

References

Arrow, K. J., and G. Debreu (1954). "Existence of an equilibrium for a competitive economy," *Econometrica* **22**, 265–290.

Auerbach, A. J., and L. J. Kotlikoff (1987). *Dynamic Fiscal Policy*. (Cambridge University Press, U.K.).

Glashoff, K., and S.-Å. Gustafson (1983). *Linear Optimization and Approximation* (Springer, New York).

Hansen, G. D. (1985). "Indivisible labor and the business cycle," *J. Monetary Econ.* **16**, 309–327.

Hildenbrand, W. (1974). *Core and Equilibria of a Large Economy* (Princeton University Press, Princeton, N.J.).

Lucas, R. E., Jr. (1978). "On the size distribution of business firms," *Bell. J. Econ.* **9**, 508–523.

Mas-Colell, A. (1975). "A model of equilibrium with differentiated commodities," *J. Math. Econ.* **2**, 263–295.

McKenzie, L. W. (1959). "On the existence of general equilibrium for a competitive market," *Econometrica* **27**, 54–71.

McKenzie, L. W. (1981). "The classical theorem on existence of competitive equilibrium," *Econometrica* **49**, 819–841.

Prescott, E. C., and R. M. Townsend (1984). "General competitive analysis in an economy with private information," *Int. Econ. Rev.* **25**, 1–20.

Rogerson, R. (1988). "Indivisible labor, lotteries and equilibrium," *J. Monetary Econ.* **21**, 3–16.

Tuck, R. H. (1954). *An Essay on the Economic Theory of Rank* (Basil Blackwell, Oxford, U.K.).

Uhlig, H. (1988). "A law of large numbers for large economies," Research Department Working Paper 342, Federal Reserve Bank of Minneapolis.

A NOTE ON BOUNDARY OPTIMAL PATHS

Henry Wan, Jr.
Department of Economics
Cornell University
Ithaca, New York 14853

1. MOTIVATION

The long-run tendencies of an economy have fascinated economists ever since the days of classical economics. As McKenzie (1987) noted, constancy of technology and constancy of the supply of primary inputs formed the basis of the Millian stationary state, yet there was no suggestion that the evolution of the economy would converge to that steady state.

It was Ramsey (1928) who modeled the evolution of the economy as decided by the rational choice over time. Superimposing this theme of dynamic optimization over the von Neumann economy, which permits balanced expansions, Samuelson (1949, 1966) and Samuelson and Solow (1956) focused on the "consumption turnpike" property of economic evolution: over a long period of time, the efficient evolution of the economy causes all produced goods to expand in approximately the same proportion, unhindered by the presence of primary goods in fixed supply. By the concerted efforts of capital theorists, the characterization of the "interior efficient paths" is now essentially complete. A major portion of this research program was undertaken by Professor McKenzie, his coworkers, his students, and others inspired by his leadership [see McKenzie (1987) for an overall review].

It is a measure of the success of such efforts that the "terra incognita" in capital theory is by now reduced to the "periphery," where *boundary efficient paths* evolve under the limitations of factors in fixed supply. In this

GENERAL EQUILIBRIUM, GROWTH, AND TRADE II

"peripheral" world, the scarcity of some primary factors forms a "limit for growth" against balanced expansions. Thus the *expansibility axiom*[1] is violated.[2] It is a world where resource shortages and environmental degradations raise their heads. Exotic though such a world appears, we shall see below that these boundary paths can also be tackled, principally by analogy with the successful analysis of the interior paths.

In the history of science, the impact of a great scholar is invariably felt beyond the research programs over which she or he personally presides to their successful completion, and over the works of those not favored with the opportunity to work closely with her or him. These are the mark of a great scientist.

This is true for von Neumann. His theory of balanced expansion has influenced the turnpike studies. His impact to economics goes far beyond his direct associates such as Oscar Morgenstern.

This is also the case for Professor McKenzie. We shall present below a prolog for a theory of "limit for growth," where the key concepts such as the "technology set," the "reduced-form felicity index" come from what is now known as the "McKenzie syntax," without which one can hardly conceptualize the crucial questions in the research program, let alone resolving them.

Presently, we focus on a world with a limit for growth, where the absence of such would have engendered unlimited physical expansion. The shortages in some primary input (e.g., land-as-site, or the carrying capacity of planet Earth) together with the presence of durable capital goods, brings back such concepts as "optimal steady state" and "optimal cycles" familiar in the work of McKenzie and his coworkers.

From the results known today,[3] efficient boundary paths also exhibit distinct differences as compared to the efficient interior paths. For the latter, optimal cycles are observable, when the time preference rate is high, for the former, the opposite is true. Optimal boundary cycles are neutrally stable so that adjacent initial conditions lead to adjacent optimal paths with the distances in between neither increasing nor decreasing over time. Perturbations of the model—provided the limits-for-growth is left alone—will displace the interior portion of the optimal path, but the latter remains to be a feeder to the class of boundary optimal paths, whose common qualitative properties will therefore remain robust.

[1]This is listed as Axiom II in McKenzie (1987). It is not required in characterizing the turnpike properties in models for capital accumulation, like in McKenzie (1963), but is needed in the generalized Ramsay setting, for constructing the comparison path, when utility is undiscounted.

[2]The expansibility axiom is not met when resources are exhaustible, but is satisfied for some renewable resource problems. This paper shows that there are other renewable resource models where the axiom is violated.

[3]For example, the entire class of tree farm examples in Wan (1989). We shall report the model and results from that source, but not the derivations.

To gauge how representative are such limit-of-growth examples for intertemporal economics, here we start with a far more general formulation, regarding both the growth and harvest processes. We then attempt to determine which properties in such examples emerge from the imposition of what conditions. We continue to use the stylized tree farm for motivation.

2. OUR BASIC MODEL

Consider a tree farm on a *unit* of land. The maximum tree life is divided into two periods of equal lengths. Reforestation follows harvest costlessly.

Land has two "microstates": 0 and 1, for being covered with young and old trees, respectively. In the latter microstate, there is *no* alternative to the process of harvesting (cum reforestation),

$$h_1 : 1 \to 0.$$

In the former microstate, the *two* choices available are a "harvesting (cum reforestation) process":

$$h_0 : 0 \to 0,$$

and a "growth process":

$$g_0 : 0 \to 1.$$

These concepts are illustrated in the flow diagram in Figure 1.

A "macrostate" x, for the tree farm, is the tree-age distribution in terms of acreage. In this example with two-period trees, x is an element in the unit interval, $X = [0, 1]$, which serves as the *state space*. The state x means that a portion x of the land is under old trees (microstate 1), and the balance, $1 - x$, is under the young ones (microstate 0). The decision in each period t is to harvest what proportion $k_t \in [0, 1]$ out of that portion,

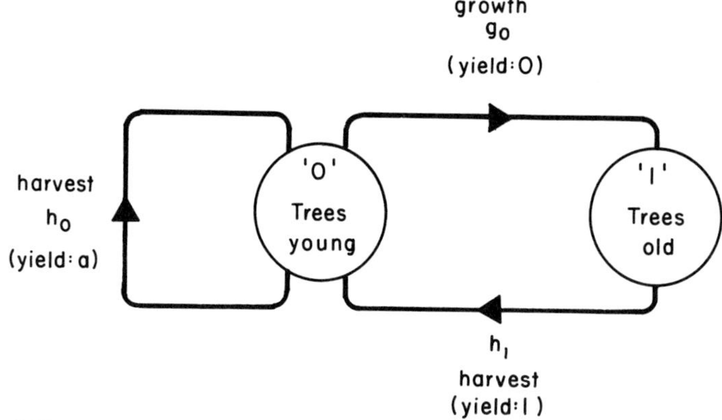

FIGURE 1 Transition in microstate for land.

$1 - x_t$, under young trees. Options may range from "cut all" ($k_t = 1$), to "keep as much (i.e., cut as little) as one can" ($k_t = \underline{k}(x)$), where the given function $\underline{k}(x) \geq 0$ is the minimum proportion of cutting. Whatever cannot be brought into maturation should obviously be harvested. The potential for growth of the sapling may well depend on the tree-age distribution at that moment. Older trees may benefit the young in providing a protective cover, or hinder the latter by drawing away water and nutrients from the common ambience.

Out of $1 - x_t$, the portion of land under young trees this period, a maximum proportion $[1 - \underline{k}(x_t)]$ may become covered with old trees, next period, e.g.,

$$0 \leq x_{t+1} \leq [1 - \underline{k}(x_t)](1 - x_t) = K(x_t),$$

the cross-vintage bound. We assume that $K(x)$ is a continuous, nonnegative function, taking a zero value only at $x = 1$.

Denoting c_t as the timber harvested at t, we can write in general.

$$c_t = G(x_t, x_{t+1}),$$

where it is expected that $G(\cdot)$ is continuously differentiable, increasing in x_t, and decreasing in x_{t+1}, and quasiconcave, with $G(0, 1) = 0$.

2.1 A Simple Example

We shall adopt the following.

Assumption 1. Old trees play a neutral role toward the growth of young trees.

Hence

$$K(x_t) = 1 - x_t,$$

where

$$x_{t+1} \leq 1 - x_t$$

will be referred to as the demographic constraint. This latter reflects the truism that the portion of land under old trees next period can never exceed the land under young trees, this period.

Assumption 2. Harvest depends linearly on areas of trees cut, by age.

We take the timber yield from a unit area under old trees harvested as unity, while the same under young trees as $a \in (0, 1)$, without losing generality. In this case,

$$G(x_t, x_{t+1}) = x_t + ak(1 - x_t),$$

with

$$x_{t+1} = (1 - k)(1 - x_t), \qquad 0 < k < 1,$$

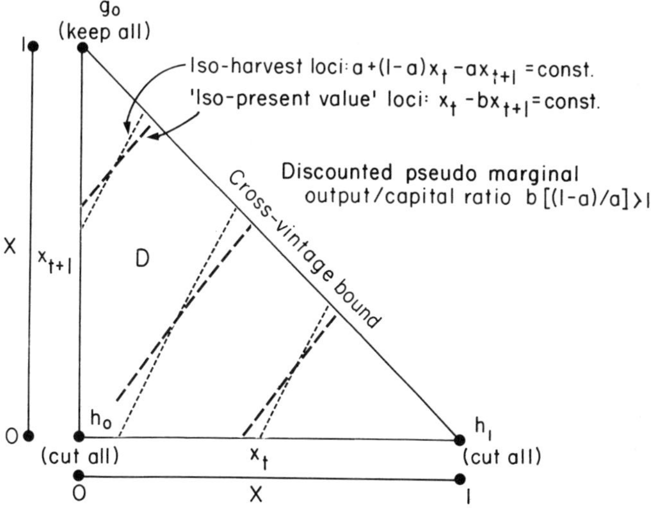

FIGURE 2 Control of macrostate for tree farm.

or

$$\begin{aligned} G(x_t, x_{t+1}) &= 1 \cdot x_t + a[(1 - x_t) - x_{t+1}] \\ &= a + (1 - a)x_t - ax_{t+1} \\ &= a(1 + hx_t - x_{t+1}), \qquad h = (1 - a)/a. \end{aligned}$$

Under this specification, the value of G is bounded by 0 and 1.

Figure 2 illustrates this simple example where both the cross-vintage bound and the isoharvest loci are linear. (For the general case, see Figure 4, presented later.)

The set of feasible pairs (x_t, x_{t+1}) in $X^2 = [0, 1]^2$ forms the *technology set D*. This is a subset of the triangle bounded by the demographic constraint and the two axes, with vertices

$$h_1 = (1, 0), \qquad h_0 = (0, 0), \qquad g_0 = (0, 1).$$

Our simple example is characterized by (a) D coincides with the triangle spanned by g_0, h_0, and h_1 and (b) the isoharvest loci take the form

$$a(1 + hx_t - x_{t+1}) = \text{constant}.$$

These are parallel lines with slope h. In Figure 2, we assume that $bh > 1$, where,

$$b = 1/(1 + \rho) \in (0, 1)$$

is the time preference factor, and ρ is the time preference rate.

Rewrite the isoharvest loci as

$$x_{t+1} = (1 + hx_t) - \text{constant}/a.$$

The term $(1 + hx_t)$ is then analytically equivalent to the production function in a Ramsey model. Thus, the expression bh is analogous to the discounted marginal output/capital ratio.

Now assume a felicity index u that is twice continuously differentiable, strictly increasing and strictly concave for all positive harvest levels, then the reduced-form felicity index is

$$\begin{aligned} V(x_t, x_{t+1}) &= u[G(x_t, x_{t+1})] \\ &= u(c_t). \end{aligned}$$

By our assumptions on G and u, V is quasiconcave.

An example for u is logarithmic. This is used to compute some numerical examples below. In this case, V is bounded everywhere except in the neighborhood of (0, 1). This property of V poses some technical complexities to the proof of the existence of an optimal policy. But these problems can be overcome in a routine manner.

The objective of the maximization problem is to find

$$\max_{\substack{0 \le x_t \le 1 - x_{t-1} \\ t \ge 1}} \sum_{t=0}^{\infty} b^t V(x_{t-1}, x_t) = W(x_0),$$

where W is the value function over the state space.

$$\begin{aligned} W(x_0) &= \max \sum_{t=0}^{\infty} b^t \log[a(1 + hx_t - x_{t+1})] \\ &= (\log a)/(1-b) + \sum_{t=0}^{\infty} b^t \log[(1 + hx_t - x_{t+1})], \end{aligned}$$

subject to

$$0 \le x_t \le 1 - x_{t-1}, \qquad t \ge 1.$$

Without the *cross-vintage bound*, $x_t \le 1 - x_{t-1}$, the optimal policy can be easily shown to be

$$\underline{P}(x) = ab/(1+b) + bhx.$$

For $bh > 1$, this case clearly admits neither an optimal steady state (OSS), nor any optimal cycle. This is shown in Figure 3(a).

The inclusion of the cross-vintage bound makes all the difference. It can be shown (Wan, 1989) that the optimal policy is piecewise linear, with a positive vertical intercept and rises monotonically up to $x = (\frac{1}{2}) - \psi$, for some $\psi \in (0, \frac{1}{2})$. From then on it takes the form of $1 - x$. The optimal cycles arise along the boundary of D, and the degenerate cycle is the boundary optimal stationary state. This is illustrated in Figure 3(b) with $a = \frac{1}{5}$ and $b = \frac{1}{2}$.

Note that in the usual discrete-time Ramsey literature, it is assumed that the production function $F(\cdot)$ is such that there exists some bounding state $x_B > 0$, where $x > x_B$, $F(x) < x$. We deal with cases where either the equivalent production function is not associated with any bounding

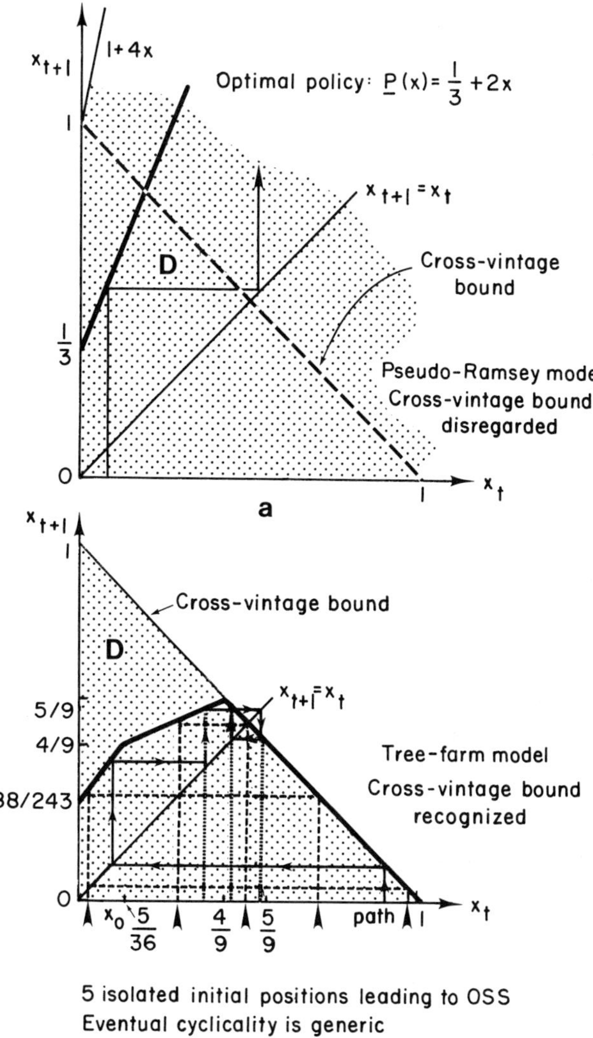

FIGURE 3 Optimal policy with and without cross-vintage bound. (a) Pseudo-Ramsey model; cross-vintage bound disregarded. (b) Tree-farm model; cross-vintage bound recognized.

state [see Figure 3(a)], or such a bounding state x_B is irrelevant, since it lies beyond the cross-vintage bound.

3. KEY ASSUMPTIONS AND THEIR IMPLICATIONS

The conditions we introduce are associated with both the cross-vintage bound and the family of isoharvest loci, to be discussed below.

Since $K(\cdot)$ is both continuous and bounded above by $1 - x \leq 1$, by the Brouwer's fixed-point theorem, there must be at least one value,[4] $\underline{x} = K(\underline{x})$.

Remark. The preceding formulation is quite general and allows various reinterpretations. For illustration, see below the simple point-input, flow-output orchard model as studied in Mitra *et al.* (1991), where the yield of a tree in fruits in the ith year is $\psi_i \geq 0$ with $i = 0, 1$, and the timber of a fallen tree has no value. A tree-age distribution x_t yields a harvest in fruits of

$$\begin{aligned} c_t &= G(x_t, x_{t+1}) \\ &= \psi_0 + (\psi_1 - \psi_0)x_t. \end{aligned}$$

This yields the optimization problem of

$$\max_{[0, 1 - x_{t-1}]} \sum_{t=0}^{\infty} b^t u[\psi_0 + (\psi_1 - \psi_0)x_t], \qquad x_0 \text{ given}, \qquad t = 1, 2, \ldots,$$

with the solution $x_t \equiv 1 - x_{t-1}$ [respectively, $x_t \equiv 0$], if $(\psi_1 - \psi_0) > 0$ [respectively, if $(\psi_1 - \psi_0) < 0$]. The control variable x_t is irrelevant, if $(\psi_1 - \psi_0) = 0$.

We now introduce a sequence of conditions for the generalized problem above and examine their respective implications.

3.1 Condition on the Maximand

Define the family of *isoharvest loci*:

$$G(x_t, x_{t+1}) = \text{constant}$$

and the family of *iso-present-value* loci:

$$x_t - bx_{t+1} = \text{constant}.$$

[4]As shown below, x is unique (Result 1) if K is strictly decreasing (Postulate 2).

We can then state the following:

Postulate 1 (single-crossing). At any point (y, z), $[b + G_2(y, z)/G_1(y, z)] \geq \delta > 0$.

Remarks. Geometrically, for the pair of loci $G(y, z) = C_1$ and $y - bz = C_2$ pass through any point (y, z), the former always cuts the latter from below, by Postulate 1. In economic terms, this means the discounted marginal output/capital ratio always exceeds unity:

$$-bG_1(y, z)/G_2(y, z) \geq b/(b - \delta) > 1.$$

3.2 Conditions on the Cross-Vintage Bound: $x_{t+1} \leq K(x_t)$

Postulate 2 (inverse association). K is strictly decreasing in x_t.

Postulate 3 (self-inversion over some interval). There exists an interval $[x', x'']$, $0 < x' < x'' < 1$, over which the function $K(\cdot)$ coincides with its inverse, $K^{-1}(\cdot)$.

Remark. Postulate 3 means that the graph of $K(\cdot)$ is symmetric with respect to the ray:

$$x_{t+1} = x_t.$$

All these properties are represented in Figure 4.

For the ease of discussion, we denote $(\underline{x}, \underline{x}) \in \partial D$ as a boundary fixed point, $(x, P(x)) \in \partial D$ as a *boundary optimal policy*, and $(x, P(x)) \notin \partial D$ as an *interior optimal policy*.

It is straightforward to prove the following.

Result 1 (the uniqueness of the boundary fixed point). If Postulate 2 holds, then there is only a unique value $\underline{x}$ such that

$$\underline{x} = K(\underline{x}).$$

Result 2 (the properties of fluctuation-proneness). If both Postulates 1 and 2 hold, then

(i) (Interval for boundary optimal policy.) There is a neighborhood $\underline{X}$ of $\underline{x}$, defined as above, such that for any $x' \in \underline{X}$,

$$P(x') = K(x').$$

(ii) (Monotonicity, up to $\underline{x}$.) For any $x < \underline{x}$,

$$P(x) > x.$$

(iii) (Instant return, beyond $\underline{x}$.) For any $x > \underline{x}$,

$$P(x) < \underline{x}.$$

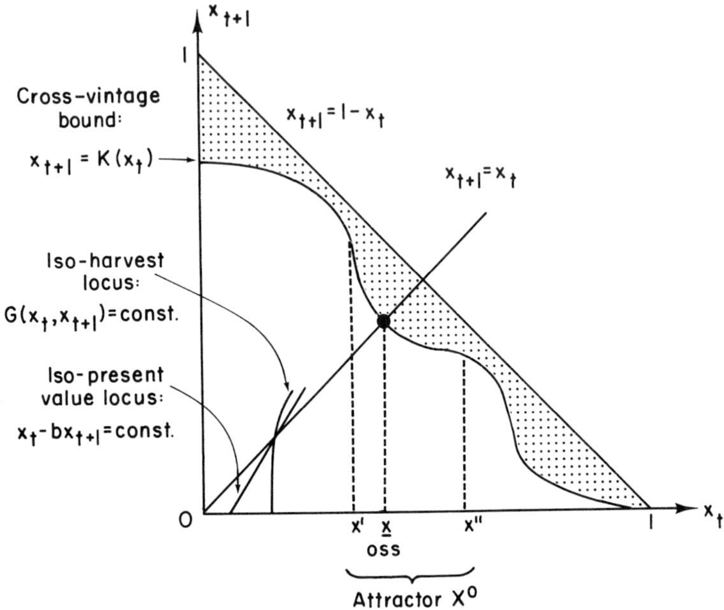

FIGURE 4 Cross-vintage bound, general case.

COROLLARY. *There exists a unique optimal steady state* $\underline{x}$ *that is a boundary optimal steady state.*

For verification, we shall first establish the following.

LEMMA 1 (*upper boundary policy near a fixed point*). *If*

$$P(x) = x$$

then for all x' *within some neighborhood of* x, $P(x') = K(x')$.

Proof of Lemma 1. If Lemma 1 is false, one can construct a sequence $\{x^q\} \to x$, such that either (a) (interiority),

$$0 < P(x^q) < K(x^q), \quad \text{all } q,$$

or (b) (lower boundary policy),

$$P(x^q) = 0, \quad \text{all } q.$$

Case a. In the interior of D, the Euler equation holds, so that

$$0 = u'\{G[x^q, P(x^q)]\}G_2[x^q, P(x^q)]$$

$$+ bu'\{G[P(x^q), P^2(x^q)]\}G_1[P(x^q), P^2(x^q)],$$

or equivalently,

$$0 = b + u'\{G[x^q, P(x^q)]\}G_2[x^q, P(x^q)]/$$
$$u'\{G[P(x^q), P^2(x^q)]\}G_1[P(x^q), P^2(x^q)],$$

for all q. Both $P(\cdot)$ and $K(\cdot)$ are continuous. Thus, passing to the limit, and using the fact that $P(x) = x$, one obtains,

$$0 = b + G_2(x,x)/G_1(x,x),$$
$$> 0, \qquad \text{(by Postulate 1)}$$

a contradiction.

Case b. $P(\cdot)$ being continuous, passing to the limit, $P(x) = 0$. So this case needs to be considered only if $x = 0$. In that instance, consider a two-period variation that (i) reduces the current consumption by $\eta > 0$, (ii) increases the value of $P(0)$ by $\eta G_2(0,0) > 0$, (iii) increases the consumption of the next period by $-\eta G_2(0,0)/G_1(0,0)$ and (iv) leaves everything else as before. This would have improved on the optimal solution: an impossibility. Thus, one can observe $P(0) = 0$, only if no increment of $P(0)$ is feasible, i.e., $P(0) = 0 = K(0)$. But this again contradicts an assumption about $K(\cdot)$, namely, $K(\cdot) > 0$, for all $x < 1$.

Proof of Result 2.

(i) By Lemma 1 and Result 1.

(ii) If the assertion is false, there exists some $x' \in (0, \underline{x})$, such that $P(x') \le x'$. First, the case $P(x') = x'$ may be readily dismissed. This is because by Lemma 1, $P(x') = x'$ means $K(x') = x' < \underline{x} = K(\underline{x})$, which contradicts Result 1. Consider next the case of $P(x') < x'$. By the proof for Lemma 1, it is known that $P(0) > 0$. Now the continuous function $[P(x) - x]$ takes opposite signs at 0 and x'. By the intermediate value theorem, there must be x'' such that $x'' < x' < \underline{x}$, with $P(x'') = x'' < \underline{x}$. Again this leads to the same kind of contradiction, substituting x'' for x'.

(iii) This is proved by the chain of inequalities:

$$P(x) \le K(x)$$
$$< K(\underline{x}) \qquad \text{(by Postulate 2)}$$
$$= \underline{x}. \qquad \blacksquare$$

Figure 5(a) illustrates the essence of the preceding proof. There is an "exclusion zone," containing that segment of the $x_{t+1} = x_t$ ray within D, which has an empty intersection with the graph of the interior optimal policy.

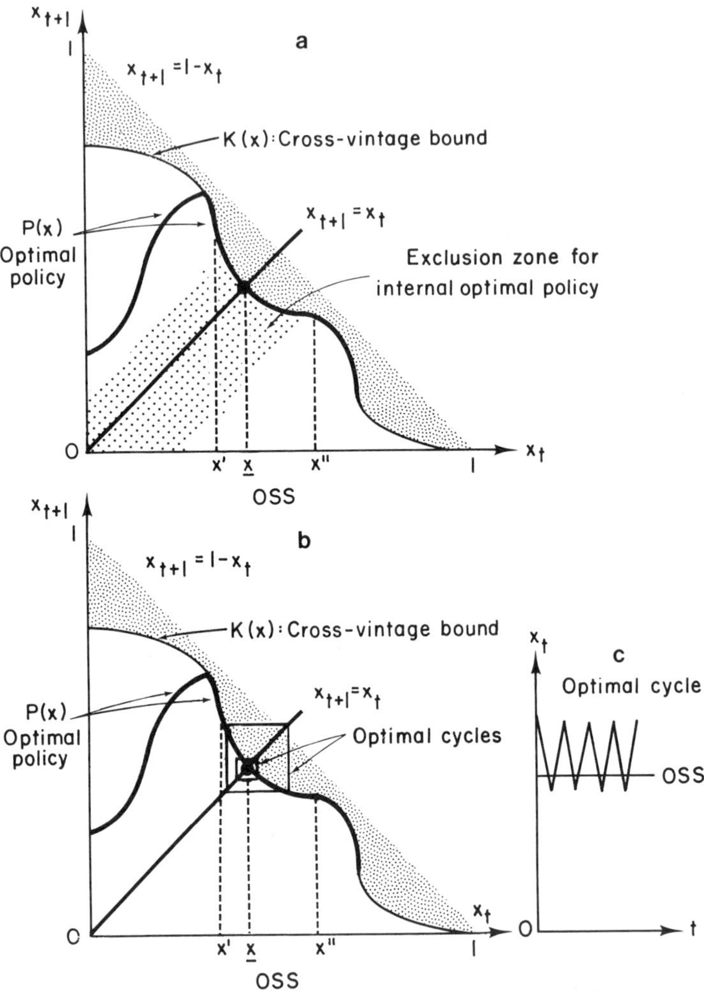

FIGURE 5 Structure of optimal policy.

Remark. Result 2 suggests that unless the initial position belongs to some denumerable subset of the state space, so that the system either (i) is initially at the unique optimal steady state or (ii) will eventually be there in finitely many periods, the optimal path is *generically* "fluctuation-prone," in that it oscillates forever, with the "down turn" completed in a single period.

Result 3. Postulate 3 implies the coexistence of a continuum of two-period, neutrally stable orbits for any initial state $x \in X^0$, where $X^0 = \underline{X} \cap [x', x'']$, x', and x'' are as in Postulate 3.

Sketch of a Proof. $K^2(\cdot)$ is the identity map, $I(\cdot)$.

Figure 5(b) illustrates how boundary optimal cycle occurs. Figure 5(c) illustrates that a typical optimal cycle does not need to be symmetric toward the optimal steady state.

Remarks

1. The cycles under Result 3 need not be symmetric toward $\underline{x}$, it depends on the curvature of K over X^0, [see Figure 5(b) and (c)].
2. It is now obvious that Postulates 1, 2, and 3 are satisfied by the class of examples we studied earlier, when $K(x_t) = 1 - x_t$, and $G(x_t) = a(1 + hx_t - x_{t+1})$.

It is appropriate now to discuss the robustness of the above results. First, concerning the cyclicality of the optimal path, note that, in general, perturbations of $G(\cdot)$ or $u(\cdot)$—but not $K(\cdot)$—will not affect cyclicality. The exception is that the optimal cycle is located at the "ends" of X^0. Results from the linear limit-of-growth models[5] are robust precisely because there $K(\cdot)$ coincides with the linear function $1 - x_t$, and thus not subject to perturbation. Perturbations of $K(\cdot)$ will affect the robustness of cyclicality but not the weaker property of fluctuation-proneness, since such perturbations affect Postulate 3 but not Postulate 2.

4. ADDITIONAL RESULTS

In the linear limit-of-growth models, all states are "eventually periodic," reaching either an optimal steady state or an optimal two-cycle in finite periods, but no state is "asymptotically periodic," converging to either an optimal steady state or a limit cycle [see definitions in Li and Yorke (1975)]. This unusual property offers us the simplicity for constructing and verifying the preceding examples, yet it may also lead to unwarranted interpretations. They are not the necessary consequences of the boundary efficient paths in general. Yet some generally valid implications of the limit-of-growth constraint, such as the properties of fluctuation-proneness may be dismissed as curiosa, simply because they appear in our examples with other "strong" properties. Thus, a clarification is in order.

From the analysis presented here, it is readily seen that the property of "all paths are eventually periodic" in the known examples is, first, a consequence of the fact that

$$K(x) = 1 - x,$$

[5]Wan (1989) as well as Mitra *et al.* (1991).

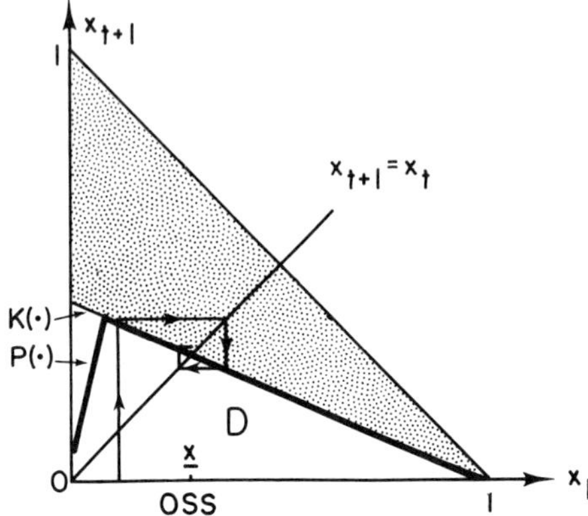

FIGURE 6 Cyclical convergence.

and second, generally valid[6] only under the slightly weaker condition of Postulate 3.

If Postulate 3 does not hold, the behavior of the optimal path can take a variety of alternative forms, such as (i) cyclical convergence and (ii) chaos. The former is depicted in Figure 6, where

$$K(x) = m(1 - x), \qquad 0 < m < 1.$$

Apparently, it is not linearity, but the symmetry toward the 45° ray, which excludes cyclical convergence.

To illustrate the existence of an optimal chaotic path, we display a simple example in Figure 7, where both Postulates 2 and 3 are violated. Here the graph of $K(x)$ first rises and then falls. This is true, for example, if some mature trees are needed for the maturation of saplings by shielding the latter from the wind. The existence of a period 3 cycle implies that optimal paths exist that are chaotic in the sense of Li and Yorke (1975). Whether the set of initial positions leading to chaos can be larger than measure zero deserves further inquiry.

Now if the monotonically decreasing graph of $K(\cdot)$ in Figure 5(b) lies sufficiently close to the origin, then a falling segment of it may join a rising branch of the graph of $P(x)$ to its left and form a "single-peaked" arch below the $x_{t+1} = 1 - x_t$ line. It seems then that the period 3 cycle of Figure 7 may reemerge, with two "rising" steps anchored on the graph of $P(x)$ and the declining step anchored on the graph of $K(\cdot)$. Thus, Postulate 2 may not rule out chaos. But an actual example needs to be constructed to clinch the issue.

[6]That is, "generically" valid and not requiring gratuitous values as initial conditions.

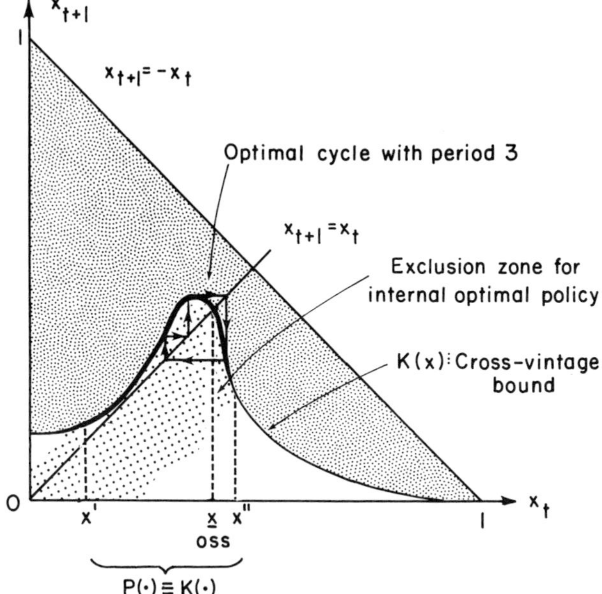

FIGURE 7 A chaotic optimal policy.

If Postulate 1 is replaced with the following:

Postulate 1' (single-crossing alternative form). At any point (y, z), $-[b + G_2(y, z)/G_1(y, z)] \geq \delta > 0$.

Then Result 2 can also be replaced with the following.

Result 2'

(a) There exists a unique optimal steady state, $x = 0$, with a neighborhood over which $P(x) = 0$.
(b) $P(x) < x$ for all $x > 0$ (global asymptotic stability property for the optimal steady state).

The derivation is analogous to the above.

In addition, one may also assume that the functions $u(\cdot)$ and $G(\cdot)$ are piecewise continuously differentiable, rather than differentiable, to allow for the presence of kinks in these functions. Nothing of substance is changed, although the discussion will have to be somewhat longer.

Finally, we shall only remark that the preceding analysis can also be extended to models where the maximum asset life is divided into more than two equal periods.

5. CONCLUSION

Methodologically, our main departure from most other works[7] (with the exception of the study of chaos) is to focus on the "topological" properties of the system, such as the single-crossing property, the "exclusion zone," which survive perturbations. A consequence of this is that we no longer rely on the construction of the support prices.[8] Even here, we are inspired by Professor McKenzie, whose example in seeking deeper insight through topological methods serves as a role model for all theorists.

Acknowledgments

The author appreciates the most helpful comments and suggestions by an anonymous referee and Professor Robert Becker, especially concerning the various ramifications of this study, which is an outgrowth of his earlier works with Tapan Mitra (Mitra and Wan, 1985, 1986). He alone is responsible for the remaining shortcomings.

References

Dechert, D. (1984). "Does optimal growth preclude chaos? A theorem on monotonicity," *Zeitscrift fur Nationalokonomie* **44**, 57–61.

Li, T. Y., and J. A. Yorke (1975). "Period 3 implies chaos," *Am. Math. Monthly* **82**, 985–992.

McKenzie, L. W. (1963). "Turnpike theorems for a generalized Leontief model," *Econometrica* **31**, 165–180.

McKenzie, L. W. (1981). "Optimal growth and turnpike theorems," in *Handbook in Mathematical Economics*, K. J. Arrow and M. Intriligator (eds.) (North Holland, Amsterdam).

McKenzie, L. W. (1987). "Turnpike theory," in *The New Palgrave, a Dictionary of Economics*, J. Eatwell, M. Millgate, and P. Newman (eds.) (Macmillan, London).

Mitra, T. and H. Y. Wan, Jr. (1985). "Some theoretic results on the theory of forestry," *Rev. Econ. Studies* **52**, 263–282.

Mitra, T. and H. Y. Wan, Jr. (1986). "On the Faustmann solution to the forest management problem," *J. Econ. Theory* **40**, 229–249.

Mitra, T., D. Ray, and R. Roy (1991). "The economics of orchards: an exercise in point-input, point-output capital theory," *J. Econ. Theory* **53**, 12–50.

Ramsey, F. P. (1928). "The mathematical theory of savings," *Econ. J.* **38**, 543–559.

Samuelson, P. A. (1949). "Market mechanism and maximization, Part III," memo, Rand Corp., Santa Monica, Calif.

Samuelson, P. A. (1966). "A catenary turnpike theorem involving consumption and the golden rule," *Am. Econ. Rev.* **55**, 486–496.

Samuelson, P. A. and R. M. Solow (1956). "A complete capital model involving heterogeneous capital goods," *Quart. J. Econ.* **70**, 537–562.

Wan, H. Y., Jr. (1989). "Optimal evolution of tree-age distribution for a tree farm," in *Mathematical Approaches to Ecological and Environmental Problems, Lecture Notes in Bio-Mathematics*, C. Castillo-Chavez *et al.* (eds.) (Springer-Verlag, Berlin).

Wan, H. Y., Jr. (1993). "Revisiting the Mitra-Wan tree farm," *Int. Econ. Rev.* forthcoming.

[7]Including Wan (1989;) as well as Mitra *et al.* (1991).

[8]In any case, if the cross-vintage bound renders the set D nonconvex, then support prices may not exist. The implication of a nonconvex D is explored by Dechert (1984).

PART III

INTERNATIONAL TRADE

THE STOLPER–SAMUELSON THEOREM: LINKS TO DOMINANT DIAGONALS

Ronald W. Jones
Department of Economics
University of Rochester
Rochester, New York 14627

Sugata Marjit
Department of Economics
Jadavpur University
Calcutta, India

Tapan Mitra
Department of Economics
Cornell University
Ithaca, New York 14853

Over 30 years ago Lionel McKenzie (1960) prepared an eloquent statement exposing the important role of matrices with dominant diagonals in economic theory. These matrices were shown to be directly relevant to issues such as the existence of positive solutions in a Leontief system, the stability of a competitive equilibrium in the case of gross-substitutes, and the unique determination of factor rewards by goods prices. Regarding this latter issue, it is, of course, well known in the field of international trade that the Stolper–Samuelson result, whereby a rise in any commodity's price lowers all factor returns save that of the factor "intensively" used in producing that commodity, requires much stronger restrictions on the production matrix than does the factor-price equalization theorem.[1] Nonetheless, we intend to show in this article that there exists a link between matrices that exhibit the dominant diagonal property and the Stolper–Samuelson theorem. Such a link emerges naturally from a new set of conditions on production technology which are shown to be *sufficient* to establish the Stolper–Samuelson results. These new conditions are, in

[1]For earlier contributions exploring this issue, see Minabe (1967), Kemp and Wegge (1969), Chipman (1969), and Uekawa (1971). Of special interest is Chipman's demonstration that diagonal dominance of the share matrix is neither necessary nor sufficient for the strong Stolper–Samuelson results.

GENERAL EQUILIBRIUM, GROWTH, AND TRADE II

turn, related to the stronger set of sufficient conditions exemplified by the Produced Mobile Factor (PMF) structure laid out in Jones and Marjit (1985, 1991), the older set of necessary conditions discussed by Kemp and Wegge (1969), and a theorem on sufficiency established in the mathematics literature by Willoughby (1977).

1. THE STRONG FACTOR-INTENSITY CONDITION

The standard setting in which the Stolper–Samuelson theorem is discussed involves the active production in competitive markets of n commodities, each produced nonjointly by the use of n distinct factors in processes that are linearly independent of each other at prevailing factor prices. The existence of any "holes" in the input–output technology matrix, whereby there exists one or more factors not used in one or more industries, plays havoc with the strong Stolper–Samuelson results.[2] Therefore we assume that the distributive share of factor i in industry j, θ_{ij}, is strictly positive for all i, j.

To proceed with our investigation we assume that a single commodity price p_s, rises, with all other commodity prices held fixed. Using "hat" terminology to indicate relative changes in variables, we are assuming

$$\hat{p}_s > 0, \quad \text{with} \quad \hat{p}_i = 0 \ \forall_i \neq s.$$

In such a case we know that some factor return must rise (and by relatively more than $\hat{p}_s$) and, since some sectors have experienced no price change, at least one other factor must have its return lowered. But this could be the return to factor s, instead of some off-diagonal term, $\hat{w}_k$, $k \neq s$.[3] The following Factor Intensity (FI) condition, due to Kemp and Wegge (1969), we now impose on the technology, and then use to show that when p_s rises, at least one off-diagonal w_k, $k \neq s$, must fall.

Definition. The matrix of distributive factor shares, $[\theta]$, satisfies the *Factor Intensity* (FI) condition if for any pair of distinct production factors, s and r, and distinct industries, s and t,

$$\frac{\theta_{ss}}{\theta_{rs}} > \frac{\theta_{st}}{\theta_{rt}}.$$

[2]That is, if some $a_{ik} = 0$ for an input–output coefficient, the matrix A^1 cannot exhibit strictly positive diagonal elements and negative off-diagonal elements. For explanation, see Jones (1987).

[3]Inada (1971) explores in some detail the case in which all diagonal elements of the inverse of the share matrix are negative and all off-diagonal elements are positive. Our Factor Intensity condition rules out this kind of behavior.

Factor s is said to be used intensively in industry s if its share there, relative to that of any other factor r, is greater than the corresponding ratio of s to r distributive shares in any other industry. With this restriction in mind we establish a weak-sounding lemma that, nonetheless, is of value in establishing our principal theorem:

LEMMA. *If the $[\theta]$ matrix of distributive factor shares satisfies the Factor-Intensity (FI) condition and one price, p_s, rises with all other commodity prices constant, at least one factor return, w_k, must fall for $k \neq s$.*

This lemma is easily established by considering the competitive profit equations of change for commodity s and any other commodity, j:

$$\theta_{ss}\hat{w}_s + \sum_{i \neq s} \theta_{is}\hat{w}_i = \hat{p}_s, \tag{1}$$

$$\theta_{sj}\hat{w}_s + \sum_{i \neq s} \theta_{ij}\hat{w}_i = 0. \tag{2}$$

Solve for $\hat{w}_s$ in each equation and equate to obtain

$$\frac{\hat{p}_s}{\theta_{ss}} = \sum_{i \neq s} \left(\frac{\theta_{is}}{\theta_{ss}} - \frac{\theta_{ij}}{\theta_{sj}} \right) \hat{w}_i. \tag{3}$$

Since the matrix of factor shares satisfies the FI conditions, each bracketed term in the summation must be negative. Therefore, a rise in p_s requires at least one $\hat{w}_i$, $i \neq s$, to be negative.

The Factory Intensity condition posits the importance of diagonal terms in the $[\theta]$ matrix relative to off-diagonal terms. Indeed, as demonstrated in Kemp and Wegge, the Factor Intensity condition is always necessary for the Stolper–Samuelson theorem to hold, but is not sufficient if $n \geq 4$. As discussed in Jones and Marjit (1985, 1991), more structure is generally required in order to guarantee strong Stolper–Samuelson results. For example, the Produced Mobile Factor (PMF) structure, so called because it can be derived from the $(n + 1) \times n$ specific factors model (Jones, 1975) by letting the single mobile input itself be produced by all the "specific" factors, implies that all the ratios of off-diagonal terms in any pair of rows, θ_{sj}/θ_{ij}, be equal for all industries, $j \neq s, i$. And this condition suffices to establish the Stolper–Samuelson result. The idea behind the Strong Factor Intensity (SFI) condition, to be defined below, is to allow these off-diagonal ratios to differ from each other, but to set an aggregate limit on the extent of these discrepancies.[4]

[4]In Section 2 an alternative characterization of the SFI condition will be provided, one that fits more closely the concept of diagonal dominance used by McKenzie (1960).

DEFINITION. A matrix of distributive factor shares satisfies the *Strong Factor Intensity* SFI condition if for any pair of distinct productive factors, s and r, and distinct industries s and t $(t \neq r)$,

$$\left(\frac{\theta_{ss}}{\theta_{rs}} - \frac{\theta_{st}}{\theta_{rt}}\right) > \sum_{i \neq r, s, t} \left|\frac{\theta_{is}}{\theta_{rs}} - \frac{\theta_{it}}{\theta_{rt}}\right|.$$

Consider two industries, s and t, and focus on some factor, $r \neq s, t$. By the (FI) condition the left-hand side of the (SFI) criterion is positive, and features the excess of the s to r input share ratio in industry s (where factor s is the intensive factor used in industry s) over that for industry t. The right-hand side collects the absolute values of the discrepancy between the ratio of other factor inputs, $i \neq s$, to r in industry s compared to industry t. The SFI criterion posits that the sum of such absolute values still falls short of the excess of θ_{ss}/θ_{rs} over the comparable ratio in the tth sector, θ_{st}/θ_{rt}.

Armed with the lemma previously established, we now prove the basic theorem.

THEOREM. *If the $n \times n$ productive structure satisfies the SFI condition, the Stolper–Samuelson results hold.*

Let p_s rise, keeping all other commodity prices constant. This leads to an array of factor price changes $\hat{w}_i$, and let k, j be such that

$$\hat{w}_k = \min_i \hat{w}_i; \qquad \hat{w}_j = \max_i \hat{w}_i \quad \text{over all } i \neq s.$$

The lemma ensures that $\hat{w}_k$ is negative. Denote by set Q the values for $i \neq s, k$ or j.

The competitive profit conditions for commodities j and k are shown in equations (4) and (5):

$$\theta_{sj}\hat{w}_s + \theta_{kj}\hat{w}_k + \theta_{jj}\hat{w}_j + \sum_{i \in Q} \theta_{ij}\hat{w}_i = 0, \tag{4}$$

$$\theta_{sk}\hat{w}_s + \theta_{kk}\hat{w}_k + \theta_{jk}\hat{w}_j + \sum_{i \in Q} \theta_{ik}\hat{w}_i = 0. \tag{5}$$

Following our earlier procedure, solve each equation for $\hat{w}_s$ and equate to obtain

$$\sum_{i \in Q} \frac{\theta_{ij}}{\theta_{sj}}\hat{w}_i + \frac{\theta_{kj}}{\theta_{sj}}\hat{w}_k + \frac{\theta_{jj}}{\theta_{sj}}\hat{w}_j = \sum_{i \in Q} \frac{\theta_{ik}}{\theta_{sk}}\hat{w}_i + \frac{\theta_{kk}}{\theta_{sk}}\hat{w}_k + \frac{\theta_{jk}}{\theta_{sk}}\hat{w}_j. \tag{6}$$

Rewrite this equation so as to isolate the terms in $\hat{w}_j$ and $\hat{w}_k$, noting that $\hat{w}_k$ is negative:

$$\left[\frac{\theta_{jj}}{\theta_{sj}} - \frac{\theta_{jk}}{\theta_{sk}}\right]\hat{w}_j + \left[\frac{\theta_{kk}}{\theta_{sk}} - \frac{\theta_{kj}}{\theta_{sj}}\right]|\hat{w}_k| = \sum_{i \in Q}\left[\frac{\theta_{ik}}{\theta_{sk}} - \frac{\theta_{ij}}{\theta_{sj}}\right]\hat{w}_i. \tag{7}$$

By the FI condition note that the coefficients of $\hat{w}_j$ and $|\hat{w}_k|$ on the left-hand side are both positive.

Now consider possible values for $\hat{w}_j$. We prove that $\hat{w}_j$ must be negative, and we do this by showing, first, that $\hat{w}_j$ cannot exceed the positive value $|\hat{w}_k|$, and second, that $\hat{w}_j$ cannot lie in the range $0 \leq \hat{w}_j \leq |\hat{w}_k|$. If $\hat{w}_j$ were to exceed $|\hat{w}_k|$, and therefore also exceed the absolute value of any $\hat{w}_i$, the right-hand side of (7) would be less than or equal to

$$\hat{w}_j \sum_{i \in Q}\left|\frac{\theta_{ij}}{\theta_{sj}} - \frac{\theta_{ik}}{\theta_{sk}}\right|.$$

(In the PMF structure discussed below, all these absolute values are zero.) The left-hand side of equation (7) exceeds

$$\hat{w}_j\left[\frac{\theta_{jj}}{\theta_{sj}} - \frac{\theta_{jk}}{\theta_{sk}}\right],$$

so that if $\hat{w}_j$ were positive, the resulting inequality would violate SFI. If $\hat{w}_j$ were nonnegative but less than or equal to $|\hat{w}_k|$, the right-hand side of (7) would be less than or equal to

$$|\hat{w}_k| \sum_{i \in Q}\left|\frac{\theta_{ik}}{\theta_{sk}} - \frac{\theta_{ij}}{\theta_{sj}}\right|,$$

and the left-hand side of (7) would exceed or equal

$$|\hat{w}_k|\left[\frac{\theta_{kk}}{\theta_{sk}} - \frac{\theta_{kj}}{\theta_{sj}}\right].$$

Once again a contradiction with SFI is involved. Therefore, $\hat{w}_j$ must be negative. A rise in p_s lowers all w_i for $i \neq s$. ($\hat{w}_s$ must therefore exceed unity.) This is the Stolper–Samuelson result.

Remark. While our strong factor-intensity condition and our generalized Stolper–Samuelson theorem are phrased in terms of economic magnitudes (the factor shares), we have actually established the following purely mathematical result: Suppose an $n \times n$ positive nonsingular matrix, $\alpha = (\alpha_{ij})$ satisfies the following condition. For every triple s, t, r of distinct indices,

$$\left(\frac{\alpha_{ss}}{\alpha_{rs}} - \frac{\alpha_{st}}{\alpha_{rt}}\right) > \sum_{i \neq r,s,t} \left|\frac{\alpha_{is}}{\alpha_{rs}} - \frac{\alpha_{it}}{\alpha_{rt}}\right|.$$

Then, the diagonal terms of α^{-1} are positive while the off-diagonal terms of α^{-1} are negative.

2. A DOMINANT DIAGONAL MATRIX

The SFI condition, if satisfied by the matrix of distributive factor shares, allows the construction of a new matrix of order $(n - 2) \times (n - 2)$, which has (a) a positive diagonal if the FI condition is satisfied and (b) a dominant diagonal if the SFI condition is satisfied.

From the original $[\theta]$ matrix of distributive shares we select an arbitrary rth row and tth column $(t \neq r)$ and construct a new matrix, $B(r, t)$, which will be $(n - 2) \times (n - 2)$. The procedure involves several steps:

(i) For each column s, divide all elements by θ_{rs}. (Thus the rth row becomes the unit vector.)

(ii) In this new matrix subtract the tth column (consisting of elements such as θ_{jt}/θ_{rt}) from all columns. (This subraction makes both the tth column and the rth row consist entirely of zeros.)

(iii) Delete the rth row *and* column and the tth row *and* column to obtain $B(r, t)$. Retain the original numbering of rows and columns so that, for example, the $(n - 2)$nd row index of $B(r, t)$ is n.

The typical diagonal element of $B(r, t)$ is

$$b_{ss} \equiv \frac{\theta_{ss}}{\theta_{rs}} - \frac{\theta_{st}}{\theta_{rt}}.$$

If (FI) is satisfied, all the diagonal elements are positive. The typical off-diagonal element in the sth column is

$$b_{is} \equiv \frac{\theta_{is}}{\theta_{rs}} - \frac{\theta_{it}}{\theta_{rt}}.$$

The usual definition of diagonal dominance requires

$$b_{ss} > \sum_{i \neq r,s,t} |b_{is}|,$$

which is precisely the condition for SFI. That is, diagonal dominance of all the $B(r, t)$ matrices implies that the underlying production structure satisfies the Stolper–Samuelson conditions.

In the subsequent section we find it convenient to use an alternative characterization of diagonal dominance, the one which McKenzie employed (1960). Applied to the SFI condition, this leads to the following definition.

Definition. A matrix of distributive shares satisfies the generalized SFI condition if there exists a set of positive numbers $d_1, \ldots, d_n$ such that for any pair of distinct productive factors, s and r and distinct industries s and t $(t \neq r)$,

$$d_s\left(\frac{\theta_{ss}}{\theta_{rs}} - \frac{\theta_{st}}{\theta_{rt}}\right) > \sum_{i \neq r, s, t} d_i \left|\frac{\theta_{is}}{\theta_{rs}} - \frac{\theta_{it}}{\theta_{rt}}\right|.$$

Suppose that the nonsingular matrix of distributive shares θ satisfies the generalized SFI condition. We can then define a diagonal matrix μ satisfying $\mu_{ii} = d_i$ for $i = 1, \ldots, n$ and a matrix, $\nu = \mu\theta$. Then, $\nu_{ij} = d_i\theta_{ij}$ for all i, j, and so we have for any pair of distinct productive factors s and r, and distinct industries s and t $(t \neq r)$,

$$d_s\left[\frac{(\nu_{ss}/d_s)}{(\nu_{rs}/d_r)} - \frac{(\nu_{st}/d_s)}{(\nu_{rt}/d_r)}\right] > \sum_{i \neq r, s, t} d_i \left|\frac{(\nu_{is}/d_i)}{(\nu_{rs}/d_r)} - \frac{(\nu_{it}/d_i)}{(\nu_{rt}/d_r)}\right|$$

which simplifies to

$$\left[\frac{\nu_{ss}}{\nu_{rs}} - \frac{\nu_{st}}{\nu_{rt}}\right] > \sum_{i \neq r, s, t} \left|\frac{\nu_{is}}{\nu_{rs}} - \frac{\nu_{it}}{\nu_{rt}}\right|$$

This means that the matrix ν is nonsingular, and (by the remark following our theorem) ν^{-1} has positive diagonal and negative off-diagonal elements. Since $\nu^{-1} = \theta^{-1}\mu^{-1}$ and μ^{-1} is a positive diagonal matrix, clearly θ^{-1} has positive diagonal and negative off-diagonal elements. This is the Stolper–Samuelson result.

3. THE WILLOUGHBY THEOREM

In Willoughby (1977) there is a theorem that states sufficient conditions that, in effect, guarantee the Stolper–Samuelson result. Here we present a version of his result phrased in terms of the distributive share matrix.

There are two strands to Willoughby's result. First is the dominance of any diagonal element over all off-diagonal elements (assumed positive) in the same row and the positivity of the θ matrix:

$$0 < m \equiv \min_{i \neq j} \frac{\theta_{ij}}{\theta_{ii}} \leq \max_{i \neq j} \frac{\theta_{ij}}{\theta_{ii}} \equiv M < 1 \tag{8}$$

Such dominance was shown by Kemp and Wegge (1969) to be a necessary consequence of a share matrix exhibiting the Stolper–Samuelson property. More generally, it follows from the FI condition, and thus may hold in larger-dimensional cases even when Stolper–Samuelson does not.[5]

The second strand of Willoughby's result, as reflected in the following statement of his theorem, is that if m and M are sufficiently close together, the Stolper–Samuelson result holds.

THEOREM (Willoughby). *Suppose* (8) *holds for an* $(n \times n)$ *distributive share matrix and, furthermore,*

$$(n-2)\frac{(M^2 - m^2)}{(m - m^2)} < 1. \tag{9}$$

Then the matrix of distributive shares must be such that θ^{-1} *has negative off-diagonal elements (and diagonal elements all exceeding unity).*

The proof involves showing that the generalized characterization of the SFI condition is satisfied with positive weights $d_i = 1/\theta_{ii}$, $i = 1, \dots, n$. We begin by observing that

$$\frac{m}{M} \le \frac{\theta_{is}/\theta_{ii}}{\theta_{rs}/\theta_{rr}} \le \frac{M}{m} \quad \text{and} \quad \frac{m}{M} \le \frac{\theta_{it}/\theta_{ii}}{\theta_{rt}/\theta_{rr}} \le \frac{M}{m} \tag{10}$$

for $i, r \neq s, t$ since m is less than or equal to the smallest θ_{ij}/θ_{ii} and M exceeds or equals the largest θ_{ij}/θ_{ii}, $i \neq j$. From this follow the bounds set on the difference between ratios of distributive shares:

$$\frac{\theta_{rr}}{\theta_{ii}}\left[\frac{\theta_{is}}{\theta_{rs}} - \frac{\theta_{it}}{\theta_{rt}}\right] \le \frac{M}{m} - \frac{m}{M} = \frac{M^2 - m^2}{mM}, \tag{11}$$

$$\frac{\theta_{rr}}{\theta_{ii}}\left[\frac{\theta_{it}}{\theta_{rt}} - \frac{\theta_{is}}{\theta_{rs}}\right] \le \frac{M}{m} - \frac{m}{M} = \frac{M^2 - m^2}{mM}. \tag{12}$$

[5]Rewrite the FI condition as $\theta_{ss}\theta_{ij} > \theta_{sj}\theta_{is}$. For given s there are $(n-1)$ inequalities of this type, for $i \neq s$. Adding them yields

$$\theta_{ss}\left(\sum_{i \neq s} \theta_{ij}\right) > \theta_{sj}\left(\sum_{i \neq s} \theta_{is}\right).$$

Since $\Sigma_{i \neq s}\theta_{ij} = (1 - \theta_{sj})$ and $\Sigma_{i \neq s}\theta_{is} = (1 - \theta_{ss})$, substitution reveals

$$\theta_{ss} > \theta_{sj} \quad \text{for all } j \neq s.$$

Thus even though a share matrix that satisfies FI may not have a dominant diagonal, it does have a "dominating" diagonal over other row elements.

Since there are $(n - 3)$ values for $i \neq r, s, t$, addition over factors $i(\neq r, s, t)$ yields

$$\theta_{rr} \sum_{i \neq r,s,t} d_i \left| \frac{\theta_{is}}{\theta_{rs}} - \frac{\theta_{it}}{\theta_{rt}} \right| \leq (n-3)\left[\frac{M^2 - m^2}{mM}\right]. \tag{13}$$

Turning to the discrepancy between the ratio of the diagonal share (θ_{ss}) to an off-diagonal share (θ_{rs}) in an industry and the comparable ratio in another industry, we obtain

$$\theta_{rr} d_s \left[\frac{\theta_{ss}}{\theta_{rs}} - \frac{\theta_{st}}{\theta_{rt}}\right] \geq \frac{1}{M} - \frac{M}{m}$$

$$= \frac{m - M^2}{mM} = \frac{(m - m^2)}{mM} - \frac{(M^2 - m^2)}{mM}. \tag{14}$$

Finally, Willoughby's condition (9) can be restated as

$$(n-2)\frac{(M^2 - m^2)}{mM} < \frac{(m - m^2)}{mM} \tag{15}$$

Now, subtract $(M^2 - m^2)/mM$ from each side of (15) to obtain

$$(n-3)\frac{(M^2 - m^2)}{mM} < \frac{(m - m^2)}{mM} - \frac{(M^2 - m^2)}{mM}. \tag{16}$$

The right-hand sides of (14) and (16) are equivalent, so that from (13), (14) and (16),

$$d_s\left[\frac{\theta_{ss}}{\theta_{rs}} - \frac{\theta_{st}}{\theta_{rt}}\right] > \sum_{i \neq r,s,t} d_i \left| \frac{\theta_{is}}{\theta_{rs}} - \frac{\theta_{it}}{\theta_{rt}} \right|. \tag{17}$$

That is, Willoughby's restriction (9) implies that the matrix of distributive factor shares satisfies the generalized SFI condition and thus leads to Stolper–Samuelson results.

The preceding proof established that a matrix satisfying the Willoughby conditions must also satisfy SFI. But we now provide an example to show that the converse does not hold: Consider the following A matrix, which is the product of a share matrix and the diagonal matrix D where $d_{ii} = 1/\theta_{ii}$:

$$A = \begin{bmatrix} 1 & 0.1 & 0.1 & 0.1 \\ 0.3 & 1 & 0.3 & 0.3 \\ 0.3 & 0.3 & 1 & 0.3 \\ 0.1 & 0.3 & 0.1 & 1 \end{bmatrix}$$

The inverse of A has a positive diagonal and strictly negative off-diagonal elements. Furthermore, the Factor Intensity condition is satisfied, as is SFI. But the Willoughby condition is not: $M = 0.3$, $m = 0.1$, $n = 4$, and $(n - 2)[(M^2 - m^2)/(m - m^2)] = 16/9 > 1$.

4. THE PRODUCED MOBILE FACTOR (PMF) STRUCTURE

Jones and Marjit (1985, 1991) develop a simple structure based on the $(n + 1)$-factor-, n-sector-specific factor model, modified so that the single "mobile" factor in such a setting is itself the output of a linear homogeneous production function with all other factors as inputs. In effect, each productive activity is a positive convex combination of an activity using only the factor "intensively" used and a common activity used in all sectors. In each industry there is one (intensive) factor that is used in two ways—in helping to produce an intermediate good used in all sectors and in combining with this intermediate good (the "produced mobile factor") to help produce the final output in that industry. All other factors enter only indirectly through their employment in producing the intermediate good. This leads to a natural additive decomposition of the share matrix into the direct factor use in the final stage (a positive diagonal matrix) and the indirect use (matrix of rank one since all sectors use varying amounts of the same intermediate good).

Such a structure must satisfy the SFI conditions. To see this consider the ratio of a pair of off-diagonal shares. As shown by (18), this ratio must be the same for all industries:

$$\frac{\theta_{is}}{\theta_{rs}} = \frac{w_i a_{is}}{w_r a_{rs}} = \frac{w_i a_{im} a_{ms}}{w_r a_{rm} a_{ms}} = \frac{w_i a_{im}}{w_r a_{rm}} \quad \text{for all } s. \tag{18}$$

The term a_{ms} refers to the input of the produced mobile factor required per unit of commodity s, whereas a_{im} and a_{rm} denote input requirements to produce a unit of the "mobile" factor. Thus the right-hand side of the SFI criterion vanishes, and the left-hand side is positive by construction.

In Jones and Marjit (1991) use is made of the geometrical apparatus employed recently by Leamer (1987) and earlier by McKenzie (1955) to depict the composition of factor input requirements in a triangle (for the case of three inputs) or an $(n - 1)$-dimensional tetrahedron (for the case of n inputs), with the use of barycentric coordinates.[6] A feature of the PMF structure is that rays from each factor origin passing through the point representing the activity level for the industry intensive in its use of

[6]This geometric apparatus for the 3×3 case is further developed in Jones (1992).

that factor all pass through a common point. That point represents the composition of inputs for the produced "mobile" factor. The weaker conditions provided by the SFI criterion provide a measure of how far apart such rays can be without sacrificing the Stolper–Samuelson result. It is as if the PMF structure combines in each activity a single factor and a common "off-the-rack" input (the common mobile factor), whereas the more general structure exhibiting SFI combines each factor with a "tailor-made" input that may differ somewhat from the tailor-made input used in any other sector.

Reconsider condition (9) required for the Willoughby result. As the number of distinct productive sectors n expands, the discrepancy between minimal and maximal relative off-diagonal elements m and M must get smaller and smaller. Thus the PMF structure represents the limiting case of the Willoughby condition.

The PMF structure yields a particularly simple form of the dominant diagonal $B(r, t)$ matrices; these matrices reduce to pure diagonal matrices since ratios of off-diagonal shares are equal. The most simple case of the PMF structure is the one in which the share of the factor used intensively in any industry is the same d over all industries and all unintensive factor shares have a common value c, where $c < d$. Such a matrix clearly has only two types of factors and supports Stolper–Samuelson conclusions since when p_j alone rises, at least one factor return must rise by a magnified amount ($\hat{w}_j$) and one (or more) factor return must fall ($\hat{w}_i$, the same value for all $i \neq j$). This special matrix will exhibit a "dominating" diagonal as long as d exceeds c, but not a dominant diagonal unless $d > (n - 1)c$. Conversely, suppose d does exceed $(n - 1)c$ in all industries save one, and that in that special sector the diagonal term is $(d + c)$ and one of the off-diagonal terms is zero. Such a matrix has a (weakly) larger diagonal than the straightforward case with all diagonal elements possessing value d and off-diagonal elements, c. Nonetheless, it cannot exhibit Stolper–Samuelson properties. The latter characteristic of a production structure depends not only on the degree of intensity in the use of a single factor in each sector but also on a limitation in the divergence of factor shares of the nonintensive factors.

5. CONCLUDING REMARKS

Relatively few production structures have been developed that are sufficient to lead to Stolper–Samuelson results. The Produced Mobile Factor (PMF) structure is an example that does support Stolper–Samuelson. The Factor Intensity (FI) condition by itself has been shown by Kemp and Wegge (1969) not to be sufficient to yield Stolper–Samuelson results in dimensions greater than three, although it is a necessary condition. The

Strong Factor Intensity (SFI) condition developed in this paper, which imposes more constraints on factor intensities than simple (FI) alone, has been shown to be sufficient for Stolper–Samuelson. Indeed, it encompasses the mathematical theorem due to Willoughby as well as the PMF structure. In imposing extra constraints on the degree of asymmetry in off-diagonal terms it provides yet another example of the concept of dominant diagonals, whose applications in economic theory were pioneered over 30 years ago by Lionel McKenzie.

It is important to emphasize that although some forms of strong symmetry are required to obtain Stolper–Samuelson results, the direction taken in the SFI condition is not the only route that is possible. An alternative path was suggested by Willoughby in his example of a *circulant* matrix. Before appropriate scaling to render it a share matrix, the circulant structure has value unity along the diagonal, values equal to some fraction a to the immediate right of the diagonal (with a_{n1} also equal to a), the smaller fraction a^2 to the right of that, and so on until the term a^{n-1} lies in the position immediately to the left of the diagonal (with a_{1n} equal to a^{n-1}). Such a matrix does not satisfy the Willoughby conditions discussed earlier nor, indeed, the SFI conditions, yet the inverse matrix is "borderline" Stolper–Samuelson in that although no positive off-diagonal elements appear, there are many zeros. Thus the kind of symmetry imposed is genuinely different from the SFI structure in that every sector looks like every other sector except for a renumbering of the most intensively used factor, etc.[7] It is the former (SFI) structure that makes use of the bounds on asymmetry provided by the concept of diagonal dominance of the differences between ratios of factor shares.

Acknowledgments

Mitra's research was supported, in part, by a grant from the National Science Foundation.

References

Chipman, J. (1969). "Factor price equalization and the Stolper–Samuelson theorem," *Int. Econ. Rev.* **10**, 399–406.

Inada, K. (1971). "The production coefficient matrix and the Stolper–Samuelson condition," *Econometrica* **39**, 219–240.

Jones, R. W. (1987). "Heckscher–Ohlin trade theory," in Eatwell et al. eds. *The New Palgrave, A Dictionary of Economics*, J. Eatwell, M. Milgate, and P. Newman (eds.) (Macmillan, New York).

[7]In associated work Jones and Mitra investigate the significance of the shape of such "share ribs," which are assumed to be similar in structure from sector to sector. For example, Stolper–Samuelson results emerge only if the typical schedule of shares from highest to lowest is sufficiently bowed in. A linear "rib" will not do (see Jones and Mitra 1992).

Jones, R. W. (1992). "Factor scarcity, factor abundance, and attitudes towards protection: The 3×3 model," *J. Int. Econ. Integration* **7**, 1–19.

Jones, R. W., and S. Marjit (1985). "A simple production model with Stolper–Samuelson properties," *Int. Econ. Rev.* **26**, 565–567.

Jones, R. W., and S. Marjit (1991). "The Stolper–Samuelson theorem, the Leamer triangle and the produced mobile factor structure," Chapter 6 in *Trade, Policy, and International Adjustments*, A. Takayama, M. Ohyama, and H. Ohta (eds.) (Academic Press, San Diego).

Jones, R. W., and T. Mitra (1992). "Share ribs and income distribution," unpublished paper.

Kemp, M. C., and L. Wegge (1969). "On the relation between commodity prices and factor rewards," *Int. Econ. Rev.* **10**, 407–413.

Leamer, E. (1987). "Paths of development in the three-factor n-good general equilibrium model," *J. Pol. Econ.* **95**, 961–999.

McKenzie, L. (1955). "Equality of factor prices in world trade," *Econometrica* **23**, 239–257.

McKenzie, L. (1960). "Matrices with dominant diagonals and economic theory," in *Mathematical Methods in the Social Sciences*, K. Arrow, S. Karlin, and P. Suppes (eds.) (Stanford University Press, Stanford, Calif.), pp. 47–60.

Minabe, N. (1967). "The Stolper–Samuelson Theorem, the Rybczynski effect, and the Heckscher–Ohlin theory of trade pattern and factor price equalization: The case of many-commodity, many-factor country," *Can. J. Econ. Political Sci.*, **33**, 401–419.

Uekawa, Y. (1971). "Generalization of the Stolper–Samuelson theorem," *Econometrica* **39**, 197–213.

Willoughby, R. A. (1977). "The inverse M-matrix problem," *Linear Algebra Appl.* **18**, 75–94.

LABOR MOBILITY AND WAGE RATE EQUALIZATION

Eric Bond
Department of Economics
The Pennsylvania State University
University Park, Pennsylvania 16802

1. INTRODUCTION

This paper examines the question of whether the mobility of labor will equalize the wage rate between locations when there are goods (such as housing and services) that are not traded. Workers are assumed to consume in the location where they work, so that workers move to the location that offers the highest utility level (including the effects of both wage rates and prices of nontraded goods). Free mobility of labor will thus lead to the equalization of utility levels, so that locations with high prices of nontraded goods must pay higher wage rates to compensate for the higher cost of living. The pressure to equalize wage rates comes from the fact that there may be other mobile factors of production or production activities that will move to take advantage of differences in wage rates. High-wage locations will lose mobile capital and labor-intensive industries to locations with low wage rates.

This paper addresses the problem using techniques developed by Lionel McKenzie (1955) for dealing with the question of whether trade in goods will lead to the equalization of factor prices when factors are immobile. McKenzie showed that if technologies are identical and there are at least as many linearly independent activities as there are immobile factors, then factor prices will be equalized for all countries whose endowments are consistent with diversified production. In the present problem, factors of production are owned by households, some of which

GENERAL EQUILIBRIUM, GROWTH, AND TRADE II

are mobile and consume where labor is supplied and some of which are immobile. The expenditure function for mobile households will be utilized to treat the mobility of labor in a manner similar to other production activities.[1] The export of labor owned by mobile households can be treated as an activity which uses a unit of labor and negative amounts of other factors of production (factors released from the production of nontraded goods when a unit of labor is exported).[2] The analysis in this paper will use some simple low-dimension models to illustrate the conditions under which wage rates will equalize, and to examine the relationship between wage rates and prices of immobile factors when factor prices do not equalize.

It will be shown that wage rates might fail to equalize for two reasons, even when technologies and expenditure functions of workers are identical across locations. The first reason is that the number of traded goods may be less than the number of nontraded factors of production. The dimensionality condition requiring that the number of traded goods be at least as large as the number of nontraded factors with labor mobility is identical to that obtained for trade in goods alone, because labor mobility adds both an additional traded activity and a factor price to be determined. The second reason for failure of wage rate equalization is that when a location is endowed with sufficiently large purchasing power (in terms of mobile capital owned by households that are immobile), the price of nontraded goods may be driven above the level consistent with the production of any traded goods. High incomes create congestion in local markets for nontraded goods, and this congestion cannot be relieved by the export of factors of production when it is owned by immobile households. This explanation is unique to the case of factor mobility with nontraded goods.

Section 2 presents a simple model with three factors of production, one traded good, and one nontraded good. Mobile households own mobile factors of production (capital and labor) and consume where labor is employed, while immobile households own immobile land and mobile capital. The one immobile factor model is the simplest one for illustrating the role played by congestion in markets for nontraded goods in creating a failure of factor price equalization. In this case, locations with high wage rates will also have high land prices and will specialize in the production of nontraded goods. Wage rates below the level associated with diversified

[1] Ethier and Svensson (1986) have shown that factor price equalization results apply to models without nontraded goods when factor mobility is introduced. In the absence of nontraded goods, the mobility of labor will automatically equalize wage rates. The export of labor can then be treated as an activity that uses one unit of labor, and factor price equalization results will be obtained using the same approach as with immobile factors.

[2] Bond (1993) shows how the expenditure function approach can be used to obtain modified versions of the principle of comparative advantage and the Stolper–Samuelson and Heckscher–Ohlin theorems with labor mobility.

production will never be observed in the one-factor model, because these wage rates would allow positive profits from production of traded goods.

Section 3 deals with the case of two goods and two immobile factors of production, and shows that a cone of diversification can be obtained such that factor prices are equalized for all locations whose endowments lie within the cone. It is shown that this cone depends on both the demand for nontraded goods and the unit input requirements for traded and nontraded goods. Since the demand for nontraded goods depends on the endowment of mobile factors in immobile households, the cone may not exist for some high-income locations. It is also shown that with two immobile factors, wage rates below the level associated with diversified production may be observed. These low wage rates are not arbitraged away by the production of traded goods (as they would be in the one factor model) because of the presence of a high price for an immobile factor used in the production of traded goods.

These results indicate how differences in demand and supply conditions in markets for traded goods across locations can lead to the failure of wage rate equalization with labor mobility.

2. ONE IMMOBILE FACTOR

In this section we examine a simple model in which there are three factors of production, which will be referred to as *land*, *labor*, and *capital*. Land represents the factor of production that is immobile between locations. Labor is assumed to be mobile between locations, but labor must consume in the location where it works. Capital is assumed to be mobile between locations, and owners of capital may locate their capital in a different location than the one in which they consume. A location can be thought of as representing a state or region within a country, or as a country within a customs union.

It will be assumed that these factors of production are owned by two types of households: mobile households and immobile households. Each immobile household is assumed to own one unit of land and k_T units of capital, and each mobile household owns one unit of labor and k_L units of capital. The endowment capital in immobile households, k_T is assumed to be the same for all households within a region, but may differ across regions, while k_L will be assumed to be the same for all mobile households regardless of location. The effect of allowing k_L to vary across mobile households will be discussed below.

It will be assumed that there are two goods: a traded good (good 1) that is chosen as numeraire and a nontraded good (good N). The traded good can be exchanged on a world market for the services of mobile capital goods. These goods are assumed to be competitively produced with a constant returns to scale production technology. The unit cost function for good i ($i = 1, N$) will be denoted $c_i(w, v, r)$, where w is the wage rate, v is the rental on land, and r is the rental on capital. Letting p_N denote the price of the nontraded good, the competitive profit conditions for the two goods will be

$$1 \leq c_1(w, v, r), \tag{1a}$$

$$p_N = c_N(w, v, r), \tag{1b}$$

where (1a) will hold with strict equality when the location produces some of the traded good. Assuming that the nontraded good is essential in consumption, the competitive profit condition for the nontraded good must hold with strict equality.

Since the location of capital can be separated from the consumption decision (for both mobile and immobile households), free mobility of capital ensures that the return to capital in each location will be equated to the world return r^*. For mobile households, consumption must take place in the location where labor is supplied, so the utility level obtained in a location will depend on both the wage rate and the price of nontraded goods in that location. Free mobility of labor equalizes the utility level of a mobile household in all locations. Letting $e(p_N, U)$ be the expenditure function associated with the mobile household utility function, the mobility of capital and labor imposes the following conditions on local factor prices

$$r = r^*, \tag{2a}$$

$$w = e(p_N, U^*) - r^* k_L, \tag{2b}$$

where U^* is the utility level available in the rest of the world. The expenditure function is assumed to be increasing and concave in p_N and increasing in U. Condition (2b) will hold with equality under the assumptions that labor is essential in the production of nontraded goods and that all labor is owned by mobile households.

Figure 1 illustrates the conditions on the local factor prices (w, v) imposed by the competitive profit and factor mobility conditions. The competitive profit condition for traded goods ensures that factor prices must lie on or above the $c_1 = 1$ locus. The ee' locus represents the values of w at v at which $w = e(c_N(w, v, r^*), U^*) - r^* k_L$. The slope of this curve is $dw/dv = a_{TN} d_{LN}/(1 - a_{LN} d_{LN})$, where $d_{LN}(p_N, U^*) = \partial e/\partial p_N$ is the compensated demand function for nontraded goods by mobile households. The ee' locus will be upward-sloping as long as $\theta_{LN} p_N d_{LN}/w < 1$, where $\theta_{LN} = w a_{LN}/p_N$. Since $\theta_{LN} < 1$ and $p_N d_{LN} < w + r^* k_L$, this inequality must be satisfied unless mobile households receive a large

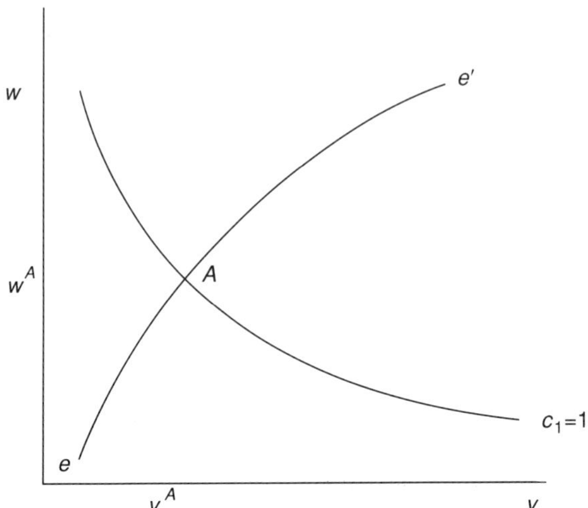

FIGURE 1 Diversified production (A) with one immobile factor.

share of their income from capital. It will be assumed in what follows that this condition is satisfied. Note also that the ee' locus must be concave in v.[3]

Conditions (1) and (2) will be satisfied for $w \geq w^A$ along the ee' locus. Point A is the point of diversified production, at which both traded goods and nontraded goods are produced. For points on the ee' locus with wages exceeding w_A, only nontraded goods are produced, with traded goods being obtained in return for the services of capital located abroad. Following McKenzie (1955), the factor-price equalization argument will be made in two steps. First, it will be shown that a set of endowments exist at which markets for factors and nontraded goods clear factor prices are given by (w^A, v^A). Second, it will be shown that this is the unique set of factor prices consistent with equilibrium for those endowments.

We first examine the conditions under which (w^A, v^A) will be consistent with equilibrium in goods and factor markets. The equilibrium condi-

[3]Consider two points (w^1, v^1) and (w^0, v^0) that lie on the ee' schedule, and let e^1 and e^0 denote the corresponding values of the expenditure function. By the concavity of the cost function for nontraded goods, we have $c_N(tw^0 + (1-t)w^1, tv^0 + (1-t)v^1, r^*) \geq tc_N(w^0, v^0, r^*) + (1-t)c_N(w^1, v^1, r^*)$ for $0 \leq t \leq 1$. By the concavity of the expenditure function in p_N, it follows that $e(tc_N(w^0, v^0, r^*) + (1-t)c_N(w^1, v^1, r^*)) \geq te^0 + (1-t)e^1$. Since the expenditure function is nondecreasing in p_N, we have $e(c_N(tw^0 + (1-t)w^1, tv^0 + (1-t)v^1, r^*) \geq e(tc_N(w^0, v^0, r^*) + (1-t)c_N(w^1, v^1, r^*))$. Combining the last two inequalities establishes that ee' is concave in v. For the case where the ee' schedule is downward-sloping ($a - a_{LN}d_{LN} < 0$), the only equilibrium will be at a tangency between the ee' schedule and the unit cost curve for the traded goods.

tion in the market for nontraded goods is

$$X_N = d_{TN}T + d_{LN}(L - Z), \tag{3}$$

where L is the endowment of labor, Z is the quantity of exported labor, T is the endowment of land, and $d_{TN}(p_N, v + r^*k_T)$ is the (uncompensated) demand for nontraded goods by immobile households. Demand functions of immobile households are assumed to be derived from identical and homothetic preferences. Equilibrium conditions for the factor markets are given by

$$T = a_{T1}X_1 + a_{TN}X_N, \tag{4a}$$

$$L - Z = a_{L1}X_1 + a_{LN}X_N, \tag{4b}$$

where $a_{Li}(w, v, r^*) = \partial c_i/\partial w$ is the unit labor requirement for good i, a_{Ti} is the unit land requirement for good i, and Z is the export of labor. A capital market equilibrium condition could also be included. However, the demand for nontraded goods depends only on the amount of capital owned by residents, not by the amount located domestically. Thus, the local capital employment is $a_{K1}X_1 + a_{KN}X_N$ and can be determined from the output levels that satisfy (4).

The equilibrium with diversified production will occur if the full employment conditions (3) and (4) are satisfied with $X_1 \geq 0$ and $Z \leq L$. Substituting (3) into (4) and solving yields

$$X_1/T = (1 - a_{LN}d_{LN} - a_{TN}d_{TN})/\Delta, \tag{5a}$$

$$(L - Z)/T = ((1 - a_{TN}d_{TN})a_{L1} + a_{LN}d_{TN}a_{T1})/\Delta, \tag{5b}$$

where $\Delta = a_{T1}(1 - a_{LN}d_{LN}) + a_{L1}a_{TN}d_{LN} > 0$. If $(1 - a_{LN}d_{LN} - a_{TN}d_{TN}) > 0$, then there will exist an equilibrium with diversified production in which factor prices are given by (w^A, v^A). The a_{ij} are determined by factor prices and d_{LN} is determined by the expenditure function (2b) and exogenously given endowment of mobile workers, k_L. The only remaining element that could vary across locations is the demand for nontraded goods by immobile households, $d_{TN}(p_N, v + r^*k_T)$, which depends on the capital endowment of immobile households. If k_T is identical across all locations, then $(1 - a_{LN}d_{LN} - a_{TN}d_{TN}) > 0$ must be satisfied in any world equilibrium in which traded goods are produced. Locations will then differ only in scale.

If k_T differs across locations, then locations with higher per capita income of immobile households will have lower relative outputs of traded goods. Relative employment of labor will be higher iff nontraded goods are labor-intensive. If it is assumed that all factor owners have identical tastes, with $\alpha = p_N d_{TN}/(v + r^*k_T) = p_N d_{LN}/(w + r^*k_L)$, the condition for $X_1 \geq 0$ is

$$(1 - a_{LN}d_{LN} - a_{TN}d_{TN}) = 1 - \big[1 - \theta_{KN} + \theta_{LN}(r^* k_L/w) + \theta_{TN}(r^* k_T/v)\big]\alpha \geq 0. \qquad (6)$$

Since $\alpha < 1$, this condition must be satisfied if $k_L = k_T = 0$. The condition is more likely to be satisfied the smaller is the share of nontraded goods in the consumption bundle, the larger is the share of capital costs in unit costs for the nontraded good, and the smaller are the endowments of capital.

In the case where k_T differs across locations, there will be a critical value $\bar{k}_T$ such that (6) will hold for all locations with $k_T \leq \bar{k}_T$. This result can be interpreted in terms of the cones of diversification discussed by McKenzie for the case in which all factors of production are immobile. Since the number of conditions obtained from markets open to trade and factor mobility (capital, labor, and traded goods) is equal to the number of factor prices to be determined in this model (r, v, and w), factor-price equalization will obtain for all locations whose endowments lie within a cone of diversification. The difference is that in this case the cone of diversification refers to the endowment of capital owned by the immobile households, because of the congestion in markets for nontraded goods created by a high level of income in immobile households. A location's endowment of labor does not matter, because the congestion created in markets for nontraded goods by mobile labor can be relieved by exporting the labor. However, even if the capital owned by immobile households is exported, the congestion in markets for nontraded goods remains because consumption is tied to the home location.

The preceding discussion has established that if (6) is satisfied, then there exists a diversified equilibrium for the region in which factor prices are (w^A, p^A). It remains to establish that this is the only equilibrium, so that factor prices will indeed be equalized if (6) is satisfied. It is clear from Figure 1 that there cannot be two diversified equilibria, but it must also be shown that there cannot be both a diversified equilibrium and one in which only nontraded goods are produced. Suppose that the market-clearing conditions (3) and (4) are satisfied for two sets of factor prices (w^0, v^0) and (w^1, v^1). It follows from the conditions for cost minimization in production of the traded good that

$$\big[(v^1 - v^0)a^1_{K1} + (w^1 - w^0)a^1_{L1}\big]X^1_1 = (v^1 - v^0)\big(T - a^1_{TN}X^1_N\big) + (w^1 - w^0)\big(L - Z^1 - a_{LN}X^1_N\big) \leq 0. \qquad (7)$$

The second equality in (7) follows from substitution from the full-employment conditions (4). Using (1b), (7) can be rewritten as

$$(v^1 - v^0)T + (w^1 - w^0)(L - Z^1) - (p_N^1 - p_N^0)X_N^1$$
$$+ \left[v^0(a_{TN}^1 - a_{TN}^0) + w^0(a_{LN}^1 - a_{LN}^0) + r^*(a_{KN}^1 - a_{KN}^0)\right]X_N^1 \le 0. \tag{8}$$

The vector in brackets in (8) must be positive by the conditions for cost minimization, and can be eliminated without affecting the inequality. If (3) is then substituted in (8), we get

$$\left[(v^1 - v^0) - (p_N^1 - p_N^0)d_{TN}^1\right]T$$
$$+ \left[(w^1 - w^0) + d_{LN}^1(p_N^1 - p_N^0)\right](L - Z^1) \le 0. \tag{9}$$

Since (2b) holds with equality and the expenditure function is concave in p_N, we have $(w^1 - w^0) \ge d_{LN}^1(p_N^1 - p_N^0)$. Equation (9) then reduces to

$$\left[(v^1 - v^0) - (p_N^1 - p_N^0)d_{TN}^1\right]T = (d_{T1}^1 - d_{T1}^0) + p_N^0(d_{TN}^1 - d_{TN}^0) \le 0, \tag{10}$$

where the second equality in (10) follows from the budget constraint of immobile households. A similar analysis starting from input usage at (w^0, v^0) yields $[(v^1 - v^0) - (p_N^1 - p_N^0)d_{TN}^0]T = (d_{T1}^1 - d_{T1}^0) + p_N^1(d_{TN}^1 - d_{TN}^0) \ge 0$. However, the weak axiom of revealed preference (which must hold under the assumption of identical and homothetic preferences for immobile factor owners) would be violated if either of these inequalities is strict. Therefore, the only possibility is $(w^0, v^0) = (w^1, v^1)$ and the equilibrium factor prices must be unique. The intuitive explanation of this argument is that an equilibrium with specialization in nontraded goods requires both higher prices for nontraded goods and a greater supply of nontraded goods than that given by the diversified equilibrium A. However, since nontraded goods markets must clear locally, an increase in price and increase in consumption is inconsistent with the weak axiom of revealed preference.

We now examine the effect of relaxing some of the assumptions regarding the endowments of mobile and immobile households.

2.1 Heterogeneous Labor

We first suppose there are two types of mobile households, high (h) income and low (l) income, with income differences due to differences in

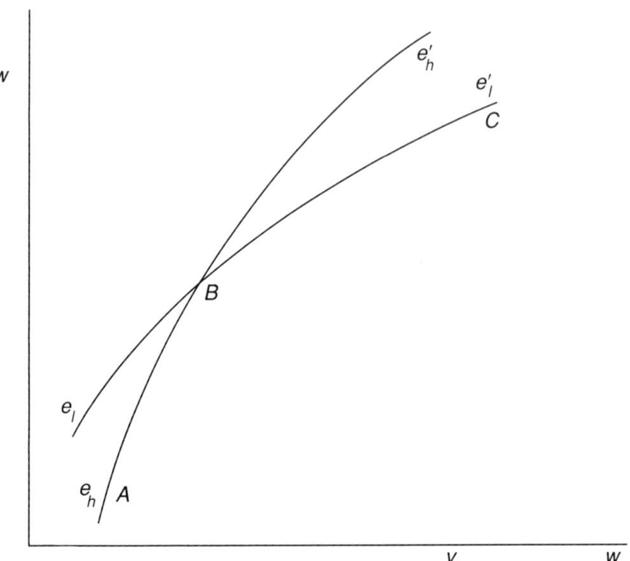

FIGURE 2 Expenditure functions for high- $(e_h e'_h)$ and low- $(e_l e'_l)$ income households.

the endowment of capital income $(k_h > k_l)$. In a free-mobility equilibrium, the utility level of each household type U_i^* will be exogenously given by world market conditions. The free mobility condition becomes

$$w \leq e(p_N, U_i^*) - r^* k_i, \qquad i = h, l. \tag{11}$$

This is illustrated in Figure 2, which shows the equilibrium w–v combinations for each household type. Assuming tastes of each household type are the same, we have $d_{hN} > d_{lN}$ and the expenditure function of high-income households must be steeper than that of low-income households at any intersection. The locus of possible w–v combinations consistent with labor mobility will then be given by the ABC locus in Figure 2. High-income households place a relatively higher value on land rents because a larger share of their income is nonwage income.

As in the case with homogeneous households, diversified production will occur where the $c_1 = 1$ locus cuts the labor mobility schedule. If k_T is the same in all immobile households, this must occur at point B and factor prices will be equalized in all locations and all household types will be indifferent between locations. The $c_1 = 1$ locus can never intersect the labor mobility locus to the right of point B, since there would be no locations in which high-income households would locate. If k_T differs across locations, then it is possible that there are locations where production is specialized to that of nontraded goods and only low income mobile households locate.[4]

2.2 Labor Endowments of Immobile Households

Now suppose that immobile households have an endowment of labor, with l_T indicating the labor endowment per unit land in immobile households. The demand for nontraded goods by immobile households becomes $d_{TN}(p_N, v + r^* k_T + w l_T)$ and the condition for labor market equilibrium is

$$(L - Z) + l_T T = a_{L1} X_1 + a_{LN} X_N. \tag{12}$$

Solving (3), (4b), and (12) yields

$$X_1/T = (1 - a_{LN} d_{LN} + (l_T - 1) a_{TN} d_{TN})/\Delta, \tag{13a}$$

$$(L - Z)/T = ((1 - a_{TN} d_{TN}) a_{L1} - (l_T - a_{LN} d_{TN}) a_{T1})/\Delta, \tag{13b}$$

where Δ as defined in (5). The introduction of labor endowments makes it less likely that the $X_1 \geq 0$ constraint binds, but raises the possibility that the $L \geq Z$ constraint is binding. This means that there may be locations in which there are no mobile households if the endowment of labor per immobile household is high enough. In regions with no mobile households, the relationship between wage rates and land prices is determined by the competitive profit conditions for producing traded goods, as indicated by the region on $c_1 = 1$ for wage rates less than w^A in Figure 1.

2.3 Location-Specific Expenditure Functions

The preceding discussion has assumed that the utility level obtained from a given bundle of goods and services is independent of the location in which it is consumed. We now allow for the possibility that there are location-specific amenities, such as clean air and warm climate, which affect the utility level of households. Letting A denote the level of the amenities (which positively affect household utility), the expenditure function of mobile households can be written as $e(p_N, A, U^*)$, where $\partial e/\partial A < 0$. Since expenditure functions consistent with free mobility will differ across locations in Figure 1, the wage rate in the diversified equilibrium will be lower and the land rents higher in locations where there is a higher

[4]A similar outcome would occur if households were identical in terms of their endowment of capital income, but high-productivity households are endowed with $\gamma > 1$ units of labor. The expenditure function of high-productivity households will be flatter than that of low-income households at any intersection, because high-productivity households place a relatively larger value on wage rates than do low-productivity households.

level of the amenity. The presence of location-specific amenities has an impact on factor-price equalization results similar to that of technological differences, since diversification will no longer be sufficient to ensure factor-price equalization. Note that if the level of amenities across locations is controlled, then the analysis of factor-price equalization will be identical to that discussed above.

In summary, these results show that with one immobile factor, the price of the immobile factor cannot fall below that associated with diversified production. If all labor is owned by mobile households, then there must be a positive relationship between land rents and wage rates for locations that do not have diversified production. If some labor is owned by immobile households, then the possibility exists that there is a negative relationship between wage rates and land rents for locations where all mobile households have gone.

3. TWO IMMOBILE FACTORS

We now examine the conditions under which factor prices will equalize when there are two traded goods and two immobile factors. It will be shown that a cone of diversification exists, such that factor-price equalization will hold for locations whose endowments lie within the cone. This analysis can be extended by introducing more goods and/or factors along the lines pursued in Dixit and Norman (1980, Chapter 4) for the case of trade in goods alone. The supplies of the mobile factors are exogenously given and denoted T_i $(i = 1, 2)$, and the respective factors prices are v_i. The two immobile factors of production could be thought of as two different types of land (varying fertility or resource abundance) or land and a type of labor that has skills that are specific to a particular location.

Factor-price equalization requires that the domestic prices of factors and nontraded goods be determined from given world market conditions for traded goods and mobile factors. Assuming that there are n traded goods, the competitive profit conditions and factor mobility conditions can be expressed as

$$p_i \leq c_i(w, v_1, v_2, r), \qquad i = 1, 2, \tag{14a}$$

$$r^* = r, \tag{14b}$$

$$w = e(c_N(w, v_1, v_2, r), U^*) - rk_L, \tag{14c}$$

where the competitive profit condition for the nontraded good has been substituted into (2b) to obtain (14c).

If the condition for capital mobility is substituted into the remaining equations, (14) can be expressed as a system of three equations in the three unknowns (w, v_1, v_2). This system can be expressed in matrix form as

$$\begin{bmatrix} p_I - r^* A'_{KI} \\ D_{LI} p_I \end{bmatrix} \leq A' \begin{bmatrix} v \\ w \end{bmatrix} \quad \text{where } A' = \begin{bmatrix} A'_{TI} & A'_{LI} \\ -d_{LN} A'_{TN} & (I - d_{LN} a_{LN}) \end{bmatrix}, \tag{15}$$

where p_I is the vector of prices of internationally traded goods, D_{LI} is the z vector of demands for traded goods by mobile households, and $A_{TI}(A_{LI})$ is the 2×2 (1×2) matrix of requirements of immobile factor i (labor) per unit of traded good j. A similar definition holds for A_{TN} and A_{KI}. The matrix A is the 3×3 matrix of requirements of the factors of production in producing the traded goods and exported factor services. Note that exported factor services are considered here as being produced by using a unit of the traded factor, less the services of all other factors required to produce the nontraded goods consumed by the factor if it remains in the home country.

In order for factor-price equalization to occur, the system (15) must yield a solution for factor prices independently of the supplies of factors of production, which requires that the rank of the matrix A be equal to 3.[5] Note that this rank condition does not depend on the endowments of immobile households, since only the demands of mobile households enter A. In addition, it is required that the technologies be identical across countries and that the expenditure functions be identical across countries, so that every country is facing the same set of equations.

3.1 The Cone of Diversification

Given that the matrix A has rank 3, factor-price equalization will hold for all locations with endowments such that there is full employment of immobile factors and labor and markets for nontraded goods clear. As in the previous section it will be assumed that nontraded factors are owned by immobile households. Type i immobile households own one unit of immobile factor i and k_i units of mobile capital, so the demand function for nontraded goods by type i households will be $d_{iN}(p_N, v_i + r^* k_i)$. Letting D_{TN} be the vector of demands for nontraded goods by immobile households and T the vector of supplies of immobile factors, we can express the equilibrium condition in the market for nontraded goods as

$$X_N = D'_{TN} T + d_{LN}(L - Z) \tag{16}$$

[5]The requirement for factor price equalization that the number of traded goods be at least as large as the number of nontraded factors generalizes to greater numbers of factors (both immobile and mobile) and greater numbers of goods. This can be seen by considering the effects of these modifications on the dimension of the A matrix.

If (16) is substituted into the full-employment conditions for factor markets, we obtain the three-equation system

$$B\begin{bmatrix} T \\ L \end{bmatrix} = A\begin{bmatrix} X_I \\ Z \end{bmatrix} \quad \text{where } B = \begin{bmatrix} I - A_{TN}D'_{TN} & -A_{TN}d_{LN} \\ -a_{LN}D'_{TN} & 1 - a_{LN}d_{LN} \end{bmatrix}, \tag{17}$$

where A is defined as in (15). The left-hand side of (17) can be thought of as the net supply of factors to the traded goods sector, which is the endowment of the factor less the usage in production of nontraded goods.

The off-diagonal elements in B are negative, since increases in the endowment of one factor raises the demand for all other factors to produce nontraded goods. The diagonal elements $(1 - a_{iN}d_{iN})$ represent the effect of an increase in the supply of a factor on the net supply of that factor to the traded goods sector. The increase in net supply is smaller than the increase in supply to the extent that some of the factor is used to satisfy the increased demand for nontraded goods. The determinant of B is $|B| = (1 - a_{1N}d_{1N} - a_{2N}d_{2N} - a_{LN}d_{LN})$. If $|B| > 0$, then the diagonal elements must all be positive and $B^{-1} \geq 0$. The latter result follows from the fact that the diagonal element of B^{-1} is of the form $c_{ii} = (|B| + a_{iN}d_{iN})/|B|$ and the off-diagonal elements are $c_{ij} = -b_{ij}/|B|$. As in the discussion of (6) for the one immobile factor case, $|B| > 0$ if households own no capital and tastes are identical and homothetic. However, in the general case with capital income, it is possible that the determinant of B is negative if the capital income of immobile households is sufficiently large.

Factor-price equalization will be possible for all locations whose endowments are consistent with a solution to (17) with $X_I \geq 0$ and $L \leq Z$. If the inverse of the matrix B exists, (17) can be written as

$$\begin{bmatrix} T \\ L \end{bmatrix} = B^{-1}A\begin{bmatrix} X_I \\ Z \end{bmatrix} = \begin{bmatrix} \tilde{A}_{TI} & 0 \\ \tilde{A}_{LI} & 1 \end{bmatrix}\begin{bmatrix} X_I \\ Z \end{bmatrix} \tag{18}$$

The partitioning of $B^{-1}A$ in the second equality in (18) follows from the fact that the last column of the A and B matrices are identical. The matrix $\tilde{A}_{TI}$ is a 2×2 matrix with the entry $\tilde{a}_{ij}$ in the ith row and jth column being interpreted as the direct plus indirect use of factor i in the production of traded good j. The indirect demand for factors results from the demand for nontraded goods generated by employment of productive factors, which leads to demand for additional factors to produce nontraded goods. If $|B| > 0$, then $B^{-1}A \geq 0$ and the full-employment conditions will be satisfied for any country whose endowment of nontraded factors of production lies in the cone spanned by the columns of the $\tilde{A}_{TI}$ matrix. Note in particular that the condition for factor price equalization is independent of the initial endowment of labor. This occurs because the effects of the labor force endowment can be fully offset by importing or exporting the factor, since the mobile labor households consume in the location where they work.

If $|B| < 0$, then there may not exist a diversified equilibrium with $X_I > 0$ for any endowment of the nontraded factors. As noted above, this possibility occurs if the location has an unusually large endowment of mobile capital owned by immobile households. The effect of the large capital endowment on local markets for nontraded goods cannot be eliminated by exporting capital, because immobile households continue to consume in the home location when capital is exported.

The preceding discussion has established the existence of a cone of diversification when there are two traded goods and two non-traded factors as long as the matrix A is nonsingular and $|B| > 0$. Two points should be made regarding the relationship between this cone and that obtained when factors are immobile and all goods are traded. First, the cone depends on the tastes for nontraded goods as in cases where some goods are nontraded and factors are immobile (Woodland, 1982). Second, the matrix B depends on the endowment of capital in a location because this endowment affects the demand for nontraded goods by immobile households in B. Thus, the same cone will apply for all locations only if the k_i $(i = 1, 2)$ are the same in all locations.

In order to complete the proof of factor-price equalization, it must be shown that the solution (w, v_1, v_2) satisfying full-employment conditions is unique. This can be done using the arguments similar to those of (7)–(10) for the one factor case. It should also be noted that in the two-immobile-factor case, the possibility of factor-intensity reversals exists. This means that there may be more than one set of factor prices solving the conditions (15), so that there may be more than one set of factor prices consistent with diversified production. The uniqueness result ensures that if two such sets of factor prices exist, the cones of diversification do not overlap.

3.2 Factor Prices with Specialization

We now turn to the case in which endowments are not consistent with equilibrium in the fully diversified equilibrium. We do this by starting from the factor prices consistent with a diversified equilibrium, and then perturbing the price of nontraded goods by a small amount to determine whether there will be a solution to the competitive profit conditions with specialization in production in the neighborhood of the diversified equilibrium. In particular, it was shown in the one-immobile-factor model that the prices of nontraded goods could never fall below that associated with a diversified equilibrium. With two immobile factors, the price of nontraded goods may fall below that associated with the diversified production in

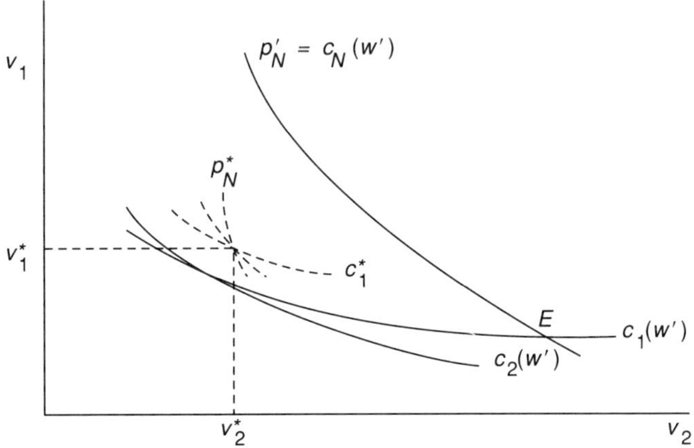

FIGURE 3 Diversified production (v_1^*, v_2^*) and specialization (E) with $p_N^* < p_N$.

some cases, depending on the relative factor intensities of traded and nontraded goods.

Figure 3 illustrates isocost curves in (v_1, v_2) space for the three production activities. The point (v_1^*, v_2^*) is the point at which production is diversified and all three isocost curves (illustrated by dotted lines) must go through this point. Since the slope of the isocost curve is a_{2i}/a_{1i}, Figure 3 is the case in which the nontraded good is most intensive in use of factor 2 (relative to factor 1) with diversified production.

Now consider the effect of an increase in the price of nontraded goods, which from the labor mobility condition requires a compensating wage increase of $dw = a_{LN} dp_N$. This leads to an outward shift in the isocost curve for the nontraded good, since the return to immobile factors must rise $(1 - a_{LN} d_{LN} > 0)$ in the production of nontraded goods. The rise in the cost of labor must reduce returns to immobile factors in the traded goods industry, leading to an inward shift in isocost curves for goods 1 and 2. The magnitude of the inward shift depends on the intensity with which labor is used in each traded good activity. Since the locus of feasible factor prices for immobile factors is given by the upper envelope of the isocost curves, Figure 3 illustrates a case in which good 2 will not be produced at the higher price of nontraded goods (point E). The effect of the increase in nontraded goods price is to drive up the cost of labor and immobile factor 2 sufficiently that production of good 2 (which uses these factors intensively relative to the other traded good) cannot be produced profitably. Note that the determination of which traded good is produced depends on both the labor intensity of the two goods and the relative usage of the immobile factors. For this case, there will be wage rates above (below) the prices associated with factor-price equalization at which the

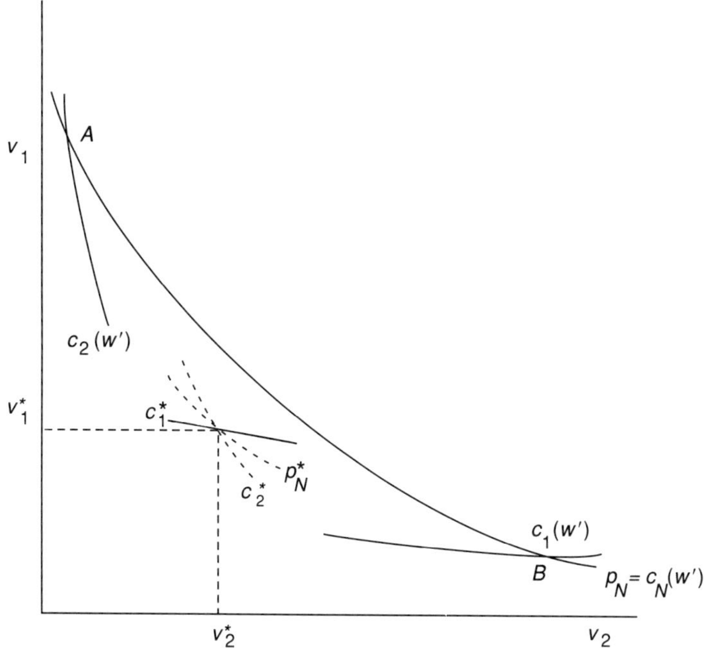

FIGURE 4 Diversified production (D) and two possible specializations with $p_N^* < p_N$.

location produces goods 1 and N (2 and N). The possibility of a low wage rate does not lead to entry of other factors to take advantage of the cheap labor because of the high price of one of the non-traded factors in this equilibrium.

Figure 4 illustrates a case in which the relative intensity a_{2N}/a_{1N} is between that of the other two goods at the diversified production point. An increase in the price of the nontraded goods (and corresponding rise in the wage rate) leads to two possible patterns of specialization in production. Point A is a high v_1/v_2 ratio in which goods 2 and the nontraded are produced, and point B is a low v_1/v_2 ratio at which the nontraded good and good 1 are produced. Which of these specialization points would be an equilibrium will depend on the factor supplies. However, a price of nontraded goods below that associated with diversification cannot be an equilibrium in this case, since both traded goods would earn positive profits. This case yields a result similar to that for the one-immobile-factor model.

In each of these cases, an increase in the price of nontraded goods must reduce the return to one of the nontraded factors and increase the return to the other factor. This follows from the fact that the net return to nontraded factors has increased in the nontraded sector and has decreased in the traded sector (because of the increase in the wage rate), so Stolper–Samuelson logic from the 2×2 case implies that one-factor return must increase and one-factor return must decrease.

The introduction of an additional traded good and nontraded factor has added two elements to the discussion of factor-price equalization of the previous section. In the 2×2 model, factor price equalization will not automatically occur if the restriction on demands for nontraded goods is satisfied ($|B| > 0$), since factor supplies must also be such that an equilibrium with diversified production is possible. Second, a richer pattern of relationships between the price of mobile labor and the price on nontraded goods is possible for the case in which factor prices do not equalize.

4. CONCLUSIONS

This paper has illustrated how the techniques of international trade theory can be applied to the issue of wage rate equalization when some households are mobile between locations. The analysis has emphasized the importance of the endowments of immobile households in determining the conditions for factor price equalization when there are nontraded goods. The presence of nontraded goods which enter the utility function of mobile factors of production thus introduce new elements into the analysis of factor-price equalization.

These results can be applied to the empirical literature that uses wage rate and land rent differences across urban areas to measure differences in the quality of life (Roback, 1982). The theoretical results generating these empirical tests assumes that the levels of location-specific attributes uniquely determine wage rates in equilibrium. Wage rates will then be negatively related to the level of desirable attributes and land rents will be positively related to attribute levels. In terms of the analysis of this paper, this is equivalent to assuming that the conditions for factor-price equalization are met for all locations with the same level of attributes. The results of this paper indicate that the relationship between attribute levels and factor prices may be affected by conditions in the local market for nontraded goods. Differences in local demand conditions (due to differences in purchasing power of immobile households) or differences in supply conditions (nonequalization of other factor prices when production is not fully diversified) may lead to the failure of wage rate equalization.

References

Bond, E. W. (1989). "The theorems of international trade with labor mobility and compensating wage differentials," Penn State Univ. Working Paper.

Bond, E. W. (1993). "Trade, factor mobility, and income distribution in a regional model with compensating wage differentials," *Reg. Sci. Urban Econ.*, **23**, 67–84.

Dixit, A. and V. Norman (1980). *Theory of International Trade* (Cambridge University Press, London).

Ethier, W. J., and L. Svensson (1986). "The theorems of international trade with factor mobility," *J. Int. Econ.* **21** 1–42.

McKenzie, L. (1955). "Equality of factor prices in world trade," *Econometrica* **23**, 239–257.

Roback, J. (1982). "Wages, rents, and quality of life," *J. Political Econ.* **90**, 1257–1278.

Woodland, A. D. (1982). *International Trade and Resource Allocation* (North-Holland, Amsterdam).

BORROWING CONSTRAINTS AND INTERNATIONAL COMOVEMENTS

Antoine Conze
CEREMADE
Université Paris—Dauphine
Paris 75116, France

Jean-Michel Lasry
CEREMADE
Université Paris—Dauphine
Paris 75116, France

José Scheinkman
Department of Economics
University of Chicago
Chicago, Illinois 60637

1. INTRODUCTION

It is now well understood how the presence of borrowing constraints can affect the time series properties of aggregate economic data. In particular, the results in Scheinkman and Weiss [9] show that borrowing constraints may cause the appearance of economic fluctuations in an economy where, if the perfect risk sharing implied by a full set of contingent claims markets was available, no aggregate fluctuations would be observed.

Departures from perfect risk sharing across countries would also have several implications for the behavior of the international comovements of economic time series. Scheinkman [8] suggested that correlation of consumption series across countries could be used to test for the presence of a full set of contingent claims markets. Also, as it is shown formally below, if the output of different countries are Pareto substitutes in consumption, in a complete markets setting, the correlation of output series should be smaller (algebraically) than that of the corresponding productivity series. In this paper we construct a formal model of a two-country economy that allows us to derive implications of the presence of borrowing constraints on the behavior of economic time series. Simulations of the model reveal that it is capable of generating significant positive correlation across output series even in the presence of uncorrelated productivity shocks. This result suggests that borrowing constraints can be used to explain the substantial positive correlation of output growth across countries in the presence of almost no correlation of productivity growth series (cf. Costello [5]). Further, the model can generate a much lower consumption correlation than that implied by a complete set of contingent claims market what again seems to be in accordance with empirical observations.

The model we use is a version of the one developed in Scheinkman and Weiss [9]. Agents in each country are engaged in the production of a single consumption good using labor as its sole input but labor productivity is random. Their utility depends on the consumption of the two goods and on leisure. They can trade their output for the other country's production or for a single durable "asset." This asset is assumed to have a fixed nominal return of zero and is thus held solely to permit higher consumption level in "lean" times. The absence of complete contingent claims markets gives rise to a precautionary demand for wealth and, in particular to a nonzero price for the asset.

The qualitative features of the equilibrium can be described simply, especially in the case where the utility function of each agent is separable and the marginal utility of leisure is constant. Suppose each country has a high and a low level of productivity. Consider an increase in the productivity of labor in country 1. If complete insurance were present, the price of good 1 would drop enough so that the consumption of good 2 would not be altered. In our case the only form of insurance available is the holding of the asset. On the average, when the productivity of country one goes from low to high, country 1 individuals would have a small share of asset holdings and will now try to increase their holding of the asset and this results is an increase in the price of the asset in term of good one. Hence country 2's individuals will have a capital gain if we measure their wealth with good 1 as the numeraire, and thus their holdings of money does serve as partial insurance. However, individuals in country 2 still face the same tradeoff between leisure and consumption of good 2 and hence the shock has no effect on their demand for good 2. Individuals in country 1 on the other hand, will, at fixed prices, consume more of both goods. The net result is an increase in output in country 2 as well as an increase in the relative price of good 2 in terms of good 1, although weaker than the relative price change in a complete market economy. Thus the productivity shock in country 1 causes, through its effect on the equilibrium price of good 2 an increase in the output of good 2 generating a positive correlation of output across countries.

There are, of course, other ways in which one could generate these comovements. If intermediate goods were introduced, then an increase in the productivity in one country could cheapen inputs in the other country sufficiently to generate an increase in output. This would, of course, imply that these intermediate goods would have countercyclical prices what seems to be contrary to the available evidence (cf. Murphy *et al.* [6]).

The model has other implications for economic time series. Since increases in productivity lead to a cheapening of the output in a country net exports are, in the model, procyclical. This seems to be at odds with the data (see, e.g., Bachus *et al.* [1]). Also the model generates a negative correlation between the value of exports and the relative price of exportables in terms of importables. Though the data on aggregate export and import prices is by nature unreliable this doesn't seem to be rejected for the United States.[1] In any case, the mechanism proposed here is, at best, responsible for a fraction of the observed patterns and deviations are to be expected.

The simulations also show that at least for certain parameter values the utility losses incurred are small relative to the changes in output correlation observed. Individuals' optimization seems to lead to large effects on quantities while avoiding big utility losses. Since this model is too unrealistic to be matched quantitatively to actual data, this should not be taken to mean that actual markets display, in fact, allocations that are almost optimal, but rather that relative large changes in some observed statistics relative to what would prevail in complete markets do not necessarily imply that large improvements are feasible.

The proof of existence of an equilibrium is entirely constructive and allows us to simulate paths as well as to compute numerical statistics for sample economies. The particular algorithm we devised satisfy monotonicity properties that are used to compare equilibria when parameter values are changed.

The paper is organized as follows. In Section 2 we present the formal model and discuss the competitive equilibrium with complete markets as well as the equilibrium in the presence of borrowing constraints. As in Scheinkman and Weiss [9] and Conze *et al.* [4] the equilibrium under borrowing constraints is shown to be characterized by a martingale property. In Section 2 we also state the main propositions that are used to show the existence of an equilibrium. Section 3 discusses the stationary distribution of asset holdings, while Section 4 presents simulations of the model. Section 5 discusses some conclusions and the appendix contains the formal proofs.

2. THE MODEL

There are two countries of equal size and one good produced in each country. In each country production displays constant returns and involves

[1] The correlation between quarterly changes in GNP between 1948 and 1987 and changes in the logarithm of the price of exports divided by the price of imports is essentially zero but equals −.24 if we omit the years of 1974 and 1979/80 when the two big "oil shocks" happened.

only the use of labor input. The amount produced in country $a(a = 1, 2)$ by one unit of labor at time t is given by a random variable θ_t^a that may assume any of a finite number of values α_j^a, $j = 1, \ldots, J_a$. More precisely we postulate the existence of a probability space $(\Omega, \mathcal{F}, P)$ and of two stochastic processes $\{\theta_t^1\}, \{\theta_t^2\}$ defined on this space.

To simplify notation, we set $I = J_1 J_2$ and $s_t = (\theta_t^1, \theta_t^2)$. The process $\{s_t\}$ takes values in

$$\{s_i, i = 1, \ldots, I\} \equiv \left\{\left(\alpha_j^1, \alpha_k^2\right), j = 1, \ldots, J_1, k = 1, \ldots, J_2\right\}.$$

We assume that the transition probability of $\{s_t\}$ is given by[2]

$$P\left(s_{t+\tau} = s_j | s_t = s_i\right) = \lambda_{i,j}\tau + o(\tau), j \neq i. \tag{1}$$

The consumer's utility function for stochastic streams of consumption and labor is given by

$$U^a = E\left[\int_0^{+\infty} e^{-rt} u^a(c_{1,t}^a, c_{2,t}^a, l_t^a)\, dt\right] \tag{2}$$

where $c_{1,t}^a$ (resp. $c_{2,t}^a$) is the consumption at time t by the ath agent of the good produced in country 1 (resp. country 2), and l_t^a is the amount of labor at time t of the ath agent. The function u^a, $a = 1, 2$ is assumed to be twice continuously differentiable on $R_{+,*}^3$, strictly increasing in its first two arguments and strictly decreasing in its third argument.

Agents observe the history of the process $\{s_t\} = \{(\theta_t^1, \theta_t^2)\}$ and make their choices conditional on these observations. We write $\mathcal{F}_t$ for the information available at time t.[3]

2.1 The Competitive Equilibrium with Complete Markets

Before proceeding further with the competitive equilibrium under borrowing constraints, we will briefly discuss some properties of the market allocation if there was a complete set of Arrow–Debreu contingent markets. Such markets would allow agents to purchase at time 0 at a price

[2] In all numerical simulations, we will consider the particular case where $J_1 = J_2 = 2$ and $\{\theta_t^1\}$ and $\{\theta_t^2\}$ are independent, with transition probabilities given by

$$P\left(\theta_{t+\tau}^a = \alpha_2^a | \theta_t^a = \alpha_1^a\right) = P\left(\theta_{t+\tau}^a = \alpha_1^a | \theta_t^a = \alpha_2^a\right) = \lambda^a\tau + o(\tau), a = 1, 2.$$

In other words, in this particular case, productivities in the two countries are independent, can take two values, and their switches are governed by independent Poisson counting processes.

[3] In other words, consumer's choices are $\mathcal{F}_t$-measurable where $\mathcal{F} = \{\mathcal{F}_t\}$ is the minimal filtration generated by $\{s_t\}$, $\sigma(s_u, 0 \leq u \leq t)$.

$\pi_{1,t}(\omega)$ [resp. $\pi_{2,t}(\omega)$] the right to delivery of one unit of consumption of the good produced in country 1 (resp. country 2) at time t in state $\omega \in \Omega$.

The problem faced by agents of type a is to maximise (2) subject to the budget constraint

$$E\left[\int_0^{+\infty} (\pi_{1,t} c_{1,t}^a + \pi_{2,t} c_{2,t}^a)\, dt\right] \leq E\left[\int_0^{+\infty} \pi_{a,t} \theta_t^a l_t^a \, dt\right].$$

Since the competitive equilibrium is Pareto-optimal, we know that its allocation solves

$$\max\{E[U^1] + \gamma E[U^2]\}$$

subject to[4]

$$c_{1,t}^1 + c_{1,t}^2 = \theta_t^1 l_t^1,$$

$$c_{2,t}^1 + c_{2,t}^2 = \theta_t^2 l_t^2,$$

with $\gamma > 0$. Since the U^a have not been specified, we can assume without loss of generality that $\gamma = 1$. Notice that in (2) the discount rate r is the same for both types of individuals. Therefore the competitive equilibrium allocation $\{(c_{1,t}^1, c_{2,t}^1, c_{1,t}^2, c_{2,t}^2)\}$ actually solves at each instant t

$$\max_{(c_1^1, c_2^1, c_1^2, c_2^2)} \left\{ u^1\left(c_1^1, c_2^1, \frac{c_1^1 + c_1^2}{\theta_t^1}\right) + u^2\left(c_1^2, c_2^2, \frac{c_2^1 + c_2^2}{\theta_t^2}\right)\right\}.$$

We wish to show that if labor and consumption are separable in the utility functions, and if we assume that an increase in consumption of one good lowers the one-period marginal utility of the other good, an increase in one country's productivity leads to a fall in the other country's output. This in particular shows that, under these assumptions, if complete markets prevails any positive output correlation must be explained by a positive correlation of productivities. We assume that

$$u^a(c_1, c_2, l) = v^a(c_1, c_2) - w^a(l).$$

Let K_1 (resp. K_2) denote output of country 1 (resp. country 2). (K_1, K_2) solves

$$\max_{K_1, K_2} V(\theta^1, \theta^2, K_1, K_2), \tag{3}$$

[4]Here and in what follows equalities and inequalities are assumed to hold with probability 1.

with

$$\begin{aligned} V(\theta^1, \theta^2, K_1, K_2) &= \max_{c_1^1, c_2^1} \left\{ v^1(c_1^1, c_2^1) - w^1\left(\frac{K_1}{\theta^1}\right) \right. \\ &\qquad \left. + v^2(K_1 - c_1^1, K_2 - c_2^1) - w^2\left(\frac{K_2}{\theta^2}\right) \right\} \qquad (4) \\ &= -w^1\left(\frac{K_1}{\theta^1}\right) - w^2\left(\frac{K_2}{\theta^2}\right) \\ &\quad + \max_{c_1^1, c_2^1} \left\{ v^1(c_1^1, c_2^1) + v^2(K_1 - c_1^1, K_2 - c_2^1) \right\} \\ &= -w^1\left(\frac{K_1}{\theta^1}\right) - w^2\left(\frac{K_2}{\theta^2}\right) + U(K_1, K_2). \end{aligned}$$

We also assume that the two goods are substitutable for both types of individuals, that is,

$$v_{12}^1 = \frac{\partial^2 v^1}{\partial c_1 \partial c_2} \leq 0, \qquad v_{12}^2 = \frac{\partial^2 v^2}{\partial c_1 \partial c_2} \leq 0,$$

and that v^1 and v^2 are strongly concave, w^1 and w^2 are convex. Then in (3) and (4) the maximum is strictly interior, so that the optimum (K_1, K_2) satisfies $\partial V / \partial K_1 = 0$ and $\partial V / \partial K_2 = 0$. Differentiating with respect to θ^1, we get

$$\begin{bmatrix} -U_{11} + w^{1''}/(\theta^1)^2 & -U_{12} \\ -U_{12} & -U_{22} + w^{2''}/(\theta^2)^2 \end{bmatrix} \begin{bmatrix} \partial K_1/\partial\theta^1 \\ \partial K_2/\partial\theta^1 \end{bmatrix} = \begin{bmatrix} w^{1'}/(\theta^1)^2 \\ 0 \end{bmatrix}, \qquad (5)$$

where $U_{ij} = \partial^2 U / (\partial K_i \partial K_j)$.

We want to show that $\partial K_1/\partial\theta^1 \geq 0$ and $\partial K_2/\partial\theta^1 \leq 0$. From (5) a sufficient condition is that $U_{11} \leq 0$, $U_{22} \leq 0$ and $U_{12} \leq 0$. It is clear that U is strictly concave, so we have the two first inequalities. Now let $(\bar{c}_1^1, \bar{c}_2^1)$ be the pair such that

$$U(K_1, K_2) = v^1(\bar{c}_1^1, \bar{c}_2^1) + v^2(K_1 - \bar{c}_1^1, K_2 - \bar{c}_2^1).$$

Then

$$\frac{\partial U}{\partial K_1} = \frac{\partial v^1}{\partial c_1}(\bar{c}_1^1, \bar{c}_2^1),$$

$$U_{12} = v_{11}^1 \frac{\partial \bar{c}_1^1}{\partial K_2} + v_{12}^1 \frac{\partial \bar{c}_2^1}{\partial K_2}.$$

Also for $a = 1, 2$,

$$\frac{\partial v^1}{\partial c_a}\left(\bar{c}_1^1, \bar{c}_2^1\right) - \frac{\partial v^2}{\partial c_a}\left(K_1 - \bar{c}_1^1, K_2 - \bar{c}_2^1\right) = 0,$$

which implies

$$\begin{bmatrix} v_{11}^1 + v_{11}^2 & v_{12}^1 + v_{12}^2 \\ v_{12}^1 + v_{12}^2 & v_{22}^1 + v_{22}^2 \end{bmatrix} \begin{bmatrix} \partial\bar{c}_1^1/\partial K_2 \\ \partial\bar{c}_2^1/\partial K_2 \end{bmatrix} = \begin{bmatrix} v_{12}^2 \\ v_{22}^2 \end{bmatrix}.$$

It is then easy to show that

$$U_{12} = \frac{v_{12}^1\left[v_{11}^2 v_{22}^2 - \left(v_{12}^2\right)^2\right] + v_{12}^2\left[v_{11}^1 v_{22}^1 - \left(v_{12}^1\right)^2\right]}{\Delta},$$

where $\Delta = (v_{11}^1 + v_{11}^2)(v_{22}^1 + v_{22}^2) - (v_{12}^1 + v_{12}^2)^2$ is strictly positive from the strong concavity of v^1 and v^2. Therefore $U_{12} \leq 0$.

Notice that when $U_{12} = 0$, $\partial K_2/\partial\theta^1 = 0$ and $\partial K_1/\partial\theta^2 = 0$. In this case the correlation between K_1 and K_2 is zero if the shocks θ^1 and θ^2 are uncorrelated. This limit case corresponds to the case where both v^1 and v^2 are separable in (c_1, c_2).

2.2 The Competitive Equilibrium and Borrowing Constraints

We assume the existence of a fixed stock of "money" whose units are chosen such that the average per capita holdings equals one half. Agents are assumed to know the initial distribution of "money" holdings.

The typical individual in country a takes as given the stochastic processes of prices $\{p_{1,t}\}$ and $\{p_{2,t}\}$ for the good produced in countries 1 and 2 respectively, and solve problem (P^a) [equations (6) to (9) below] in order to choose, among other things, the amount y_t^a of "money" that he will hold:

$$\max E\left[\int_0^{+\infty} e^{-rt} u^a(c_{1,t}^a, c_{2,t}^a, l_t^a)\, dt\right], \tag{6}$$

subject to

$$y_0^a \text{ given}, \tag{7}$$

$$\dot{y}_t^a = \theta_t^a p_{a,t} l_t^a - p_{1,t} c_{1,t}^a - p_{2,t} c_{2,t}^a, \tag{8}$$

$$y_t^a \geq 0,\ l_t^a \geq 0,\ c_{1,t}^a \geq 0,\ c_{2,t}^a \geq 0. \tag{9}$$

Notice that (9) implies that no borrowing is allowed. An equilibrium is a pair of stochastic processes $\{(p_{1,t}, p_{2,t})\}$ such that if $\{(y_t^a, c_{1,t}^a, c_{2,t}^a, l_t^a)\}$ solves (P^a), then for all $t \geq 0$,

$$y_t^1 + y_t^2 = 1, \tag{10}$$

$$c_{1,t}^1 + c_{1,t}^2 = \theta_t^1 l_t^1, \tag{11}$$

$$c_{2,t}^1 + c_{2,t}^2 = \theta_t^2 l_t^2. \tag{12}$$

We will also assume that the marginal utilities of consumption at zero consumption are infinite. This guarantees that $c_{1,t}^a > 0$, $c_{2,t}^a > 0$ and $l_{1,t}^a > 0$ for all t and $a = 1, 2$.

Let $\{z_t\}$ be the stochastic process representing the average amount of "money" held by agents in the first country.

As in Scheinkman and Weiss [9] and Conze *et al.* [4], we will first motivate heuristically a candidate equilibrium. We should then prove that our candidate is in fact an equilibrium. The proof here would be completely similar to the proof of this result for the models in Scheinkman and Weiss [9] and Conze *et al.* [4], to which the reader is referred.

Any competitive equilibrium at each instant t, conditional on the amount of "money" received by the typical individual of country one from the typical individual of country two, is Pareto-optimal. Hence the competitive allocation $\{(c_{1,t}^1, c_{2,t}^1, c_{1,t}^2, c_{2,t}^2)\}$ must solve at each instant t

$$\max_{(c_1^1, c_2^1, c_1^2, c_2^2)} \left\{ u^1\left(c_1^1, c_2^1, \frac{c_1^1 + c_1^2}{\theta_t^1}\right) + \gamma_t u^2\left(c_1^2, c_2^2, \frac{c_2^1 + c_2^2}{\theta_t^2}\right)\right\}.$$

Further, if

$$q_t^1 = \frac{1}{p_{1,t}} \frac{\partial u^1}{\partial c_1}\left(c_{1,t}^1, c_{2,t}^1, \frac{c_{1,t}^1 + c_{1,t}^2}{\theta_t^1}\right), \tag{13}$$

$$q_t^2 = \frac{1}{p_{2,t}} \frac{\partial u^2}{\partial c_2}\left(c_{1,t}^2, c_{2,t}^2, \frac{c_{2,t}^1 + c_{2,t}^2}{\theta_t^2}\right), \tag{14}$$

that is, $\{q_t^a\}$ is the stochastic process describing the marginal utilities of money of individual a, then

$$\gamma_t = \frac{q_t^1}{q_t^2}. \tag{15}$$

We will assume that u^1 and u^2 are such that the function

$$V(c_1^1, c_2^1, c_1^2, c_2^2) = u^1\left(c_1^1, c_2^1, \frac{c_1^1 + c_1^2}{\theta_t^1}\right) + \gamma_t u^2\left(c_1^2, c_2^2, \frac{c_2^1 + c_2^2}{\theta_t^2}\right)$$

is strongly concave, i.e., D^2V is negative definite. Since by assumption its maximum is interior, it follows from the implicit functions theorem that

$$c^1_{1,t} = c^1_1(\theta^1_t, \theta^2_t, \gamma_t), \tag{16}$$

$$c^1_{2,t} = c^1_2(\theta^1_t, \theta^2_t, \gamma_t), \tag{17}$$

$$c^2_{1,t} = c^2_1(\theta^1_t, \theta^2_t, \gamma_t), \tag{18}$$

$$c^2_{2,t} = c^2_2(\theta^1_t, \theta^2_t, \gamma_t), \tag{19}$$

and that all these functions are, at least, continuously differentiable.

We will look for an equilibrium in which (almost all) sample paths of $\{z_t\}$ are absolutely continuous functions of t, that is, $z_t = \int_0^t \dot{z}_u \, du$ for some process $\{\dot{z}_t\}$. Further, we only consider equilibria in which each individual of a given type starts with the same amount of "money." With strict concavity, this implies that y^1_t equals z_t and y^2_t equals $1 - z_t$. Since

$$\dot{z}_t = p_{1,t}c^2_{1,t} - p_{2,t}c^1_{2,t},$$

we may write, using equations (13)–(15) as well as equations (16)–(19),

$$\begin{aligned} \dot{z}_t &= f(s_t, q^1_t, q^2_t), \\ &= \frac{1}{q^1_t\theta^1_t} g^1\left(\theta^1_t, \theta^2_t, \frac{\theta^2_t}{\theta^1_t}\right) - \frac{1}{q^2_t\theta^2_t} g^2\left(\theta^1_t, \theta^2_t, \frac{q^1_t}{q^2_t}\right), \end{aligned} \tag{20}$$

where

$$\begin{aligned} g^1(\theta^1, \theta^2, x) = \theta^1 \frac{\partial u^1}{\partial c_1} &\left(c^1_1\left(\theta^1, \theta^2, \frac{1}{x}\right), c^1_2\left(\theta^1, \theta^2, \frac{1}{x}\right), \right. \\ &\left. \qquad \frac{c^1_1(\theta^1, \theta^2, 1/x) + c^2_1(\theta^1, \theta^2, 1/x)}{\theta^1} \right), \\ &\times c^2_1\left(\theta^1, \theta^2, \frac{1}{x}\right), \\ g^2(\theta^1, \theta^2, x) = \theta^2 \frac{\partial u^2}{\partial c_2} &\left(c^2_1(\theta^1, \theta^2, x), c^2_2(\theta^1, \theta^2, x), \right. \\ &\left. \qquad \frac{c^1_2(\theta^1, \theta^2, x) + c^2_2(\theta^1, \theta^2, x)}{\theta^2} \right) \\ &\times c^1_2(\theta^1, \theta^2, x). \end{aligned}$$

Notice that from (20), f is homogeneous of degree -1 in (q^1, q^2).

We will look for an equilibrium in which $q_t^1 = q^1(s_t, z_t)$ and $q_t^2 = q^2(s_t, z_t)$. In this case, from (20) we can infer that the process $\{(s_t, z_t)\}$ is Markovian. We will now proceed to further characterize this equilibrium.

As money yields no direct utility it is natural to guess that, in equilibrium, the expected discounted marginal utility of money at $t + dt$, conditional on the information available at time t, equals the marginal utility of money at time t, i.e., the processes $\{e^{-rt}q_t^a\}$, $a = 1, 2$ are $\mathcal{F}$-martingales. From the Markov property of $\{(s_t, z_t)\}$ and (1) we get

$$\begin{aligned}
&E\left[e^{-r(t+\tau)}q_{t+\tau}^a | \mathcal{F}_t\right] \\
&\quad = E\left[e^{-r(t+\tau)}q_{t+\tau}^a | s_t, z_t\right] \\
&\quad = e^{-rt}q^a(s_i, z_t) + e^{-rt}\left\{\frac{dq^a}{dz}(s_i, z_t)f\left(s_i, q^1(s_i, z_t), q^2(s_i, z_t)\right)\right\}\tau \\
&\qquad + e^{-rt}\left\{\sum_{j\neq i}\lambda_{i,j}\left[q^a(s_j, z_t) - q^a(s_i, z_t)\right] - rq^a(s_i, z_t)\right\}\tau + o(\tau),
\end{aligned}$$

with $s_i = s_t$. When $\tau \to 0$, the martingale condition implies that

$$\begin{aligned}
&\frac{dq^a}{dz}(s_i, z_t)f\left(s_t, q^1(s_i, z_t), q^2(s_i, z_t)\right) \\
&\qquad + \sum_{j\neq i}\lambda_{i,j}\left[q^a(s_j, z_t) - q^a(s_i, z_t)\right] - rq^a(s_i, z_t) = 0.
\end{aligned}$$

Also the no-borrowing condition implies that $\dot{z}_t|_{z_t=0} \geq 0$ and $\dot{z}_t|_{z_t=1} \leq 0$, that is, for all $i \in \{1, \ldots, I\}$,

$$\begin{aligned}
f\left(s_i, q^1(s_i, 0), q^2(s_i, 0)\right) &\geq 0, \\
f\left(s_i, q^1(s_i, 1), q^2(s_i, 1)\right) &\leq 0.
\end{aligned}$$

For simplicity of notations, we set $\nu_i = r + \Sigma_{j\neq i}\lambda_{i,j}$, $q_i^1(z) = q^1(s_i, z)$ and $q_i^2(z) = q^2(s_i, z)$. Writing the previous results together, we obtain system (S) [equations (21)–(24)] on [0, 1]: for all $i \in \{1, \ldots, I\}$,

$$\frac{dq_i^1}{dz}(z)f\left(s_i, q_i^1(z), q_i^2(z)\right) + \sum_{j\neq i}\lambda_{i,j}q_j^1(z) - \nu_i q_i^1(z) = 0, \tag{21}$$

$$\frac{dq_i^2}{dz}(z)f\left(s_i, q_i^1(z), q_i^2(z)\right) + \sum_{j\neq i}\lambda_{i,j}q_j^2(z) - \nu_i q_i^2(z) = 0, \tag{22}$$

$$f\left(s_i, q_i^1(0), q_i^2(0)\right) \geq 0, \tag{23}$$

$$f\left(s_i, q_i^1(1), q_i^2(1)\right) \leq 0, \tag{24}$$

where $f(s, q^1, q^2)$ is C^1 and homogeneous of degree -1 in $(q^1, q^2) \in \mathbf{R}^2_{+,*}$. For simplicity of notation, we denote by q the vector of the $2I$ functions $(q_i^1, q_i^2)_{i \in \{1, \ldots, I\}}$.

Notice first that system (S) always has the trivial solution $q_i^a = 0$, $i = 1, \ldots, I$, $a = 1, 2$. This corresponds to the case where money has no value. In order to guarantee the existence of a nontrivial solution, we need Assumptions 1–3 (below). As we explain below Assumptions 1 and 2 are satisfied in the separable case with constant marginal utility of leisure whenever relative risk aversion is not too big.

Theorem 1 that follows states the existence of at least one nontrivial solution to system (S) under certain conditions. Before going further, we make the following assumptions.

Assumption 1

- $\forall s \in \{s_i,\ i = 1, \ldots, I\}$, $\forall q^2 \in \mathbf{R}_{+,*}$, the function $q^1 \in \mathbf{R}_{+,*} \mapsto f(s, q^1, q^2)$ is strictly increasing.
- $\forall s \in \{s_i,\ i = 1, \ldots, I\}$, $\forall q^1 \in \mathbf{R}_{+,*}$, the function $q^2 \in \mathbf{R}_{+,*} \mapsto f(s, q^1, q^2)$ is strictly decreasing.

Since we will look to solutions q such that q_i^1 is decreasing and q_i^2 is increasing, Assumption 1 implies that $\dot{z}$ will be decreasing as a function of z.

Assumption 2

- $\forall i \in \{1, \ldots, I\}$, $f(s_i, x, 1) > 0$ for $x \in \mathbf{R}_{+,*}$ big enough.
- $\forall i \in \{1, \ldots, I\}$, $f(s_i, x, 1) < 0$ for $x \in \mathbf{R}_{+,*}$ small enough.

Assumption 2 is necessary in order for equations (23) and (24) to be satisfied.

We can get an idea of the restrictions imposed by Assumptions 1 and 2 by examining the separable case, with constant marginal utility of leisure and same utility function for both groups. Without loss of generality, we can take the marginal utility of leisure equal to 1, and the utility functions is

$$u(c_1, c_2, l) = v(c_1) + w(c_2) - l.$$

In this case, we get

$$f(\theta^1, \theta^2, q^1, q^2) = \frac{1}{q^1\theta^1} g^1\left(\frac{q^2}{q^1\theta^1}\right) - \frac{1}{q^2\theta^2} g^2\left(\frac{q^1}{q^2\theta^2}\right),$$

with $g^1 = (v')^{-1}$ and $g^2 = (w')^{-1}$. Since marginal utilities of consumption at zero consumption are infinite, it is clear that Assumption 2 is satisfied. Now since g^1 and g^2 are strictly decreasing, Assumption 1 is satisfied if and only if $x \mapsto xg^1(x)$ and $x \mapsto xg^2(x)$ are strictly decreasing functions, that is if and only if

$$\forall c > 0, c\frac{v''(c)}{v'(c)} > -1 \quad \text{and} \quad c\frac{w''(c)}{w'(c)} > -1. \tag{25}$$

Equation (25) says that the relative risk aversion is less than one.

From Assumptions 1 and 2 and the fact that $f(s, q^1, q^2)$ is homogeneous in (q^1, q^2), there exist for every $s \in \{s_i,\ i = 1, \dots, I\}$ a unique $h(s) > 0$ such that $f(s, q^1, q^2) = 0$ is equivalent to $q^2 = q^1 h(s)$. Moreover, $f(s, q^1, q^2) > 0$ if and only if $q^2 < q^1 h(s)$ and $f(s, q^1, q^2) < 0$ if and only if $q^2 > q^1 h(s)$.

To every application K: $\{1, \dots, I\} \to \{1, 2\}$ we associate the real matrix $I \times I$ defined by $M(K) = (m_{i,j})$ where $m_{i,i} = 0$, and if $j \neq i$,

$$m_{i,j} = \frac{\lambda_{i,j}}{\nu_i}\mathbf{1}_{K(i)=K(j)} + \frac{\lambda_{i,j}}{\nu_i}\frac{1}{h(s_j)}\mathbf{1}_{K(i)=1,\,K(j)=2} + \frac{\lambda_{i,j}}{\nu_i}h(s_j)\mathbf{1}_{K(i)=2,\,K(j)=1}.$$

For every K, we denote by $\rho(K)$ the greatest positive eigenvalue of $M(K)$, which is well defined by the Perron–Frobenius theorem (see, e.g., Nikaido [7]). Also, we set $\rho = \sup_K \rho(K)$.

THEOREM 1. *System* (S) *has at least one solution* q *satisfying*

$$\forall i \in \{1, \dots, I\},\ q_i^1 \in C^0([0,1]) \cap C^1([0,1] \setminus \{z_i^*\}), \tag{26}$$

$$\forall i \in \{1, \dots, I\},\ q_i^2 \in C^0([0,1]) \cap C^1([0,1] \setminus \{z_i^*\}), \tag{27}$$

$$\forall i \in \{1, \dots, I\},\ q_i^1 \text{ is strictly positive and strictly decreasing}, \tag{28}$$

$$\forall i \in \{1, \dots, I\},\ q_i^2 \text{ is strictly positive and strictly increasing}, \tag{29}$$

if and only if $\rho > 1$, *where* z_i^* *is the only point in* $[0,1]$ *such that*

$$z_i^* = 0 \quad \text{if } f\big(s_i, q_i^1(0), q_i^2(0)\big) < 0,$$

$$z_i^* = 1 \quad \text{if } f\big(s_i, q_i^1(1), q_i^2(1)\big) > 0,$$

$$f\big(s_i, q_i^1(z_i^*), q_i^2(z_i^*)\big) = 0 \quad \text{otherwise}.$$

Notice that in Theorem 1, uniqueness of z_i^* follows from the fact that $z \mapsto f(s_i, q_i^1(z), q_i^2(z))$ is strictly decreasing. The proof of the theorem is in the Appendix. It is very similar to the proof of the main result in Conze *et al.* [4]. We will refer to this paper as much as possible.

In Section 2.3 we state the main propositions needed to establish Theorem 1. The proofs are in the Appendix.

The condition $\rho > 1$ does not hold in all cases even under Assumptions 1 and 2. Intuitively if agents discount the future heavily or if their productivities does not vary enough across states then money commands a zero price. The fact that productivities vary enough can be stated as follows.

Assumption 3. There exist i and j in $\{1, \dots, I\}$ such that $h(s_i) > 1$ and $h(s_j) < 1$.

In the separable case mentioned above, when $w = v$, it is easy to check that $h(\theta, \theta) = 1$ and that $\partial h / \partial \theta^1 > 0$. Hence Assumption 3 is verified provided there are two states with relative productivities respectively greater and less than 1.

THEOREM 2. *Assume* 1–3. *Then there exist* $\bar{r} > 0$ *such that* $\rho > 1$ *if and only if* $r < \bar{r}$.

The proof of Theorem 2 is given in the Appendix.

2.3 Existence of an Equilibrium

The proof of existence of a solution to system (S) when $\rho > 1$ is entirely constructive. This allows us to establish results concerning the comparison of solutions as parameters change as well as to obtain numerical simulations of the model that can be used to compute the correlations among the different equilibrium prices and quantities.

The argument consists in transforming the problem of solving system (S) into a fixed point problem. In order to do this let E (resp. F) be the space of strictly positive and strictly decreasing (resp. increasing) functions that are defined in $[0, 1]$ and continuous. Let $s \in]0, 1[\times]0, 1[$ and $\nu > 0$ be constants. Let $(\tilde{u}, \tilde{v}) \in E \times F$. We define the switch point associated to $(s, \tilde{u}, \tilde{v})$ by

$$z^* = 0 \quad \text{if } f(s, \tilde{u}(0), \tilde{v}(0)) \leq 0,$$

$$z^* = 1 \quad \text{if } f(s, \tilde{u}(1), \tilde{v}(1)) \geq 0,$$

$$f(s, \tilde{u}(z^*), \tilde{v}(z^*)) = 0 \text{ otherwise}.$$

We introduce the following system, which we call reduced system [equations (30)–(34)]:

$$\frac{du}{dz}(z)f(s,u(z),v(z)) - \nu u(z) + \tilde{u}(z) = 0, \tag{30}$$

$$\frac{dv}{dz}(z)f(s,u(z),v(z)) - \nu v(z) + \tilde{v}(z) = 0, \tag{31}$$

$$u(z^*) = \frac{\tilde{u}(z^*)}{\nu} \quad \text{if } z^* > 0, \tag{32}$$

$$v(z^*) = \frac{\tilde{v}(z^*)}{\nu} \quad \text{if } z^* < 1, \tag{33}$$

$$f(s,u(z^*),v(z^*)) = 0. \tag{34}$$

Notice that if $0 < z^* < 1$, then $v(z^*)/u(z^*) = \tilde{v}(z^*)/\tilde{u}(z^*) = h(s)$ and (34) actually follows from (32) and (33).

Given functions $(q_i^1, q_i^2) \in E \times F$ for each $i = 1, \dots, I$, Proposition 1 (below) shows existence and unicity of $(q_i^1, q_i^2) \in E \times F$ the solution to system (30)–(34) with $s = s_i$, $\nu = \nu_i$ and

$$\tilde{u}(z) = \sum_{j \neq i} \lambda_{i,j} \tilde{q}_j^1(z),$$

$$\tilde{v}(z) = \sum_{j \neq i} \lambda_{i,j} \tilde{q}_j^2(z).$$

We may think of this as defining a map Φ on $(E \times F)^I$. Obviously a fixed point of Φ is a solution to (S).

The next four propositions establish the existence of at least one fixed point for Φ and a constructive method to compute the fixed point. Proposition 1 shows that in fact Φ maps $(E \times F)^I$ into $(E \times F)^I$ and further that Φ is increasing; i.e., if $\tilde{q} \geq \tilde{p}$, then $\Phi(\tilde{q}) \geq \Phi(\tilde{p})$.[5] Proposition 2 shows that there exists a $\bar{q}$ such that $\Phi(\bar{q}) \leq \bar{q}$, i.e., $\bar{q}$ is a supersolution. Proposition 3 establishes the existence of a subsolution, i.e. of $\underline{q}$ such that $\Phi(\underline{q}) \geq \underline{q}$. Finally, Proposition 4 shows that if we let $\bar{q}_n = \Phi(\bar{q}_{n-1})$ and $\bar{q}_0 = \bar{q}$ then $\bar{q}_n$ is a decreasing sequence that converges to a $\bar{q}_*$ that satisfies $\Phi(\bar{q}_*) = \bar{q}_*$. Also, if we let $\underline{q}_n = \Phi(\underline{q}_{n-1})$ and $\underline{q}_0 = \underline{q}$ then $\underline{q}_n$ is an increasing sequence that converges to a $\underline{q}_*$ that is also a fixed point of Φ. Further $\bar{q}_*$ and $\underline{q}_*$ are solutions of (S) satisfying conditions (26) to (29).

[5]Here, $q \geq p$ means that for each $a \in \{1, 2\}$, for each $i \in \{1, \dots, I\}$, for each $z \in [0, 1]$, $q_i^a(z) \geq p_i^a(z)$.

Notice that we have thus obtained two solutions to (S). In all simulations we found that $\bar{q}_* = \underline{q}_*$ but we have no proof that this equality always holds.

The precise results are as follows.

Proposition 1. *System (30)–(34) has a unique solution $(u, v) \in E \times F$ with u and v in $C^1([0,1] \setminus \{z^*\})$. Moreover, let $(\tilde{u}_1, \tilde{v}_1) \in E \times F$ and $(\tilde{u}_2, \tilde{v}_2) \in E \times F$ with $\tilde{u}_1 \geq \tilde{u}_2$ and $\tilde{v}_1 \geq \tilde{v}_2$. Let (u_1, v_1) and (u_2, v_2) be the corresponding solutions of system (30)–(34). Then $u_1 \geq u_2$ and $v_1 \geq v_2$.*

Proposition 2. *For all $(q^1, q^2) \in \mathbf{R}^2_{+,*}$, let*

$$\tilde{f}(q^1, q^2) = \min\left\{ \min_i f(s_i, q^1, q^2), -\frac{2}{q^1} + \frac{1}{q^2} \right\}.$$

There exist a function $y \in E \cap C^1([0,1])$ such that

$$\frac{dy}{dz}(z)\tilde{f}(y(z), y(0)) - ry(z) = 0,$$

$$\frac{y(1)}{y(0)} < \min_{i \in \{1,\ldots,I\}} \left\{ h(s_i), \frac{1}{h(s_i)} \right\}.$$

Define $\bar{q} = (\bar{q}_i^1, \bar{q}_i^2)_{i \in \{1,\ldots,I\}}$ by $\bar{q}_i^1(z) = y(z)$ and $\bar{q}_i^2 = y(1-z)$ for all $i = 1, \ldots, I$. Then $\bar{q}$ is a supersolution, that is with $q = \Phi(\bar{q})$, $q_i^1(z) \leq \bar{q}_i^1(z)$ and $q_i^2(z) \leq \bar{q}_i^2(z)$ for all $z \in [0,1]$ and $i \in \{1, \ldots, I\}$.

Proposition 3. *Assume $\rho > 1$. Let $K: \{1, \ldots, I\} \to \{1, 2\}$ such that $\rho(K) = \rho$. There exist a strictly positive eigenvector $[a_i] \in \mathbf{R}^I$ (i.e. $a_i > 0$ $\forall i$) associated to $(M(K), \rho)$. Define $(a_i^1, a_i^2)_{i \in \{1,\ldots,I\}} \in \mathbf{R}^{2I}_{+,*}$ by $a_i^1 = a_i$ if $K(i) = 1$, $a_i^2 = a_i$ if $K(i) = 2$ and $a_i^2 = a_i^1 h(s_i)$. Then for ε and η small enough, $\underline{q} = (\underline{q}_i^1, \underline{q}_i^2)_{i \in \{1,\ldots,I\}}$ defined by $\underline{q}_i^1(z) = \varepsilon(a_i^1 - \eta z)$ and $\underline{q}_i^2(z) = \varepsilon(a_i^1 - \eta(1-z))$ is a subsolution, that is with $q = \Phi(\underline{q})$, $q_i^1(z) \geq \underline{q}_i^1(z)$ and $q_i^2(z) \geq \underline{q}_i^2(z)$ for all $z \in [0,1]$ and $i \in \{1, \ldots, I\}$.*

Proposition 4. *Let the sequence $\bar{q}_n = (\bar{q}_{i,n}^1, \bar{q}_{i,n}^2)_{i \in \{1,\ldots,I\}} \in (E \times F)^I$ be defined by $\bar{q}_0 = \bar{q}$ and $\bar{q}_n = \Phi(\bar{q}_{n-1})$. Let the sequence $\underline{q}_n = (\underline{q}_{i,n}^1, \underline{q}_{i,n}^2)_{i \in \{1,\ldots,I\}} \in (E \times F)^I$ be defined by $\underline{q}_0 = \underline{q}$ and $\underline{q}_n = \Phi(\underline{q}_{n-1})$. Then the first sequence is decreasing and converges to $\bar{q}_* = (\bar{q}_{i,*}^1, \bar{q}_{i,*}^2)_{i \in \{1,\ldots,I\}} \in (E \times F)^I$, the second sequence is increasing and converges to $\underline{q}_* = (\underline{q}_{i,*}^1, \underline{q}_{i,*}^2)_{i \in \{1,\ldots,I\}} \in (E \times F)^I$. Moreover the convergence of $(\bar{q}_{i,n}^1, \bar{q}_{i,n}^2)$ [resp. $(\underline{q}_{i,n}^1, \underline{q}_{i,n}^2)$] to $(\bar{q}_{i,*}^1, \bar{q}_{i,*}^2)$ [resp. $(\underline{q}_{i,*}^1, \underline{q}_{i,*}^2)$] is uniform* *on* $[0,1]\setminus\{\bar{z}_i^*\}$ [*resp.* $[0,1]\setminus\{\underline{z}_i^*\}$] *where* $\bar{z}_i^*$ [*resp.* $\underline{z}_i^*$] *is the switch point associated to* $(s_i, \bar{q}^1_{i,*}, \bar{q}^2_{i,*})$ [*resp.* $(s_i, \underline{q}^1_{i,*}, \underline{q}^2_{i,*})$], *and* $(\bar{q}^1_{i,*}, \bar{q}^2_{i,*})$ [*resp.* $(\underline{q}^1_{i,*}, \underline{q}^2_{i,*})$] *is* C^1 *on* $[0,1]\setminus\{\bar{z}_i^*\}$ [*resp.* $[0,1]\setminus\{\underline{z}_i^*\}$]. $\bar{q}$ *and* $\underline{q}$ *are solutions to system* (S) *satisfying conditions* (26)–(29).

The method used to obtain the existence of a solution to system (S) yields several results concerning comparison of solutions. These are illustrated by the following result:

PROPOSITION 5. *If* $\bar{r} > \hat{r} \geq r$ *and if* q *is a solution to* (S) *satisfying* (26)–(29) *when the discount rate is* r, *then there exists a solution* $\hat{q}$ *to* (S) *satisfying* (26)–(29) *when the discount rate is* $\hat{r}$ *such that* $\hat{q}_i^a(z) \leq q_i^a(z)$, $a \in \{1,2\}$, $i \in \{1,\dots,I\}$, $z \in [0,1]$.

Proof. Let Φ_r denote the application Φ defined above when the dependence to r is made explicit. Since q solves system (S), it is straightforward to check that (q_i^1, q_i^2) solves the reduced system (30)–(34) with $\nu = \hat{q} + \sum_j \lambda_{i,j}$, and

$$\tilde{u}(z) = (\hat{r} - r)q_i^1(z) + \sum_j \lambda_{i,j} q_j^1(z),$$

$$\tilde{v}(z) = (\hat{r} - r)q_i^2(z) + \sum_j \lambda_{i,j} q_j^2(z)$$

Furthermore, $\tilde{u} \geq \sum_j \lambda_{i,j} q_j^1$ and $\tilde{v} \geq \sum_j \lambda_{i,j} q_j^2$, so that by Proposition 1 $\Phi_{\hat{q}}(q) \leq q$, i.e., q is a supersolution to the fixed-point problem associate with $\Phi_{\hat{q}}$. Since $\bar{r} > \hat{r}$, Theorem 2, Proposition 3, and Proposition 4 imply the existence of a solution to (S) when the discount rate is $\hat{r}$. From Proposition 4 this solution $\hat{q}$ satisfies $\hat{q} \leq q$. Hence the result. ■

3. THE STATIONARY DISTRIBUTION OF ASSET HOLDING

Starting from an initial distribution of asset holdings and state of labor productivity at time t_0, the distribution of asset holdings and labor productivity at time t_1 is random, as it depends on the realization of the random path of labor productivity.

A characteristic of the model is that the process $\{(z_t, s_t)\}$ has a strong ergodic property, that is there exist a unique probability measure π on $[0,1] \times \{s_1, \dots, s_I\}$ (together with the Borel σ-algebra) such that for all bounded function f on $[0,1] \times \{s_1, \dots, s_I\}$,

$$\lim_{t \to +\infty} E[f(z_t, s_t) | z_0, s_0] = \int f(z,s)\, d\pi(z,s) \tag{35}$$

independently of the initial distribution of (z_0, s_0). This property is proved in Conze [3], Theorem 1. In particular, (35) implies the mean-ergodic property

$$\lim_{T \to +\infty} E\left[\frac{1}{T}\int_0^T f(z_t, s_t)\, dt | z_0, s_0\right] = \int f(z, s)\, d\pi(z, s),$$

which enables us to use space averages to compute time averages. The ergodic distribution π is, of course, also invariant for the process $\{(z_t, s_t)\}$, that is for all $t \geq 0$,

$$\int E[f(z_t, s_t) | z_0 = z, s_0 = s]\, d\pi(z, s) = \int f(z, s)\, d\pi(z, s).$$

Further, π can be characterized by a set of equations. Let $p_i = \pi([0, 1] \times \{s_i\})$ and $F_i(z) = \pi([0, z] \times \{s_i\})$. Conditional on $s_{t+dt} = s_i$, the state s_t takes value s_i with probability $1 - \lambda_i\, dt$ and value s_j, $j \neq i$, with probability $\lambda_{j,i}\, dt$. Hence,

$$p_i = p_i(1 - \lambda_i\, dt) + \sum_{j \neq i} p_j \lambda_{j,i}\, dt,$$

that is

$$\lambda_i p_i - \sum_{j \neq i} \lambda_{j,i} p_j = 0. \tag{36}$$

Now if $s_t = j$, then $z_t = z_{t+dt} - f(s_j, q_j^1(z_t), q_j^2(z_t))$, and a first-order expansion leads to

$$F_i(z) = \left[F_i(z) - \frac{dF_i}{dz}(z) f\big(s_i, q_j^1(z), q_i^2(z)\big)\, dt\right](1 - \lambda_i\, dt) + \sum_{j \neq i} F_j(z) \lambda_{j,i}\, dt.$$

Hence

$$\frac{dF_i}{dz}(z) f\big(s_i, q_j^1(z), q_i^2(z)\big) + \lambda_i F_i(z) - \sum_{j \neq i} \lambda_{j,i} F_j(z) = 0. \tag{37}$$

Moreover

$$F_i(0) = 0 \quad \text{if } z_i^* > 0, \tag{38}$$

$$F_i(1) = p_i. \tag{39}$$

Here the derivation of system (36)–(39) was heuristic. Nevertheless, it is shown in Conze [3], Theorem 2 that there is a unique solution to this system satisfying $p_i > 0$ for all $i \in \{1, \ldots, I\}$, $\Sigma_i p_i = 1$, F_i positive, increasing and continuous on $[0, 1] \setminus \{z_i^*\}$, and that $(p_i, F_i)_{i \in \{1, \ldots, I\}}$ corresponds to the invariant probability measure π. The discontinuity of F_i at z_i^* means that the invariant distribution associates a strictly positive mass with the event $s_t = s_i$ and $z_t = z_i^*$. The explanation is that conditional on the productivity state being s_i, the point z_i^* plays the role of an attractor for the dynamics of $\{z_t\}$.

4. SIMULATIONS OF THE MODEL

In this section we present the results of the numerical simulations of the model that are used to compute the correlation among the different equilibrium prices and quantities.

All the results exhibited here were computed in the following manner. First we apply the fixed-point algorithm that is used to prove the existence of a solution to system (S) to calculate numerically the equilibrium marginal utility functions of the asset $q_i^a(z)$. Once we have obtained the functions $q_i^a(z)$, we are able to compute all the relevant equilibrium quantities or prices as a function of the productivity vector s and the average amount of the asset held by agents in the first country z. In order to compute the relevant correlations, it now suffices to compute the ergodic distribution of the pair (s_t, z_t). This is accomplished by using a fixed-point algorithm, as described in the proof of Theorem 2 in Conze [3].

The simulations are for the utility function $u(c_1, c_2, l) = (c_1^\delta + c_2^\delta)/2 + l$, two states of productivity for each "country" and independence of productivity changes across countries.

In the complete markets case, the output correlation is, as we proved above, zero. At zero discount rates we have essentially complete markets (cf. Bewley [2]), and hence output correlation is also zero. As the discount rate increases, output correlation also increases but is a concave function of the discount rate (see Figure 1). Although we do not have a way of changing the stringency of the borrowing constraint, it seems intuitive that the effect of increasing the severity of the borrowing constraint should be similar to that of increasing the discount rate. Hence it is reasonable to conjecture that a relatively mild borrowing constraint would lead to a large level of output correlation. In Figure 1 we also plot the effect of a change in the discount rate on average utility. A higher discount rate leads individuals to be less willing to work today in exchange for money to be spent in lean times and this leads to a fall in the average utility.

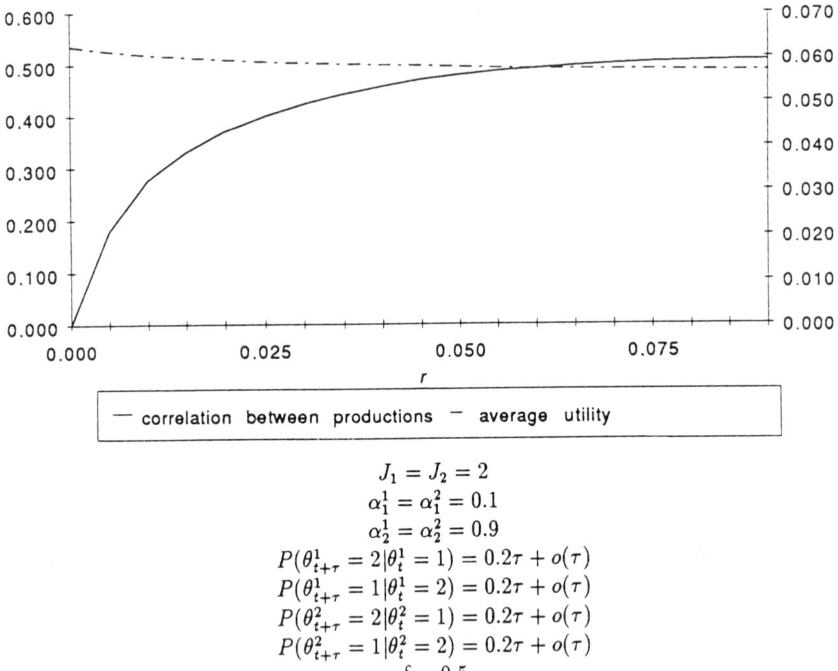

$$J_1 = J_2 = 2$$
$$\alpha_1^1 = \alpha_1^2 = 0.1$$
$$\alpha_2^1 = \alpha_2^2 = 0.9$$
$$P(\theta_{t+\tau}^1 = 2|\theta_t^1 = 1) = 0.2\tau + o(\tau)$$
$$P(\theta_{t+\tau}^1 = 1|\theta_t^1 = 2) = 0.2\tau + o(\tau)$$
$$P(\theta_{t+\tau}^2 = 2|\theta_t^2 = 1) = 0.2\tau + o(\tau)$$
$$P(\theta_{t+\tau}^2 = 1|\theta_t^2 = 2) = 0.2\tau + o(\tau)$$
$$\delta = 0.5$$

FIGURE 1 Output correlations and average utility versus discount rate.

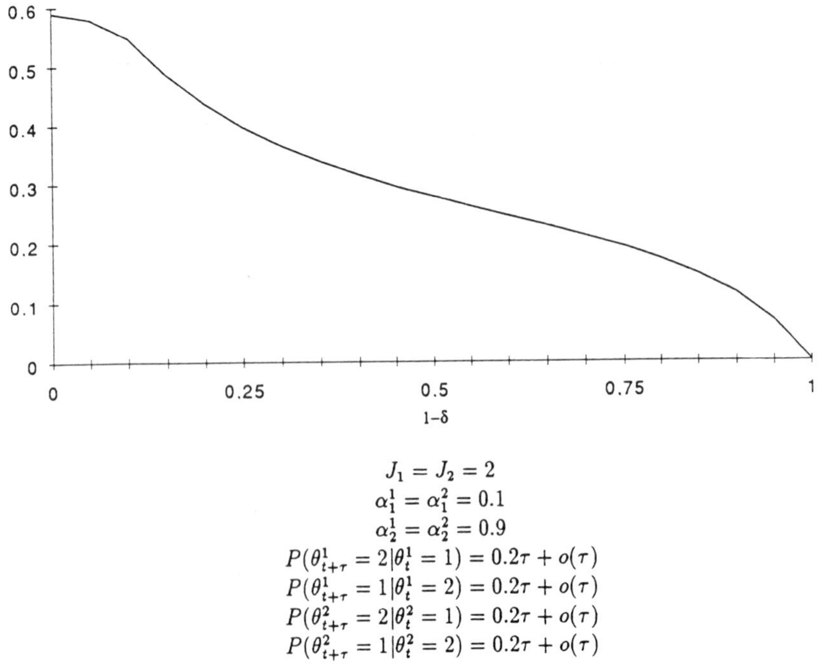

$$J_1 = J_2 = 2$$
$$\alpha_1^1 = \alpha_1^2 = 0.1$$
$$\alpha_2^1 = \alpha_2^2 = 0.9$$
$$P(\theta_{t+\tau}^1 = 2|\theta_t^1 = 1) = 0.2\tau + o(\tau)$$
$$P(\theta_{t+\tau}^1 = 1|\theta_t^1 = 2) = 0.2\tau + o(\tau)$$
$$P(\theta_{t+\tau}^2 = 2|\theta_t^2 = 1) = 0.2\tau + o(\tau)$$
$$P(\theta_{t+\tau}^2 = 1|\theta_t^2 = 2) = 0.2\tau + o(\tau)$$
$$r = 0.01$$

FIGURE 2 Output correlations versus relative risk aversion.

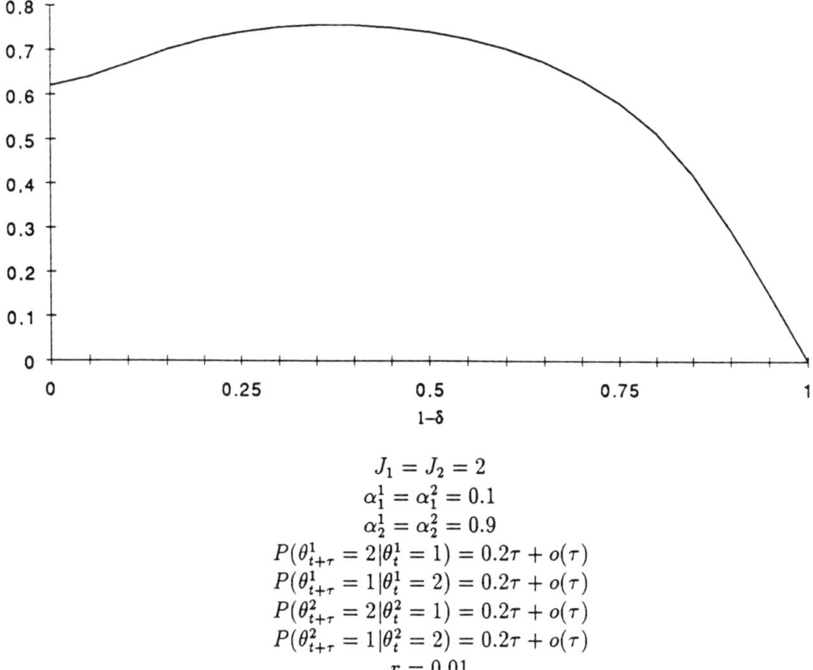

FIGURE 3 Correlation between consumption across countries and relative risk aversion.

Figure 2 shows that the higher the relative risk-aversion coefficient $(1 - \delta)$, the lower the output correlation obtained. The tendency toward risk neutrality lowers, in equilibrium, the value of money and hence increases the correlation of output.

Figure 3 plots the effect of risk aversion on the correlation of (the value of) consumption across countries. It is clear that in a complete markets equilibrium the correlation of consumption across countries is unity. Here lower risk aversion may lead to a higher or lower correlation of consumption across countries. This results from a higher correlation in output combined with less insurance across countries in equilibrium, the lower the risk aversion. This last point is illustrated in Figure 4, where we plot the ratio of utility of type 1 in equilibrium to the utility of the same type in a complete markets equilibrium, as a function of the relative risk-aversion parameter. The results of the simulations used to derive Figure 4 also point out to the fact that, at least for a range of parameters values, large output correlations can be associated with very small losses in utility. Individuals' optimization as well as market mechanisms seem to avoid much of the utility losses while at the same time causing big changes in certain quantities.

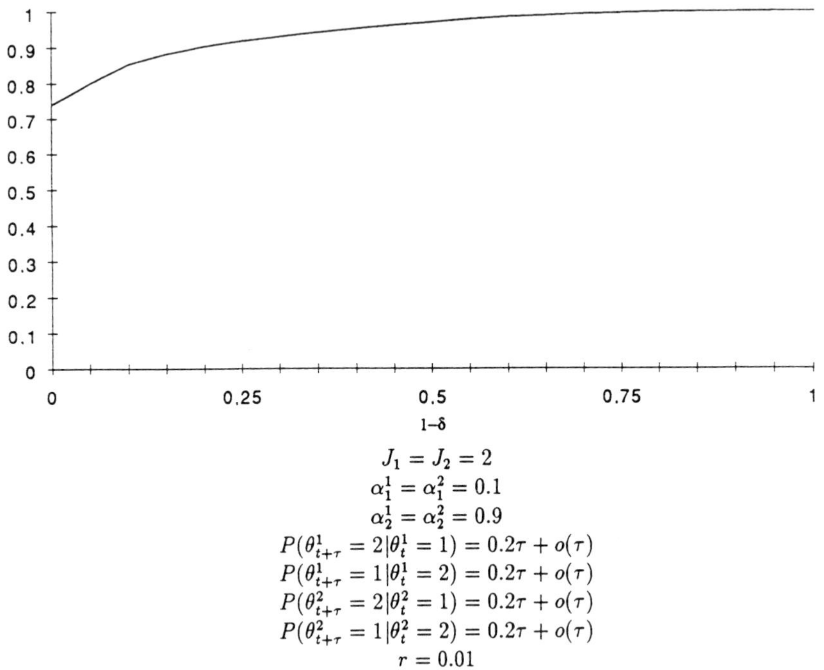

FIGURE 4 Ratio of utility under borrowing constraints to the utility in a complete market versus relative risk aversion.

Simulations also show that in the model "exports" are positively correlated with output and negatively correlated with the relative price of the exported good.

5. CONCLUSION

This paper has presented a model where failure of perfect risk sharing across countries can be used to explain a positive correlation of output series in the presence of independent productivity shocks.[6] In the model, the distribution of financial assets across countries evolves endogenously and in turn affects the distribution of outputs even after controlling for the productivity shocks.

In order to focus on the effect of the borrowing constraints we considered the case where the productivity shocks were independent and

[6]The fact that no migration is allowed also plays an important role in generating the comovements. In fact, in our model, the only risks that need to be shared are the shocks to the productivity of labor in the different countries, and if migration were costless, wages in each country would equalize. Murphy *et al.* [6] used, in a static model, immobile labor to generate an increase in output in one sector in response to an increase in productivity in another sector.

the utility functions in both countries were identical and separable. In this case we showed that the model was capable of generating substantial positive cross-country correlation of output and a lower consumption correlation than that implied under complete markets. Simulations also revealed that the model generates a negative correlation between the value of output and the relative price of exportables in terms of importables. This should not be surprising since most of the output changes in one country would be the result of a change in productivity in that same country. As mentioned in footnote 1 in the introduction, the correlation between quarterly changes in U.S. GNP between 1948 and 1987 and changes in the logarithm of the price of exports divided by the price of imports[7] is not significantly distinct from zero, but if we omit the years 1974 and 1979/1980 when the two "oil shocks" occurred, it equals $-.24$.

Our model cannot accommodate the presence of intermediate goods as oil or any of the monetary aspects that are surely important in determining the transmission of output shocks. Nonetheless, we believe it is useful in illustrating how incomplete markets can help explain some of the aspects of this international transmission. Further, the mathematical techniques discussed here should be useful in dealing with the missing ingredients.

APPENDIX

Proof of Proposition 1

Here we prove Proposition 1. The proof will first be done in the case $0 < z^* < 1$ and then extended to the general case by using an approximation procedure.

When $0 < z^* < 1$, the reduced system (30)–(34) is equivalent to the two following differential systems: a forward problem on $[z^*, 1]$

$$\begin{cases} \dfrac{du}{dz}(z)f(s, u(z), v(z)) = \nu u(z) - \tilde{u}(z), \ z \in]z^*, 1] \\ \dfrac{dv}{dz}(z)f(s, u(z), v(z)) = \nu v(z) - \tilde{v}(z), \ z \in]z^*, 1] \\ \qquad u(z^*) = \dfrac{\tilde{u}(z^*)}{\nu} \\ \qquad v(z^*) = \dfrac{\tilde{v}(z^*)}{\nu}, \end{cases} \tag{40}$$

[7]The data are from the International Financial Statistics.

and a backward problem on $[0, z^*]$

$$\begin{cases} \dfrac{du}{dz}(z)f(s,u(z),v(z)) = \nu u(z) - \tilde{u}(z),\ z \in [0, z^*[\\ \dfrac{dv}{dz}(z)f(s,u(z),v(z)) = \nu v(z) - \tilde{v}(z),\ z \in [0, z^*[\\ u(z^*) = \dfrac{\tilde{u}(z^*)}{\nu} \\ v(z^*) = \dfrac{\tilde{v}(z^*)}{\nu}. \end{cases} \tag{41}$$

We will deal only with system (40). The resolution of system (41) follows by changing z in $1 - z$ in (40).

Since $f(s, u(z^*), v(z^*)) = 0$, system (40) is degenerate. Let $\varepsilon > 0$. We consider the following system on $[z^*, 1]$:

$$\begin{cases} \dfrac{du_\varepsilon}{dz}(z)f_\varepsilon(s,u_\varepsilon(z),v_\varepsilon(z)) = \nu u_\varepsilon(z) - \tilde{u}(z) \\ \dfrac{dv_\varepsilon}{dz}(z)f_\varepsilon(s,u_\varepsilon(z),v_\varepsilon(z)) = \nu v_\varepsilon(z) - \tilde{v}(z) \\ u_\varepsilon(z^*) = \dfrac{\tilde{u}(z^*)}{\nu} \\ v_\varepsilon(z^*) = \dfrac{\tilde{v}(z^*)}{\nu} \end{cases} \tag{42}$$

with $f_\varepsilon(s, u, v) = f(s, u, v) - \varepsilon$. Notice that $f_\varepsilon(s, u_\varepsilon(z^*), v_\varepsilon(z^*)) = -\varepsilon < 0$.

LEMMA 1. *System* (42) *has a unique solution* $(u_\varepsilon, v_\varepsilon)$ *with* u_ε (*resp.* v_ε) *in* $C^1([z^*, 1])$, *strictly positive and strictly decreasing* (*resp. increasing*). *Moreover, for all* $z \in]z^*, 1]$,

$$\frac{\tilde{u}(z^*)}{\nu} > u_\varepsilon(z) > \frac{\tilde{u}(z)}{\nu}$$

$$\frac{\tilde{v}(z^*)}{\nu} < v_\varepsilon(z) < \frac{\tilde{v}(z)}{\nu}$$

Proof. System (42) is a standard Cauchy problem. The proof follows the proof of Proposition 5 in Conze *et al.* [4], and is left to the reader. ∎

LEMMA 2. *The family* (u_ε) [*resp.* (v_ε)] *is increasing* (*resp. decreasing*) *with* ε.

Proof. Let $\varepsilon' > \varepsilon > 0$. For all real pair $(u, v) \in [\tilde{u}(1)/\nu, \tilde{u}(z^*)/\nu] \times [\tilde{v}(z^*)/\nu, \tilde{v}(1)/\nu]$,

$$f_{\varepsilon'}(s, u, v) < f_\varepsilon(s, u, v) < 0.$$

Hence

$$\frac{du_\varepsilon}{dz}(z) \leq \frac{\nu u_\varepsilon(z) - \tilde{u}(z)}{f_{\varepsilon'}(s, u_\varepsilon(z), v_\varepsilon(z))},$$

$$\frac{dv_\varepsilon}{dz}(z) \geq \frac{\nu v_\varepsilon(z) - \tilde{v}(z)}{f_{\varepsilon'}(s, u_\varepsilon(z), v_\varepsilon(z))}.$$

Let $x(z) = (u_\varepsilon(z) - u_{\varepsilon'}(z))_+^2 + (v_{\varepsilon'}(z) - v_\varepsilon(z))_+^2$ where $(\cdot)_+ = \max(\cdot, 0)$. Then

$$\frac{dx}{dz} = 2(u_\varepsilon - u_{\varepsilon'}) + \left(\frac{du_\varepsilon}{dz} - \frac{du_{\varepsilon'}}{dz}\right) + 2(v_{\varepsilon'} - v_\varepsilon) + \left(\frac{dv_{\varepsilon'}}{dz} - \frac{dv_\varepsilon}{dz}\right).$$

Since $(u, v) \mapsto (\nu u - \tilde{u}(z))/f_{\varepsilon'}(s, u, v)$ and $(u, v) \mapsto (\nu v - \tilde{u}(z))/f_{\varepsilon'}(s, u, v)$ are Lipschitz on $[\tilde{u}(1)/\nu, \tilde{u}(z^*)/\nu] \times [\tilde{v}(z^*)/\nu, \tilde{v}(1)/\nu]$ uniformly in $z \in [z^*, 1]$, there exist $R > 0$ such that

$$\frac{du_\varepsilon}{dz} - \frac{du_{\varepsilon'}}{dz} \leq R(|u_\varepsilon - u_{\varepsilon'}| + |v_{\varepsilon'} - v_\varepsilon|),$$

$$\frac{du_\varepsilon}{dz} - \frac{du_{\varepsilon'}}{dz} \leq R(|u_\varepsilon - u_{\varepsilon'}| + |v_{\varepsilon'} - v_\varepsilon|),$$

and we obtain $dx/dz \leq 3Rx$. From $x(z^*) = 0$ and Gronwall's lemma $x(z) = 0$ for all z in $[z^*, 1]$. ■

Since $u_\varepsilon(z) \geq \tilde{u}(z)/\nu$ and $v_\varepsilon(z) \leq \tilde{v}(z)/\nu$ for all z in $[z^*, 1]$, the families (u_ε) and (v_ε) converge pointwise to u and v respectively, satisfying for $z \in]z^*, 1]$

$$\frac{\tilde{u}(z^*)}{\nu} > u(z) \geq \frac{\tilde{u}(z)}{\nu},$$

$$\frac{\tilde{v}(z^*)}{\nu} < v(z) \leq \frac{\tilde{v}(z)}{\nu}.$$

LEMMA 3. *Let* $\bar{z} > z^*$. *Then* (u_ε) *and* (v_ε) *are Lipschitz on* $[\bar{z}, 1]$ *uniformly in* ε.

Proof. The proof is quite simple, and is left to the reader. ■

Using Ascoli's theorem, Lemma 3 and the pointwise convergence of (u_ε) and (v_ε) imply their uniform convergence to u and v on $[\bar{z}, 1]$. It is then straightforward to check that (u, v) is a solution of (40) with u decreasing, v increasing, and both in $C^0([z^*, 1]) \cap C^1(]z^*, 1])$. Also, the inequalities $u(z) \geq \tilde{u}(z)/\nu$ and $v(z) \leq \tilde{v}(z)/\nu$ are in fact strict for $z > z^*$. Therefore,

$$\frac{\tilde{u}(z^*)}{\nu} > u(z) > \frac{\tilde{u}(z)}{\nu}, \tag{43}$$

$$\frac{\tilde{v}(z^*)}{\nu} < v(z) < \frac{\tilde{v}(z)}{\nu}. \tag{44}$$

The strict monotonicity of u and v then follows. Similarly, we obtain a solution of (41) on $[0, z^*]$ with u strictly decreasing, v strictly increasing, and both in $C^0([0, z^*]) \cap C^1([0, z^*[)$, and

$$\frac{\tilde{u}(z)}{\nu} > u(z) > \frac{\tilde{u}(z^*)}{\nu}, \tag{45}$$

$$\frac{\tilde{v}(z)}{\nu} < v(z) < \frac{\tilde{v}(z^*)}{\nu}. \tag{46}$$

Hence a solution to the reduced system (30)–(34) with $u \in E \cap C^1([0,1] \setminus \{z^*\})$ and $v \in F \cap C^1([0,1] \setminus \{z^*\})$.

LEMMA 4. *(u, v) is unique.*

Proof. Let $(\bar{u}, \bar{v})$ be another solution. We will prove that $\bar{u} = u$ and $\bar{v} = v$ on $[z^*, 1]$. The proof is similar on $[0, z^*]$. We start by proving $\bar{u} \leq u$ and $\bar{v} \geq v$. Let $\varepsilon > 0$. For all $(a, b) \in \mathbf{R}^2_{+,\,*}$, $f_\varepsilon(s, a, b) < f(s, a, b)$. As in Lemma 2's proof, we get $\bar{u} \leq u_\varepsilon$ and $\bar{v} \geq v_\varepsilon$. Taking the limit in ε, $\bar{u} \leq u$ and $\bar{v} \geq v$. This implies $f(s, \bar{u}, \bar{v}) \leq f(s, u, v) \leq 0$, and finally

$$\frac{d\bar{u}}{dz} - \frac{du}{dz} \geq \frac{\nu\bar{u} - \nu u}{f(s, u, v)} \geq 0, \qquad \forall z \in]z^*, 1].$$

Hence, since $\bar{u}(z^*) = u(z^*)$, $\bar{u} \geq u$. Also $\bar{v} \leq v$. ■

Hence the first part of Proposition 1 in the case $0 < z^* < 1$. We now turn to the second part of Proposition 1. Let $(\tilde{u}_1, \tilde{v}_1) \in E \times F$ and $(\tilde{u}_2, \tilde{v}_2) \in E \times F$ with $\tilde{u}_1 \geq \tilde{u}_2$ and $\tilde{v}_1 \geq \tilde{v}_2$. Let z_1^* (resp. z_2^*) be the switch point associated to $(s, \tilde{u}_1, \tilde{v}_1)$ [resp. $(s, \tilde{u}_2, \tilde{v}_2)$], and assume that $0 < z_1^* < 1$ and $0 < z_2^* < 1$. Let (u_1, v_1) and (u_2, v_2) be the solutions of (30)–(34) corresponding to respectively $(\tilde{u}_1, \tilde{v}_1)$ and $(\tilde{u}_2, \tilde{v}_2)$.

LEMMA 5. *For all z in $[0, 1]$, $u_1(z) \geq u_2(z)$ and $v_1(z) \geq v_2(z)$.*

Proof. As in Conze *et al.* [4], we only have to consider the case $\tilde{v}_1 = \tilde{v}_2 = \tilde{v}$. It is easy to obtain

$$z_1^* \geq z_2^*$$

$$\tilde{u}_1(z_1^*) \geq \tilde{u}_2(z_2^*)$$

$$u_1(z_2^*) \geq u_1(z_1^*) \geq u_2(z_2^*) \geq u_2(z_1^*)$$

$$u_1(z) \geq u_2(z), \forall z \in [z_2^*, z_1^*]$$

$$v_1(z) \geq v_2(z), \forall z \in [z_2^*, z_1^*].$$

We want to prove $u_1 \geq u_2$ and $v_1 \geq v_2$ on $[0, z_2^*]$ and on $[z_1^*, 1]$. The proof will be done for $z \in [z_1^*, 1]$. Consider $(u_{1,\varepsilon}, v_{1,\varepsilon})$ [resp. $(u_{2,\varepsilon}, v_{2,\varepsilon})$] solutions of (42) with $z^* = z_1^*$ and $(\tilde{u}, \tilde{v}) = (\tilde{u}_1, \tilde{v}_1)$ [resp. $z^* = z_2^*$ and $(\tilde{u}, \tilde{v}) = (\tilde{u}_2, \tilde{v}_2)$]. As in Conze et al. [4], one can prove $u_{1,\varepsilon} \geq u_{2,\varepsilon}$ and $v_{1,\varepsilon} \geq v_{2,\varepsilon}$ on $[z_1^*, 1]$, for all $\varepsilon > 0$. Taking limit in ε leads to the desired result. ■

To obtain Proposition 1 in the general case, we use the following approximation procedure. Let

$$e > \max\left\{\frac{\tilde{v}(0)}{h(s)}, \tilde{u}(1)h(s)\right\},$$

and set

$$\tilde{u}_{e,n}(z) = \tilde{u}(z) + \max\{e - enz, 0\}$$

$$\tilde{v}_{e,n}(z) = \tilde{v}(z) + \max\{e - en(1 - z), 0\}$$

for all $n \in \mathbf{N}_*$. It is easy to check that the switch point z_n^* associated to $(\tilde{u}_{e,n}, \tilde{v}_{e,n})$ satisfies $0 < z_n^* < 1$. Let (u_n, v_n) be the solution of (30)–(34) for $\tilde{u} = \tilde{u}_{e,n}$ and $\tilde{v} = \tilde{v}_{e,n}$. Then as in Conze et al. [4], Section 5.2, (u_n, v_n) converges to (u, v), satisfying Proposition 2.

Proofs of Propositions 2, 3, and 4

To prove Proposition 2, one may first check that $\tilde{f}$ is still homogeneous of degree -1, locally Lipchitz and that $\tilde{f}(1, 1) < 0$, and then proceed as in Conze et al. [4], Proposition 2.

We now prove Proposition 3. The existence of the vector $[a_i]$ follows from the Perron–Frobenius theorem (see for instance Nikaido [7]). From $[a_i] < M(K)[a_i]$ we get

$$\forall i \in \{1, \ldots, I\}, \qquad a_i^{K(i)} < \frac{1}{\nu_i} \sum_{j \neq i} \lambda_{i,j} a_j^{K(i)}. \tag{47}$$

Let

$$a_{i,\eta}^1(z) = a_i^1 - \eta z,$$

$$a_{i,\eta}^2(z) = a_i^2 - \eta(1 - z),$$

$$\tilde{u}_{i,\eta}(z) = \sum_{j \neq i} \lambda_{i,j} a_{i,\eta}^1(z),$$

$$\tilde{v}_{i,\eta}(z) = \sum_{j \neq i} \lambda_{i,j} a_{i,\eta}^2(z),$$

$$q_{\varepsilon,\eta} = \left(q_{i,\varepsilon,\eta}^1, q_{i,\varepsilon,\eta}^2\right)_{i \in \{1,\ldots,I\}} = \Phi(\underline{q}),$$

and $z_{i,\eta}^*$ be the switch point associated to $(s_i, \tilde{u}_{i,\eta}, \tilde{v}_{i,\eta})$. Assume, for instance, $K(i) = 1$. We start with the case $z_{i,\eta}^* = 1$. From (47), we get for η small enough

$$\frac{1}{\varepsilon} q_{i,\varepsilon,\eta}^1(1) = \frac{1}{\nu_i} \sum_{j \neq i} \lambda_{i,j} a_{j,\eta}^1(1) \geq a_{i,\eta}^1(z) + \delta, \forall z \in [0,1],$$

with $\delta > 0$ independent of ε and η. Since $q_{i,\varepsilon,\eta}^1$ is decreasing,

$$\frac{1}{\varepsilon} q_{i,\varepsilon,\eta}^1(z) \geq a_{i,\eta}^1(z) + \delta \ \forall z \in [0,1]. \tag{48}$$

In particular, $q_{i,\varepsilon,\eta}^1(z) \geq \underline{q}_i^1(z)$. From (48), we get

$$\begin{aligned} \frac{1}{\varepsilon} q_{i,\varepsilon,\eta}^2(1) &= \frac{1}{\varepsilon} q_{i,\varepsilon,\eta}^1(1) h(s_i) \\ &\geq a_{i,\eta}^1(1) h(s_i) + \delta h(s_i) \\ &\geq a_{i,\eta}^2(1) + \delta', \end{aligned}$$

with $\delta' = \delta h(s_i) > 0$. Let

$$\bar{z}_\varepsilon = \inf\left\{ z \in [0,1] / \forall y \in [z,1], \frac{1}{\varepsilon} q_{i,\varepsilon,\eta}^2(y) \geq a_{i,\eta}^2(y) + \frac{\delta'}{2} \right\}.$$

If $\bar{z}_\varepsilon = 0$, then $q^2_{i,\varepsilon,\eta}(z) \geq \varepsilon a^2_{i,\eta}(z)$ for all z in $[0,1]$. If not, then for $z \in [0, \bar{z}_\varepsilon]$,

$$\frac{1}{\varepsilon}\frac{dq^2_{i,\varepsilon,\eta}}{dz}(z) = \frac{1}{\varepsilon}\frac{\nu_i q^2_{i,\varepsilon,\eta}(z) - \tilde{v}_{i,\eta}(z)}{f\left(s_i, q^1_{i,\varepsilon,\eta}(z), q^2_{i,\varepsilon,\eta}(z)\right)}$$

$$= \varepsilon\frac{\nu_i q^2_{i,\varepsilon,\eta}(z)/\varepsilon - \tilde{v}_{i,\eta}(z)/\varepsilon}{f\left(s_i, q^1_{i,\varepsilon,\eta}(z)/\varepsilon, q^2_{i,\varepsilon,\eta}(z)/\varepsilon\right)}.$$

Also for $z \in [0, \bar{z}_\varepsilon]$,

$$\frac{1}{\varepsilon}q^2_{i,\varepsilon,\eta}(z) \leq \frac{1}{\varepsilon}q^2_{i,\varepsilon,\eta}(\bar{z}_\varepsilon) = a^2_{i,\eta}(\bar{z}_\varepsilon) + \frac{\delta'}{2} \leq a^2_{i,\eta}(1) + \frac{\delta'}{2},$$

hence

$$\frac{1}{\varepsilon}q^2_{i,\varepsilon,\eta}(z) \leq \frac{1}{\varepsilon}q^2_{i,\varepsilon,\eta}(1) + \frac{\delta'}{2} - \delta' \leq \tilde{v}_{i,\eta}(1) - \frac{\delta'}{2}.$$

This implies for $z \in [0, \bar{z}_\varepsilon]$

$$f\left(s_i, q^1_{i,\varepsilon,\eta}(z), q^2_{i,\varepsilon,\eta}(z)\right) \geq f\left(s_i, \tilde{u}_{i,\eta}(1), \tilde{v}_{i,\eta}(1) - \frac{\delta'}{2}\right) > Q,$$

with $Q > 0$ independent of ε and η, and we finally obtain for $z \in [0, \bar{z}_\varepsilon]$,

$$\frac{1}{\varepsilon}q^2_{i,\varepsilon,\eta}(z) \geq \frac{1}{\varepsilon}q^2_{i,\varepsilon,\eta}(\bar{z}_\varepsilon) - R\varepsilon = a^2_{i,\eta}(\bar{z}_\varepsilon) + \frac{\delta'}{2} - R\varepsilon$$

$$\geq a^2_{i,\eta}(z) + \frac{\delta'}{2} - R\varepsilon,$$

with R independent of ε and η. Hence, for ε and η small enough, $q^2_{i,\varepsilon,\eta}(z) \geq \underline{q}^2_i(z)$. If $z^*_{i,\eta} = 0$, then

$$\tilde{v}_{i,\eta}(z) = \sum_{j \neq i}\lambda_{i,j}a^2_{j,\eta}(z) \geq \tilde{u}_{i,\eta}(z)h(s_i) = \sum_{j \neq i}\lambda_{i,j}a^1_{j,\eta}(z)h(s_i),$$

and we get from (47) that

$$a^2_{i,\eta}(z) \leq \sum_{j \neq i}\lambda_{i,j}a^2_{j,\eta}(z) + \delta, \qquad \forall z \in [0,1],$$

with $\delta > 0$ independent of ε and η. We then proceed as in the first case $z^*_{i,\eta} = 1$. Finally, if $0 < z^*_{i,\eta} < 1$, then we proceed as in the first case for $z \leq z^*_{i,\eta}$ and as the second case when $z \geq z^*_{i,\eta}$.

From the monotonicity of Φ and the existence of a subsolution and a supersolution, Proposition 4 is a well-known result when Φ maps a compact into itself. But here $(E \times F)^I$ is not compact. Nevertheless, the proof doesn't present any particular difficulty, and is completely similar to the proof of Proposition 4 in Conze *et al.* [4], to which the reader should refer.

The Case $\rho \leq 1$

PROPOSITION 6. *If $\rho \leq 1$, there is no solution to system (S) satisfying* (26)–(29).

Proof. Assume that $\rho \leq 1$ and that there is a solution q to (S) satisfying (26)–(29). For all i in $\{1, \dots, I\}$, let $a_i = q_i^1(\frac{1}{2})$ if $z_i^* \geq \frac{1}{2}$ and $a_i = q_i^2(\frac{1}{2})$ otherwise. If $z_i^* \geq \frac{1}{2}$, then $f(s_i, q_i^1(\frac{1}{2}), q_i^2(\frac{1}{2})) \geq 0$ and from $(dq_i^1/dz)(\frac{1}{2}) \leq 0$ and equation (21), we get

$$\nu_i q_i^1\left(\frac{1}{2}\right) \leq \sum_{j \neq i} \lambda_{i,j} q_j^1\left(\frac{1}{2}\right). \tag{49}$$

Also

$$q_i^2\left(\frac{1}{2}\right) \leq q_i^1\left(\frac{1}{2}\right) h(s_i). \tag{50}$$

If $z_i^* < \frac{1}{2}$, then $f(s_i, q_i^1(\frac{1}{2}), q_i^2(\frac{1}{2})) \leq 0$ and from $(dq_i^2/dz)(\frac{1}{2}) \geq 0$ and equation (22), we get

$$\nu_i q_i^2\left(\frac{1}{2}\right) \leq \sum_{j \neq i} \lambda_{i,j} q_j^2\left(\frac{1}{2}\right). \tag{51}$$

Also

$$q_i^2\left(\frac{1}{2}\right) \geq q_i^1\left(\frac{1}{2}\right) h(s_i). \tag{52}$$

Let K: $\{1, \dots, I\} \to \{1, 2\}$ be defined by $K(i) = 1$ if $z_i^* \geq \frac{1}{2}$ and $K(i) = 2$ otherwise. From (49)–(52), we obtain

$$[a_i] \leq M(K)[a_i] \tag{53}$$

where inequality between two vectors means inequality between their coordinates. If $\rho < 1$, then $M(K)^n$ is a contraction for n big enough (see Nikaido [7]) and (53) implies that for all i, $a_i = 0$, i.e. $q_i^1(\frac{1}{2}) = q_i^2(\frac{1}{2}) = 0$, which contradicts (28) and (29). If $\rho = 1$ and $[a_i] \neq M(K)[a_i]$, there exist $\varepsilon > 0$ and $m \in \mathbf{N}_*$ such that $(1 + \varepsilon)[a_i] \leq M(K)^m[a_i]$. Also $(M(K)^m/(1 + \varepsilon))^n$ is a contraction for n big enough (again see Nikaido [7]) and $q_i^1(\frac{1}{2}) = q_i^2(\frac{1}{2}) = 0$ for all i. At least, if $\rho = 1$ and $[a_i] = M(K)[a_i]$, then from $\nu_i > \sum_{j \neq i} \lambda_{i,j}$ we have that $q_i^1(\frac{1}{2}) = q_i^2(\frac{1}{2}) = 0$ for all i. ■

Proof of Theorem 2

Here we prove Theorem 2. From the definition of the matrices $M(K)$, it is obvious that the $\rho(K)$, and therefore ρ itself, are continuous and decreasing functions of r. By continuity, it is sufficient for Theorem 2 to prove that $\rho > 1$ when $r = 0$.

Let K: $\{1, \ldots, I\} \to \{1, 2\}$ and $M(K) = (m_{i,j})$. From the Perron-Frobenius theorem, the existence of $a \in R^I_{+,*}$ such that $M(K)a \geq a$ and $M(K)a \neq a$ is a sufficient condition to have $\rho(K) > 1$.

Let a be the vector with all coordinates equal to 1. To get $\rho > 1$, it suffices to prove that there exist K: $\{1, \ldots, I\} \to \{1, 2\}$ such that

$$\forall i \in \{1, \ldots, I\}, \sum_j m_{i,j} \geq 1 \tag{54}$$

with strict equality for at least one $i \in \{1, \ldots, I\}$. Let K be defined by $K(i) = 1$ if $h(s_i) > 1$ and $K(i) = 2$ otherwise. It is easy to check that $m_{i,j} \geq \lambda_{i,j}/\nu_i$ for all $(i, j) \in \{1, \ldots, I\}^2$, $j \neq i$. If none of these inequalities is strict, then for all $(i, j) \in \{1, \ldots, I\} \times \{1, \ldots, I\}$ either $K_j = K_i$ or $h(s_j) = 1$, which implies that $h(s_i) \geq 1$ for all $i \in \{1, \ldots, I\}$ or $h(s_i) \leq 1$ for all $i \in \{1, \ldots, I\}$. This contradicts Assumption 3.

Acknowledgments

This research was supported by a NSF U.S.–France binational grant INT H4 13966 and by a NSF grant SES 8420930. Some of this work was done while Scheinkman was visiting Université Paris-Dauphine and some while Conze was visiting the University of Chicago.

References

1. D. Backus, P. Kehoe, and F. Kydland (1989). "International borrowing and world business cycles," unpublished paper.
2. T. Bewley (1977). "The permanent income hypothesis: A theoretical formulation," *J. Econ. Theory* **16**.
3. A. Conze (1990). "Propriété ergodique d'un système dynamique stochastique," unpublished paper, CEREMADE, Université Paris-Dauphine.
4. A. Conze, J.-M. Lasry, and J. Scheinkman (1990). "A system of non-linear functional differential equations arising in an equilibrium model of an economy with borrowing constraints," *Annales de l'Institut Henri Poincaré*, November, 1991.
5. D. Costello (1989). "A cross-country cross industry comparison of the behavior of Solow residuals," unpublished paper.
6. K. Murphy, A. Schleifer and R. Vishny (1989). "Building blocks of market clearing business cycle models," unpublished paper.
7. H. Nikaido (1972). *Convex Structures and Economic Theory* (Academic Press, New York).
8. J. Scheinkman (1984). "General equilibrium models of economic fluctuations," unpublished paper, Department of Economics, Univ. Chicago.
9. J. Scheinkman and L. Weiss (1986). "Borrowing constraints and aggregate economic activity," *Econometrica* **54**.

MULTINATIONAL CORPORATIONS AND ABSOLUTE ADVANTAGE: THE ASYMMETRIC CASE

Fumio Dei
School of Business Administration
Kobe University
Rokko, Kobe 657, Japan

1. INTRODUCTION

Although it is conventional for trade theorists to regard multinational corporations (MNCs) as international factor movements,[1] Helpman (1984, 1985) and Helpman and Krugman (1985, Chapters 12 and 13) have developed an innovative approach to MNCs. They modify the Heckscher–Ohlin model so as to involve Chamberlinian monopolistic competition, assume no factor mobility between countries, and stress the idea that an MNC is a firm within which the parent exports headquarter services to overseas subsidiaries. They conclude that under the assumption that there is no technological gap between countries, MNCs can arise from differences in factor endowment proportions.

While differences in factor endowment proportions may be one determinant of MNCs, in this paper we highlight an alternative determinant: technological superiority possessed by MNCs. Since the Ricardian model is the simplest tool to analyze technological differences, we utilize the two-country, two-good Ricardian model under perfect competition. In this model, MNC superiority is interpreted as absolute advantage. To consider headquarter services explicitly, we divide labor coefficients into two parts, coefficients for headquarter activity and those for plant activity. By assuming two goods and perfect competition, we neglect the aspect of differen-

[1]See, for example, Caves (1971, pp. 17–19).

GENERAL EQUILIBRIUM, GROWTH, AND TRADE II

tiated products and monopolistic competition. This alteration in model structure eases the task of deriving the world transformation curve and reveals the patterns of MNCs along this curve.

In the present paper, we shall examine the "asymmetric case," in which one country has an absolute advantage in both goods and the other country has an absolute disadvantage in both goods. This case would be important in explaining MNCs in the North–South setting. The "symmetric case," in which one country has an absolute advantage in one good and an absolute disadvantage in the other good, is discussed in Dei (1991).

The remainder of this paper is organized as follows. In Section 2 we describe the basic structure of the model. We draw the locus of the commodity price ratio against the relative wage rate. Using this locus, we trace out the world transformation curve in Section 3. Concluding remarks are provided in Section 4.

2. THE BASIC STRUCTURE OF THE MODEL

Consider a Ricardian world of two countries, home and foreign. There are two goods, good 1 and good 2, which are produced using only one factor, labor. We assume that the configuration of constant labor requirements per unit output of good i, a_i and a_i^*, is given by

$$a_1/a_2 < a_1^*/a_2^*, \tag{1}$$

$$a_1 < a_1^* \quad \text{and} \quad a_2 < a_2^*, \tag{2}$$

where an asterisk denotes the foreign country. In the traditional case where MNCs are not allowed to exist, (1) implies that the home country has a comparative advantage in good 1, and (2) implies that she has an absolute advantage both in good 1 and in good 2.

Let us assume that total labor requirements are divided into two parts. One is the requirements for headquarter activity, and the other is the requirements for plant activity:

$$a_i = a_i^H + a_i^P;\, a_i^* = a_i^{*H} + a_i^{*P}, \qquad i = 1, 2, \tag{3}$$

where superscripts H and P stand for headquarters and plants, respectively. Headquarters employ labor to produce headquarter services such as management and marketing, and send them to plants that produce goods using these services and labor. Suppose that MNCs are permitted to exist. It is assumed that MNCs cannot move their headquarters abroad but their plants are mobile internationally, and that MNCs undertaking headquarter activity at home and plant activity abroad face the same input coefficients of labor for each activity as before. The latter assumption implies

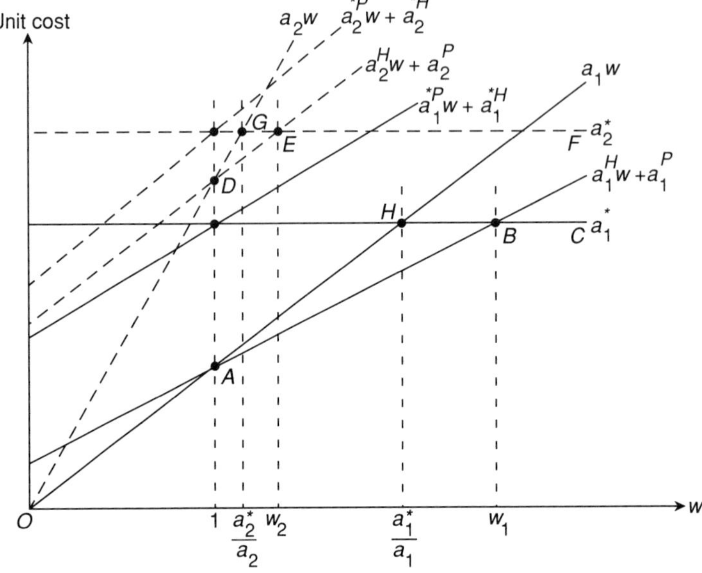

FIGURE 1

that becoming an MNC does not affect absolute advantage at all. We think of an MNC as a firm that exports headquarter services to its overseas plants.

Taking foreign labor (services) as numeraire, and denoting by w the relative wage rate on home labor in terms of foreign labor, we obtain cost conditions illustrated in Figure 1. Unit cost lines are drawn as solid lines for good 1 and as broken lines for good 2. For example, $a_2^Hw + a_2^P$ is the unit cost of good 2 when home local firms in industry 2 decide to become MNCs. Minimum unit cost locus for good 1 is *OABC*, and that for good 2 is *ODEF*. Unit cost lines $a_1^{*P}w + a_1^{*H}$ and $a_2^{*P}w + a_2^{*H}$ are located above loci *OABC* and *ODEF*, respectively. Hence, foreign local firms with an absolute disadvantage in good 1 and good 2 cannot appear as MNCs. This suggests that MNCs must have an absolute advantage. That is, absolute advantage is a necessary condition for firms to become MNCs. Although foreign local firms producing good 2 have a comparative advantage if no MNCs are allowed to exist, they cannot compete as MNCs nevertheless. Thus, we can say that comparative advantage in the absence of MNCs has nothing to do with the emergence of MNCs.

In Figure 1, $w_1(w_2)$ is the relative home wage rate at which foreign local firms are on an equal footing with home MNCs in the cost of producing good 1 (good 2), so that w_1 and w_2 satisfy

$$a_1^Hw_1 + a_1^P = a_1^*; \qquad a_2^Hw_2 + a_2^P = a_2^*. \tag{4}$$

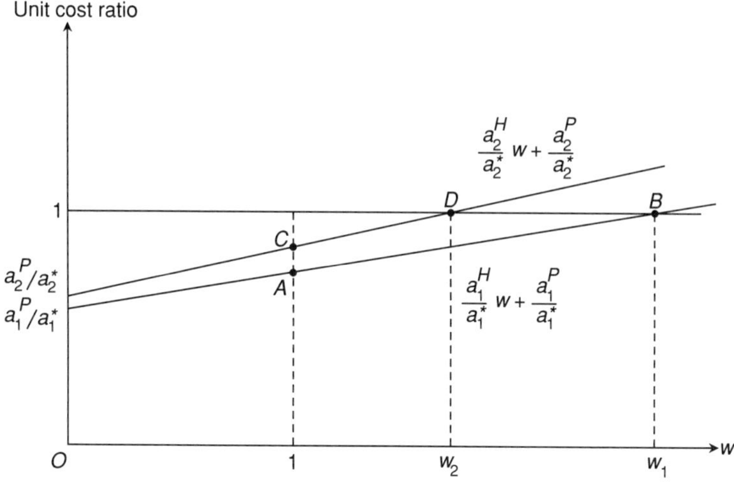

FIGURE 2

Equations (4) can be rewritten as

$$\frac{a_1^H}{a_1^*}w_1 + \frac{a_1^P}{a_1^*} = 1; \qquad \frac{a_2^H}{a_2^*}w_2 + \frac{a_2^P}{a_2^*} = 1. \tag{5}$$

Figure 2 shows how to determine w_1 and w_2. The vertical axis measures the ratio of unit cost of each good in home MNCs to that in foreign local firms. Line AB representing $(a_1^H/a_1^*)w + a_1^P/a_1^*$ intersects at point B with horizontal line DB that is unity in height. Point B gives w_1. Similarly, point D yields w_2. Points A and C are below line DB because of absolute advantage ranking (2). Comparative advantage ranking (1) locates point A below point C. As is clear from Figure 2, w_2 must be smaller than w_1 if line AB is flatter than line CD, that is, if $a_1^H/a_1^* < a_2^H/a_2^*$. On the other hand, if $a_1^H/a_1^* > a_2^H/a_2^*$ then w_2 may be larger than w_1. Let us assume that $a_1^H/a_1^* \neq a_2^H/a_2^*$.

Consider the case in which $a_1^H/a_1^* < a_2^H/a_2^*$. We have $1 < w_2 < w_1$. As will be shown later, the range within which w can vary depends on the relative labor endowment between the two countries. However, suppose for the moment that w is given exogenously. We have only to look at w such that $1 \leqq w \leqq w_1$. w can be neither lower than 1 nor higher than w_1. If w were outside this range, one country would produce nothing, and unemployment would push w back to the range between 1 and w_1.

Figure 3 illustrates how home-labor intensity relative to foreign labor in the production of each good changes as w changes. When $w = 1$, it is seen from Figure 1 that each good is produced by home MNCs and/or

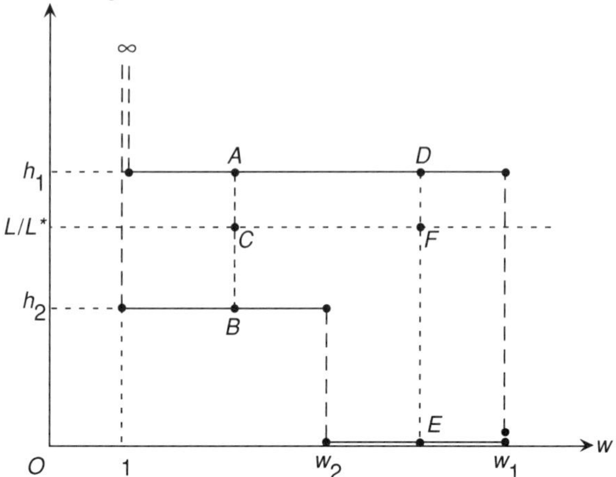

FIGURE 3 $a_1^H/a_1^* < a_2^H/a_2^*$ and $h_2 < L/L^* < h_1$.

home local firms. Home MNCs adopt home-labor intensity h_1 for good 1 and h_2 for good 2, where

$$h_1 \equiv a_1^H/a_1^P; h_2 \equiv a_2^H/a_2^P. \tag{6}$$

Since home local firms do not use foreign labor at all, home-labor intensity for each good becomes infinite.

Inequality (1) can be rewritten as

$$\frac{a_1^H}{a_1^*}\left(1 + \frac{1}{h_1}\right) < \frac{a_2^H}{a_2^*}\left(1 + \frac{1}{h_2}\right). \tag{7}$$

Inequality (7) implies that it is ambiguous whether h_1 is larger or smaller than h_2 if $a_1^H/a_1^* < a_2^H/a_2^*$. But

$$h_1 \text{ must exceed } h_2 \text{ if } a_1^H/a_1^* > a_2^H/a_2^*. \tag{8}$$

Note that

$$\text{there is no case where } w_1 < w_2 \text{ and } h_1 < h_2. \tag{9}$$

The reason is as follows. Suppose that $w_1 < w_2$. We must have $a_1^H/a_1^* > a_2^H/a_2^*$ (see Figure 2). Relationship (8) leads to $h_2 < h_1$. Then we obtain (9).

Let us assume that $h_1 \neq h_2$. Supposing that $a_1^H/a_1^* < a_2^H/a_2^*$, we display the case where $w_2 < w_1$ and $h_2 < h_1$ in Figure 3. When $1 < w < w_2$, good 1 is produced only by home MNCs as shown by Figure 1. Similarly, home MNCs drive other producers out of the good 2 market.

Home-labor intensity is fixed at h_1 for good 1 and h_2 for good 2. When $w = w_2$, two home-labor intensities, h_2 and zero, are available to the good 2 production. There is no change in h_1. In the case where $w_2 < w < w_1$, good 2 is produced only by foreign local firms. Home-labor intensity for good 2 is zero. h_1 is still used in the good 1 production. When $w = w_1$, foreign local firms can compete with home MNCs in the good 1 production. Hence, h_1 and zero can appear as home-labor intensities. Good 2 has zero home-labor intensity.

We can find the analogy between Figure 3 and a diagram showing that capital/labor ratio in each industry decreases as the rental/wage ratio rises in the simple 2 × 2 Heckscher–Ohlin model.[2] It is well known that in this model the economy's factor endowment proportion specifies the range of factor price ratio that can be observed and that the aggregate factor endowment ratio is equal to a weighted average of factor input ratio in each industry. These properties will hold in our Ricardian model if the two countries as a whole are regarded as one economy.

Suppose that L and L^* are given so that $h_2 < L/L^* < h_1$ in Figure 3. $L(L^*)$ represents the total amount of home (foreign) labor, which is immobile internationally. If $1 < w < w_2$, good 1 (good 2) is produced only by home MNCs under home-labor intensity $h_1(h_2)$. The full-employment conditions in the two countries imply that

$$\frac{L_1^*}{L^*}h_1 + \left(1 - \frac{L_1^*}{L^*}\right)h_2 = \frac{L}{L^*}, \tag{10}$$

where L_1^* is the amount of foreign labor used for the good 1 production. L_1^*/L^* is given by BC/AB in Figure 3. Since $0 < L_1^*/L^* < 1$, each weight in (10) is positive. This means that both goods must be produced. This production structure when $1 < w < w_2$ can be denoted by $H_1, H_2|P_1, P_2$ because home MNCs undertake headquarter activity at home (H_1, H_2) and plant activity abroad (P_1, P_2) to produce both goods. A line dividing H_1, H_2 and P_1, P_2 represents a border. Note that L_1^*/L^* in (10) is uniquely determined, so that output of each good is also uniquely determined for any w such that $1 < w < w_2$.

If $w_2 < w < w_1$ in Figure 3, then h_2 in (10) reduces to zero. But (10) holds again in the sense that $L_1^*/L^* = EF/DE$ in Figure 3. Since $0 < L_1^*/L^* < 1$, some foreign labor is employed by foreign local firms to produce good 2. Thus there is incomplete specialization. The production pattern in this case can be written as $H_1|P_1, X_2^*$ because good 1 is produced only by home MNCs $(H_1|P_1)$ and good 2 is produced only by

[2]A classic literature is Johnson (1957), where the wage/rental ratio instead of the rental/wage ratio is measured horizontally.

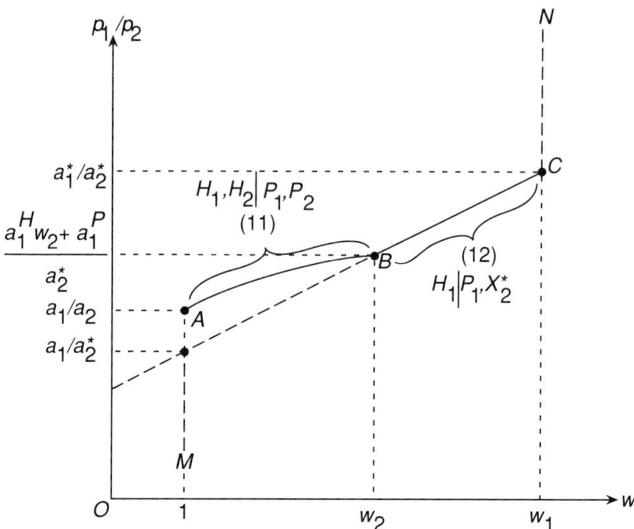

FIGURE 4 $a_1^H/a_1^* < a_2^H/a_2^*$ and $h_2 < L/L^* < h_1$.

foreign local firms (X_2^*). Since L_1^*/L^* is constant, output of each good is unchanged for any w such that $w_2 < w < w_1$.

As shown above, both goods are produced when $1 < w < w_2$ or $w_2 < w < w_1$ in Figure 3. Our next task is to draw in Figure 4 the locus of p_1/p_2 against w, where p_i is the relative price of good i in terms of foreign labor. p_1/p_2 is determined by the zero profit conditions as in (11) and (12):

$$p_1/p_2 = \left(a_1^H w + a_1^P\right)/\left(a_2^H w + a_2^P\right) \quad \text{when} \quad 1 < w < w_2, \tag{11}$$

$$p_1/p_2 = \left(a_1^H w + a_1^P\right)/a_2^* \quad \text{when} \quad w_2 < w < w_1. \tag{12}$$

In Figure 4, curve AB representing (11) and line BC relating to (12) are upward sloping. This reflects that good 1 is home-labor-intensive good for all w such that $1 < w < w_1$ in Figure 3.[3] We obtain from (11) that $(p_1/p_2)' = (h_1 - h_2)a_1^P a_2^P/(a_2^H w + a_2^P)^2 \gtrless 0$ and $(p_1/p_2)'' \lesseqgtr 0$ as $h_1 \gtrless h_2$.

In the case where $L/L^* < h_2 < h_1$, w can vary between w_2 and w_1 in Figure 3. Only line BC in Figure 4 is relevant. If $h_2 < h_1 < L/L^*$, Figure 3 reveals that w is nailed to 1. As is clear from Figure 1, $p_1/p_2 = a_1/a_2$ as long as both goods are produced. We assume that L/L^* equals neither h_1 nor h_2.

[3]Because of Jones' magnification effect, curve AB has the elasticity of p_1/p_2 with respect to w less than unity. Since line BC, if extended, has a positive intercept on the p_1/p_2 axis, its elasticity is also less than unity.

The relationships between L/L^* and the range of w are summarized as follows. Let us measure country size by the labor endowment. If the home country is extremely larger than the foreign country, the home wage rate is depressed to the foreign wage rate in spite of the home country's technological advantage in both goods. Note that in a standard Ricardian trade model without MNCs, overall technological superiority of the home country leads to a higher home wage rate. If the relative country size of the home country is extremely small, then we have $1 < w_2 \leqq w \leqq w_1$. Such relative country size reinforces the effect of home technological advantage on w, in the sense that the range of w between a_2^*/a_2 and a_1^*/a_1 in the case of no MNCs shifts to the right as in Figure 1. If relative country size is given at an intermediate level, the range of w spreads to the right and left. This is the mixture of two extreme cases discussed above. Allowing firms to become MNCs makes room for relative country size to affect the range of w.

So far we have examined the case in which $a_1^H/a_1^* < a_2^H/a_2^*$ and $h_2 < h_1$. As seen from (7), there may be the case in which $a_1^H/a_1^* < a_2^H/a_2^*$ and $h_1 < h_2$. In such a case, $w_2 < w_1$ as in Figure 3, but the positions of h_1 and h_2 are opposite. Hence, a factor-intensity reversal occurs. The critical w is w_2. Good 2 is home-labor-intensive when $1 < w < w_2$, while good 1 is home-labor-intensive when $w_2 < w < w_1$. The curve corresponding to *AB* in Figure 4 will be negatively sloped.

If $a_1^H/a_1^* > a_2^H/a_2^*$, then $h_2 < h_1$ from (8). w_1 may be larger or smaller than w_2. Assuming that $w_1 \neq w_2$, we have two cases: (i) $h_2 < h_1$ and $w_2 < w_1$, and (ii) $h_2 < h_1$ and $w_1 < w_2$. Case (i) will yield the same diagram as in Figure 3. In case (ii) we will find a factor-intensity reversal. The locus of p_1/p_2 against w to be drawn in Figure 4 is upward-sloping first and downward-sloping next as w rises.

3. THE WORLD TRANSFORMATION CURVE

In this section, we derive the world transformation curve. We are concerned mainly with the case in which $a_1^H/a_1^* < a_2^H/a_2^*$ and $h_2 < L/L^* < h_1$, so that most of our analysis is based on Figures 3 and 4. In Figure 4, we can attach to the locus of *ABC* two vertical dashed lines *AM* and *CN* that indicate complete specialization. Such an extended locus permits us to delineate the world transformation curve. Constant-returns-to-scale technology in our model makes the world production possibilities set convex, so that parametric changes in p_1/p_2 along the extended locus *MABCN* will yield the world transformation curve.

The locus *MABCN* gives us the transformation curve *ABCD* with two kinks and three flats as shown in Figure 5. At sufficiently low p_1/p_2, the world economy is completely specialized in good 2. Figure 4 implies that w

is set at 1, its lowest level. At this wage rate, good 2 can be produced only by home local firms and/or home MNCs. All foreign labor is employed by home MNCs. Since $h_2 < L/L^*$, some of home labor must be used by home local firms in order to guarantee full employment in both countries. The production pattern at A in Figure 5 is $X_2, H_2|P_2$. A sufficiently high p_1/p_2 causes complete specialization in good 1. The pattern is $H_1|P_1, X_1^*$ because $w = w_1$ and $L/L^* < h_1$. As discussed above, the pattern $H_1, H_2|P_1, P_2$ or $H_1|P_1, X_2^*$ freezes world output of each good. As is clear from Figure 4, price changes do not alter world outputs under these patterns. This means that the transformation curve has two kinks. Kink $B(C)$ in Figure 5 corresponds to curve AB (line BC) in Figure 4, so that there is the pattern $H_1, H_2|P_1, P_2$ at $B(H_1|P_1, X_2^*$ at $C)$ in Figure 5. Of course, slopes of the transformation curve reflect commodity price ratios. For example, the slope of AB is equal to $-1/(a_1/a_2)$. We know production patterns at two ends and two kinks, but do not know those along the linear segments. Now let us introduce the minimum-types-of-MNC assumption, as in Dei (1991). That is, we assume that the minimum number of types of MNC comes out from among potential types of MNC. In this paper, there are two potential types of MNC, home MNCs producing good 1 and home MNCs producing good 2. Thus, we have to consider which part of the curve $ABCD$ can be traced out without one type or both types of MNC.

Consider first the production pattern along the linear segment AB in Figure 5. We know from Figure 4 that $w = 1$ on this segment. As is clear from Figure 1, when $w = 1$, good 1 can be produced only by home MNCs and/or home local firms. Combining X_1 with $X_2, H_2|P_2$ at point A in Figure 5, we have the pattern $X_1, X_2, H_2|P_2$. The full-employment condi-

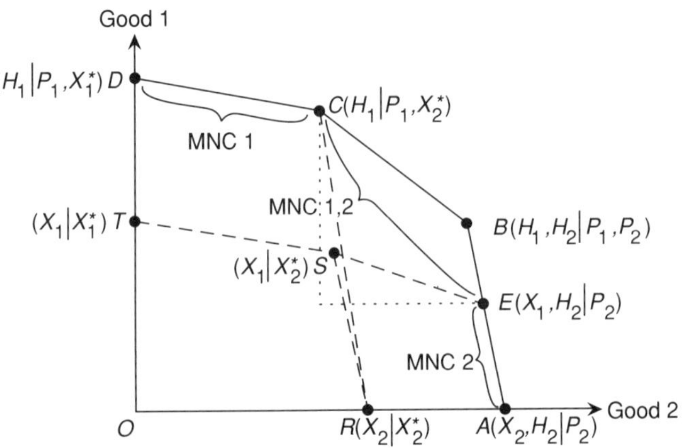

FIGURE 5 $a_1^H/a_1^* < a_2^H/a_2^*$ and $h_2 < L/L^* < h_1$.

tions for this pattern are

$$a_1 X_1 + a_2 X_2 + a_2^H X_2^M = L; a_2^P X_2^M = L^*, \tag{13}$$

where $X_i(X_i^M)$ is the output of good i home local firms (home MNCs) produce. We easily find that a production point moves from A to E along AB as X_1 increases from zero level, where point E has the pattern $X_1, H_2|P_2$. In (13), X_2^M is fixed. Thus the movement from A to E causes reallocation of home labor from X_2 to X_1 between local firms in the home country. The output of good 2 is larger at E than at B, because all foreign labor is devoted to the plant activity for good 2 at E, but fewer foreign labor is employed in this activity at B. This implies that point E must lie southeast of point B. Hence AE which is a part of segment AB can be attained without home MNCs producing good 1.

Without home MNCs producing good 2, the pattern $H_1|P_1, X_1^*, X_2^*$, which is the mixture of patterns at C and D, reproduces the linear segment CD. Since $w = w_2 < w_1$ on the linear segment BC, Figure 1 reveals that good 1 is produced only by home MNCs and that good 2 is produced only by foreign local firms and/or home MNCs. If the emergence of home MNCs producing good 2 cannot be allowed on the linear segment BC, we can reach only point C, whose pattern is $H_1|P_1, X_2^*$. Thus the portion EBC needs home MNCs of both types except E and C.

As shown in Figure 5, the world transformation curve can be separated into three parts:

1. The part where home MNCs appear only in sector 1 (MNC 1)
2. The part where home MNCs appear only in sector 2 (MNC 2)
3. The part where home MNCs appear in both sectors (MNC 1, 2)

There are MNCs of either type at every point of the transformation curve. Using the basic theorem in activity analysis that competitive equilibrium yields an efficient point of production,[4] we can say that a production point that would be obtained without any MNCs is inefficient. Allowing MNCs of both types to exist pushes the whole of the transformation curve outward. The Appendix provides the derivation of the world transformation curves in the cases in which no MNCs or MNCs of one type only are allowed to exist.

We now discuss the case where L/L^* is given so that $h_2 < h_1 < L/L^*$ in Figure 3. w is fixed at unity, and p_1/p_2 under incomplete specialization is fixed at a_1/a_2. The transformation curve is just a line with the slope, $-1/(a_1/a_2)$. As shown in Figures 6 and 7, point $E(G)$, which has the pattern $X_1, H_2|P_2(X_2, H_1|P_1)$, lies on the transformation curve. The out-

[4]See McKenzie (1953–1954, p. 168).

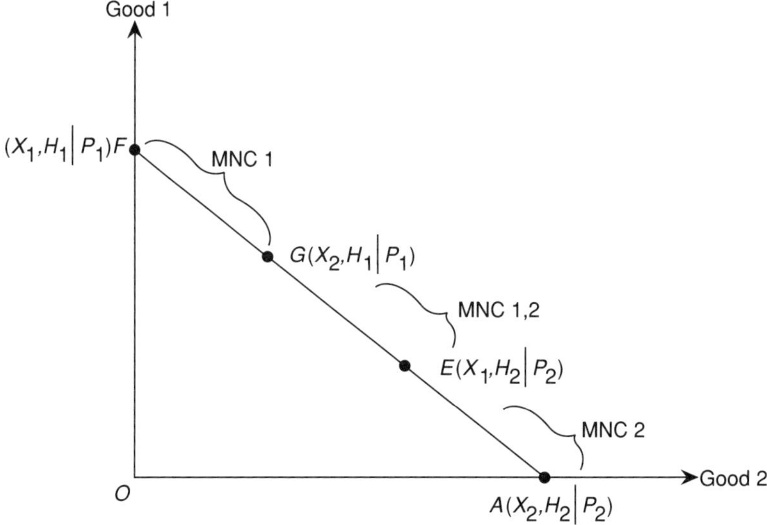

FIGURE 6 Presence of MNC 1, 2: $a_1^H/a_1^* < a_2^H/a_2^*, h_2 < h_1 < L/L^*$ and $h_1 + h_2 + 1 > L/L^*$.

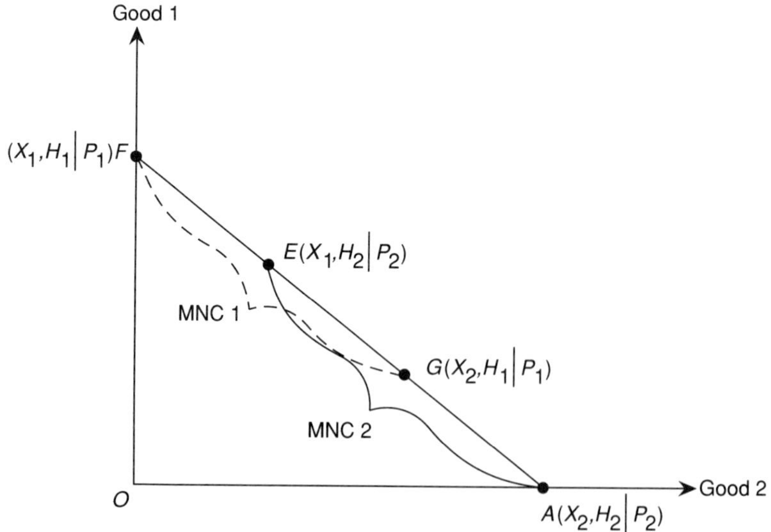

FIGURE 7 Absence of MNC 1, 2: $a_1^H/a_1^* < a_2^H/a_2^*, h_2 < h_1 < L/L^*$ and $h_1 + h_2 + 1 < L/L^*$.

puts of good 1 at E and G are given by

$$X_1 = \left(L - L^* a_2^H / a_2^P\right) / a_1 \quad \text{at } E,$$

$$X_1^M = L^* / a_1^P \quad \text{at } G.$$

Then we have

$$X_1^M \text{ at } G \gtreqless X_1 \text{ at } E \quad \text{as } h_1 + h_2 + 1 \gtreqless L/L^*.$$

Figure 6 illustrates the case in which X_1^M at $G > X_1$ at E. Points in between E and G are contained neither by MNC 1 part nor by MNC 2 part. If no MNCs are assumed to exist, we know from $w = 1$ and Figure 1 that local firms appear only in the home country. Thus, the full-employment conditions in the foreign country are not satisfied. This implies that MNC 1, 2 part emerges in between E and G. In Figure 7, X_1^M at $G < X_1$ at E. MNC 1 part overlaps with MNC 2 part between E and G. We have to decide a priori which of MNC 1 and MNC 2 appears in this overlap. Suppose that in Figure 7, L is extremely larger than L^*. Foreign labor does not relatively contribute so much to world outputs. The output of good 1 (good 2) produced by home local firms at $E(X_1, H_2|P_2)$ (at $G(X_2, H_1|P_1)$) will be very close to its world output under complete specialization. This means that MNC 1 part or MNC 2 part covers most of the transformation curve and that MNC 1, 2 part is excluded from the curve.

For the case where L/L^* is given so that $L/L^* < h_2 < h_1$ in Figure 3, the relevant locus of p_1/p_2 against w under incomplete specialization is BC in Figure 4. Figure 8 displays the transformation curve ICD. Along IC good 1 is produced only by home MNCs, since $w = w_2 < w_1$. Thus only

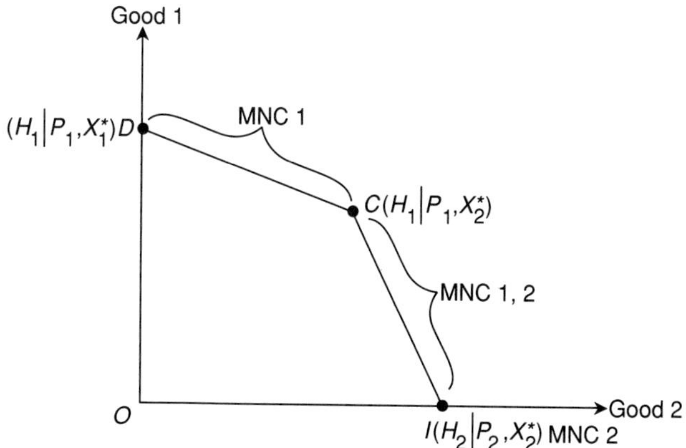

FIGURE 8 $a_1^H/a_1^* < a_2^H/a_2^*$ and $L/L^* < h_2 < h_1$.

the pattern $H_1, H_2|P_1, P_2, X_2^*$ can trace out the linear segment IC, and MNC 1, 2 part covers IC except points I and C. The linear segment CD is MNC 1 part.

We can relate Figure 8 with Figure 5 as follows. Suppose that in Figure 5 there is an increase in L^*, with L held constant. Point D moves upward and point C shifts to the right. Point B moves southeast along the L constraint

$$a_1^H X_1^M + a_2^H X_2^M = L,$$

because the L^* constraint

$$a_1^P X_1^M + a_2^P X_2^M = L^*$$

is steeper than the L constraint when $h_2 < h_1$, and shifts outward.[5] This movement is identical to the Rybczynski effect on outputs in the simple Heckscher–Ohlin model. An increase in L^* expands the output of foreign-labor-intensive good, good 2 and reduces the output of home-labor-intensive good, good 1. A large increase in L^* will move point B to the horizontal axis, and kink point B disappears. We will obtain Figure 8.

It is evident that MNC 2 (1) part is assigned to the right (left) end of the transformation curve. When there is complete specialization, home MNCs with superior technology must emerge. From Figures 5–8, we obtain the following patterns of MNCs:

$$\left.\begin{array}{c}\text{As relative world output of good 1 to good 2}\\ \text{increases under incomplete specialization,}\\ \text{there happens one pattern from among}\\ \text{MNC } 2 \to 1, 2 \to 1\\ \text{MNC } 2 \to 1\\ \text{MNC } 1, 2 \to 1.\end{array}\right\} \qquad (14)$$

As (14) shows, it is not true that home MNCs of both types always emerge, although they have an absolute advantage in both goods. In particular, MNC 1, 2 part never occurs in Figure 7 that corresponds to the second pattern in (14).[6]

Relationship (14) also suggests that home local firms in each sector have a chance to become MNCs. Strong demand for good 1 will encourage the emergence of home MNCs producing good 1. Now let us inspect changes in outputs produced by home MNCs, X_1^M and X_2^M, in the case shown in Figure 5. As is clear from (13), $X_1^M = 0$ and X_2^M is fixed when

[5]The L constraint is flatter than the segment BC in Figure 5. This is verified by comparing $(a_1^H w_2 + a_1^P)/a_2^*$ with a_1^H/a_2^H and replacing a_2^* with $a_2^H w_2 + a_2^P$.

[6]There is another typical pattern, MNC $2 \to 1, 2$. This occurs when $1 < w_1 < w_2$ and $h_2 < L/L^* < h_1$ or when $1 < w_1 < w_2$ and $L/L^* < h_2 < h_1$.

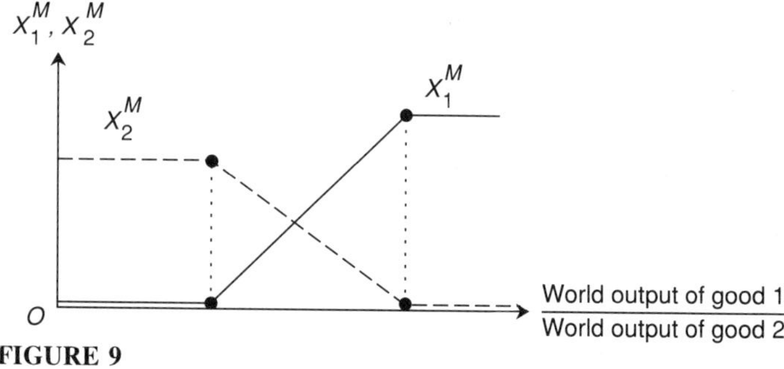

FIGURE 9

the production point moves from A to E. When it moves from E to B, the production pattern is $X_1, H_1, H_2|P_1, P_2$ in between E and B. A decrease in world output of good 2 implies a decrease in X_2^M. The full employment of foreign labor needs an increase in X_1^M. In between B and C, there is the pattern $H_1, H_2|P_1, P_2, X_2^*$. In order to increase world output of good 1, X_1^M must increase. This reduces home labor devoted to the headquarter activity of home MNCs producing good 2, leading to a decrease in X_2^M. On the linear segment CD, X_1^M is fixed and $X_2^M = 0$. Thus, in Figure 9, we can draw two curves which show how X_1^M and X_2^M change as the production point moves from right to left.[7] As illustrated in Figure 9, X_1^M tends to increase and X_2^M tends to decrease as relative world supply of good 1 to good 2 increases. There are, in general, such tendencies in other cases, also.[8]

4. CONCLUDING REMARKS

We traced out the world transformation curve and assigned the patterns of MNCs along this curve. One of our conclusions is that shifts in world demand toward one good tend to promote international operation of MNCs that have an absolute advantage in this good. The same conclusion is obtained in Dei (1991). A new feature the "asymmetric case" introduced is that MNCs may appear in both sectors simultaneously. It is quite possible that in the country with an absolute advantage in both goods,

[7]Although nonhorizontal parts of these curves are drawn as straight lines, they need not be so.

[8]We must treat Figure 6 carefully. The pattern $X_1, X_2, H_1, H_2|P_1, P_2$, which is the combination of patterns at E and G, can realize any point in between E and G on the transformation curve. Under this pattern, however, X_1^M and X_2^M are indeterminate. In order to pin them down, we now impose the minimum-types assumption on local firms as we did on MNCs. Then the production pattern becomes either $X_1, H_1, H_2|P_1, P_2$ or $X_2, H_1, H_2|P_1, P_2$ and we can see that tendencies discussed above work again.

import-competing firms as well as exporting firms under the situation where no MNCs are allowed to exist become MNCs when the world economy moves to the situation where MNCs are allowed to exist in both sectors.

As in Helpman (1984, 1985) and Helpman and Krugman (1985, Chapters 12 and 13), we assumed that there are no factor movements between countries. One who wants to make the factor movement approach might use the model in which internationally mobile capital is sector-specific and embodies technology. As is easily expected, it would be very difficult to draw the world transformation curve in such a model. In this sense, the present paper provides a very simple framework to consider MNCs. Helpman (1984, 1985) and Helpman and Krugman (1985, Chapters 12 and 13) emphasized differences in factor endowment proportions as a determinant of MNCs, but we focused on a technological gap, so that this paper is a complement to their contributions

APPENDIX: THE WORLD TRANSFORMATION CURVES WITH NO MNCs OR MNCs OF ONE TYPE ONLY

We limit our attention to the case of Figure 5 in which $a_1^H/a_1^* < a_2^H/a_2^*$ and $h_2 < L/L^* < h_1$. It will be straightforward to consider other cases which are shown by Figures 6–8.

Suppose first that MNCs can appear only in sector 1. Minimum unit cost locus for good 1 is the same as before, that is, *OABC* in Figure 1. However, the locus for good 2 is not *ODEF*, but *OGF* in Figure 1. In the case where $L/L^* < h_1$, world complete specialization in good 1 yields the production pattern $H_1|P_1, X_1^*$ at $w = w_1$, which has already been indicated by point D in Figure 5. On the other hand, when the world economy is completely specialized in good 2, point G in Figure 1 must be chosen, and $w = a_2^*/a_2$. The production point is $R(X_2|X_2^*)$ to the left of A in Figure 5, because home firms cannot utilize their absolute advantage in good 2 internationally via multinationalization.

As p_1/p_2 rises, w rises from a_2^*/a_2 to w_1. When $a_2^*/a_2 < w < w_1$, Figure 1 tells us that good 1 (2) is produced only by home MNCs (foreign local firms). This corresponds to $C(H_1|P_1, X_2^*)$ in Figure 5. Thus, the world transformation curve is *RCD*. When $w = a_2^*/a_2$, $p_1/p_2 = \{a_1^H(a_2^*/a_2) + a_1^P\}/a_2^*$ under incomplete specialization, which is smaller than a_1/a_2. This implies that *RC* is steeper than *AE*. Recall that the slope of *AE* is $-1/(a_1/a_2)$.

Consider next the transformation curve with no MNCs. As is easily expected, the transformation curve is given by *RST* in Figure 5. There is one kink $S(X_1|X_2^*)$ under our assumption that the home country has a comparative advantage in good 1 in the absence of MNCs. T must be below D. We can easily check that RS and AE (ST and CD) are parallel each other. It should be noted that the length of RS (ST) is longer than that of AE (CD), because good 1 (2) is produced more at S than at E (C). It is clear that the possibility that home firms in sector 1 become MNCs shifts the transformation curve RST outward except point R.

Finally, consider the transformation curve when MNCs can emerge only in sector 2. Minimum unit cost locus is OHC for good 1 and $ODEF$ for good 2. The restriction that $h_2 < L/L^*$ implies that the production pattern must be $X_2, H_2|P_2$ at $w = 1$ under complete specialization in good 2. This gives again point A in Figure 5. Complete specialization in good 1 yields the production pattern $X_1|X_1^*$ at $w = a_1^*/a_1$ and the production point T in Figure 5. As p_1/p_2 increases, w varies from 1 to a_1^*/a_1. Note that w_2 may or may not be larger than a_1^*/a_1. Figure 5 illustrates the case in which $w_2 < a_1^*/a_1$.

Suppose that $w_2 < a_1^*/a_1$. When $1 < w < w_2$, good 1 (2) is produced only by home local firms (home MNCs). The production pattern is $X_1, H_2|P_2$, so that the production point is E in Figure 5. When $w_2 < w < a_1^*/a_1$, good 1 (2) is produced only by home local firms (foreign local firms). We have the production point $S(X_1|X_2^*)$ in Figure 5. The transformation curve is $AEST$. We can say that allowing home MNCs to appear only in sector 2 expands the production possibility as shown by the portion AES.

When $a_1^*/a_1 < w_2$, it is easily seen that the transformation curve is AET (not drawn in Figure 5). For $1 < w < a_1^*/a_1$, the production pattern is $X_1, H_2|P_2$. Thus the transformation curve has one kink $E(X_1, H_2|P_2)$. ET is flatter than ST.

We have derived three kinds of the transformation curves, RST, RCD, and $AEST$ (AET). These clearly show that MNC 1, 2 part such as the portion EBC in Figure 5 cannot be attained unless MNCs of both types appear simultaneously, and that the transformation curve with no MNCs lies everywhere exactly inside the transformation curve when we allow MNCs of both types to exist.

Acknowledgment

I wish to thank Prof. Ronald W. Jones for helpful comments on an earlier version of this paper.

References

Caves, R. E. (1971). "International corporations: The industrial economics of foreign investment," *Economica* **38**, 1–27.

Dei, F. (1991). "Multinational corporations and absolute advantage: The symmetric case," in *Trade, Policy, and International Adjustments*, A. Takayama, M. Ohyama, and H. Ohta, (eds.) (Academic Press, San Diego), pp. 77–91.

Helpman, E. (1984). "A simple theory of international trade with multinational corporations," *J. Political Econ.* **92**, 451–471.

Helpman, E. (1985). "Multinational corporations and trade structure," *Rev. Econ. Studies* **52**, 443–457.

Helpman, E., and P. R. Krugman (1985). *Market Structure and Foreign Trade* (MIT Press, Cambridge, Mass.).

Johnson, H. G. (1957). "Factor endowments, international trade, and factor prices," *Manchester School Econ. Soc. Studies* **25**, 270–283.

McKenzie, L. W. (1953–1954). "Specialisation and efficiency in world production," *Rev. Econ. Studies* **21**, 165–180.

VARIABLE RETURNS TO SCALE AND DYNAMIC ADJUSTMENTS: THE MARSHALL–LERNER CONDITION RECONSIDERED

T. Ide
Faculty of Economics
Fukuoka University
Fukuoka 814-01, Japan

A. Takayama
Department of Economics
Southern Illinois University
Carbondale, Illinois 62901

1. INTRODUCTION

As is well known, the Marshall–Lerner (ML) condition plays an important role in the pure theory of international trade. All comparative statics results such as the effects of tariffs, transfer payments, and productivity changes obtained in the literature depend on the ML condition. The ML condition in these discussions is obtained as a stability condition of the goods market via the Walrasian price adjustment process.

On the other hand, it is known that the "Marshall–Lerner condition" is due to neither Marshall nor Lerner (cf. Kemp, 1987), and that Marshall's (1879) own discussion of this issue is via the output adjustment process instead of the price adjustment process. The rehabilitation of the Marshallian approach from this viewpoint is attempted by Amano (1968). By now, it is also known that while the price adjustment process is appropriate for the pure exchange economy, it is not appropriate for the long-run problem.[1]

[1]See, for example, Yasui (1940), Newman (1965, esp. pp. 106–108), Amano (1968), Takayama (1985, pp. 298–300), and Ide and Takayama (1991b). Given this, the description of an equilibrium as Walrasian stable but Marshallian unstable (or vice versa) is meaningless. It contains a "serious substantive error of muddling up exchange with production." (Newman, 1965, p. 107). Both Marshall (1920) and Walras (1926) had theories of production as well as those of pure exchange, and they both recognized that the price adjustment process is

GENERAL EQUILIBRIUM, GROWTH, AND TRADE II

On the other hand, no one has clarified the reason why the output adjustment process is appropriate for the long-run analysis. Our first motive of this analysis then is to narrow this gap. Among other results, we shall show, under a general equilibrium framework, that the Marshallian long-run equilibrium (LRE) is stable under the Marshallian output adjustment process *if and only if* it is stable under the capital adjustment process.[2] This then justifies the use of the stability criterion via Marshallian output adjustment, and leads us to discard the traditional ML condition. Comparative statics theorems must then be revised accordingly.

This paper proposes to rewrite that part of the pure theory of trade that deals with the "ML condition" and related comparative statics questions. In so doing, we incorporate *variable returns to scale* (VRS) that have been attracting a great deal of attention recently, as is exemplified by survey articles by Helpman (1984) and Krugman (1987).[3] This is important, since scale economies can yield a negatively sloped supply price curve,[4] in which case the stability criterion is different depending on whether we use the output adjustment process or the price adjustment process. We introduce VRS in such a way as to incorporate its recent progress. We obtain

---

appropriate for the theory of exchange and that the output adjustment process is appropriate for the theory of production. Walras emphasized the theory of exchange, while Marshall emphasized the theory of production and coined the celebrated concepts of short-run and long-run equilibria. See also Aoki (1970) for Marshallian stability. For a more complete discussion on Walrasian-vs.-Marshallian stability, see Ide and Takayama (1990).

[2]This corresponds to the results obtained elsewhere by the present authors (Ide and Takayama, 1991b), in which a similar conclusion is obtained for a small open economy with factor market distortions and/or variable returns to scale. In the present paper, prices are not given exogenously, but rather are determined endogenously.

[3]See also Jones (1968), Markusen and Melvin (1980), Panagariya (1980, 1986), Ide and Takayama (1991a, 1991b), for example. A seminal article by Graham (1923) has recently been rehabilitated by Ethier (1982) and Helpman (1984).

[4]Supposing that England exports cloth in exchange for Germany's linen, Marshall (1879, pp. 12–13) writes:

> This case has its origin in the fact that the wares which a country exports may be such that the difficulty of producing them diminishes very rapidly when their amount increases... the production of a commodity on a large scale for home consumption precedes the development of any considerable foreign trade in it... Adam Smith mentioned as one of the chief advantages of foreign trade.."
> "... it is conceivable that ... the fall in the price of cloth in England may be greater than the fall in the price of linen. Thus it is possible that an increase in Germany's demand for English cloth may cause each yard of linen to be sold here on such terms as to give command over a larger amount of cloth than before; it is possible that an increase in Germany's demand of English cloth may cause hereto obtain an import of English cloth increased *in a greater ratio* than is her export of linen to England.

Thus, the supply price curve of cloth vis à vis linen is negatively sloped.

the proper stability condition for the international equilibrium that replaces the traditional ML condition,[5] and then we obtain comparative statics results. We illustrate this by way of a shift of tastes and a unilateral transfer. The former was discussed by Marshall (1879) following Adam Smith's discussion in his *Wealth of Nations*. We show that the Smith–Marshall result is correct, *if* we use the Marshallian stability criterion. Our transfer results are quite different from the traditional ones. For example:

(a) The terms of trade can move *against* the recipient country when the transfer condition is satisfied.
(b) The donor (resp. recipient) country can become *better off* (resp. *worse off*).

Unlike the traditional discussion, we shall show that these conclusions can be obtained even when the equilibrium is stable.

A brief summary of the paper is in order now. Section 2 presents the basic model. Section 3 analyzes the stability of temporary equilibrium and LRE. Section 4 relates the stability of the LRE under the output adjustment process to that under the capital adjustment process. Section 5 obtains the stability condition for the international equilibrium. Sections 6 and 7 analyze comparative statics questions, the effects of a change in tastes and of a transfer. The paper is completed with two technical appendices.

2. MODEL[6]

Write the production functions of two outputs, X and Y, as

$$X = F(L_X, K_X, X), \qquad Y = G(L_Y, K_Y, Y), \tag{1}$$

where L_j and K_j, respectively, denote labor and capital inputs in the jth sector ($j = X, Y$). Functions F and G are linear homogeneous in labor and capital inputs. The arguments X and Y in F and G capture VRS, which we assume to be exogenous to the individual firms but internal to the industry. Let a_{ij} denote the quantity of factor i required to produce one unit of good j. Then, the full-employment conditions are given by

$$a_{LX}X + a_{LY}Y = L, \qquad a_{KX}X + a_{KY}Y = K. \tag{2}$$

Let w and r, respectively, denote the real wage rate and the real rate of return on capital, and let p be the relative price of X, where Y is taken

[5] Amano (1968) clarifies Chipman's (1965) question as to the logical consistency of Marshall's analysis. Amano (1968) also offers a critical review of Kemp's study on this topic (1964, chapter 5).

[6] The model and notations are more or less standard (see Jones, 1965, 1968).

as the numéraire. Then the zero profit conditions are written as

$$a_{LX}w + a_{KX}r = p, \qquad a_{LY}w + a_{KY}r = 1. \tag{3}$$

The coefficients of production, a_{ij} values are chosen via the usual cost minimization procedure. Let σ_j signify the elasticity of factor substitution of industry $j(j = x, y)$, and let ω denote the wage–rental rate (w/r). Then letting θ_{ij} denote the ith cost share of industry j, and denoting the rate of change by $(\hat{\ })$, we have

$$\hat{a}_{LX} = -\theta_{KX}\sigma_x\hat{\omega} - R_{LX}\hat{X}, \qquad \hat{a}_{KX} = \theta_{LX}\sigma_x\hat{\omega} - R_{KX}\hat{X}, \tag{4a}$$

$$\hat{a}_{LY} = -\theta_{KY}\sigma_y\hat{\omega} - R_{LY}\hat{Y}, \qquad \hat{a}_{KY} = \theta_{LY}\sigma_y\hat{\omega} - R_{KY}\hat{Y}, \tag{4b}$$

where $R_{iX} \equiv -(X/a_{ix})(\partial a_{ix}/\partial X)$ and $R_{iY} \equiv -(Y/a_{iY})(\partial a_{iY}/\partial Y)$, $i = L, K$. Let AC_j and MC_j, respectively, denote the average cost and marginal cost of industry j. Then $\rho_j \equiv AC_j/MC_j > 0$ signifies the output elasticity of cost for industry j. Increasing or decreasing returns to scale prevail in industry j, depending on whether $\rho_j > 1$ or $\rho_j < 1$. (cf. Ide and Takayama, 1989). Constant returns to scale prevail if and only if $\rho_j = 1$. We call ρ_j the *degree of returns* for the industry j. Under the assumption of cost minimization, we may compute[7]

$$\rho_j = 1/(1 - R_j), \quad \text{where } R_j \equiv \theta_{Lj}R_{Lj} + \theta_{Kj}R_{Kj}.$$

It is evident that R_j is monotonically related to ρ_j, where R_j $(j = X, Y)$ is the measure of degree of returns introduced by Jones (1968).

Equations (2)–(4) exhaust all the important conditions that describe the supply side of the model. The basic relations among price and outputs are obtained as (see Appendix A):

$$\hat{p} = A\hat{Z}/\mu, \tag{5a}$$

$$\hat{X} = (\mu_X/\mu)\hat{Z}, \qquad \hat{Y} = -(\mu_Y/\mu)\hat{Z}, \tag{5b}$$

where $Z \equiv X/Y$, $\mu_X > 0$, $\mu_Y > 0$, and $\mu \equiv \mu_X + \mu_Y > 0$. Equation (5a) states that p increases or decreases as Z increases or decreases if and only if $A > 0$. Equation (5b) states that X increases and Y decreases as Z increases.

[7]Let $C_X(w, r, X)$ and $AC_X(w, r, X)$, respectively, denote the total and the average cost functions of industry X. Then noting $C_X(\cdot) = AC_X(\cdot)X$ and $AC_X(\cdot) = wa_{LX}(w, r, X) + ra_{KX}(w, r, X)$, a simple calculation yields $\rho_X = 1/(1 - R_X)$. Similarly, we can obtain $\rho_Y = 1/(1 - R_Y)$. To ensure $MC_j > 0$, we require $\rho_j > 0$. It is evident that $R_j < 0$ and $0 < R_j < 1$ depending on whether $0 < \rho_j < 1$ or $\rho_j > 1$, and that $R_j = 0$ if and only if $\rho_j = 1$. We can further show that $\rho_j > 1$ if and only if the AC_j curve is falling as the output of j increases. Namely, the definition of VRS in terms of ρ_j corresponds to Marshall's (1920) definition of scale economies in terms of falling average cost curves.

To obtain a graphic representation of (5), we recall the usual production possibility frontier (PPF), which we write as

$$Y = Y(X), \bar{Y} \equiv Y(0), 0 = Y(\bar{X}), \tag{6}$$

where $\bar{X}$ and $\bar{Y}$, respectively, signify the complete specialization values of X and Y. The relation $Y = Y(X)$ signifies the PPF for the case of incomplete specialization. The *marginal rate of transformation* (MRT) between the two commodities is defined by MRT $\equiv -dY/dX > 0$.

We can obtain the following relation (cf. Ide and Takayama, 1991b, p. 151).

$$p = \rho \cdot \text{MRT}, \quad \text{where } \rho \equiv \rho_X/\rho_Y > 0. \tag{7}$$

Similar relations have been obtained in the literature under much more restrictive assumptions.

Equation (7) implies that the price line is no longer tangent to the PPF except for the case of $\rho = 1$, i.e., when the degree of returns is the same between the two industries (e.g., Heckscher–Ohlin models); ρ need *not* be constant.[8]

When ρ *is* constant, the value of p can easily be inferred from MRT by (7). In this case, the PPF is strictly concave (resp. convex) to the origin, p and MRT increase (resp. decrease) as the value of X increases. The shape of the PPF can change from strictly concave to strictly convex, or conversely, at certain points (called the *inflection points*) of the PPF. In this case, $\hat{p}/\hat{X}$ and $\hat{p}/\hat{Z}$ change their sign. If constant returns to scale prevail in both industries, then the PPF is strictly concave for *all* $X > 0$ and $Y > 0$.

Observation. Assume that ρ is constant. Then the PPF is locally strictly concave (resp. convex) to the origin if and only if $A > 0$ (resp. $A < 0$).

The shape of the PPF under VRS is studied in the literature. For example, Herberg and Kemp (1969) showed that if both production functions are homothetic, and if increasing returns to scale prevail in sector X (with a constant ρ_X) and constant returns to scale prevail in section Y, then the PPF is bowed in toward the origin in a neighborhood of $X = 0$. Markusen and Melvin (1981, p. 458) noted that if the elasticities of factor substitution are different between the two industries, then there can be more than one inflection point.

In Figure 1, we illustrate the relation between p and the MRT, assuming that $\rho > 1$ always (so that $p >$ MRT) and that the PPF is uniformly bowed in toward the origin. In this case, the MRT decreases as X (or Z) increases.

[8]This is the source of Panagariya's (1980) criticism of Jones (1968). See Ide and Takayama (1991b, p. 132) for a clarification of the issue in this debate.

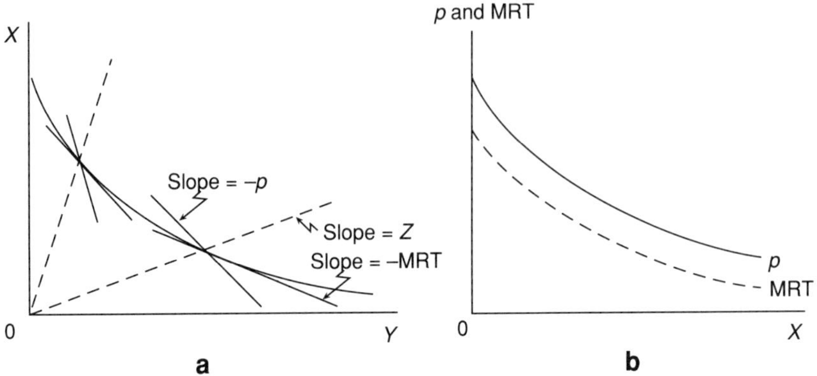

FIGURE 1 The relation between p and MRT.

The p value shown in Figure 1 is obtained from the supply side of the economy, and we call it the *long-run* (LR) supply price. It is that p that is compatible with the conditions of full employment (2), efficient allocation of resources (4), and zero profit (3). It is the price at which producers are just breaking even. It corresponds to Marshall's long-run supply price except that the our p is obtained in a general equilibrium framework. It is "long-run" in the sense that the wage rate and the rate of return on capital are equalized between the sectors. Denoting the LR supply relation by $p_L(X)$, we obtain

$$\hat{p}_L = A\hat{X}/\mu_X. \tag{8}$$

The inverse relation of $p_L(X)$, $X = X_L(p)$, signifies the usual "long-run supply curve." Since $\mu_X > 0$, it follows from (8) that $\hat{p}_L/\hat{X} \gtrless 0$ according to whether $A \gtrless 0$. We define the elasticity of LR supply price by

$$e \equiv (dp_L/p)/(dX/X) = A/\mu_X. \tag{9}$$

thus, $e > 0$ or $e < 0$, depending on whether $A > 0$ or $A < 0$.

3. STABILITY OF TEMPORARY AND LONG-RUN EQUILIBRIUM

We now introduce the demand side of the economy. Let $D_i(p, I)$ denote the demand for the ith commodity ($i = x, y$), where I signifies income, i.e., $I \equiv pX + Y$. The budget condition of this economy is written as

$$pD_x(p, I) + Dy(p, I) \equiv pX + Y(\equiv I). \tag{10}$$

The equilibrium conditions are given by $D_x = X$ and $D_y = Y$, one of which is superfluous by virtue of (10).

Following Marshall (1920), we define the temporary equilibrium as the equilibrium in which the adjustment time is short enough so that the output levels can be taken as a constant. For the adjustment process, both Walras and Marshall assert that the price adjustment process is appropriate. Thus

$$\dot{p} = a_0[D_x(p, pX + Y)/X - 1] \equiv f(p), \tag{11}$$

where X and Y are constants, and a_0 is a positive adjustment coefficient. Assume that there exists a $p^* > 0$ such that $f(p^*) = 0$. Such a p^* signifies the temporary equilibrium. Note that p^* is globally stale if $f'(p) < 0$ for all p.

To obtain the stability property of the temporary equilibrium, we first define the elasticity of temporary demand by

$$\eta^* \equiv -\frac{p}{D_x}\frac{\partial D_x}{\partial p}_{|X, Y = \text{const.}} \tag{12}$$

p^* is globally stable if $\eta^* > 0$ for all p. By definition of η^*, we may assert

$$\eta^* = -\frac{p}{D_x}\left[\frac{\partial D_x}{\partial p} + X\frac{\partial D_x}{\partial I}\right]. \tag{13}$$

Let $D_x^*(p, u)$ be the compensated demand function of good X for a given level of utility u. Then consider the following identity for duality.

$$D_x^*(p, u) = D_x[p, E(p, u)],$$

where $E(p, u)$ is the minimum expenditure function. Differentiating this with respect to p and utilizing the Shephard (–McKenzie) lemma,[9] we obtain

$$\partial D_x^*/\partial p = \partial D_x/\partial p + D_x(\partial D_x/\partial I). \tag{14}$$

Since $D_x = X$ in equilibrium, we may obtain from (13) and (14):

$$\eta^* = -\frac{p}{D_x}\frac{\partial D_x^*}{\partial p}, \tag{15}$$

where $\eta^* > 0$ for all p since $\partial D_x^*/\partial p < 0$ for all p. From this, we may conclude the following.

PROPOSITION 1. *The temporary equilibrium is asymptotically globally stable.*

[9]The Shephard (–McKenzie) lemma states that $\partial E/\partial p = D_x^*$ (see Takayama, 1985, Section 1.F). Note that (14) corresponds to the Slutsky equation.

We now introduce the adjustment process that involves changes in output levels. To this end, write the demand function as

$$D_x[p, pX + Y(X)],$$

where $Y(X)$ is the usual PPF relation. The difficulty of specifying the demand function here is that income I depends on the output levels, and, without specifying such levels, income becomes indeterminate, and so does the amount demanded. To avoid this difficulty, which can lead to circular reasoning, we assume that the public expects the realization of equilibrium in the market and obtains the value of X from which the public obtains the value of income by $I \equiv pX + Y(X)$. This means the public obtains the value of X from

$$D_x[p, pX + Y(X)] = X. \tag{16}$$

We then ask the question of whether such expectations will indeed be realized, i.e., whether the equilibrium based on such expectations will actually happen. If the answer to this is affirmative, we obtain rational expectations.[10]

Relating X and p by (16), we obtain

$$p = p_D(X), \tag{17}$$

which we call the *demand price*. It corresponds to Marshall's demand price, the maximum price that consumers are willing to pay, except that it is recast into a general equilibrium framework. Define the elasticity of demand price by

$$\eta \equiv -\frac{X}{p}\frac{dp_D}{dX}. \tag{18}$$

Differentiating (16) and utilizing (7), we may obtain the relation

$$\eta = \alpha/\eta^*, \quad \text{where } \alpha \equiv 1 - m + m/\rho, \tag{19}$$

and where $m \equiv p\,\partial D_x/\partial I$.[11] The parameter m signifies the marginal propensity to consume commodity X. Since $1 - m > 0$[12] and $\rho > 0$, α is always positive. Then $\eta > 0$ by (19), since $\eta^* > 0$. Namely, the demand price curve, which incorporates changes in the output levels, is also

[10]This corresponds to the approach taken by Amano (1968). An alternative approach is to assume homothetic demands. In this case, there is no income term, and the procedure of utilizing an equilibrium condition to obtain the demand condition can be avoided. The results for such a case are completely analogous to those in the present analysis.

[11]Since I is defined in terms of commodity Y, $p(\partial D_x/\partial I)$ is a quantity that has no dimensions. Since ρ has no dimensions, m/ρ has no dimensions, either.

[12]Differentiating (10) with respect to I, we obtain $m + (\partial D_y/\partial I) = 1$. Hence, assuming that Y is not an inferior good, we obtain $1 - m > 0$.

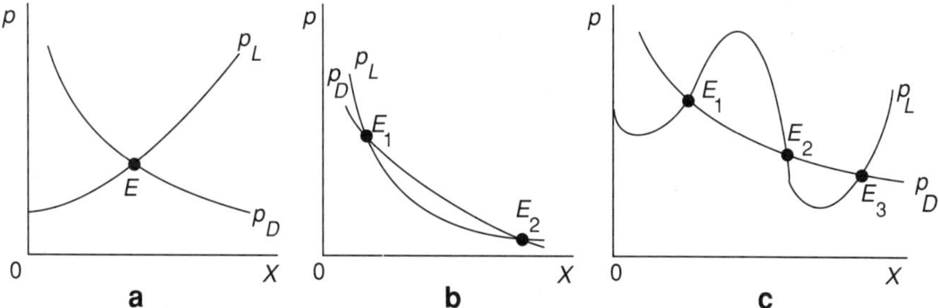

FIGURE 2 Marshallian stability of long-run equilibria.

negatively sloped. If the degree of returns is the same between the two industries, then $\rho = \alpha = 1$, and $\eta = 1/\eta^*$.

We now consider the Marshallian output adjustment process[13]

$$\dot{X} = a_1[p_D(X)/p_L(X) - 1] \equiv \phi(X), \tag{20}$$

where a_1 is a positive adjustment coefficient. Assume that there exists an $X^* > 0$ such that $\phi(X^*) = 0$. Note that X^* signifies a *long-run equilibrium* (LRE). Assuming away the knife-edge case of $\phi'(X^*) = 0$, LRE is asymptotically locally stable under (20) if and only if $\phi'(X^*) < 0$. Such stability is called the *Marshallian stability*. Recalling (9) and (18), we may easily conclude that $\phi'(X^*) < 0$ if and only if $\eta + e > 0$. Thus we may obtain the following result.

PROPOSITION 2. *The LRE X^* is locally Marshallian stable if and only if $\eta + e > 0$, where η and e are evaluated at X^*.*

We illustrate Marshallian stability in Figure 2, where p_D and p_L signify the demand price and the supply price curves, respectively. The p_D curve is always negatively sloped since $\eta > 0$ always. The p_L curve is positively or negatively sloped depending on whether $e > 0$ or $e < 0$. In Figure 2(a), E is a unique equilibrium that is globally Marshallian stable. In Figure 2(b), E_1 is Marshallian unstable, and E_2 is locally Marshallian stable. In Figure 2(c), E_1 and E_3 are locally Marshallian stable, whereas E_2 is unstable.

[13]This corresponds to Aoki's (1970) exposition of the Marshallian process, where he states, "Suppose that an industry with excess of supply price over demand price expands and an industry with excess of demand price over supply price contracts" (p. 100). His actual formulation (p. 106) is more complicated.

4. OUTPUT ADJUSTMENT AND CAPITAL ADJUSTMENT PROCESSES

In the very short-run, output levels stay constant, and Walrasian price adjustment will bring the economy to the temporary equilibrium. Then reflecting sectoral gap in the wage rates, the labor moves between the sectors and the output levels change accordingly. The economy is thus brought into the short-run equilibrium (SRE). Then, reflecting the sectoral gap in the rates of return on capital, capital moves between the sectors and the output levels change accordingly, where it is assumed that SRE is achieved instantaneously along this process, if this process is stable, the economy is brought into the LRE. Letting r_x and r_y, respectively, denote the real rates of return in the X and Y industries, we postulate the following capital adjustment process leading to the LRE.

$$\dot{K}_X = a_2\left[r_x/r_y - 1\right], \tag{21}$$

where a_2 is a positive adjustment coefficient. When this adjustment process is allowed to work itself out, the real rate of return on capital (as well as the wage rate) is equalized between the sectors, i.e., we obtain a LRE.[14]

Our task now is to relate the stability of process (21) to the Marshallian stability condition. Using the model in Section 2, we may express the right-hand side of (21) as a function of K_X alone. We may then define the function Φ by

$$\Phi(K_X) \equiv a_2\left[r_x(K_X)/r_y(K_X) - 1\right]. \tag{22}$$

Assume that there exists a $K_X^* > 0$ such that $\Phi(K_X^*) = 0$. K_X^* is a LRE value of K_X. Assuming away the knife-edge case of $\Phi'(K_X^*) = 0$, we may assert that K_X^* is asymptotically locally stable if and only if $\Phi'(K_X^*) < 0$. The expression for $\Phi'(K_X^*)$ can be obtained as shown in Appendix B [cf. equation (B.15)] as

$$\Phi'(K_X^*) = a_2\left[\hat{r}_x/\hat{K}_X - \hat{r}_y/\hat{K}_X\right]\Big/K_X^*$$

$$= -a_2(\eta + e)\mu_X\rho_X\rho_Y/(\lambda_{KY}B_0K_X^*), \tag{23}$$

where the expression for B_0 is given in (B.11). Given $B_0 > 0$, $\Phi'(K_X^*) < 0$ if and only if $\eta + e > 0$. Hence, recalling Proposition 2, we may obtain the following.

[14]The use of the term "long-run" is perfectly consistent with the Marshallian sense (e.g., see Neary, 1978, p. 672).

PROPOSITION 3. *Assume $B_0 > 0$. Then the LRE is stable under process* (20) *if and only if it is stable under process* (21). *The stability condition of these two processes is both given by $\eta + e > 0$.*

In Appendix B, we shall show that $B_0 > 0$ under a plausible assumption. Then Proposition 3 states that the LRE is stable under the Marshallian output adjustment process if and only if it is stable under the capital adjustment process. The Marshallian adjustment process via the LR supply price curve can be viewed as the shadow of the capital adjustment process projected onto the screen of the output space. The capital adjustment mechanism thus provides a micro foundation for the Marshallian adjustment process leading to the LRE.[15]

5. REHABILITATION OF THE MARSHALLIAN APPROACH

5.1 Preliminaries: International Equilibrium

We consider two countries (A and B) and assume that country A exports good Y and imports good X. Let D_{ij} denote country j's demand for good $i(=x, y)$, and let X_j and Y_j, respectively, denote country j's output of X and Y. Let M_i be country i's import demand, i.e., $M_a \equiv D_{xa} - X_a$, $M_b \equiv D_{yb} - Y_b$. The equilibrium conditions of the two commodities are written as[16]

$$D_{xa} + D_{xb} = X_a + X_b, \qquad D_{ya} + D_{yb} = Y_a + Y_b,$$

one of which is superfluous by Walras' law. Using the budget condition of each country, the preceding equilibrium conditions can equivalently be written as

$$pM_a = M_b. \tag{24}$$

[15]Following Neary's (1978) analysis of factor market distortions (FMDs), we may consider the adjustment process in which both factors adjust. Namely,

$$\dot{L}_X = c_0\left[w_x(L_X, K_X)/w_y(L_X, K_X) - 1\right], \qquad \dot{K}_X = c_1\left[r_x(L_X, K_X)/r_y(L_X, K_X) - 1\right].$$

Taking a linear approximation of this system, we can show that the determinant condition is satisfied if and only if $\eta + e > 0$, while the trace condition is *not* satisfied. Thus, the stability of the capital adjustment process is necessary but *not* sufficient for the stability of the two-factor adjusting process. This conclusion can be contrasted to Neary's (1978) result (in the context of factor market distortions) that the stability conditions of the two processes are equivalent, which in turn implies that the Marshallian distinction of short run and long run is *not* important.

[16]The budget conditions, $pD_{xa} + D_{ya} = pX_a + Y_a$, $pD_{xb} + D_{yb} = pX_b + Y_b$, yield "Walras' law," namely, $p[(D_{xa} + D_{xb}) - (X_a + X_b)] + [(D_{ya} + D_{yb}) - (Y_a + Y_b)] = 0$.

Country A's and country B's demand functions of imported goods are specified by

$$D_{xa} = D_{xa}(p, I_a),\ D_{yb} = D_{yb}(1/p, I_b), \tag{25}$$

where I_a and I_b are defined by $I_a \equiv pX_a + Y_a$, $I_b \equiv X_b + Y_b/p$. Note that I_a is measured in terms of commodity Y, and I_b is measured in terms of commodity X; i.e., each country's income is measured in terms of its exports. Assuming incomplete specialization, we write the PPF relations as

$$X_a = X_a(Y_a), \qquad Y_b = Y_b(X_b), \tag{26}$$

Now recall (7), and write country j's long-run supply price as p^j, where we omit subscript L for simplicity. Then we have the relations

$$p^a = -\rho_a/X_a'(Y_a), \qquad p^b = -\rho_b Y_b'(X_b), \quad \text{where } \rho_j \equiv \rho_X^j/\rho_Y^j, \tag{27}$$

where $\rho_a = \rho_a(Y_a)$ and $\rho_b = \rho_b(X_b)$, so that we have $p^a = p^a(Y_a)$ and $p^b = p^b(X_b)$.

5.2 The Temporary Equilibrium

The temporary (international) equilibrium is the one in which $pM_a = M_b$ holds when the output levels of both commodities in each country stay constant. We consider the following Walrasian price adjustment process.[17]

$$\dot{p} = b_0(M_a - M_b/p), \tag{28}$$

where b_0 is a positive adjustment coefficient. Since X_a, Y_a, X_b, and Y_b are constants, M_a and M_b are functions of p alone. Thus we have

$$\dot{p} = b_0[M_a^*(p) - M_b^*(1/p)/p] \equiv M^*(p). \tag{29}$$

Assume that there exists a $p^* > 0$ such that $M^*(p^*) = 0$, where p^* signifies the temporary equilibrium price ratio. Assuming away the knife-edge case of $dM^*/dp = 0$, p^* is asymptotically locally stable if and only if $dM^*/dp < 0$. Define the elasticities of import demand *with constant outputs* for countries A and B by

$$\eta_a^* \equiv -\frac{p}{M_a}\frac{dM_a^*}{dp}, \qquad \eta_b^* \equiv -\frac{1/p}{M_b}\frac{dM_b^*}{d(1/p)}. \tag{30}$$

[17]We may note that $M_a - M_b/p = (D_{xa} + D_{xb}) - (X_a + X_b)$.

The expressions for η_a^* and η_b^* are obtained as

$$\eta_a^* = -\frac{p}{M_a}\left(\frac{\partial D_{xa}}{\partial p} + X_a \frac{\partial D_{xa}}{\partial I_a}\right), \qquad \eta_b^* = -\frac{(1/p)}{M_b}\left[\frac{\partial D_{yb}}{\partial(1/p)} + Y_b \frac{\partial D_{yb}}{\partial I_b}\right]. \tag{31}$$

From the definition of η_a^* and η_b^* in (30), we can easily assert that $dM^*/dp < 0$ if and only if $\eta_a^* + \eta_b^* - 1 > 0$. Thus, we obtain the following result.

PROPOSITION 4. *The temporary international equilibrium is stable if and only if* $\eta_a^* + \eta_b^* - 1 > 0$.

Since it is meaningless to discuss the Marshallian stability unless the temporary equilibrium is achieved, we henceforth assume $\eta_a^* + \eta_b^* > 1$.

5.3 Marshallian Stability for the Long-Run Equilibrium

To investigate the output adjustment process, we need to obtain the demand price relation. Using the same argument as that used earlier, we consider the following equilibrium condition by way of (24):

$$p\{D_{xa}[p, pX_a(Y_a) + Y_a] - X_a(Y_a)\}$$
$$= D_{yb}[1/p, X_b + Y_b(X_b)/p] - Y_b(X_b). \tag{32}$$

This equation determines p for given values of Y_a and X_b. We call such a p the *demand price* for the two-country model. We then assume that (32) yields the following functional relation, which is the desired demand price relation:

$$p = p_D(Y_a, X_b). \tag{33}$$

Differentiating (32) and recalling (27) and (31), we obtain

$$\Delta^* dp = (\alpha_a\, dY_a - p\alpha_b\, dX_b)/M_a. \tag{34}$$

Here Δ^*, α_a, and α_b are defined by[18]

$$\Delta^* \equiv \eta_a^* + \eta_b^* - 1 > 0, \tag{35a}$$

$$\alpha_a \equiv m_a + (1 - m_a)\rho_a > 0, \qquad \alpha_b \equiv m_b + (1 - m_b)/\rho_b > 0, \tag{35b}$$

$$m_a \equiv p(\partial D_{xa}/\partial I_a), \qquad m_b \equiv (1/p)(\partial D_{yb}/\partial I_b),^{19} \tag{35c}$$

[18]Note that if the degrees of return are the same between the two industries, we have $\rho = 1$. If $\rho_a = 1$, then $\alpha_a = 1$; and if $\rho_b = 1$, then $\alpha_b = 1$.

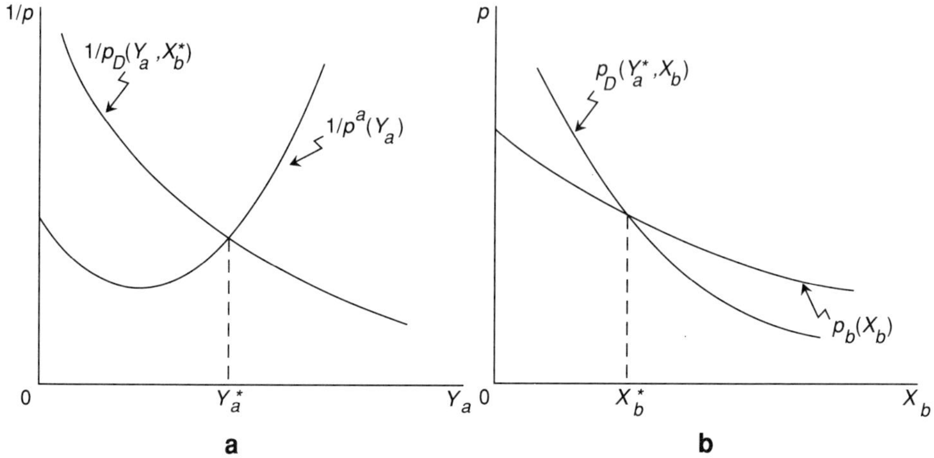

FIGURE 3 An illustration of international equilibrium for (a) country A and (b) country B.

where m_i signifies the country i's marginal propensity to consume the imported good. If the degree of returns is the same between the two industries for each country ($\rho_a = \rho_b = 1$), then $\alpha_a = 1$ and $\alpha_b = 1$, which corresponds to the traditional result. From (34) and (35), we may obtain the following result:

$$\partial p_D/\partial Y_a = \alpha_a/(\Delta^* M_a) > 0, \qquad \partial p_D/\partial X_b = -p\alpha_b/(\Delta^* M_a) < 0. \quad (36)$$

Using (36) and the supply curve relations, we may illustrate the international equilibrium. Figure 3(a) illustrates the equilibrium for country A, while Figure 3(b) illustrates the equilibrium for country B. Note that we have $\hat{Y}_a/\hat{p}^a < 0$ and $\hat{X}_b/\hat{p}^b < 0$ at the point of international equilibrium.

We now write the Marshallian output adjustment process as[20]

$$\dot{Y}_a = b_{1a}\left[\frac{1}{p_D(Y_a, X_b)} - \frac{1}{p^a(Y_a)}\right] \equiv \pi_a(Y_a, X_b), \qquad (37a)$$

$$\dot{X}_b = b_{1b}\left[p_D(Y_a, X_b) - p^b(X_b)\right] \equiv \pi_b(Y_a, X_b), \qquad (37b)$$

[19]The multiplication or division by p here is to make m_a and m_b dimensionless. Note also that since we have $pD_{xa}(p, I_a) + D_{ya}(p, I_a) = I_a$ and $D_{xb}(1/p, I_b) + D_{yb}(1/p, I_b)/p = I_b$, we can assert $1 - m_a = \partial D_{ya}/\partial I_a$ and $1 - m_b = \partial D_{xb}/\partial I_b$. Hence assuming away inferior goods, we have $1 - m_a > 0$ and $1 - m_b > 0$.

[20]Here we follow Amano (1968) in stating the adjustment process to facilitate the comparison. Alternatively, we may write it in the "ratio" form as before:

$$\dot{Y}_a = b_{1a}\left[p^a(Y_a)/p_D(p_a, X_b) - 1\right], \qquad \dot{X}_b = b_{1b}\left[p_D(Y_a, X_b)/p^b(X_b) - 1\right].$$

The stability conditions of (37) and the above system are equivalent.

where b_{1a} and b_{1b} are positive adjustment coefficients. Performing the Taylor expansion on the right-hand side of (37a) and (37b) about the equilibrium point (Y_a^*, X_b^*) and ignoring the second-order or higher-order terms, we obtain a system of linear differential equations. Setting $b_{1a} = b_{1b} = 1$ by the choice of units, the coefficient matrix of such a system can be written as

$$J = \begin{bmatrix} -\dfrac{1}{p^2}\dfrac{\partial p_D}{\partial Y_a} + \dfrac{1}{p^2}\dfrac{dp^a}{dY_a} & -\dfrac{1}{p^2}\dfrac{\partial p_D}{\partial X_b} \\ \dfrac{\partial p_D}{\partial Y_a} & \dfrac{\partial p_D}{\partial X_b} - \dfrac{dp^b}{dX_b} \end{bmatrix}. \tag{38}$$

Define the *elasticities of export supply* in the usual manner by

$$\epsilon_a \equiv -\frac{p}{M_b}\frac{dY_a}{dp}, \qquad \epsilon_b \equiv \frac{p}{M_a}\frac{dX_b}{dp}. \tag{39}$$

For the traditional constant-returns-to-scale case, $A > 0$ for both countries, so that we obtain $\epsilon_a > 0$ and $\epsilon_b > 0$ by (8). In general, ϵ_i can be either positive or negative. Figure 3 depicts the cases of $\epsilon_a > 0$ and $\epsilon_b < 0$.

Using (27), (31), and (39), we may rewrite (38) as

$$J = \begin{bmatrix} -(1/\epsilon_a + \alpha_a/\Delta^*)/(pM_b) & \alpha_b/(M_b\Delta^*) \\ \alpha_a/(M_a\Delta^*) & -p^2(1/\epsilon_b + \alpha_b/\Delta^*)/M_b \end{bmatrix}. \tag{40}$$

The trace and the determinant of J can be obtained as

$$\text{trace } J = -\frac{1}{M_b}\left[\frac{1}{p}\left(\frac{\alpha_a}{\Delta^*} + \frac{1}{\epsilon_a}\right) + p^2\left(\frac{\alpha_b}{\Delta^*} + \frac{1}{\epsilon_b}\right)\right], \tag{41a}$$

$$\det J = \frac{1}{M_a M_b}\left[\frac{1}{\Delta^*}\left(\frac{\alpha_a}{\epsilon_b} + \frac{\alpha_b}{\epsilon_a}\right) + \left(\frac{1}{\epsilon_a\epsilon_b}\right)\right]. \tag{41b}$$

The equilibrium (Y_a^*, X_b^*) for the linear system is stable if and only if

$$\text{trace } J < 0 \quad \text{and} \quad \det J > 0. \tag{42}$$

Now define the familiar "elasticity of offer curve." To this end, observe

$$M_a \equiv D_{xa}[p, pX_a(Y_a) + Y_a] - X_a(Y_a), \tag{43a}$$

$$M_b \equiv D_{yb}[1/p, X_b + Y_b(X_b)/p] - Y_b(X_b). \tag{43b}$$

Since Y_a and X_b are related to p by the supply price curve relations, we may consider M_a and M_b to be functions of p alone. We then define the elasticities of import demand (elasticities of offer curve) for countries A and B (in the usual way) by[21]

$$\eta_a \equiv \frac{-p}{M_a}\frac{dM_a}{dp}, \qquad \eta_b \equiv \frac{-(1/p)}{M_b}\frac{dM_b}{d(1/p)}. \tag{44}$$

Using (27), (31), (35), (39), and (43), we may obtain the relations

$$\eta_a = \eta_a^* + \alpha_a \epsilon_a, \qquad \eta_b \equiv \eta_b^* + \alpha_b \epsilon_b, \tag{45}$$

where $\alpha_a > 0$ and $\alpha_b > 0$. Define $\Delta \equiv \eta_a + \eta_b - 1$. Then from (45), we obtain

$$\Delta = \Delta^* + \alpha_a \epsilon_a + \alpha_b \epsilon_b. \tag{46}$$

Using this, we may rewrite (trace J) and (det J) as follows:

$$\text{trace } J = \frac{-1}{M_b \Delta^*}\left[\frac{1}{p\epsilon_a}(\Delta - \alpha_b \epsilon_b) + \frac{p^2}{\epsilon_b}(\Delta - \alpha_a \epsilon_a)\right], \tag{47a}$$

$$\det J = \Delta/(M_a M_b \epsilon_a \epsilon_b \Delta^*). \tag{47b}$$

From this, we may obtain the following important conclusion.

Proposition 5. *The equilibrium* (Y_a^*, X_b^*) *for the linear approximation system for* (37) *is stable if and only if either of the following two conditions holds*:

$$\epsilon_a > 0 \quad \text{and} \quad \epsilon_b > 0, \tag{48a}$$

$$\epsilon_a \epsilon_b < 0 \quad \text{and} \quad \Delta < 0. \tag{48b}$$

Proof. Suppose that (48a) holds. Then $\Delta > 0$ by (46), so that trace $J < 0$ by (47a) and det $J > 0$ by (47b). Now suppose that (48b) holds. Suppose further that $\epsilon_a < 0$ and $\epsilon_b > 0$. Then we have det $J > 0$, and

$$(\Delta - \alpha_b \epsilon_b)/\epsilon_a > 0 \quad \text{and} \quad (\Delta - \alpha_a \epsilon_a)/\epsilon_b = (\Delta^* + \alpha_b \epsilon_b)/\epsilon_b > 0.$$

Therefore, trace $J < 0$. The same argument applies when $\epsilon_a > 0$ and $\epsilon_b < 0$.

To prove the converse, we show that an equilibrium is *un*stable if either of the following two conditions is satisfied:

$$\epsilon_a < 0 \quad \text{and} \quad \epsilon_b < 0, \tag{49a}$$

$$\Delta > 0 \quad \text{and} \quad \epsilon_a \epsilon_b < 0. \tag{49b}$$

[21]Notations η_a and η_b do not correspond to η for the closed economy; η_a and η_b are defined in the usual manner that appears in the literature.

First suppose that (49a) holds, in which case $\epsilon_a \epsilon_b > 0$. Then by (47b), $\det J > 0$ requires $\Delta > 0$. Then by (44), we must have

$$\Delta^* + \alpha_a \epsilon_a > -\alpha_b \epsilon_b > 0, \qquad \Delta^* + \alpha_b \epsilon_b > -\alpha_a \epsilon_a > 0,$$

which implies trace $J > 0$, and hence the equilibrium is unstable. Next, suppose that (49b) holds; then $\det J < 0$, and the equilibrium is unstable. ■

Remarks

1. Barring the possibility of equalities, there is one more possible case when we take the negation of (48), i.e., the case of $\Delta < 0$ and $\epsilon_a \epsilon_b > 0$. However, if $\epsilon_a > 0$ and $\epsilon_b > 0$, then $\Delta > 0$ by (46). If $\epsilon_a < 0$ and $\epsilon_b < 0$, then the equilibrium is unstable by (49a).

2. Condition (48) is sufficient for the local stability of the original system. If the eigenvalues of J are neither zero nor pure imaginary, and there are no multiple roots, condition (48) is also necessary for the stability of the original system. Recall the so-called "Poincaré theorem."[22]

3. Proposition 5 is similar to, but different from, the Marshall–Amano results. For example, neither of them is aware of our α_a and α_b.

Proposition 5 asserts that there are two cases: (a) the case of $\epsilon_a > 0$ and $\epsilon_b > 0$ and (b) the case of $\epsilon_a \epsilon_b < 0$. In case *a*, we automatically have $\Delta > 0$, which corresponds to the usual ML condition, and the traditional comparative statics results hold. In case *b*, the stability condition requires $\Delta < 0$: i.e., the usual ML condition need to be *reversed*, and hence the usual comparative statics results no longer hold. In the constant-returns-to-scale (CRS) case, $\epsilon_a > 0$ and $\epsilon_b > 0$, and the equilibrium is *always* Marshallian stable. In the traditional analysis, the stability condition is obtained via the Walrasian process, and it is *assumed* that such a condition holds. Also, in such an analysis very little is said about the relation between CRS and stability.

We may now obtain the decomposition formula for η_a. Letting $D_{xa}^*(p, u)$ denote the compensated demand of X in country A, we consider the identity,

$$D_x^*(p, u) = D_x[p, E(p, u)],$$

where $E(p, u)$ is the minimum expenditure function. Differentiating this with respect to p and utilizing the Shephard (–McKenzie) lemma, we

[22]The Poincaré theorem states that the behavior of the trajectory of a system of nonlinear differential equations on the plane in a neighborhood of the equilibrium can be approximated by that of its corresponding linear system, unless the characteristic roots are both pure imaginary, or are real and equal (see, e.g., Simmons, 1972, pp. 325–327; Cesari, 1959, pp. 156–163).

obtain

$$\partial D_{xa}^*/\partial p \equiv \partial D_{xa}/\partial p + D_{xa}(\partial D_{xa}/\partial I_a). \tag{13'}$$

Recalling (31), we then obtain

$$\eta_a^* = \eta_a' + m_a, \quad \text{where } \eta_a' \equiv -\frac{p}{M_a}\frac{\partial D_{xa}^*}{\partial p}. \tag{50a}$$

Repeating the same argument for country B, we may obtain

$$\eta_b^* = \eta_b' + m_b, \quad \text{where } \eta_b' \equiv -\frac{(1/p)}{M_b}\frac{\partial D y_b^*}{\partial(1/p)}. \tag{50b}$$

Here η_a' and η_b', respectively, signify the elasticities of compensated import demand for countries A and B. Using (45) and (50), we may conclude the following.

PROPOSITION 6. *The elasticities of offer curves can be decomposed into*

$$\eta_a = \eta_a' + m_a + \alpha_a \epsilon_a, \qquad \eta_b = \eta_b' + m_b + \alpha_b \epsilon_b. \tag{51}$$

This corresponds to Jones' formula (1961), except that he did not deal with variable returns to scale. Equation (51) is reduced to Jones' formula under CRS.

6. A SHIFT IN TASTES

Following Marshall (1879), we consider the effect of a change in tastes on the terms of trade. To this end, we rewrite country B's demand function for commodity Y as $D_{yb} = D_{yb}(1/p, I_b, \tau)$, where τ is a shift parameter representing a change in country B's tastes. Then (32) and (33) become

$$p\{D_{xa}[p, pX_a(Y_a) + Y_a] - X_a(Y_a)\}$$
$$= D_{yb}[1/p, X_b + Y_b(X_b)/p, \tau] - Y_b(X_b). \tag{32'}$$

$$p = p_D(Y_a, X_b, \tau). \tag{33'}$$

Differentiating (32′) and using (27), (31), (35), and (39), we obtain

$$dp/d\tau = -\gamma/(M_a\Delta), \quad \text{where } \gamma \equiv \partial D_{yb}/\partial\tau.$$

Here $\gamma > 0$ signifies a change in tastes in favor of good Y (and hence against X due to the budget condition) in country B. We may then conclude

$$dp/d\tau < 0 \quad \text{if} \quad \epsilon_a > 0 \quad \text{and} \quad \epsilon_b > 0, \qquad dp/d\tau > 0 \quad \text{if } \epsilon_a \epsilon_b < 0,$$

where we may recall that $\epsilon_a \epsilon_b < 0$ requires $\Delta < 0$ for stability. Thus we obtain the following.

PROPOSITION 7. *Country B's increase in tastes for her imported good* (Y) *will increase the relative price of* Y, $1/p$ (*i.e., the terms of trade will move against country* B) *if* $\epsilon_a > 0$ *and* $\epsilon_b > 0$. *It will reduce the relative price of* Y (*i.e., the terms of trade will move in favor of country* B), *if* $\epsilon_a \epsilon_b < 0$.

Remark. As in Marshall (1879), consider the world as consisting of England and Germany, where England exports cloth in exchange for German linen. Let A and B, respectively, denote England and Germany. Suppose that there is an upward shift in Germany's demand for English cloth (Y). If $\epsilon_a \epsilon_b < 0$, then such a change in tastes in Germany will move the terms of trade in favor of Germany and against England, and with $\epsilon_a < 0$, the output of English cloth increases. This corresponds to the conclusion obtained by Marshall, in which he cites Adam Smith. For a succinct discussion of Smith on the issue of increasing returns to scale, see Negishi (1981). Note that the Marshallian result can*not* be obtained if we use the Walrasian stability criterion.

7. THE TRANSFER PROBLEM

Consider a unilateral transfer from country A to country B by the amount of T measured in terms of commodity Y. The budget conditions are written as

$$pD_{xa} + D_{ya} = pX_a + Y_a - T(\equiv I_a),$$

$$D_{xb} + D_{yb}/p = X_b + Y_b/p + T/p(\equiv I_b).$$

Thus the same Walras' law as before holds. Equation (24) is rewritten as

$$pM_a = M_b - T, \tag{24'}$$

which is equivalent to the equilibrium conditions for the markets for X and Y. Incorporating the behavioral relations, we can rewrite (24′) as

$$\begin{aligned} p[D_{xa}(p, pX_a + Y_a - T) - X_a] \\ = D_{yb}(1/p, X_b + Y_b/p + T/p) - Y_b - T. \end{aligned} \tag{52}$$

Differentiating this and setting $T = 0$ initially, we obtain

$$M_a \Delta^* \, dp = \alpha_a \, dY_a - p\alpha_b \, dX_b + (1 - m_a - m_b) dT, \tag{53}$$

where Δ^*, α_a, α_b, m_a, and m_b are defined as before. Define ϵ_a and ϵ_b again by (39). Since $\alpha_a \, dY_a - p\alpha_a \, dX_b = -(\alpha_a \epsilon_a + \alpha_b \epsilon_b) M_a \, dp$, (53) becomes

$$M_a(\Delta^* + \alpha_a \epsilon_a + \alpha_b \epsilon_b) dp = (1 - m_a - m_b) dT. \tag{54}$$

We have (44), (45), and (46) as before. Substituting (46) into (54), we obtain

$$\frac{dp}{dT} = \frac{1}{M_a \Delta}(1 - m_a - m_b). \tag{55}$$

Using (55) with Proposition 5, we may at once obtain the following result.

PROPOSITION 8

(*i*) *Supposing* $\epsilon_a > 0$ *and* $\epsilon_b > 0$, *a unilateral transfer will move the terms of trade against the donor country if and only if* $1 - m_a - m_b > 0$.

(*ii*) *Supposing* $\epsilon_a \epsilon_b < 0$, *a unilateral transfer will move the terms of trade in favor of the donor country if and only if* $1 - m_a - m_b > 0$.

Remark. Condition $(1 - m_a - m_b > 0)$ is known as the *transfer condition* in the traditional analysis. (ii) Says that the traditional conclusion regarding the direction of the terms of trade will completely be reversed if $\epsilon_a \epsilon_b < 0$.

A further understanding may be obtained as follows. A unilateral transfer from A to B lowers A's income I_a and increases B's income I_b. This, ceteris paribus, lowers D_{xa} and increases D_{xb}. Since $1 - m_b = \partial D_{xb}/\partial I_b$, the transfer condition $(1 - m_a - m_b > 0)$ means that an increase in D_{xb} exceeds a fall in D_{xa}. This, in turn, shifts up the demand price curve, or the p_D curve. More precisely, setting $dY_a = dX_b = 0$ in (53), we obtain

$$dp_D/dT_{|Y_a,\, X_b = \text{const.}} = (1 - m_a - m_b)/M_a \Delta^*.$$

Thus, given the stability of temporary equilibrium $(\Delta^* > 0)$ and the transfer condition, the transfer T shifts the p_D curve up. Assume $\epsilon_a > 0$. Then there are two cases to consider: (a) $\epsilon_b > 0$ and (b) $\epsilon_b < 0$. If $\epsilon_b > 0$, an upward shift of the p_D curve induces a rise in the equilibrium price p^* as illustrated in Figure 4(a) as in the conventional result. On the other hand, if $\epsilon_b < 0$, then the upward shift of the p_D curve induces a fall in p^* as

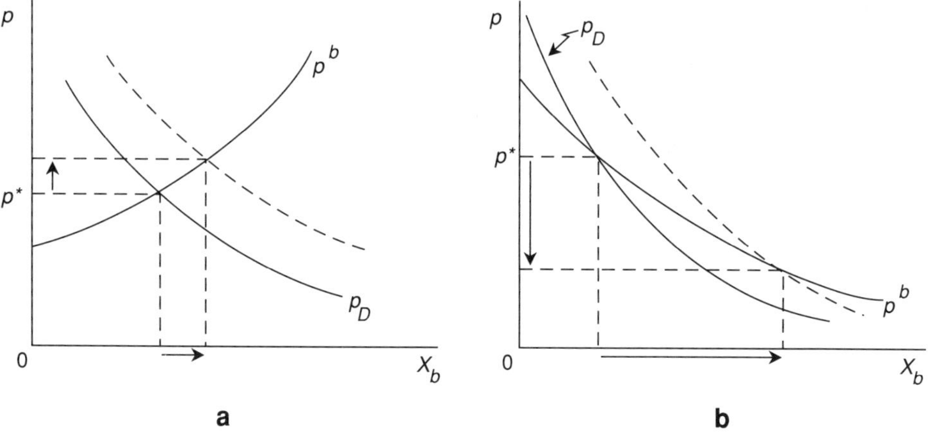

FIGURE 4 The effects of a unilateral transfer: (a) $\epsilon_b > 0$; (b) $\epsilon_b \leq 0$.

shown in Figure 4(b). Namely, the terms of trade will move *in favor of* the donor country.

Also, using the definition of ϵ_i in (39), we may obtain

$$dY_a/dT = -M_a\epsilon_a(dp/dT), \qquad dX_b/dT = (M_a/p)\epsilon_b(dp/dT). \quad (56)$$

Hence utilizing (55), we obtain

$$dY_a/dT = -\epsilon_a(1 - m_a - m_b)/\Delta, \quad (57a)$$

$$dX_b/dT = \epsilon_b(1 - m_a - m_b)/(p\Delta). \quad (57b)$$

The stability condition requires $\epsilon_a > 0$ and $\epsilon_b > 0$ (which implies $\Delta > 0$), *or* $\epsilon_a\epsilon_b < 0$ (which in turn requires $\Delta < 0$). Thus from (57), we obtain the following.

PROPOSITION 9. *Assume the transfer condition.*

(i) If $\epsilon_a > 0$ and $\epsilon_b > 0$, a transfer will reduce the export industry's output in the donor country, and increases that of the recipient country.

(ii) If $\epsilon_a > 0$ and $\epsilon_b < 0$, a transfer will increase the export industry's outputs of both countries.

(iii) If $\epsilon_a < 0$ and $\epsilon_b > 0$, a transfer will reduce the export industry's outputs of both countries.

We now consider the effect of a transfer on welfare. Following the usual convention, assume that the welfare of a country can be represented by a real-valued function, and denote the indirect utility function of country A by U_a:

$$U_a = U_a(p, I_a) = U_a(p, pX_a + Y_a - T). \tag{58}$$

Differentiating this, and dividing the resulting expression by U_{aI} ($\equiv \partial U_a/\partial I_a$), and using Roy's identity, we obtain

$$dU_a/U_{aI} = -M_a dp + (pdX_a + dY_a - dT).$$

Utilizing (27), we may rewrite this as

$$\frac{1}{U_{aI}}\frac{dU_a}{dT} = -1 - M_a\frac{dp}{dT} + (1 - \rho_a)\frac{dY}{dT}a. \tag{59}$$

Substituting (55) into this, and recalling (51), we obtain

$$\frac{1}{U_{aI}}\frac{dU_a}{dT} = \frac{-1}{\Delta}(\eta'_a + \eta'_b + \alpha_a\epsilon_a + \alpha_b\epsilon_b) + (1 - \rho_a)\frac{dY_a}{dT}. \tag{60}$$

Using (56) and the definition of α_a in (35b), the right-hand side (RHS) of (60) reduces to

$$-(\eta'_a + \eta'_b + \alpha'_a\epsilon_a + \alpha_b\epsilon_b)/\Delta, \quad \text{where } \alpha'_a \equiv (1 - m_b) + m_b\rho_a > 0. \tag{61}$$

Country B's welfare may be represented by

$$U_b = U_b(1/p, I_b) = U_b(1/p, X_b + Y_b/p + T/p). \tag{58'}$$

Repeating an argument similar to that used for country A, we obtain

$$\frac{p}{U_{bI}}\frac{dU_b}{dT} = 1 + M_a\frac{dp}{dT} + (1 - 1/\rho_b)\frac{dX_b}{dT}, \tag{59'}$$

$$\frac{p}{U_{bI}}\frac{dU_b}{dT} = \frac{1}{\Delta}(\eta'_a + \eta'_b + \alpha_a\epsilon_a + \alpha_b\epsilon_b) + (1 - 1/\rho_b)\frac{dX_b}{dT}, \tag{60'}$$

where $U_{bI} \equiv \partial U_b/\partial I_b$. Utilizing (56) and (35b), the RHS of (60′) reduces to

$$(\eta'_a + \eta'_b + \alpha_a\epsilon_a + \alpha'_b\epsilon_b)/\Delta, \qquad \text{where } \alpha'_b \equiv (1 - m_a) + m_a/\rho_b > 0. \tag{61}$$

To obtain a further insight into the welfare effect of a transfer, it would be useful to recall (59) and (59′). From these, it is easy to see that the effect of a transfer on each country's welfare can be decomposed into three effects: (a) the direct effect of transfer, (b) the terms of trade effect, and (c) the scale effect. The first, second, and third terms of the RHS of (59), respectively, capture these three effects for country A. Similarly, the three terms of the RHS of (59′) capture these three effects for country B.

In the traditional CRS case, $\rho_a = \rho_b = 1$, and the scale effect vanishes. Thus the welfare effect of a transfer is confined only to the direct and the terms of trace effects. Substituting $\rho_a = \rho_b = 1$ into (60) and (60′), we can obtain the usual formulas. To proceed further with our analysis, we assume that the transfer condition is satisfied, and impose the following assumption.

Assumption 1. The production functions are identical between the countries, and the degrees of returns are constant regardless of the output levels.[23]

In the traditional Heckscher–Ohlin model, in addition to this, the assumption of CRS ($\rho_X = \rho_Y = 1$) is imposed. Under Assumption 1, we have

$$\rho_X^a = \rho_X^b (\equiv \rho_X), \qquad \rho_Y^a = \rho_Y^b (\equiv \rho_Y), \qquad \rho_a = \rho_b (\equiv \rho).$$

If $\rho_Y > \rho_X$, then country A exports good Y whose degree of returns is greater than that of the other good. If $\rho_X > \rho_Y$, then country A exports Y whose degree of returns is less than that of B. Note that $\rho_Y > \rho_X$ if and only if $1 - \rho > 0$.

Since the traditional welfare effect holds for the case of $\epsilon_a > 0$ and $\epsilon_b > 0$, we may focus our attention on the case of $\epsilon_a \epsilon_b < 0$. In this case there are two subcases: (a) $\epsilon_a > 0$ and $\epsilon_b < 0$ and (b) $\epsilon_a < 0$ and $\epsilon_b > 0$. In both cases, we must have $\Delta < 0$ to obtain stability. Let $S_a \equiv (1 - \rho_a)(dY_a/dT)$ and $S_b \equiv (1 - 1/\rho_b)(dX_b/dT)$. Namely, S_i signifies the *scale effect* of country i as indicated in equations (59) and (59′). Then utilizing (55) and (57) together with $\Delta < 0$, the transfer condition, and Assumption 1, we obtain

(i) The case of $\epsilon_a > 0$, $\epsilon_b < 0$, $1 - \rho > 0$:

$$S_a > 0 \quad \text{and} \quad S_b < 0. \tag{62a}$$

(ii) The case of $\epsilon_a > 0$, $\epsilon_b < 0$, $1 - \rho < 0$:

$$S_a < 0 \quad \text{and} \quad S_b > 0. \tag{62b}$$

[23] It is often assumed that production functions take the following form:

$$X = X^T F(L_X, K_X), \qquad Y = G(L_Y, K_Y), \qquad 0 < T < 1, \quad T = \text{contant}.$$

In this case, $\rho_X[= 1/(1 - T)]$ and $\rho_Y(= 1)$ are constants.

(iii) The case of $\epsilon_a < 0$, $\epsilon_b > 0$, $1 - \rho > 0$:

$$S_a < 0 \quad \text{and} \quad S_b > 0. \tag{62c}$$

(iv) The case of $\epsilon_a < 0$, $\epsilon_b > 0$, $1 - \rho < 0$:

$$S_a > 0 \quad \text{and} \quad S_b < 0. \tag{62d}$$

Using (62a) and (62d) together with (ii) of Proposition 8, we may obtain the following.

PROPOSITION 10. *Under Assumption* 1 *and the transfer condition, both the terms of trade effect and the scale effect are favorable to the donor country, and are adverse to the recipient country, if* (*a*) $\epsilon_a > 0$, $\epsilon_b < 0$ *and* $\rho_Y > \rho_X$, *or if* (*b*) $\epsilon_a < 0$, $\epsilon_b > 0$ *and* $\rho_X > \rho_Y$.

We may now graphically illustrate the effect of a transfer, where we choose the case of $\epsilon_a > 0$ and $\epsilon_b < 0$. We assume that the production functions are identical between the two countries. If we measure p on the vertical axis and the output of each country's exportable in the horizontal axis as in Figure 5, this assumption implies that the supply price curves of both countries have a similar shape. The initial terms of trade are denoted by p_0 in Figure 5. Note that at the initial equilibrium points A and B, we have $\epsilon_a > 0$ and $\epsilon_b < 0$.

Now consider a unilateral transfer from country A to country B. Assume that the transfer condition is satisfied. Recall (ii) of Propositions 8 and 9, which state that if $\epsilon_a > 0$ and $\epsilon_b < 0$, the terms of trade will move in favor of the *donor* country ($dp/dT < 0$), and that the outputs of exportable (Y_a and X_b) will increase in both countries. In Figure 5 the terms of trade after the transfer is denoted by p_1, and it is less than its initial value p_0. Also, Y_a and X_b will both increase by the transfer as

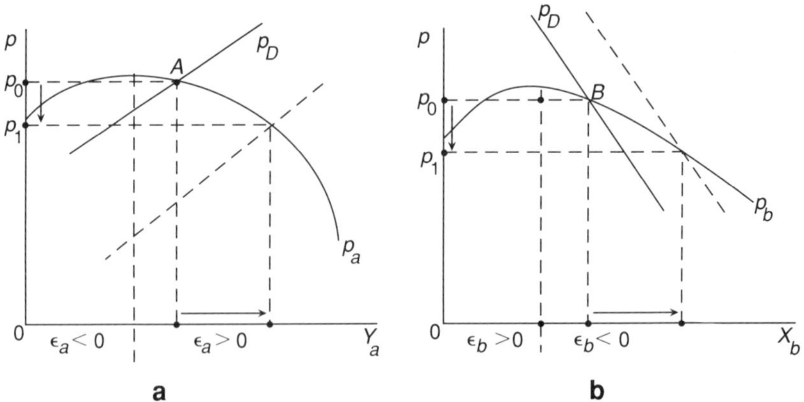

FIGURE 5 A unilateral transfer when $\epsilon_a > 0$ and $\epsilon_b < 0$: (a) country A; (b) country B.

indicated in Figure 5. In this case, the terms of trade effect of a transfer on welfare is favorable to the donor country and adverse to the recipient country. If $\rho_Y > \rho_X$, then the scale effect is also favorable to country A and adverse to country B.

The intuition behind such scale effects may be stated as follows. Suppose that industry Y, say, the manufacturing sector, enjoys scale economies; and that in industry X, say, the agricultural sector, constant or decreasing returns to scale prevail. By assumption, country A exports good Y, and country B exports good X. Suppose that the transfer expands the export industries of both countries as seen in Figure 5. Then country A expands the production of the good that enjoys scale economies, and hence shrinks the output of the other good that is produced under no scale economies. In country B, completely the opposite happens, i.e., the output of the increasing-returns-to-scale industry shrinks, and the output of the good that is produced under constant or decreasing returns to scale increases. Namely, the transfer induces the scale effect that is favorable to country A and adverse against country B. In this case, the terms-of-trade effect is also favorable to the donor country and adverse to the recipient country. For example, if Japan gives aid to Southeast Asian countries, and exports goods with scale economies to these countries and imports those goods that enjoy no scale economies, then Japan can become better off and the other countries can become worse off.

We now consider the effect of a transfer on world welfare. Define the change in the world welfare due to a unilateral transfer by[24]

$$\frac{dW}{dT} \equiv \frac{1}{U_{aI}} \frac{dU_a}{dT} + \frac{p}{U_{bI}} \frac{dU_b}{dT}.$$

Substituting (59) and (59′) into this, we obtain

$$dW/dT = (1 - \rho_a)(dY_a/dT) + (1 - 1/\rho_b)(dX_b/dT). \qquad (63)$$

Namely, the scale effects are the only factors that determine a change in the level of the world welfare. For the traditional CRS case, $\rho_a = \rho_b = 1$, so that we have $dW/dT = 0$ by (63); i.e., the welfare of the world will remain unchanged by a unilateral transfer.[25] However, under VRS, the world welfare can either improve or deteriorate.

[24]The multiplication of the second term on the right-hand side by p is to obtain the same dimension throughout the equation.

[25]Then the transfer question can be considered a zero-sum game. Such a view is behind the neoclassical analysis of transfer. If there is a third country, then both the recipient and the donor countries *can* gain by the sacrifice of the third country under the zero-sum game situation. This is the essence of the three-agent transfer question by Yano (1983), Bhagwati *et al.* (1984) and others, all of which are discussed in terms of the Walrasian stability criterion.

Again impose Assumption 1, and assume $\rho_Y > \rho_X$. We may then obtain from (63),

$$dW/dT > 0 \quad \text{if } dY_a/dT > 0 \quad \text{and} \quad dX_b/dT < 0, \tag{64a}$$

$$dW/dT < 0 \quad \text{if } dY_a/dT < 0 \quad \text{and} \quad dX_b/dT > 0. \tag{64b}$$

From Proposition 9, Y_a and X_b move in the opposite direction only when $\epsilon_a > 0$ and $\epsilon_b > 0$. Hence let us assume this to proceed further with our discussion. In this case, using (i) of Proposition 9 together with (64b), we may conclude $dW/dT < 0$. On the other hand, if $\rho_X > \rho_Y$, we obtain $dW/dT > 0$.

In summary, we obtain the following results.

PROPOSITION 11

(*i*) *If constant returns to scale prevail in both industries, the welfare of the world as a whole will remain unchanged by a unilateral transfer.*

(*ii*) *Assume* $\epsilon_a > 0$, $\epsilon_b > 0$, *the transfer condition, and Assumption* 1. *Then a unilateral transfer from country A to country B will deteriorate the world welfare if* $\rho_Y > \rho_X$, *and it will improve the world welfare if* $\rho_X > \rho_Y$.

Remark. In statement (ii) of Proposition 11, the output of country A's export industry (Y) decreases and the output of country B's export industry (X) increases by (i) of Proposition 9. This means that the world output of good Y decreases and that of good X increases. If the degree of returns for good Y is greater than that for good X, then the world will become worse off by the transfer. On the other hand, if the degree of returns for good X is greater than that for good Y, the world will become better off by the transfer.

8. SOME FURTHER DISCUSSIONS

In Proposition 1, we show that the temporary equilibrium is always stable, where stability is defined in terms of the Walrasian price adjustment process. Proposition 3 asserts that the LRE is stable under the Marshallian output adjustment process if and only if it is stable under the capital adjustment process. There is one important concept, i.e., SRE, missing in this analysis. When the temporary equilibrium is reached, the sectoral gap of the wage rates exists, and labor moves between the two sectors in which capital remains sector specific. We can then consider the two processes.

$$\dot{X} = a_3[\, p_D(X)/p_S(X) - 1] \equiv \psi(X),$$

$$\dot{L}_X = a_4\big[w_x(L_X)/w_y(L_X) - 1\big] \equiv \Psi(L_X),$$

where $p_S(X)$ signifies the short-run supply price curve, in which the wage rates are equalized between the sectors while the sectoral gap of the rates of return on capital exists. The first process is the *output* adjustment process leading to the SRE, and the second process is the *labor* adjustment process leading to the SRE. It can be shown that the SRE is stable in one process if and only if it is stable in the other process.[26] When the SRE is achieved, the sectoral gap of the rates of return on capital remains, and this sets in the capital adjustment process. We then have two processes (20) and (22) discussed earlier, and the stability condition of LRE for one process implies the other.

In Proposition 5, we obtained the correct stability condition of international equilibrium under VRS, and subsequently illustrated its applications to the questions of a shift of tastes and a unilateral transfer. Needless to say, its applications are not limited to these two. In fact, there can be many applications. One important such example would be the question of tariffs. Roughly speaking, the traditional theory of tariffs runs as follows. Starting with the free trade situation, the imposition of an import tariff will always move the terms of trade in favor of the tariff-imposing country, will raise the domestic relative price of the imported good if and only if the Metzler condition is satisfied, and will improve the welfare of the tariff-imposing country at the expense of the other country. We can show that with the correct stability condition, *none* of these results hold under VRS, although they are all valid under CRS. Another well-known traditional result is that free trade is always optimal for a small country. We can show that under VRS this is no longer correct, while such holds under CRS. Namely, if the country exports the good whose returns is relatively greater (resp. less) than that of her imports, export promotion or subsidies (resp. some protection) is better than free trade (i.e., the optimal tariff policy requires promoting expansion of the output whose scale merit is greater). In fact, this has been the policy of Japan throughout her rapid growth after World War II, for example. For such results in the theory of tariffs, see Ide and Takayama (1992).

APPENDIX A

The Supply Side of the Economy

Differentiating (2) and (3) in the text, we obtain

$$\lambda_{LX}\hat{X} + \lambda_{LY}\hat{Y} = \hat{L} - \left[\lambda_{LX}\hat{a}_{LX} + \lambda_{LY}\hat{a}_{LY}\right], \tag{A.1a}$$

$$\lambda_{KX}\hat{X} + \lambda_{KY}\hat{Y} = \hat{K} - \left[\lambda_{KX}\hat{a}_{KX} + \lambda_{KY}\hat{a}_{KY}\right], \tag{A.1b}$$

$$\theta_{LX}\hat{w} + \theta_{KX}\hat{r} = \hat{p} - \left[\theta_{LX}\hat{a}_{LX} + \theta_{KX}\hat{a}_{KX}\right], \tag{A.2a}$$

$$\theta_{LY}\hat{w} + \theta_{KY}\hat{r} = -\left[\theta_{LY}\hat{a}_{LY} + \theta_{KY}\hat{a}_{KY}\right]. \tag{A.2b}$$

[26]See Ide and Takayama (1990).

Substituting (4) in the text into (A1), we obtain

$$\lambda'_{LX}\hat{X} + \lambda'_{LY}\hat{Y} = \hat{L} + \delta_L\hat{\omega}, \qquad \lambda'_{KX}\hat{X} + \lambda'_{KY}\hat{Y} = \hat{K} - \delta_K\hat{\omega}, \tag{A.3}$$

where $\lambda'_{ij} \equiv \lambda_{ij}(1 - R_{ij})$, $\delta_L \equiv \lambda_{LX}\theta_{KX}\sigma_x + \lambda_{LY}\theta_{KY}\sigma_y$, and $\delta_K \equiv \lambda_{KX}\theta_{LX}\sigma_x + \lambda_{KY}\theta_{LY}\sigma_y$. δ_L and δ_K are weighted sums of elasticities of substitution. The economic significance of δ_L and δ_K is given in Jones (1965). Following Jones (1968, p. 264), we impose the following assumption.

Assumption A1. At constant factor prices, the expansion of any industry results in an increased demand for each factor of production.

By (A.3), this is equivalent to assuming each $\lambda'_{ij} > 0$, which in turn is equivalent to assuming each $(1 - R_{ij}) > 0$. Solving (A.3) for $\hat{X}$ and $\hat{Y}$, we may obtain

$$\hat{X} = \mu_X\hat{\omega}/|\lambda'|, \qquad \hat{Y} = -\mu_Y\hat{\omega}/|\lambda'|, \tag{A.4a}$$

where $|\lambda'| \equiv \lambda'_{LX}\lambda'_{KY} - \lambda'_{LY}\lambda'_{KX}$, and

$$\mu_X \equiv \lambda'_{KY}\delta_L + \lambda'_{LY}\delta_K > 0 \quad \text{and} \quad \mu_Y \equiv \lambda'_{KX}\delta_L + \lambda'_{LX}\delta_K > 0. \tag{A.4b}$$

Substituting (4) into (A2), we may obtain

$$\theta_{LX}\hat{w} + \theta_{KX}\hat{r} = \hat{p} + R_X\hat{X}, \qquad \theta_{LY}\hat{w} + \theta_{KY}\hat{r} = R_Y\hat{Y}. \tag{A.5}$$

Substituting (A.4a) into (A.5), we obtain

$$\theta'_{LX}\hat{w} + \theta'_{KX}\hat{r} = \hat{p}, \qquad \theta'_{LY}\hat{w} + \theta'_{KY}\hat{r} = 0, \tag{A.6}$$

where θ'_{ij} values are defined by

$$\theta'_{LX} \equiv \theta_{LX} - R_X\mu_X/|\lambda'|, \qquad \theta'_{KX} \equiv \theta_{KX} + R_X\mu_X/|\lambda'|, \tag{A.7a}$$

$$\theta'_{LY} \equiv \theta_{LY} + R_Y\mu_Y/|\lambda'|, \qquad \theta'_{KY} \equiv \theta_{KY} - R_Y\mu_Y/|\lambda'|. \tag{A.7b}$$

We also assume the following, which is again due to Jones (1968, p. 264).

Assumption A2. In an economy with a fixed set of factor endowments, an increase in any factor price must increase the (average) cost of producing each commodity.

By (A.6), this assumption is equivalent to assuming that each θ'_{ij} is positive.

Solving (A.6) for $\hat{w}$ and $\hat{r}$, we obtain

$$\hat{\omega} = |\lambda'|\hat{p}/A, \tag{A.8}$$

$$A \equiv |\lambda'||\theta'| = |\lambda'||\theta| - (R_X\mu_X + R_Y\mu_Y), \tag{A.9}$$

where $|\theta'| \equiv \theta'_{LX}\theta'_{KY} - \theta'_{LY}\theta'_{KX}$. Using (A.4a) and (A.8), we obtain

$$\hat{p} = A\hat{Z}/\mu, \qquad \hat{X} = (\mu_X/\mu)\hat{Z}, \qquad \hat{Y} = -(\mu_Y/\mu)\hat{Z}. \tag{A.10}$$

If both functions are homothetic ($R_j = R_{Lj} = R_{Kj}$), (A.9) can be rewritten as

$$A = (1 - R_X)(1 - R_Y)|\lambda||\theta| - (R_X\mu_X + R_Y\mu_Y). \tag{A.11}$$

Hence, if constant returns to scale prevail in both industries ($R_X = R_Y = 0$), then $A = |\lambda||\theta|$, which is positive. In this case, (A.10) means the usual price–output response. Namely, an increase in p accompanies a rise in Z and X and a fall in Y. This yields the usual Stolper–Samuelson effects.

APPENDIX B

The Stability of LRE and the Significance of $B_0 > 0$

Along the adjustment process toward the LRE, it is assumed that the SRE holds instantaneous, while the sectoral gap in the real rates of return on capital remain until the economy reaches the LRE. Let r_x and r_y be such rates in sectors X and Y, respectively. Then (A.2) and (4) can be written as

$$\theta_{LX}\hat{w} + \theta_{KX}\hat{r}_x = \hat{p} - \left[\theta_{LX}\hat{a}_{LX} + \theta_{KX}\hat{a}_{KX}\right], \tag{B.1a}$$

$$\theta_{LY}\hat{w} + \theta_{KY}\hat{r}_y = -\left[\theta_{LY}\hat{a}_{LY} + \theta_{KY}\hat{a}_{KY}\right], \tag{B.1b}$$

$$\hat{a}_{LX} = -\theta_{KX}\sigma_x\hat{\omega}_x - R_{LX}\hat{X}, \hat{a}_{KX} = \theta_{LX}\sigma_x\hat{\omega}_x - R_{KX}\hat{X}, \tag{B.2a}$$

$$\hat{a}_{LY} = -\theta_{KY}\sigma_y\hat{\omega}_y - R_{LY}\hat{Y}, \qquad \hat{a}_{KY} = \theta_{LY}\sigma_y\hat{\omega}_y - R_{KY}\hat{Y}, \tag{B.2b}$$

where $\omega_x \equiv w/r_x$ and $\omega_y \equiv w/r_y$. Substituting (B2) into (B1), we obtain

$$\theta_{LX}\hat{w} + \theta_{KX}\hat{r} = \hat{p} + R_X\hat{X}, \qquad \theta_{LY}\hat{w} + \theta_{KY}\hat{r}_y = R_Y\hat{Y}. \tag{B.3}$$

Using (B.2) and recalling $\rho_j = 1/(1 - R_j)$, $j = X, Y$, we obtain

$$\hat{X} = \left(\theta_{LX}\hat{L}_X + \theta_{KX}\hat{K}_X\right)\rho_X, \tag{B.4a}$$

$$\hat{Y} = \left(\theta_{LY}\hat{L}_Y + \theta_{KY}\hat{K}_Y\right)\rho_Y. \tag{B.4b}$$

Here we recall (17), which specifies the demand side of the economy. This yields

$$\hat{p} = -\eta\hat{X}.$$

Using this together with (B.3) and (B.4), we obtain

$$\theta_{LX}\hat{w} + \theta_{KX}\hat{r}_x = \left(\theta_{LX}\hat{L}_X + \theta_{KX}\hat{K}_X\right)(\rho_X - 1)/(R_X - \eta), \tag{B.5a}$$

$$\theta_{LY}\hat{w} + \theta_{KY}\hat{r}_y = \left(\theta_{LY}\hat{L}_Y + \theta_{KY}\hat{K}_Y\right)(\rho_Y - 1). \tag{B.5b}$$

Also, from (B.2), we may obtain

$$\sigma_x\left(\hat{w} - \hat{r}_x\right) = \left[(1 - R_{LX})\hat{K}_X - (1 - R_{KX})\hat{L}_X\right]\rho_X, \tag{B.6a}$$

$$\sigma_y\left(\hat{w} - \hat{r}_y\right) = \left[(1 - R_{LY})\hat{K}_Y - (1 - R_{KY})\hat{L}_Y\right]\rho_Y. \tag{B.6b}$$

Rewrite (2) as $\lambda_{LX} + \lambda_{LY} = 1$, $\lambda_{KX} + \lambda_{KY} = 1$. From this, we obtain

$$\lambda_{LX}\hat{L}_X + \lambda_{LY}\hat{L}_Y = 0, \qquad \lambda_{KX}\hat{K}_X + \lambda_{KY}\hat{K}_Y = 0. \tag{B.7}$$

Solving (B.5a) and (B.6a) for $\hat{w}$ and $\hat{r}_x$, we obtain

$$\hat{w} = \left[\{\alpha_1 - \theta_{KX}(1 - R_{KX})\}\hat{L}_X + \{\alpha_2 + \theta_{KX}(1 - R_{LX})\}\hat{K}_X\right]\rho_X/\sigma_x, \tag{B.8a}$$

$$\hat{r}_x = \left[\{\alpha_1 + \theta_{LX}(1 - R_{KX})\}\hat{L}_X + \{\alpha_2 - \theta_{LX}(1 - R_{LX})\}\hat{K}_X\right]\rho_X/\sigma_x, \tag{B.8b}$$

where $\alpha_1 \equiv \theta_{LX}(R_X - \eta)\sigma_x$, $\alpha_2 \equiv \theta_{KX}(R_X - \eta)\sigma_x$. Solving (B.5b) and (B.6b) for $\hat{w}$ and $\hat{r}_y$, we obtain

$$\hat{w} = \left[\{\alpha_3 - \theta_{KY}(1 - R_{KY})\}\hat{L}_Y + \{\alpha_4 + \theta_{KY}(1 - R_{LY})\}\hat{K}_Y\right]\rho_Y/\sigma_y, \tag{B.9a}$$

$$\hat{r}_y = \left[\{\alpha_3 + \theta_{LY}(1 - R_{KY})\}\hat{L}_Y + \{\alpha_4 - \theta_{LY}(1 - R_{LY})\}\hat{K}_Y\right]\rho_Y/\sigma_y, \tag{B.9b}$$

where $\alpha_3 \equiv \theta_{LY}R_Y\sigma_y$ and $\alpha_4 \equiv \theta_{KY}R_Y\sigma_y$. Equating (B.8a) and (B.9a) and using (B.7), we obtain

$$\lambda_{KY}B_0\hat{L}_X = \lambda_{LY}B_1\hat{K}_X, \tag{B.10}$$

where B_0 and B_1 are defined by

$$B_0 \equiv \lambda_{LY}\sigma_y\rho_X[\theta_{KX}(1 - R_{KX}) - \theta_{LX}(R_X - \eta)\sigma_x] + \lambda_{LX}\sigma_x\rho_Y[\theta_{KY}(1 - R_{KY}) - \theta_{LY}R_Y\sigma_y], \tag{B.11}$$

$$B_1 \equiv \theta_{KX}\lambda_{KY}\sigma_y\rho_X[(R_X - \eta)\sigma_x + (1 - R_{LX})] + \theta_{KY}\lambda_{KX}\sigma_x\rho_Y[R_Y\sigma_y + (1 - R_{LY})]. \tag{B.12}$$

Substituting (B.10) into (B.8b), we obtain

$$\hat{r}_x = \rho_X[(R_X - \eta)\sigma_x(\lambda_{LY}\theta_{LX}B_1 + \lambda_{KY}\theta_{KX}B_0) + \theta_{LX}\{\lambda_{LY}B_1(1 - R_{KX}) - \lambda_{KY}B_0(1 - R_{LX})\}]\hat{K}_X/(\lambda_{KY}B_0\sigma_x). \tag{B.13}$$

Also substituting (B.10) into (B.9b), we obtain

$$\hat{r}_y = -\rho_Y[R_Y\sigma_y(\lambda_{LX}\theta_{LY}B_1 + \lambda_{KX}\theta_{KY}B_0) + \theta_{LY}\{\lambda_{LX}B_1(1 - R_{KY}) - \lambda_{KX}B_0(1 - R_{KY})\}]\hat{K}_X/(\lambda_{KY}B_0\sigma_y). \tag{B.14}$$

Using (B.13) and (B.14), we may compute

$$\hat{r}_x/\hat{K}_X - \hat{r}_y/\hat{K}_X = -(\eta + e)\mu_X\rho_X\rho_Y/(\lambda_{KY}B_0). \tag{B.15}$$

From this, we may obtain (23) in the text.

The Significance of $B_0 > 0$

As argued in the text and as is evident from (B.15), the sign of B_0 plays a key role in the stability of the LRE. Here we show that the sign of B_0 is deeply related to the nature of the model. Substituting (B.10) into (B.4a) to obtain

$$\hat{X} = \rho_X B_2\hat{K}_X/(\lambda_{KY}B_0), \tag{B.16}$$

$$B_2 \equiv \lambda_{LY}\theta_{LX}B_1 + \lambda_{KY}\theta_{KX}B_0 = \lambda_{LY}\lambda_{KY}\theta_{KX}\sigma_y + \theta_{KY}(\lambda_{KX}\lambda'_{LY}\theta_{LX} + \lambda_{LX}\lambda'_{KY}\theta_{KX})\sigma_x\rho_Y. \tag{B.17}$$

Since $\lambda'_{LY} > 0$ and $\lambda'_{KY} > 0$ by Assumption A1, we have $B_2 > 0$. Hence we may conclude

$$\hat{K}_X/\hat{X} > 0 \quad \textit{if and only if } B_0 > 0. \tag{B.18}$$

Using (B.10) and (B.16), we obtain

$$\hat{X} = \rho_X \hat{B}_2 L_X / (\lambda_{LY} B_1). \tag{B.19}$$

Since $B_2 > 0$ always, we may conclude from (B-19)

$$\hat{L}_X/\hat{X} > 0 \quad \textit{if and only if } B_1 > 0. \tag{B.20}$$

Next, using (B.7), we may rewrite (B.10) as

$$\lambda_{KX} B_0 \hat{L}_Y = \lambda_{LX} B_1 \hat{K}_Y. \tag{B.10$'$}$$

Substituting (B.10′) into (B.4b), we obtain

$$\hat{Y} = \rho_Y B_3 \hat{K}_Y / (\lambda_{KX} B_0), \tag{B.21}$$

$$\begin{aligned} B_3 &\equiv \lambda_{LX}\theta_{LY}B_1 + \lambda_{KX}\theta_{KY}B_0 \\ &= \lambda_{LX}\lambda_{KX}\theta_{KY}\sigma_x + \theta_{KX}(\lambda'_{LX}\lambda_{KY}\theta_{LY} + \lambda'_{KX}\lambda_{LY}\theta_{KY})\sigma_y\rho_X. \end{aligned} \tag{B.22}$$

Since $\lambda'_{LX} > 0$ and $\lambda'_{KX} > 0$ by Assumption A1, we have $B_3 > 0$. Thus we may conclude

$$\hat{K}_Y/\hat{Y} > 0 \quad \textit{if and only if } B_0 > 0. \tag{B.23}$$

Using (B.10′) and (B.21), we may also obtain

$$\hat{Y} = \rho_Y B_3 \hat{L}_Y / (\lambda_{LX} B_1). \tag{B.24}$$

Since $B_3 > 0$ always, we may conclude from (B.24)

$$\hat{L}_Y/\hat{Y} > 0 \quad \text{always } \textit{if and only if } B_1 > 0. \tag{B.25}$$

We now introduce the following assumption.

Assumption A3. The expansion of any industry results in an increased demand for each factor of production.

In terms of symbols, this assumption means

$$\hat{K}_X/\hat{X} > 0, \qquad \hat{L}_X/\hat{X} > 0, \qquad \hat{K}_Y/\hat{Y} > 0, \qquad \hat{L}_Y/\hat{Y} > 0. \tag{B.26}$$

Using (B.18), (B.20), (B.23), (B.25), and (B.26), we obtain the following result.

PROPOSITION A. *$B_0 > 0$ (and $B_1 > 0$)* if and only if *Assumption A3 holds.*

Acknowledgments

We appreciate this opportunity to present a paper for the volume in honor of Professor Lionel W. McKenzie. In early years of the Rochester Ph.D. program, Lionel taught a one-year course on modern value theory, where he emphasized Marshall in the first semester and Walras in the second semester. The present paper is concerned with both Marshall and Walras. It deals with the stability question and international trade: Lionel has significant contributions in both fields. It also revives the contribution by Professor Frank Graham, Lionel's teacher. Earlier versions of this paper were presented at various universities in United States and Japan and several conferences by the second author. The former includes Yale University, Columbia University, Princeton University, and Tulane University in April 1991 and the latter includes the Midwest Economics Conference at Washington University in October 1989 and the Far Eastern Meeting of the Econometric Society at Seoul National University in July 1991. We are indebted to comments provided in these occasions.

References

Amano, A. (1968). "Stability conditions in the pure theory of international trade: A rehabilitation of the Marshallian approach," *Quart. J. Econ.*, **82**, 326–339.

Aoki, M. (1970). "A note on the Marshallian process under increasing returns," *Quart. J. Econ.* **84**, 100–112.

Bhagwati, J. N., R. A. Brecher, and T. Hatta (1984). "The generalized theory of transfers and welfare: Bilateral transfers in a multilateral world," *Am. Econ. Rev.* **73**, 606–618.

Cesari, L. (1959). *Asymptotic Behavior and Stability Problems in Ordinary Differential Equations* (Springer-Verlag, Berlin).

Chipman, J. S. (1965). "A survey of the theory of international trade: Part 2, The neoclassical theory," *Econometrica* **33**, 685–760.

Ethier, W. J. (1982). "Decreasing costs in international trade and Frank Graham's argument for production," *Econometrica* **50**, 1243–1268.

Graham, F. (1923). "Some aspects of protection further considered," *Quart. J. Econ.* **37**, 199–227.

Helpman, E. (1984). "Increasing returns to scale, imperfect markets, and trade theory," in *Handbook of International Economics*, R. W. Jones and P. B. Kenen, (eds.) (North-Holland, Amsterdam), pp. 325–365.

Herberg, H., and M. C. Kemp (1969). "Some implications of variable returns to scale," *Can. J. Econ.* **2**, 403–415.

Ide, T., and A. Takayama (1989). "Returns to scale under non-homotheticity and homotheticity, and the shape of average costs," *Zeitschrift für die gesamte Staatswissenschaft* **145**, 367–388.

Ide, T., and A. Takayama (1990). "Factor market distortions and variable returns to scale in the theory of international trade: Walrasian and two Marshallian criteria," paper presented at an International Economics Symposium, University of Pennsylvania, November.

Ide, T., and A. Takayama (1991a). "The Marshall–Lerner condition reconsidered," *Econ. Lett.* **35**, 201–207.

Ide, T., and A. Takayama (1991b). "Variable returns to scale, Marshallian stability, and global correspondence in the pure theory of international trade," in *Trade, Policy, and International Adjustments*, A. Takayama, *et al.* (eds.) (Academic Press, San Diego), pp. 108–154.

Ide, T., and A. Takayama (1991c). "Variable returns to scale, comparative statics paradoxes, and the theory of comparative advantage," in *Current Issues in International Trade*, H. Herberg and N. V. Long (eds. Univ. Michigan Press, Ann Arbor).

Ide, T., and A. Takayama (1992). "Marshallian stability and the theory of tariffs under variable returns to scale," (unpublished manuscript).

Jones, R. W. (1961). "Stability conditions in international trade: A general equilibrium approach," *Int. Econ. Rev.* **2**, 199–209.

Jones, R. W. (1965). "The structure of simple general equilibrium models," *J. Political Econ.* **73**, 261–272.

Jones, R. W. (1968). "Variable returns to scale in general equilibrium theory," *Int. Econ. Rev.* **9**, 261–272.

Kemp, M. C. (1964). *The Pure Theory of International Trade* (Prentice-Hall, Englewood Cliffs, N.J.), Chapters 5 and 8, pp. 59–71, 110–131.

Kemp, M. C. (1987). "Marshall–Lerner condition," *The New Palgrave a Dictionary of Economids*, Vol. 3, J. Eatwell, M. Milgate, and P. Newman (eds.) (Macmillan, London) pp. 450–469.

Krugman, P. R. (1987). "Increasing returns and the theory of international trade," in *Advances in Economic Theory: Fifth World Congress*, T. F. Bewley (ed.) (Cambridge Univ. Press, U.K.).

Markusen, J. M., and J. M. Melvin (1981). "Trade, factor prices, and the gains from trade with increasing returns to scale," *Can. J. Econ.* **14**, 450–469.

Marshall, A. (1879). *The Pure Theory of Foreign Trade* (privately printed: published by the London School of Economics and Political Science, 1930; also Appendix J of his *Money, Credit and Commerce*, (Macmillan, London) pp. 330–360.

Marshall, A. (1920). *Principles of Economics*, London, Macmillan, 8th ed. (1st ed. 1890) (Macmillan, London).

Neary, J. P. (1978). "Dynamic stability and the theory of factor market distortion," *Am. Econ. Rev.* **68**, 671–682.

Negishi, T. (1981). "Adam Smith and increasing returns to scale under competition," in his *Classical Economics and Contemporary Economics*, (Iwanami, Tokyo), pp. 51–64 (in Japanese).

Newman, P. (1965). *The Theory of Exchange* (Prentic-Hall, Englewood Cliffs, N.J.)

Panagariya, A. (1980). "Variable returns to scale in general equilibrium theory once again," *J. Int. Econ.* **10**, 499–526.

Panagariya, A. (1986). "Increasing returns, dynamic stability, and international trade," *J. Int. Econ.* **20**, 43–63.

Simmons, G. F. (1972). *Differential Equations* (McGraw-Hill, New York).

Smith, A. (1976). *An Inquiry into the Nature and Causes of the Wealth of Nations*, (1st ed. 1776, 6th e. 1791) R. H. Campbell, A. S. Skinner, and W. B. Todd, (eds.) (Clarendon Press, Oxford).

Takayama, A. (1972). *International Trade: An Approach to the Theory* (Holt, Reinhart, and Winston, New York).

Takayama, A. (1985). *Mathematical Economics*, 2nd ed. (Cambridge Univ. Press, New York).

Walras, L. (1926). *Elements of Pure Economics* (transl. W. Jaffe) (George Allen & Unwin, London, 1954; 1st ed., 1874 and 1877; 4th ed. 1900).

Yano, M. (1983). "Welfare aspects of transfer problem," *J. Int. Econ.* **15**, 277–289.

Yasui, T. (1940). "Equilibrium analysis and process analysis," *Keizaigaku Ronshu* (University of Tokyo) (January, February, March, and June issues), [reprinted in *Collected Works*, Vol 1, T. Yasui (ed.), Tokyo, (Sobunsha, Tokyo, 1970, pp. 353–472 (in Japanese)].

TARIFF PROTECTION WITH IMPERFECT COMPETITION AND EXISTENCE OF THE GENERAL EQUILIBRIUM SOLUTION WITH INTRAINDUSTRY TRADE

Yasuo Uekawa
Department of Economics
Chukyo University
Nogoya 466, Japan

1. INTRODUCTION

There are many competing trade models of imperfect competition. The analysis of intraindustry trade between two countries containing an imperfectly competitive industry has received the attention of several economists (Brander, 1981; Brander and Krugman, 1983; Brander and Spencer, 1984a, 1984b; Dixit, 1984; Venables, 1985).

Consider the following trade model. There are two goods (Z and Y) and a single factor of production, say, labor. Good Z is competitively produced under constant returns to scale and good Y is produced under increasing returns to scale by imperfectly competitive firms (one domestic firm and one foreign firm), with each firm following Cournot behavior. Both countries charge tariffs.

How do firms interact with one another, and how can a tariff be used to extract rent from the foreign rival? In considering these questions it is very important to analyze the existence conditions for the general equilibrium solution involving intraindustry trade between two countries. However, it is not surprising that the use of the existence conditions appears to have been simply ignored. Constancy of marginal costs has often been assumed for algebraic simplicity by many economists analyzing this problem.

The studies of Brander and Spencer (1984a) on the effects of domestic tariff changes on world welfare are particularly significant in this connec-

GENERAL EQUILIBRIUM, GROWTH, AND TRADE II

tion. Brander and Spencer (1984a, 1984b) have noted that the noncooperative solution to the profit-maximizing problem faced by the firms involves intraindustry trade between two countries, and have presented several important propositions. However, it is very important to analyze the conditions required for the general equilibrium solution involving intraindustry trade between two countries to exist uniquely, and to examine the effect of domestic tariff changes on world welfare.

In the present paper we consider the same model as that of Brander and Spencer. To begin with, we establish a necessary and sufficient condition for the general equilibrium solution involving intraindustry trade between two countries to exist uniquely. Using this condition we examine the effects of domestic tariff changes on domestic and the world welfare.

2. MODEL

The two-country trade model to be discussed is as follows. Each country produces two goods (Z and Y) using a single factor (labor) that is taken as the numeraire in the both countries. The production functions for good Z in the two countries are

$$Z = L_z \quad \text{and} \quad Z^* = L_z^*, \tag{1}$$

where L_z is the amount of labor used in the domestic production of good Z and Z is the output of good Z, and starred qualities denote the corresponding entities in the foreign country. On the other hand, good Y is produced by one imperfectly competitive domestic firm and one imperfectly competitive foreign firm. The production functions for good Y by the firms are

$$F + cY = L_y \quad \text{and} \quad F^* + c^*Y^* = L_y^*, \tag{2}$$

where L_y is the amount of labor used in the domestic production of good Y, $Y = y + x$; $Y^* = y^* + x^*$, and y and x are domestic sales and foreign sales, respectively, by the domestic firm. F and c are a fixed cost and constant marginal cost, respectively, in the domestic firm. Labor is supplied inelastically to the domestic (or foreign) country in amount L (or L^*), so that

$$L_z + L_y = L \quad \text{and} \quad L_z^* + L_y^* = L^*. \tag{3}$$

The social utility functions in both countries are

$$U = u(X) + m \quad \text{and} \quad U^* = u^*(X') + m^*, \tag{4}$$

where m and X are consumptions of good Z and good Y, respectively, in the domestic country so that $X = y + x^*$ and $X^* = y^* + x$. We assume that

$$u'(X) > 0; \quad u''(X) < 0 \quad \text{and} \quad u^{*\prime}(X^*) > 0; \quad u^{*\prime\prime}(X^*) < 0. \tag{5}$$

Thus we see from (4) and (5) that the inverse demand functions for good Y are

$$p(X) = u'(X) \quad \text{and} \quad p^*(X^*) = u^{*\prime}(X^*), \tag{6}$$

and therefore,

$$p'(X) = u''(X) < 0 \quad \text{and} \quad p^{*\prime}(X^*) = u^{*\prime\prime}(X^*) < 0. \tag{7}$$

3. EXISTENCE OF GENERAL EQUILIBRIUM SOLUTION WITH INTRAINDUSTRY TRADE BETWEEN TWO COUNTRIES

In this section a necessary and sufficient condition for the general equilibrium solution involving intraindustry trade between two countries to exist uniquely is presented.

Each country charges a tariff. Let t and t^* denote the domestic tariff and the foreign tariff, respectively. We assume that t and t^* are arbitrarily given such that $0 \le t < \tilde{t}$ and $0 \le t^* < \tilde{t}^*$, where $\tilde{t}$ and $\tilde{t}^*$ are prohibitive tariffs to be determined later. The total profit of the domestic firm producing X is

$$V = yp(X) + xp^*(X^*) - cy - (c + k + t^*)x - F, \tag{8}$$

where k is transport cost, the same amount in both directions. The total profit of the foreign firm is

$$V^* = y^*p^*(X^*) + x^*p(X) - c^*y^* - (c^* + k + t)x^* - F^*. \tag{9}$$

The first-order conditions are

$$V_y = 0; \quad V_x = 0; \quad V^*_{y^*} = 0; \quad V^*_{x^*} = 0. \tag{10}$$

Cournot behavior is assumed for each market separately. For example, when deciding on domestic sales y, the home firm takes as given foreign sales at home x^*, as well as home exports x. Therefore we have the following system of equations:

$$
\begin{aligned}
p(X) + yp'(X) - c &= 0 \\
p^*(X^*) + xp^{*\prime}(X^*) - (c + k + t^*) &= 0 \\
p^*(X^*) + y^*p^{*\prime}(X^*) - c^* &= 0 \\
p(X) + x^*p'(X) - (c^* + k + t) &= 0
\end{aligned} \tag{A}
$$

for any given t and t^* such that $0 \leq t < \tilde{t}$ and $0 \leq t^* < \tilde{t}^*$. The second-order conditions are

$$
\begin{aligned}
V_{yy} &= 2p'(X) + yp''(X) < 0 && \text{for any given } x^* \geq 0, \\
V_{xx} &= 2p^{*\prime}(X^*) + xp^{*\prime\prime}(X^*) < 0 && \text{for any given } y^* \geq 0, \\
V^*_{y^*y^*} &= 2p^{*\prime}(X^*) + y^*p^{*\prime\prime}(X^*) < 0 && \text{for any given } x \geq 0, \\
V^*_{x^*x^*} &= 2p'(X) + x^*p''(X) < 0 && \text{for any given } y \geq 0.
\end{aligned} \tag{11}
$$

Note that the first expression of (11), for example, implies the second-order condition for maximization by a monopolist in an autarkic state of the domestic economy, so that $y = X$, and so on for the rest as well.

Throughout this paper we assume that

$$
\begin{aligned}
&V_{yx^*} = p' + yp'' < 0; \qquad V_{xy^*} = p^{*\prime} + xp^{*\prime\prime} < 0, \\
&V^*_{y^*x} = p^{*\prime} + y^*p^{*\prime\prime} < 0; \qquad V^*_{x^*y} = p' + x^*p'' < 0.
\end{aligned} \tag{12}
$$

From (8) and (9), we obtain

$$
\begin{aligned}
V_{yx} &= V_{yy^*} = V_{xy} = V_{xx^*} = V^*_{y^*y} = V^*_{y^*x^*} = V^*_{x^*x} = V^*_{x^*y^*}, \\
&= 0.
\end{aligned} \tag{13}
$$

Thus the Jacobian matrix of equation system (A) is

$$
\Delta \equiv \begin{bmatrix} V_{yy} & 0 & 0 & V^*_{x^*y} \\ 0 & V_{xx} & V^*_{y^*x} & 0 \\ 0 & V_{xy^*} & V^*_{y^*y^*} & 0 \\ V_{yx^*} & 0 & 0 & V^*_{x^*x^*} \end{bmatrix}. \tag{14}
$$

We see from (11)–(14) that

$$
\det \Delta = \delta \cdot \delta^* > 0, \tag{15}
$$

where from (11) and (12),

$$\delta \equiv V_{yy}V^*_{x^*x^*} - V_{yx^*}V^*_{x^*y} = (p')^2 + p' \cdot (2p' + Xp'') > 0,$$

$$\delta^* \equiv V_{xx}V^*_{y^*y^*} - V_{xy^*}V^*_{y^*x} = (p^{*\prime})^2 + p^{*\prime} \cdot (2p^{*\prime} + X^*p^{*\prime\prime}) > 0. \qquad (16)$$

We see from (11)–(16) that the Jacobian matrix of system (A) is an N–P matrix.[1] Therefore, we have the following proposition.

PROPOSITION 1. *The solution to system* (A) *is unique if system* (A) *has a solution* (*see Nikaido*, 1968, *p*. 371).

The reaction functions of the domestic and the foreign firms, $h(x^*)$ and $f(y)$, in the domestic market are defined as follows:

$$h(x^*) \equiv \{y: p + yp' - c = 0 \text{ for any given } x^* \geq 0\}, \qquad (17)$$

$$f(y) \equiv \{x^*: p + x^*p' - (c^* + k + t) = 0 \text{ for any given } y \geq 0\}. \qquad (18)$$

We obtain from (12), (17), and (18) that

$$h'(x^*) = -(p' + yp'')/(2p' + yp'') < 0, \qquad (19)$$

$$f'(y) = -(p' + x^*p'')/(2p' + x^*p'') < 0. \qquad (20)$$

Similarly, the reaction functions of the foreign and the domestic firms, $h^*(x)$ and $f^*(y^*)$ in the foreign market are defined as follows:

$$h^*(x) \equiv \{y^*: p^* + y^*p^{*\prime} - c^* = 0 \text{ for any given } x \geq 0\}, \qquad (21)$$

$$f^*(y^*) \equiv \{x: p^* + xp^{*\prime} - (c + k + t^*) = 0 \text{ for any given } y^* \geq 0\}. \qquad (22)$$

Differentiation of (21) and (22) yields

$$h^{*\prime}(x) = -(p^{*\prime} + y^*p^{*\prime\prime})/(2p^{*\prime} + y^*p^{*\prime\prime}) < 0, \qquad (23)$$

$$f^{*\prime}(y^*) = -(p^{*\prime} + xp^{*\prime\prime})/(2p^{*\prime} + xp^{*\prime\prime}) < 0. \qquad (24)$$

Let us define

$$h(0) \equiv y^a; \quad h^*(0) \equiv y^{a^*} \text{ and } f(0) \equiv \tilde{x}^*; \quad f^*(0) \equiv \tilde{x} \qquad (25)$$

and

$$p(\bar{x}^*) \equiv c; \quad p^*(\bar{x}) \equiv c^*; \quad p(\bar{y}) \equiv c^* + k + t;$$
$$p^*(\bar{y}) \equiv c + k + t^*. \qquad (26)$$

[1]A matrix is termed an N–P matrix if it has all the principal minors of odd orders negative and those of even orders positive.

Then we have from the definitions of the reaction functions in both markets that

$$h(\bar{x}^*) = 0; \qquad h^*(\bar{x}) = 0 \quad \text{and} \quad f(\tilde{y}) = 0; \qquad f^*(\tilde{y}^*) = 0. \tag{27}$$

Notice that y^a (or y^{a^*}) is the autarkic equilibrium consumption of good Y in the domestic (or foreign) country.

We shall show the following proposition.

PROPOSITION 2. *A necessary and sufficient condition that system of equations* (A) *for any given t and t^* (such that $0 \le t < \tilde{t}$ and $0 \le t^* < \tilde{t}^*$) have a unique positive solution with $y^0 > 0$, $x^0 > 0$, $y^{*0} > 0$, $x^{*0} > 0$ is that*

$$\text{(a)} \quad \tilde{y} > y^0, \quad \bar{x}^* > \tilde{x}^*; \qquad \text{(b)} \quad \tilde{y}^* > y^{a^*}, \quad \bar{x} > \tilde{x}. \tag{28}$$

Proof:

Necessity. Suppose that there exists a unique positive solution to equation system (A) but condition (28) does not hold. Suppose that (28) (a) does not hold. That is, $\tilde{y} \le y^a$ and/or $\bar{x}^* \le \tilde{x}^*$. Suppose that either $\tilde{y} = y^a$ or $\bar{x}^* = \tilde{x}^*$ holds. Then $h(x^*)$ and $f(y)$ have exactly one point of intersection such that either $y^0 = y^a > 0$ and $x^{*0} = 0$ or $y^0 = 0$ and $x^{*0} = \bar{x}^* > 0$holds, a contradiction. Suppose that $\tilde{y} < y^a$. Then

$$-y^a p'(y^a) + c < c^* + k + t, \tag{2.1}$$

since $p(y^a) = -y^a p'(y^a) + c$ and $p(\tilde{y}) = c^* + k + t$. On the other hand, from (2.1),

$$\bar{x}^* > \tilde{x}^*, \tag{2.2}$$

since $p(\bar{x}^*) = c < -\tilde{x}^* p'(\tilde{x}^*) + c^* + k + t = p(\tilde{x}^*)$. Hence we see from (2.1) and (2.2) that $h(x^*)$ and $f(y)$ have exactly one point of intersection such that $(y^0, x^{*0}) > 0$ and $h'(x^{*0}) = 1/f'(y^0)$ (see Figure 1). But from

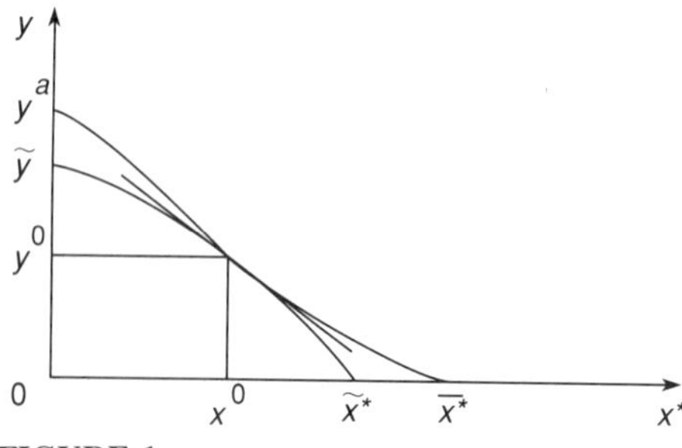

FIGURE 1

(19) and (20),

$$h'(x^{*0}) - 1/f'(y^0)$$

$$= \frac{\left[(p')^2 + p' \cdot (p' + x^{*0}p'') + p' \cdot (p' + y^0 p'')\right]}{(2p' + y^0 p'')(p' + x^{*0}p'')} > 0, \qquad (2.3)$$

a contradiction, since (2.3) holds from (11) and (12).

Suppose that $\tilde{x}^* > \bar{x}^*$. Then

$$c > -\tilde{x}^* p'(\tilde{x}^*) + c^* + k + t, \qquad (2.4)$$

since $p(\bar{x}^*) = c$ and $p(\tilde{x}^*) = -\tilde{x}^* p'(\tilde{x}^*) + c^* + k + t$. On the other hand, from (2.4),

$$\tilde{y} > y^a, \qquad (2.5)$$

since $p(y^a) = -y^a p'(y^a) + c > c^* + k + t = p(\tilde{y})$. Hence we see from (2.4) and (2.5) that $h(x^*)$ and $f(y)$ have exactly one point of intersection such that $(y^0, x^{*0}) > 0$ and $h'(x^{*0}) = 1/f'(y^0)$, a contradiction, since (2.3) holds.

Suppose that (28) (b) does not hold. Then we have contradictions similar to those obtained above.

Sufficiency. Suppose that condition (28) holds. Then we have from Proposition 1 that two continuous functions $h(x^*)$ and $f(y)$ have exactly one point of intersection such that $y^0 > 0$ and $x^{*0} > 0$ (see Figure 2).

Similarly, $h^*(x)$ and $f^*(y^*)$ have exactly one point of intersection such that $y^{*0} > 0$ and $x^0 > 0$ (see Figure 3). ■

Condition (28) is equivalent to

$$-y^a p'(y^a) + c > c^* + k + t > c + \tilde{x}^* p'(\tilde{x}^*)$$

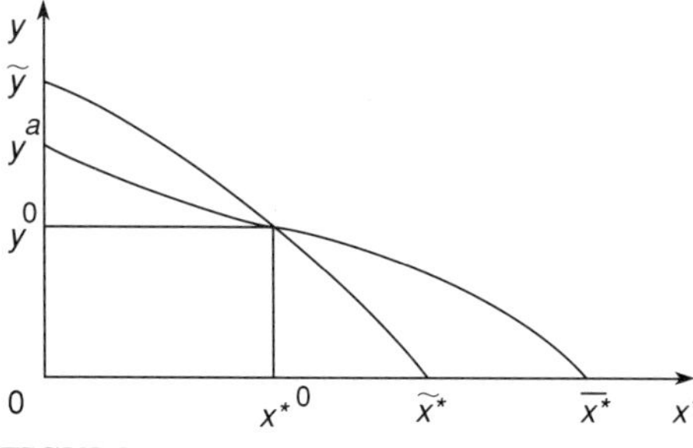

FIGURE 2

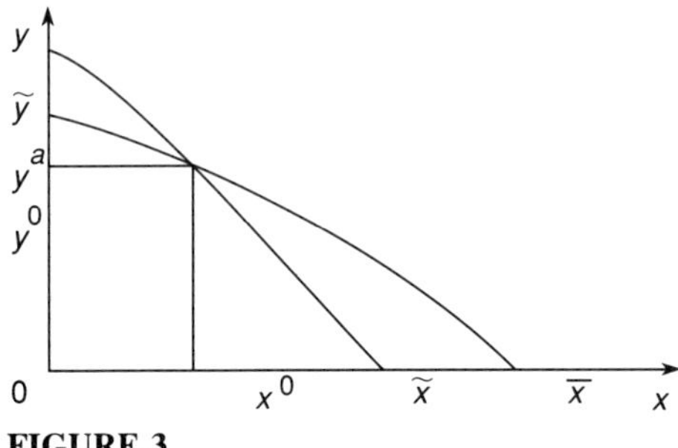

FIGURE 3

and

$$-y^{a^*}p^{*\prime}(y^{a*}) + c^* > c + k + t^* > c^* + \tilde{x}p^{*\prime}(\tilde{x}) \tag{29}$$

for any t and t^* such that $0 \leq t < \tilde{t}$ and $0 \leq t^* < \tilde{t}^*$.

Throughout this paper we assume that condition (28) [and therefore condition (29)] holds. We shall show that condition (29) plays important roles in the following analyses.

4. TARIFF AND INDIVIDUAL COUNTRIES

In this section we examine the effects of tariff changes on each country's consumption of good Y and welfare.

First let us consider the effects on each country's consumption of tariff changes. The unique positive solution to system (A) is determined depending on t and t^*. Therefore the solution to system (A) will have to be written as $y(t, t^*)$, $x(t, t^*)$, $y^*(t, t^*)$, $x^*(t, t^*)$. But for simplicity of notations we will use y^0, x^0, y^{*0}, x^{*0}, as seen in Proposition 2.

Differentiating system (A) partially with respect to t or t^* yields

$$(y_t \quad x_t \quad y_t^* \quad x_t^*) \cdot \Delta = (0 \quad 0 \quad 0 \quad 1) \tag{30}$$

or

$$(y_{t^*} \quad x_{t^*} \quad y_{t^*}^* \quad x_{t^*}^*) \cdot \Delta = (0 \quad 1 \quad 0 \quad 0) \tag{31}$$

where $y_t \equiv \partial y^0/\partial t$, etc.

As long as condition (28) holds, system (A) has a unique positive solution for any given t and t^* such that $0 \leq t < \tilde{t}$ and $0 \leq t^* < \tilde{t}^*$. Therefore, we see from the solution to system (A) that

$$\lim_{t \to \tilde{t}} y(t, t^*) = y^a; \qquad \lim_{t \to \tilde{t}} x^*(t, t^*) = 0$$

and

$$\lim_{t^* \to \tilde{t}^*} y^*(t, t^*) = y^{a^*}; \qquad \lim_{t^* \to \tilde{t}^*} x(t, t^*) = 0. \tag{32}$$

Now the solution to equation system (30) or (31) is obtained from the following inverse matrix of the Jacobian matrix Δ for system (A):

$$\Delta^{-1} = (\delta \cdot \delta^*)^{-1} \begin{bmatrix} V^*_{x^*x^*} \cdot \delta & 0 & 0 & -V^*_{x^*y} \cdot \delta^* \\ 0 & V^*_{y^*y^*} \cdot \delta & -V^*_{y^*x} \cdot \delta & 0 \\ 0 & -V_{xy^*} \cdot \delta & V_{xx} \cdot \delta & 0 \\ -V_{yx^*} \cdot \delta^* & 0 & 0 & V_{yy} \cdot \delta^* \end{bmatrix}. \tag{33}$$

Thus we obtain from (11)–(16) that

$$y_t = -(p' + y^0 p'')/\delta > 0; \qquad x_t = 0$$

and

$$y^*_t = 0; \qquad x^*_t = (2p' + y^0 p'')/\delta < 0 \tag{34}$$

and therefore,

$$X_t = y_t + x^*_t = p'/\delta < 0,$$
$$X^*_t = y^*_t + x_t = 0. \tag{35}$$

Similarly from (31),

$$y^*_t = 0; \qquad x_{t^*} = (2p^{*\prime} + y^{*0} p^{*\prime\prime})/\delta^* < 0,$$
$$y^*_{t^*} = -(p^{*\prime} + y^{*0} p^{*\prime\prime})/\delta^* > 0; \qquad x^*_{t^*} = 0, \tag{36}$$

and therefore,

$$X_{t^*} = y_{t^*} + x^*_{t^*} = 0,$$
$$X^*_{t^*} = y^*_{t^*} + x_{t^*} = p^{*\prime}/\delta^* < 0. \tag{37}$$

Thus we obtain from (32), (35), and (37) the following two propositions.

PROPOSITION 3. *Each country's consumption of good Y is greater under intraindustry trade between two countries containing tariffs t and t^* than under autarky.*

PROPOSITION 4. *An increase of t (or t^*) reduces the domestic (or foreign) country's consumption of good Y and the foreign (or domestic) firm's production, and increases the domestic (or foreign) firm's production.*

In the social utility function (4) each country's consumptions m and m^* of good Z are determined as follows. Let

$$L_z = m + z \quad \text{and} \quad z = x^{*0} p(X^0) - x^0 p^*(X^{*0}), \tag{38}$$

where z is positive or negative according to whether the domestic country imports or exports good Y. Therefore,

$$L_z = x^{*0}p(X^0) - x^0p^*(X^{*0})$$

and

$$L_z^* = m^* + x^0p^*(X^{*0}) - x^{*0}p(X^0). \tag{39}$$

Since $L_z = L - L_y$ and $L_z^* = L^* - L_y^*$, we have from (2) that

$$U(t,t^*) = u(X^0) + L - F - c(y^0 + x^0) - x^{*0}p(X^0)$$
$$+ x^0p^*(X^{*0}) - kx^0 + tx^{*0} - t^*x^0 \tag{40}$$

and

$$U^*(t,t^*) = u^*(X^{*0}) + L^* - F^* - c^*(y^{*0} + x^{*0}) + x^{*0}p(X^0)$$
$$- x^0p^*(X^{*0}) - kx^{*0} + t^*x^0 - tx^{*0}. \tag{41}$$

Differentiating (40) partially with respect to t yields

$$U_t = (p - c)y_t + x^{*0}(1 - p' \cdot X_t) + tx_t^*. \tag{42}$$

Let us examine the sign of $(1 - p' \cdot X_t)$. Using (16) and (35), we have that

$$1 - p' \cdot X_t = p' \cdot (2p' + x^{*0}p'')/\delta > 0. \tag{43}$$

Hence we obtain from (42) and (43) the following proposition.

PROPOSITION 5. *An increase in the domestic tariff increases the domestic welfare if initially t is sufficiently small.*

Maximizing U with respect to t yields a first-order condition, that is, $U_t = 0$. Thus the optimal tariff $\bar{t}$ in the domestic country yields

$$\bar{t} = -\left[(p - c)y_t + x^{*0}(1 - p' \cdot X_t)\right]/x_t^* > 0. \tag{44}$$

PROPOSITION 6. *The optimal profit-shifting tariff is positive.*[2]

Remark. Brander and Spencer (1984a) have also considered the optimal rent seeking specific tariff in a setting of Cournot competition among domestic and foreign firms, but concluded only that the optimal tariff may be positive, zero, or negative. An increase in tariff decreases the level of domestic consumption in their model as well as in ours. It may be

[2]Brander and Spencer (1984a, Proposition 2) have insisted: "With both domestic and foreign firms, $p_t < 1$ is sufficient but not necessary for the optimal profit-shifting tariff to be positive. In particular, a positive tariff is optimal if $p_t < 1 + (p - c)y_t/x^{*0}$" using our notations.

harmful for domestic welfare to impose a tariff. However, unlike in the Brander–Spencer model, our domestic firm supplies both home and foreign markets, and it keeps an opportunity to gain more in the foreign country even if the domestic consumption decreases as the result of tariff imposition.

Differentiating (41) partially with respect to t yields

$$U_t^* = x^{*0}(p' \cdot y_t - 1) < 0,$$

since y_t is negative. Thus we have the following proposition.

PROPOSITION 7. *An increase in the domestic tariff decreases necessarily the foreign welfare.*

5. TARIFF AND WORLD WELFARE

In this section we examine the effect on the world welfare of a change in the domestic tariff.

The total world welfare is represented as $U^w = U + U^*$. We have from (40) and (41) that

$$U^w(t, t^*) = u(X^0) + L - F - c(y^0 + x^0) - kx^0 + u^*(X^{*0}) + L^* - F^* - c^*(y^{*0} + x^{*0}) - kx^{*0}. \tag{45}$$

Let us assume free trade between two countries in the beginning for simplicity of exposition, that is, $t = t^* = 0$. Differentiating (45) partially with respect to t yields

$$U_t^w = (p - c)y_t + (p - c^* - k)x_t^* + \left[(p - c^* - k)p' + (c - c^* - k)(p' + y^0 p'')\right]/\delta. \tag{46}$$

On the other hand, from condition (29),

$$y^a p'(y^a) < c - c^* - k < -\tilde{x}^* p'(\tilde{x}^*). \tag{29'}$$

Now either $c - c^* - k \geq 0$ or $c - c^* - k < 0$ holds. Suppose that $c - c^* - k \geq 0$. Then either

$$-\tilde{x}^* p'(\tilde{x}^*) < c - c^* - k \tag{47}$$

or

$$0 \leq c - c^* - k < -\tilde{x}^* p'(\tilde{x}^*) \tag{48}$$

holds.

Suppose that (47) holds. Then we see from Proposition 2 that intra-industry trade between two countries does not exist. Thus we obtain the following proposition.

PROPOSITION 8. *If condition* (48) *holds, then an increase in the domestic tariff decreases the world welfare.*[3]

Suppose that $c - c^* - k < 0$. Consider the following two equations:

$$p(y^a) + y^a p'(y^a) - c = 0, \tag{49}$$

$$p(X^0) + y^0 p'(X^0) - c = 0. \tag{50}$$

Subtracting (50) from (49) yields

$$p(y^a) - p(X^0) + y^a p'(X^0) = 0,$$

Hence,

$$y^a p'(y^a) < y^0 p'(x^0), \tag{51}$$

since $p(y^a) > p(X^0)$ from Proposition 3. Therefore, either

$$y^0 p'(X^0) < c - c^* - k < 0 \tag{52}$$

or

$$y^a p'(y^a) < c - c^* - k < y^0 p'(X^0). \tag{53}$$

Now we have from (46) that

$$U_t^w = \left[\left(-y^0 p'(X^0) + c - c^* - k \right) p' + (c - c^* - k)\left(p' + y^0 p'' \right) \right] / \delta. \tag{54}$$

Suppose that (52) holds. Then the sign of (54) is indeterminate. Suppose that (53) holds. Then we see from (54) that $U_t^w > 0$. Hence we obtain the following proposition.

PROPOSITION 9. *If condition* (53) *holds, then an increase in the domestic tariff increases world welfare.*

Now let us interpret Propositions 8 and 9 economically. Condition (48) implies that production technology of the domestic firm is inferior to that of the foreign firm. Increase of domestic tariff increases inefficient domestic production and reduces efficient foreign production of good Y by Proposition 4, and therefore decreases the world welfare if condition (48) holds.

[3]Brander and Spencer (1984a, Proposition 4) have insisted: "If foreign marginal cost (including transport cost) is less than or equal to domestic marginal cost, an increase in the domestic tariff decreases world welfare." However, the domestic firm will not be able to enter into both markets if $-x^* p'(x^*) < c - c^* - k$.

On the other hand, condition (53) implies that production technology of the domestic firm is greatly superior to that of the foreign firm. Increase of domestic tariff increases much efficient domestic production and decreases inefficient foreign production and therefore increases the world welfare if condition (53) holds.[4]

Next consider the following two equations:

$$p(y^a) + y^a p'(y^a) - c = 0, \tag{55}$$

$$p(X^0) + x^{*0} p'(X^0) - (c^* + k) = 0. \tag{56}$$

Subtracting (56) from (55) yields

$$p(f^a) - p(X^0) + y^a p'(y^a) - x^{*0} p'(X^0) = c - c^* - k < 0. \tag{57}$$

Hence we have from (57) that

$$x^{*0} p'(X^0) > y^a p'(y^a), \tag{58}$$

since $p(X^a) > p(X^0)$ from Proposition 3.

On the other hand, from (46),

$$U_t^w = \left[\left(-x^{*0} p'(X^0) + c - c^* - k\right) p'(X^0) + (c - c^* - k) y^0 p''(X^0)\right] \big/ \delta. \tag{59}$$

Now either $p'' > 0$ or $p'' \leq 0$ holds. We have the following two conditions:

$$x^{*0} p'(X^0) < c - c^* - k < 0 \quad \text{and} \quad p'' > 0. \tag{60}$$

$$y^a p'(y^a) < c - c^* - k < x^{*0} p'(X^0) \quad \text{and} \quad p'' \leq 0. \tag{61}$$

Thus we see that $U_t^w < 0$ if condition (60) holds, and $U_t^w > 0$ if condition (61) holds.

Proposition 10. *An increase in the domestic tariff decreases world welfare if condition* (60) *holds.*

Proposition 11. *An increase in the domestic tariff increases world welfare if condition* (61) *holds.*

Acknowledgments

The author is indebted to Professors M. C. Kemp and R. W. Jones for their helpful comments and suggestions. I also thank Professors E. Bond and K. Okuguchi.

[4]This economic interpretation was suggested by Professor Jones.

References

Brander, J. A. (1981). "Intra-industry trade in identical commodities," *J. Int. Econ.* **11**, 1–14.

Brander, J. A., and P. R. Krugman (1983). "A reciprocal dumping model of international trade," *J. Int. Econ.* **15**, 313–321.

Brander, J. A., and B. J. Spencer (1984a). "Tariff protection and imperfect competition," in *Monopolistic Competition and International Trade*, H. Kierzkowski, (ed.) (Oxford Univ. Press, London).

Brander, J. A., and B. J. Spencer (1984b). "Trade warfare, tariff and cartels," *J. Int. Econ.* **16**, 227–242.

Dixit, A. K. (1984). "International trade policy for oligopolistic industries," *Econ. J.* **94**, 1–16.

Nikaido, H. (1968). *Convex Structures and Economic Theory* (Academic Press, New York).

Venables, A. J. (1985). "Trade and trade policy with imperfect competition: The case of identical products and free entry," *J. Int. Econ.* **19**, 1–19.

INTERNATIONAL TRANSFERS IN DYNAMIC ECONOMIES

Makoto Yano
Faculty of Economics
Yokohama National University
Yokohama, Japan
and
Department of Economics
University of Southern California
Los Angeles, California 90089

1. INTRODUCTION

This study analyzes the effect of an international transfer in a dynamic general equilibrium model. In a static general equilibrium model, as is well known, an exogenous change has substitution effects on both production and consumption and income effects on consumption. Counterparts to these effects, naturally, exist in a dynamic model. Substitution effects work both intersectorally and intertemporally. Income effects work on the consumption side. Moreover, what may be called *capital accumulation effects* work on the production side, because an exogenous change generally affects the path of capital accumulation. The existing literature has, however, not yet built a comparative dynamic method, comparable to the standard method of local comparative statics, that can capture these effects in a unified manner. The main part of this study is devoted to presenting the first step toward building the method of local comparative dynamics for a simple dynamic general equilibrium model.

My local comparative dynamics establishes several conclusions with respect to the dynamic effects of an international transfer. First, a transfer can cause what I call an *intertemporal welfare effect reversal*; in other words, after a once-and-for-all transfer is made in the initial period, a participant's discounted utility sum and its utility in the stationary state to which an equilibrium path will converge may change in opposite directions. Second, an intertemporal welfare effect reversal can occur even if a

GENERAL EQUILIBRIUM, GROWTH, AND TRADE II

transfer has the normal overall welfare effect, i.e., increases its recipient's discounted utility sum and reduces that of its donor. This suggests that a country might wish to receive a transfer even if it knows that it will be worse off with respect to long-run utility. Although Yano (1991) demonstrates this possibility, it was limited to the case in which consumptions in different periods are perfect substitutes. This study demonstrates that the intertemporal welfare effect reversal is not a pathological phenomenon specific to that case but can occur in a general setting in which intertemporal substitutability of consumptions is imperfect. Second, it demonstrates that an international transfer can cause "real business cycles," i.e., that the equilibrium path after a transfer may fluctuate around a trend even if the economy is in a stationary equilibrium before the transfer.

The model of this study features market equilibrium by assuming that markets are complete for all the future goods. It also features optimal capital accumulation by assuming that producers must make investment one period before output will be produced. The study of a model with these features was pioneered by Wan (1971), which was concerned with the case of a finite time horizon and a single good. In contrast, a growing number of studies have been concerned with the case of an infinite time horizon and multiple goods, on which also this study focuses.

The comparative dynamics of this study is based on the turnpike property that a perfect foresight equilibrium path will converge to a stationary state with time. In general, the convergence is not guaranteed if von Neumann facets are nontrivial (see McKenzie, 1983). Moreover, von Neumann facets are generally nontrivial in models with constant-returns-to-scale technologies. This study builds a two-sector model that allows each sector to have a standard neoclassical production function (which is of constant returns to scale) and, at the same time, excludes the existence of nontrivial von Neumann facets.[1]

This study develops a method of local comparative statics that can characterize the effect of an exogenous change in terms of intertemporal and intersectoral substitution effects, income effects, and capital accumulation effects. Although, in the existing literature, the dynamic effect of a transfer has not been related to these effects, it has been analyzed by several studies. Bewley (1982) demonstrates that a transfer affects the stationary state to which an equilibrium path will converge. Yano (1984b) demonstrates that this fact can be attributed to the discounting of future

[1]In order to trivialize von Neumann facets, Bewley (1982) and Marimon (1989) assume decreasing returns technology, and Yano (1984a) assumes that the social production set is a laterally strictly convex cone. Coles (1985) allows for nontrivial von Neumann facets and proves the convergence of an equilibrium path to a neighborhood of a von Neumann facet by extending the method of McKenzie (1983).

utilities; if the discount factor is exogenously shifted so that future utilities may become as important as present utilities, a transfer has no effect on the stationary state. Lipton and Sachs (1983) analyze the dynamic effect of a transfer by simulation. Epstein (1987) characterizes the welfare effect of a transfer by a local comparative statics. That study, however, focuses intertemporal substitutability in a single-good model with recursive utility functions so that the interaction between intertemporal and intersectoral substitution effects is not taken into account.

In what follows, Section 2 sets up the model. Section 3 states the main theorems. Section 4 discusses their interpretations. Section 5 through Section 10 are devoted to proving the theorems.

2. MODEL

There are two countries, $h = \alpha, \beta$, and two goods, $i = 1, 2$. Good 1 is the pure consumption good; good 2 can be used as input as well as consumed. Let R_+^2 be the nonnegative orthant of the two-dimensional real space, R^2. Denote by $\varphi_t = (\varphi_{1t}, \varphi_{2t}) \in R_+^2$ the sequences of *present* value prices of goods in period t.

Country h's periodwise preference is summarized by a single utility function, $u^h : R_+^2 \to R$, $u_t^h = u^h(D_t^h)$, where $D_t^h = (D_{1t}^h, D_{2t}^h)$ is h's consumption vector in period t. Define the following functions:

$$\mathbf{v}^h(q, Y^h) = \max u^h(D_1, D_2) \quad \text{s.t. } qD_1 + D_2 = Y^h;$$

$$\left(\mathbf{D}_1^h(q, u^h), \mathbf{D}_2^h(q, u^h)\right) = \operatorname{argmin} qD_1 + D_2 \quad \text{s.t. } u^h(D_1, D_2) = u^h.$$

Function $\mathbf{v}^h$ is an indirect utility function, which is defined with respect to the relative price of good 1, q, and income Y^h. Function $\mathbf{D}_i^h$ is a compensated demand function, which is defined with respect to the relative price and utility u^h. Denote by $\mathbf{v}_q^h$ and $\mathbf{v}_Y^h$ the partial derivatives of $\mathbf{v}^h(q, Y)$ with respect to q and Y, respectively; moreover, denote by $\mathbf{D}_{iq}^h$ and $\mathbf{D}_{iu}^h$ the partial derivatives of $\mathbf{D}_i^h(q, u^h)$ with respect to q and u^h, respectively. Assume $\mathbf{v}_Y^h > 0$, $\mathbf{v}_{YY}^h < 0$ and $\mathbf{D}_{lq}^h < 0$.

The optimization of country h's consumers can be summarized as $\max_{\{Y_t\}} \Sigma_{t=1}^{\infty} \rho^t \mathbf{v}^h(q_t, Y_t)$ subject to $\Sigma_{t=1}^{\infty} \varphi_t Y_t = W^h$, where ρ, $0 < \rho < 1$, is the discount factor of the future utilities,[2] q_t is the relative price of the

[2]Becker (1980) and Fukao and Hamada (1989) consider the case in which agents have different discount factors. In that case, the agents eventually consume nothing except those who have the weakest discount factor.

period t good 1 in terms of the period t good 2, φ_t is the present value price of the period t good 2, and W^h is h's wealth. (The wealth will be defined below.) By the first-order condition of optimization,

$$\mathbf{v}_Y^h(q_t, Y_t^h) = \gamma^h \rho^{-t} \varphi_t, \tag{2.1}$$

where γ^h is country h's marginal utility of wealth (a Lagrangean multiplier). Equation (2.1) indicates that $\rho^{-t}\varphi_t$ may be regarded as the current value price of the period t good 2; denote it by $p_t \equiv \rho^{-t}\varphi_t$. Since, by (2.1), consumption demand Y_t^h can be written as $Y_t^h = Y^h(q_t, \gamma^h p_t)$, u_t^h can also be expressed indirectly as a function of q_t and $\gamma^h p_t$,

$$u_t^h = v^h(q_t, \gamma^h p_t) \equiv \mathbf{v}^h(q_t, Y^h(q_t, \gamma^h p_t)). \tag{2.2}$$

This implies that h's demands for the period t good i can be written as a Frisch demand function,

$$D_{it}^h = D_i^h(q_t, \gamma^h p_t) \equiv \mathbf{D}_i^h(q_t, v^h(q_t, \gamma^h p_t)). \tag{2.3}$$

To produce output in period t, good 2 must be used in period $t-1$ and the primary goods in period t. In this sense I call good 2 the *capital good*. The relationship between capital input and outputs is captured by what I call a *capital input function*, $k^h : R_+^2 \to R$; $K = k^h(X)$ indicates that country h needs K units of good 2 in order to produce outputs $X = (X_1, X_2)$. Define the following functions:

$$\mathbf{c}^h(q, Z^h) = \min k^h(X_1, X_2) \quad \text{s.t. } qX_1 + X_2 = Z^h;$$

$$(\mathbf{X}_1^h(q, K^h), \mathbf{X}_2^h(q, K^h)) = \operatorname{argmax} qX_1 + X_2 \quad \text{s.t. } k^h(X_1, X_2) = K^h.$$

Function c^h may be called a *capital cost function* (note the difference between capital cost and capital input functions). Given a relative price of good 1, q, the minimum amount of capital that country h needs to produce $qX_1 + X_2$ units of gross output is $\mathbf{c}^h(q, qX_1 + X_2)$. Function $\mathbf{X}_i^h$ may be called a *compensated supply function*, which is defined parallel to the compensated demand functions above; if capital input K^h are kept constant, country h would supply $\mathbf{X}_i^h(q, K^h)$ units of good i, given a relative price, q. Denote by $\mathbf{c}_q^h$ and $\mathbf{c}_Z^h$ the partial derivatives of $\mathbf{c}^h(q, Z^h)$ with respect to q and Z^h, respectively; moreover, denote by $\mathbf{X}_{iq}^h$ and $\mathbf{X}_{iK}^h$ those of $\mathbf{X}_i^h(q, K^h)$ with respect to q and K^h, respectively. Assume $\mathbf{c}_Z^h > 0$, $\mathbf{c}_{ZZ}^h < 0$, and $\mathbf{X}_{1q}^h > 0$.

Remark 1. Behind a capital input function, production processes of industries may be considered, in which industries use primary good inputs, such as labor, as well as the produced good input (capital). In the Kemp–Khang model (see Kemp and Khang, 1974), in which the existence of two primary goods is assumed, the above conditions on function $\mathbf{c}^h$ and $\mathbf{X}_{1q}^h$ can be guaranteed. In the Heckscher–Ohlin–Samuelson model, in contrast, it is well known that $\mathbf{c}_{ZZ}^h = 0$ and that, by the Rybcyzski theorem, $\mathbf{X}_{1k}^h < 0$ and $\mathbf{X}_{2k}^h > 0$ if sector 1 is capital intensive. This case can be, as seen below, captured as a limit case of the present model. Note that in the Kemp-Khang model, $\mathbf{X}_{1K}^h$ and $\mathbf{X}_{2K}^h$ can take any combination of signs.

The optimization of h's industries gives rise to

$$\max_{\{Z_t\}} \sum_{t=1}^{\infty} \left(\varphi_t Z_t - \varphi_{t-1}\mathbf{c}^h(q_t, Z_t)\right).$$

By the first-order condition of optimization,

$$\mathbf{c}_Z^h\left(q_t, Z_t^h\right) = \varphi_t/\varphi_{t-1} = \rho p_t/p_{t-1}. \tag{2.4}$$

Thus, h's supply of gross output, Z_t^h, can be written as a function of $q_t, p_t, \rho^{-1}p_{t-1}$,

$$Z_t^h = \mathbf{Z}^h\left(q_t, p_t, \rho^{-1}p_{t-1}\right). \tag{2.5}$$

Thus, h's demand for the period $t-1$ capital can be written as

$$K_{t-1}^h = K^h\left(q_t, p_t, \rho^{-1}p_{t-1}\right) \equiv \mathbf{c}^h\left(q_t, Z^h\left(q_t, p_t, \rho^{-1}p_{t-1}\right)\right), \tag{2.6}$$

and its supply of the period t good i can be written as

$$X_{it}^h = \mathbf{X}_i^h\left(q_t, p_t, \rho^{-1}p_{t-1}\right) \equiv \mathbf{X}_i^h\left(q_t, K^h\left(q_t, p_t, \rho^{-1}p_{t-1}\right)\right). \tag{2.7}$$

Denote by T^h country h's transfer payment ($T^\alpha = -T^\beta \equiv T$) and by $K_0^h \in R_+$ country h's capital endowments at time 0. Then, country h's wealth W^h consists of the value of initial asset, $p_0\overline{K}_0^k$, the present value of the returns from the production sector, $\Sigma_{t=1}^{\infty}\rho^t(p_t Z_t - \rho^{-1}p_{t-1}\mathbf{c}^h(q_t, Z_t))$, and transfer T^h; that is,

$$W^h = -T^h + p_0\overline{K}_0^h + \sum_{t=1}^{\infty}\rho^t\left(p_t Z_t - \rho^{-1}p_{t-1}\mathbf{c}^h(q_t, Z_t)\right). \tag{2.8}$$

An economy is in a *perfect foresight equilibrium* if there is a sequence of prices (q_t, p_t) and marginal utilities of wealth γ^h that satisfy the market clearing conditions,

$$\left.\begin{aligned} &\sum_h \left(D_1^h(q_t, \gamma^h p_t) - X_1^h(q_t, p_t, \rho^{-1}p_{t-1})\right) = 0 \\ &\qquad \sum_h \left(D_2^h(q_t, \gamma^h p_t) - X_2^h(q_t, p_t, \rho^{-1}p_{t-1})\right. \\ &\qquad\qquad\qquad \left. +K^h(q_{t+1}, p_{t+1}, \rho^{-1}p_t)\right) = 0 \\ &\qquad\qquad\qquad\qquad\qquad t = 1, 2, \ldots, \end{aligned}\right\} \tag{2.9}$$

as well as the wealth constraints,

$$\begin{aligned} &\sum_{t=1}^{\infty} \rho^t p_t\left(q_t D_1^h(q_t, \gamma^h p_t) + D_2^h(q_t, \gamma^h p_t)\right) \\ &\quad = -T^h + -p_0 \bar{K}_0^h + \sum_{t=1}^{\infty} \rho^t\left(p_t Z_t(q_t, p_t, \rho^{-1}p_{t-1})\right. \\ &\qquad\qquad \left. -\rho^{-1}p_{t-1}K^h(q_t, p_t, \rho^{-1}p_{t-1})\right), \end{aligned} \tag{2.10}$$

$h = \alpha, \beta$. (If (2.9) and (2.10) are satisfied, the market for the period 0 good 2 is also cleared, i.e., $\Sigma_h(K^h(\varphi_0, \varphi_1) - K_0^h) = 0$ holds, by the Walras law.) Because this is a standard general equilibrium system, I may choose one good as the numeraire and set its price identically equal to 1; let

$$p_0 \equiv 1. \tag{2.11}$$

The equilibrium system, (2.9) and (2.10), features both market equilibrium and optimal capital accumulation. As an equilibrium system, this system is very similar to that considered by Negishi (1960) for the static case. The idea is to take two steps. First, given transfer $T^\alpha = -T^\beta$, pick marginal utilities of wealth γ^α and γ^β, arbitrarily, and find the allocation of discounted utility sums that maximizes $\Sigma_h \Sigma_{t=1}^{\infty} \rho^t u_t^h / \gamma^h$ over all feasible allocations of discounted utility sums. Because the path of capital accumulation that achieves the maximum $\Sigma_h \Sigma_{t=1}^{\infty} \rho^t u_t^h / \gamma^h$ is an optimal path, there is a price path that supports the optimal path (see McKenzie, 1986).

System (2.9) captures such a support price path, p_t. In the capital theoretic terminology, system (2.9) may be viewed as a system of Euler equations. By using the first equation of (2.9), q_t can be erased from the second equation. This results in a second-order recursive system of p_{t-1}, p_t, and p_{t+1}, which may be thought of as the dual of Euler equations. The path that starts from $p_0 = 1$ and converges to the saddlepoint of the recursive system supports an optimal path. In this way, price paths p_t and q_t can be determined for the arbitrarily chosen γ^α and γ^β.

In general, these price paths and the γ^α and γ^β do not satisfy budget equations. The second step is, therefore, to pick γ^α and γ^β so that together with the corresponding prices they satisfy the budget equations (2.10).

My comparative dynamic takes the same steps as those explained above. Denote by $\hat{x} = dx/x$ the relative change in variable x. By applying an infinite-dimensional implicit function theorem to (2.9), relative changes $\hat{p}_1, \hat{p}_2, \ldots$ and $\hat{q}_1, \hat{q}_2, \ldots$ can be related to $\hat{\gamma}^\alpha$ and $\hat{\gamma}^\beta$.[3] Then, by substituting those results into the total differentiation of (2.10), $\hat{\gamma}^\alpha$ and $\hat{\gamma}^\beta$ can be related to infinitesimal transfer $dT^\alpha = -dT^\beta$. By using these relationships, we can characterize the welfare effect of a transfer.

3. COMPARATIVE DYNAMICS AND STATICS: MAIN THEOREMS

In general, an equilibrium path, satisfying the system of (2.9) and (2.10), converges to a stationary state; $\hat{p}_\infty = \lim_{t\to\infty} \hat{p}_t$ and $\hat{q}_\infty = \lim_{t\to\infty} \hat{q}_t$ are well defined. Thus, the effect of a transfer can be analyzed from two viewpoints, comparative dynamics and statics. As in the standard literature on growth theory, I refer as *comparative dynamics* to the analysis of an equilibrium path as a whole, i.e., of such variables as $\hat{p}_t$ and $\hat{q}_t$, and as *comparative statics* to that of a stationary state to which an equilibrium path converges, i.e., of such variables as $\hat{p}_\infty$ and $\hat{q}_\infty$.

In order to make the comparison between pre- and posttransfer stationary states more meaningful, I assume that before a transfer, the economy is in a stationary equilibrium. If the pretransfer equilibrium path were not stationary, such a comparison would be of less significance, for the stationary state that the pretransfer equilibrium path would have reached in the infinitely far future is less relevant once a transfer has been made.

[3] Araujo and Scheinkman (1978) have developed a method of local comparative dynamics for an optimal growth model. Their method is similar in nature to the analysis of system (2.9) in this study. Because, $\hat{q}_t$, $\hat{p}_t$, $\hat{\gamma}^\alpha$, and $\hat{\gamma}^\beta$ must be determined consistently with the wealth constraints, (2.10), this study deals with a structure more complicated than that of Araujo and Scheinkman (1978).

Assumption 1. The pretransfer equilibrium path is stationary.

Moreover, in order to simplify my analysis, I make the following assumption (this assumption can be dispensed with).

Assumption 2. In the pretransfer stationary equilibrium, each country's trade account is balanced.

In the pretransfer stationary equilibrium, under Assumption 2, the following holds for $t = 1, 2, \ldots$:

$$q_t\left(D_{1t}^h - X_{1t}^h\right) + \left(D_{2t}^h - X_{2t}^h + K_t^h\right) = 0; \tag{3.1}$$

$$p_t = 1. \tag{3.2}$$

It is important to note that (3.1) and (3.2) hold only in the pretransfer equilibrium; once a transfer is made, the equilibrium price and balances of trade will change. Denote by q the relative price of good 1 in terms of good 2 in the pretransfer stationary equilibrium and by M^α and M^β, respectively, α's volume of imports and β's volume of imports in the pretransfer stationary equilibrium. Assume that α imports good 1 in the pretransfer stationary equilibrium. By (3.1),

$$M^\alpha = M^\beta / q > 0. \tag{3.3}$$

As noted above, $\mathbf{v}_{YY}^h$ and $\mathbf{c}_{ZZ}^h$ capture intertemporal substitutability on the consumption and production sides, respectively. Thus, I define $\sigma^h \equiv -v_Y^h/(M^\beta \mathbf{v}_{YY}^h) > 0$ and $\sigma_X^h \equiv \mathbf{c}_Z^h/(M^\beta \mathbf{c}_{ZZ}^h) > 0$ and call them *indices of intertemporal substitution in consumption and in production*, respectively. As explained above, $\mathbf{D}_{1q}^h$ and $\mathbf{X}_{1q}^h$ capture intersectoral substitutability on the consumption and production sides, respectively. Hence, I define $\eta^h \equiv -q(\mathbf{D}_{1q}^h - \mathbf{X}_{1q}^h)/M^\alpha > 0$ and call it an *index of intersectoral substitution*. Because $\eta^\beta = q(\mathbf{D}_{2q}^\beta - \mathbf{X}_{2q}^\beta)/M^\beta$, η^h may be viewed as an elasticity of doubly compensated import demand. (I say "doubly" in the sense that h's utility and h's capital input are both compensated.)

Define $m^h \equiv q\mathbf{D}_{1u}^h v_y^h$, which is the standard *marginal propensity to consume good* 1. In parallel, define $m_X^h \equiv q\mathbf{X}_{1K}^h \mathbf{c}_Z^h$, which I call the *marginal propensity to expand sector* 1. This parameter captures the effect on sector 1's output of an increase in gross output $Z^h = qX_1^h + X_2^h$. In order to increase gross output Z^h, given primary inputs, it is necessary to increase capital input K^h, which $\mathbf{c}_Z^h$ captures. Given a relative price q, the increase in capital input affects sector 1's output, which $\mathbf{X}_{1K}^h$ captures. Therefore, the increase in the value of sector 1's output per unit gross output increase is captured by m_X^h. Sector 1 may be called a *normal sector* if $m_X^h > 0$ and an *inferior sector* if $m^h < 0$; these concepts parallel to the normality and inferiority on the consumption side.

Define $\sigma \equiv \Sigma_h \sigma^h$, $\sigma_X \equiv \Sigma_h \sigma_X^h$, $\eta \equiv \Sigma_h \eta^h$, $m = \Sigma_h \omega^h m^h$, $m_X \equiv \Sigma_h \omega_X^h m_X^h$, $\omega \equiv \omega^\alpha \omega^\beta$ and $\omega_X \equiv \omega_X^\alpha \omega_X^\beta > 0$, where $\omega^h \equiv \sigma^h/\sigma$ and $\omega_X^h \equiv \sigma_X^h/\sigma_X$. Parameters σ and σ_X capture aggregate intertemporal substitutability, respectively, in consumption and in production; η captures aggregate intersectoral substitutability; and, m and m_X capture average income effects, respectively, on the consumption side and on the production side. Moreover, define the following parameters:

$$s^h \equiv \eta^h + \sigma_X^h \left(m_X^h\right)^2 > 0; \tag{3.4a}$$

$$s \equiv \eta + \sigma_X \omega_X \left(m_X^\alpha - m_X^\beta\right)^2 + \sigma_X m_X^2 \left(= \sum_h s^h\right) > 0; \tag{3.4b}$$

$$s_* \equiv s + \sigma\omega\left(m^\alpha - m^\beta\right)^2 > 0; \tag{3.4c}$$

$$s_{**} \equiv s + \sigma\omega\left(m^\alpha - m^\beta\right)^2 + \sigma m^2 > 0; \tag{3.4d}$$

$$\Delta \equiv s + m^\alpha - m^\beta; \tag{3.4e}$$

$$\mu^h \equiv (1-\rho)\sigma_X^h m_X^h; \tag{3.4f}$$

$$\mu \equiv \sum_h \mu^h; \tag{3.4g}$$

$$c_2 \equiv \rho\sigma_X\left[\varphi + \sigma m(m - m_X)\right]; \tag{3.4h}$$

$$c_1 \equiv -\left[(\sigma + (1+\rho)\sigma_X)\varphi + \sigma_X\sigma\left((m - m_X)^2 + \rho m^2\right)\right]; \tag{3.4i}$$

$$c_0 \equiv \rho^{-1} c_2; \tag{3.4j}$$

$$\varphi \equiv \eta + \sigma_X\omega_X\left(m_X^\alpha - m_X^\beta\right)^2 + \sigma\omega\left(m^\alpha - m^\beta\right)^2 > 0. \tag{3.4k}$$

Take the recursive system

$$c_2 x_{t+1} + c_1 x_t + c_0 x_{t-1} = 0, \tag{3.5}$$

and denote by λ and λ' its characteristic roots, satisfying

$$|\lambda| \le |\lambda'|. \tag{3.6}$$

Assumption 3.

$$\Delta\left[\frac{(1-\rho)\lambda}{1-\lambda}\sigma(s_* - \mu m) + \mu\left(\sigma m + \mu\left(1 - \frac{s_{**}}{\Delta}\right)\right)\right] \neq 0.$$

The main results of this studies are as follow.

THEOREM 1. *If* $-1 \leq \lambda < 1$, *there are constants* C_p *and* C_q *such that the following holds*:

$$\hat{p}_t = C_p(1 - \lambda^t)\, dT^\alpha; \tag{3.7}$$

$$\hat{q}_t = C_q(1 - \lambda^t)\, dT^\alpha. \tag{3.8}$$

THEOREM 2. (*Adjustment-path effects.*) *Suppose* $-1 \leq \lambda < 1$. *Let* $\gamma \equiv \gamma^\beta/\gamma^\alpha$, $Q \equiv (\rho^{-1} - 1)\Sigma_{t=1}^\infty \rho^t q_t$, $P \equiv (\rho^{-1} - 1)\Sigma_{t=1}^\infty \rho^t p_t$ *and* $d\tau^h \equiv (\rho^{-1} - 1)\, dT^h$. *Then*,

$$d\gamma/dT^\alpha < 0 \Leftrightarrow \sum_{t=1}^\infty \rho^t\, du_t^\alpha/dT^\alpha < 0 \quad \text{and} \quad \sum_{t=1}^\infty \rho^t\, du_t^\beta/dT^\alpha > 0. \tag{3.9}$$

Moreover,

$$\hat{\gamma} = -\frac{1}{\omega\delta\Delta}(s_* - \mu m)\left(\frac{(1-\rho)\lambda}{1-\lambda}s_* + \mu m\right)\frac{d\tau^\alpha}{M^\beta}, \tag{3.10}$$

where

$$\delta \equiv \frac{(1-\rho)\lambda}{1-\lambda}\sigma(s_* - \mu m) + \mu\left(\sigma m + \mu\left(1 - \frac{s_{**}}{\Delta}\right)\right). \tag{3.11}$$

Remark 2. Assumption 3 is crucial in my comparative dynamics; it implies $\delta\Delta \neq 0$, which is necessary for relating $d\gamma$ to $d\tau^\alpha$ in (3.10). Mathematically speaking, Assumption 3 makes it possible to apply an inverse function theorem to the equilibrium system so that the endogenous variables can be locally expressed as functions of transfer τ^α. Because the equilibrium system is infinite dimensional, in principle, an infinite dimensional inverse function theorem is necessary (see Araujo and Scheinkman, 1978a, and Yano, 1989b, which employ such theorems in the analysis of infinite-dimensional systems). Under my assumptions, however, it is possible to derive the local characterization, (3.10), without explicitly considering the invertibility of an infinite-dimensional derivative.

THEOREM 3. (*Stationary-state effects.*) *Suppose* $-1 \leq \lambda < 1$. *Limits* $u_\infty^h \equiv \lim_{t\to\infty} u_t^h$ *and* $q_\infty \equiv \lim_{t\to\infty} q_t$ *are well defined. For the* $\hat{\gamma}$ *in Theorem* 1, *the following holds*:

$$du_\infty^\alpha/u_2^\alpha = M^\beta\frac{\sigma\omega}{s_* - \mu m}(s - \mu m^\beta)\hat{\gamma}; \tag{3.12}$$

$$du_\infty^\beta/u_2^\beta = -M^\beta\frac{\sigma\omega}{s_* - \mu m}(s - \mu m^\alpha)\hat{\gamma}. \tag{3.13}$$

THEOREM 4.

$$\left.\begin{aligned} -1 \le \lambda < 0 \quad &\Leftrightarrow \quad -(1+\rho) \ge \frac{(\sigma + (1+\rho)\sigma_X)\varphi + \sigma_X\sigma\big((m-m_X)^2 + \rho m^2\big)}{\sigma_X(\varphi + \sigma m(m-m_X))} \\ \lambda = 0 \quad &\Leftrightarrow \quad \varphi = -\sigma m(m-m_X) \\ 0 < \lambda \le 1 \quad &\Leftrightarrow \quad 1+\rho \le \frac{(\sigma + (1+\rho)\sigma_X)\varphi + \sigma_X\sigma\big((m-m_X)^2 + \rho m^2\big)}{\sigma_X(\varphi + \sigma m(m-m_X))} \end{aligned}\right\} \tag{3.14}$$

THEOREM 5. *Suppose* $-1 \le \lambda < 1$. *Then,*

$$-\frac{(1-\rho)\lambda}{1-\lambda}s_* < \mu m < s_*. \tag{3.15}$$

4. INTERPRETATION OF THE THEOREMS

This section is devoted to interpretation of the theorems.

4.1 International Business Cycles

Theorems 1 and 4 indicate that an international transfer may induce business cycles to a world economy. In order to explain this, I say that time series x_t exhibit weak business cycles if there are constants x, c, and ξ such that $|x_t - x| < c(-\xi)^t$ and $-1 < \xi < 0$. In the preceding definitions, x may be thought of as a trend. If time series x_t exhibit weak business cycles, the variable fluctuates around a trend, and the fluctuations will eventually disappear. By Theorems 1 and 4, the following holds.

PROPOSITION 1. *After an infinitesimal transfer, the time series of every economic variable exhibit weak business cycles if*

$$\eta + \sigma_X\omega_X\big(m_X^\alpha - m_X^\beta\big)^2 + \sigma\omega(m^\alpha - m^\beta)^2 < \sigma m(m - m_X). \tag{4.1}$$

Proposition 1 indicates that it is not so unlikely that a transfer causes weak real business cycles. A necessary condition is that, given the normality of goods and sectors ($0 < m <$ and $0 < m_X < 1$), the average income effect on the pure consumption good, captured by $m = \Sigma_h \omega^h m^h$, is larger than the average capital accumulation effect on the pure consumption good sector (1), captured by $m_X = \Sigma_h \omega_X^h m_X^h$. Provided that this condition is satisfied, a transfer causes weak business cycles if both capital accumulation effects, captured by m_X^α and m_X^β, and income effects, captured by m^α

and m^{β}, are similar between the two countries and if intersectoral substitution effects, captured by η^{h}, are smaller.

Theorem 4 suggests that if $\lambda = -1$, there is a chance in which strict business cycles appear, i.e., the fluctuation of business cycles may persist. Such a chance is, however, not large; by Theorem 1, $\lambda = -1$ requires the following condition to be satisfied.[4]

$$(\sigma + 2(1+\rho)\sigma_X)\left(\eta + \sigma_X\omega_X\left(m_X^{\alpha} - m_X^{\beta}\right)^2 + \sigma\omega\left(m^{\alpha} - m^{\beta}\right)^2\right)$$
$$+ \sigma_X\sigma\left((2+\rho)m^2 - 3mm_X + m_X^2\right) = 0. \tag{4.2}$$

4.2 Normality in Overall Welfare Effect

In the literature on the transfer problem (e.g., Yano, 1983), it is often said that a transfer is normal if it increases its recipient's welfare at a cost to its donor. In this study, I say that a transfer has the *normal overall welfare effect* if it increases its recipient's discounted utility sum and reduces that of its donor at the same time; I call such a transfer simply a normal transfer. By Theorems 1 and 2, the following holds.

PROPOSITION 2. *A transfer has the normal overall welfare effect if and only if*

$$\Delta\delta > 0, \tag{4.3}$$

where δ and Δ are defined as follows:

$$\delta = \frac{(1-\rho)\lambda}{1-\lambda}\sigma(s_* - \mu m) + \mu\left(\sigma m + \mu\left(1 - \frac{s_{**}}{\Delta}\right)\right); \tag{4.4}$$

$$\Delta = \eta + \sigma_X\omega_X\left(m_X^{\alpha} - m_X^{\beta}\right)^2 + \sigma_X m_X^2 + m^{\alpha} - m^{\beta}. \tag{4.5}$$

Proposition 2 indicates that a transfer may or may not have the normal overall welfare effect, although (4.3) is far too complicated to say

[4]The real business cycles considered here are "local cycles" that occur in a neighborhood of a stationary state. In nature, however, they are similar to the real business cycles that are observed by the global analysis of an optimal path of capital accumulation [see Benhabib and Nishimura (1985) for the analysis of such a case]. If neither (4.2) nor (4.3) is satisfied, the new stationary state is totally unstable, i.e., $1 < |\lambda| \leq |\lambda'|$. In that case, the posttransfer equilibrium path does not stay in a neighborhood of the pretransfer stationary equilibrium and follows a complicated nonlinear dynamics that might involve chaos (see Boldrin and Montrucchio, 1986).

anything conclusive in the general setting.[5] However, there are several interpretable characterizations in the special cases in which parameters $\eta > 0$, $\sigma > 0$ and $\sigma_X > 0$ take extreme values.

Case 1a ($\eta = \infty$). This is the case in which intersectoral substitutability is infinitely large; in other words, goods 1 and 2 in a period are perfect substitutes on the production or consumption sides. Since $0 < \lambda' \equiv \lim_{\eta \to \infty} \lambda < 1$, it holds that

$$\lim_{\eta \to \infty} \delta\Delta/\eta^2 = \frac{(1-\rho)\lambda'\sigma}{1-\lambda'} > 0. \tag{4.6}$$

Therefore, *if intersectoral substitutability is sufficiently large, a transfer always has the normal overall welfare effect.*

Case 1b ($\eta = 0$). This is the case in which there is no intersectoral substitutability. In this case, neither the expression for δ nor that for Δ becomes very simplified.

Case 2a ($\sigma = 0$). This is the case in which there is no intertemporal substitutability on the consumption side. As shown in the Appendix (in Section 6), it holds that

$$\lim_{\sigma \to 0} \frac{\sigma\lambda}{1-\lambda} = \frac{(1-\rho)\sigma_X\left(\eta + \sigma_X\omega_X\left(m_X^\alpha - m_X^\beta\right)^2\right)}{\eta + \sigma_X\omega_X\left(m_X^\alpha - m_X^\beta\right)^2 + \sigma_X m_X\left(m_X - (1-\rho)m\right)}. \tag{4.7}$$

By (4.4), (4.5), and (4.7), I have

$$\lim_{\sigma \to 0} \delta\Delta = (1-\rho)^2\sigma_X\left(\eta + \sigma_X\omega_X\left(m_X^\alpha - m_X^\beta\right)^2 + \sigma_X m_X^2\right) \times\left(\eta + \sigma_X\omega_X\left(m_X^\alpha - m_X^\beta\right)^2 + m^\alpha - m^\beta\right). \tag{4.8}$$

This implies that *in the limit case in which consumptions in different periods are perfect complements, a transfer has the normal overall welfare effect if and only if*

$$\eta + \sigma_X\omega_X\left(m_X^\alpha - m_X^\beta\right)^2 + m^\alpha - m^\beta > 0. \tag{4.9}$$

[5] In a model with recursive preference, Epstein (1987) demonstrates that a transfer may not have the normal overall welfare effect.

Case 2b ($\sigma = \infty$). This is the case in which intertemporal substitutability is infinitely large on the consumption side.[6] The Appendix demonstrates

$$\lim_{\sigma \to \infty} \frac{\sigma\lambda}{1-\lambda} = \frac{\sigma_X\left(\omega(m^\alpha - m^\beta)^2 + m(m - m_X)\right)}{\omega(m^\alpha - m^\beta)^2}. \tag{4.10}$$

By (4.4), (4.5), and (4.10),

$$\lim_{\sigma \to \infty} \frac{\delta\Delta}{\sigma} = (1-\rho)\sigma_X\left(\omega(m^\alpha - m^\beta)^2 + m^2\right) \times\left(\eta + \sigma_X\omega_X(m_X^\alpha - m_X^\beta)^2 + \rho\sigma_X m_X^2 + m^\alpha - m^\beta\right). \tag{4.11}$$

Thus, if *consumptions in different periods are sufficiently close to perfect substitutes, a transfer has the normal overall welfare effect if*

$$\eta + \sigma_X\omega_X(m_X^\alpha - m_X^\beta)^2 + \rho\sigma_X m_X^2 + m^\alpha - m^\beta > 0. \tag{4.12}$$

Case 3a ($\sigma_X = 0$). This is the case in which there is no intertemporal substitutability on the production side. As shown in the Appendix, it holds that

$$\lim_{\sigma_X \to 0} \frac{\sigma\lambda}{\sigma_X(1-\lambda)} = \frac{\eta + \sigma\omega(m^\alpha - m^\beta)^2 + \sigma m(m - m_X)}{\eta + \sigma\omega(m^\alpha - m^\beta)^2}. \tag{4.13}$$

By (4.4), (4.5), (4.13), and $\mu \equiv (1-\rho)\sigma_X m_X$, I have

$$\lim_{\sigma_X \to 0} \frac{\delta\Delta}{\sigma_X} = (1-\rho)\left(\eta + \sigma\omega(m^\alpha - m^\beta)^2 + \sigma m^2\right)(\eta + m^\alpha - m^\beta). \tag{4.14}$$

Thus, *if intertemporal substitutability is sufficiently small on the production side, a transfer has the normal overall welfare effect if*

$$\eta + m^\alpha - m^\beta > 0. \tag{4.15}$$

[6]This is the case considered by Yano (1991).

Case 3b ($\sigma_X = \infty$). This is the case in which intertemporal substitutability is infinitely large. As shown in the Appendix, it holds that

$$\lim_{\sigma_X \to \infty} \frac{\sigma\lambda}{\sigma_X(1-\lambda)} = \frac{(1-\rho)\omega_X\left(m_X^\alpha - m_X^\beta\right)^2}{\omega_X\left(m_X^\alpha - m_X^\beta\right)^2 + m_X\left(m_X - (1-\rho)m\right)}. \tag{4.16}$$

By this, it may be shown that

$$\lim_{\sigma_X \to \infty} \delta/\sigma_X^2 = (1-\rho)^2\omega_X\left(m_X^\alpha - m_X^\beta\right)^2 > 0; \tag{4.17}$$

$$\lim_{\sigma_X \to \infty} \Delta/\sigma_X = \omega_X\left(m_X^\alpha - m_X^\beta\right)^2 + m_X^2 > 0. \tag{4.18}$$

Thus, *if intertemporal substitutability is sufficiently large on the production side, a transfer has the normal overall welfare effect.*

One notable feature in the limit cases above is that, except in Case 1b, the following holds. If the donor's marginal propensity to consume its import is larger than the recipient's marginal propensity to consume the donor's import, a transfer has the normal overall welfare effect. In the static model, as is well known, this is the case in which the "antiorthodox" presumption holds, i.e., a transfer turns the terms of trade in favor for its donor. In that case, as is emphasized in Jones (1970), an exogenous change tends to have normal effects in various respects. The preceding analysis demonstrates that this nature is carried over to my dynamic setting if indices of intertemporal substitution take the extreme values, 0 or ∞. Moreover, it poses the validity of the following proposition as an open question. (*Conjecture*: A transfer always has the normal overall welfare effect if its donor's marginal propensity to consume its import is smaller than the recipient's marginal propensity to consume the donor's imports.)

4.3 Intertemporal Welfare Effect Reversals

This section characterizes what I call an *intertemporal welfare effect reversal*, i.e., the phenomenon that a transfer changes a country's discounted utility sum and its stationary state utility level in directions opposite to each other. Theorems 2, 3, and 5 imply the following.

PROPOSITION 3. *Let* $\{h, h'\} = \{\alpha, \beta\}$. *Take a transfer that has the normal overall welfare effect. An intertemporal welfare effect reversal occurs in country* h' *if and only if*

$$\eta + \sigma_X\omega_X\left(m_X^\alpha - m_X^\beta\right)^2 + \sigma_X m_X^2 < (1-\rho)\sigma_X m_X m^h. \tag{4.19}$$

Proposition 3 implies that there are two main factors to which intertemporal welfare effect reversals may be attributed. One factor is the international difference in marginal propensity to consume. Suppose that there is no such difference ($m^\alpha = m^\beta$). Then, $s = s^*$ by (3.4b) and (3.4c). Thus, by Theorem 5, $s^* = s > \mu m = \mu m^h$ for $h = \alpha, \beta$. Thus, (4.19) cannot hold.

The other factor is consumers' myopia, i.e., future discounting. If futures utilities are not discounted, i.e., if $\rho = 1$, (4.19) cannot hold.

Proposition 3 and the preceding discussions of the limit cases indicate that a transfer that has the normal overall welfare effect may cause intertemporal welfare effect reversals. Expressions (4.12) and (4.19) indicate that in the case in which intertemporal substitutability is sufficiently large on the consumption side (σ near ∞), a necessary condition is

$$m^\beta - m^\alpha < \eta + \sigma_X \omega_X \left(m_X^\alpha - m_X^\beta\right)^2 + \rho \sigma_X m_X^2$$
$$< (1-\rho)\sigma_X m_X \left(m^h - m_X\right). \tag{4.20}$$

In the case in which there is no intersectoral substitutability ($\eta = 0$) and in which intertemporal substitutability is sufficiently small on the production side (σ_X near 0), a necessary condition is

$$\omega_X \left(m_X^\alpha - m_X^\beta\right)^2 + m_X^2 < (1-\rho) m_X m^h \quad \text{and} \quad m^\alpha - m^\beta > 0. \tag{4.21}$$

5. PROOF OF THEOREMS

5.1 Proof of Theorem 1

First, I locally expand the system of equations (2.9) and (2.10); Lemma 3 expands (2.9), and Lemma 4 expands (2.10). To start with, note the following.

LEMMA 1. *$D_1^h = D_1^h(q_t, \gamma^h p_t)$ can be expanded as follows:*

$$dD_{1t}^h = \left(qD_{1q}^h - M^\alpha \sigma^h (m^h)^2\right)\hat{q}_t - M^\alpha \sigma^h m^h \hat{p}_t - M^\alpha \sigma^h m^h \hat{\gamma}^h. \tag{5.1}$$

Proof. Let $dy_t^h \equiv qdD_{1t}^h + dD_{2t}^h$ [dy_t^h captures a change in "real income" (see Caves and Jones, 1985)]. Then, $u_t^h = v^h(q_t, q_t D_{1t}^h + D_{2t}^h)$ implies

$$du_t^h = v_Y^h \, dy_t^h, \tag{5.2}$$

since $v_q^h = -v_Y^h D_{1t}^h$ by Roy's identity (see Varian, 1978). Totally differentiate $v_Y^h(q_t, q_t D_{1t}^h + D_{2t}^h) = p_t \gamma^h$, which follows from (2.1). Since Roy's identity implies $v^h_{qY} = -D^h_{1t}v^h_{YY} - m^h v^h_Y/q_t$,

$$dy^h_t/M^\beta = -\sigma^h m^h \hat{q}_t - \sigma^h \hat{p}_t - \sigma^h \hat{\gamma}^h. \tag{5.3}$$

By the definition of $u^h_t = u^h(q_t, \gamma^h p_t)$ [see (2.3)] and by $m^h \equiv qD^h_{1u}v^h_Y$, (5.2) and (5.3) imply (5.1). ■

LEMMA 2. *$X^h_{1t} = X^h_1(q_t, p_t, p_{t-1})$ and $K^h_{t-1} = K^h(q_t, p_t, p_{t-1})$ can be expanded as follows*:

$$dK^h_{t-1} = \rho\left(\sigma^h_X m^h_X \hat{q}_t + \sigma^h_X \hat{p}_t - \sigma^h_X \hat{p}_{t-1}\right); \tag{5.4}$$

$$dX^h_{1t} = \left(qX^h_{1q} + M^\alpha \sigma^h_X \left(m^h_X\right)^2\right)\hat{q}_t + M^\alpha \sigma^h_X m^h_X \hat{p}_t - M^\alpha \sigma^h_X m^h_X \hat{p}_{t-1}. \tag{5.5}$$

Proof. Denote by $dz^h_t = q_t\, dX^h_{1t} + dX^h_{2t}$ the change in "real gross output." Then, because $K^h_{t-1} = \mathbf{c}^h(q_t, q_t X^h_{1t} + X^h_{2t})$,

$$dK^h_{t-1} = \mathbf{c}^h_Z\, dz^h_t, \tag{5.6}$$

by $\mathbf{c}^h_q = -\mathbf{c}^h_Z X^h_{1t}$. (This corresponds to Roy's identity.) Totally differentiate $\mathbf{c}^h_Z(q_t, q_t X^h_{1t} + X^h_{2t}) = \rho p_t/p_{t-1}$, which directly follows from (2.5). By using $\mathbf{c}^h_{qZ} = -X^h_{1t}\mathbf{c}^h_{ZZ} - m^h_X \mathbf{c}^h_Z/q_t$, which follows from $\mathbf{c}^h_q = -\mathbf{c}^h_Z X^h_{1t}$ (Roy's identity on the production side),

$$dz^h_t/M^\beta = \sigma^h_X m^h_X \hat{q}_t + \sigma^h_X \hat{p}_t - \sigma^h_X \hat{p}_{t-1}. \tag{5.7}$$

Since, by (2.3) and Assumption 1, $\mathbf{c}^h_Z = \rho$ in the pretransfer stationary equilibrium, (5.6) and (5.7) imply (5.4). By (5.4) and $m^h_X \equiv q\mathbf{X}^h_{1K}\mathbf{c}^h_Z$, the definition of $X^h_{1t} = \mathbf{X}^h_1(q_t, K^h_{t-1})$ [see (2.7)] implies (5.5). ■

LEMMA 3. *System* (2.9) *can be expanded as follows*:

$$\left.\begin{aligned} -\Big(\eta + \sigma_X\omega_X\left(m^\alpha_X - m^\beta_X\right)^2 + \sigma\omega\left(m^\alpha - m^\beta\right)^2 \\ + \sigma_X m^2_X + \sigma^h\left(m^h\right)^2\Big)\hat{q}_t \\ -(\sigma_X m_X + \sigma m)\hat{p}_t + \sigma_X m_X \hat{p}_{t-1} - \sum_h \sigma^h m^h \hat{\gamma}^h = 0; \\ -(\sigma_X m_X + \sigma m)\hat{q}_t + \rho\sigma_X m_X \hat{q}_{t+1} \\ +\sigma_X \hat{p}_{t-1} - (\sigma + (1+\rho)\sigma_X)\hat{p}_t + \rho\sigma_X \hat{p}_{t+1} - \sum_h \sigma^h \hat{\gamma}^h = 0. \end{aligned}\right\} \tag{5.8}$$

Proof. Since $\Sigma_h(D_{1t}^h - X_{1t}^h) = 0$, (5.1) and (5.5) imply the first equation. Since $\Sigma_h(D_{1t}^h - X_{1t}^h) = 0$ and $\Sigma_h(D_{2t}^h - X_{2t}^h + K_t^h) = 0$, $\Sigma_h(dy_t^h - dz_t^h + dK_t^h) = 0$, which implies the second equation by (5.3), (5.4), and (5.7). ■

Next, I expand equations (2.10) in order to relate changes in prices and marginal utilities of wealth, $\hat{p}_t$, $\hat{q}_t$ and $\hat{\gamma}^h$, to transfer $dT^\alpha = -dT^\beta$. To this end, define $\hat{P} \equiv (\rho^{-1} - 1)\Sigma_{t=1}^{\infty}\rho^t\hat{p}_t$, $\hat{Q} \equiv (\rho^{-1} - 1)\Sigma_{t=1}^{\infty}\rho^t\hat{p}_t$, and $d\tau^h \equiv (\rho^{-1} - 1)\, dT^h$.

LEMMA 4. *Equations* (2.10) *can be expanded as follows*:

$$(\sigma^\alpha m^\alpha - 1)\hat{Q} + \sigma^\alpha\hat{P} + \sigma^\alpha\hat{\gamma}^\alpha = \frac{d\tau^\alpha}{M^\beta}; \tag{5.9}$$

$$(\sigma^\beta m^\beta + 1)\hat{Q} + \sigma^\beta\hat{P} + \sigma^\beta\hat{\gamma}^\beta = -\frac{d\tau^\alpha}{M^\beta}. \tag{5.10}$$

Proof. Since $q\, dX_{1t}^h + dX_{2t}^h = \rho^{-1}\, dK_{t-1}^h$ by optimization, (2.10) implies

$$\begin{aligned}\sum_{t=1}^{\infty}\rho^t p_t\big(q_t\, dD_{1t}^h + dD_{2t}^h + q_t D_{1t}^h\hat{q}_t\big) + \sum_{t=1}^{\infty}\rho^t p_t\big(q_t D_{1t}^h + D_{2t}^h\big)\hat{p}_t \\ = p_0\big(K_0^h - K_0^h\big)\hat{p}_0 + \sum_{t=1}^{\infty}\rho^t p_t q_t X_{1t}^h\hat{q}_t \\ + \sum_{t=1}^{\infty}\rho^t p_t\big(q_t X_{1t}^h + X_{2t}^h - K_t^h\big)\hat{p}_t - dT^h.\end{aligned} \tag{5.11}$$

By (2.11), $\hat{p}_0 = 0$. By (3.1) and (3.2), $q_t D_{1t}^h + D_{2t}^h - (q_t X_{1t}^h + X_{2t}^h - K_t^h) = 0$ and $p_t = 1$ in the pretransfer stationary equilibrium. Moreover, by $\Sigma_h\, dT^h \equiv 0$, $d\tau^\alpha \equiv -d\tau^\beta$. By (5.3), $q_t\, dD_{1t}^h + dD_{2t}^h \equiv dy_t^h = -M^\beta(\sigma^h m^h\hat{q}_t + \sigma^h\hat{p}_t + \sigma^h\hat{\gamma}^h)$. Therefore, (5.11) implies Lemma 4. ■

I now prove Theorem 1. By $\hat{p}_0 = 0$ and by the first equation of (5.8),

$$-s_{**}\hat{Q} - (\mu + \sigma m)\hat{P} - \sum_h \sigma^h m^h\hat{\gamma}^h = 0. \tag{5.12}$$

Next, erase q_t from the second equation of (5.8) by using the first. Then, with the c_0, c_1, and c_2 defined by (3.4h)–(3.4j), the following holds:

$$c_2\big(\hat{p}_{t+1} - \hat{p}_\infty\big) + c_1\big(\hat{p}_t - \hat{p}_\infty\big) + c_0\big(\hat{p}_{t-1} - \hat{p}_\infty\big) = 0, \tag{5.13}$$

where

$$\hat{p}_{\infty} = \frac{-s_{**}\sum_h \sigma^h \hat{\gamma}^h + (\mu + \sigma m)\sum_h \sigma^h m^h \hat{\gamma}^h}{\sigma(s_* - \mu m)}. \tag{5.14}$$

Suppose that $-1 < \lambda < 1$. Then, the change in price sequence, $\hat{p}_t$, to the posttransfer equilibrium can be characterized by

$$\hat{p}_t = (1 - \lambda^t)\hat{p}_{\infty}, \tag{5.15}$$

since $\hat{p}_0 \equiv 0$.[7] By (5.14) and (5.15),

$$\frac{1-\rho\lambda}{1-\lambda}\hat{P} = \frac{-s_{**}\sum_h \sigma^h \hat{\gamma}^h + (\mu + \sigma m)\sum_h \sigma^h m^h \hat{\gamma}^h}{\sigma(s_* - \mu m)} (\equiv \hat{p}_{\infty}). \tag{5.16}$$

The system of equations (5.12)–(5.16) determines $\hat{P}$, $\hat{Q}$, $\hat{p}_{\infty}$, $\hat{\gamma}^{\alpha}$, and $\hat{\gamma}^{\beta}$ for given $d\tau^{\alpha}$. Thus, Theorem 1 is proved.

5.2 Proof of Theorem 2

First, I prove (3.9). To this end, note the following.

LEMMA 5. $\Sigma_h \Sigma_{t=1}^{\infty} \rho^t \, dy_t^h = 0$.

Proof. By (2.11), $\hat{p}_0 = 0$. By (2.9), $\Sigma_h (D_{1t}^h - X_{1t}^h) = 0$ and $\Sigma_h (D_{2t}^h - X_{2t}^h + K_t^h) = 0$. Moreover, $\Sigma_h \, dT^h = 0$ by definition. Thus, by $q \, dD_{1t}^h + dD_{2t}^h \equiv dy_t^h$ and (5.11), the lemma holds since $p_t = 1$ and $q_t = q$ in the pretransfer stationary equilibrium. ■

Let $U^h = \Sigma_{t=1}^{\infty} \rho^t u_t^h$. Then, by (5.2) and (2.1), Lemma 5 implies $dU^{\beta}/dU^{a} = \Sigma_{t=1}^{\infty} \rho^t \, du_t^{\beta} / \Sigma_{t=1}^{\infty} \rho^t \, du_t^{a} = \mathbf{v}_Y^a \Sigma_{t=1}^{\infty} \rho^t \, dy_t^h / (\mathbf{v}_Y^{\beta} \Sigma_{t=1}^{\infty} \rho^t \, dy_t^{\beta}) = -\gamma$, i.e., $dU^{\alpha}/dU^{\beta} = -\gamma$. Since the curvature conditions imposed on functions $\mathbf{v}^h$, $\mathbf{D}_1^h$, $\mathbf{c}^h$, and $\mathbf{X}_1^h$ imply the strict concavity of utility function u^h and the strict convexity of capital input function k^h, the set of feasible welfare allocations, (U^{α}, U^{β}), is strictly convex. Thus, (3.9) holds.

To complete the proof, recall that the equilibrium condition can be expressed as the system of (5.12), (5.13), (5.14), (5.15) and (5.16), which can

[7]This is because the perfect foresight equilibrium path can be regarded as an optimal path in the capital theoretic sense (see Bewley, 1982) and because an optimal path lies on the stable manifold (see McKenzie, 1986). Even if $\lambda = -1$, the effect of a transfer can be characterized in the same way, as (5.15) suggests.

be transformed into

$$\begin{pmatrix} 1-(m^{\alpha}-m^{\beta}-1/(\sigma\omega)) & & 0 \\ 0 & \Delta & \mu \\ 0 & \mu s_{**} & \dfrac{(1-\rho)\lambda}{1-\lambda}\sigma(s_{*}-\mu m)+\mu(\alpha m+\mu) \end{pmatrix}$$

$$\times \begin{pmatrix} \hat{\gamma} \\ \hat{Q} \\ \hat{P} \end{pmatrix} = \begin{pmatrix} -1/(\sigma\omega) \\ -(m^{\alpha}-m^{\beta}) \\ 0 \end{pmatrix} \frac{d\tau^{\alpha}}{M^{\beta}}. \tag{6.1}$$

This readily implies Theorem 2.

5.3 Proof of Theorem 3

The stationary effect of a transfer can be captured by setting q_t and p_t time-independent in (5.8), i.e., $q_t = q_\infty$ and $p_t = p_\infty$ for all t. Then, by $\hat{\gamma}^{\beta} - \hat{\gamma}^{\alpha} = \hat{\gamma}$, it holds that

$$\begin{pmatrix} s_{**} & \sigma^{\alpha}m^{\alpha} & \sigma^{\beta}m^{\beta} \\ \sigma m+\mu & \sigma^{\alpha} & \sigma^{\beta} \\ 0 & -1 & 1 \end{pmatrix} \begin{pmatrix} \hat{q}_\infty \\ \hat{\gamma}^{\alpha}+\hat{p}_\infty \\ \hat{\gamma}^{\beta}+\hat{p}_\infty \end{pmatrix} = \begin{pmatrix} 0 \\ 0 \\ \hat{\gamma} \end{pmatrix}. \tag{7.1}$$

Since $du^h_\infty/v^h_Y = -M^{\beta}(\sigma^h m^h \hat{q}_\infty + \sigma^h(\hat{\gamma}^h + \hat{p}_\infty))$ by (5.2) and (5.3), Theorem 3 follows from (7.1).

5.4 Proof of Theorem 4

The characteristic equation of (3.5) is $c_2\lambda^2 + c_1\lambda + c_0 = 0$. Thus, $\varphi = -\sigma m(m - m_X)$ implies $c_2 = c_0 = 0$ by (3.4h) and (3.4j) and, thus, $\lambda = 0$. Assume $\varphi \neq -\sigma m(m - m_X)$. Then, by (3.4h)–(3.4j), λ must satisfy

$$C \equiv (1/\lambda)^2 - 2x(1/\lambda) + \rho = 0, \tag{8.1}$$

where x is defined as follows:

$$x = \frac{(\sigma + (1+\rho)\sigma_X)\varphi + \sigma_X\sigma\big((m-m_X)^2 + \rho m^2\big)}{2\sigma_X(\varphi + \sigma m(m-m_X))}. \tag{8.2}$$

(I focus on $1/\lambda$ in order to simplify my discussion below.) Figure 1 illustrates curve $C = 0$, which consists of two parts, C_+ and C_-; if $x > 0$, curve $C = 0$ coincides with C_+; if $x < 0$, with C_-. By Figure 1, $|\lambda| \le 1$ if and only if $|x| > (1+\rho)/2$, which readily implies the theorem (see Boyd, 1990).

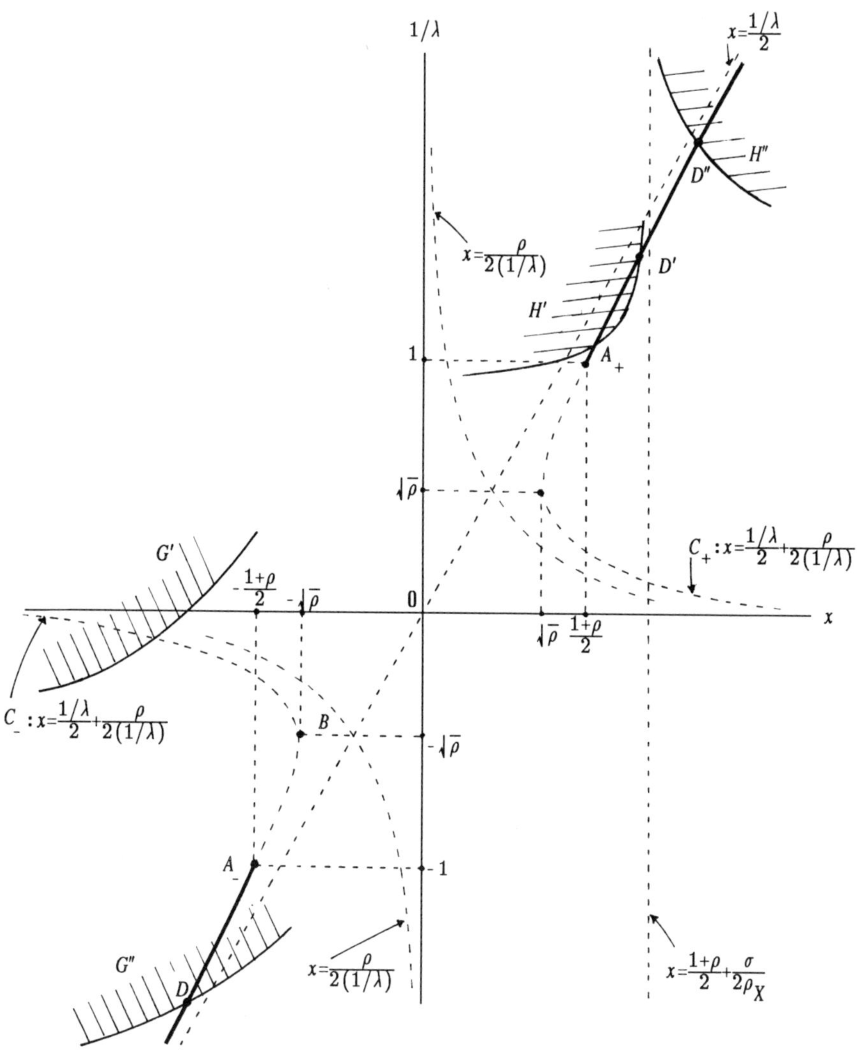

FIGURE 1

5.5 Proof of Theorem 5

I now prove Theorem 5. In addition to the above result, by using Figure 1, I may establish the following, which will be used for the proof below.

LEMMA 6. *If* $\varphi = -\sigma m(m - m_X)$, $\lambda = \lambda' = 0$. *If* $\varphi \neq -\sigma m(m - m_X)$, *either* $-\sqrt{\rho}/\rho \leq \lambda < 0$ *and* $\lambda' \leq -\sqrt{\rho}/\rho$, *or* $0 < \lambda \leq \sqrt{\rho}/\rho$ *and* $\lambda' \geq \sqrt{\rho}/\rho$. *Moreover,* $|\lambda| < 1$ *if and only if* $|x| > (1+\rho)/2$. *In particular, if* $|(m - m_X)/m| > 1$, $|\lambda| < 1$ *always hold.*

Proof. Define $\overline{X} \equiv (\bar{x}, 1/\bar{\lambda})$ as follows:

$$\overline{X} \equiv (\bar{x}, 1/\bar{\lambda}) \equiv \left(\frac{(m - m_X)/m}{2} + \frac{\rho}{2(m - m_X)/m}, (m - m_X)/m \right). \tag{8.3}$$

Note that point $\overline{X}$ is on curve $C = 0$. Note that $\varphi \geq 0$ and (8.2) imply

$$\varphi = \frac{-2\sigma\sigma_X m(m - m_X)x + \sigma\sigma_X\left((m - m_X)^2 + \rho m^2\right)}{2\sigma_X x - (\sigma + (1 + \rho)\sigma_X)} \geq 0, \tag{8.4}$$

which implies

$$m(m - m_X)(x - \bar{x})\left(x - \left(\frac{1 + \rho}{2} + \frac{\sigma}{2\sigma_X}\right)\right) \leq 0 \quad \text{and}$$

$$x \neq \frac{1 + \rho}{2} + \frac{\sigma}{2\sigma_X}. \tag{8.5}$$

If $m(m - m_X) < 0$, $\bar{x} < 0$ by (8.3), and by (8.5) x must satisfy one of the following conditions:

$$x \leq \bar{x}(< 0); \tag{8.6}$$

$$x > \frac{1 + \rho}{2} + \frac{\sigma}{2\sigma_X}. \tag{8.7}$$

If $m(m - m_X) = 0$, by (8.2) and $\varphi > 0$, x must satisfy

$$x \geq \frac{1 + \rho}{2} + \frac{\sigma}{2\sigma_X}. \tag{8.8}$$

If $m(m - m_X) > 0$, $\bar{x} > 0$ by (8.3), and by (8.5) x must satisfy one of the following conditions:

$$(0 <)\bar{x} \leq x < \frac{1 + \rho}{2} + \frac{\sigma}{2\sigma_X}; \tag{8.9}$$

$$\frac{1 + \rho}{2} + \frac{\sigma}{2\sigma_X} < x \leq \bar{x}. \tag{8.10}$$

Note

$$\frac{1 + \rho}{2} + \frac{\sigma}{2\sigma_X} - \bar{x} = \frac{\theta}{2\sigma_X m(m - m_X)}, \tag{8.11}$$

where θ is defined as follows:

$$\theta \equiv (\sigma m + \sigma_X m_X)(m - m_X) - \rho \sigma_X m_X m. \tag{8.12}$$

Conditions (8.6)–(8.10) imply that

$$\text{either} \quad x > \frac{1+\rho}{2} + \frac{\sigma}{2\sigma_X} \quad \text{or} \quad |x| \geq |\bar{x}|. \tag{8.13}$$

Note $[(1+\rho)/2] + (\sigma/2\sigma_X) > \sqrt{\rho}$, and $|\bar{x}| \geq \sqrt{\rho}$ because $(\bar{x}, 1/\bar{\lambda})$ is on curve $C = 0$. Thus, by (8.13), $|x| \geq \sqrt{\rho}$, which implies the first conclusion. By Figure 1, if and only if $|x| \geq (1+\rho)/2$, the characteristic roots are separated by 1. If $|(m - m_X)/m| > 1$, $|\bar{x}| > (1+\rho)/2$ and, thus, $|x| > (1+\rho)/2$ by (8.13). ■

In order to prove Theorem 5, let $\Gamma_1 \equiv s_* - \mu m$ and $\Gamma_2 \equiv$

$$\left(\frac{(1-\rho)\lambda}{1-\lambda} s_* + \mu m\right) \Big/ (1-\rho).$$

It suffices to prove $\Gamma_1 > 0$ and $\Gamma_2 > 0$. By (3.4), I have the following:

$$\Gamma_1 = \varphi - \sigma_X m_X (m - m_X - \rho m); \tag{9.1}$$

$$\Gamma_2 = \frac{\lambda}{1-\lambda}(\varphi + \sigma_X m_X^2) + \sigma_X m_X m. \tag{9.2}$$

I first prove $\Gamma_1 > 0$. Suppose $\varphi + \sigma m(m - m_X) > 0$. Then, by (8.2), $x > (1+\rho)/2$ means $0 < \varphi - \sigma_X m_X (m - m_X - \rho m) = \Gamma_1$. By Lemma 6 and Figure 1, $x > (1+\rho)/2$ also means $0 < \lambda < 1$; $\Gamma_1 > 0$ if and only if $0 < \lambda < 1$. Suppose $\varphi + \sigma m(m - m_X) \leq 0$. Then, $m(m - m_X) \leq \varphi/\sigma < 0$ and $0 \leq m^2 < m_X m$, which implies $m_X(m - m_X) < 0$. Thus, by (9.1), $\Gamma_1 > 0$. In the following part, I prove $\Gamma_2 > 0$.

Suppose $\varphi = -\sigma m(m - m_X)$. Then, $\lambda = 0$ by Lemma 6, and $m_X m > m^2 \geq 0$ by $\sigma > 0$ and $\varphi > 0$. Thus, by $\sigma_X > 0$ and (9.2), $\Gamma_2 > 0$. Thus, in the following part, I may focus on the case of $\varphi \neq -\sigma m(m - m_X)$; thus, by Lemma 6, $\lambda \neq 0$ in the following part. Suppose $m^2 = m_X m$, i.e., $m(m - m_X) = 0$. Then, (8.8) holds. Thus, $x > 0$, which implies $0 < \lambda < 1$ by Figure 1. Thus, by $\varphi > 0$ and $m_X m = m^2 \geq 0$, (9.2) implies $\Gamma_2 > 0$. If $m^2 < m_X m$, either (8.6) or (8.7) holds. Suppose (8.7) and $m^2 < m_X m$ hold. By (8.7), $x > 0$, which implies $0 < \lambda < 1$ by Figure 1. Thus, by $m m_X = m^2 > 0$ and $\varphi > 0$, (9.2) implies $\Gamma_2 > 0$. If $m^2 > m_X m$, either $m_X m \geq 0$ or $m_X m < 0$. Suppose $m^2 > m_X m \geq 0$. By $m(m - m_X) > 0$, either (8.9) or (8.10) holds. Thus, $x > 0$, which implies $0 < \lambda < 1$ by Figure 1. Thus, by $m_X m \geq 0$, $\varphi > 0$, and (9.2), $\Gamma_2 > 0$. This discussion implies that it suffices to prove $\Gamma_2 > 0$ in the following two cases: *Case A*, (8.6) and $m^2 < m_X m$ holds; *Case B*, $m_X m < 0$.

If (8.6) is satisfied, $x < 0$, which implies $-1 < \lambda < 0$ by Figure 1. If $m_X m < 0$, $m(m - m_X) > 0$. Thus, by (8.9) and (8.10), $x > 0$, which implies $0 < \lambda < 1$. Thus, $-1 < \lambda < 0$ and $m_X m > 0$ hold in Case A, and $0 < \lambda < 1$ and $m_X m < 0$ hold in Case B. Then, by (9.2), in either case, $\Gamma_2 \leq 0$ is equivalent to

$$(1/\lambda) \geq -\frac{\varphi}{\sigma_X m_X m} + (1/\bar{\lambda}). \tag{9.3}$$

Let $R_C = \{(x, 1/\lambda) | C = 0 \text{ and } |\lambda| < 1\}$ and $R_2 = \{(x, 1/\lambda) | \Gamma_2 \leq 0\}$. Note that, in order to prove $\Gamma_2 > 0$, it suffices to prove $R_C \cap R_2 = \phi$.

Note that $\Gamma_2 = 0$ is equivalent to

$$\begin{aligned}(1/\lambda) &= -\frac{\varphi}{\sigma_X m_X m} + (1/\bar{\lambda}) \\ &= \frac{\sigma\theta}{\sigma_X m_X m\big(2\sigma x - (\sigma + (1+\rho)\sigma_X\big)} + \frac{\theta}{\sigma_X m_X m} + \rho,\end{aligned} \tag{9.4}$$

where θ is defined by (8.12). Thus, curve $\Gamma_2 = 0$ is a rectangular hyperbola of which the asymptotes are vertical and horizontal and intersect at point

$$O_2 \equiv \left(\frac{1+\rho}{2} + \frac{\sigma}{2\sigma_X}, \frac{\theta}{\sigma_X m_X m} + \rho\right). \tag{9.5}$$

Since $x = \bar{x}$ implies $\varphi = 0$ by (8.4), by (9.3) curve $\Gamma_2 = 0$ intersects curve $C = 0$ at point $\overline{X} \equiv (\bar{x}, 1/\bar{\lambda})$. The slope of curve $\Gamma_2 = 0$ at $\overline{X}$ is

$$\left.\frac{d(1/\lambda)}{dx}\right|_{\Gamma_2 = 0} = -\frac{2\sigma m(m - m_X)^2}{\theta m_X}. \tag{9.6}$$

By (8.1), the slope of curve $C = 0$ at point $\overline{X}$ is

$$\left.\frac{d(1/\lambda)}{dx}\right|_{C=0} = \frac{2(m - m_X)^2}{(m - m_X)^2 - \rho m^2}. \tag{9.7}$$

Between the slopes, at $\overline{X}$, of curve $C = 0$ and $\Gamma_2 = 0$, I have

$$\begin{aligned}&\left.\frac{d(1/\lambda)}{dx}\right|_{\Gamma_2=0} - \left.\frac{d(1/\lambda)}{dx}\right|_{C=0} \\ &\quad = -\frac{(\sigma m^2 + \sigma_X m_X^2)(m - m_X)^2\big(m(m - m_X) - \rho m^2\big)}{\theta m m_X\left[(m - m_X)^2 - \rho m^2\right]}.\end{aligned} \tag{9.8}$$

Case A. In this case, $\bar{x} < 0$ by (8.6), and $m(m - m_X) < 0$. Thus, by (8.11), $\theta < 0$. Since $m_X m > 0$, by (9.4) the boundary of R_2, i.e., curve $\Gamma_2 = 0$, is a rectangular hyperbola that lies in the second quadrant around point O_2. Since $m(m - m_X) < 0$, in Figure 1, the intersection between curves $C = 0$ and $\Gamma_2 = 0$, $\bar{X}$, lies on curve C_-, and R_C must lie on curve C_- below point A_-. If $\bar{X}$ lies above point B, R_2 may be shown by region G'; thus, $R_C \cap R_2 = \phi$. Suppose $\bar{X}$ lies below B. Then, $(m - m_X)/m < -\sqrt{\rho}$. Thus, by $m(m - m_X) < 0$, $(m - m_X)^2 - \rho m^2 > 0$ and $m(m - m_X) - \rho m^2 < 0$. Since $\theta < 0$ as noted above, by these facts, (9.8) implies that the slope of curve C_- is steeper than that of curve $\Gamma_2 = 0$ at $\bar{X}$. Thus, R_2 may be shown by G'' in Figure 1., and $\bar{X}$ by point D. Since, by (8.6), R_C is on curve C_- below point D, $R_C \cap R_2 = \phi$. Thus, $\Gamma_2 > 0$ in Case A.

Case B. By $m_X m < 0$, the following holds:

$$1/\bar{\lambda} \equiv (m - m_X)/m > 1; \tag{9.9}$$

$$(m - m_X)^2 - \rho m^2 > 0. \tag{9.10}$$

Note that by (9.9), the intersection of curves $\Gamma_2 = 0$ and $C = 0$, $\bar{X}$, must lie on curve C_+ above point A_+. Since $m_X m < 0 \leq m^2$, $m(m - m_X) > 0$. Thus, either (8.9) or (8.10) holds. Suppose (8.9) holds. Then, (8.12) implies $\theta > 0$. By (8.9) and (9.5), curve $\Gamma_2 = 0$ must lie on the left of the vertical asymptote. Since $\theta > 0$ and $m m_X < 0$ as noted above, by (9.4), curve $\Gamma_2 = 0$ lies on the second quadrant around point O_2. By (9.9), (9.10), $m m_X < 0$, and $\theta > 0$, (9.8) implies that curve $\Gamma_2 = 0$ is steeper than curve $C = 0$ at $\bar{X}$. Thus, R_2 may be shown by region H', and $\bar{X}$ by point D'. Since, by (8.9), R_C must be on curve C_+ above point D', $R_C \cap R_T = \phi$. Suppose (8.10) holds. Then, (8.12) implies $\theta < 0$. By (8.10) and (9.5), curve $\Gamma_2 = 0$ must lie on the right of the vertical asymptote. Since $\theta < 0$ and $m m_X < 0$, by (9.4), curve $\Gamma_2 = 0$ lies on the first quadrant around O_2. Thus, R_2 may be shown by region H'', and $\bar{X}$ by point D''. Since, by (8.10), R_C must be on curve C_+ below point D'', $R_C \cap R_\Gamma = \phi$. Thus, $\Gamma_2 > 0$ in Case B.

APPENDIX

This appendix derives (4.7), (4.10), (4.13), and (4.16). Let $c \equiv -(1 + \rho^{-1})c_2 - c_1$. Then, by (3.4h) and (3.4i), I have

$$c = \sigma\left(\eta + \sigma\omega(m^\alpha - m^\beta)^2 + \sigma_X m_X\left(m_X^\alpha - m_X^\beta\right)^2\right) + \sigma\sigma_X m_X\left(m_X - (1 - \rho)m\right), \tag{A.1}$$

and the characteristic equation of (22) may be written as $c_2\lambda^2 - ((1 +$

$\rho^{-1})c_2 + c)\lambda + \rho^{-1}c_2 = 0$. By Figure 1, λ, $-\sqrt{\rho}/\rho < \lambda < \sqrt{\rho}/\rho$, satisfies

$$\lambda = \frac{(1+\rho^{-1})C_2 + C - \sqrt{(1-\rho^{-1})^2(C_2)^2 + C^2 + 2(1+\rho^{-1})C_2 C}}{2C_2} \tag{A.2}$$

for $C_2 = \xi c_2$ and $C = \xi c$ and for any number ξ. Define the following:

$$f \equiv (1+\rho^{-1})C_2 + C - \sqrt{(1-\rho^{-1})^2(C_2)^2 + C^2 + 2(1+\rho^{-1})C_2 C}\,; \tag{A.3}$$

$$g \equiv (1-\rho^{-1})C_2 - C + \sqrt{(1-\rho^{-1})^2(C_2)^2 + C^2 + 2(1+\rho^{-1})C_2 C}\,. \tag{A.4}$$

In the case of $\sigma \to \infty$, define $x \equiv 1/\sigma$ and the following:

$$C_2 \equiv c_2/\sigma^2 = \rho\sigma_X\Big(\eta + \sigma_X\omega_X\big(m_X^\alpha - m_X^\beta\big)^2\Big)x^2 + \rho\sigma_X\Big(\omega\big(m^\alpha - m^\beta\big)^2 + m\big(m - m_X\big)\Big)x; \tag{A.5}$$

$$C \equiv c/\sigma^2 = \Big(\eta + \sigma_X\omega_X\big(m_X^\alpha - m_X^\beta\big)^2 + \sigma_X m_X\big(m_X - (1-\rho)m\big)\Big)x + \omega\big(m^\alpha - m^\beta\big)^2. \tag{A.6}$$

In the case of $\sigma_X \to 0$, define $x = \sigma_X$ and the following:

$$C_2 \equiv c_2 = \rho\omega_X\big(m_X^\alpha - m_X^\beta\big)^2 x^2 + \rho\Big(\eta + \sigma\omega\big(m^\alpha - m^\beta\big)^2 + \sigma m\big(m - m_X\big)\Big)x; \tag{A.7}$$

$$C \equiv c = \sigma\Big(\omega_X\big(m_X^\alpha - m_X^\beta\big)^2 + \sigma m_X\big(m_X - (1-\rho)m\big)\Big)x + \sigma\Big(\eta + \sigma\omega\big(m^\alpha - m^\beta\big)^2\Big). \tag{A.8}$$

Then, in both cases, as $x \to 0$, $C_2 \to 0$, $C'' \to 0$, and $f \to 0$. Thus, since $\lambda/x = f/(2C_2 x)$, and since $C > 0$ at $x = 0$, by L'Hopital's rule I have

$$\lim_{x\to 0}(\lambda/x) = \lim_{x\to 0} f'' \Big/ \lim_{x\to 0}(2C_2 x)'' = \rho^{-1}C_2'/C. \tag{A.9}$$

Thus, (4.10) and (4.13) follow immediately from (A.5)–(A.8).

In the case of $\sigma \to 0$, define $x = \sigma$ and the following:

$$C_2 \equiv c_2 = \rho\sigma_X\Big(\omega(m^\alpha - m^\beta)^2 + m(m - m_X)\Big)x + \rho\sigma_X\Big(\eta + \sigma_X\omega_X\big(m_X^\alpha - m_X^\beta\big)^2\Big); \tag{A.10}$$

$$C \equiv c = \omega(m^\alpha - m^\beta)^2 x^2 + \Big(\eta + \sigma_X\omega_X\big(m_X^\alpha - m_X^\beta\big)^2 + \sigma_X m_X\big(m_X - (1-\rho)m\big)\Big)x. \tag{A.11}$$

In the case of $\sigma_X \to \infty$, define $x = 1/\sigma_X$ and the following:

$$C_2 \equiv c_2/\sigma_X^2 = \rho\Big(\eta + \sigma\omega(m^\alpha - m^\beta)^2 + \sigma m(m - m_X)\Big)x + \rho\omega_X\big(m_X^\alpha - m_X^\beta\big)^2; \tag{A.12}$$

$$C \equiv c/\sigma_X^2 = \sigma\Big(\eta + \sigma\omega(m^\alpha - m^\beta)^2\Big)x^2 + \sigma\Big(\omega_X\big(m_X^\alpha - m_X^\beta\big)^2 + m_X\big(m_X - (1-\rho)m\big)\Big)x. \tag{A.13}$$

Then, in both cases, as $x \to 0$, $C \to 0$, and $g \to 0$. Thus, since $x/(1-\lambda) = 2C_2x/g$, and since $(1-\rho^{-1})C_2 < 0$ at $x = 0$, by L'Hopital's rule I have

$$\lim_{x\to 0} x/(1-\lambda) = 2\lim_{x\to 0}(C_2x)'/\lim_{x\to 0} g' = (\rho^{-1} - 1)C_2/C'. \tag{A.14}$$

Thus, (4.7) and (4.16) follow immediately from (A.10)–(A.13).

Acknowledgments

This paper is based on a part of my paper "A Comparative Dynamic Method for General Equilibrium Models and Its Application to the Transfer Problem" (Discussion Paper 89-1, Yokohama National University). That paper was presented in the Conference on General Equilibrium and Growth: The Legacy of Lionel McKenzie, held at the University of Rochester, May 5–7, 1989, and in the Department of Economics, New York University. I am grateful to all the participants in the presentations; to M. Kemp, L. McKenzie, and T. Negishi for their encouragment at early stage of this research; to K. Nishimura for conversations; and to H. Wan and an anonymous reviewer of this paper for valuable comments. A travel grant from the Japan–U.S. Friendship Council, which made my presentations at Rochester and NYU possible, and a grant from the Japanese Ministry of Education, which supported part of this research, are gratefully acknowledged.

References

Araujo, A., and J. Scheinkman (1978). "Smoothness, comparative dynamics, and the turnpike property," *Econometrica* **45**, 601–620.

Becker, R. (1980). "On the long-run steady state in a simple dynamic model of equilibrium with heterogeneous households," *Quart. J. Econ.* **95**, 375–382.

Benhabib, J., and K. Nishimura (1985). "Competitive equilibrium cycles," *J. Econ. Theory* **35**, 284–306.

Bewley, T. (1982). "An integration of equilibrium theory and turnpike theory," *J. Math. Econ.* **10**, 233–267.

Boldrin, M., and L. Montrucchio (1986). "On the indeterminacy of capital accumulation paths," *J. Econ. Theory* **40**, 26–39.

Boyd, J. (1990). "Reciprocal roots, paired roots and the saddlepoint property," mimeograph, University of Rochester, N.Y.

Caves, R., and R. Jones (1985). *World Trade and Payments: An introduction*, 4th ed. (Little, Brown, Boston).

Coles, J. (1985). "Equilibrium turnpike theory with constant returns to scale and possibly heterogeneous discount factors," *Int. Econ. Rev.* **26**, 671–680.

Epstein, L. (1987). "A simple dynamic general equilibrium model," *J. Econ. Theory* **41**, 68–95.

Fukao, K., and K. Hamada (1989). "International trade and investment under different rates of time preference," mimeograph, Hitotsubashi University.

Jones, R. (1970). "Transfer problem revisited," *Economica* **37**, 178–184.

Kemp, M., and C. Khang (1974). "A note on steady-state price: Output relationships," *J. Int. Econ.* **2**, 187–197.

Lipton, D., and J. Sachs (1983). "Accumulation and growth in a two-country model," *J. Int. Econ.* **15**, 135–159.

Marimon, R. (1989). "Stochastic turnpike property and stationary equilibrium," *J. Econ. Theory* **47**, 282–306.

McKenzie, L. (1983). "Turnpike theory, discounted utility, and the von Neumann facet," *J. Econ. Theory* **30**, 330–352.

McKenzie, L. (1986). "Optimal economic growth and turnpike theorems," in *Handbook of Mathematical Economics*, K. Arrow and M. Intriligator, (eds.) (North-Holland, Amsterdam).

Negishi, T. (1960). "Welfare economics and existence of an equilibrium for competitive economy," *Metroeconomica* **12**, 92–97.

Samuelson, P. (1952). "The transfer problem and transport costs: The terms of trade when impediments are absent," *Econ. J.* **62**, 278–304.

Varian, H. (1978). *Micro Economic Analysis* (Norton, New York).

Wan, H. (1971). "A simultaneous variational model for international capital movement," in *Trade, Balance of Payments, and Growth*, J. Bhagwati *et al.* (eds.) (North-Holland, Amsterdam), pp. 261–287.

Yano, M. (1983). "Welfare aspects of the transfer problem," *J. Int. Econ.* **15**, 277–289.

Yano, M. (1984a). "Competitive equilibria on turnpikes in a McKenzie economy, I: A neighborhood turnpike theorem," *Int. Econ. Rev.* **25**, 695–717.

Yano, M. (1984b). "The turnpike of dynamic general equilibrium paths and its insensitivity to initial conditions," *J. Math. Econ.* **13**, 235–254.

Yano, M. (1991). "Temporary transfers in a simple dynamic trade model," *J. Econ. Theory* **54**, 372–388.

Yano, M. (1989b). "Comparative statics in dynamic stochastic models," *J. Math. Econ.* **18**, 169–185.

Yano, M. (1990). "Von Neumann facets and the dynamic stability of perfect foresight equilibrium paths in neo-classical trade theory," *Zeitschrift fur Nationalokonomie* **51**, 27–69.

INDEX

Absolute advantage, multinational corporations
  overview, 490–491
  Ricardian model structure, 491–497
  world transformation curve, 497–505
Abstract market, competitive equilibrium
  irreducibility, 22–26
  weak irreducibility, 36–37
Accumulation equations, *see also* Capital accumulation
  turnpike properties, 355–358
ADDMMM-economy, competitive equilibrium, irreducibility, 36–37
Adjustment-path effects theorem, international transfers
  equations, 564
  proof, 573–574
Aggregate consumption, volatility testing, 315–317
Aggregate demand
  externalities and, 15–17
  Graham–McKenzie economy, competitive equilibrium, 4–5, 13
Aggregate interiority assumption
  continuum economies, 104–105
  irreducibility, 89–90
Aggregate production, vintage capital, 272–274
Allocation
  competitive equilibrium, irreducibility, 24–26
  volatility testing, asset pricing model, 310–311
Altruism function, endogenous fertility, 237–238
Approximation theory
  borrowing constraints and international comovements, 481–485
  Brouwer fixed-point theorem, 28–34
  competitive equilibrium, 4
Arbitrage equations, volatility testing, 312–317
Arc-connectedness, bona fide fiscal policies, 174–175
Arrow–Debreu economic model, *see also* Walrasian economic model
  borrowing constraints and international comovements, 463–466
  distribution of asset holdings, 318–322
  general equilibrium theory, firm and plant aspects, 393–395
  irreducibility, 96–97
  volatility testing, 302–303
Arrow economic model
  exceptional case, irreducibility, 81
  futures trading, 203–206
Arrow securities
  asymptotic inefficiency, genericity, 222–226
  security market model, defined, 215–221
Ascoli's theorem, borrowing constraints and international comovements, 484–485
Asset holdings
  borrowing constraints and international comovements, 475–477
  distribution, 318–322

Asset prices
defined, 207
infinite horizons, incomplete financial markets, 121–122
volatility testing
commodities and, 308
distribution of wealth and, 323
with insurance, 311–317
without insurance, 317–327
intertemporal model, 302–329
Asset sequences
asymptotic efficiency, infinite matrices, 220–221
asymptotic inefficiency
defined, 207
genericity, 221–226
infinite matrices, 220–221
securities market equilibrium, 209–213
Asymptotic completeness
defined, 204–205
multinational corporations, absolute advantage
overview, 490–491
Ricardi model structure, 491–497
world transformation curve, 497–503
security market model, 214
Asymptotic efficiency
asset sequences, infinite matrices, 219–220
defined, 204
security market model, 214
Asymptotic inefficiency
asset sequences, infinite matrices, 220–221
behavior with security growth, 213–221
genericity, 221–226
model components, 206–209
securities market equilibrium, 204, 209–213
unconstrained consumption, 227–230
Attainable sets, economy with externalities, 15–17
Aumann's proof, competitive equilibrium, 34–35
Autarky, lump-sum taxes, 179
Autocorrelation estimations, vintage capital model, 280–285

Backlog transactions
competitive economies, optimizing price choices, 187–189
Scarf's economy
multiperiod horizons, 195–197
single–period horizons, 191–192
Baire category theorem, asymptotic inefficiency, 222–226
Balanced fiscal policies
defined, 168
lump-sum taxes, 170–171
equilibrium money prices, 176–178
Banach lattice, commodity pair desirability
Core–Walras equivalence, 162–164
definitions, 152–153
extremely desirability commodities, 160–162
Banach space, commodity pair desirability
definitions, 152–153
dynamic game strategies, resource exploitation, 335–339
model and preliminary theorem, 155–160
Bankruptcy condition
budget set continuity, 127–138
discontinuity of budget correspondences, 131–138
modeling strategy, 127–131
infinite horizons, incomplete financial markets, 126–127
Barro–Becker model of endogenous fertility
background, 237–238
basic assumptions, 238–241
Bayes' rule, disturbance densities, 373–375
Beato equilibrium notion, Graham–McKenzie economy, 10–13

Bellman's equation
 Cyert–DeGroot–Maskin–Tirole duopoly games, 340–344
 disturbance densities, experimental consumption, 374–375
 dynamic game strategies, resource exploitation, 334–339
Berge's maximum theorem
 competitive equilibrium, Hausdorff continuity, 30
 disturbance densities, experimental consumption, 374–375
 Graham–McKenzie economy, 8
Best-reply payoff, reaction function equilibria, 348
Billingsley's theorem, disturbance densities, 371–375
Blackwell's theorem
 Cyert–DeGroot–Maskin–Tirole duopoly games, 340
 dynamic game strategies, 349–350
Bochner integrable function, commodity pair desirability, 154
 Core–Walras equivalence, 163–164
 definitions, 153–154
 model and preliminary theorem, 155–160
Bona fide fiscal policies
 defined, 168
 lump-sum taxes, 172–175
Borel σ-algebra
 commodity pair desirability, 154
 competitive equilibrium, firm-specific and plant-specific aspects, 403–410
 subsets, disturbance densities, 371–372
Borrowing constraints, international comovements
 background, 460–462
 competitive equilibrium, 466–472
 with complete markets, 463–466
 equilibrium existence, 472–475
 model components, 462–475
 model simulations, 477–480
 stationary distribution of asset holdings, 475–477
Boundary optimal paths
 motivation, 411–413
 reforestation model, 413–418
  assumptions, 418–423
  cross-vintage bound conditions, 419–423
  maximand condition, 418–419
  results, 423–425
Bounded convergence theorem, disturbance densities, 376–377, 384–385
Boundedness
 asset returns, 207
  security market model, 205–206
 asymptotic inefficiencies, security market equilibrium, 211–213
 bona fide fiscal policies, lump-sum taxes, 174–175
 competitive equilibrium
  externalities, 19
  mapping, 19–20
Brouwer's fixed-point theorem
 boundary optimal paths, 418–423
 competitive equilibrium, 26–34
  separating hyperplane theorem, 34–35
Budget correspondence discontinuity, bankruptcy condition, 131–138
Budget set
 asymptotic inefficiencies, 208
 irreducibility, equilibrium, 79
Budget vector, Slutsky coefficients, 53–55

Capital
 boundary optimal paths, 411–412
 endogenous fertility model, 244–246
 international transfer model, 558
  cost function, 558
  input function, 558–559
 as production factor, labor mobility and wage rate equalization, 444–452

Capital accumulation
  boundary optimal paths, 412
  capital accumulation games, 352–355
  international transfers, 555–557
  turnpike properties
    comparative statics and dynamics, 362–363
    existence and stability properties, 358–362
    formulation and notation, 355–358
    overview, 352–355
Capital adjustment process, long-run equilibrium (LRE), 516–517
Capital/output ratio, vintage capital model, 253–254
Capital string, vintage capital model, 251
  consumption paths, 297
  efficient production, 253–254
Cartesian product, competitive equilibrium, 4
Cauchy problem, borrowing constraints and international comovements, 482–483
Cheaper point theorem, irreducibility
  aggregate interiority, 89–90
  compensated to uncompensated equilibrium, 87–89
  nonconvex feasible sets, 83–85
  outside agents, independent coalitions, 107
Chebyshev set, competitive equilibrium, 28–30
Circulant matrix, Stolper–Samuelson theorem, dominant diagonals, 440
Clarke–Rockafellar theorem, Graham–McKenzie economy, 9–10
Classical integrability conditions, Slutsky coefficients, 55
Clipped Edgeworth box economy
  Gale's linear exchange model, 94–95
  irreducibility, generalized interdependence, 100–102
Closed-loop stationary strategies, 344–349
Coalition, irreducibility
  defined, 105
  outside agents, 107
Cobb–Douglas production function
  endogenous fertility model, 242–246
  exchange economy, price adjustments, 199–200
  general equilibrium theory, 399–403
  stochastic model, 272–274
  vintage capital model, 258
    policy function, 262–266
    value function, 258–259
Commodities
  asset prices
    infinite horizons, 122
    volatility testing, 308
  bundles, asymptotic inefficiency, 206–207
  commodity pair desirability, 160–162
  prices
    asymptotic inefficiencies, 209
    defined, 207–208
    Graham–McKenzie economy, 7
    price vectors, lump-sum taxes, 178–179
  space
    asymptotic inefficiency, 206–207
    equilibrium allocations, 231
    irreducibility, 78
      aggregate interiority, 89–90
Commodity pair desirability
  Banach lattices, 152–154
  Core–Walras equivalence in Banach lattices, 162–164
  defined, 151–152
  extremely desirable commodities, 160–162
  lemmas, 154–155
  model and preliminary theorem, 155–160
  notation, 152
Common portfolio restrictions, indeterminacy, 62
Comparative dynamics
  capital accumulation games, turnpike properties, 362–363
  international transfers, 561–565
Comparative statics
  capital accumulation games, turnpike properties, 362–363

international transfers, 556–557, 561–565
long-run equilibrium (LRE)
changes in taste, 524–525
transfer problems, 525–532
Compensated demand function
international transfer model, 557–558
irreducibility, 79
Compensated equilibrium, irreducibility
continuum economies, 104
feasible allocation, 80
Honkapohja's theory, 80
necessity theorems, 110–112
sufficiency theorems, 107–110
to uncompensated equilibrium, 74–77
Compensated supply function, international transfer model, 558
Competitive equilibrium
background, 3–4
borrowing constraints and international comovements
complete markets, 463–466
proof of existence, 472–475
stochastic markets, 466–472
commodity pair desirability, 156
compensated to uncompensated equilibrium, 74–77
development of classical theorem, 36–44
existence with externalities, 15–22
Arrow–Debreu economy versus McKenzie economy, 21–22
versus Graham–McKenzie economy, 15–17
proof of survival assumption, 17–20
subsequent work on, 20–21
survival assumption, 15–17
firm-specific and plant-specific aspects, 403–410
geometric applications, 39–44
Graham's model, 4–14
continuity of demands, 14
influence on subsequent work, 10–13
proof with Kakutani fixed-point theorm, 5–10
restricted demand functions, 14
results in Graham–McKenzie economy, 4–5
interiority, irreducibility and irreversibility, 22–36
abstract markets, 22–23
Debreau–Gale–Nikaido lemma, 34–35
digression on irreducibility, 23–26
proof with Brouwer fixed-point theorem, 26–34
irreducibility in abstract markets, 36–37
lump-sum taxes, 168–169
balanced fiscal policies, 171
ordered structures, versus geometric applications, 44–46
Pareto-efficiency, general theory, 73–74
price adjustments
examples, 185–186
Gale's economy, 197–200
optimizing price maker, 187–189
overview, 181–185
Scarf's economy, multiperiod horizon, 193–197
Scarf's economy, single-period horizon, 189–192
survival conditions, proofs, 37–44
viability issues, 39–44
Complete market economy, indeterminacy, 67–71
Completeness, asymptotic inefficiency, 222–226
Cone of diversification, labor mobility and wage rate equalization, 453–455
Cones, irreducibility, 84–85
Constant elasticity of substitution (CES), vintage capital model
linearity of policy function, 262–266
one Hoss–Shay model, 258
production, 252–253
stochastic optimization problem, 273–274
value function, 258–259
wage-output behaviors, 269–270

Constant–returns-to-scale (CRS)
long-run equilibrium (LRE), 523–524
tariffs, 533
transfer conditions, 528–532
vintage capital model, 253
Consumers
bona fide fiscal policies, lump-sum taxes, 173–175
competitive equilibrium
convexity assumptions, 40–44
Kakutani fixed-point theorem, 31–34
defined, 208
infinite horizons
incomplete financial markets, 122–124
irreducibility,
continuum economies, 104
feasible sets, 78
learning, 367–368
Scarf's economy, multiperiod horizons, 196–197
volatility testing
asset prices with insurance, 314–317
continuum of, 308–309
distribution of asset holdings, 318–322
Consumption
aggregate, *see* Aggregate consumption
asymptotic inefficiencies, 208, 227–230
bundles
security market model, 205
unconstrained consumption, 227–230
dynamic game strategies, resource exploitation, 332–333
endogenous fertility, background, 237–238
experimental, *see* Experimental consumption
incomplete financial markets, 131
labor mobility and wage rate equalization, 446–449
long-run equilibrium (LRE), changes in taste, 524–525
myopic, *see* Myopic consumption
unconstrained, *see* Unconstrained consumption
volatility testing
covariation with asset prices, 327–329
covariation with stock returns, 306–307
market efficiency, 306–307
Consumption beta theory, 305
Continuity
bona fide fiscal policies, lump–sum taxes, 174–175
commodity pair desirability, 156
competitive equilibrium, 18–22
Continuous function, vintage capital model, 272
Continuum economies, irreducibility, 104–107
Contrapositives, security market model, 217–218
Convexified nonoligarchy condition, 76–77
Convexified oligarchy, Gale's linear exchange model
cheapest points theorem, 93
nonoligarchic allocations, 92–93
Convexity assumptions, competitive equilibrium, 36–37
Core allocation
compensated to uncompensated equilibrium, 75–77
competitive equilibrium, 73–74
Core equivalence theorem, *see* Core–Walras equivalence
Core theory, competitive equilibrium, 23–26
Core–Walras equivalence
commodity pair desirability
Banach lattices, 162–164
model and preliminary theory, 155–160
infinite-dimensional commodity space, 150–152
Cournot–Nash best response
Cyert–DeGroot–Maskin–Tirole duopoly games
linear-quadratic case, 343

Cournot–Nash equilibria
competitive equilibrium, 20
reaction function equilibria, 345–349
tariffs, imperfect competition, 550–551
Covariation, volatility testing, 327–329
Cross-vintage bound
boundary optimal paths, 416–417
inverse association, 419–420
Cyclical convergence, boundary optimal paths, 423–425
Cyert–DeGroot–Maskin–Tirole duopoly games
chaotic MPE, 343–344
linear-quadratic case, 342–343
Markovian strategies, 399–344

Date–event budget constraints, infinite horizons, 125–126
Debreu–Gale–Nikaido lemma, 34–35
Debreu's theorem, *see also* Arrow–Debreu economic model
competitive equilibrium, 20
Graham–McKenzie economy, 8
Demand continuity, Graham–McKenzie economy, 7
Demand elasticity
endogenous fertility, 237–238
fertility rate changes, 242–246
Demand function
competitive equilibrium
continuity of demands, 14
price-dependent preferences, 20–21
restriction, 14
long-run equilibrium (LRE), 524–525
lump-sum taxes, balanced fiscal policies, 172
Slutsky coefficients, 52–55
volatility testing, asset pricing model, 309–310
Demand price, temporary and long-run equilibrium stability, 514–515
Demand sets, irreducibility, 79–80
Demographic constraint, boundary optimal paths, 414–418
Density functions, disturbance densities, 384–385
Depreciation case, vintage capital model, 255
Detrended investments, vintage capital model
growth theory, 256
linearity of policy function, 263–266
stochastic model, time-dependent technologies, 292–296
wage-output behaviors, 269–270
Diffeomorphism, reaction function equilibria, 346
Difference equations
capital accumulation games, turnpike properties, 357–358
vintage capital model, linearity of policy function, 265–266
Differentiability assumption
capital accumulation games, 353
infinite horizons, 123–124
Dimensionality condition, labor mobility factors, 443
Discount factor, volatility testing, 306–307
Discount rates
bankruptcy condition, 136–138
borrowing constraints and international comovements, 477–479
Discrete time analysis, competitive economies, 187–189
Distributive factor matrix
factor intensity (FI) condition, 431–434
structure, 434–435
Distributive share matrix, Willoughby theorem, 435–438
Disturbance densities, experimental consumption
extensions for exponential, and truncated-normal distributions, 382–385
main results, 375–382
MLRP disturbances, 385–392
model components, 370–375
overview, 367–370
Divisible goods, irreducibility, 85–87

Dominant diagonals
capital accumulation games, 358–362
Stolper–Samuelson theorem
matrix structure, 434–435
overview, 429–430
strong factor intensity (FI) control, 430–434
Willoughby theorem, 435–438
Dubovickii–Milyutin cone of interior displacement, 12–13
Dynamic game strategies
Bellman's equation for, 349–350
Cyert–DeGroot–Maskin–Tirole duopoly games, 339–344
overview, 331–332
reaction function equilibria, 344–349
resource exploitation model, 332–339
Dynastic utility function, 238–241

Echo principle, vintage capital model, 250
Economic agents, irreducibility, 77–79
Economic profits, volatility testing, 303–304
Edgeworth process, *see also* Clipped Edgeworth box economy
competitive economies, 186
price adjustments, 186
Efficiency mapping
competitive equilibrium, 18–19
vintage capital model, 253–254
Efficiency price mappings, competitive equilibrium
infinite commodities, 35
tangent spaces and normal cones, 44
Elasticity of offer curve, long-run equilibrium (LRE), 521–524
Embodiment hypothesis, vintage capital model, 249
Endogenous fertility, growth theory and
Barro–Becker model, 238–241
fertility rate changes, 241–246
overview, 237-238
schooling modification, 246–247
Endowments
asymptotic inefficiencies, 208
initial, *see* Initial endowments
Envelope theorem, endogenous fertility model, 240–241
Equilibrium, *see also specific types of equilibrium*
allocation, asymptotic inefficiency, unconstrained consumption, 227–230
without insurance, volatility testing, 311
labor mobility and wage rate equalization, 446–449
prices
incomplete financial markets, 119–120
lump-sum taxes, 169, 176–178
securities market, 204–205
asymptotic inefficiencies, 209–213
defined, 208–209
Euclidean distance
disturbance densities, 383–385
vintage capital stochastic model, 297–300
Euclidean space
commodity pair desirability, 153
competitive equilibrium
Brouwer fixed-point theorem, 30
consumer satiation, 31–34
firm-specific and plant-specific aspects, 406–410
Kakutani's theorem, 31–32
general equilibrium theory, plant-specific aspects, 398–403
Euler equation
boundary optimal paths, 420–421
dynamic game strategies, 337–339
international transfer model, 560–561
vintage capital model
linearity of policy function, 263–266
stochastic model, 299–300
Exchange economies
competitive equilibrium, 24–26
linear, *see* Linear exchange economies
Existence properties, capital accumulation games, 358–362
Existence theorem, compensated to uncompensated equilibrium, 75–77
Expansibility axiom, boundary optimal paths, 412

Expenditure function
labor mobility and wage rate equalization, 443
location-specific, 451–452
Experimental consumption
defined, 367–368
disturbance densities, 367–370
Extended demand mapping, Graham–McKenzie economy, 6–7, 12–13
Externalities
competitive equilibrium, 15–22
infinite commodities and economies, 20–21
Extremely desirability commodities, commodity pair desirability, 160–162

Factor intensity (FI) condition, Stolper–Samuelson theorem,
dominant diagonals, 430–434
Factor market distortions, output and capital adjustment processes, 517
Factor price equalization, labor mobility and wage rate equalization, 443
cone of diversification, 454–455
two immobile factors, 452–458
Factor price specialization, labor mobility and wage rate equalization, 455–458
Fan–Glicksberg fixed-point theorem, 35
Farkas' lemma, normalized nominal systems, 124–126
Fatou's lemma
commodity pair desirability, Core–Walras equivalence, 165–166
vintage capital model
labor, 251
stochastic model, 286
Feasible allocations, irreducibility, 78–79
continuum economies, 104
necessity theorems, 111–112
Felicity index, boundary optimal paths, 416–417
Fershtman–Muller game, capital accumulation, 352–355
Fertility rate changes, endogenous fertility model, 241–246
Financial assets, incomplete financial markets, 118–120
Financial equilibrium
indeterminacy, 59–62, 68–71
infinite horizons, incomplete financial markets, 121–122, 127
Finite-dimensional linear programs
general equilibrium theory, plant-specific aspects, 400–403
Graham–McKenzie economy, competitive equilibrium, 7–8
Finite-horizon economies
incomplete financial markets
bankruptcy condition, 130–131
short-run equilibrium, 143–146
lump-sum taxes
balanced fiscal policies, 170–171
bona fide fiscal policies, 173–175
Finite-state securities, asymptotic inefficiencies, 210–213
Finite transition times, vintage capital stochastic model, 287–288
Firm, role in general equilibrium theory, 395–397
First efficiency theorem, compensated to uncompensated equilibrium, 74–75
First order conditions, volatility testing, 314–317
Fiscal policies, lump-sum taxes, 170–175
Fixed-point algorithm, borrowing constraints and international comovements, 477–480
Fixed-point theorems, *see specific theorems*
Flexible accelerator theory, 248
Fluctuation-proneness, boundary optimal paths, 421–423
Foreign labor, multinational corporations and absolute advantage, Ricardian model, 492–494

Friedman's theorem, capital accumulation games, 361–362
Frobenius' theorem, Slutsky coefficients, 55

Gale's economic model
  irreducibility, nonoligarchic allocations, 91–92
  price adjustments, 197–200
General equilibrium theory, 73–74
  compensated to uncompensated equilibrium, 74–77
  firm and plant as factors in competitive equilibrium and, 403–410
    firm-specific aspects, 395–397
    overview, 393–395
    plant-specific aspects, 397–403
  irreducibility, 79–80
  intraindustry trade
    tariff protection with imperfect competition, 541–553
    two-country model, 543–548
Genericity, asymptotic inefficiency, 221–226
Geometric problems, competitive equilibrium
  convexity assumptions, 39–44
  ordered structures, 44–46
Giffen good, competitive economies, 184–185
Global integral, Slutsky coefficients, 54–55
Good faith expectation, lump-sum taxes, 172–175
Goods, general equilibrium, 541–542
Government bonds, volatility testing, 309
Graham's model, competitive equilibrium, 4–14
Graham–McKenzie economy
  competitive equilibrium, 4–5
  and economy with externalities, 15–17
Gronwall's lemma, borrowing constraints and international comovements, 483
Grossman, Kihlstrom, and Mirman (GKM) model, disturbance densities, 368–370
Growth theory
  overview, 237
  vintage capital model, 248–300

Hahn process, competitive economies' price adjustments, 182
Harrot-neutral technical process
  endogenous fertility
    model, 237–238
    production function, 238–239
  vintage capital model
    efficient production, 2253–254
    labor, 251
Hausdorff continuity, competitive equilibrium, 30
Hausdorff space, commodity pair desirability, 153–154
Heckscher–Ohlin model
  Chamberlinian monopolistic competition, 490–491
  labor mobility, 443
  multinational corporations and absolute advantage
    rental/wage ratio, 495–497
    world transformation curve, 497–503
  transfer conditions, constant-returns-to-scale (CRS), 529–532
Heckscher–Ohlin–Samuelson model, 559
Hemicontinuity, competitive equilibrium, 31–32
Henon's attractor, reaction function equilibria, 347
Hessian matrices, capital accumulation games
  dominant diagonal properties, 358–362
  turnpike properties, 353
Hicks's distinction of income and substitution effects, 54–55
Hilbert space, competitive equilibrium, 31–34

Hildenbrand's theory, commodity pair desirability, 155
Home labor, multinational corporations and absolute advantage, Ricardian model, 493–494
Homeomorphism, Graham–McKenzie economy, 11–13
Homoethic demands, temporary and long-run equilibrium stability, 514
Homogeneity property, vintage capital model, 261–262

Identity mapping, competitive equilibrium, 18–19
Immobile households, labor mobility and wage rate equalization
  endowment of labor, 451
  production factors, 444–452
Imperfect competition, tariff protection, intraindustry trade equilibrium, 541–553
Implicit function theorem, disturbance densities, experimental consumption, 380–381
Inada-type conditions, capital accumulation games, turnpike properties, 356–358
Incomplete financial markets
  defined, 116–120
  infinite horizons
    bankruptcy condition, 126–127, 127–138
    commodities, 122
    consumers, 122–124
    financial equilibrium, 127
    financial structure, 121–122
    indeterminacy, 141–146
    normalized nominal systems, 124–126
    price space, 138–141
Incomplete markets model
  indeterminacy, 61–62
    indeterminacy terminal tax model, 64–67
Indeterminacy
  Cyert–DeGroot–Maskin–Tirole duopoly games, 342
  imperfections in, 67–71
    financial markets, 55–113
  incomplete markets, infinite horizons, 141–146
  incomplete markets model, 61–62
  nominal, *see* Nominal indeterminacy
  outside money, 62–67
  restricted participation model, 57–62
Infinite dimensional commodity space, 150–152
Infinite dimensional inverse function theorem, 564
Infinite horizons
  games
    duopoly game, resource exploitation, 332–339
    dynamic game, turnpike properties, 353
    reaction function equilibria, 346–349
  incomplete financial markets
    bankruptcy condition, 126–127, 127–138
    commodities, 122
    consumers, 122–124
    financial equilibrium, 127
    indeterminacy, 141–146
    normalized nominal systems, 124–126
    overview, 116–120
    price space, 138–141
    stochastic environment, 120–121
Inflation beta theory of asset prices, 315–317
Inflection points, production possibility frontier (PPF), 511–512
Initial endowments, irreducibility, 81–83
Insurance, volatility testing
  absence of asset pricing model, 317–327
  presence of asset pricing model, 311–317
Interdependent agents, *see also* Strong interdependence
  irreducibility, 98–103, 106–107

Interiority
bona fide fiscal policies, lump-sum taxes, 175
competitive equilibrium, 22–36
infinite commodities, 35
irreducibility, 81–83
aggregate interiority, 89–90
initial endowments, 81–83
particular allocation, 81
Interior optimal paths
boundary optimal paths, 411–412
cross-vintage bound, 419–420
Intermediate value theorem, competitive equilibrium, 30
International business cycles, international transfers, 565–566
International equilibrium, Marshallian approach to, 517–518
Intersection mapping
competitive equilibrium, 44
Graham–McKenzie economy, 6, 9, 11
Intersectoral substitutability, international transfers
comparative dynamics and statics, 562–563
normal overall welfare effect, 567–569
Intertemporal optimization, vintage capital model, 255–256
Intertemporal substitutability, international transfers
comparative dynamics and statics, 562–563
normal overall welfare effect, 567–569
Intertemporal welfare effect reversal
defined, 555–557
international transfers, 569–570
Intraindustry trade, general equilibrium model for tariff protection, 542–543
tariff protection with imperfect competition, 541–553
Inventory accumulation
price adjustments, Gale's economy, 197–200
Scarf's economy, multiperiod horizons, 193–197
Inventory costs, competitive economies, 187–189
Inverse supply mapping, competitive equilibrium
externalities, 18–19
survival condition, 37–39
Irreducibility
Arrow's exceptional case, 81
basic assumptions, 77–79
cheaper feasible points, 83–89
cheaper point theorem, 87–89
desirability of divisible goods, 85–87
nonconvex feasible sets, 83–85
compensated to uncompensated equilibrium, 76–77
competitive equilibrium, 22–36
abstract market, 22–26
nonsatiation of consumer, 32–34
strong viability assumption, 42–44
continuum economies, 104–107
interdependence, 106–107
nonoligarchic allocations, 105
preliminary conditions, 104–105
equilibrium conditions, 79–80
generalized form, 102–103
interdependent agents
generalized interdependence, 100–102
resource relatedness, 98–100
interiority
aggregate interiority, 89–90
overview, 81–83
McKenzie's economic model, 97–98
nonoligarchic allocations, 90–96
agents at cheapest points, 93
clipped Edgeworth box exchange economy, 94–95
convex allocations, 92–93
definitions, 90–91
Gale's linear exchange model, 91–92
triangular Edgeworth box economy, 95–96
proofs of propositions, 107–112
necessity theorems, 110–112
sufficiency theorems, 107–110
survival assumptions, 103
weak, *see* Weak irreducibility
Irreversibility, competitive equilibrium, 22–36

Jacobian matrix, imperfect competition, individual countries, 549–551
Jones' magnification effect, 496–497

Kakutani fixed-point theorem, competitive equilibrium
  consumer satiation, 31–32
  Graham–McKenzie economy, 5–10, 12
  mappings, 18
  validity conditions, 43–44
Kemp–Khang model, international transfers, 559
Kuhn–Tucker theorem
  infinite horizon economy, 139–141
  vintage capital stochastic model, 286–287

Labor
  endowment of immobile households, 451
  foreign, *see* Foreign labor
  general equilibrium, tariff protection
    with imperfect competition, 541–543
  heterogeneous labor, mobility and wage
    rate equalization, 449–451
  home, *see* Home labor
  indivisibility constraint, general equilibrium theory, 397–403
  mobility wage rate equalization
    diversification cone, 453–455
    factor price specialization, 455–458
    heterogeneous labor, 449–451
    labor endowments of immobile households, 451
    location-specific expenditure functions, 451–452
    one immobile factor, 444–452
    overview, 442–444
    production factor, 444–452
    two immobile factors, 452–458
  multinational corporations and absolute advantage, 492–494
  vintage capital model, 251
    efficient production, 253–254
    linearity of policy function, 266–267
    optimal allocations, 257
    stochastic model, lemmas, 285–300
Lagrange conditions
  competitive equilibrium, firm-specific and plant-specific aspects, 408–410
  general equilibrium theory, plant-specific aspects, 400–403
  Slutsky coefficients, 52–55
Land as production factor, labor mobility and wage rate equalization, 444–452
Large trades, asymptotic inefficiency, 226
Learning consumer, defined, 367–368
Lebesgue measure
  bounded measurable functions, 150–152
  competitive equilibrium, firm-specific and plant-specific aspects, 404–410
  disturbance densities, experimental consumption, 370–375, 383–385
Leisure, marginal utility, 470–472
L'Hopital's rule, international transfers, 580–581
Likelihood function, vintage capital, 275–276
Limit-of-growth models, boundary optimal paths, 423–425
Linear approximation system, long-run equilibrium (LRE), 522–524
Linear exchange economies
  compensated to uncompensated equilibrium, 76–77
  nonoligarchic allocations, 92
Linear independence, asymptotic inefficiencies
  asset sequences, 223–226
  security market equilibrium, 211–213
Linearity, vintage capital model, 262–266

Lipschitz equations
borrowing constraints and international comovements, 483–484
competitive equilibrium, Brouwer fixed-point theorem, 29–30
vintage capital model, 272
Local factor prices, labor mobility and wage rate equalization, production factors, 445–446
Location-specific amenities, labor mobility and wage rate equalization, 451–452
Log-likelihoods, vintage capital stochastic model, 274–277
Long-run (LR) supply price, model, 512
Long-run equilibrium (LRE)
Marshallian stability, 519–524
origins of theory, 508
output and capital adjustment processes, 516–517
stability, 512–515
significance of B_0 greater than 0, 535–539
Lump-sum redistribution
competitive equilibrium, 73–74
irreducibility, Arrow's exceptional case, 81
Lump-sum taxes
balanced fiscal policies, 170–171
bona fide fiscal policies, 172–175
extensions, 178–179
fiscal policy and, 168–169
preliminaries, 169–172
volatility testing, asset pricing model, 309
Lyapunov's theorem
commodity pair desirability, 154–155
Core–Walras equivalence, 165–166

Macrostate model, boundary optimal paths, 414–418
Managerial span-of-control theory
firm in general equilibrium theory, 395–397
firm-specific and plant-specific aspects, 403–410
Mapping, competitive equilibrium
externalities, 18–19
firm–specific and plant-specific aspects, 405–410
Marginal cost pricing equilibria, 10–13
Marginal propensity to consume goods, 562
Marginal propensity to expand sector, 562
Marginal rate of transformation (MRT), 511–512
Marginal utility of wealth, international transfer model, 558, 560
Market efficiency, volatility testing
definition, 303–305
review of existing tests, 305–307
Markov perfect equilibrium (MPE)
chaotic MPE, 343–344
Cyert–DeGroot–Maskin–Tirole duopoly games, 340–344
linear-quadratic case, 342–343
Markov strategies
borrowing constraints and international comovements, 469–470
reaction function equilibria, 346–349
pseudo-trigger strategies, 348
turnpike properties, 354
volatility testing, market efficiency, 306–307
Marshallian output adjustment process
long-run equilibrium (LRE), 520-524
temporary and long-run equilibrium stability, 515
Marshallian stability
long-run equilibrium (LRE)
international equilibrium, 519–524
output and capital adjustment processes, 516–517
temporary equilibrium, 513–515
transfer results, overview, 509
Marshall-Lerner (ML) condition, variable returns to scale (VRS)
international equilibrium, 517–518
long-run equilibrium stability, 512–515, 519–524, 535–38
model structure, 509–512

output adjustment and capital adjustment, 516–517
overview, 507–509
shifting consumer tastes, 524–525
supply side economy, 533–535
temporary equilibrium stability, 512–515, 518–519
transfer problems, 525–532
Martingale condition, borrowing constraints and international comovements, 469–470
Maximal accumulation path, vintage capital stochastic model, 291–293
Maximand condition, boundary optimal paths, 418–419
Maximizing hypotheses, competitive equilibrium, 16
Maximum-likelihood estimation, vintage capital, 274–285
Maximum theorem, dynamic game strategies, 350
McKenzie economic theory
boundary optimal paths
overview, 411–412
syntax, 412
competitive equilibrium
Arrow–Debreu economy, 21–22
Brouwer fixed-point theorem, 26–34
mapping, 27–28
externalities, 16–17
firm-specific and plant-specific aspects, 403–410
infinite commodities, 35
influence on subsequent research, 34–35
irreducibility, 23–26
price-dependent preferences, 20–21
general equilibrium theory
firm-specific aspects, 393–397
plant-specific aspects, 393–395
irreducibility, *see* Irreducibility
Slutsky coefficients and, 51–55
survival assumption, 37–39
Mean-ergodic property, borrowing constraints and international comovements, 476–477
Measurability, commodity pair desirability, 156
Measure space of consumers, irreducibility, 104
Measure theory, disturbance densities, 371–375
Mehra and Prescott's model, volatility testing, 323–325
Microstate model, boundary optimal paths, 413–418
Millian stationary state, 411
Mobile households, labor mobility and wage rate equalization
heterogeneous labor, 449–451
production factors, 444–452
Modified demand mapping, competitive equilibrium, 18–19
Monotone likelihood ratio property (MLRP)
disturbance densities, 369–370
experimental consumption, 377–378
Monotonicity
borrowing constraints and international comovements, 487–488
commodity pair desirability, 156–160
Graham–McKenzie economy, competitive equilibrium, 13
irreducibility
overriding desirability of divisible goods, 85–87
preferences, 83
Multinational corporations, absolute advantage, asymmetric case
overview, 490–491
Ricardian model structure, 491–497
world transformation curve, 497–503
Multiperiod horizons, price adjustments, 193–197
Multiple trading dates, asymptotic inefficiency, 231
Myopic consumption, disturbance densities, 368–370

Naive accelerator theory, vintage capital model, 248
Nash equilibrium
capital accumulation games
comparative statics and dynamics, 362–363
existence and stability properties, 358–362
turnpike properties, 354–358
dynamic game strategies, 333–334
incomplete financial markets, 141–146
reaction function, 345–349
Necessity theorems
irreducibility, 110–112
nonoligarchy, 105
Negative diagonal elements, capital accumulation games, 364–365
Net trade vector, irreducibility, 101–102
No-arbitrage conditions, infinite horizons, 125–126
No favorable surprise assumption, price adjustments, 182–183
Nominal indeterminacy, 59–62
Nonconvexity
feasible sets, compensated to uncompensated equilibrium, 75–77
general equilibrium theory
firm-specific aspects, 395–397
plant-specific aspects, 397–403
Noncooperative equilibrium, capital accumulation games, 356–358
Nonlinear utility functions, vintage capital model, 270–272
Nonmonotonicity properties, vintage capital model, 259–260
Nonnegative orthant consumptions, irreducibility, 83
Nonnegative prices, competitive economies, 189
Nonoligarchic allocations, irreducibility, 90–96, 105
cheapest point theorem, convexified examples, 93–96
convexified oligarchy, 92–93
definitions, 90–91
Gale's linear exchange model, 91–92
sufficiency theorems, 107–110
Nonresidential fixed investments, vintage capital
estimation results, 277–278
stochastic model, 274–285
Nonsatiation, irreducibility, 79–80
Nonsmooth analysis
competitive equilibrium and, 4
Graham–McKenzie economy, 8–9
Nonsymmetric stationary equilibria, 337–339
Nontâtonnement process, competitive economies, 181–185
Nontraded goods, labor mobility and wage rate equalization, 443
cone of diversification, 453–455
factor price specialization, 456–457
production factors, 444–449
Nonuniqueness, Cyert–DeGroot–Maskin–Tirole duopoly games, 344
Normalized nominal systems, infinite horizons, 124–126
Normal overall welfare effect, international transfers, 566–569
Normal vector square, commodity pair desirability, 152–153
Norm topology, vintage capital stochastic model, 288–289
Null matrix, Slutsky coefficients, 51–55
Numeraire securities
asymptotic inefficiencies
contrapositives, 217–218
unconstrained consumption, 229–230
security market model, 205–206
Numerical simulations, borrowing constraints and international comovements, 477–480

Off-diagonal elements, labor mobility and wage rate equalization, 453–455
Oligarchy, irreducibility, 105
One Hoss–Shay model, growth theory, 257–258

One-shot games, reaction function equilibria, 346–349
Open-loop strategies, capital accumulation games, 354–358
Operator distance, asymptotic inefficiency, 221–226
Optimizing price maker
  competitive economies, 187–189
  Scarf's economy
    multiperiod horizons, 193–197
    single-period horizons, 191–192
Output
  adjustment process
    exchange theory and, 508
    long-run equilibrium (LRE), 516–517
  correlations versus discount rate, 477–479
  vintage capital model, behavior over time, 267–269
Outside money, indeterminacy, 62–67
Overlapping-generations model, distribution of asset holdings, 320–322
Overridingly desirable goods, irreducibility, 84–85

Pareto-efficient allocation
  compensated to uncompensated equilibrium, 75–77
  competitive equilibrium, 73–74
  Gale's linear exchange model
    nonoligarchic allocations, 92
  irreducibility
    Arrow's exceptional case, 81
    interiority, 81-83
Pareto-optimal allocation
  asymptotic inefficiencies, 213–221
    asset sequences, 223–226
    equilibrium allocations, 218–219, 230–231
  borrowing constraints and international comovements
    competitive equilibrium, 467–472
    contingent markets, 464–466
  competitive equilibrium, Brouwer fixed-point theorem, 27–28
  general equilibrium theory, plant-specific aspects, 399–403
  lump-sum taxes, 168–169
    bona fide fiscal policies, 173–174
    equilibrium money prices, 176–178
  security markets, 203–206
Partial derivatives, vintage capital model, 257
Perfect competition, commodity pair desirability, 156
Perfect foresight equilibrium, international transfers, 560
  proof, 570
  theorem, 564
Perron-Frobenius theorem, borrowing constraints and international comovements
  competitive equilibrium, 471–472
  proofs, 486–487
Plant, role in general equilibrium theory, 397–403
Poincaré theorem, long-run equilibrium (LRE), 523–524
Pointwise convergence, vintage capital stochastic model, 286–300
Poisson counting, borrowing constraints and international comovements, 464–466
Policy function, vintage capital model, 262–272
  examples, 269–270
  labor allocation, 266–267
  linearity, 262–266
  nonlinear utility functions, 270–272
  stochastic optimization problem, 273–274
  wage and output behavior over time, 267–269
Positivity constraints, asymptotic inefficiency, 227–228
Posterior probability, disturbance densities, 373–375
Preferences
  elasticities, endogenous fertility, 238
  firm in general equilibrium theory, 395–397
  incomplete financial markets, price space, 138–141
  lump-sum taxes, 170

Preferences (*continued*)
ordering
infinite horizons, incomplete financial markets, 123–124
irreducibility, consumers' preferences, 78
vintage capital model, 255
Prescott model, disturbance densities, 368
Prescott–Townsed private information economies, 395–397
Price adjustments
competitive economies
examples, 185–186
Gale's economy, 197–200
optimizing price maker, 187–189
overview, 181–185
Scarf's economy multiperiod horizons, 193–197
single period horizon, 189–192
convergence, bankruptcy condition, 136–138
exchange theory and, 507–508
Price-dependent preferences, 20–21
Prices, *see also specific types of prices*
domain, irreducibility, 79
space, incomplete financial markets, 138–141
volatility testing, asset pricing model, 309
Prisoner's dilemma, nonuniqueness, 344
Probability distribution
asymptotic inefficiency, 206–209
volatility testing, market efficiency and, 303–305
Produced Mobile Factor (PMF)
Stolper–Samuelson theorem, dominant diagonals, 438–439
strong factor intensity (SFI) condition, 431–434
Producer durable equipment investment, vintage capital stochastic model, 278–285
Product convergence, bankruptcy condition, 134–138
Production function
diversification
factor price specialization, 455–458
labor mobility and wage rate equalization, 444–452
two immobile factors, 452–458
endogenous fertility model, 238–239
vintage capital model, 251–253
efficiency, 253–254
stochastic model, lemmas, 286–287
Production possibility frontier (PPF), 511–512
Production possibility set
general equilibrium theory, plant-specific aspects, 397–403
Graham–McKenzie economy, competitive equilibrium, 4–5, 13–14
Productivity
competitive equilibrium
McKenzie economies, externalities, 16–17
strong survival assumption, 20
endogenous fertility model, schooling, 246–247
Profit-sharing tariffs, imperfect competition, individual countries, 550–551
Pseudo-trigger strategies, reaction function equilibria, 348

Quantity theory, lump-sum taxes, 172
Quasiconcavity, disturbance densities, 375–378, 381–382, 386–389
Quasiconvexity
disturbance densities, 375–378
Slutsky coefficients, 54–55

Ramsey model, boundary optimal paths, 415–418
Rates of return, volatility testing, 323–325

Reaction function equilibria
  Henon's attractor as, 347
  Markovian strategies, 344–349
  one-parameter family of chaotic RFE, 347
  plethora of, 346–347
  pseudo-trigger strategies, 348–349
Real-valued function, Graham–McKenzie economy, 7–8
Reducibility, Gale's linear exchange model, 91–92
Regular paths, capital accumulation games, 356–358
Reisz representation theorem
  commodity pair desirability, 153–154
    Core–Walras equivalence, 163–165
  competitive equilibrium, 45
    nonsatiation of consumer, 32–33
    space structures
Residual depreciation, vintage capital, 275–276
Residual space, asymptotic inefficiency, 222–226
Resource availability
  commodity pair desirability, Banach space, 156
  dynamic game model, 332–339
Resource relatedness
  competitive equilibrium, 73–74
    irreducibility, 24–26
  extensions, 178–179
  irreducibility, 99–100
Restricted participation, indeterminacy, 59–62
Reward function, vintage capital model, 271–272
Ricardian economic model, multinational corporations and absolute advantage
  basic structure, 491–497
  overview, 490–491
Ricardo–Viner trade theory model, competitive equilibrium, 22
Risk aversion
  borrowing constraints and international comovements versus output correlations, 477–479
  volatility testing
    asset prices and distribution of wealth, 323
    burden of risk, 322–323
    covariation as factor, 327–329
    distribution of assets, 318–322
    market efficiency, 305
    Mehra and Prescott's results, 323–325
    risk-free assets, 325–327
Risk-free assets
  security market model, 205–206
  volatility testing, 325–327
Roy's identity, international transfers, 570
Rudin's theorem, disturbance densities, 382–385
Rybcyzski theorem
  international transfers, 559
  multinational corporations and absolute advantage, 497–503

Savings, volatility testing, 306–307
Scale effect of transfer condition, 529–530
Scarf's economy, price adjustments
  multiperiod horizon, 193–197
  single-period horizon, 189–192
Schauder and Tychonoff's theorem, dynamic game strategies, 336
Scheffe's theorem, disturbance densities, 383–385
Schooling, endogenous fertility model, 246–247
Second welfare theorem, competitive equilibrium, 35
Security market model
  asymptotics, 213–221
  components, 206–209
  equilibrium in, 209–213
  genericity, 221–226
  overview, 203–206
  unconstrained consumption, 227–230
Self-sufficiency
  compensated to uncompensated equilibrium, 76–77
  Gale's linear exchange model, 92

Semicontinuity, bankruptcy condition, 134–138
Separating hyperplane theorem, 34–35
Sequential properties, dynamic game strategies, 336–339
Set-theoretic subtraction, competitive equilibrium, 4
Shephard (–McKenzie) lemma
  long-run equilibrium (LRE), 513–515
    international stability conditions, 523–524
  temporary equilibrium stability, 513–515
Short-run equilibrium (SRE)
  incomplete financial markets, 143–146
  labor adjustment, 533
  origins of theory, 508
  output and capital adjustment processes, 516–517
    stability, 532–533
Single-agent economy, incomplete markets, 140–141
Single-period horizons, Scarf's economy, 189–192
Single-valued demands, Graham–McKenzie economy, 13–14
Six-period price cycle, Scarf's economy, 195–197
Slutsky coefficients
  McKenzie economy, 51–55
  symmetry condition, 52–55
Social utility function, imperfect competition, individual countries, 549–550
Span condition, asymptotic inefficiency, 224–226
Specialist systems, price adjustments, 200–201
Splitting property, commodity pair desirability
  Core–Walras equivalence, 162–164
  extremely desirability commodities, 161–162
Spot markets
  commodities, 203–206
  restricted participation model, 58–62
Square-integrable functions, measure space, 150–152
Stability properties, capital accumulation games, 358–362
State space, boundary optimal paths, 413–418
Stationary distribution, asset holdings, 475–477
Stationary equilibrium, dynamic game strategies, 333–339
Stationary-state effects theorem, international transfers
  equations, 564
  proof, 574
Steady-state capital shock, vintage capital model, 260–262
  labor allocation, 266–267
Steady-state values
  boundary optimal paths, 420
  endogenous fertility model
    fertility rate changes, 242–246
    model components, 240–241
Stochastic model
  incomplete financial markets, 120–121
  vintage capital, 272–274
    empirical results, 274–285
  volatility testing, asset pricing model, 308
Stock returns, volatility testing, 306–307
Stolper–Samuelson theorem
  dominant diagonals linked with
    matrix, 434–435
    overview, 429–430
    produced mobile factor (PMF) structure, 438–439
    strong factor intensity (FI) condition, 330–334
    Willoughby theorem, 435–438
  labor mobility, 443
  variable returns to scale, 535
Strange attractor, reaction function equilibria, 347
Strategy spaces, capital accumulation games, 353–354
Strictly positive equilibrium prices, 34–35

Strict survival assumption, irreducibility, 82
Strong factor intensity (SFI) condition, 430–434
Strong interdependence, irreducibility, 100
Strong oligarchy, irreducibility, 90–91
Strong survival assumption, competitive equilibrium
  Aumann's research, 34–35
  Brouwer fixed-point theorem, 28
  McKenzie economy, externalities, 19–20
  nonsatiation of consumer, 32–34
  relaxation to viability, 45–46
Strong viability, competitive equilibrium
  externalities, 15–17
  relaxation to viability, 45–46
  viability and irreducibility conditions, 42–44
  weakening, 22
Sufficiency
  disturbance densities, 369–370
  intraindustry trade, tariff protection with imperfect competition, 545–548
  irreducibility, 107–110
    nonoligarchic allocations, 105
Supply side of economy, variable returns to scale, 533–535
Support functions, Graham–McKenzie economy, 8
Survival assumption
  competitive equilibrium
    consumer satiation, 33–34
    McKenzie economies, externalities, 16–17
    viability, 37–39
    viability and, 45–46
  irreducibility, 103
  McKenzie economy's omission of, 36–44
  strong, *see* Strong survival assumption

Tac-functions, Graham–McKenzie economy, 8
Tarafdar fixed-point theorem, 34–35
Tariffs
  imperfect competition
    individual countries, 548–551
    intraindustry trade equilibrium, 541–553
  variable returns to scale, 533
  world welfare, 551–553
Temporary equilibrium
  output and capital adjustment processes, 518–519
  stability, 512–515
  transfer condition, 526–532
Terminal tax model, indeterminacy, 63–67
Terminal utility model, indeterminacy, 63–67
Terminal wealth constraints, security market model, 205
Three-period price cycle, Scarf's economy, 193–197
Topological space, competitive equilibrium, 30
Townsend's volatility model, 329
Trace norm, asymptotic inefficiency, 222–226
Traded goods, labor mobility and wage rate equalization, 443–444
  production factors, 444–449
  two immobile factors, 452–458
Trade effect of transfer condition, 528, 530–531
Traders' income, competitive equilibrium, 25–26
Trading sets, asymptotic inefficiencies, 208
Transfer conditions
  direct effects, 528
  international transfers in dynamic economies
    business cycles, 565–566
    comparative dynamics and statics, 561–565
    intertemporal welfare effect reversals, 569–570
    normality in overall welfare effect, 566–569
    overview, 555–557

Transfer conditions (*continued*)
theorem proofs, 570–580
two-country/two-good model, 557–561
long-run equilibrium (LRE), 525–532
scale effect, 529
trade effect, 528, 530–531
Transivity, commodity pair desirability, 157–158
Transversality condition
dynamic game strategies, 338–339
infinite horizons, incomplete financial markets, 118–120, 123–124
Triangular Edgeworth box economy, 95–96
Truncation time, vintage capital model
efficient production, 254
maximal accumulation path, 291–292
nonmonotonicity properties, 259–260
Turnpike properties
capital accumulation games
comparative statics and dynamics, 362–363
existence and stability, 358–362
formulation and notation, 355–358
overview, 352–355
Cyert–DeGroot–Maskin–Tirole duopoly games, 342
international transfers, 556–557
T-values, vintage capital stochastic model, 277–282

Uncertainty, volatility testing, 307–312
Uncompensated equilibrium
demand set, 79
irreducibility
to compensated equilibrium, 74–77
continuum economies, 104
feasible allocation, 80
generalized interdependence, 107
sufficiency theorems, 107–110
Unconstrained consumption, asymptotic inefficiency, 227–230
Uniform approximation, security market model, 215–221
Uniform properness, asymptotic inefficiencies, 213–214
Uniform topology, security market model, 215–221
Upper hemicontinuity, Graham–McKenzie economy, 13
Utility functions
borrowing constraints and international comovements, 477–480
competitive economies, price adjustments, 185–186
endogenous fertility model, 239–240
fertility rate changes, 241–246
general equilibrium theory, plant-specific aspects, 399–403
international transfer model, 557–558
Slutsky coefficients, 52–55
vintage capital model
nonlinearity, 270–272
nonmonotonicity properties, 260
preferences, 255

Value functions
dynamic game strategies, 335–339
reaction function equilibria, 348
vintage capital model, 258–259, 271–272
Variable returns to scale (VRS), Marshall–Lerner (ML) condition
international equilibrium, 517–518
long-run equilibrium stability, 512–515, 519–524, 535–38
model structure, 509–512
output adjustment and capital adjustment, 516–517
overview, 507–509
shifting consumer tastes, 524–525
supply side economy, 533–535
temporary equilibrium stability, 512–515, 518–519
transfer problems, 525–532
Viability assumptions, competitive equilibrium
consumer satiation, 33–34
strong viability assumption, 42–44

Vintage capital model
growth theory
alternative one Hoss–Shay model, 257–258
capital, 251
efficiency, 253–254
intertemporal optimization problem, 255–256
labor, 251
nonmonotonicity properties, optimal path, 259–260
optimality lemmas, 285–300
overview, 248–251
preferences, 255
production, 251–253
steady-state values, 260–262
technical results, 256–259
value function, 258–259
policy function
examples, 269–272
growth theory, 262–272
labor allocation, 266–267
linearity, 262–266
wage-output behavior over time, 267–269
stochastic variant, 272–274
empirical results, 274–285
Volatility tests
intertemporal asset pricing model
allocations, 310–311
commodities and assets, 308
consumers, 308–309
covariation as factor, 327–329
demand function, 309–310
equilibrium without insurance, 311, 317–327
government bonds or money, 309
insurance, 311–317
market efficiency
defined, 303–305
testing, 305–307
overview, 302–303
prices, 309
underlying stochastic processes, 308
von Neumann economy, boundary optimal paths, 411–412
von Neumann facets, international transfers, 556–557
Von Neumann–Morgenstern utility
disturbance densities, experimental consumption, 370–375
incomplete financial markets
price space, 138–141
infinite horizons, 123

Wage rate equalization
labor mobility
diversification cone, 453–455
factor price specialization, 455–458
heterogeneous labor, 449–451
labor endowments of immobile households, 451
location-specific expenditure functions, 451–452
one immobile factor, 444–452
overview, 442–444
two immobile factors, 452–458
multinational corporations and absolute advantage, Ricardian model, 492–494
vintage capital model, behavior over time, 267–269
Walrasian economic model
assumptions, 203–206
asymptotic inefficiencies, 209, 213–221
competitive equilibrium
and McKenzie economy, 21–22
separating hyperplane theorem, 34–35
Gale's linear exchange model, 94–96
indeterminacy, 57, 68–71
tâtonnement, competitive economies, 181–185
Weak compensated demand set, irreducibility, 79–80
Weak convergence, asymptotic inefficiency, 227–228

Weak irreducibility
competitive equilibrium
abstract market, 36–37
relaxation to viability in presence of, 45–46
interdependence, resource relatedness, 100
survival assumption, viability, 39
Weak oligarchy, irreducibility, 90–91
Wealth
direct and indirect utility for, 302–303
distribution of asset holdings, 318–322
endogenous fertility model, 238
fertility rate changes, 245–246
volatility testing, 322–323
Weierstrass' theorem, disturbance densities, 374–375
Welfare
effect of transfer, equilibrium conditions, 527–532
overall effect, international transfers, 566–569
tariff increases
imperfect competition, individual countries, 550–551
total world welfare, 551–553
Willoughby theorem
Produced Mobile Factor (PMF), 438–439
Stolper–Samuelson theorem, dominant diagonals, 435–438
World transformation curve
multinational corporations and absolute advantage, 497–503
with no MNCs or limited MNCs, 504–505

Zero-sum game, transfer condition as, 531–532

Economic Theory, Econometrics, and Mathematical Economics

Edited by Karl Shell, *Cornell University*

Previous Volumes in the Series

Erwin Klein, *Mathematical Methods in Theoretical Economics: Topological and Vector Space Foundations of Equilibrium Analysis*

Paul Zarembka, editor, *Frontiers in Econometrics*

George Horwich and Paul A. Samuelson, editors, *Trade, Stability, and Macroeconomics: Essays in Honor of Lloyd A. Metzler*

W. T. Ziemba and R. G. Vickson, editors, *Stochastic Optimization Models in Finance*

Steven A. Y. Lin, editor, *Theory and Measurement of Economic Externalities*

Haim Levy and Marshall Sarnat, editors, *Financial Decision Making under Uncertainty*

Yasuo Murata, *Mathematics for Stability and Optimization of Economic Systems*

Jerry S. Kelly, *Arrow Impossibility Theorems*

Fritz Machlup, *Methodology of Economics and Other Social Sciences*

Robert H. Frank and Richard T. Freeman, *Distributional Consequences of Direct Foreign Investment*

Elhanan Helpman and Assaf Razin, *A Theory of International Trade under Uncertainty*

Edmund S. Phelps, *Studies in Macroeconomic Theory*, Volume 1: *Employment and Inflation*, Volume 2: *Redistribution and Growth*

Marc Nerlove, David M. Grether, and José L. Carvalho, *Analysis of Economic Time Series: A Synthesis*

Michael J. Boskin, editor, *Economics and Human Welfare: Essays in Honor of Tibor Scitovsky*

Carlos Daganzo, *Multinomial Probit: The Theory and Its Application to Demand Forecasting*

L. R. Klein, M. Nerlove, and S. C. Tsiang, editors, *Quantitative Economics and Development: Essays in Memory of Ta-Chung Liu*

Giorgio P. Szegö, *Portfolio Theory: With Application to Bank Asset Management*

M. June Flanders and Assaf Razin, editors, *Development in an Inflationary World*

Thomas G. Cowing and Rodney E. Stevenson, editors, *Productivity Measurement in Regulated Industries*

Robert J. Barro, editor, *Money, Expectations, and Business Cycles: Essays in Macroeconomics*

Ryuzo Sato, *Theory of Technical Change and Economic Invariance: Application of Lie Groups*

Iosif A. Krass and Shawkat M. Hammoudeh, *The Theory of Positional Games: With Applications in Economics*

Giorgio P. Szegö, editor, *New Quantitative Techniques for Economic Analysis*

Murray C. Kemp, editor, *Production Sets*

Andreu Mas-Colell, editor, *Noncooperative Approaches to the Theory of Perfect Competition*

Jean-Pascal Benassy, editor, *The Economics of Market Disequilibrium*

Tatsuro Ichiishi, *Game Theory for Economic Analysis*

David P. Baron, *The Export–Import Bank: An Economic Analysis*

Réal P. Lavergne, *The Political Economy of U.S. Tariffs: An Empirical Analysis*

Halbert White, *Asymptotic Theory for Econometricians*

Thomas G. Cowing and Daniel L. McFadden, *Microeconomic Modeling and Policy Analysis: Studies in Residential Energy Demand*

V. I. Arkin and I. V. Evstigneev, translated and edited by E. A. Medova-Dempster and M. A. H. Dempster, *Stochastic Models of Control and Economic Dynamics*

Svend Hylleberg, *Seasonality in Regression*

Jean-Pascal Benassy, *Macroeconomics: An Introduction to the Non-Walrasian Approach*

C. W. J. Granger and Paul Newbold, *Forecasting Economic Time Series*, Second Edition

Marc Nerlove, Assaf Razin, and Efraim Sadka, *Household and Economy: Welfare Economics of Endogenous Fertility*

Thomas J. Sargent, *Macroeconomic Theory*, Second Edition

Yves Balasko, *Foundations of the Theory of General Equilibrium*

Jean-Michel Grandmont, editor, *Temporary Equilibrium: Selected Readings*

J. Darrell Duffie, *An Introductory Theory of Security Markets*

Ross M. Starr, editor, *General Equilibrium Models of Monetary Economics: Studies in the Static Foundations of Monetary Theory*

S. C. Tsiang, *Finance Constraints and the Theory of Money: Selected Papers*

Masanao Aoki, *Optimization of Stochastic Systems: Topics in Discrete-Time Dynamics*, Second Edition

Peter Diamond and Michael Rothschild, editors, *Uncertainty in Economics: Readings and Exercises*, Revised Edition

Martin J. Osborne and Ariel Rubinstein, *Bargaining and Markets*

Tatsuro Ichiishi, Abraham Neyman, and Yair Tauman, editors, *Game Theory and Applications*

E. L. Presman and I. N. Sonin, translated and edited by E. A. Medova-Dempster and M. A. H. Dempster, *Sequential Control with Incomplete Information*

Motoshige Itoh, Kazuharu Kiyono, Masahiro Okuno-Fujiwara, and Kotaro Suzumura, *Economic Analysis of Industrial Policy*

Akira Takayama, Michihiro Ohyama, and Hiroshi Ohta, editors, *Trade, Policy, and International Adjustments*

John M. Letiche, editor, *International Economic Policies and Their Theoretical Foundations: A Sourcebook*, Second Edition

Peter B. Linhart, Roy Radner, and Mark A. Satterthwaite, editors, *Bargaining with Incomplete Information*

ISBN 0-12-084655-1